INDUSTRIAL CONFLICT

Industrial
Conflict

EDITED BY   ARTHUR KORNHAUSER

ROBERT DUBIN

ARTHUR M. ROSS

McGRAW-HILL BOOK COMPANY, INC. 1954

New York   Toronto   London

INDUSTRIAL CONFLICT

Library of Congress Catalog Card Number: 53-12870

PREFACE

THIS volume was conceived as an integrated and genuinely interdisciplinary approach to the issues of industrial conflict in the United States. We were interested not only in examining the dimensions of the problem but also in bringing the entire field into focus to provide perspective and insights for students and all persons actively concerned with labor-management affairs. This book aims primarily to give a mountain-peak view of the problems, with a comprehensive analysis of the determining influences and conditions that give rise to conflict and an assessment of efforts at solution. Specific research inquiries and detailed techniques employed in the conduct and control of conflict behavior remain secondary. The central purpose is rather to provide a frame of reference for thinking and research.

Since this volume is published under the auspices of the Society for the Psychological Study of Social Issues (SPSSI) many persons—including the members of SPSSI—may be surprised that it is not more heavily psychological in its emphasis. The decision against this was a deliberate one, dictated principally by a conviction that current social and psychological research on industrial problems suffers particularly from lack of adequate background knowledge and broad understanding of the relationships. As a matter of fact, there is extremely little writing or research by psychologists that seriously gets into the matters here examined. This we believe to be both unfortunate and temporary—unfortunate, because psychologists have distinctive potential contributions to make, and temporary, because the pressing importance of the problems is bound to exert increasing pulls upon psychologists as well as upon other social scientists. It is our hope that this book will help to accelerate psychological interest in labor-management relations. Particularly, we hope that it will stimulate thought and promote research planning oriented toward broad and realistic formulations of problems instead of research so largely at the level of finding improved techniques to augment the administrative skills of industrial management.

With these broader purposes in view, it was necessary to organize the contents of the book on a different basis from that of the usual symposium. The three editors started with the assumption that a psychologist, a sociologist, and an economist, each having special interests in the field of industrial relations, could map out the contents of the book. Accordingly, they proceeded to draw up an extensive outline of the volume which was completed in a 2-day conference. The outline was then submitted to the board of advisory editors, also interdisciplinary in composition, for a review and revision. There resulted a twelve-page single-spaced typescript that represented the editors' judgment of what should go into the volume.

Upon recommendation of the editors and the members of the Editorial Advisory Board, a group of scholars, considered among the leading authorities in their respective fields, were invited to undertake the task of writing the individual chapters.

The authors are drawn principally from academic circles, though a few are connected with either organized labor or business groups. Many have had extensive experience in dealing with labor problems, particularly in governmental posts and as independent arbitrators; almost all have carried on significant research undertakings. The contributors were selected in terms of their special competence to deal with the topics assigned them; none was chosen as representative of any partisan viewpoint.

In securing the cooperation of the contributors, the editors indicated that the chapter outlines were designed to show the areas to be covered rather than to prescribe views to be adopted in writing the chapters. The prospectus contained the following statement:

> The book will be directed toward advanced college students and the serious-minded public, including those in labor and management organizations. The volume is to consist principally of contributed chapters prepared specially to fit together in an integrated manner as far as possible. The book will be oriented within a broad and liberal social frame of reference as contrasted with a one-sided approach from the standpoint of management, organized labor, or any particular ideology.

Each chapter as it was received was carefully read by all the editors and by at least two members of the Editorial Advisory Board. The editors then held another 2-day meeting to pool their thinking in regard to final revision of the manuscripts. The authors then prepared final drafts of their chapters based upon the resulting comments and suggestions. It is worth noting that only two authors were lost in this process, there being failure to agree that the chapters as originally submitted covered the subjects and topics sought. The editors were unanimous in asking for extensive revisions, which the two authors declined to undertake.

We feel it is particularly important that the full measure of recognition be accorded the group of scholars whose joint efforts give this volume its value and significance. They have had the vision to see the advantages of an interdisciplinary approach such as this one; they have displayed the discipline necessary to fill out smaller segments of the total picture in order that the whole intellectual endeavor might be organized and integrated; and they have evidenced the highest measure of intellectual integrity in pursuing the truth. It is a significant commentary on the liberal tradition of contributing to, and sharing, knowledge that there was a willing acceptance of responsibility and an enthusiastic participation in the preparation of the book. Neither authors nor editors stood to benefit financially since the entire proceeds from the book go to SPSSI. This volume is literally a labor of love for all those who have had an active hand in its creation.

The editors wish to express their sincere gratitude to the many persons who cooperated in producing the book. The contributing authors have already been singled out for the special vote of appreciation that SPSSI and the editors owe them. Our hearty thanks go also to the members of the Editorial Advisory Board and to the officers and board of SPSSI who have been generous and helpful in their support and facilitation of the editorial work. A special word of thanks is directed to the two representatives of SPSSI, Marie Jahoda and Rensis Likert, who accepted the time-consuming task of reading the entire manuscript.

It should be explicitly stated that neither the Society nor its representatives are responsible for views expressed in this book. On the complex and unsettled issues of industrial conflict, there are bound to be disagreements even among the doctors. No attempt has been made to hide these points of difference; they are a true reflection of the present state of scholarly thought in this area. Each individual author has expressed his own considered judgments on the topic assigned him. In the editorial sections of the book, the three coeditors have similarly tried to bring together the conclusions and the unanswered questions they consider most relevant and in accord with present knowledge. No careful reader can possibly accept every idea that is presented in the various sections of the book. The differing interpretations demand critical appraisal by each reader—and this means not only consideration of alleged facts but steady reexamination of value assumptions as well. But beneath the differences, a very substantial body of agreed-upon knowledge will be found. Taking the present volume in its entirety, it is our hope that it offers a well-balanced view of industrial conflict in the United States, portraying both established knowledge and issues that are still debated.

Arthur Kornhauser
Robert Dubin
Arthur M. Ross

CONTENTS

3 *DEALING WITH INDUSTRIAL CONFLICT*

PART *1* **BASIC ISSUES CONCERNING INDUSTRIAL CONFLICT**

CHAPTER 1 PROBLEMS AND VIEWPOINTS

The Editors

Among the troublesome problems of our industrial age, relations between labor and management occupy a prominent place. Owners and managers of industry and the wage workers whom they hire and direct can be expected to develop different orientations toward industry and different perceptions of their own interests. Despite heavy accent in recent years on *common* goals and on the virtues of industrial peace and harmony, the pursuit of opposed aims continues to cause strife. General agreement as to the desirability of high-level and continuous production does not prevent sharp disagreements over the way in which the production is to be achieved, the human costs it justifies, and the relative rewards due the participants. Constant efforts are required to mitigate conflict in regard to the issues that arise on these matters, to create and preserve smooth-working relationships, and to provide acceptable mechanisms of compromise, accommodation, and adjudication to settle disagreements and to deal with organized group conflict which explodes, or threatens to explode, into open warfare. It should be specifically noted that "industrial conflict" is not to be construed as equivalent to the use of violence. While violence does occur on occasion, it has come to be an unusual rather than a usual mark of labor-management conflict.

The problems are not new. They have bedeviled labor-management relationships throughout the history of modern capitalism. The growth of the factory system has been accompanied step by step by painful gropings toward more satisfactory human relations. Slowly and haltingly the men who manage and those who labor have sought to make industrial work more acceptable as a way of life and to evolve more satisfactory and appropriate forms of government in industry. The changes have not come smoothly and without struggle. The record of the past century is thickly dotted with intense and often violent industrial disputes. These conflicts arose from the organized effort of working people to improve their lot, even when it led them to transgress the accepted rules and the rights of property. Resistance by employers expressed itself sharply in opposition to the trade-unions which groups of workers attempted to form to force concessions from unwilling managements. In the effort to combat unions and to curtail their power, large corporations used the instruments of government, in so far as these were available to maintain "law and order" and to "protect the public interest," and also built up their own special means of self-defense in the form of elaborate spy systems, the hiring of thugs and strikebreakers, and the domination of local communities. Until recent decades, the courts, the police, and the militia could be depended upon by the corporations to prevent any important or sustained gains in power by unions. This long fight for the right to organize and to bargain collectively has extended into the present period; in some regions of the country and in certain industrial situations, this fundamental battle is not yet fully concluded.

While this history of bitter conflict is undeniable, it must be seen in proper perspective. Many corporations have succeeded in carrying on peaceful labor relations for decades and have steadily improved the wages and conditions of their employees without being clubbed into it. Strikes and lockouts are spectacular and consequently command public attention. For the most part, however, industry proceeds more or less smoothly to solve its problems and to meet its prosaic tasks of production. The occasional instances of overt conflict must not be assigned exaggerated importance. At the same time, they need to be evaluated realistically. They offer convincing evidence of persistent oppositions strongly enough felt to cause workers and companies to undergo the costs and personal sacrifices of prolonged work stoppages.

It is now generally understood that important changes have occurred in labor-management relations in the United States during the past two decades. Organized labor has made unprecedented gains both in numbers and in power. Labor unions have grown to a point where they exercise a telling influence upon the economic and political affairs of the nation. This new position of labor has greatly changed the nature of the struggles between management and working people. Corporations are no longer as able to use the old methods, either governmental or private, for resisting the demands of unions. Great aggregates of power now find themselves opposed to each other, each wielding enough influence to keep from being "pushed around" and each being able to prevent the machinery of government from being used in a highly one-sided manner. At the same time, the consequences of unresolved disputes threaten from time to time to impose intolerable hardships on the society and hence lead to increased pressures for governmental measures to enforce settlements.

Not less significant than organized labor's growth is the remarkable change which has occurred, both in management circles and among the general public (white-collar, professional, and other non-wage-earning groups), in the acceptance of unions. Perhaps most astonishing is the readjustment that has been taking place in the thinking of management executives themselves. There can be little question that most of them now recognize that unions are here to stay. Neither they nor the middle class are opposed to the existence of labor unions, even though large numbers object to particular actions and policies. The fight for recognition has been won in most industries. Management's resistance to further union advances is now carried on within a framework of organized dealings. It seems highly questionable whether the violent outbreaks of the past will be repeated in this new period. The spirit of desperation on the part of labor groups is disappearing as is the imperious refusal of powerful management to tolerate any opposition to its dictates. Antagonisms are now more likely to work themselves out through procedures of orderly collective bargaining, public relations, psychological appeals to working people, and pressures on government.

The Purpose of This Book

It is against the background of these historical changes, especially of the recent changes, that the contributors to this volume reexamine present-day industrial conflict. Attention is directed primarily to the American scene. Comparisons with experience abroad are introduced for the light they throw on industrial conflict at home and not as a basis for world-wide generalizations. The book aims to deal with the essential features of present-day labor-management strife in the United States in a comprehensive manner, covering the nature and meaning of the conflict relationship—its causes and conditions and attempted methods for reducing and dealing with it—the unsolved problems that remain, and the alternative roads ahead. The treatment is analytical rather than descriptive, and its purpose is to provide interpretation, insight, and understanding rather than to offer procedures or formulas.

This focus on industrial conflict is rather unusual in the present social climate. It is more popular to write about cooperation than about conflict. To give attention to economic group conflict seems to some people to sanction and approve it—and to border on the "subversive." The tendency seems to be growing to deal with such matters only as evils to be overcome and to concentrate exclusively on the "positive" or "constructive" question of how to reduce or remove conflict. These tendencies are not absent from the chapters of this book. At the same time, however, the reader will find that much of the treatment simply considers industrial conflict as a part of the social process to be understood and then dealt with in whatever manner commends itself to society as a whole. For some groups, desirable solutions may lie in the direction of eliminating conflict—for example, by using education, government, and other social controls to produce allegiance to the ideals of harmony and unity without modification of existing social relationships. But others will find in their understanding of conflict reasons for wishing to preserve the conflict and will seek more effective methods for channeling the opposed strivings toward desirable social change as they see it. It is not for social scientists to adopt one value orientation and to deal with the matter under study exclusively within that frame of values. What is needed is as true and balanced an understanding of labor-management relations as possible, and this must be based upon impartial inquiry into both conflict and harmony and into the social gains as well as the social losses resulting from each.

The book brings together the scholarly thinking of specialists representing a variety of approaches. The time is past when questions of labor and industry were considered the exclusive province of the economist. It is now recognized that the problems are challenging ones for all the social sciences and that all can contribute to the answers. Accordingly, the present volume has deliberately called on experts from several disciplines, notably economics, psychology, and sociology. At the same time, the reader will also discover that few of the contributors remain within the confines of a particular specialty. In tackling concrete social issues, each specialist tends to cross disciplinary lines. It is perhaps especially noteworthy that economists, whose field this has traditionally been, are compelled to carry their inquiries far beyond the limits of economic analysis as such and to employ concepts and methods more familiar to the sociologist, the political scientist, and the social psychologist. Partly, then, because the following chapters are contributed by specialists from different fields of knowledge and partly because each writer utilizes whatever intellectual tools he believes appropriate, the book as a whole takes on an interdisciplinary tone and reflects views current in the several social sciences.

The viewpoint of the analyses is neither that of labor nor of management but that of social scientists attempting to see the problems within the context of the whole society. Industrial conflict is a significant part of the social process, a salient aspect of our day-to-day world, to be studied and understood and intelligently dealt with. Some of its consequences are ones that most people in America would approve; other consequences they find bad. But wholesale praise or condemnation certainly provides no solution. The problems and the alternative answers are much too intricate to be left to offhand emotional decisions. Whatever else the chapters in this book do or fail to do, they unmistakably point to the need for vastly greater knowledge than we now possess, as a basis for wise social action in regard to conflict in industry.

A tendency is discernible in many discussions of industrial conflict to adopt one or the other of two extreme positions: an alarmist view or a complacent view. The former typically plays up the injurious effects of "labor trouble" and demands vigorous remedies, especially coercive action by government. The other, perhaps with equal exaggeration, contends that there really is no reason to be disturbed, that no serious harm is being done by conflict in industry, that existing procedures of collective bargaining and disputes settlement are working well, and that there is no indication of significant shifts of power that would be at all revolutionary. Neither of these positions seems justified. It is well to guard against both undue optimism and unwarranted pessimism. The comfortably optimistic orientation tends to build overconfidently on short-run successes and special cases; the pessimists tend to overemphasize the inevitability of historic trends and the assumed impossibility of finding happy middle-ground solutions utilizing moderate but effective democratic controls.

A more tentative, skeptical, and inquiring approach appears wisest in the present state of knowledge. It is not the intent of this book to offer settled conclusions but to suggest lines of thought that may be helpful in the ongoing search for better answers. Where no good answers exist, it is well to recognize the limitations of knowledge and to place large question marks beside those popular beliefs and accepted principles that are of doubtful validity. But the demands of action require that we proceed on the basis of the best judgments available at the time. The quest for more firmly established conclusions likewise needs to be informed about the present state of knowledge and then to push on from there. It is with these needs in mind that the authors who have contributed to this volume have set down their conclusions and reflections in regard to labor-management conflict. Their views are by no means always in agreement, and each reader will encounter statements that he finds unconvincing and lacking adequate support. All that can be claimed is that this is where we are; here is where the thinking of a selected group of experts on these matters now stands. It is from this point that further steps must be taken toward more penetrating analyses, deeper understandings, and better practical solutions in the area of labor-management affairs.

Three main sets of questions are considered in this introductory section of the book: (1) How serious is the problem of industrial strife in the United States? What are the principal current views as to what should be done? (2) What is the general nature of industrial conflict? What significant forms does it assume apart from strikes? What is the broad conditioning context within which labor-management relationships are to be viewed? (3) What is the place of industrial conflict in a free, democratic society? What are the predominant goals in regard to industrial conflict in our society? What are the alternatives to conflict?

The remainder of this chapter discusses these questions in a preliminary manner. The other chapters of Part 1 spell out several interpretations that bear particularly on the first and last of the three sets of questions.

The Problem of Strikes

How serious is industrial conflict in the United States? It would be out of place to answer this question definitively here, since a major purpose of the present volume is to pave the way for an informed judgment on the reader's part. By way of orientation, however, it may be helpful to discuss the frequency and significance of strikes, since the strike is the principal overt manifestation of conflict.

There are three standard measurements of strike activity: the number of strikes (defined as stoppages involving at least six workers for a period of at least one working shift); the number of workers directly involved; and the number of man-days of idleness on the part of workers directly involved. In the quarter century since 1927, there have been more than 75,000 strikes, 40,000,000 workers involved, and 600,000,000 man-days of idleness in the United States.

These numbers, particularly the last one, are large, but the reader should be warned that statistics on man-days of inactivity do not provide a reliable basis for measuring the magnitude of economic loss because of strikes. On the one hand, the substantial indirect effects of certain strikes are not included, for example, curtailment of output in automobile plants when steel supplies become exhausted. On the other hand, there is sufficient slack in the economy to absorb the effect of most strikes without enduring loss of any great consequence. Production is shifted from one point of time to another or from one establishment to another or from one area to another. That is, employers may build up inventories in anticipation of the strike or step up production to fill delayed orders after it has terminated, or consumers may obtain the goods from competing producers in the area or in some other area. In general, the less durable is a commodity (and the less adapted to stockpiling) and the more nearly is the whole market area included in the scope of a strike, the greater is the likelihood that a real economic cost is involved. Compare, for example, a strike in a shoe factory with a strike in an electrical utility. In the first case, the commodity can be stockpiled, purchases can be postponed, and alternative sources of supply can be utilized. In the second, none of these "offsets" are available.

Of course, even when strikes involve no enduring economic loss to society as a whole, they often involve financial losses to particular employers, workers, and communities. There may be corresponding gains to other employers, workers, and communities, but these are smaller or less obvious and less traceable. Some strikes do not even have these limited economic effects because they are merely substitutes for curtailments of work which would otherwise take the form of layoffs. This is probably true of all but a few of the many coal strikes which have taken place during the past 25 years. Because of excess capacity in the industry and declining demand for coal, orders have been insufficient to provide steady employment in nonstrike periods throughout many of these years.

Among the various sources of economic loss, therefore, strikes must be regarded as relatively minor. Certainly there are more important reasons why work is not performed and output not produced. For example, the number of man-days lost because of unemployment in the single year 1933 was more than five times as great as the loss from all strikes from 1927 up to the present time. The judgment of most specialists is that the economic consequences of strikes are overrated.

Probably the basic explanation for this exaggerated view lies in the *overtness* of the strike. Glaring and palpable, it thrusts itself rudely above the surface of society. Although not the most significant source of economic loss, it is certainly the most conspicuous. The number of workers participating in strikes is roughly of the same order of magnitude as the number suffering industrial accidents. The accidents occur quietly, however, generally one by one, whereas strikes are showy mass phenomena. Similarly, strikes are not the only expression of industrial discontent, and probably not the most dangerous, but they are the most spectacular. They are not the only form of economic conflict but merely the most conspicuous. They involve face-to-face primary relationships between mutually identified antagonists, whereas some forms of conflict (*e.g.*, competition in the market place) are so impersonal that the antagonists may not even be known to each other. A legal dispute is an open adversary proceeding, but one which is carried on through paid professionals who are governed more or less rigidly by a prescribed code of polite conduct. The same institutional sublimation of conflict is yet to be achieved in the case of strikes, although some progress has been made.

But the popular view of the strike problem cannot be dismissed lightly on the ground that the conspicuousness of strikes is out of proportion to their "real" significance. Society defines its own problems without much regard for the judgments of the social scientist. As Thomas and Znaniecki [1] stated a generation ago, "If men define situations as real, they are real in their consequences." And Robert K. Merton [2] recently observed that

[1] W. I. Thomas and Florian Znaniecki, *The Polish Peasant in Europe and America*, Vol. 1, Chicago, University of Chicago Press, 1918.

[2] Robert K. Merton, "The Self-fulfilling Prophecy," *Antioch Review*, 8 (Summer, 1948), 194–195.

. . . men respond not only to the objective features of a situation, but also, and at times primarily, to the meaning this situation has for them. And once they have assigned some meaning to the situation, their consequent behavior and some of the consequences of that behavior are determined by the ascribed meaning. . . . Public definitions of a situation . . . become an integral part of the situation and affect subsequent developments.

Attempted solutions to the strike problem tend to be based more on the public perception of the strike than on its objective features. The real importance of strikes, therefore, is the public reaction which they provoke. The real danger is that such reaction will be hostile to the institution of collective bargaining. We rely on collective bargaining as a system for establishing and administering terms of employment and as an alternative to unilateral domination by one party or the other and to government dictation. Despite conventional obeisance to collective bargaining, the lay public is uneasy with it. Although compulsory arbitration is clearly antithetical to collective bargaining and is opposed by labor and management alike, opinion polls indicate that the notion of submitting unresolved contract disputes to the test of impartial adjudication is dear to the public. We do not have compulsory arbitration in the United States, but we have seen the beginning of another development hostile to collective bargaining: the use of legislation for determining what should or should not be included in collective agreements. Union security, checkoff, health and welfare plans, allowable employer payments, and termination clauses are now regulated in this manner. Public uneasiness is reflected in the time-worn clichés of industrial relations: There is no substitute for free and unfettered collective bargaining between free management and free labor, sitting around the conference table, etc.; *but* the public is the silent third party and the public interest is paramount over the special interests of management and labor. In an atomic age, workers and employees must eschew the law of the jungle; *but* the right to strike is sacred and inviolable. And so it goes. Thus the collective-bargaining system is at one and the same time celebrated with the deepest reverence and tolerated on the shortest sufferance. This is the real strike problem.

As noted above, more than 600 million man-days of idleness have been incurred in strikes since statistics of this type became available in 1927. Strike activity has not been spread out evenly throughout this 25-year period, however, nor throughout the economy. Up to 1944, there was a pronounced correlation between strike activity and two other phenomena: spurts of union organization and rapid increases in the cost of living. The years 1927, 1937, and 1941 were high-water marks, with from 23 to 28 million man-days of idleness in each of the 3 years. Beginning with 1945, however, there have been more than 34 million man-days of idleness in every year but one (1951), with an average of about 48 million. Prices have been rising and employment has been high during most of the recent period, of course. (The relationship between strikes and the business cycle is discussed by Rees in Chap. 15.)

In appraising the trend of strike activity we should recognize that employment and union membership have both been increasing. Nonagricultural employment doubled between 1933 and 1952; union membership expanded four or five times over. Thus higher totals of strike activity do not necessarily demonstrate a greater "propensity to strike." Table 1.1 shows man-days idle, as a per cent of total working time and as a multiple of union membership, from 1927 through 1950. The figures are annual averages for eight 3-year periods. When strike statistics are related to union membership, it is not at all clear that an upward trend in the propensity to strike can be perceived.

Table 1.1   **Man-days Idle Compared with Working Time and Union Membership**

Period	Man-days idle, as per cent of working time (1)	Man-days idle, as multiple of union membership (2)
1927–1929	0.20	4.1
1930–1932	0.13	2.1
1933–1935	0.34	5.4
1936–1938	0.26	2.8
1939–1941	0.23	1.7
1942–1944	0.10	0.7
1945–1947	0.77	4.2
1948–1950	0.47	2.7

SOURCES: Column (1) computed from data collected by U.S. Bureau of Labor Statistics; column (2) from Arthur M. Ross and Donald Irwin, "Strike Experience in Five Countries, 1927–1947," *Industrial and Labor Relations Review,* 4 (1951), 332 (carried forward to 1950).

Strike activity is concentrated in limited sectors of the economy. About 60 per cent of the total man-days of idleness during the past 25 years has been incurred in mining, textiles and apparel, iron and steel, automobiles, and food manufacturing. In addition, the construction industry has seen many strikes, but of small size, whereas the lumber industry has had a moderate number of strikes, of average size but small duration. Other industry groups may be noted in which strike activity has been conspicuously small. Some of these have been largely unorganized during most or all of the period. Since nonunion workers rarely strike, it is not surprising that there have been few stoppages in chemicals, petroleum products, agriculture, wholesale and retail trade, and finance. However, there has also been relatively little strike activity in certain unionized industries such as printing and publishing, aircraft manufacturing, paper and allied products, rubber products, nonferrous metals, and machinery. (In Chap. 14, Kerr and Siegel note that certain centers of industrial conflict are common to numerous countries and discuss the reasons for this fact.)

To a considerable extent, the strike problem centers in a relatively few large stoppages. Strikes involving more than 10,000 workers have accounted for less than one-half of one per cent of all strikes since 1927 but have accounted for more than one-third of all workers affected. These major disputes clearly have the greatest economic impact of all and evoke the most sizable public reaction. They frequently have a pace-setting character in fixing patterns of adjustment as well as the tone of industrial relations over large segments of the economy.

The issues in strikes are as numerous as the matters on which companies and unions can agree or disagree. Basically, these issues can be classified as either economic or organizational. The Bureau of Labor Statistics has a somewhat more elaborate classification, however, and distributes the 4,737 strikes which occurred in 1951 into the categories shown in Table 1.2.

Table 1.2 **Strike Issues in the United States, 1951**

1. Wages, hours, and fringe benefits	44.4% *
2. Union organization (recognition, strengthening bargaining position, discrimination, closed or union shop, and others)	14.4
3. Union organization plus wages, hours, and fringe benefits (as issues in the same strike)	4.3
4. Other working conditions (job security, shop conditions and policies, work load, and others)	28.3
5. Interunion or intraunion matters (sympathy, union rivalry or factionalism, jurisdiction, union regulations, and others)	6.9
6. Not reported	1.7
Total	100.0 %

* Percentages from *Monthly Labor Review*, 74 (May, 1952), 517 ff.

The strikes involving "wages, hours, and fringe benefits" tended to be the larger ones, however, and accounted for 62.5 per cent of man-days of idleness during 1951.

As time goes on the importance of particular strike issues rises and falls. Many strikes during the early 1930's were in protest against wage reductions. With unprecedented unemployment and falling membership, unions were on the defensive and were not in a position to press for recognition in new territory. Organizational issues rose in prominence during 1933, however, and remained predominant until 1941. (Demands for recognition were often accompanied by demands for higher wages and other economic benefits.) During World War II most unions were covered by the "no-strike, no-lockout" pledge, and unsettled disputes were adjudicated by the National War Labor Board (NWLB). For this reason strikes over labor-contract issues were rare except in the coal-mining industry (the United Mine Workers refused to be bound by the no-strike pledge). There were numerous "outlaw" strikes over work loads, disciplinary disputes, shop conditions, and other plant grievances, particularly in the automobile industry. These wartime strikes, which were not formally sanctioned by union leadership, were generally terminated quickly, so that man-days of strike idleness were low during the 1942–1944 period. Since the end of World War II, union demands for higher wages and fringe benefits have been the predominant strike issues.

The *formal issues* in strikes should not be identified with the *causes* of strikes. Questions and disagreements arise in almost every contract negotiation, but most negotiations are completed without recourse to a work stoppage. The proportion of successful negotiations cannot be stated precisely, since reliable statistics on the number of collective agreements are lacking, but probably it exceeds 95 per cent. Therefore the causes of strikes are not the issues on which the parties negotiate but the reasons for their failure to reach agreement in a small percentage of cases.

Thus the strike in present-day American society is a component of the collective-bargaining system, which in turn is an essential feature of the enterprise system. Collective bargaining would have little meaning were it not for the possibility of a strike, with attendant losses on both sides, since there would be little pressure on the parties to modify their positions and reach agreements. It follows that the strike and the lockout are really two-sided contests and that there are two parties to every stoppage, equally in disagreement with each other. The difference between the union's position and the employer's position is always mathematically equal to the difference between the employer's position and the union's position. The fact of a lockout does not necessarily mean that the employer is at fault, nor the fact of a strike that the union is to blame. As one of the editors [3] has observed in another connection,

> The public tends to think of the strike as a union weapon and the lockout as the corresponding employer weapon. Many authors in the field of labor economics follow the same practice. . . . The only essential difference between a strike and a lockout is that the union takes the first overt step in one case and the employer in the other. But ordinarily the union must take the initiative if the issue is to be forced, because . . . almost all the provisions of the collective agreement are administered by the employer. To levy blame for a stoppage requires a more sophisticated analysis than one which merely identifies the party making the first move.

As the strike has become "institutionalized" in recent decades, most of the violence and much of the excitement have disappeared. The strike is no longer an improvident emotional outburst nor a pitched battle between opposing armies intent on gaining unconditional surrender but rather a cold-blooded and hardheaded bargaining maneuver conducted by professional negotiators.

The foregoing observations have been designed to put the strike into perspective as an incident of the collective-bargaining system. They do not at all detract from efforts to reduce the quantity and intensity of strikes—efforts which are described in Part 3 of this volume. The social cost of work stoppages, although overrated, is nevertheless considerable; the private cost to particular individuals and business firms is even greater; and the creative and constructive potentialities of collective bargaining cannot be realized in a relationship dominated by conflict. Other things being equal, collective bargaining is most successful when economic pressure is used least frequently. Moreover, strike activity in the United States is relatively great in comparison with other countries. This is shown in Table 1.3, which consists of five comparative measurements of strike activity, in terms of annual averages for the period 1927 to 1950.

The Larger Dimensions of Industrial Conflict

Complete work stoppages and outbreaks of violence due to industrial disputes are certainly the most dramatic expressions of industrial conflict. For the general public they are also the most disturbing. In the minds of many

[3] A. M. Ross, *Trade Union Wage Policy*, Berkeley, University of California Press, 1948, pp. 106–107.

industrial conflict has come to *mean* strikes. It is the phenomenon of strikes that most compellingly leads people to call for remedial measures.

Table 1.3 **Comparative Measures of Strike Activity, Annual Averages, 1927–1950**

Measure	Aus- tralia	Canada	Great Britain	Sweden	United States
I. Workers involved in strikes, as per cent of nonagricultural employment	8.6%	2.4%	2.4%	1.4%	3.6%
II. Workers involved in strikes, as per cent of union membership	15.7%	11.6%	6.0%	3.1%	17.3%
III. Working days lost, as multiple of workers involved in strikes	8.3	11.0	7.0	48.8	18.5
IV. Working days lost, as multiple of nonagricultural employment	0.6	0.3	0.2	0.8	0.6
V. Working days lost, as multiple of union membership	1.1	1.3	0.5	1.5	3.0

SOURCE: Arthur M. Ross and Donald Irwin, "Strike Experience in Five Countries, 1927–1947," *Industrial and Labor Relations Review*, 4 (1951), 332 (carried forward to 1950).

But a true understanding of industrial strife and what should be done about it demands consideration of related, less-spectacular manifestations as well. It may even be suggested that the general object of study is not the labor dispute, the strike or the lockout, but the total range of behavior and attitudes that express opposition and divergent orientations between industrial owners and managers on the one hand and working people and their organizations on the other hand. To the extent that a conflict relationship exists, each side strives to win relative advantage and to protect and advance the individual and organizational welfare of its own group against the resistance of the opposed group—and in the process each may try to inflict loss or injury on the other. Labor disputes occur within this larger context; they are part of a complex total relationship and can be understood only as the entire relationship is held in view.

The foregoing statements assume the existence of underlying oppositions. The crucial question must be faced whether this is justified. Is industrial conflict necessary? Are the interests of the two "parties" in fact opposed or harmonious? Even casual analysis of the matter leaves no doubt that the answer to this last question must be "both." No one could well argue that there are no important common goals of production, high earnings, and survival, shared by all groups in industry. But equally clearly, there are divergent interests with respect to the division of the pie and, more generally, in the weight to be given in decisions to considerations of production costs and profits as against direct human satisfactions of working people. Conflict regarding the relative weight assigned these factors is seen not only in union-management disputes over wages and working rules but likewise in the unorganized antagonisms and personal dissatisfactions concerning job assignments, agreeableness and safety of work conditions, opportunities for personal participation and self-expression, and innumerable other such points at which workers may feel that their legitimate aspirations are thwarted, that they are unjustly treated, or that unreasonable deprivations and unnecessary sacrifices are imposed upon them. Beneath all the specific points of conflict lies the issue of whether the prerogatives of management, the power relations in industry, are to be maintained as they now exist or whether they are subject to modification in the interests of fuller participation by working people and their unions.

The reality of opposed interests *as seen by the parties* is, of course, the decisive fact. And the *perceived* relationship obviously depends not only on the "economic facts of life" but also on the social interpretations current among the people involved. It is possible that, at least for limited periods of time, workers and managers may falsely believe that they have conflicting interests when, in fact, no objective basis for such beliefs exists. Conversely, they may accept a doctrine of complete harmony even though genuine grounds for conflict are present. Realistic study of the problem must certainly give attention to the way each group perceives its relationship to the other and to the attitudes and beliefs that prevail and govern the actions of each vis-à-vis the other, along with economic analyses of their material interests.

We return now to the question of how the conflict orientations of the parties find expression. What are these varied manifestations of conflict earlier referred to? Perhaps the listing of some principal categories will best give the answer, for example, a classification such as the following:

Manifestations of organized group conflict (union-management conflicts)
> In industry
>> Interruptions of production—strikes, lockouts, and removal of plant
>> Organized restrictions of output—work limitations, slowdowns, sabotage, and unilateral changes of work standards, piece rates, etc.
>> Conflicts in contract negotiations, grievance cases, dealings between foremen and stewards, etc., without work stoppages
> In the larger society
>> Political oppositions—local and national
>> Other community and social oppositions—conflicting pressures on newspapers and radio, rivalries over recreational, educational, and other services for workers, etc.

Manifestations of individual and unorganized conflict
> In industry—employee behavior
>> Unorganized withholding of effort, intentional waste and inefficiency, etc.
>> Labor turnover and absenteeism
>> Complaints, friction, infractions of rules, and similar evidences of low morale and discontent
> In industry—management behavior
>> Autocratic supervision and overstrict discipline and penalties
>> Unnecessary and discriminatory firing, layoffs, and demotions
>> Unofficial speed-ups, etc.
> In the larger society
>> Employee expressions of opposition in everyday talk, voting behavior, consumer choices, etc.

Owner and management expressions of opposition in use of political influence against unions, support of one-sided educational and propaganda programs, etc.

The mere listing of these varied types of labor-management conflict behavior calls attention to the serious limitation inherent in looking at industrial conflict as if it were confined to strikes and formal disputes. Moreover, it is apparent that the different expressions of conflict are important not only as they throw additional light on open warfare in industry; they are vastly significant in themselves—possibly more important in their effects than overt union-management conflict itself. Even in terms of lost production, the interferences and costs of restrictive practices, absenteeism, and turnover far exceed total losses from work stoppages due to strikes. In directly human terms, too, the persistent interpersonal and intergroup tensions undoubtedly produce greater ill effects in the form of anxieties and "nervous symptoms" than do the occasional work interruptions. Moreover, it appears especially important to underscore the operation of industrial conflict outside the walls of industry as well as the various consequences of conflict inside the industrial structure itself. Industrial conflict, considered as a whole, increasingly finds expression in the sociopolitical sphere, in elections, lobbying, public-relations activities, and educational and propaganda drives to win approval and support from workers, leaders of community opinion, and the general public. It may turn out, indeed, that the course of labor-management relations over the next decades will be determined more by happenings on the political and public-opinion front than by anything done in industry.

In the larger view of industrial conflict the problems call for study in broad sociopsychological and political terms rather than study solely in reference to relations occurring directly between unions and management in industry. Particularly, the foregoing considerations indicate the inadequacy of evidence confined to specific industrial-relations cases as a basis for conclusions concerning the future of industrial peace or conflict. An understanding of trends and forces at work cannot neglect the analysis of changing sociopolitical conditions and the shifting interpretations and expectations that occur in the society as a whole and in subdivisions of the society. It is imperative here to guard against a "provincialism in time" that uncritically accepts current conditions and norms as if they were permanent. It is precarious in the extreme to assume that "good solutions" to industrial-relations problems in recent years and in particular companies can validly be generalized as applicable to other times and places. Questions of a fundamental nature remain unanswered—questions pertaining to the effects, for example, of a business recession or even a disappointing slowing down of the rate of improvement, of changes in the world situation and the amount of concern over national security and need for unity, and of long-run changes in the relative effectiveness of propaganda and educational influences by business groups and by labor and liberal groups. Such reminders simply dictate caution about our statements of present knowledge. We always need to ask under what conditions given conclusions hold true. And this question itself leads on to thinking and research that will help our society understand and deal with industrial conflict in its larger dimensions.

Place of Industrial Conflict in a Free Society

Is continued industrial conflict threatening to the interests of the larger society? This is a value-laden question that has no immediate yes or no answer. But the question is somewhat differently viewed if we try to minimize the value overtones and seek out an answer in functional terms. We might well consider a prior question: What are the functions of conflict in a free society? From our answer to such a question it should be possible to seek the grounds for a consideration of how industrial conflict relates to the interests of a free society.

Social Functions of Organized Group Conflict. We can suggest at least four general functions of group conflict in a free society. We will examine each of these briefly with special emphasis upon industrial-relations illustrations.

The most obvious function of group conflict is to make explicit the grounds that separate the groups in opposition. It is a venerable sociological proposition that the "we" group always characterizes its virtues explicitly in contrast to the equally concretely stated vices of the "they" group. In terms of the larger society, this concrete expression of the differing goals and objectives of competing and conflicting groups is useful. It suggests that overt conflict cannot be carried out without each side's striving for some kind of public justification of its position. Now the significance of having to justify publicly a disputed position lies in the fact that elements underlying the dispute are given some kind of affirmative expression. Each side comes to know its own mind and that of its opponent. There is no guarantee that, because the grounds for conflict are made explicit, these will necessarily represent the "true" basis of conflict. All that we are suggesting is that the group conflict serves to rally the forces of the groups in conflict around some explicit goals. This facilitates group action by enhancing group unity. It need hardly be urged that a period of conflict in union-management relations is typically a time when union membership coalesces around union leadership and the symbolic goals of the union. Usually the same kind of unity is also brought to a climax within the ranks of management under similar circumstances.

A second function of group conflict in a free society is to bring issues out into the open, where they become sensitive to the pressures of public opinion and subject to social control. To give a disputed position its most favorable appearance, great effort is often made to have it appear reasonable and socially legitimate. Strenuous efforts are often made by both unions and managements to advertise publicly the virtues of their respective positions. It is not our purpose here to question whether such efforts really do influence public opinion. It is more important to emphasize that these activities are group responses to public opinion and give concrete evidence that a group in conflict at least takes cognizance of the existence of public opinion.

At another level, the public exposure of conflict issues makes possible the application of social controls. The legal and administrative actions of government and the less formal efforts at social control by private organizations can come into play only when the appropriate occasion is evident. A conciliator does not enter a labor dispute until there is a dispute and something to conciliate. The National Labor Relations Board (NLRB) does not take action until there is a complaint before it based upon an existing labor dispute. In short, a labor dispute has to be exposed to public knowledge before the more direct forms of social control can become operative.

A third function of open and direct conflict between groups in our society is to force the rapid resolution of the conflict. This may seem paradoxical on the face of it. Yet it is true that open conflict demands its own resolution. Certainly, in the field of labor relations, it is not possible to point to a single situation where open conflict has gone unresolved for a substantial period of time. This does not mean that the particular solution to a given conflict issue is mutually satisfactory or that the issue may not be raised again in the future. It does mean, however, that some kind of working arrangement is achieved that makes possible the continuation of the ongoing activity that has been interrupted or disrupted by the dispute. In continuous union-management relations particularly, there is a tremendous pressure for rapid resolution of present conflict issues so that the relationship between the parties can have a basis for continuity. To put this point in more general form, the social structure cannot function effectively on a day-to-day basis when there are points of controversy within it over how it is to function. Thus there is stress on resolution of publicly recognized conflict between groups to preserve the operating efficiency of the social structure. Society cannot function satisfactorily if there is disagreement as to the rules by which it operates. Nor can two groups continue a satisfactory relationship if there is conflict about the basis of the relationship. It is perhaps in this sense that we can understand W. G. Sumner's phrase "antagonistic cooperation" as being particularly relevant to union-management relations.

A fourth function of open group conflict is that it serves to stabilize the social structure by clarifying the identity of the power-holding groups at strategic points in the society. Ours is preeminently an industrial society. What happens in the industrial sphere may have far-reaching impact upon the total society. With the rise of labor unionism fundamental changes have occurred in our society, changes that are reflected in the new definitions of "a fair day's pay," "a fair day's work," the length of the working day and week, personal security, and social responsibility, just to mention a few of the more dramatic aspects of these changes. Indeed, Sumner Slichter has been moved to summarize these fundamental changes in societal practices and values as symbolizing the "laboristic society." However one characterizes these changes, it is clear that they have been wrought through industrial conflict and the emergence of a strong labor movement that has wrested important concessions from management and has used its industrial power to influence the course of government policy. It seems reasonably certain that collective relations between management and labor and the conflict that has characterized these relations have clarified the relative strength of the two groups within the total society.

How, then, can we tentatively answer the following question: Is continued industrial conflict threatening to the interests of the larger society? The general answer that suggests itself is that when conflict becomes institutionalized it becomes an integral part of the society's way of daily functioning. In outlining some of the functions that group conflict plays in a free society we have been suggesting aspects of the institutionalization of this conflict. We do not have reason to believe that the daily industrial conflict of our society is automatically a threat to social stability; the continued vitality of our society is at least short-run evidence to the contrary. In later sections of this volume, we shall see more fully the significant ways in which industrial conflict has been increasingly institutionalized to bring it into more organized and stabilized relationship with the total social structure.

Moral Foundations of Union and Management Positions

As simple as it may seem, it is desirable to point out why industrial conflict must be analyzed in terms of union-management relations. It is organized management and organized labor that give substance to industrial conflict. It is only through the group that socially effective goals, directed at affecting the larger social structure, can be pursued. This point is developed particularly in Chap. 17.

It is, of course, possible to characterize organized management and organized labor as special-interest groups in our society. It is possible to point to the private and selfish character of some of their collective goals. But more important from our standpoint is the fact that every organized group seeks to orient itself significantly toward the larger society within which it operates. Each group fits its collective action to the range of acceptable behavior of the society. Each group, furthermore, develops a programmatic outlook and moral justification for its purposes and goals. In the examination of the self-defined moral positions of management and labor, we can find still another dimension of industrial conflict.

For management, the moral justification of its goals and policies in industrial relations takes two courses: The first is the broad contention that the stability of our society is dependent upon management's stout defense of the principles of free enterprise in the collective-bargaining relationship. The second course is to assert that supervisory and managerial techniques are designed to maximize the status of the individual worker and provide him with psychological as well as material security. Thus individual integrity and social stability are the twin moral pillars of management's position respecting collective bargaining.

American industrial management necessarily identifies itself as both the product and protector of a free-enterprise system. Many management pronouncements identify the basic welfare of our society with the strengthening of the free-enterprise system. Indeed, Chap. 12 clearly indicates how the manager's own view of his moral position has shifted from emphasis on individual opportunity and responsibility to one of social responsibility and industrial statesmanship. Bendix relates this shifting perspective to the bureaucratization of business organizations and to the complex interdependence they have with an industrial society.

At the same time, we see elaborated in Chaps. 24 through 29 the types of supervisory and managerial techniques designed to provide for the material and psychological security of the employees of industry. The moral position underlying these practices is the managerial concern for individual integrity. This is variously labeled "the new personnel philosophy," "the human-relations approach," or "scientific management" in terms much broader than Taylor implied in that phrase. There are those who would argue that management is really not interested in the individual's personal welfare, but only in getting the most out of a worker and making him like it. This cynical view ignores the fact that a self-image as an exploiter still cannot find a respectable place in our morality. While some managers may hope that social science will prove an important ally for scientific worker exploitation, other managers hold to the more generous moral position that the management and manipulation of employees is most productive when their cooperation is willingly forthcoming. Enlightened management grounds its actions to improve individual productivity in the moral precept that individual security and feelings of personal security are the foundation of willing and enthusiastic participation in the enterprise. It is notable that this represents a fundamental transformation of the Puritan ideology (see Chap. 12), in which the individual is viewed as duty-bound to give to his job and to his employer the full measure of his efforts and diligence. Now the burden of duty is seen as falling upon the employer to provide the kind of environment in which the employee is able to reach the fullest self-realization and, thereby, his highest level of performance in the interests of the enterprise. The moral imperative has shifted from the shoulders of the worker to the hands of management.

On the union side there are also two moral positions that represent self-justifications of union objectives. The one of largest scope is the contention that trade-unions are instruments of social justice. The second moral justification underlying American labor unionism is that it protects the individual worker in his immediate work environment from exploitation and degradation. These self-justifications are interrelated but serve to give moral sanction to union policies at different levels of action.

As the social balance wheel to managerial power, unions are viewed by their officials and members as the most effective curb upon the societal dominance of management. The unions see themselves as the only effective force in the society capable of checking the growing social power of a managerial class. Government may respond to the direct or indirect blandishments of the managerial elite to serve their private or special interests; the industrial and commercial middle class is relatively unorganized and impotent as a social force; the farmers are organized largely in the pursuit of very narrow interests; but labor unions are locked in direct battle with the managerial class and have the social power to checkmate or at least to balance the power of organized capital. Organized labor is fighting the battle for social justice at the only effective point in the social system, in the industrial arena itself. So goes the general tenor of one moral self-image of the union movement.

At the plant level and at the level of the individual worker-member, the union sees itself as the champion of the individual enmeshed in a bureaucratic structure over which he can exercise no control. But for the collective power of the union, the employer would have almost unrestricted opportunity to exploit his work force. Through all the instruments of collective bargaining the union seeks to minimize the exploitation of the individual worker at one of the most sensitive points of his contact with the social order, his job and means of livelihood.

In some of the classic interpretations of the American labor movement (*e.g.*, Commons and Perlman), it is concluded that only the radical unions perceived themselves as instruments of social justice, since they intended to have an articulated program of social change. The labor union rooted in American industrialism was seen as amoral and materialistic, as job conscious and striving toward the simple goal of "more, more, more." What was not so readily perceived was that, in order to achieve job control and gain more, organized labor had to enter into direct power contests with industrial management. These contests served to test the relative strength of the parties. But the conflict also required that each party seek the approbation of legitimacy from the larger society for its goals. In short, each side had to provide moral justifications for its immediate goals and tactics in order to secure, if not approval, at least the neutrality of public opinion and of the governmental instruments of social control. Thus, as one consequence of the restructuring of social power through collective bargaining, each side found it necessary to erect moral shoring for its goals and policies in the industrial power struggle.

How do the self-justifications of management and organized labor match up? Particularly, how do they relate to the issue of industrial conflict? Both groups see their goals satisfied within the structure of a free-enterprise system. While management insists that the system has reached its mature and effective form, unions contend that further development still lies ahead. Management wants to consolidate the system and urges its course on the grounds that social stability will bring tranquility and permanent order to the social system. The union movement wants additional steps as the fulfillment of social justice for working men and, therefore, seeks to shift the centers of social power in the direction of organized labor.

At the plant level, management finds at its disposal a wide range of managerial techniques for adjusting people to jobs or jobs to people in the interests, at least in part, of preserving the individual's psychological and material integrity. The union justifies much of its plant-level activities as being motivated by the same values. Here the difference between labor and management turns on means, in relation to the moral self-images that each has.

Does it not seem clear that conflict will be the most probable outcome of the differing moral convictions of the parties to industrial relations? We tend to see positions in any conflict as being polarized. Management is conservative, labor is radical; management champions free enterprise, labor is the instrument of statism or socialism; management wants to increase productivity, labor to restrict it. On any given issue these polarizations may be accurate, or, indeed, their reverse may even be true. But what we are likely to overlook is that a moral self-justification represents the sentiments, the beliefs, the ideology of a group, and these transcend immediate goals and tactical moves. The fundamental moral values of a group run deep, are resistant to change, and persistently guide the strategy and tactics of the group. It is the moral values of a group that give it its "main drift" (to utilize one of Mills's phrases of Chap. 10) within the social system.

What about cooperation? Homans, in Chap. 4, makes an eloquent plea and a substantial case for cooperation in industry. He points to this as one of the great frontiers of our society where tremendous unrealized potentials remain to be explored and exploited.

It is perhaps important to see that cooperation is a genuine possibility in every union-management relationship. The union contract is one product of such cooperation, as are the grievance procedure, joint time study, common support of tariffs to protect a given industry, and the like. The range of potential areas of cooperation is limited only by the range of potential interests of the parties. There is no sociological or psychological principle that precludes the possibility of cooperation in some elements of the union-management relationship.

The crucial question, however, is whether or not the entire relationship can be grounded in cooperation. For example, is the given instance of cooperation the product of the resolution of basic conflicts at some other point in the economy, as in the case of a crucial bargain being followed in a dependent industry or plant? Is the cooperation a consequence of a highly protected position, in which it takes the form of collusion against third parties? Does it result when the management of a marginal or depressed company abdicates its managerial direction and, at least temporarily, places the union in the unaccustomed role of codirector of the enterprise for mutual survival? Does cooperation take the limited form of a suggestion system in which either the individual or the union is the agency for forwarding suggestions, the product of which is at least partially shared with the suggestor? These are the common situations underlying the instances of cooperation reported in the literature. We are sometimes tempted to take the existence of these forms of cooperation as evidence to support the generality of the principle of union-management or management-men cooperation. These points are well illustrated in Chap. 27 on union-management cooperation.

But perhaps there are important aspects of the social structure that at least complicate the development of cooperative relationships. Homans himself points to some of the elements of an industrial organization that are universal in character, regardless of the nature of the socioeconomic system. These are features at the company and plant level that make cooperation between management and men difficult.

At the level of the social system, we would have to consider the implication of the existence of power and the use of power instruments as group weapons. As Blumer points out in Chap. 17, power relations are a basic social process in a free society. He suggests that power relations are conflictful in character. Does this necessitate the translation of power relations into other kinds of social process (such as "codified" or "sympathetic" relations, in Blumer's terms) before general cooperation is possible? Could this conceivably be accomplished within the framework of our society? Were all the basic relationships in a society codified, we would have a highly static society. If the fundamental relationships were sympathetic in character, we would have anarchy.

In Chap. 3 it is suggested that industrial conflict is a consequence of the emergent character of our society. The conflicts in the industrial arena signalize the developing, dynamic, and delicately balanced features of our industrial economy. The resolution of these conflicts symbolizes a new equilibrium in social relationships and social structures, ready to change, in turn, in still newer directions. In short, is it really an either-or choice between conflict and cooperation with which we are faced? Perhaps the most realistic position is to suggest that conflict is functional in a free society and that the direction of the social change which is its product will leave greater room in the future for cooperative relations.

All the later sections of the book contribute further to the exploration and answering of the questions that have been considered in a preliminary way in this chapter. The remainder of Part 1 deals with industrial relations in terms of the changing history and significance of the strike and in reference to differing philosophies concerning the place of industrial conflict in a democratic society.

Part 2 is concerned with the nature and causes of industrial conflict. The authors there examine major determinants and conditions responsible for conflict: the psychological factors, the structure and functioning of labor unions and corporate organizations involved in conflict, and the broad social and economic contexts which are conducive to conflict or peace.

Part 3 turns explicitly to the problems of social policy and social action. What are the ways in which industrial conflict is dealt with, and how may it be better dealt with? Here the contributors summarize the conclusions that now appear to them best supported by experience and research pertaining to collective bargaining and related processes for handling disagreements; to the efforts of management, unions, and government to remove causes of conflict; and to the activities of government in regulating and controlling labor-management affairs.

Part 4, in four brief chapters, highlights certain experiences in other nations. This material affords opportunity for interesting and useful comparisons with the American scene.

Finally, in Part 5, the editors attempt to pull together the principal suggestions and the chief questions that emerge from the entire volume. What light does the series of chapters throw on present trends, alternative roads ahead, and social policy decisions that are still in the making?

CHAPTER 2 THE NATURAL HISTORY OF THE STRIKE *

Arthur M. Ross   *University of California (Berkeley)*

THE theme of this chapter is that the meaning of the strike, as a "weapon of labor," is largely dependent on the nature of the organization sponsoring it. The outstanding fact about the strike in the United States is that one kind of organization, the business union, has been able to achieve a prescriptive, although not uncontested, right to the use of this weapon and a proprietary interest in the discontent it represents. The union did not create the community of interest among workers; the factory system did that. The union did not originate industrial unrest but merely sharpened and took advantage of it. The union did not invent the strike but only sought to appropriate it for its own purposes. This it was able to achieve because of the fact that, in structure and orientation, it was best equipped for strategic employment of the strike weapon. What has the strike become in the hands of business unionism and what might it have become in other hands?

The Strike as an Opportunity

Discontent is the prime mover of economic and social change. Ever since the emergence of a numerous wage-earning class, groups and movements of quite diverse tendencies have claimed the right to exploit this discontent and convert it into a vehicle for change. Labor unrest is commonly centered on specific grievances, which have to be remedied after a fashion if any organization is to become the chosen instrument. Nevertheless, it can be turned in more than one direction and used for more than one purpose; and indeed many different kinds of organization have gone fishing in the troubled waters of rank-and-file discontent. Clearly it makes a great deal of difference which kind of organization has had the best luck.

In the United States the business union has achieved a virtual monopoly of the labor strike. We take this fact for granted today and thereby fail to recognize its significance. A century ago it was not clear by any means that this would happen. What was the situation then? A multitude of workers

* Readers who are familiar with the traditional literature of labor economics (Commons, Hoxie, Perlman, etc.) will recognize that some of the ideas in this essay are not particularly original. Inasmuch as the volume is addressed to a wider audience, such material is appropriately included here.

I am glad to acknowledge my indebtedness to Chancellor Clark Kerr and the late Prof. L. H. Fisher of the University of California for advice and counsel in preparing this manuscript.—A. M. R.

had been brought together, out of the isolation of the countryside and the village, into the factories and cities of the new industrial society. One kind of cooperation and one form of discipline were demanded by the logic of the productive process. But the habits of cooperation and discipline could be used in other ways. The workers had been organized for division of labor. They could be organized for other purposes. Their labor was applied collectively and could be withheld collectively.

These were the necessary conditions for the use of the strike. It is signifi-- cant that the existence of unions is not among these conditions. A strike is a temporary withholding of function, whereas a union is a continuing associa- tion whose life is always somewhat distinct from the lives of the individuals who happen to make up its membership at any one time. Every strike has leaders, but a union has officials; and there is a world of difference between the two. Every strike comes to an end and is succeeded by a settlement of some kind, but this is not necessarily the same as collective bargaining as we know it.

Some of the early strikes in England and the United States were similar to present-day industrial conflicts. They were sponsored by continuing labor organizations, they had well-defined objectives, and they showed evidence of carefully formulated strategy. Many, however, had an essentially different character. Rather than organized, they were unorganized; or, to be more accurate, the striking workers were thrown together into an *ad hoc* organiza- tion, with or without a name, which often disappeared when the strike had ended. Rather than calculated, they were impulsive; and although based on deeply felt grievances, they were not marked by clear notions of how the grievances were to be remedied or of how the remedies were to be obtained. G. D. H. Cole has described some of the improvident revolts which occurred during the early decades of the Industrial Revolution in England.[1] Desperate outbursts of this kind were not so common in the United States, where the factory system was introduced under somewhat different circumstances. How- ever, John R. Commons and his associates have shown that a large number of the early strikes among skilled workers were spontaneous (in the sense that they were not sponsored by any continuing organization). They have also shown that the incidence of violence in the early strikes was inversely proportional to the degree of organization.[2] There is evidence that the virtually exclusive proprietorship over the strike which trade-unions presently exercise in the United States was not achieved until after World War I and that more than one-third of all strikes were "unorganized" as late as the turn of the century. During many of the years between 1880 and 1900, the number of workers involved in strikes was greater than the number of union members.[3] A report issued by the Commissioner of Labor in 1907 showed that from 38 to 48 per cent of all strikes were "not ordered by labor organizations" during

---

[1] G. D. H. Cole, *A Short History of the British Working Class Movement, Vol. 1, 1789–1848*, London, G. Allen, 1925, pp. 12–110, *passim*.

[2] John R. Commons *et al.*, *History of Labor in the United States*, Vol. 1, New York, Macmillan, 1918, pp. 109–155, 412–416.

[3] This statement is based upon Leo Wolman, *Growth of American Trade Unions, 1880–1923*, New York, National Bureau of Economic Research, 1924; and upon various bulletins of the U.S. Bureau of Labor Statistics.

each of the 5-year periods between 1880 and 1900.[4] From reports of the Bureau of Labor Statistics it is possible to calculate the proportion of strikes among nonunion workers from 1916 up to the present. This proportion, which stood at 17.4 per cent in 1916, fell steadily until about 1921. It rose again between 1925 and 1933, when unionism was in the doldrums and then declined once more as trade-union membership grew. During the past decade the proportion has been nominal.

Thus trade-unions devoted to the practice of collective bargaining have now achieved a virtual monopoly of strikes in the United States (as well as in England). A century ago it was not at all clear that the strike weapon could be appropriated so successfully by the business union.

The Grand National and the Knights of Labor

There were some who were not inclined to make use of the strike or did not know how. These groups could not achieve lasting leadership of the labor movement. Consider the fate of Robert Owen's Grand National Consolidated Trades Union in the 1830's. It enlisted more than half a million members within a few weeks after being established.

> Workers of every sort flocked into the new organization. It enrolled not only skilled craftsmen and factory operatives in the major trades, but workers in every conceivable occupation. Agricultural labourers were enrolled in many districts. . . . Lodges of "Industrious Females" were formed in many centres, and "Miscellaneous Lodges" enlisted not only manual workers in the scattered trades, but also many sympathisers from the professional classes. The aim of the Union, in Owen's mind, was nothing less than the inclusion in one great body of the whole of the "productive classes." [5]

Owen, as is well known, was chiefly concerned with education and cooperation. He was interested in strikes as a medium for organizing producers' cooperatives, and he had a vague project for a general strike of the whole working class with the object of securing the universal 8-hour day or perhaps of achieving an immediate peaceful revolution, but he could not see himself as a run-of-the-mill strike leader. He fell out with some of his associates whom he believed to be stirring up class hatred; and after a number of disastrous strikes and lockouts, which were not of Owen's making, the Consolidated Union dwindled away.

The essential difficulty was that Owen could not do business with the trade-unionists of the time. He "disapproved of sectional (*i.e.*, non-general) strikes, and was by temperament unfitted for leadership in a militant working-class campaign. . . . He had hoped by the power of union to achieve a bloodless and painless revolution; he certainly had never meant to become the leader of a mere strike agitation." [6]

The career of the Knights of Labor in the United States was not very

[4] *Annual Report of the Commissioner of Labor*, Washington, Government Printing Office, 1910.

[5] G. D. H. Cole, *The Life of Robert Owen*, London, Macmillan & Co., 1930, pp. 278–279.

[6] Cole, *A Short History of the British Working Class Movement*, p. 127.

different. The Order was founded in 1869 as a trade-union. It was similar to other unions except for its principle of universal solidarity. The first Master Workman, Uriah Stephens, was a garment cutter and a trade-unionist. But in the later years the Master Workman (Terence V. Powderly) and the General Executive Board were out of sympathy with the use of the strike. Their opposition stemmed partly from the failure of most strikes during the 1873 depression and partly from their emphasis on education, cooperation, and arbitration. A defense fund established in 1880 was to be distributed 10 per cent for education, 60 per cent for cooperation, and 30 per cent for strikes. The Board declared that strikes cause more injury than benefit and that all attempts to "foment" them should be discouraged. Before a strike could be supported, four different "arbitration committees" of the Order had to act upon it.

Ironically, it was a series of successful strikes which made the name of the Order a household word and a series of unsuccessful strikes which brought it to ruin. After 15 years of existence the Order had a membership of only 50,000 in 1883. By 1886 it had grown to 700,000 members, and by 1890 it had fallen to 100,000.[7] Four out of the five large railway strikes in 1884 and 1885 were victorious, but

> . . . it cannot be said that the successful strike activity of the Knights . . . was due to the new Assistance Fund or the policy of the Order. . . . Strikes were won not by careful planning but by spontaneous revolt which caught the employers unprepared. The first success on the railroads in the case of the Union Pacific was so sudden and complete as to create an illusion that it was easy and could be repeated at will. Others followed but each one found the employers better prepared until finally the Southwestern System turned on the Order and utterly defeated it. None of these strikes was managed by the Order from beginning to end. They began with locals or districts and drew in the general officers only when they showed signs of failure.[8]

The greatest victory was against the Wabash System, and yet Powderly and the executive board settled for a promise that members would not be discriminated against. Neither recognition nor collective bargaining was even requested. Ware [9] states that

> . . . nothing could reveal more clearly Powderly's ineptitude as a bargainer than his failure to demand something more realistic. The fact is that Powderly was essentially a pedagogue and had no interest in, nor equipment for, the major trade union job of negotiation. The general executive board simply wanted to avoid trouble.

The fiasco of the Southwestern strike in March of 1886 and the snatching of defeat out of the jaws of victory in the meat-packing strike of the same year hastened the demise of the organization.

Revolutionary Groups

Organizations, like the Consolidated Union and the Knights of Labor, which wanted to lead the working class without using the strike could not

[7] Wolman, *op. cit.*, p. 32.

[8] Norman J. Ware, *The Labor Movement in the United States, 1860–95*, New York, Appleton, 1929, p. 135.

[9] *Ibid.*, p. 145.

survive. But there were others who were willing to accept it and had a use for it. Of these the most notable have been the various groups of revolutionaries on the one hand and the business unionists on the other.

In Chap. 19 of this volume Prof. Taft describes the doctrines of the syndicalists and communists relating to industrial conflict. Consequently there is no need for a full recital of these doctrines at this point. All revolutionary groups have agreed that trade-unions are schools and organizing centers of revolution and that strikes are a means of preparing for the violent overthrow of capitalism. The value of the strike, they have held, is that it arouses the workers from their lethargy, sharpens their awareness of class conflict, and (in Bakunin's words) "fuses them into a molten state" from which they can be formed "in accordance with their demands and instincts." The great danger in the strike, they have insisted, is that it *may* be settled in such a fashion as to diminish, rather than intensify, the revolutionary potential of the workers. Thus Sorel complained of "all the well-intentioned people, all the 'progressives' and friends of the Republic . . . the preachers of ethics and sociology" who attempt to mediate disputes; and he suggested that the proper response was "to repay with black ingratitude the benevolence of those who would protect the workers, to meet with insults the homilies of the defenders of human fraternity, and to reply by blows to the advances of the propagators of social peace." [10] For the same reason the communists developed an elaborate technique of denouncing as "sellouts" all strike settlements made by noncommunist union officials, and cultivated the technique to such a high degree of perfection that it could be applied with equal assurance whether the strike was actually successful or unsuccessful.[11]

Professor Taft points out that the life process of many syndicalist and communist labor organizations has been largely dissociated from their formal ideology. The career of the Industrial Workers of the World (IWW) in the United States must be reckoned an exception and demonstrates the fatal weakness in the syndicalist theory of industrial conflict when taken seriously. As a syndicalist union, the IWW had nothing but contempt for conventional business-union objectives: recognition, collective bargaining, and labor agreements. Bill Haywood reasoned that "as all is fair in love and war, industrial unionists should abrogate all agreements which would compel them to violate the principles of unionism." [12] As late as 1916, the by-laws of the organization prohibited "(*a*) any agreement wherein any specified length of time is mentioned for the continuance of said agreement" and "(*b*) any agreement wherein the membership is bound to give notice before making demands affecting hours, wages or shop conditions." [13] Most contemptible of all was the strike for recognition; in fact the IWW took the position that it was unwilling to recognize the employer.

For an action group, the IWW retained a remarkable ideological purity.

[10] Georges Sorel, *Reflections on Violence*, 3d ed., trans. T. E. Hulme, New York, B. W. Huebsch, 1912, p. 6.

[11] For skillful examples of the technique, see Earl Browder, *Communism in the United States*, New York, International Publishers, 1935, pp. 218–219, 251–257.

[12] Paul F. Brissenden, *The I. W. W., A Study of American Syndicalism*, Columbia University Studies in History, Economics, and Public Law, 83 (1919), 324.

[13] *Ibid.*

It scorned not only collective bargaining but all the other encumbrances of an institutionalized labor movement: local organizations, paid officers, dues of more than nominal size, treasuries, and strike funds. It was never able to raid the membership of functioning unions but had considerable success with unorganized workers, particularly the immigrant workers of the East and the migratory workers of the West. It was primarily interested in capitalizing upon spontaneous strikes as a medium for revolutionary propaganda. As Saposs has observed, the IWW did not organize the unorganized but merely supplied leadership where spontaneous strikes occurred.[14]

The strike tactics of the IWW had many advantages.

> The I. W. W. could be as sensational and reckless as it saw fit. It was not confronted with the problem of explaining intricate practices such as collective bargaining and trade agreements. It could make the wildest demands and accusations against employers since it paid slight heed to public sentiment and did not expect to negotiate directly with the employers. . . .[15]

Immigrant and migratory workers were not alone in responding to the IWW's strike leadership. The organization was temporarily quite successful in Southern cotton-mill towns, for example. Moreover, most of the strikes led by the IWW were victorious.

Still there was obviously something missing in the formula. The IWW aroused the greatest enthusiasm among unorganized workers but was unable to hold their confidence. The local "militants" eventually became disillusioned. Twenty years after being established, the IWW was disintegrating.

What was wrong was quite evidently the failure to build unions in the wake of successful strikes. Outside of strike periods, IWW leaders were not directly concerned with the immediate economic interests of their followers. Permanent unions were not established to protect these economic interests. After the prominent IWW leaders had withdrawn from the scene of the strike, local leaders were not equal to the task of perpetuating the jerry-built organization. The policy of discouraging the employment of paid officials and the accumulation of treasures was an additional handicap. Concessions won in strikes were gradually whittled away. If another strike was to be conducted, the workers had to be organized all over again.[16] "Thus," Saposs concludes, "while at first the I. W. W. gripped the imagination of the immigrant and other unorganized workers so that they regarded it as a Messiah come to deliver them from their economic servitude, as they became somewhat oriented and conversant with practical trade union achievements, they began to sense the defects in its policies and tactics. . . ."[17]

In a way, the place of the IWW in the revolutionary movement corresponds with that of the Shakers among religious sects. The Shakers made a practice of total celibacy in their communal settlements. This merely reflected, in somewhat extreme fashion, the high regard in which the virtue of continence is held by all Protestant groups, but it raised a serious obstacle in

[14] David J. Saposs, *Left Wing Unionism,* New York, International Publishers, 1926, pp. 142–143.

[15] *Ibid.,* pp. 144–145.

[16] *Ibid.,* pp. 148–149.

[17] *Ibid.,* p. 152.

the way of survival. The IWW had a total disdain for the appurtenances of business unionism. This was good syndicalist doctrine, but it meant that the IWW could have only a temporary lease on the discontent of unorganized workers.

The Communists have never carried dialectical materialism to the point of interfering with practical activity. At the core of their ideology is the proposition that the proletariat is endowed with its own motive power in the form of an inherent revolutionary drive; but this conception has not stood in the way of recognizing the true significance of leadership. Thus in a highly orthodox exegesis of Marx's views on trade-unions, Lozovsky [18] states that

> . . . the political significance of the strike depends on the size and scope of the movement. . . . If the leaders from the very outset lead it into narrow craft channels, the political edge of the strike is blunted and it is immediately deprived of its chief content. . . . If a strike which has purely economic demands as its point of departure is from the very beginning consciously directed along the lines of combining it with the political struggle, it yields maximum effects.

Furthermore the Communists have shown a healthy respect for the value of an "apparatus." They have had no prejudice against organization, discipline, bureaucracy, or financial provision and have never made the characteristic IWW mistake of winning strikes and then leaving the workers to their own devices. Once in control of an organization, trade-union or otherwise, they have hung on with iron persistence, usually preferring to follow a scorched-earth policy rather than to relinquish control of a functioning apparatus.

Communist strategy in the field of economic conflict is clearly more powerful than the utopian or syndicalist, yet it also contains a major dilemma. Unless we recognize this dilemma we cannot understand the working out of the strategy in practice nor appreciate the difficulties under which the Communists have labored in the more industrialized nations. After all, none of the Communist victories has been won in the manner anticipated by Marx, who certainly expected that England and Germany would fall before Russia or China. Obviously the movement has had much better success in feudal agricultural societies than in industrial societies. Czechoslovakia is the only nation which was well industrialized when it passed into Communist control, and the circumstances under which this occurred were not those which Marx predicted.

The problem is created by the conjunction of the agitational motive and the organizational motive in the same body of strategy. The agitational motive dictates the use of the strike as an instrument of propaganda, for sharpening class lines, instilling revolutionary sentiments, etc. It demands that the grievances of the rank and file should not be settled conclusively within the framework of capitalism. The organizational motive emphasizes the value of a functioning trade-union apparatus (subservient to the political apparatus, of course) and dictates the use of the strike as a means of building and maintaining a stable union. The IWW was governed solely by the agitational motive. Although this may have been unwise in the long run, at least there were no insoluble problems

---

[18] A. Lozovsky, *Marx and the Trade Unions,* New York, International Publishers. 1935, pp. 134–135.

of choice. Business unions, influenced mainly by the organizational motive, are likewise in a position to proceed single-mindedly. But the Communists have had to carry water on both shoulders; and as if this were not enough, at times they have been subject to a third set of requirements, the requirements of Russian foreign policy. Under these circumstances, the life of a revolutionary becomes difficult indeed.

So long as the Communist group is operating from the outside or as a militant minority faction on the inside, the procedure is clear enough. It consists of the following five steps, which are all compatible with one another: (1) agitate the workers' grievances and catalyze their discontent; (2) show the effectiveness of Communist strike leadership and tactics; (3) expose the weakness of the existing union officials (the "labor lieutenants of the capitalist class"); (4) "deepen the political character of the struggle"; and (5) denounce the settlement as a sellout. This much is easy enough.

The really serious dilemmas are encountered when Communists cooperate with other elements in a united-front program or come into full control of a union. The older and more firmly established is the union, the more difficult does it become to give priority to the agitational motive. The union is encumbered with contract commitments. A more conciliatory type of leadership is rising to the top in the local units. The workers, protected by seniority, have grown older and feel more secure; some of their pressing grievances have been adjusted; and having become educated in the ways of business unionism, they are not interested in embarking on improvident strikes. But if priority is given indefinitely to the organizational motive, then the revolutionary purpose is sacrificed and the economic struggle is robbed of all of its political significance. Eventually the point is reached when the officials hold their positions on sufrance. They must continue to behave like good trade-unionists or they will be displaced. Should the Communist movement then take a turn to the left and demand a renewal of agitational activity, the moment of crisis has arrived. A fundamental choice can no longer be avoided. If the officials break with the Party, they can retain their position as effective trade-union leaders. If they remain loyal to the Party, they will be voted out of office, or the members will desert to some other union, or the organization will go under in the wake of disastrous strikes.

Essentially this has been the career of communism in the CIO (I am using the term loosely and without regard to the question of formal Party membership). The Communists were good organizers and tireless workers and cooperated vigorously in building the new industrial unions. They rose to power in many local unions and a number of international unions. There were some difficulties during the period of the Russo-German pact (such as the Allis-Chalmers and North American Aviation strikes), but the implicit conflict between the agitational and organizational motives did not come to a head until after the war, when the Communist movement turned to the left once more and the popular front collapsed. This occurred in 1946; and a few years later the center of Communist strength in the CIO had been eliminated.

Developments in France are even more instructive. In 1946 the Communists were firmly in control of the General Confederation of Labor and of all its important national unions except for those representing teachers, office workers, and government employees. With about 5 million members, this was the most valuable apparatus ever possessed by the Communists in any capitalist nation. They had acquired it by virtue of their record during the resistance period, their freedom from the taint of Nazi collaboration, their energy and discipline as union leaders and organizers, and their popular-front policy. By the end of 1948 many of these advantages had been squandered away in strikes: the vast strike movement of November and December of 1947, involving more than 2 million workers; the violent coal strike during the autumn of 1948; and a number of additional industry-wide and multi-industry strikes. Although there were genuine rank-and-file grievances in each of these stoppages, the results were quite disastrous from any organizational standpoint. A large section of the Confederation broke away to form the *Force Ouvrière*. As time went on, workers responded to strike orders with diminishing enthusiasm. The total strength of the labor movement declined and repressive legislation was enacted.

The only explanation for this reckless program is that the organizational motive has been superseded by other considerations. Of these there were two. First was the renewal of revolutionary agitation. With uncontrolled inflation, black markets, inequitable tax policies, etc., conditions were ideal for agitational strikes. Second, and probably more important, was the influence of Russian foreign policy and the conflict over the European Recovery Plan.

Thus postwar strikes in France were conducted in a highly sophisticated context. They were at one and the same time a protest on the part of the rank and file against the deterioration of living standards, a means of pushing forward the domestic propaganda program of the Communist Party, and a response to the problems of Russian foreign policy in Western Europe. These purposes could all be served simultaneously, but only at the price of serious organizational losses. The besetting problem of revolutionary strike strategy has not yet been satisfactorily solved.

Business Unionism

In a classic volume, *Trade Unionism in the United States,* Robert F. Hoxie distinguished five types of unionism: business, uplift, revolutionary, predatory, and dependent. Business unionism, he said,[19]

> . . . is essentially trade-conscious, rather than class-conscious. . . . It is conservative in the sense that it professes belief in natural rights, and accepts as inevitable, if not as just, the existing capitalistic organization and the wage system, as well as existing property rights and the binding force of contract. It regards unionism mainly as a bargaining institution and seeks its ends chiefly through collective bargaining, supported by such methods as experience from time to time indicates to be effective in sustaining and increasing its bargaining power. In harmony with its business character it tends to emphasize discipline within the organization, and is prone to develop strong leadership and to become somewhat autocratic in government, although government and leaders are ordinarily held pretty strictly accountable to the pragmatic test.

[19] Robert F. Hoxie, *Trade Unionism in the United States,* New York, Appleton, 1917, pp. 45–46.

Hoxie's definition was influenced by the fact that the craft-union structure and "voluntaristic" philosophy of the AFL were then predominant. But Hoxie's definition can accommodate industrial unions if "industry" is substituted for "craft" and if allowance is made for ancillary political action on a somewhat broader front. If primary reliance upon collective bargaining and a belief in "industrial partnership" under capitalism can be regarded as the central features of business unionism, then the advent of industrial unions has not brought any essential change. Business unionism is still the dominant strain in the American labor movement.

Our major thesis is that the meaning of industrial conflict is largely dependent on the nature of the sponsoring organization. Let us now examine what the strike has become in the hands of the business union.

The first contribution of the business union has been to rationalize the conduct of the strike. It has attempted with great success to eliminate the irrational emotional outburst. Anger and resentment are dampened when the moment is inappropriate and accentuated when the time is ripe; emotion is stored up and paid out in the light of cold strategical requirements. An essential part of the union leader's basic equipment is the mastery of strike strategy and tactics. He must know when to strike and when not to strike, how to mobilize the rank and file, how to conduct a propaganda offensive, how to use the strike as an organizing medium, how to form alliances, how to deal with strikebreakers, and how to handle public relations, legal matters, strike relief, etc.[20] Unless he is committed to securing an unconditional surrender (which is highly unlikely inasmuch as the strike is a part of the bargaining process), he must maintain contact with the adversary during the period of the conflict.

An essential ingredient in the task of union management is the enforcement of discipline. The "eager beaver" and the "hothead" are the natural enemies of the union official. They have a disconcerting tendency to assume that every grievance must be settled here and now. The union official insists that there is a time and place for everything, including the settlement of grievances and the alleviation of discontent. It is up to the professional and not the amateur to select the time and place. Improvident protest movements must be avoided. Valuable contracts and relationships must not be sacrificed for a mess of pottage. Workers must not jump the gun even when strike action is indicated. When the call is sounded, however, they must respond to the last man. Conscientious objectors and nonresisters are accorded little sympathy. While the conflict persists, strikers must observe the rules of war, to a reasonable extent. And when the armistice has been signed, they must lay down their arms. Naïve and quixotic notions of absolute justice are useful as propaganda weapons but the business-union official does not make the error of swallowing his propaganda whole.

In the hands of the business union the strike has not only been invested with rationality, strategy, and discipline but has also been adjusted to the economic and political mores of the community. This is seen most clearly in the ready acceptance by union leaders of the doctrine that a collective-bargaining agreement is a binding contract to be observed as a matter of sacred honor and

---

[20] See *Handbook of Trade Union Methods*, New York, International Ladies' Garment Workers' Union, Education Department, 1937, pp. 37–56.

good business practice. Among the few points of agreement in President Truman's unsuccessful Labor-Management Conference of November, 1945, was the one affirming the sanctity of contract. "Collective bargaining agreements should contain provisions that grievances and disputes involving the interpretation or application of the terms of the agreement are to be settled without resort to strikes, lockouts, or other interruptions. . . ." [21] This has become standard practice throughout most of the industry. It is true that union leaders objected when the Taft-Hartley Act made them liable in court for breach of contract, but primarily because they were doubtful of their ability to control all the members and nonmembers employed in the bargaining units which were covered by collective agreements.

By virtue of the adherence to the contract system, strikes have been localized not only in time but in scope as well. This is shown by the decline in the relative importance of the sympathetic strike as collective bargaining and contracting have become more prevalent. One might surmise that the growth of unions would increase the incidence of secondary action by instilling greater solidarity among the workers and providing better channels of communication and better means of collaboration. But this would be to misinterpret the real meaning of business unionism, and the facts are exactly opposite. Many of the early strikes in the United States, such as the 10-hour-day strikes, were not well defined by trade or industry and spilled over into a variety of local activities. Available statistics for the period since 1880 show that the incidence of secondary strikes, although never very great, has declined continuously. These statistics are summarized in Table 2.1.

Table 2.1 **Sympathetic Strikes, as Percentage of All Strikes**

Period	Number of strikes	Workers involved	Man-days of idleness
1881–1905	3.7	4.7	n.a.
1906–1915	n.a.	n.a.	n.a.
1916–1926	1.9	n.a.	n.a.
1927–1936 *	1.5	3.1	1.3
1937–1947 *	0.9	1.7	0.6

SOURCE: Publications of U.S. Bureau of Labor Statistics.

* Averages of annual percentages. If the war years (1942–1944) are eliminated, the percentages for 1937–1947 are as follows: 1.1, 1.9, and 0.8.

n. a.—not available.

The business-union strike, in contrast with the syndicalist or communist strike, is conducted so as to minimize unnecessary damage to the industry, inconvenience to the community, and loss of public opinion. The delivery of milk to schools and hospitals is one example of the special arrangements that are made. It is an unwritten law that any strike which threatens to paralyze the economy (*e.g.,* the railroad strike of 1946) will be dealt with summarily. The militant, left-wing International Longshoremen's and Warehousemen's Union temporarily interrupted its strike on the Pacific Coast during 1948 to unload

[21] *President's National Labor-Management Conference, Summary and Committee Reports,* Washington. U.S. Department of Labor, Division of Labor Standards, 1946, p. 45.

an elephant for the Sacramento zoo, as well as various other perishable cargoes. Unions and employers often enter into informal understandings concerning the conduct of strikes. Sometimes these understandings are set down in writing as formal agreements. For example, The Lionel Corp. and the Playthings, Jewelry and Novelty Workers International Union (CIO) signed a joint stipulation in April, 1948, at the outset of a strike. It was agreed by and between the parties that nonunionists could enter the plant, that the union would supply members to carry on maintenance and unload raw materials, that the company would not attempt to perform regular production work, and that shipments would not be made from the plant. At one point the union sent in enough employees to run out 100 samples of toy locomotives for use by distributors. In January, 1946, on the eve of the nationwide strike in the steel industry, the International Policy Committee of the United Steelworkers passed a resolution providing as follows:

> Staff Representatives and Local Union Officers, under the direction of the District Directors, shall make all necessary arrangements with local plant, mill or mine managements for the continued employment of necessary stand-by men or service forces during the strike. Such stand-by men or service forces shall be employed for the sole purpose of preventing deterioration of production equipment or absolutely necessary community utility services.

Pursuant to this agreement oral or written arrangements were made at all plants.

In the adjustment of strikes to the requirements of the enterprise system, much of the heat and emotion have disappeared, as well as most of the violence. This is particularly true after recognition has been won and collective bargaining has been established. Occasionally a bread-and-butter strike breaks out into real violence (*e.g.*, the meat-packing and West Coast oil-refinery disputes in 1948) but the typical modern strike is a cold business proposition. The rhetorical forays and rebuttals between Walter Reuther and C. E. Wilson leading to the General Motors strike in 1946 made headlines, but the strike front itself presented a scene of unbroken quiet. It was hard to believe that the dramatic sit-down strikes of 1936 and 1937 had taken place in these same plants. At the outset of the 1948 maritime strike on the West Coast, longshoremen and seamen, like a group of Civil War veterans at a GAR reunion, eagerly rehearsed their memories of the 1934 San Francisco general strike; but after the first 2 or 3 days, picket-line duty became a steady bore. Of course, it would be wrong to imply that business unionism alone has transformed the strike into a highly conventionalized form of conflict. This could not have happened without profound changes in employer attitudes and practices and in the legal framework of collective bargaining. The important point here is that the business union has willingly participated in the process of transformation, to the point where the auto workers did not bother even to mobilize pickets and the longshoremen forbade gambling on the picket line in order not to alienate public opinion.

Although the growth in trade-union strength might have been the basis for a policy of industrial *Schrecklichkeit,* such a policy has not developed. In a recent study, "Strike Experience in Five Countries," [22] the author has shown, on the basis of considerable statistical evidence, that

> . . . although patterns of industrial conflict differ from place to place, a common chain of developments is apparent in the majority of the countries. . . . (*a*) Labor unions have been growing in size and strength. (*b*) An increasing percentage of the employed labor force has been drawn into strikes. (*c*) Over the years such strikes have been growing shorter. (*d*) Consequently, despite higher rates of participation, the loss of working time per wage and salary earner has been diminishing.

(The last-mentioned development has not yet come to pass in the United States but is clearly evident in statistics relating to Australia, Great Britain, and Sweden.) It was concluded that

> . . . if loss of working time is any basis for judgment, then the amount of damage occasioned by strikes has been growing less rather than greater. The shortening of the average length of strike indicates that a process of accommodation has taken place between the practice of industrial conflict, on the one hand, and the requirement that intolerable interruption of output be avoided, on the other. [23]

These conclusions are worth reiterating here.

But the most significant influence of business unionism has been to draw the revolutionary sting out of strikes. Every one of the prescriptions of Sorel and Marx has been violated. Whereas, according to the revolutionaries, the strike should serve to sharpen class lines and accentuate class conflict, it is now conducted as an integral part of an effort to achieve industrial partnership. Instead of outraging the middle class and isolating the workers, the business-union leader spares no effort to make the strike as quiet, dignified, and respectable as circumstances will permit. The powerful symbolism of labor conflict, with its heroes, martyrs, and battle memories, is employed not to build the revolution but to build a social institution which increasingly insulates the workers against the proponents of revolutionary change.

Thus the business-union leader, the "merchant of discontent," puts a price tag on the class struggle. He is equipped to make peace as well as to declare war, and he makes it possible for the employer to purchase labor peace for a 10-cent increase and a union shop. The great advantage of business unionism, from the standpoint of survival and growth, is that by establishing these terms of sale it is able to avoid the conflict between organizational and agitational motives—a conflict which, as we have seen, has been the besetting and insuperable problem of syndicalist and communist unionism. The safety and health of the organization are given top priority, and the long-run economic change is left to take care of itself.

Conclusion

It is true enough that labor peace has to be purchased over and over again, that there are strong inflationary pressures in a democratic society, and that

---

[22] *Industrial and Labor Relations Review*, 4 (April, 1951), 323–342.

[23] *Ibid.*, pp. 334–335.

each time the price is apt to be higher. The business-union leader must hold his men in line and keep himself in office, and therefore every generation of leaders must strike a new and stiffer bargain with the managers of industry. Over the years substantial changes are wrought in economic life regardless of the wishes or intentions of the individuals involved. There are many who point to these changes and argue that the insatiable demands of the business union for "more and more and more" will accomplish obliquely the revolutionary transformation which, as a direct objective, would be wholly repugnant. But the evidence to date is by no means convincing. It indicates rather that abundant resources and a dynamic technology have made it possible to accommodate the union's minimum demands without altering the essential framework of the economic system in the United States. When all is said and done, the relative positions of the economic classes have not been reversed. The period of highest corporate profits and of greatest union strength is one and the same period. Labor's share of the national income varies within narrow limits whether the labor movement is strong or weak. Changes in wages and productivity move diversely over short periods but consistently over longer terms. The central core of managerial control over production policies, employment levels, and prices has not been penetrated to any substantial extent.

If it is granted, and labor history appears conclusive on the point, that the discontent of workers is a phenomenon which grows naturally out of the master-servant relationship and that the organization of this discontent owes more to the factory system than to the labor union, then it becomes difficult indeed to share certain contemporary concerns about a "laboristic age." For this mistakes both the character and the function of the labor movement, in America at least. The strike, which is the expression of labor's power, is clearly no invention of the labor movement nor any product of trade-union strategy. It is more correctly viewed as one of the data of the industrial situation and the relevant question is not whether there will be strikes but for what objects the striking power of organized workers will be used. From this standpoint the business union has received less than the conservative recognition which is its due. The striking power of workers has been a prize sought by other groups with other purposes. The syndicalists and the communists would have used it for a total alteration in the structure of American society. The demands of the business union, in contrast, are compatible with a profit system. Business unionism is the natural enemy of revolutionary unionism and a more effective adversary perhaps than the capitalist manager himself. If, and the forecast seems a dubious one, we in America are indeed on the threshold of the laboristic age, the collective-bargaining strategy and weapons of the trade-union movement will have had relatively little responsibility for its advent.

CHAPTER 3 CONSTRUCTIVE ASPECTS OF INDUSTRIAL CONFLICT

Robert Dubin   *University of Oregon*

It is perhaps axiomatic that industrial conflict has a negative meaning for most people. In its most visible form industrial conflict tends to be associated with the strike. To the employer whose plant is on strike, to the workers who have ceased working, and to the consumers who are dependent upon an uninterrupted flow of goods or services, the strike represents an obvious disturbance. The employer finds his organization at a standstill and, therefore, temporarily useless. The worker finds that his wages and, therefore, his way of life are interrupted. The consumer can no longer expect a necessary flow of goods and services upon which he may have become dependent. For all the parties involved there is a serious interruption in the continuity of tasks, expectations, and normal operations. This very interruption in the continuity and stability of an ongoing flow of production is viewed by all parties with relative distaste.

Before we can conclude, however, that industrial conflict is invariably undesirable and that it is so viewed by all the parties affected, it is necessary for us to place industrial conflict into a larger framework. We have two basic questions for which answers have to be sought: (1) How does industrial conflict fit into the broad societal context in which it is found? (2) Is it possible to distinguish meaningfully between industrial disorder and social change as alternative consequences of industrial conflict?

Democracy and Conflict

The way in which industrial relations are carried on is inevitably a reflection of the societal norms. We have to take the existence of a democratic form of government and the democratic norms of our society as the background against which American industrial conflict must be viewed. Consequently, a brief description seems to be in order of the features of the democratic norms that are relevant to the problems of conflict within a democracy.

One of the basic rights that the concept of democracy assumes is the right of freedom of expression. Implicit in the idea of freedom of expression is the belief that individuals and groups will have differing notions, differing perceptions, and differing ideas about the nature of the world in which they operate. The guarantee of freedom of expression is a guarantee that these differing viewpoints will, in fact, be expressed by individuals and by the groups with whom they are associated. In addition, there is the expectation that, where differences of outlook exist, it is the responsibility and duty of those holding divergent viewpoints to express them. The consequence of the right of freedom of expression is, therefore, the actual and conscious expression of such differences as exist or are presumed to exist between individuals and groups in the society.

It is not necessary for us to examine the causes of differences in point of view and outlook. It is sufficient to emphasize that the democratic framework is based upon the assumption that such differences will, in fact, exist and that there will be freedom for expressing these differences.

A society would obviously be torn asunder if differences were never resolved or if the majority of differences failed of resolution. Therefore the right to differ has associated with it the responsibility to determine at what point differences become destructive of the basic stability of the society itself. If major differences go unresolved for a period of time, the very basis of the society may be threatened. In the political field we therefore find the device of "majority rule" to be the mode by which differences may be resolved. It does not mean that the minority necessarily gives up its divergent point of view. Majority rule does mean, however, that the group that commands the largest allegiance is capable of carrying out its point of view in a program of governmental action in spite of the differing outlook and viewpoint of the minority. Thus the democratic process has built into it devices for permitting the ongoing business of society to be carried forward without total consensus on the goals and the means for achieving these goals.

When we translate the problem of conflict into the area of industrial relations, we find that majority rule does not constitute the operating principle for the resolution of such conflicts. For example, it would be meaningless to say that we would resolve a strike by counting noses and determining how everyone immediately involved in the strike feels the issue ought to be resolved. Should such a process be adopted, it seems clear that the workers, constituting the largest single group within the enterprise, would ordinarily outvote all other groups. We do not, therefore, depend upon the principle of "one person—one vote" as the basis for resolving industrial conflict. Nevertheless, there are other devices, and there is the basic underlying expectation that industrial conflict will be resolved.

Indeed, we can go one step further and specify at least one broad condition that constitutes a basic criterion for determining methods for resolving industrial conflicts.

The key concept is that of disorder. By disorder we mean behavior that interrupts the normal business of the society. We also mean that, if this behavior continues for a sufficient length of time, the fundamental ideas of right and wrong in the society could potentially be subject to serious challenge as a consequence. Let us examine these two aspects of disorder.

The legislative and legal history of industrial relations can be written from the standpoint of the concept of disorder. Legislation and its judicial interpretation has been largely concerned with confirming the contemporary ideas of right and wrong in industrial relations, as the power-holding groups of the society interpret these ideas. The early conspiracy doctrine, in terms of which self-organization of workers was viewed as a conspiracy against the property rights of the employer, was a product of the judicial belief that such challenge would create fundamental disorder in a free-enterprise economy. The right to strike and to picket have been viewed from the legislative and legal standpoint in terms of their effect upon the stability and continuity of going concepts of right and wrong. The sit-down strike dramatized this in a most forceful manner, and the highest court was constrained to hold that property rights of owners outweighed the workers' nebulous rights to a job. The basic challenge of the sit-down strike was viewed as a potential threat to the whole notion of property rights. The legal emphasis upon peaceful picketing is another evidence of concern with minimizing violence in the society, since violence, as a means for resolving conflict, can be readily translated into other areas of social action. If condoned in the area of the strike, it may provide the basis for potential disorder in other areas of the society and thereby threaten the very stability of the society itself.

The Taft-Hartley law reemphasized the concern that legislators had with the possible impact of disorder on the larger society. The provisions of the law, preventing Communists from holding union office if the union sought the services of the NLRB, is strong evidence of this point. The proscription against Communist union leaders was a device intended by the legislators to minimize the potential power of Communists to use labor-union organizations as a means for creating disorder in the society through violence and sabotage.

The time factor enters into our view of disorder in several ways. In the case of those industries producing goods and services that are "affected with the public interest," tolerance with respect to the length of time during which this disorder will be acceptable in the society is very narrowly limited. While we might be willing to go without electric, water, gas, and other utility services temporarily, as a consequence of natural disasters, there is a strong expectation that repairs will be immediately forthcoming and that the interrupted service will be restored as rapidly as possible. The emphasis is upon speed in restoring the interrupted services. A strike affecting the public interest has the potential of continuing for a considerable length of time and as a consequence interrupting, during the period of the strike, the flow of essential goods and services. There is an underlying assumption that the longer these goods and services fail to enter into the main stream of the society, the greater will be the consequent disorder. As a result, we tend to view strikes in industries and occupations affected with the public interest as having a permeating influence on the spread of disorder the longer the interruption in goods and services is permitted to continue.

In periods of national emergency such as a war, the economy becomes exceptionally sensitive to the imbalance created by industrial disorder. It was no accident that the major labor unions of the United States made a no-strike pledge during the last war. This pledge was a recognition that even temporary interruption in the flow of goods and services could have a very rapid impact on the sensitive balance of the economy as a whole, geared as it was to war production. In the instance of the no-strike pledge and the attempt to enforce it, the limits of tolerance measured in a time dimension came to be viewed within a very narrow perspective. It was believed that the whole productive scheme might become disordered very rapidly in the face of even a short strike.

Consequently, the time dimension played an important role in defining the limits of acceptable disorder in our society under conditions of war.

In a democratic society we can conclude that conflict is never eliminated. Indeed, conflict is accepted as an inevitable consequence of the functioning of a complex society based upon an equally complex culture. The amount of conflict and the issues involved will differ in historical periods as will the techniques for carrying out conflict.

Within a democracy we can also conclude that the continuity of the society and its stability depend upon a common set of criteria for determining when conflict becomes disorder. In the area of industrial relations we can see a historical change in the definition of the limits of conflict. But that there has always been a going conception which has set the limits upon industrial conflict cannot be denied. We have as one of our tasks, then, to examine the present viewpoints about the relationships between conflict and disorder in the area of industrial relations.

Industrial Disorder and Industrial Conflict

The larger society defines the contemporary limits of disorder by proscribing behavior that may have unacceptable social consequences because it means the use of violence, defies existing government policy, injures public health and safety, or jeopardizes established legal rights and positions of social power. But this sets only the outside limits of allowable conflict. In order to see where the practical limits are likely to be set and to analyze the relationships between conflict and disorder in industry, it will be profitable to examine the problem with the individual enterprise or firm as the unit upon which attention will be focused. It is only at the operating level of the economy that we will be able to observe how disorder becomes a tactic and a weapon in the broader institutionalization of industrial conflict. We will then be able to determine how the disorder attendant upon industrial conflict is to be evaluated in relation to the social change that is one of its consequences.

Disorder in industry can be defined as the breakdown of an ordered organizational structure and the human relationships that are prescribed by the organization pattern. Every enterprise has a more or less well-defined structure and a pattern of expected behavior that govern the actions of each individual contributing his services to the organization. For a wide variety of reasons an enterprise may not be able to fulfill its daily operating functions. This inability of the organization to function, as planned on a daily basis, in producing the goods or providing the services for which it is established is evidence of lack of order within the enterprise. Indeed, it is one of the marks of capable organization management to be able either to anticipate the disordering influences that will play upon the organization or to maintain a degree of managerial flexibility that will make possible rapid adjustment to the disordering influences. It is almost axiomatic that no organization has such a high degree of stability that it is never subject to at least minor disordering situations. For business organizations in particular the dynamic influences that play upon operations make disorder an almost daily, commonplace occurrence. The "problems" of business management are largely to be found in maintaining the daily flow of work in the firm and in protecting operations from influences that will interrupt or disrupt the ongoing activities.

Industrial disorder has special meanings for management and workers in an enterprise. There are factors contributing to disorder that are directly controlled by the parties. There are other factors that are less amenable to control by the parties. Furthermore, there are factors contributing to industrial disorder that are the consequence of the relations between management and men, while some factors have their origins at other points. It will be useful to sort out several of the major factors making for industrial disorder in order to see at what points industrial conflict contributes to it.

Management and Industrial Disorder. The managerial concept of order is grounded in three characteristics of organization. To management the business firm operates in an orderly fashion when it exhibits (1) continuity with its past, (2) controlled direction and amount of change in the present, and (3) predictability in the future.

These three elements of industrial order are bound together and operate simultaneously. On some occasions management may give special attention to only one aspect, but generally no single element can be emphasized to the exclusion of the others. Thus a forecast of sales predicts the future; but the forecast must inevitably take into account and affect the changes in current operations necessary to fulfill the forecast of output; and the prediction must also be realistic with respect to past availability of men, materials, and machines —it must have a logical continuity with past performance.

It is clear that industrial order in the individual firm represents a delicate balance of many factors. A change in the market for goods or services may require major adjustment to keep the firm on an even keel. Important operation shifts may occur in response to changing availability of raw material, parts, and subassemblies, of long- and short-term credit, and of capital equipment. Special crises like fire or storm damage and machine or equipment breakdown often require immediate and drastic decision to restore order. These illustrations serve to emphasize that business firms operate in a dynamic environment that creates constant demands for managerial action to maintain continuity, stability, and, hence, order in the enterprise.

This changing environment, as the previous illustrations suggest, often lies beyond the scope of direct control by any individual management. The typical response to unbalancing influences is internal accommodation and adjustment to these influences. Ordinarily it is not possible or feasible to exercise direct control over disordering factors that are external to the enterprise.

When we turn to the relationships between management and men, we find a different condition. Management typically views its function as that of directing and controlling the work force. The manager-worker relationship lies especially within the realm of direct control, in the view of management. This gives us the key to understanding the special significance that management attaches to disordering influences originating in the work force.

The conditions of worker participation in a business firm are established by management. In a very literal sense management was there first. The rules governing worker behavior, output, and discipline are a product of a set of managerial decisions. These decisions establish the ordered set of relationships between men in the enterprise.

So long as the violations of rules and common understandings governing worker behavior are subject to established systems of sanctions and penalties, the basic order in the organization remains undisturbed. The order in the relationships between management and men is then a product of an established code and of a system of discipline that polices the observation of the code. Mere disobedience is not sufficient to threaten the established order if its punishment is certain and swift.

The real root of worker-centered industrial disorder, from management's standpoint, lies in an overt or covert threat to the management-determined system of rules governing worker behavior. When the rules themselves are open to question and, indeed, modification, then either disorder results or the rules get changed. This is typically the situation in collective bargaining.

A union is not primarily concerned with organizing and channeling mass flouting of existing work rules. The union's central concern is with changing these rules in a desired direction. In pursuit of this goal union militancy and management resistance may produce the most public evidence of industrial disorder, the strike. But there are many other weapons open to both management and union in the contest to determine the content of the code of work.

To a management unwilling to share decision with a union in determining major portions of the work code, the mere existence of union organization among its employees is a disordering influence. To such management the failure by employees to accept a management-determined work code is an ever-present threat to order in the establishment. For this kind of management the only effective curb upon employee-originated industrial disorder is the elimination of any possibility of unionization. There are still sectors of the American economy where this management view prevails.

It is the contention here that violent management opposition to unions is not grounded primarily in economics. It is rather the consequence of a managerial picture of established order in an enterprise that appears, in the eyes of the management architects of this order, to be threatened by unionism.

When collective bargaining prevails, the management view of industrial disorder more nearly approximates the situation where management accommodates its business decisions to influences over which it exerts much less direct control. Thus collective bargaining tends to place the management-worker relationship in the same arena with those disordering influences that are part of the external environment to which management is constantly making routine accommodations and adjustments. Before we consider this important consequence of the institutionalization of employer-employee relationships, let us briefly examine industrial disorder from the workers' viewpoint.

Employees and Industrial Disorder. The employees' view of industrial disorder differs significantly from that of management. To an employee, the organization that hires him is an important segment of the total social environment in which he lives. Participation in the organization may be the source of great satisfaction or the cause of great dissatisfaction. Whether the employing firm will be viewed from either of these standpoints by the majority of its employees is not primarily a consequence of their personality idiosyncrasies. It is rather the result of the way in which order and stability are established to define the major dimensions of the organization environment. The sources of general dissatisfaction or satisfaction are in the organization, not in the individuals employed by it.

In this organizational setting the individual reacts to his work environment as largely external to himself and only partially subject to his direct control. Indeed, the very evidence of his daily work life brings home to the manual worker the degree to which he is directed in his behavior with only limited free choices available. From the moment of starting work by punching a time clock, through work routines that are established at fixed times, until the day ends at the same mechanical time recorder, there is impressed upon the industrial worker his narrow niche in a complex and ordered system of interdependency. But it is a system over which he, as an individual, exercises little direct control.

The very standardization of work routines and social behavior in the work place is the highest expression of order in the enterprise. Were the routinization of work life to remain largely fixed or were it even to change in an orderly fashion, the work environment would constitute a relatively stable social structure within which the individual worker could establish an effective and well-defined workday life.

From the worker's standpoint, many sources of instability in his work environment are either a consequence of managerial action or are perceived as originating with management. Obvious things like technological change and changes in work schedule originate with management. Less obvious changes, like a shift in managerial attitude toward employees, may have an equally disordering impact upon workers. The fact is that workers view management as the primary source of the disorder in their working life.

Workers, then, tend to view industrial disorder as having an immediate, *personal* impact upon them. Management tends to view industrial disorder as having an institutional impact rather than a personal one. How can these two views of industrial disorder be mediated so that the impact of disorder is minimized?

Management can attempt to react to disorder in noninstitutional terms. We often find this expressed in the so-called human-relations or clinical approach, in which there is an attempt to find the roots of organizational problems in the behavior of individuals. This approach will always be inadequate, for the very requirements of organizational stability and continuity necessitate minimizing the attention given to personal considerations that are in conflict with the institutional interests.

The primary mode for mediating the worker and management views of industrial disorder is through collective bargaining. Collective bargaining maintains the focus upon organization or institutional factors. The emphasis is upon making rules for the class of employees. The common meeting ground is collective bargaining, where the institutional outlook is paramount for both union and management. In collective relations there is a joint rule-making responsibility through which the working code of management-men relations is established. The individual worker finds that his personalization of the disordering aspects of his work life is given expression in group power through the union. Thus it is the worker's personalized reaction to industrial disorder that is translated into organizational terms to make the worker reaction to disorder comparable to that of management. Collective bargaining is the social process that provides a common framework within which management and worker views of the disputed matters that lead to industrial disorder can be considered, with the aim of eliminating the causes of the disorder.

Institutionalizing Industrial Conflict

Collective bargaining is the great social invention that has institutionalized industrial conflict. In much the same way that the electoral process and majority rule have institutionalized political conflict in a democracy, collective bargaining has created a stable means for resolving industrial conflict.

Collective relations between management and union are grounded in the conscious and deliberate use of power and force. Power is marshaled and force is used to gain the immediate ends of the contending parties as they are formalized in the bargaining agreement. The union agreement sets forth the final resolution of the current conflicts in a body of policies and rules that govern the management-men relationships. It is not of central significance that these rules be arrived at by peaceful means. More important is the fact that the collective agreement represents a compromise between what management wants and what the union wants. It is the fact of both the expectation of compromise and its actual achievement that is most relevant in delineating collective bargaining as a mode for institutionalizing industrial conflict.

Both union and management enter into a contract negotiation with the full expectation that an acceptable contract will result. A great deal of indeterminacy exists, however, as to what exactly will be the content of the contract. Management does not know how far the union will press a particular demand. The union does not have precise knowledge of how important a given issue is to management. Within the range of this indeterminacy, persuasion and trading are typically accompanied by force. The union may threaten or actually carry out a strike to gain a particular set of demands. Management willingness to meet the threat with an acceptance of the consequences of a strike is its own use of power and force. Management power in collective bargaining has come more and more to be displayed in its willingness to accept a strike and in its staying power during the period of the strike, for once the strike commences, after a relatively short period of a build-up in union power, there is usually a gradual loss in the effectiveness of the strike on the union's side and a consequent gain in power by management. In general, the longer a strike lasts, the greater is the probability that management will emerge as the relative victor in that particular power struggle.

The union weapons of the strike, the slowdown, and the jamming of the grievance procedure, the management weapons of the lockout, arbitrary reinterpretation of a bargaining agreement, and "tough" grievance decisions—all have one element in common. They are weapons for maximizing industrial disorder. It is obvious that the strike and lockout halt production completely. This is complete industrial disorder from our standpoint. The slowdown introduces disorder while the organization continues to function (the strike on the job). An arbitrary management reinterpretation of the union agreement will also be disorder-producing for the union and its members while the organization continues to function. When either or both parties use the grievance machinery as an instrument of power, they are attempting to convert machinery for social adjustment into an instrument of force, again while the organization continues to function on a daily basis.

We can then distinguish three levels of industrial disorder that sometimes accompany collective bargaining: (1) Disorder designed to halt the regular functioning of the enterprise. (2) Disorder designed to be disruptive while the organization continues to operate. (3) Disorder directed at redefining an existing institutional practice to the advantage of the party creating the disorder.

Thus the use of power and force in collective bargaining, by both parties, has as its immediate function the creation of industrial disorder. Force and power are the instruments for introducing temporary chaos into the enterprise. The chaos is deliberately sought. It is the weapon by which management and union each seek to secure the most favorable terms in the rules that govern their relationships.

It is clear that, if the analysis up to this point is accurate, industrial disorder as a feature of industrial conflict is always temporary and limited. The strategic end of industrial conflict is to establish a new basis of order, a new set of rules governing management-men relationships. The tactics for carrying on collective bargaining at points where conflict arises may necessitate maximizing industrial disorder. But every industrial conflict is resolved, and with its resolution comes a new working code that guides the relationships during the period of the resulting agreement.

One of the consequences of the institutionalization of industrial conflict through collective bargaining is that the limits of industrial disorder come to be institutionally determined. For any given conflict there is inevitably introduced a long-time perspective, a vista of continuing relations between company and union regardless of the outcome of the current controversy. This time perspective can have an important tempering influence toward limiting disorder. It is significant that in the United States strike violence has been inversely related to the permanence of unionism. As collective bargaining becomes an established feature of our society both sides come to recognize that each conflict-created disorder is inevitably succeeded by a reestablished order and that permanently disruptive disorder may materially impede the resolution of the conflict. Thus collective bargaining tends to produce self-limiting boundaries that distinguish permissible from subversive industrial disorder.

A second consequence of the institutionalization of industrial conflict is that there is a significant shift in the managerial view of relations with employees. This shift is in the direction of seeing employee relations as responding increasingly to factors of influence external to the enterprise. Certainly a market view of wage and "fringe" benefits of the contract takes into account important external factors, such as area and industry practices, as the basis for decisions. Industry-wide collective bargaining has been a natural outgrowth of the shifting locus of influences playing upon management-men relationships. The consequence, particularly for management, of the growing importance of factors external to the enterprise in determining the collective bargain is obvious. To the degree that direct control over the working code by management is lessened, to that degree is management in a position to make its industrial-relations decisions as a process of accommodation. Management bargaining decisions then come to be made within the same framework of accommodation as many other kinds of business decisions.

Social Change and Industrial Conflict

The third great consequence of institutionalizing industrial conflict is its stabilizing influence upon the whole society. Collective bargaining provides the means for systematic social change in the working code governing management-men relations. The means for carrying out and resolving industrial conflict becomes established, limited, and defined.

We can appreciate the importance of stabilizing the basis of social change in industry when we recall that ours is an industrial society. It is industry that constitutes one of the most basic or central elements of our total social structure. What happens in the society is, to an important degree, a direct or indirect consequence of developments in the industrial sector.

It follows, then, that the very stability of the total social structure is significantly affected by stability in the industrial segment of that social structure. However, industrial stability is more accurately portrayed as a moving equilibrium rather than a static one. New industries arise, old ones are modified or disappear; technology is constantly changing; markets shift; raw materials exhibit shifting sources of supply and substitution of man-made for natural material; the population grows, and with it come increases in the work force and changes in its composition; and the nature of industrial organization itself is constantly undergoing modification. These are only some of the more important dynamic forces compounding the difficult problem of maintaining a moving equilibrium in industry.

Most of these sources of change in industry are treated as impersonal factors when decisions are made in the individual enterprise. In management-men relationships we have persons and groups involved whose sentiments, loyalties, and satisfactions are intimately bound up in the relationship itself. It is all the more remarkable, therefore, that we have invented the institutional practice of collective bargaining for regulating the conflict process in industrial relations.

Indeed, we can go further and say that the relatively unstructured conflict of early collective bargaining has been supplanted by antagonistic cooperation in its present development. The antagonistic element highlights the continued existence of areas of conflict whose resolution produces social change. The cooperation element points to the fact that the function of conflict is to establish a new basis of order, not to continue disorder.

It may not reflect reality accurately to assert that we have solved the technological problems of an industrial civilization but have made a mess of the human problems. It is, perhaps, more accurate to conclude that we have invented a moderately successful process for ordering the way in which the working code of management-men relationships is defined and thereby have produced reasonable stability in this important area of human problems. We can also add that collective bargaining is consonant with, and fortifies, the democratic principles of the society in which it is practiced.

Conclusion

In answer to the first question with which we started, How does industrial conflict fit into the broad societal context in which it is found? we must conclude that in the industrial sphere the democratic ethos of our society finds its natural expression in industrial conflict. That there are conflicts of interests in industry today seems scarcely questionable. That we have institutionalized the mode of this conflict through collective bargaining is also clear. We have thus built, in the institutional practice of collective bargaining, a social device for bringing conflict to a successful resolution. This has been accomplished within the framework of a democratic society. We have not, through collective bargaining, eliminated the causes of differences and conflicts.

The answer to our second basic question, Is it possible to distinguish meaningfully between industrial disorder and social change as alternative consequences of industrial conflict? gives us the basis for understanding why collective bargaining has not eliminated industrial conflict. Our industrial society is a highly dynamic one. Furthermore, it is a highly interdependent one. As a consequence, stability and order are ever threatened by either too rapid change in one sector of the society or by the impact of a single change upon a delicately balanced equilibrium at some other point in the social fabric. The one constant in our society seems to be change itself. This makes all the more remarkable the fundamental achievement of collective bargaining. The bargaining contracts of union-management relations give stability and order to these relations. However temporary the period of a given contract—and some may hold that a year is temporary indeed—the fact remains that the union contract symbolizes order and stability. Union-management relations typically exhibit a high degree of disorder when the contract is under negotiation, often reaching the strike stage. But the disorder of the strike has the aim of establishing a new basis of order. Collective bargaining underpins the social structure of management-men relations, always in terms of a commonly agreed-to working code.

A problem that lies deep in the moral roots of our American society is the determination of what a "just" working code, establishing the relations between employer and employee, should be. That very material changes have been wrought in the code in the past century is confirmed by even superficial observation of history. That more rapid changes in the working code have come in the past two decades, with a powerful labor movement bargaining for industrial workers, can hardly be gainsaid. Collective bargaining and the industrial conflict with which it deals have certainly been instruments of social change. At only limited points, and for only temporary periods of time, has industrial disorder become an important element in industrial conflict.

CHAPTER 4 INDUSTRIAL HARMONY AS A GOAL

George C. Homans   *Harvard University*

I<small>N THIS</small> chapter, I shall first say what I mean by industrial harmony, then show why it is a goal that a modern society must try to attain, and lastly suggest some of the conditions that must be met if it is to be attained. In doing this, I shall not limit myself to the individual factory but rather consider the factory in relation to the general economy, the governments, and the ideologies of our time, for only in this relation does industrial harmony become a goal of paramount importance.

The Meaning of Industrial Harmony

Harmony, like conflict, is a symptom and not a basic condition. Conflict does not exist just because people like to fight (though they do) or are told they must (though they often are). It is an expression of real discontents. No doubt these discontents are sometimes different from the ones that get stated in the formal programs. A man may well be angry and yet not be able to say just why. Nevertheless, the real discontents are there, and since the American workingman is intelligent, we can count on him, by and large, to know what he really wants. By the same token, harmony is an expression of a relative decline in discontent.

Industrial harmony means harmony *between* persons or groups of persons. Conflict may arise, and harmony can conceivably be achieved, within a number of different pairs of opponents in industry, and conflict within any one may influence the course of conflict within the others, as when the demand of a certain job-group for higher pay than others may crosscut and imperil the unity of the workers as a whole in their relations with management. The parties to conflict are many, and their disputes intersect; yet when we speak of industrial conflict we usually mean conflict between management and workers. In this major conflict, indeed, many of the minor ones find expression. When speaking of industrial harmony, I shall mean harmony between these major parties.

Industrial harmony is certainly not perfect harmony. If industrial harmony means that every person and every group in industry gets just what he wants—or even something less than what he wants—without having to put up a fight for it, we shall never achieve industrial harmony; and we had better not set up a goal so illusory. The pursuit of the ideal of perfect harmony can too easily lead to the harmony of silence, where raising one's voice in protest brings in the secret police and ends in a visit to the salt mines.

But if industrial harmony is something less than perfect harmony, it is also something more than total war between the parties. When either management or labor, in the factory or the nation at large, wishes to destroy the other, harmony certainly does not exist. What is more, neither side in the long run will succeed in its aim. Management—the present group or its successors—will certainly survive. Free labor unions might not survive a totalitarian regime brought on by industrial disorder. Sooner or later, management and labor will have to live with one another.

But what I have described are only the preconditions of industrial harmony. For industrial harmony, the two parties must, to an indefinite but recognizable degree and in spite of differences of opinion, be willing to work together actively—not simply to hold the other at arm's length and say no to his proposals—to increase the effectiveness of the organization in producing goods and services *and* to increase the human development and satisfactions of persons in the plant. This stresses the direction that cooperation should take rather than the amount of increased effectiveness or personal satisfaction that can be achieved. Further than this a definition cannot go. If you are not satisfied with it, all I can do is point to examples of what I consider industrial harmony, for instance, the union-management relations of the Inland Steel Container Co. in the years 1947–1950, as described in W. F. Whyte's *Pattern for Industrial Peace.* In this plant, both my conditions were met, though not without struggle; effectiveness increased, and so did personal satisfactions, measured in money if in no other way.

This definition of harmony allows room, as it must, for plenty of conflict. It certainly allows for the existence of a union, with its full panoply of weapons, well oiled, in the background, in stand-by status, as a protection for the workers in case active cooperation breaks down. This is, I think, the status of union organization in many American factories today. In any event, we must remember that conflict is not an all-or-nothing matter. My definition of harmony embraces conflict within the arms of common code and common purpose, and there is nothing strange about this. It is a reality of everyday existence; it is, in fact, the essence of democracy.

The aim of increased personal satisfaction we shall all agree on, but there seems to be some doubt about the aim of industrial effectiveness. By my values, it is not an ignoble one. All discussions of the profit motive, begun by businessmen themselves in an attempt to appear hard-boiled and abetted by emotional intellectuals, have obscured the fact that an automobile is manufactured as much *for use* in a capitalistic economy as in a totalitarian one and that the job of any industrial system is to produce useful goods and get them in the hands of consumers. Aside from this test of effectiveness from the consumer's point of view, effectiveness is vital within the organization. I have come to the conclusion that no single nonmaterial factor is more responsible for employee dissatisfaction within a factory than sheer confusion and disorganization.

Do not tell me I am neglecting conflicts of interest. There is no group and no person in an organization whose interests do not conflict at some point with those of others. In a world where no one's interests can be furthered indefinitely, a society holds these interests in check or is replaced by one that does. Moreover, management and unions have some interests in common: the preservation of the organization and its jobs and, if I may mention it, the preservation of a free society. They have equally important common duties: the provision of cheap goods and services to the consumer. Industrial harmony requires a community of reasonably responsible men.

Alternative Goals and the Consequences

There would be no point in urging the attainment of industrial harmony if we already had it, but we do not. A great deal of dissatisfaction on the part of workers in industry exists and expresses itself in industrial conflict. Whether the dissatisfaction is in some sense "natural" or arises because workers have learned to expect more of industry than they used to is immaterial, as we probably would not want to destroy the great expectations. The assumption of dissatisfaction made, I assert that the reason why industrial harmony is a goal worth striving for is that no other goal for industry is *in the long run* open to us. And if we do not look at the long run, it will be upon us anyhow, all the more menacing for our ignorance of it.

I can put my argument best by considering what would happen if we took the opposite course, so far as it was within our power, and encouraged the spread and violence of industrial conflict. Let us suppose that we tried to increase the dissatisfaction of workers with, and their psychological alienation from, the present industrial system and tried to increase the extent and turbulence of strikes and other forms of conflict between labor and management. The end result, if we look not at what might conceivably be but at the evidence of recent history and the dissident groups that, in fact, exist in the Western world, would probably be the appearance of some form of state socialism or totalitarianism on communist or fascist models.

Either of these changes would probably mean the removal of the present occupants from positions of industrial power. But changes in personnel aside, and I am not committed to personnel, what sort of industrial order would these political changes leave us with? By answering this question we arrive at the need for industrial harmony.

1. The dominant part of industry would still be organized in large-scale units, because there is little evidence that, in an important number of industrial activities, large-scale units are not functionally necessary for the maintenance of our present standard of living. It is, in fact, the existence of large units that makes the nationalization and central control of industry under socialism or totalitarianism possible. With all their condemnation of monopoly, the socialists make monopoly their principle of organization. Do you think that under socialism General Motors—the actual machinery, factories, and organization —would disappear, except in name?

2. The productive units would still be organized hierarchically. I believe a great deal could, and can, be done to decentralize decision and give the workingmen who are doing a particular job more control over their industrial environment than they have now, but I do not conceive, and nobody has in fact proposed, that there would not still be a large number of decisions made at

the top and sent down as orders. The evidence is that communism, at least, would increase the centralization of decision rather than relax it.

3. There would still be differences in the material rewards received by workers in industry, and there would, therefore, still be relatively poor people, whom the intellectuals of the time, if they dared to open their mouths, could call "underprivileged" and "exploited." The differences might well be smaller than exist at present, though communist society tends to increase them, but of the fact that they would exist there is no question or doubt whatever. They would exist because, if there are felt differences in responsibility between jobs, the persons with more responsibility demand and get more pay (or automobiles and *dacha*'s). Let anyone who has observed a joint union-management job-evaluation program deny the heavy pressure for wage differentials.

4. Probably there would also be absolutely poor people. If the real wages of American workingmen are averaged over long enough time spans, say, spans of a quarter century, they appear to have risen fairly steadily for 100 years or more. Even in the United States we cannot count on this continuing indefinitely under any possible political and economic system, especially when our mineral resources are being used up at the present rate and the possibilities of atomic power as cheap energy have been oversold. It is wholly irresponsible to go on talking about the wealth that will be ours in the future. If we do get richer, we shall manage to worry along somehow under almost any industrial system, buying off the workers' discontent. But the wise man plans for the worst, not the best, contingency. Many workingmen must already realize, as the rest of us do, that pay raises are almost immediately wiped out by the rising cost of living, and they must wonder whether they are not caught in a rat race.

5. There would still be profits, in the sense that all the income of an industrial organization would not go to its employees. The profits might not go to private persons and private organizations, but profits and reinvestment there would certainly be, because there would have to be profits for the maintenance, modernization, and expansion of plant. There would be a nice little surplus value for the Marxists of the future to theorize about.

6. There would still be an emphasis on productivity, an emphasis that has been greater in socialist society (Great Britain) and in communist society (the Soviet Union) than in the United States. In the first two societies, special reasons exist for the emphasis on production, but the underlying reasons are present in all three. It is not just the money-mad, slave-driving capitalist that demands hard work from labor, but the situation. All three societies set as a goal a higher standard of living for the citizen, and higher standards of living depend on productivity, either in the form of high investment for machinery and plant (more surplus value taken from the worker) or in more work (more energy taken from him). In the society of the future, the worker would still have to work.

7. There would still be—perhaps I should whisper it—a certain amount of compulsion for people to take certain jobs. For in any society we can envisage there are going to be dirty jobs. They may well be less dirty than some present jobs, but they will be dirtier than other jobs of their own time, and people will

be loath to take them. Yet they will be necessary jobs, and people will *have* to take them. Great Britain is already having trouble recruiting workers for the coal mines. In theory this difficulty could be postponed indefinitely. One solution might be continuous immigration in the form of people for whom any job in the new country is better than any job open to them in the old, such as Algerians in France, Poles and Italians in Belgium, Poles in England, and Puerto Ricans, Mexicans, and Negroes in the United States. We have never considered how far a caste system—a body of men that can be forced by caste barriers into dirty work—is a functional necessity of modern Western industry. Another theoretically possible solution is an increase in wages in the dirty jobs until they become attractive enough for people to take them. But in an age of labor unions, when no one union likes to see another get ahead of it in pay raises, this method becomes increasingly more difficult to use. No doubt the planners would like to do it, but will politics allow the planners to plan? And outside of immigration of a caste type, and high pay for dirty work, the solutions remain economic coercion in the form of a certain amount of unemployment, which is abhorrent to the welfare state, or direct coercion on the Soviet model, which is abhorrent to most of us. But some coercion there will probably be because it is probably necessary. The question is whether it would be better to have a little coercion of an indirect kind in order to avoid a great deal more coercion of an extremely direct kind. Assuredly, whether we gag at the means or not, the problem is going to be solved.

What does all this mean? It means, in the first place, that if an increase in industrial conflict only leads to changes in the politicoeconomic "system," any new system we can realistically expect will be, *as far as the everyday environment of the workingman is concerned,* extraordinarily like the present one. If, therefore, the workingman is discontented in the present system, he will, I apprehend, be discontented in the new one unless—and this is an important *unless*—we cut down his expectations, and this, I fear, would demand sitting on him for some time with force.

If we ever took the totalitarian alternative, the workingman would probably be even more discontented than he is now, because the amount of coercion and spying would probably increase; and he would not like these things any more than I would. As for socialism, the assumption used to be that the worker's knowledge under socialism that he now "owns" the factory he works in would change his attitude toward the boss. Whether the recent experience of the Labor government of Great Britain bears out the assumption is very doubtful. In fact, the problem of industrial relations may become more difficult under socialism instead of less so, when the former leaders of labor become, as members of national boards, responsible for the efficient management of factories. The workingmen will look for leaders to represent them against the bosses, and since the union leaders are now the bosses, the new labor leaders will tend to come from a different group, the Communists often being available for the purpose. Developments of this kind might have been predicted from studies of labor-management cooperation in some American factories where, as the labor leaders took increasing responsibility for the management of a plant, they lost their control over their followers. The change in "ownership" is, in fact, personnel changes aside, a purely verbal change and does not affect the actual behavior of people in a factory or the functional requirements of the factory.

We desperately need to create a more humanly satisfactory industrial order, but our difficulties are radical and run deeper than we thought. They are not to be solved just by a change of politicoeconomic system. If this is all we do, we shall find that the "brave new world" bears a shocking family likeness to the bad old one, that it presents problems no less stubborn than those of the old, and that there is no system without "contradictions." Easy methods—and changing a system is, to my mind, an easy method—will not be enough. We must go back to the hard old way of changing human behavior at the grass roots.

The Goal of Harmony within the Plant

In the second place, what I have said means that, if the workingman is not humanly satisfied with the conditions he lives under, we shall not forever be able to buy his acquiescence by increases in real wages, by the leveling of material rewards, by a decrease in the pressure for production, or by the elimination of hierarchical authority. These I shall call the external determinants of workers' behavior, the ones that some students of industrial relations accuse people like myself, who emphasize the internal collaborative environment of the plant, of forgetting. Our emphasis is not misplaced, for the external determinants are the ones that, in the long run, under capitalism, socialism, or totalitarianism, we shall be least able to change. The strategic determinants, the ones we might be able to change in order to create a new industrial society, are the internal.

When you have put a new group in power, calling itself representative of labor or the proletariat, and when you have given the workingman all the money he can get in your society, you will still find him at his lathe or on the assembly line. He will still be *there*. He will still be subjected to authority in a big organization, still paid less than some other people in the plant. You will have to convince him—because it will be necessary—to cooperate with others in the system in order to produce goods and services for the public. You will be able to convince him only by showing him that the system he lives under is a just system, just and righteous because (in the absence of further material rewards that can be given him) he is, inside the plant and in his day-to-day life, treated in a way he finds humanly satisfactory. However much you may want to escape it, you will not in fact be able to escape working on the internal environment of the plant, because that is the environment of daily life. You will have to do these things eventually. I might almost add, though my argument does not require it, Why not now?

Why Is the Goal Worth Striving For?

Let me review briefly. I start with the assumption that the workers in modern industry are often discontented with both the material and the other conditions of their life and that this discontent breeds conflict. From this assumption I have argued that no other course than the advancement of industrial harmony is open to us. Suppose we took the opposite course and encouraged industrial conflict. The result would probably be a change in the politicoeconomic system which would, in fact, since it would hardly affect the ordinary working environment, not remove the sources of discontent, especially as buying off discontented workers with material rewards is not indefinitely possible.

I still have not proved my point, for logically there is a third course open, besides either increased conflict or increased harmony. We might do nothing. We might try to preserve the *status quo,* with about the present level of industrial conflict, which would be all right with me if it were possible, since, taken all in all, I think humanity has never "had it so good" as it has in the United States right now. But I believe that this course would just as surely betray us. The *status quo* does not, unhappily, stay *"quo."* The sources of the workingman's discontent are endemic in our industrial technology and organization, and if left untreated, they will fester.

Ultimately the question is one of value. I value a society with a rising standard of living, a rising standard of human satisfaction in general, a low level of coercion, a society that is flexible, changing, ready to try experiments, provided they are real experiments and not, like most of our so-called experiments in social organization, irrevocable commitments. This means that they must be experiments that can be called off if they do not work. Neither the promotion of industrial conflict nor what is, in effect, a do-nothing policy will, I believe, help create or maintain such a society. A society where industrial conflict is suppressed by force can, of course, be made to work. I am under no illusion that Soviet society will fall apart by the sheer stress of its own methods. But I simply do not like that kind of society. And since I assume that my values are, by and large, those of other Americans, I say that there is no course open to us except the promotion of industrial harmony by attacking the sources of discontent.

One of the fruits—or perhaps it is a definition—of industrial harmony is confidence, confidence in the abilities and intentions of the parties at issue, be they labor, management, or any others. Confidence is a form of capital that is just as much a prerequisite for industrial change as any other form. If either party proposes a change in the technical and social organization of a plant, that change will go into effect only if the other party has enough confidence in the first to wait and see what the results of the change will be and to suspend judgment. Confidence is a form of capital that must be spent to get change, and if the change is accepted by the parties as favorable, the capital is restored. If we are to have an expanding, flexible, adaptive society, ready to take risks in the technological or social field, we need this confidence.

In some societies, and I am thinking especially of the French, this confidence seems to me to have been reduced to a low level, and one encounters the interesting and indeed amusing spectacle of a state holding theoretically great centralized power that in fact has difficulty making any move because each element in society automatically opposes anything that the others favor. We turn to the state to solve our problems; but the more power we give her, the less she is able to exercise, because there are more interests she touches. Just one more revolution, the French intellectuals cry, and the millennium will come in. Just one more—and yet they have had, depending on the definition, seven or eight already, and *plus ça change, plus c'est la même chose.* We have never solved the problem of a society with plural sources of power. Indeed we have never thought in detail about it. One advantage I see in a developing harmony between management and labor within particular plants and industries is the possibility of the appearance of centers of power sufficiently strong, because they are industrial *communities,* to resist some of the constrictions of an all-powerful but impotent state.

I have a theory that the liberal societies of the West entered the Industrial Revolution with a certain number of degrees of freedom, or opportunities for development. Today these opportunities, at least in the economic and political spheres and in different degrees in different countries, have been pretty well exploited, and society is pressing against its constraints. I am not making the usual complaint here about government interference with free enterprise. I am talking about the functional constraints of a social system which, admittedly, we know little about. But I suspect that the opportunities open to liberal society were not infinite in number and have been largely worked out. We talk a great deal about political action, but what can it do today? How can you compare the situation in the 19th century, when the enactment of a tariff or the repeal of the corn laws could bring into being or destroy a whole class of men, with the situation today, when the main action issue in a British election (aside from slogan issues) is whether or not dividends shall be limited? No great changes can be made, and no one proposes them, because the resistance they would bring into play is obviously too strong. The state is all-powerful, but only to keep things as they are. Society has, in effect, filled nearly every nook and cranny in which it was free to move. And I infer from this that, if social change is going to take place in the future, it must take place outside the old spheres of economic and political legislation. We must make not only a new start but a new kind of start.

The Prerequisites of Harmony

When we have done thrashing around with our ideological conflicts, when we have put off the evil hour for hard work on the industrial sphere as long as we dare, we shall finally have to get down to the business of creating an industrial *order* that the workingman and the manager will accept as just and in which they will be willing to collaborate. This does not mean that either party will get all it likes. Of course conflicts of interest will exist, but in any society that people have accepted as a social order, they have been kept under control. Such orders have existed in the past. They will exist again. We shall have to create one at a high level of civilization, or we shall assuredly get one at a low level.

But we shall only get this industrial order at a price, and the price may well be higher for the new social order than for any older ones. To put it crudely, a citizen of the Middle Ages may have been ready to accept as just a social order in which he took a good deal more pushing around than his modern counterpart will bear, or than we should want him to bear, now. Happily, much experience and research in the last few decades have begun to teach us some of the problems and conditions that must be solved and met in setting up an industrial order at the present time.

In general, an industrial enterprise has to solve three kinds of problems: the problem of technical effectiveness, the problem of individual motivation or social control, and the problem of social organization. Only at its peril does the enterprise neglect any one of these, and all of them interlock. I shall mention only a few of the conditions that must be met in solving the last two problems.

1. The workingman comes to his job as a man and not just as an economic man. He is driven by many motives and exposed to many irritations *besides* those connected with the desire to get good wages. The economic motives are not unimportant, but they are not the only ones.

2. In particular, he comes to his job with stronger sentiments of personal integrity than he did in the past. He probably defines some kinds of treatment as humiliating that his father would not have so defined.

3. We have heard over and over again that the modern workingman, the modern man, feels the need for security. This is not a matter of the decline of his moral fiber or of his willingness to take risks. He is in fact less secure than he used to be. In the old days a general clerk or mechanic, when he was fired, could get a job in another firm. He had a general skill he could sell to anyone. This is far less true today when he may know only one special routine used in only one company, and his danger is not that he will be out of a job but that there will be no job for him to be out of. If he does not get a new job substantially equal in pay and status to the one he has lost, he will feel that his efforts in life have had no meaning; and a society in which a large number of people feel that their efforts are meaningless is not a healthy society. Companies have tended to pass the social costs of technological unemployment on to the general community, which is not able to pay them. The companies themselves must do the job.

4. It is very easy to get sentimental about the effects of highly specialized, repetitive work and to raise the cry that man is being made slave to the machine. The fact is that work that some of us would feel to be monotonous and stultifying is not felt to be so by some kinds of workers, for instance, young women, under certain kinds of conditions, notably those that allow free social interchange. Looked at from the outside, making quilts seems a highly monotonous occupation, and yet the quilting bee was, at least in folklore, an almost romantic task. It is also true that someone has to do the dirty work. But when all this is said, it still remains true, at least by my sense of human dignity and the possibilities of personal development, that keeping a man all his life on monotonous, repetitive, unthinking work is positively immoral. And we do not have to do it.

5. The workingman comes to the factory a social person. He needs and makes an opportunity to become intimate with others. Workingmen tend to form cohesive groups of those doing the same kind of job or working at the same place. In the complex and changing technology and organization of today, these groups are put in the position of absorbing changes they have had no part in originating, and in these circumstances they behave, by restriction of output and other such practices, as if they were, by group action, trying

to recapture a lost control over the industrial environment and the conditions that affect their well-being. This is one of the strongest sources of industrial conflict. But there is also a little evidence that, if the group is in fact given some control over its environment ("allowed to participate," as it is usually called), the defensive attitude tends to disappear. We have not experimented enough with participation on a small scale, and we do not know just what participation should mean. Should it mean that the workers are consulted and express their views on all changes that affect them, or should they control change by their own decision? And in what areas should they take control? We need experiments.

6. Besides the problem of the individual working group, there is the problem of the relations between groups, between line and staff, between office and shop, and also between smaller groups doing different jobs. Such groups tend, though they would not put it in these terms, to insist that the material and other rewards of each job should be consistent with the workers' own evaluation of the importance and responsibility of the jobs in relation to others. Where pay differentials are consistent with the workers' own evaluation, they are not felt to be unjust. The same is true of promotions.

7. Some characteristics of the sheer organizational structure of modern industry bring it about that persons placed in certain positions—notably the staff specialist, the foreman, and perhaps the union steward—feel that their jobs are especially frustrating. We need to do a great deal more in studying the design of communications systems.

8. If unions did not exist, we should have to invent them. Even in non-unionized plants, a workingman feels, rather pathetically, that his boss ought to stand up for him in a pinch. A need for representation, a need for defense exists, and does not have to be created, but especially in large industries, a man's boss is not in a good position to meet the need. Some outside agency must, and it will also serve as a vehicle for collective communication between union and management. Even when workers are fairly well satisfied, do not often attend union meetings, and even feel no great enthusiasm for the union that represents them, they nevertheless feel there should be some union. At the very least, it serves as a stand-by defense, to be invoked if necessary. We must not only accept the fact that unions are here to stay but accept the idea that they need to stay.

9. When a man has a gripe—and it is he that knows whether he has one or not—he wants action on it. And a gripe against his foreman is not different from another gripe. If the foreman cannot give him satisfaction, he wants the dispute settled by some disinterested party. People are decent, and if the decision goes against him, he will accept the fact with a good grace, provided it has been reached by due process of law. All judicial systems work on this assumption. It is obviously not a question of giving the litigants all they want but of giving them due process. Whatever its delays (and we all suffer from the law's delays), whatever the amount of time it demands of managers and union stewards, our American grievance procedure, with impartial umpires, is among the most useful developments in the modern industrial scene. Here the workingman can find for his own personal gripes, irrational as others may view them, something he can recognize as justice; here both union and man-

agement are forced to take cognizance of the frictions that arise, with individual people, in the day-by-day operation of the plant, in a participation that is the first step to responsibility.

In short, the conditions for industrial harmony are the conditions of substantial justice, not justice in terms of what theoretically ought to be, but justice in terms of what is felt to be just by all sorts of persons here and now. Industrial harmony founded on justice is far more solid than that founded on "good human relations"—if good human relations means, at best, being a "good guy" and, at worst, being an "operator." I do not want a society based on nice and sensitive men. I want one based on just, responsible, and intelligent men.

Our dreams of changing the world radically by carrying out further the provisions of any one of our ideologies are perishing. Their sweet intoxication is wearing off. They will not do all we thought they would. Our monsters swim deeper than any of our harpoons will reach. But this knowledge, which has led some to despair, is in fact a strength: we are a much more realistic people than we were. We still have before us the problem of building an industrial civilization, and we must tackle it the hard way because it is a hard problem. We must go to the root of the matter, to the conditions of everyday living in the factory, for there, multiplied many thousandfold by many thousand factories, the discontents of modern society are engendered. And we have the encouragement of knowing that, at least for short time spans and for quite small groups, industrial harmony can be achieved. Witness again the relay-assembly-test room in the Western Electric researches and the case of the Inland Steel Container Co. Witness too the collaboration, armed if you will, between labor and management in many plants in dealing with grievances, job evaluation, working conditions, and other elements of the internal environment. Can we make industrial harmony the rule and not the exception? We have never really tried.

2 a · MOTIVATIONAL ANALYSIS

ROOTS OF INDUSTRIAL CONFLICT

A PRONOUNCED tendency has been evident during the past few decades for psychologists, sociologists, and anthropologists to move into the area of labor-management problems previously left to economists and "practical men." This movement has both intensified and popularized earlier reactions of social thinkers against oversimple interpretations of labor relations in terms of economic motives alone. Psychologically oriented students have long insisted that there is much more to the labor movement and industrial conflict than a fight over wages versus profits. Some have so overstressed the point, in fact, that they wind up by assigning a decidedly subordinate place to economic wants. More balanced views, however, while recognizing the basic importance of economic self-interests and material gains in our society, perceive the vital part played by a variety of other motivations as well. These views emphasize the multiplicity of goals toward which behavior is directed and their dependence on the entire range of social influences rather than on exclusively economic forces. Large parts of the two chapters in this section of the book are devoted to the elaboration of this general proposition.[1]

Of special interest is the increasing amount of attention now given to desires for status, social recognition, and human dignity and for personal freedom and independence, self-determination, and effective participation in carrying on one's own activities. As basic needs for subsistence and economic security are satisfied, these intangible self-esteem motivations that are so highly valued and encouraged as central to our democratic way of life assume new prominence. The popular "human-relations" emphasis in industry focuses on these "noneconomic" desires, sometimes to a degree that goes too far in neglecting the fundamental wants for material gain and security. But the opposite error is probably still the more common one—the failure to appreciate sufficiently working people's desires for self-determined, self-expressive activi-

---

[1] A recent book by Professor Viteles is invaluable in bringing together the widely scattered psychological research contributions pertaining to working people's motivations and attitudes. See Morris S. Viteles, *Motivation and Morale in Industry,* New York, Norton, 1953. The content of Viteles's book has special relevance to the topics in Parts 2a and 3b of the present volume.

ties. The employer too often does not see that doing something *for* employees cannot satisfy their very real psychological need that it be done *by* themselves or by an organization which they feel to be their own.

The chapters by Kornhauser and Katz develop a broad motivational approach to problems in this field. They cite illustrative examples of social and psychological thought and research, and they point out certain significant implications. The purpose of Chap. 5 is to furnish a frame of reference, a way of viewing the general phenomena of industrial conflict in our society from the standpoint of a social psychologist. The analysis suggests that industrial conflict is deeply rooted in opposed goals and expectations engendered in employers and working people in a free democratic and changing society like ours. It appears that adequate understanding of labor relations requires much more knowledge than can be derived from studies of particular labor-management cases, with analysis confined to the organizations directly involved. Likewise, it calls for more than is revealed by statistical correlations of the factors associated with number of strikes or with other indexes of conflict. A motivational approach, it is argued, forces one not only to consider changes in specified objective conditions but also to see the effects of these as dependent at the same time on pervasive cultural influences, on differential group pressures, and on organizational demands and individual determinants, as these all jointly shape people's attitudes and beliefs and govern the direction of their behavior.

Chapter 6, using the same type of motivational framework, concentrates on the question of what satisfactions and deprivations are typical for modern industrial workers and of how these affect morale and conflict. Katz analyzes evidence bearing on the effects of (1) the job itself or the content of the work, (2) the life of the worker in the plant, and (3) factors in his life outside the plant. He emphasizes that, while industrial conflict does not flow simply and directly from the general level of workers' dissatisfaction, nevertheless the amount of discontent does constitute one important condition. On the basis of the evidence, he singles out and underscores several salient sources of satisfaction and frustration in each of the three areas. The last part of the chapter elaborates especially upon the contrasting gratifications and morale effects dependent upon the different types of administrative organization developed in a company. Substantial support is found for the conclusion that decentralization of authority and responsibility, that is, granting increased opportunity for effective participation by individuals and groups at lower organizational levels, increases satisfaction. This extremely important theme is further discussed in Part 3a and in the concluding chapters of the book.

Taken seriously, we believe that a motivational approach—to be developed far beyond that sketched and illustrated in these chapters—can have far-reaching consequences for thinking and research in regard to industrial relations. It means that any valid generalizations about objective industrial conditions that affect labor-management relations must take into account the relevant motivations, which, in turn, depend upon the entire social context. Wage increases, cooperation plans, human-relations programs, and "flattened" organizational structures may indeed bring increased harmony; but at other times and places, in different contexts, and with different desires and expectations aroused, the same changes may have exactly opposite effects. This is not a counsel of despair. Rather it is a challenge to learn enough about the values, beliefs, and expectations that operate both in general and at particular times and places to be able to state within what limits, or under what social and motivational conditions, certain predicted results are probable. After all, social psychology and its sister disciplines are barely beginning to dig into these problems. It remains for the future to tell what the digging will yield.

CHAPTER 5 HUMAN MOTIVATIONS UNDER-LYING INDUSTRIAL CONFLICT

Arthur Kornhauser   *Wayne University*

INDUSTRIAL conflict is human conflict. At its core are people with certain interests and motives opposing other people with divergent interests and motives. The opposition, the warfare—"hot" or "cold"—stems from conflicting desires, incompatible objectives, goal values that are not shared by the two groups. Each perceives the achievement of its goals as interfered with by the efforts of the other. The understanding of these opposed "goal strivings" is the central problem for the social psychologist tackling the industrial-conflict relationship.

The Problem of Motivation

The conflicting goals to be considered include, but certainly reach beyond, the purposes that appear at the surface in demands for a 10-cent-an-hour wage increase and similar specific benefits. Adequate psychological understanding must concern itself with motivations that are deeper and more pervasive than those that are directly manifest in the particular points of contention in labor disputes. The more general sources of opposition spring from the whole broad range of aspirations and ungratified needs that impel people in our society to struggle restlessly toward what they think will be a more satisfying life for themselves.

A search for the roots of industrial conflict, in other words, calls for an inquiry into the wants and the frustrations of 20th-century "industrial man." What are the directions and dimensions of working people's desires, and to what extent do they feel that their needs are being satisfied? One important component of industrial conflict must be sought in the answer to such questions. The labor leader, to use C. Wright Mills's neat phrase, is a "manager of discontent."

But owners and industrial managements also have their needs and their discontent. In performing their functions, including their relations with labor, they too experience wants and expectations that are thwarted or threatened in a way that leads them to push for changes or to resist impending changes. And what is true of managers is, in great or small degree, likewise true of labor leaders, government officials, and everyone else, each in his own varied relationships to industry and labor.

Efforts to explain peaceful versus conflictful relations in industry have usually turned to investigations of the objective conditions associated with each. Is there greater or less conflict when price levels are rising or falling? How much conflict is there in industries where labor costs are large or small in proportion to other costs? How does a given piece of labor legislation affect industrial conflict? What is the effect of company size, the age of the union, the employees' skill level, and the administrative organization of the plant? While objective descriptions and statistical correlations of such factors certainly contribute valuable knowledge, it is equally clear that they leave much to be desired. It is usually recognized that the influence of each variable depends on a vast network of other conditions, past and present—upon, indeed, the entire social and economic environment, including characteristics of the particular situation such as the cohesiveness and divisive elements within the management and employee groups, the history of peace or conflict between the organizations, personalities on both sides, and many additional factors. In more human and dynamic terms, the effect of all the conditions and changes depends on the *meanings* that they have for the persons concerned; and these meanings depend on the varied structures of needs, attitudes, and beliefs of the persons.

Efforts to account for people's differing interpretations of situations and for their actions quite commonly and naturally prompt the question: "Why?" Why do workers join unions? Why do company executives oppose this or that demand? Why do union leaders decide to strike or to accept the employer's offer? Why the militancy—or its absence? Why *all* the behavior summed up in the words "industrial conflict"? The why questions are directed at the "purposive" characteristic of actions. The inquirer wishes to "understand" the behavior by ascertaining its intent or objective. The course of conduct "makes sense" in so far as it can be seen as instrumental to the fulfillment of ends. Specific actions are then explicable as means, as moves directed toward predictable goals, even though the means themselves may be varied and unpredictable. "Motives" become the key explanatory concept since they are the processes in the person that do the "directing," that function in the present to orient his behavior toward the future.

The thesis advanced in this chapter is simply that attempts to analyze the motives operating in labor-management situations represent potentially important additions to unstable generalizations based on empirical correlations and descriptive historical accounts. An examination of the nature and usefulness of the motivational interpretations available for this task constitutes the substance of what follows. This emphasis on motivation in no sense denies the importance of factors in the objective situation, past and present, as correlative determinants of behavior. Motives themselves are products of social learning in past situations, and they function now in relation to the specific present situation. To account for action by reference to motives should never imply a neglect of the changing environmental conditions with reference to which the motives operate. Conflict behavior is to be understood in terms of social motivations functioning *within the particular objective circumstances*.

In passing, it should be noted that all too frequently, when psychological analyses are offered by economists, businessmen, and others interested in labor-management relations, the interpretations are grossly oversimplified and inadequate. If the concepts of dynamic psychology are to be usefully applied to this complex field of social behavior, we need to be on guard against the errors and shortcomings of "common sense." While psychology does not stand ready with satisfactory and agreed-upon conclusions concerning motivation, at least a few guiding views appear worth setting down. In the current unsettled state of thought on these matters, it will be clear, however, that I am simply sketching what I believe to be a tenable formulation with no claims to thoroughness, orthodoxy, or originality.

Characteristics of Human Motivation

The motivation concept is a tool to help order our knowledge concerning the goal directedness of behavior. It includes all those states and processes in a person that account for the orientation of thought and action toward ends or goals. The need for such explanatory aids is clear enough: innumerable observations attest to the fact that behavior has future reference and that present actions are understandable by knowledge of what they lead to, or what they are expected to lead to, by the persons acting.

Motivation theories simply assert that this future reference of behavior is accounted for by inner tendencies or conditions existing in the present and determining the course of action toward predictable outcomes. The internal processes that function motivationally are quite varied, and different theories stress certain ones or others of these processes. In general, the motives are viewed as states of tension or disequilibrium, described either in physiological or psychological terms. They include specific chemical conditions of blood and other tissues, organic deficits and pressures, muscular sets, states of disequilibrium in the nervous system, as well as verbalized desires and purposes, thoughts, images, and other conscious processes. Motivational explanations can well utilize both types of knowledge: that which comes from self-observation as well as that detected and inferred by the outside observer.

Whatever the particular organic or mental process that functions motivationally, it does so in so far as it tends to persist and to stimulate and facilitate certain behavior, while inhibiting other behavior, until the proper tension-relieving changes are brought about. While this predisposing or directing function may depend partly on inherent physiological connections between "drive states" and appropriate responses, in human motivation it is predominantly due to the fact that tension-reducing types of action have become associated with the motive state through lifetime processes of social learning.

From what has been said it is clear that motivations include those that are "unconscious" as well as those that are "conscious." This means that we cannot rest content with the purposes and desires people report as their motives; it is necessary to go behind and beneath these. Frequently deeper, less obvious (and less socially approved) motives can be inferred from the course of the behavior itself, particularly if the current observations are supplemented by knowledge concerning behavior of the person or group in the past.

It is now widely recognized, for example, that a stated goal of higher wages may veil unverbalized strivings for self-respect and dignity or vague hostilities toward the boss, the machine, and the entire industrial discipline. The unstated motivations may be inferred at times from the fact that the discontent continues after the wage increase is granted, from the comparative satisfaction of those individuals who are given more responsible positions or symbols of status instead of wage increases, and from innumerable bits of confirmatory observation about the particular men involved and about people generally in our society.

The person who boasts or takes the offensive in interpersonal dealings rarely will assign as his motive the desire to hide his own fears and avoid facing his feeling of personal inadequacy. The employer who pleads emotionally for the protection of the workingman's rights against union coercion is not likely to acknowledge even to himself the part that his own self-interest and opposition to strong unions play in his beliefs or to admit that his heated condemnation of union tyranny may stem from hidden self-doubts about his own authoritarian tactics. The same unconscious mechanisms operate, of course, in labor leaders and all other people. Both clinical practice and everyday experience confirm the importance of the varied motivations that are only dimly recognized by the person himself or that are completely outside his awareness.

But if conscious purposes fail to provide a fully adequate understanding of motives, an attempt to turn to biological drives for the answer serves even less satisfactorily. The basic drives, or organic needs, such as hunger, sex, and fatigue, do indeed constitute significant types of motivation. But it is misleading to take them as the model for motivational explanations in general, though this is often done. A brief review of certain leading characteristics of distinctively human motivation, that is, of socially acquired motives, will indicate the differences. More important, it will call attention to aspects of motivation of particular significance for understanding complex social actions of the kind that appear in industrial conflict.

1. The goals of social behavior are more variable, less specifically fixed by the nature of the organism. In the case of bodily needs, the consummatory acts that bring relief can be specified within quite definite limits. By contrast, the end reactions which gratify desires for self-esteem or for personal security, for example, vary enormously from culture to culture, from person to person, and even from situation to situation for the same person. Thirst always requires drinking; but who can say what particular behavior will be the inevitable end result of workmanship impulses or fondness for power? Hostility toward the boss or company may manifest itself in anything from inaudible epithets to a full-scale strike. An indefinitely large array of specific actions are functionally equivalent in satisfying the socialized needs and, hence, substitutable one for another. Consequently, attempts to understand the motives that underlie industrial-conflict behavior must not be confined to some distinctive manifestation (say, the strike) but must be alert to all the varied and devious expressions of opposition.

2. In contrast to organic drives, too, the socialized motivations often operate less imperatively. They are ordinarily more readily quieted or avoided, short of fulfillment. A great deal of unjustified psychologizing about human motives and their thwarting rests on the dubious analogy that, because the physical needs, when aroused, persist and dominate behavior until the tension is relieved, the same must be true for all other motives. Actually, however, many of our socialized motivations become active and remain active without

the compelling quality of the organic needs; they may persist for a time and then subside again even when no substantial gratification has occurred. There appears no sufficient basis in fact for the view that any and all motives, once actively aroused, insistently demand gratification, with dire consequences for the personality as the alternative.

3. Organic drives typically lead to behavior that relieves a state of tension or deficit and thus permits the organism to return to the *status quo ante*. This characteristic of biological drives has become especially significant in its questionable application to motives generally. The question is whether motivated conduct as a whole can properly be described as producing a return to the antecedent state of equilibrium. While this concept of "homeostasis" may be useful in reference to physiological drives, it easily encourages fallacious conclusions if one is considering, for example, desire for power or status. The power- or status-motivated person does not merely return, after each achievement, to a previously existing condition of stability; rather the motivations persist on a new level, with newly defined goals, new worlds to conquer.

In the negotiating process between management and union representatives, for example, the gaining of an objective by either party frequently does not mean that he has now recaptured a condition of internal equilibrium that had been upset by the changes that precipitated the dispute. Rather the very process of satisfying the particular tension has changed the participants and created new interests and revised expectations that will continue to require further adjustments. Emphasis on this growing, changing, emergent quality of motivated behavior appears more realistic and enlightening than a presumed reinstatement of a preceding state of stability or equilibrium.

4. By analogy with organic drives it is also easy to slip into the belief that motives operate over relatively short time periods, that they account for behavior sequences of only very limited duration. After all, the organic needs are usually taken care of with reasonable dispatch. But it is worth emphasizing that motivational explanations are pertinent to behavior lasting through years as well as minutes. The inner directive influences that impel a man to become a lawyer, to build an industrial empire, to get revenge on the corporation that mistreated him years earlier—these are no less problems of motivation than the explanation of why the foreman impulsively fires an employee for calling him a liar.

The short and the long sequences of behavior do not really present separate sets of problems. The smaller segments of conduct are themselves parts of the larger. In moving toward long-run goals, a person seeks subgoals and sub-subgoals. When one is analyzing social actions, this hierarchical arrangement of goals becomes most significant. Frequently the motivation for the momentary behavior can be understood only through knowledge concerning its relation to the remote objectives, as perceived by the actor. Neglect of this consideration may account for the frequently expressed astonishment and charge of "irrationality" in reference to the losses that labor-union members (and companies) are willing to suffer in carrying on a strike the gains from which, it appears, cannot possibly repay the sacrifice. What is omitted is the extent to which the short-run goal in this dispute is believed to affect the long-run goals of the company and the union in their relations to each other (as well as the perceived effects on a variety of other personal and institutional objectives of the persons concerned).

5. Finally, it is most important to underscore the extent to which social learning makes human motivation different from the "animal drives." While motivation processes, like all other conditions of the human animal, are built upon biologically inherited foundations, the particular directions they take are defined by social influences. The hereditary potentialities are actualized through a lifetime of social learning, beginning in earliest infancy. Even in the case of hunger and sex, it is evident that the elementary biological drives are drastically modified to form desires for corned beef and cabbage, chop suey, or shashlik and for quite specific types of sex object and conditions for sex satisfaction. As we turn to motivations less closely related to specifiable organic drives, such as need dispositions and wants having to do with personal security or curiosity or power position, the overwhelming importance of the socially acquired (and the insignificance of the biologically given) is difficult to deny.

The goals a person seeks are those he has "absorbed" from the groups of which he has been and is a member. He comes to act, think, perceive, and feel as his social groups expect him to; he learns to accept the values, and to be the kind of person, his society calls for; and, specifically, he lives up to what is expected of persons in the status and roles he occupies. What models are set for him as worthy and unworthy goals? Especially, what do his parents and others with whom he emotionally identifies strive for? And in his own developing behavior, which courses of action are reinforced through approval and rewards, and which ones are "extinguished"? The individual learns to want and seek those things he is supposed to want according to the standards of his family, friends, and larger reference groups.

Certain broad goals are shared by the whole society; others are emphasized by particular divisions of the population, for example, by national, religious, and socioeconomic groupings. Moreover, in a diversified and changing society like ours, since everyone is exposed to incompatible standards and subjected to cross pressures from several groups, his own motivations represent combinations and resultants that do not rigidly conform to any one pattern. Industrial-conflict behavior is to be understood and dealt with by reference both to the common motivations dominant in our society and to those motivations specially characteristic of the groups and individuals involved in conflict.

The remaining sections of this chapter attempt to indicate ways in which the preceding observations bear upon problems of industrial conflict. We begin by considering the principal goal values prevalent in our culture and the possible usefulness of a working classification of these "dependable motives."

A Classification of Motives

Psychologists face a peculiar paradox in the matter of motive classifications. While the applied literature of the field and many professional practitioners continue to utilize convenient categorizations of motives, the winds of psychological doctrine have blown in an opposite direction. Classifications of motives have become increasingly rare in the formulations of recent social-psychology theory.[1] Nevertheless, I believe that such classifications are useful and that their theoretical respectability can be defended.[2]

A working classification along the following lines is suggested, though no particular classification can be considered in any sense final. The socially defined motivational categories or "goal values" are certainly not to be conceived of as "culture free"; all that is suggested here is that they are characteristic within our own culture. They may or may not correspond to the principal motivations found in other societies.

Organic drives, with specifiable physiological bases and homeostatic goals
(Hunger; thirst; escape from pain and extreme temperature; other sensory preferences; sex [at physiological level]; rest and sleep [fatigue]; exercise and release of energy; need for air and for elimination of body wastes; emotional tensions, positive and negative; etc.)
Some principal socially defined motives
Desire for security; escape from danger and threat; fear and anxiety
Desire for social approval, recognition, and admiration
Desire for power, mastery, and ascendance; self-assertive motives
Desire for personal freedom, independence, and self-expression
Desire for affection, personal response, companionship, and love (socialized sex motives)
Desire to help and protect others ("parental" motives)
Desire for effectiveness, completeness, and excellence of performance ("workmanship" and curiosity motives)
Desire to destroy whatever interferes with other desires; motives of aggression
Desire for self-esteem; pride; maintenance of feelings of personal worth

Perhaps a few other categories should be added, for example, desire to submit and be dependent; desire to acquire things; and desires to play, to have

---

[1] Evidence regarding the current unpopularity of motive classifications is supplied by an examination of social-psychology textbooks of the last few years. The use of motivational categories is either ignored or rejected, for example, in such well-known books as the following: David Krech and Richard S. Crutchfield, *Theory and Problems of Social Psychology,* New York, McGraw-Hill, 1948; M. Sherif, *An Outline of Social Psychology,* New York, Harper, 1948; Richard T. LaPiere and Paul R. Farnsworth, *Social Psychology,* New York, McGraw-Hill, 1949; A. R. Lindesmith and A. L. Strauss, *Social Psychology,* New York, Dryden, 1949; T. M. Newcomb, *Social Psychology,* New York, Dryden, 1950; S. S. Sargent, *Social Psychology,* New York, Ronald, 1950; S. E. Asch, *Social Psychology,* New York, Prentice-Hall, 1952; R. E. L. Faris, *Social Psychology,* New York, Ronald, 1952; and E. L. Hartley and R. E. Hartley, *Fundamentals of a Social Psychology,* New York, Knopf, 1952. It is interesting to note that a few books, which have greater interest in *applications,* do introduce classifications of social motives, for example: S. H. Britt, *Social Psychology of Modern Life,* rev. ed., New York, Rinehart, 1949; and R. Dewey and W. J. Humber, *The Development of Human Behavior,* New York, Macmillan, 1951.

[2] Among the leading attempts in recent years to develop a systematic psychology of human motives, incorporating a classification of social motives, are those of the following authors: H. A. Murray, *Explorations in Personality,* New York, Oxford, 1938; H. A. Murray, "Toward a Classification of Interaction," in T. Parsons and E. A. Shils (eds.), *Toward a General Theory of Action,* Cambridge, Mass., Harvard University Press, 1951, pp. 434–464; A. H. Maslow, "A Theory of Human Motivation," *Psychological Review,* 50 (1943), 370–396; and E. C. Tolman, "A Psychological Model," in Parsons and Shils (eds.), *op. cit.,* pp. 279–361, esp. pp. 321–323, 335–336.

fun, to enjoy one's self; but since there is some possibility that these can better be treated as subgoals, they are not separately listed here.

It seems clear that classifications like the above are not created out of thin air. These dependable motives represent the thoughtful inferences of many observers based upon observations of millions of purposive activities and upon the grouping of the activities according to the goals or ends toward which the behavior is oriented. Certainly, the ends of conduct are often complex, ambiguous, and difficult to discern. But the opposite is true in enough cases to provide reasonably sure footing for the student who pushes ahead cautiously. Although there is no one "right" and accepted classification of motives in our culture, a considerable amount of agreement exists concerning the major ones.

Any carefully considered list of motivational categories promises to have value as a set of working tools. At the very least, it serves to emphasize the variety of motives and warns against oversimple thinking in terms of "economic wants" alone or any other one-sided or too-restricted interpretations. But beyond this, the classification provides a beginning toward systematically organizing our knowledge concerning the directions of people's striving and thus serves as a guide for further inquiry into the particular behavior in question. The categories call attention to possible reasons for action which might easily go unnoticed but which, once one considers them, may appear well worth investigating by collecting relevant evidence. In other words, while the list of motives cannot in itself offer any useful, ready-made explanations of behavior, it does serve as a source of hypotheses or "hunches" that supply starting points for inquiry into the past and subsequent behavior and attitudes of the persons involved, as they respond to the particular situational influences and opportunities to which they are exposed. These directed observations test whether the facts support or contradict the tentative motivational explanations.

Why, for example, do so many working people join labor unions? Or why do the men in a particular place refuse to join? Answers to such questions certainly do not flow directly from a list of motive categories. These provide no easy differential explanations. But the investigator who starts by thoughtfully weighing the possibilities suggested by each motive in turn will launch his inquiries with a wealth of plausible interpretations to aid him in arriving at answers. He will also have guarded against the overlooking of interesting and perhaps important parts of a sound interpretation. He will proceed to investigate, in respect to each main goal, the extent to which the working people under study find that their present conditions and opportunities gratify or thwart their aspirations.

Since the limitations and weaknesses of mere lists of motives have so commonly been stressed by psychologists, it seems worthwhile supplementing what has been said in order to indicate the way in which such categories may properly be conceived.

In the first place, it is essential to recognize that the separate motives do not function singly. Conduct is an expression of complicated combinations, integrations, and conflicts among the different tendencies. Rarely, if ever, can a particular act be ascribed solely to this or that isolated motive. The most one can say is that a particular need or desire is primary or dominant in controlling the observed behavior. All the goal orientations exist within one person; all involve the relationships of goal objects to the actor himself. The complex set of motives centering in self-esteem becomes most notably involved along with each of the others. Moreover, the motives represented in this category include a vast elaboration of supporting motivational processes (the "defense mechanisms") which enter subtly into the dynamics of personalities striving to solve, or to escape, their problems. An individual may continue to work long, hard hours at a job after he has reached retirement age, not only because he is still trying to build up a "nest egg for old age," but because paid employment helps maintain his self-esteem, because he gets workmanship satisfactions out of his job, because he fears the dreary monotony of checker games and idleness, because he enjoys the company of his fellows on the job, and because he can't tolerate the constant companionship of his wife at home. Although one motive may be dominant in given behavior, the actions of individuals are characteristically directed by combinations of needs and wishes as these are uniquely organized within the person.

A second significant point to be noted is that the dependable motives vary greatly in strength and specific direction from person to person, from group to group, and from time to time. While these wants are more or less universal in our society, this does not mean that they are fixed and uniform for all individuals. On the contrary, their differential explanatory value lies in the fact that they differ in emphasis and specific direction for different people living under different social and economic conditions. For one person or group during a given time period, security goals may be intense and dominant; for other persons or for these same people under other conditions, needs for personal freedom or affection or some other desires may be uppermost. Motives arrange themselves in hierarchies, though relative positions within the hierarchy shift depending on the values emphasized in the current social milieu and on the degree to which conditions of life, past and present, provide gratifications or impose deprivations in respect to the several needs. Those motives that are stressed by a person's social groups and that remain inadequately satisfied tend to function as salient determinants of behavior.[3]

As a consequence, inquiry into the why of concrete industrial behavior is compelled to study the *differential* facts pertaining to the direction and intensity of the motivations operating in the particular persons or groups dealt with. There is no substitute for specific evidence concerning the aims and needs that are present in each instance of industrial conflict under study. The view advanced in the present chapter is simply that the concrete empirical research is illuminated and made more productive if it is conducted within an organizing frame of reference built around the conception of broad underlying motivations.

A third closely related consideration in regard to the use of a general

---

[3] Professors Maslow and Tolman and others note that there are observable uniformities in the hierarchic arrangement of motives. The insistent biological demands must be satisfied before other, "higher-level," needs assert themselves; and, it is argued, certain of the social needs similarly take precedence over others. See Maslow, *op. cit.*; and Tolman, *op. cit.*

motive classification is the recognition that each category comprehends within itself a range of more specific desires. The classification attempts to group the diverse tendencies in reference to ends or goals that are, in some sense, basic or ultimate for the person, that are sought each for its own sake and not as a means to something else. But the person's quest for these general objectives always takes the form of needs and desires directed toward particular objects, situations, and relationships.

These motivations directed toward particular objects can be thought of as "attitudes." An attitude is simply a learned tendency or readiness to react to a specified object in a predictable manner and direction but not with an automatic or invariable response. For example, a hostile attitude toward a company implies readiness to engage in behavior that by one means or another will injure and weaken the "adversary"; other attitudes portend approach, avoidance, destruction of the object, exalting or derogating it, supporting or opposing it, and innumerable other such orientations. Overt behavior is largely interpretable as an acting out of these socially acquired attitudinal sets or tendencies.

The variety of attitudes is unlimited. We have attitudes of friendliness, resentment, or antagonism; critical attitudes or tolerant attitudes; attitudes of disgust; capitalistic attitudes, authoritarian attitudes, or prolabor attitudes. Attitudes may be pointed quite specifically toward particular persons or objects, *e.g.,* aversion to a certain radio commentator's voice. Or the attitudes may be directed at relationships of any degree of generality, for example, receptivity toward all social change or an attitude of opposition to all political activity by labor unions. In each instance the attitude implies a disposition toward action of a somewhat definite, but still highly variable, character. The goal or direction is definite; the specific actions are not.

Attitudes may bear a simple or a complex relationship to the dependable motives with which they are associated. A friendly attitude may express a relatively direct and uncomplicated "desire for response," or it may represent a striving for security, social approval, power, and enhanced self-esteem. A hostile attitude toward the boss may be compounded of self-assertiveness, desires for independence and freedom, security, recognition, and pride—in fact, all the person's deeper motives. Some of the motives that seek gratification through a given attitude and the behavior it prompts may be prominent; others remain secondary or negligible. Moreover, motives which predominated in the origin of the attitude may later become insignificant, while new motives enter to support the attitude and its associated conduct.

These considerations lead to the practical conclusion that a psychological understanding of labor-management relations requires not only the ascertaining of relevant attitudes but also the analysis of their *current motivational significance* for the persons involved. It is not enough to learn the attitudes workers and employers have toward each other, toward unions, and toward work and employment relations. We need to know at the same time what deeper, broader motivations, such as the categories previously listed, are being gratified or thwarted in a way that engenders the particular attitudes that are expressed. It is not enough to know that a number of labor leaders feel strongly opposed to piece rates, nor even to find out how these attitudes origi-

· nated. The crucial question is what motives (and what pressures and influences) *now* dictate adherence to the stand against incentive wages.

A classification of basic motives, then, is in no sense an alternative to the study of particular attitudes. Specific attitudes and broad motive categories are both valuable motivational concepts. The broad categories are merely higher-level, more general inferences from a wider range of behavior. Thus, for example, an inquiry into attitudes may conclude that a group of workers has strong favorable feelings toward being consulted and being asked to contribute ideas concerning their jobs. But we can also go on to consider many parallel cases of participant behavior plus ten thousand other instances of reactions to personal involvement under widely varied circumstances—all of which may support the conclusion that, quite generally in our society, people are positively disposed toward any relationship that they perceive as affording opportunities for self-expression or that provides recognition and enhancement of their personal worth. These last-named motive categories, then, are very general attitudes toward *whatever* is believed to bring social approval, increased power, security, independence, affection, or others of the major goal values.

A final word, now, in regard to the usefulness of motive classifications: The outstanding criticism leveled against this approach is that it leads to empty tautological or circular explanations. People fight because they have an "instinct of pugnacity" (a generalized motive of aggression); they join unions because they are "gregarious" (that is, are joiners); and so on. The foregoing discussion has tried to make clear the reasons for rejecting this criticism. Certainly, motive labels have sometimes been used in the fashion criticized, but this misuse is not at all inevitable. The goal values can be employed as organizing concepts to guide inquiry into the concrete evidence and to interpret findings in a way that reaches toward significant generalizations. Motive categories in themselves never will explain why some companies and unions negotiate harmoniously while others quarrel, why conflict is greater in one industry than another, and why it is different this year from last year. But they *can* help in finding the answers. While they are not substitutes for hard facts about people's specific needs and acts in response to the changing conditions that affect conduct, they serve as aids for ferreting out the relevant information that provides the desired insight and understanding.

The Self—Its Inner Conflicts and Frustrations

Clearly the rich reality of complex human motivation far transcends the schematic approach sketched in the preceding pages. The oversimple picture requires at least enough supplementation to provide a hint of the complications encountered and analyzed by students of personality dynamics.[4] The supplementation can perhaps best consist of a few notes concerning the

---

[4] Some of the principal contributions of Sigmund Freud and his followers as well as those of numerous non-Freudian psychologists are discussed in G. Murphy, *Personality*, New York, Harper, 1947; and in D. C. McClelland, *Personality*, New York, William Sloane Associates, 1951. Both these books contain many references to the voluminous literature in this field.

"self" (or ego) and the typical motivational mechanisms that come into being as defenses of the self in relieving its inner conflicts, anxieties, and frustrations.

Motivated behavior may move forward smoothly to its goal or it may encounter obstacles. In so far as a kindly environment—especially in the form of a society free of severe contradictions in its values and expectations—affords individuals ready means for the fulfillment of their wants and in so far as the desires are channeled successfully toward attainable objectives, satisfying adjustments prevail. Contrariwise, where this desire clashes with that, where aroused motives persist in the face of unsurmounted difficulties either environmental or in the person himself, satisfying behavior is impossible. A condition of unrelieved tension ensues, which manifests itself as unrest, dissatisfaction, emotional irritability, and a striking about for some way out, for some means either to break through or to withdraw from the struggle. The extent to which these conditions of frustration are prevalent in different groups in present-day industry will go far in determining the occurrence of industrial conflict.

Outstandingly significant in producing human frustration and its consequent behavior are those conflicts of incompatible motives in which the self is deeply involved. The conflicts bring into play the strong systematized feelings each of us has built up toward himself, the key motives that have come to dominate our lives. Just as we have complex multimotivated attitudes toward friends, family, job, and country, so do we have them toward ourselves. These self-regarding attitudes are at the very heart of a person's makeup. They include the cluster of attitudes which have to do with self-esteem, feeling of personal worth, suspicion of one's personal inadequacy or inferiority, fear of being unloved or unwanted, doubts concerning one's moral worth or social acceptability, intense desire to be *this* sort of person, and aversion to being *that* sort.

The development of a conception of self and of the motivations associated with it is largely a process of internalizing the approval and disapproval of others with regard to one's appearance, skills, attitudes, desires, and values. Initially, the self-image and the accompanying motives reflect the manner in which parental rewards and punishments have been administered. But additional modifications take place in all the other social relationships of the person.

The point to be stressed in the present connection is the special part these self-feelings play in people's inner conflicts and the behavior that results. The key consideration is this: *Every person struggles to maintain favorable feelings toward himself.* A person thinks and acts positively toward those things which fit in with, or enhance, his self-esteem and feeling of personal security; he reacts negatively toward those that conflict with, or lower, his self-feelings. Each of us strives to hold on to his feelings of personal worth in spite of failures and in the face of insistent desires which are irreconcilable with the self he admires. The incompatible motives that conflict with the accepted self-image tend to be repressed and become inaccessible to conscious recall and verbal expression. They continue to function, but at an "unconscious" level. Repression reduces the anxiety and tension resulting from the conflicting desires, but these unconscious motives continue to press for gratification and in doing so produce further effects upon behavior.

An understanding of the devious processes people employ in resolving inner conflicts is important for an understanding of industrial conflict, since the behavior of people in industry is always partially determined by their personal patterns of self-defense. An analysis of such defensive patterns is particularly relevant to the understanding of behavior where the parties to an industrial dispute act in puzzling or unexpected ways or in a manner that appears to be contrary to their own self-interests. In such situations, as in neurosis, the apparent irrationality of the action arises from the fact that (1) the behavior in question is functioning to minimize inner conflict and anxiety rather than simply to attain the objective goal and (2) the repressed motives tend to elicit actions which have not been thought out and evaluated since the entire process remains somewhat detached from the integrated core of the personality.

A few examples of the typical mechanisms of defense by which individuals maintain their positive self-feelings in the face of threatening inner conflicts and frustrations are the following:

Fantasy. When individuals are severely frustrated by unpleasant realities or conflicting motives, they may take refuge in daydreams which provide make-believe wish fulfillments. The emphasis on happy endings in the great majority of Hollywood movies is an attempt to provide fantasy gratifications for the deprivations which people experience in the real world. The Horatio Alger fantasy that "every man can become a millionaire"—or, more modestly, the factory worker's dream of retiring to a ranch or chicken farm—has served to preserve self-esteem on many unpleasant industrial jobs, but it has frequently militated against employers and employees making an honest appraisal of the industrial situation.

Compensation. Compensatory reactions are defenses against feelings of inferiority or inadequacy growing out of real or imagined defects and failures. Such reactions usually draw attention away from the flaw and substitute more desirable characteristics. Industrial workers frequently compensate for felt inadequacies in their role as wage earners by emphasizing their achievements in other spheres, such as hunting and fishing, sex exploits, craftsmanship at home, or by rabid perusal of the accomplishments of the local athletic teams. People who feel caught in a weak or untenable position are likely to "throw their weight around" to hide the unpleasant truth from themselves. Acts of special kindness or charity may occur in compensation for past sins or in preparation for cutting new throats, not as deliberate techniques of deception, but as ways in which the actor himself is saved from facing his hateful intent.

Rationalization. When people are unable to accept the true motives for their actions or are unable to tolerate the frustration connected with an unattainable goal, they rationalize the situation by finding reasons acceptable to the self for the current predicament. Failures may be rationalized, for example, by disparaging the unattainable object ("sour-grapes" mechanism) or by pointing up the desirable features of present unimpressive attainments ("sweet-lemon" mechanism). Ruthless industrial-relations policies have sometimes been rationalized as "for the good of the employees themselves," for example, the old contention that child-labor practices really benefit the children by teaching them good habits and keeping them out of mischief through having useful work to do.

Displacement. When impulses cannot be directly expressed because their presence is inadmissible to the person's self-standards, the impulses may be displaced, with accompanying rationalizations, toward more accessible individuals or objects. The utilization of scapegoats as a displaced target for aggressive impulses is one of the more common instances of the operation of this mechanism in our society. The hostility of workers toward members of minority groups frequently represents a displacement of aggressive impulses generated by the frustrations imposed by life conditions and personal inadequacies. Or the aggression may be directed toward less skilled workers, the boss, or trivial annoyances of the job. Displacements of aggressions engendered at home on employees and fellow workers or, inversely, taking out work frustrations on the wife, have become proverbial—a "kicking-the-dog" mechanism.

These examples illustrate only a few of the manifold self-protective ways in which people handle their inner tensions that arise from conflicts of motives. In interpreting behavior in terms of these mechanisms, it is important to recognize that actions do not fall into two classes, the self-defensive and the not self-defensive. It is rather a question of the *degree* to which motivation is functioning defensively in any given act, that is, the extent to which the process serves to hide from the individual the things that it would be painful or even intolerable for him to admit to himself. Moreover, these various types of motivation must be treated as valuable suggested interpretations of conduct, to be checked upon as hypotheses, but not to be tacked on to this or that behavior as explanatory labels. It is necessary to examine evidence of their applicability in each particular instance, just as in the case of the general motive categories previously discussed. But unless one has these and many additional possible interpretations in mind, there is little likelihood that he will discover significant evidence to contribute to his understanding of people's less obvious ways of acting. The more plausible and comprehensive the motivational concepts with which one approaches the behavior to be interpreted, the greater the probability of arriving at a sound, practically useful understanding of that behavior.

Motivations of Industrial Conflict

A motivational analysis of industrial conflict is concerned with the behavior of all persons and groups significantly involved in the relationships between labor and management. The activities and attitudes of leaders and officials at all levels, in their roles as organization representatives and spokesmen, notably require attention. But no less in need of analysis are the motivations of working people, directors, bankers, merchants, legislators, opinion influencers, consumers, and voters—everyone in so far as he affects the state of labor relations. The relevant behavior is not limited to collective bargaining, strikes, and other organized dealings between the "parties." Neither is it confined, as implied in most attitude surveys, to informal and personal expressions of individual dissatisfactions and antagonisms. Keeping the central posi-

tion of organized group relationships in view, we can still profitably focus on
the actions and motivations of the interacting individuals—in the roles they
occupy and subject to the group pressures and interpersonal influences operating upon them—since it is in their behavior that the multifarious influences
in the situation converge and are screened and sorted as to the part they will
play in producing conflict or harmony. This approach seeks uniformities not
in the complex environmental conditions nor in the diversities of observed
behavior but in the *meanings* these objective factors have in reference to the
needs, attitudes, and goal orientations of the people involved.

In any analysis of the motivations that enter into industrial-conflict behavior it is essential that one make clear whether the purpose is to understand
particular cases of conflict, say, in one company versus others, this year contrasted with last year, these individuals versus others in the same situation,
or to understand generically the sources of labor-management disharmony
over large areas of industrial society and through long time periods. The conflict behavior in question, whether limited or widespread, reflects divergent
aims and attitudes between interest groups; but in the particular cases the
differential explanations pertain to peculiarities of the personalities and to the
specific pressures and influences operating in those situations, while for the
general case the paramount task is to discover the pervasive factors in "human
nature" (as found in mid-20th-century America) and in the conditions of
modern work and life (including social organization) that lead to labor-management oppositions, in so far as these characterize industry as a whole.

We shall here give primary attention to the general problem. It is the
more fundamental and necessary question from the standpoint of society as
a whole, in order both to understand more fully the present state of industrial
relations and to appreciate the broad alternatives that lie ahead. Although research on special cases, treated in considerable detachment from the world
in which they exist, is more feasible and "practical," and is currently vastly
more popular, its significance is severely restricted. Although it can contribute
valuably to the cultivation of harmony and to the cordiality of relations within
the "social system" of the company studied, it is questionable whether it does
not omit crucially important determining conditions that lie outside the local
situation, including prominently the existence of sharp and overt conflict relations at other points in the larger social system of which this firm is an inevitable part. Stated bluntly, the question is this: Do local plant studies minimize the existence of conflict and the basic causes that produce it by concentrating on the restricted situation and the peace which it enjoys and by
neglecting the extent to which this harmony occurs by reason of battles fought
elsewhere and at other times?

Motivation-oriented studies of industrial harmony and conflict cannot be
bounded by plant walls nor by a defined plant "society." People's wants and
expectations are surely not determined solely by what occurs at the work place.
The motivations that enter into labor relations reflect events in other plants
as well, and in the economic and political system generally, in the "outside"
life of individuals, in the shifting standards of the times as these are reflected
in the views of whatever leadership and reference groups the people turn to.
Relationships within a company are approved and maintained in a peaceful

state because they are perceived as comparing favorably with what went before and with other places, that is, with current expectations and specific goals. The expectations which have their roots in the big world beyond the plant are no less indispensable for an understanding of conflict or its absence than are the procedures adopted by a company in efforts to satisfy employees' current desires peacefully. If expectation levels, stimulated by gains won elsewhere through conflict, rise and threaten to overtake local achievements, then the local harmony is likely to be preserved only as the no-conflict establishment is motivated to meet the new expectations resulting from distant conflict. The essential point, for present purposes, is simply that an understanding of industrial conflict must consider relationships in the whole society. While inquiry may well focus on the particular company situation, realism requires that the behavior under study be examined in its dependence on external influences as well. Both sets of factors need to be caught up and coherently organized in a comprehensive attitude-motivation analysis that concerns itself with the basic question of why labor and management groups are in conflict to whatever extent they are.

This basic question is answerable in general terms. More detailed and specific answers are being slowly and arduously hammered out by research workers from all the social-science disciplines. The following chapter by Dr. Katz provides a view of certain significant accomplishments in this direction. In the remaining pages of this chapter, I shall sketch a few broad features of the *general* answer.

The over-all picture is this: Large numbers of working people are discontented. Many more, while not actively dissatisfied, experience desires that are less fully gratified than they have come to believe is just and possible. Consequently, both groups strive to make gains, to protect and advance their interests, and to change things to accord better with their aspirations. They turn to, and support, leaders and organizations perceived as working toward these goals. But other powerful groups oppose such changes. Owners and managers of industry, on the whole, seek to retain their traditional rights and the freedom of control which they believe necessary to the interests of production, profits, and the general welfare of society, as they see it. Basically industrial conflict arises from the persistent urge of working people to get more and from the resistance by owners and managers to many of the changes that this entails. Labor unrest is the dynamic element.

But what is the motivation of labor unrest? What causes discontent? What is it working people want more of? Correspondingly, of course, what motivates management to resist demanded changes? And, on both sides, which opposed needs are sufficiently salient and intense to precipitate the more serious consequences of conflict?

Some significant considerations bearing on the answers to these questions are the following: [5]

1. Labor unrest is part of the general disorganization and unsettlement of our time. Perhaps the most outstanding characteristic of our age is the wide-

[5] The discussion here is adapted from statements by the author in a previous publication: J. R. P. French, Jr., A. Kornhauser, and A. Marrow, "Conflict and Cooperation in Industry," *Journal of Social Issues*, 2 (1946), 13 ff.

spread social and individual insecurity and the confusion of values, which have resulted from the impact of science and the Industrial Revolution. The old loyalties and informal controls which ordered and stabilized people's lives have lost their hold. This is true of employers and employees alike. We live in a period of ideological and moral turmoil. No sanction or source of authority goes unquestioned. We have no firm faith in ourselves and our way of life and no clear personal goals and purposes to give unity and meaning to our world.

The long-run picture shows the unsettling influences of science and technology and of an enormous increase in leisure, standards of living, education, and aspirations of the masses of people everywhere. Add to this the more recent short-run convulsions of two world wars, the vast revolution in Russia and in the East, the widespread socialist movements throughout Europe, the powerful counterrevolutionary and antidemocratic forces, the unprecedented economic collapse of the 1930's, the spectacularly rapid growth of labor organization in America, now the menacing possibilities of a third world war, and the inspiring but unsettling potentialities of atomic energy. This is the backdrop against which industrial relations in America must be projected. Under these conditions, the marvel is that people do not feel even *more* insecure, confused, frustrated, and without compass or anchor.

It would be difficult to exaggerate the importance of this psychological atmosphere within which employer and employee motivations and attitudes exist today. The specific wants emphasized by employers and by working people are important primarily as indicators of their deeper insecurities and gropings for inner peace. The psychological insecurity goes far beyond the wish for economic security. The worker is likely to be more oppressed by feelings of lostness in a world beyond his comprehension and control, by a sense of not belonging, than by direct economic threats. Similarly, the industrialist who explodes emotionally against what he considers "the threat of unions" and "impending communism" is moved largely by his own uncertainties regarding his personal status and power in a vague, forbidding future in which almost anything can happen. The breakdown of old sanctions and traditional controls leads both to eager search for new elements of security and to intensified resistance to the threat of further change. Vague and confused as the search is, it is naturally markedly different for those who are at high occupational and socioeconomic levels and for the mass of wage earners who aspire to a "new deal."

2. The considerations that impel people to seek certain changes in industry and to oppose other changes—with resultant group conflicts—depend upon the extent to which their conditions of life and work impose deprivations and provide opportunities for gratifications. The major motives indicated in the classification previously outlined meet with varying degrees of satisfaction and frustration. Although the broad question of how far these motives find adequate gratification among working people, as contrasted with the top economic groups, can be answered in no conclusive fashion, there is strong indication that much greater dissatisfaction is the rule at the less-favored occupational levels. This is most patently the case in respect to desires for personal security and for all the other want satisfactions which money and a good steady job provide. But increasingly prominent, too, are unsatisfied desires in respect to the less tangible goals.

What do working people want more of? They want more of whatever they feel especially deprived of relative to other people and relative to what they believe possible: more security, more income, more personal appreciation and decent human treatment, more friendly social relations, more individual self-expression, more feeling of accomplishment and effectiveness, and more say in policies that affect them. Their wants focus upon the matters which are most frustrating or forbidding at the time. They emphasize those things about which they believe something can and should be done. Enough of them are restless and dissatisfied to furnish a substantial following for any plausible leadership that does not openly depart from their conception of what is fair and what is the American way of doing things.

The most influential sections of the employer class are doubtless much clearer in their aims. Their goal is to preserve the economic system with authority relations essentially unchanged. Yet they too have their own doubts and bewilderments. The revolutionary forces loose in the world leave them divided and disturbed regarding their specific aims. It has become obvious to most of them that they cannot resist all change and return to the "good old days." The grave problem for them is how *far* to defend the old ways, along what defense line they can best take their stand, and whether it is possible for them to preserve their positions without counteroffensives to break the growing power, economic and political, of organized labor.

In this fluid and emotional condition on the side of both labor and management, extremist leaders can readily take advantage of the confusion to push groups into positions which are not at all of their deliberate choosing. This makes it the more urgent for businessmen and working people as a whole, especially for moderate leaders, to understand the deeper feelings and frustrations which are thus exploited and accordingly to be on guard, prepared to combat the extremist leadership of both right and left.

3. The two preceding points indicate the fluidity, indefiniteness, and variety of the dissatisfactions and efforts for change that characterize labor unrest. The more that working people want takes now one form, now another. Different aspirations, frustrations, and demands and different orientations toward change follow one another in a way that undermines any stable generalizations about the relative importance either of the broad motive categories or of various objective factors in work and away from work, as causes of unrest and conflict. Defensible generalizations will deal rather with the ways in which particular desire-expectation patterns are brought into existence by specified social influences and with the relationship of the means of gratification to these socially emphasized motivations. The complex shifting social processes affecting people bring now this and now that type of discontent and set of aims into prominence. In one area and period they result in intense struggles for change, and at other times and places they bring calm satisfaction and peace.

This third point, then, in answer to our general problem as well as the two sections that follow will deal with significant aspects of the social determination processes that are shaping the motivations that lead to industrial conflict in the present-day world. First to be underscored is the set of values in our culture that emphasizes and sanctions the competitive struggle of individuals and groups to improve their lot, to get as much as they can according to the rules of the game. Our society "believes in" people's wanting more than they have and approves their efforts to advance their own interests. When this philosophy is accepted and acted upon by groups of working people, industrial conflict becomes a normal part of the social process.

There can be little question that a pronounced tendency does exist for people at middle and lower economic levels to want more than they can get and consequently to live in a perpetual state of unsatisfied aspirations. Notable in this connection is the rapid expansion of working people's expectations over recent decades. Pervasive influences have accentuated the feeling of disparity between what is and what can be. With the ordinary employee's rapid rise in education, in material conditions of life, and in leisure, and with his American background in contrast to that of the new immigrant, come sharper questions about his status relative to others and about his rights in life. Radio and television, motion pictures, newspapers and magazines, and ubiquitous advertising and selling pressures constantly stimulate larger wants. Wage workers come to have consumption standards and desires identical with those of the salaried middle class. They also come to expect security, dignity, increased independence, and the other intangibles that are stressed in 20th-century democratic states. Reports of the achievements of labor groups at home and abroad and the employees' own direct contacts with labor organizations add their effects. So also do reports of unheard-of production possibilities in the immediate future. And there is the ever-present contrast between democratic participation on the political front and its relatively slight development in industry.

At the same time, the decline in opportunities for individual success by moving out of the working class or even out of dull routine occupations leads increasing numbers to turn to collective solutions. The American tradition of unbounded opportunity creates great aspirations in the minds of youth. They have believed in the success-story pattern of life. When ambitions to get ahead are frustrated, as for large numbers they inevitably are, some naturally blame "conditions" and seek to change things.

Not to be underestimated, either, in assessing working people's motivations in the present period are the deep anxieties and resentments remaining from the depression years of the thirties. Great numbers of workers still carry the scars of that period and stand ready to support whatever social action appears necessary to prevent a return of the injury that they and their families experienced at that time. Let economic conditions deteriorate even moderately, and in all probability these deep-lying fears and hostilities will explosively assert themselves. This probability needs to be held in view at the same time as the recognition that, under current conditions of prosperity and favorable employment opportunities, no serious or widespread signs of unrest are observable. Most men are hard at work, earning good wages, and satisfied with their jobs. The crucial question is which set of facts to emphasize. Does the present period of relatively calm accommodation signify the new day of labor-management peace which optimistic experts proclaim? Or do deeper social motivations of the kind we have mentioned mean that industrial conflict is a continuing process? The psychological analysis convinces us that conflict relations between labor and management are not on the way to disappearance in the foreseeable future. Our reading of the socially defined motivations in

American society makes us profoundly skeptical of interpretations that build so hopefully on such temporary foundations as a few special cases and a few short years provide.

4. The directions in which people seek solutions for unsatisfied wants are defined by the accepted thought patterns of the times and by the interpretations circulated and approved within different sections of the population. Western society has come to place heavy emphasis on the belief that it is largely through workers' gains in industry that increased human satisfactions are to be achieved. By many, the position of workers striving to improve their lot is perceived as a *moral* position, a struggle against injustice and inequality. While the American ideals of individual self-reliance and salvation through personal effort persist, they are coupled with other beliefs that stress the limited opportunities that prevent many people from exercising these virtues and that stress the consequent need for reforms that will guarantee adequate job and life opportunities for all. Labor organizations have become a symbol and an instrument for advancing these "legitimate" aims of workers; as such they are accepted by an overwhelming majority of Americans.

It is evident that propaganda symbols and current social interpretations play a most important part in shaping such aims and expectations for management, employees, and the public. Not what is but what men believe to be the case counts in action, and what men believe turns not only on changing conditions of the world itself but most significantly also upon the meaning ascribed to these conditions. The particular demands shift and vary, depending on circumstances and leadership. It may be anything from better service in the lunchroom to nationalization of industry. The individual accepts given interpretations—Marxist doctrine, for example, belief in the harmony of employer-employee interests, the view that the management of his company is trustworthy or untrustworthy, the view that he should have greater opportunity to use his ability and to share in decisions, or the view that his union must survive and grow, that it should be active in national politics, or that it needs more militant leaders or more cooperative ones—because these views are persuasively presented to him, because they are currently accepted in his groups, and because they fit in plausibly with his own vague search for adjustment to a confusing world. These symbols, myths, and beliefs in turn color the picture of the world to which he now adjusts and help govern his further reactions to the events about him.

In like manner, labor leaders accept different views of their own roles and build up different expectations regarding the strength and survival of their union, their personal careers in the union, their social and political future, and their security and status relative to other leaders. The interpretations they adopt reflect not only the facts and pressures operating in their own situation, as they experience it, but also the views that are in circulation in the worlds in which they move. Analyses of motivations in industrial conflict must assign a large place to the social expectations and interpretations that determine the goals of the leadership.

The particular symbols and doctrines accepted by working people, union leaders, and employers are not necessarily those which best fit the individual's needs or which most truly or successfully rationalize his social position, though they must do so tolerably well. In addition, however, their acceptance is determined by their availability to the individual and by the effectiveness of their presentation. Here enter all the influences of education and propaganda and of social pressures which favor or oppose given changes. The conflicting goals of working people, leaders, and employers are in no small measure reflections of the opposing interpretations they read and hear.

A stubborn industrial dispute often appears absurd until one gets inside the minds of the opponents and learns how totally differently they construe the point at issue. Usually these divergent meanings go back into a long history of misunderstandings, with a cluster of fighting traditions about the unreasonableness and evil intentions of the other side, as evidenced in past dealings. Today's work stoppage may derive its meaning from accumulated grievances of years earlier, grievances interpreted and kept alive in a manner to serve best the purposes of the organized group and its leaders.

But what employees want and support is determined outside the factory as well as inside, by what they read in the papers and hear over the air, by what their children learn in schools, and by what their preacher and corner grocer have to say. Since newspapers and magazines and radio and television programs are controlled with few exceptions by persons having the viewpoint of employers (they are owned by businessmen and are subject to pressure from advertisers), it is natural that they exert their influence preponderantly toward preventing changes and ideologies which do not accord with the desires of business. They attempt to build and strengthen the worker's faith that the best, perhaps only, solution to his problems lies in loyal support of his employer and business leadership generally.

These efforts of management, no less than the strivings of workers, are backed by strong moral sanctions. They too are in accord with main currents of popular approval. Part of what people conceive to be "the American way of life" is firm adherence to the necessity and rightness of free enterprise, the leadership role of the businessman, the importance of not interfering with management's right to manage, and the avoidance of "creeping socialism." The observation that these divergent and even contradictory social interpretations exist side by side in our society is not new. But it is a fact that must never be lost sight of in analyzing the roots of industrial conflict. One portion or another of the inconsistent value system can readily become dominant under changing social conditions and the impact of new propaganda and new leadership. The course of labor relations over the next few decades may be determined more by events on this broad ideological and communications front than by developments in industry itself.

5. One other set of influences is particularly worth mentioning. Unsatisfied desires and expectations that motivate people to strive for social and economic improvements are partially offset by the pull of alternative gratifications. We refer to the unprecedented growth and appeal of opportunities for substitute satisfactions in present-day America, the myriad distractions and counterattractions which divert working people's attention from dissatisfying conditions. These partial and indirect gratifications serve to relieve emotional tension and to reduce pressures for change. People caught up in a dizzy whirl of activities have no time to express their restiveness in demands for change.

Sports, gambling, alcohol, religion, war, and the latest murder mystery all function to prevent more serious clamor for improvement. A home-town baseball game still has greater appeal than a union meeting for most workers.

"Solutions" to chronic thwarting may also be found in more personal types of adjustment and maladjustment, from neurotic ailments to artistic creativeness, from apathy and surrender to absorbing hobbies, and from resorting to crime to ambitiously carving out a successful career. The substitute goals include socially more ominous alternatives, too. Frustrations easily fasten upon convenient scapegoats. The discontent that might have gone into pressures for economic reform may be diverted to other targets, against Negroes, Jews, and foreigners or against Communists, intellectuals, labor bosses, and big government.

Although these alternative outlets for unrest are numerous and are adopted by many persons, more impressive is the fact that institutional developments and the 20th-century climate of opinion in America increasingly encourage direct expression of labor discontent in the form of collective demands on industry. Most notable are the expanded role of labor unionism and the prevalence of union-management contractual relations. Substitute gratifications and indirect displacements of working people's frustrations, while important, have by no means drained off all the energies that might go into efforts to protect and advance the workers' interests. Discontent finds ready channels and moral sanctions for collective expression looking toward social and industrial reforms in the interests of the common people.

Concluding Observations

This chapter has suggested some principal features of a motivational approach to industrial-conflict behavior. It appears that industrial conflict, to be adequately understood, must be seen in its multiform and widespread expressions and not viewed merely as a phenomenon of strikes nor studied merely in special cases where it is pronouncedly great or slight in the particular local situation. It is an inseparable part of the general move by the less favored in society to improve their lot. It is manifested by restricted output and unnecessary waste, by personal complaints and hostile expressions against the job, the boss, and the company, by union demands, and by support of political leaders and governmental measures believed to work in the interests of laboring people. Correlatively, it encompasses the varied efforts by management to combat and defend and stand fast against all such opposition and to weaken it by winning the loyalty of employees to management's own objectives.

The behavior of the parties in conflict is motivated by their divergent interests, as they conceive them, and by the belief that their respective interests are injured or threatened by the self-interested behavior of the other. The conflict stems from insistent wants and goal values held by the people involved, desires and expectations shaped and defined by their culture and by the group influences most significantly affecting them. Changing social conditions, moreover, produce shifting emphasis on the different goals sought and give rise to new expectations and aspirations.

In our dynamic, democratic society, the desires and expectations of the masses of people constantly outrun present opportunities for fulfillment. The consequence is unrest, be it aroused and intense or mild and dormant. People experience a discontented striving for solutions, both personal and collective. And in the present-day world, this urge for improvements focuses largely on getting more from employers, either directly or by way of government.

The particular dissatisfactions and points of controversy are diverse and variable. Consequently, generalizations about the importance or unimportance of specified objective factors as causes of unrest and conflict remain extremely vulnerable. It appears promising to seek causal generalizations formulated more in terms of expectations and desires that are aroused and ungratified than in terms of wages, labor supply, technological changes, supervisory personalities and practices, size of organization and work groups, and similar determinants. The effects of the objective factors depend too greatly on whether *other* matters in the total picture are satisfactory, what hopes and fears have been stimulated, what alternatives are available, and what accumulated hostilities exist—in sum, how the change in question is perceived and evaluated by the persons affected. Instead of a conclusion, for example, that the increasing of wages does or does not reduce conflict, more complex propositions seem necessary to the effect that wage increases perceived as satisfactorily meeting aroused desires and expectations (and not negated by counteracting changes) tend to reduce conflict behavior. The thing to be generalized about, in other words, is not the wages but the *relationship* of the wages to the motivations.

In this view, understanding of the motivations is indispensable. Each objective factor, as experienced in its total context, must be weighed to determine the extent to which it satisfies, or promises to satisfy, the strivings of the people concerned. Pressures for change, of a kind which causes industrial conflict, arise from discrepancies between what people want and the ability of their industrial situation to satisfy the wants.

What people want is described in an over-all way by the broad goal values or dependable motives of our culture (security, social approval, self-expression, etc.). While such categories are useful as general guides, adequate understanding requires that at the same time we accumulate knowledge to account for the particular goals and subgoals that are uppermost at given times and places. The study of the complex social psychological processes that contain the answer is still in its primitive stages. But the analysis surely must assign a prominent place to such variables as these: the existing and changing cultural conditions and social climate that stimulate and encourage specific expectations while discouraging others; people's exposure to differential subcultures and group influences; the current conditions of gratification and deprivation experienced in respect to aroused wants, especially the gratification-deprivation ratio relative to their own preceding conditions and relative to the lot of other people with whom they compare themselves; the availability and attractiveness of alternative and substitute gratifications; the extent to which potentially more compelling desires (physical needs, especially) are gratified; the basis people have for believing that the goals they seek are attainable by the means proposed; and the social sanctions and disapprovals that support or deter them in their struggle to achieve new gains or to protect the present position of themselves and their group. Industrial discontent and conflict, or, conversely, industrial satisfaction and harmony, have their roots in the motivations that these complex relationships bring into positions of dominance.

Social conditions of the present period clearly seem to stimulate and encourage working people's moves for change, especially changes demanded in and from industry. If this is the case, the question presents itself of whether this makes continuing conflict inevitable. Particularly, it prompts the question: Can voluntary employer actions satisfy the desires for improvement? If it is assumed that our free society will continue, it is difficult to find plausibility in the view that industrial conflict can be eliminated by peaceful concessions. The reasons are simple: first, management's role necessitates adherence to subgoals different from those of working people—productivity and profit versus direct personal satisfactions of the varied wants of workers; second, working people and their organizations will always want more—new expectations and demands will constantly push beyond what has been obtained.

The prospect is thus one of continuing conflict. This certainly need not mean violent conflict. An essential of democratic social systems is the acceptance of conflict relationships, controlled as far as feasible to insure compromise and accommodation. The alternative is some form of dictatorship or, what amounts to the same thing, a concentration of power and influence on one side of social controversies that permits this group to impose its views. The changes resulting from ongoing conflict may be small or great: trifling gains here and there for either contending party or the quiet revolution that some predict. Which type of consequence is to occur will depend largely on the structure of beliefs and expectations that people develop throughout our society. Students of labor relations cannot afford to lose sight of this fact. Taken seriously, it would mean much greater development of sociopsychological and motivational analyses in this sphere, and it would mean decidedly greater caution in generalizing about long-run trends and consequences on the basis of special cases and current conditions.

CHAPTER 6 SATISFACTIONS AND DEPRIVATIONS IN INDUSTRIAL LIFE

Daniel Katz   *University of Michigan*

THE satisfactions and deprivations which are a function of industrial life can be related to three broad areas of activity: (1) the job itself, *i.e.,* the specific nature of the content of the work, (2) the plant life of the worker, *i.e.,* the physical and social conditions of work, the factory as a social system, and (3) the out-plant life of the worker which is a consequence of his industrial employment. In the following pages this last area will be considered, after a discussion of the job itself.

The Relation of Worker Satisfaction to Industrial Conflict

This type of analysis is intended to give some of the background in which industrial struggle occurs and not to assess the weighting of specific types of psychological frustration and satisfaction in the determination of conflict. Industrial conflict is basically a struggle between two organized groups which are competing for their share of a joint product. It can occur when deprivations and frustrations have reached an intolerable point. But conflict can also occur when workers are relatively well off and when their conditions are improving. As group action, industrial conflict cannot be equated to the degree of dissatisfaction of individual workers, though dissatisfaction is one of the related factors. The level of frustration and discontent can be relatively high without manifestation of overt conflict if the channels for the expression of group action are lacking. Moreover, industrial conflict is not necessarily a pathological phenomenon to be understood as the desperation efforts of deprived and discontented people. Rather, it may be the normal antagonistic cooperation in a competitive society in which each interested group attempts to use its power to influence the societal outcome. Employers have been surprised to find their unorganized groups of workers becoming unionized, because they feel they have treated them as well as, if not better than, other employers. They fail to preceive that conflict is inherent in a democratic society in which there is a plurality of competing groups. Labor and management may be partners in production, but in a relatively free economy the distribution of returns to both parties is set only within broad limits. Hence the amount of conflict will be determined by many factors other than the satisfaction the worker finds in his job or in his life within the plant. All those aspects of the situation which contribute to a perception of differential roles for workers and management and to a belief in the common fate of one's group as opposed to an out-group are relevant here; so, too, are the perceptions of both workers and management of their own power relative to the power of the other side.

Too little attention has been paid to the exact nature of the antagonistic cooperation which exists between labor and management. The area of cooperation is basically on the side of production at a sufficient level for the company to remain in business and pay wages. This cooperative aspect has been institutionalized in the many organized patterns of the industrial setup. The division of labor, the hierarchy of supervisors and officers, and the coordination of all parts of the organization are part of the pattern of a social unit with central objectives which can be achieved only through cooperative effort. But the major conflict develops not so much on the productive side, although there can be competition for the interesting jobs, but on the side of the distribution of rewards. And the conflict can be just as great if the company earnings are huge as if they are small. In fact, since a major factor in compromising the fight over the size of the return to labor and management is the need for workers to have a job and for the company to stay in business and compete with its rivals, one might expect more conflict when productivity is high and earnings are great. Hence the notion that workers and management have a great deal in common in increasing productivity, and thus increasing the amount of return to both, is only part of the story. It is possible that increasing cooperation on the production side may open the way for more conflict on the side of the distribution of the reward. The percentage of return to the owners and workers is more flexible the greater the margin of profit and hence subject to more argument and more struggle. Some of the most militant and aggressive unions are found in companies and industries where the margin of profit is high.

Workers' deprivations and gratifications are important in furnishing the reservoir of feeling and motivation which activates the institutional patterns we have been describing. They become salient in conflict when the worker has identified their causes and perceives a solution in organized struggle with the employer. It is unwise to assume a one-to-one relationship between the area of cooperation, namely, the productive side of the process, and the area of conflict, namely, the distribution of returns. Workers can like their foreman, approve of management's practices and policies with respect to the work situation, and still fight bitterly for wages and benefits. Conversely, they may find their jobs uninteresting and their foremen arbitrary and still not channel their sources of dissatisfaction against the company in any really hostile sense. This is not to say these areas are unrelated. Rather, the relationship is not automatic, and the conditions for maximum transfer need to be specified. One condition, for example, has to do with the size of the plant. In a small business where the employee knows the boss personally, his feelings toward him as a supervisor will be definitely related to his negotiations with him over wages. In a large plant, however, where the worker is many times removed from the employer, the personal relationships with the foreman may have little relevance to the support the worker gives his union representatives in the negotiation process. Another generalization is that negative transfer is more likely than positive transfer. Workers dissatisfied with the nature of their jobs may be militant in their attitudes toward management. On the other hand, on the positive side, workers who like their jobs may still make demands for better conditions and higher wages. Similarly, the bitterness resulting from strikes may carry over to a minimal cooperation in the productive process, whereas positive feeling about a good wage settlement may not entail a corresponding degree of productive effort.

Two other generalizations can be made about labor-management relations in terms of worker frustrations and gratifications. In the first place, worker deprivation leads most directly to conflict when it is experienced as a sharp and unfavorable contrast to an existing practice, standard, or expectation. When workers see their fellows who are performing the same type of work in a similar type of company in the same community get a raise in wages or a shorter work week, their dissatisfaction is readily directed against their own management. Similarly, when management's promises to improve conditions and to raise wages stand out in sharp relief to management's performance, strikes are a likely outcome, as in the wildcat strikes in some of the shipyards during the war. In the second place, the type of dissatisfaction most relevant to conflict has to do with wages, since earnings sum up so many of the motivations of human beings in our society. It is true that other factors at times assume paramount importance—the IWW built up its strength in the Eastern silk mills some 40 years ago on the issue of the 8-hour day. Nevertheless, over time the basic struggle, almost by definition, is for wages, since this represents the most direct way of dividing the joint product. The report of the Bureau of Labor Statistics for 1952 that the dominant cause of the large strikes during the past year was the issue of wages is typical of our industrial history.

Historical Frame of Reference

Our assumption that change is progress is challenged by the contrast often drawn between the robot role of the modern industrial worker and the lot of the craftsman in the handicraft stage of production. The assembly-line worker is compared to the old craftsman, who could express his talents in his work, who could take pride in his own achievements, whose status as a skilled journeyman was high, who enjoyed a sense of self-determination in the ownership and use of his own tools, and whose work pattern had aesthetic and ceremonial as well as utilitarian aspects. Now this contrast between the machine age and the handicraft era can easily be overdone. Very few of the working population enjoyed the desirable role of the master craftsman. And it is also easy to glorify an older period and to neglect its darker side: in this case, the long, slavelike period of apprenticeship and the dependence upon the whims of a tyrannical nobility. For, as Walter Lippmann [1] has observed, "The prototype of all revivals is each man's wistful sense of his own childhood. There is something infinitely pathetic in the way we persist in recalling what is by its very nature irrevocable."

Nevertheless, the picture of gratification in the handicraft period has value in assessing worker satisfaction in our time, even if it represents something of an idealized account. Its value in furnishing a frame of reference is that

[1] W. Lippmann, "Drift," in K. A. Robinson, W. B. Pressey, and J. D. McCollum (eds.), *Essays Toward Truth*. New York, Holt, 1924, p. 177.

it points to three major sources of human satisfaction, sources generally overlooked in the standards with which unions and management are primarily concerned, for the old-time craftsman was pictured (1) as enjoying the fruits of creative activity, (2) as integrating his satisfactions of work, aesthetics, and ritual in a single pattern, and (3) as finding in his means to a living the goal of a satisfactory way of life in itself. The first major source deals with the gratifications that come from the expression of one's talents and abilities, from self-development and self-realization. This type of motivation ranges from creative objectification of an inner conflict, as in the case of the artist, to the feeling of satisfaction in the expression of some minor skill. An older ideology reserved such gratification for the gifted few, but both democratic doctrines and psychological logic can draw no line among human beings with respect to the richness of personal reward in the attaining of some degree of self-actualization. It is interesting that, while on the one hand the gradual spread of democratic values into the various spheres of life has made for recognition that all people are entitled to develop and enjoy the expression of their talents, on the other hand the growth of a machine society has simplified the skill level of jobs so that the work area in which the individual can exercise his judgment and talent has narrowed.

The second major factor suggested by the craftsman's life of the handicraft period is the integrated manner of the satisfaction of the diverse needs of the individual. At the one extreme is the integration of many needs in a single pattern of activity. On the other is a complete compartmentalization in which human wants are satisfied one at a time by activities unrelated to anything but the immediate need. For example, a person can satisfy his hunger by a leisurely meal in which the courses are aesthetically related and where there are congenial companions and good conversation with music in the background, etc.; or he can satisfy his hunger quickly and effectively by concentrating upon food alone. There are obvious advantages in either method of gratification. When a given need is very intense it is not necessarily helpful to encumber its satisfaction with irrelevant activities. Moreover, there is a certain type of freedom in compartmentalizing need satisfaction. An attempted pattern of integration entails risks in that a single wrong element can sour the whole combination. On the other hand the person is not a multiple of divorced needs but a unified organism, and the more of himself that can enter meaningfully into an activity, the greater the gratification and the more enduring the remembered happiness. Then, too, conflicts can be avoided by not compartmentalizing responses catering to different needs.

The third consideration is related to the matter of integrated activity, but it deals with a rather different dimension, the dimension of the means or end-relatedness of the activity. How far removed are the means from the desired goal both in time and in the nature or quality of the activity? The politician whose friendly outgoing personality craves human contact finds little discrepancy in reward quality between his goal of public office and the means for reaching this goal, which involve meeting and interacting with people.

These factors in human happiness deserve some consideration in assessing worker satisfaction in our time, especially since they are not necessarily explored in the usual inventory of employee morale. The salient things which workers mention and are articulate about generally concern some immediate frustration or some immediate problem, and most morale studies are not designed to bring out the deeper gratification and frustration of workers. In discussing some results from typical studies, it may be necessary, therefore, to examine findings in a fairly broad interpretative context.

The Job Itself

Since the major part of the individual's day is spent at work and since the major part of the working day is concerned with the content of the job, it is important to know the nature and degree of gratification and deprivation in job performance itself. From the objective point of view, the development of large-scale production with its increasing use of machines and its use of machinelike institutionalization of the work process has apparently undermined three possible sources of work satisfaction. The skill level of many jobs has been greatly reduced, so that intricate and complex tasks are seldom required of the worker. The variety of operations and tasks required of the individual has also greatly diminished. A skilled job, by definition, has some variety of psychological function, but it is also possible for an unskilled job to call for a variety of behaviors. Nonetheless, in the development of machine production we have also moved toward extreme specialization of function so that the worker is left not only with a low-level-skill job but also with one that is repetitive and monotonous. In the third place the job has been set up with standardized procedures so that the incumbent has little chance to do it his own way. He has been left a minimum of decisions about the work itself.

That this objective reduction in skill, variety, and spontaneity has been accompanied by resulting losses in psychological satisfaction is not universally accepted. There are those who maintain that people with low aptitude and low aspiration find work which requires no thought and little skill a great relief. It enables them to pursue a pleasant life of fantasy while on the job. The favorite example of this point of view is the man who had the task of sorting good apples from bad and complained about its difficulty because there were too many decisions to make. Another school holds that the work frustration on the modern assembly line is greatly exaggerated, since the worker himself introduces psychological variety into routine work. The outside observer sees the flow of similar materials and the replication of the same motion in dealing with these materials. The worker, however, seizes upon tiny cues and sees differences which require differential treatment. Now undoubtedly there is some truth in both these claims, but the evidence suggests strongly that they do not represent the larger truth, namely, that human beings, whether or not they have the aspirations developed in a college education, suffer genuine deprivation from a work existence which reduces their personal involvement to a single set of routinized movements. Though morale studies show many points of disagreement, they consistently report that job satisfaction is a function of occupational calling and of the job.[2] The very argument that workers introduce variety into simple mechanical jobs by searching for minimal

[2] T. W. Harrell, *Industrial Psychology*, New York, Rinehart, 1949.

points of difference or seek relief in fantasy merely suggests substitute compensatory mechanisms due to the blocking of a major motive pattern. It is of interest that after the war the millions of men in the armed services, who had been in a situation where all decisions were made for them, were now obsessed with only one thought, how to get back to civilian life as quickly as possible. Examples can be found, of course, of people who shirk responsibility and who will prefer the simpler of two tasks, but it is also possible that such instances represent cases of stunted personality development.

Comparisons of occupational groups show that the more skilled the vocation the more its members enjoy their jobs. R. Hoppock reported that more than 90 per cent of a group of 500 teachers liked their work.[3] In contrast H. M. Bell found that 98 per cent of young people working in canning factories and textile mills hated their jobs.[4] In another study by Hoppock, of 309 people in a small Pennsylvania town, the greatest dissatisfaction with work occurred among the unskilled laborers. Satisfaction increased with occupational level, with the greatest satisfaction among professional groups.[5]

Table 6.1 **Job-satisfaction Indexes of Five Occupational Groups**

Occupational Classification	N	Mean Index
I. Unskilled manual	55	401
II. Semiskilled	74	483
III. Skilled manual and white-collar	84	510
IV. Subprofessional, business, and minor supervisory	32	548
V. Professional, managerial, and executive	23	560

R. L. Hull and A. Kolstad [6] analyzed questionnaire responses of thousands of workers and report: "The results do suggest, however, that there is some relationship between skill and morale, that is, that a cross section of workers in highly skilled trades would give somewhat higher scores than a cross section of unskilled labor." The relationship between job satisfaction and occupational status has also been confirmed in studies by Thorndike [7] and by Uhrbrock.[8] In addition, Super [9] corroborated this finding and also reported that the amount of upward occupational mobility was of little importance in satisfaction but that the direction of the change had a great deal to do with job satisfaction.

In most of these studies, job satisfaction is used loosely to cover over-all liking for the job situation as well as intrinsic job satisfaction deriving from

[3] R. Hoppock, *Job Satisfaction,* New York, Harper, 1935.

[4] H. M. Bell, *Youth Tell Their Story,* Washington, American Youth Commission, 1937.

[5] Hoppock, *op. cit.*

[6] R. L. Hull and A. Kolstad, "Morale on the Job," in G. Watson (ed.), *Civilian Morale,* New York, Reynal & Hitchcock, 1942, p. 357.

[7] E. L. Thorndike, "Workers' Satisfactions: Likes and Dislikes of Young People for Their Jobs," *Occupations,* 13 (1935), 704–706.

[8] R. Uhrbrock, "Attitudes of 4,430 Employees," *Journal of Social Psychology,* 5 (1934), 365–377.

[9] D. Super, "Occupational Level and Job Satisfaction," *Journal of Applied Psychology* 23 (1939), 547–564.

the content of the work process. Hence the greater gratification of the higher occupational levels can be due to the higher pay, the greater prestige of the calling, the hours or working conditions, etc. It is important, therefore, to hold constant factors other than the nature of the work in comparing the satisfaction derived from jobs varying in level of skill and complexity. This is, of course, not possible in dealing with broad occupational groupings where wages and conditions of work are completely tied to type of occupation in the practical workaday world, where we do not find doctors whose working conditions, wages, and prestige are the same as ditchdiggers (though we find professors who sometimes earn as much as bricklayers). Within a single company, however, it is possible to make meaningful comparisons of intrinsic job satisfaction within a restricted range of differential skill level. The company may have the same working conditions and the same program of employee benefits for all workers within this range. Moreover, the wages may take account of seniority as well as of skill level. Hence it is possible to find workers at more complex tasks earning no more than workers at less skilled jobs.

Such a situation is true for clerical workers in the home office of a large Eastern insurance company, where the tasks vary from routine filing through correspondence with policy holders to moderately complicated mathematical computations. The Survey Research Center of the University of Michigan conducted a survey of employee morale in this company, in which 580 employees were intensively interviewed.[10] Intrinsic job satisfaction was measured by an index which summarized the answers to these four questions: "How well do you like the sort of work you are doing?" "Does your job give you a chance to do the things you feel you do best?" "Do you get any feeling of accomplishment from the work you are doing?" "How do you feel about your work; does it rate as an important job with you?" Not only was the score on this index of intrinsic job satisfaction significantly related to type of work, but type of work proved the single most important determinant of liking for the work itself. Employees were grouped into four classes on the basis of job level: specifically, high-level technical, semisupervisory, varied clerical, and repetitious clerical. The high-level technical group had only 7 per cent of their members who fell into the category of low intrinsic job satisfaction compared with 41 per cent of the group doing repetitive clerical work. Moreover, this relationship was not reduced when length of service or salary was held constant. These results suggest strongly that the greater gratifications found by higher-level occupational groups are not wholly a function of wages and conditions of work. People do derive important satisfaction in the expression of their skills, in interesting and challenging work, and in the sense of accomplishment from successful performance.

In the same study, the employees who were higher on intrinsic job satisfaction tended to be the people who described their jobs as having variety and as giving them some chance to make decisions. In other circumstances, this could be interpreted as a psychological phenomenon, that is, a manifestation of the ability of some people to find variety in even the most routine tasks. In

---

[10] N. C. Morse, *Employee Satisfaction, Supervision and Morale in an Office Situation*, Part II, University of Michigan, Survey Research Center Report, 1953.

this instance, however, the people who found their work varied and containing opportunities for some decision making were in fact doing more skilled and varied work. The old contention that people do not like to make decisions is also answered by the findings of this study. Only 24 per cent of the employees were satisfied with the amount of decision making in their jobs, as the following figures indicate:

Employees making no decisions who would not like to make any	11%
Employees making some decisions who would not like to make more	13
Employees making no decisions who would like to make some	30
Employees making some decisions who would like to make more	46
Total	100%
$N = 537$	

A similar finding, though not so pronounced, comes from the Survey Center's study of the production workers in a plant representative of heavy industry.[11] These factory workers do not represent so high an educational level as the home-office employees of the insurance company. Nevertheless, 51 per cent of 5,700 workers, in response to the question, "Would you like to have more or less to say about the way your work is done?" wanted to have more to say. Forty per cent wanted no more to say about their work than they had at the time, and 9 per cent failed to answer. And the majority of workers (68 per cent) felt that they had little or nothing to say about how their jobs should be carried out. Moreover, the majority (65 per cent) thought the work would be better done if the men had more chance to make suggestions about such things as design, setups, and the layout of the work. When pressed further on the problem of why the men didn't make suggestions on how the work should be done, the following reasons were given:

Men don't get credit for suggestions	50%
Top management won't use suggestions men make	28%
Foremen won't use suggestions men make	23%
Other men don't think a man should make suggestions	11%
Men don't know where to make suggestions	10%
Men don't know what suggestions to make	7%

The implication of these results is clear: in spite of the deadening of expectations about participation in the work process in large-scale mechanized production, many workers still feel deprived of the opportunity to apply their skill and knowledge in a full measure to their jobs. Furthermore, it should be noted that they are still sufficiently interested in their work to feel that they could make significant contributions if given an opportunity to participate in decisions about the work. The desire to be involved in decisions may reflect both the need for self-expression in which the individual develops his skill and the need for self-determination in which the person wants the feeling of being his own master. Purcell, in an investigation of Swift & Company, quotes one worker as follows: " 'I likes my job. I never have any trouble. I'm a shipper in the cooler. I fill orders and *there's nobody to bother me.* I like

[11] *Attitudes and Opinions of Hourly Employees,* University of Michigan, Survey Research Center Report, August, 1950.

it very good. *I only see the foreman once a week. I'm on my own.* I really likes my job.' " [12]

In spite of a culture which emphasizes speed and mechanization and an industry which makes robots its ideal, the old values of craftsmanship, of creativity, of individual initiative, and of self-determination are very much alive in millions of American workers. Men still prefer jobs which challenge their skill and which give them some measure of decision making and responsibility. The fact that the great majority of jobs offer a routinized work content is a constant source of frustration to the man who still has some craftsmanship and enterprise in his make-up.

The lack of meaningful content in the job itself, as has been indicated, is a complex matter. It includes the thwarting of both the individual's craftsmanship and his desire for self-determination. Both of these factors become important as a source of industrial conflict when there is added to them the perception that representatives of management possess these desirable functions. Moreover, the exercise of decision making about the work processes is also a matter of the power relationship between the worker and the foreman. The worker not only may be denied any chance for self-expression but also may be the puppet of those above him. It is not uncommon to have workers complain about the foreman who pushes them around and tells them, "You aren't paid to think around here." In such situations there is not only the frustration of the worker's desire for self-determination but also the perception that he is the victim of the arbitrary power monopolized by management's representatives. The worker is not going to see himself as a partner in the production process with management when there is such a clear and distinct division of decision making and power in the jobs held by the hourly paid as against the salaried members of the company. Thus the lines of the power struggle become drawn not only at the top levels in negotiations about wages but also on the floor of the plant in the very definition of the job itself.

There are, however, two other major areas in which the worker can reap rich satisfactions, even if the work itself is not rewarding. One area has to do with his *out-plant life*. If mechanization can return to the worker huge rewards in the way of more leisure, more economic security, and a better standard of living, then he may be compensated for the loss of attractiveness of the work itself. A second area has to do with the social system surrounding the job and would include the life of the worker in the plant. This broad area covers all the factors in the work situation which are not a direct function of the work itself, for example, company and union policies and programs, working conditions, and the social climate of the factory.

The Out-plant Life of the Worker

The out-plant life of the worker cannot be considered in any systematic fashion in this chapter, but any over-all evaluation of the satisfactions and deprivations of the modern worker must balance losses on the job with possible gains off the job. The remarkable reduction in working hours, which gives

[12] T. V. Purcell, "Dual Allegiance in the Industrial Plant Community," Doctor's dissertation, Harvard University, 1952.

the factory worker unprecedented leisure time to pursue his own interests, cannot be ignored. Nor can the material rewards of high wages and fringe benefits be underestimated. They make possible a fuller life, free from privation and physical suffering. Freedom from want and freedom from fear are among the most important goals of a free people. The auto-assembly-line worker may have a dull, frustrating type of job, but on the other hand his 40 hours in the factory leave him considerable time to make trips in his own car, to enjoy his radio and television set, or even to read and learn more about his world. Moreover, his frustrated craftsmanship can find expression in repairing and improving his house, which in time he may look forward to having as his own, free from mortgage. His living standard is guaranteed by the automatic adjustment provided by the union contract, and he is protected from unemployment by seniority and unemployment insurance, from sickness by a benefit program, and from the debility of age by a pension and retirement system.

Thus the deprivations and satisfactions in the life of the worker which are a function of his job and his life in the plant may be of minor importance compared to his existence outside the plant itself. The primary goals of the worker relate to economic advancement and economic security for himself and his family. His taking a job is a means to this end, and so long as the end is richly rewarded, the gratifications and frustrations in reaching the goal may be easily overemphasized. In industrial conflict, to give paramount importance to satisfaction with wages is not necessarily an acceptance of a simple economic determinism. In our society, as Veblen pointed out long ago, we have reduced all forms of motivation to a pecuniary accounting. In a free market money has been known to buy anything from men's brains to women's virtue. Since income remains the all-important means for satisfying human wants and needs, wages will continue to be a major consideration in industrial conflict.

On the other hand, the difficulty of taking satisfaction with wages as the central determinant of industrial conflict is that it is too summary a statement of the motivational factors involved. Precisely because money is the means of satisfying almost all human needs and wants, we do not know what workers are dissatisfied with when they find their earnings unsatisfactory. We are generally safe in concluding that, for the great majority, the motivation is not the money itself. An account of behavior in terms of economic interests tells us little more than that people are motivated to satisfy their wants and desires.

To understand the basis for wage dissatisfaction and industrial conflict would entail a thorough study of the worker's total life space. The worker who wants to increase his earnings may be thinking essentially in terms of protecting himself and his family against material wants, both for the present and for the future. Or he may be striving for a more comfortable way of life, with richer leisure-time activities provided by television and a fine motor car. Or he may be attempting to maintain his place in his social group with the symbols of prosperity demanded by group standards. Or he may have certain standards of his own for economic progress as he grows older. Still another important factor may be the projection of his own frustrations into the careers of his children. Higher earnings for some people may represent the one area where they still can dream and plan about the future. For some workers increased earnings may mean more recognition on the job and in the plant itself. This is far from exhausting the motivations that lie behind the desire for increased earnings. Some of these needs are not static and absolute but change with successive experiences. It is characteristic of our society that wants and needs tend to run ahead of the means for satisfying them.

One important summary measure which is relevant to existing worker satisfaction with wages concerns the worker's level of aspiration. Some of the determinants of this level of aspiration with respect to wages are (1) How does the rate of pay in the worker's factory for his type of work compare with other levels of work in the same plant? (2) How does the wage rate in his factory compare with other plants in the community? (3) How does his occupational rate compare with that of other occupations? (4) How do wages given by the company compare with dividends and profits? (5) How do his wages now compare to his wages when he was a less experienced worker? (6) How much do his wages actually buy in the market now, as compared to his purchasing power a year ago?

Other criteria which have to do with the level of wage aspiration are less relative evaluations of what others are receiving, but consist of appraisals of attainable gains in terms of their cost; for example, the worker may make some assessment of the relative chances of success of a joint struggle together with his fellow workers for a wage increase, or he may be willing to accept the cost of the privation of a strike for the long-term advantages of making a fight for his rights.

There has been little research on the criteria which determine the level of aspiration of the worker concerning his wages and on the relative importance of these criteria. Some companies have followed the policy of eliminating small wage differentials for similar jobs within the plant. The assumption is that the worker's satisfactions are readily affected by the people in psychological proximity to himself; hence, uniformity of wage rates within the company becomes desirable, even for jobs which are not identical but which can be readily perceived by workers as calling for much the same level of ability. In smaller communities, the general assumption is that the worker often compares himself with men doing the same type of work in other concerns within the community. In general, the worker seems to make the comparison more within his industry than he does on occupations within a geographic area. On the other hand, the farmer in the past has compared himself with the city worker as well as with other farmers.

Most of the research has concerned the workers' evaluation of wages and other factors relevant to the over-all job situation. These studies show considerable variation in the relative weight that employees assign to wages compared to such factors as recognition for good work, congenial working companions, type of job, and working conditions. Similar ratings by foremen and upper supervision, of factors important to workers, attach more significance to wages. The general interpretation has been that wages have been greatly overrated as a source of worker satisfaction and dissatisfaction. This interpretation is subject to qualification, however, on a number of counts. It is one thing to ask people about what they want in an ideal job and another thing to assess their major satisfactions and dissatisfactions in their current situation. Even when asked about the present job situation workers may, as Haire and Gottsdanker point out, take wages for granted if they are at an acceptable level.[13] Corroborative evidence for this point of view comes from a study of a large public utility in a metropolitan center, where job security was excellent but where wage standards fell below the going rate in the automobile plants.[14] When asked, "What do you like least about working for Detroit Edison?" the 8,075 workers gave the ranking shown in Table 6.2 to eleven factors.

Table 6.2 **Factor Liked Least**

1. Chances for promotion	22%
2. Earnings	20
3. Type of supervisor or boss	7
4. Hours of work	6
5. Benefits such as sports or recreational facilities	6
6. The job itself	5
7. Working conditions	5
8. Job security	4
9. Benefits such as sickness insurance or retirement	3
10. People worked with	2
11. Good treatment to be relied on from the company	1
Could not or would not decide	19
Total	100%

Even when satisfaction with wages is high, there are two obvious disadvantages in having worker happiness geared to the life off the job. In the first place, leisure time can too easily be filled by the same assembly-line type of process as in the factory, with ready-made daydreams provided by radio and television. The same culture which produces an institutionalized industrial machine also produces for leisure-time pursuits a uniform set of activities and commodities. For example, the broadening effect of travel is lessened by the narrowing of regional differences: the same commercialized billboards, the same radio programs, and the same slick magazines confront the traveler in all parts of the country. In the second place, there is a genuine weakness in a lack of integration between the means of earning a living and living itself. The professional person makes his job his way of life. The scientist still thinks about his problems outside the laboratory; his social life is spent largely with fellow scientists in discussion of common problems; his recreation is tied to his scientific interests. This is why the professional man cannot be put on an hourly earning schedule.

The factory worker has few such opportunities for integrating his outplant life with his job. An interesting exception can be found on a simple level among maintenance-of-way gangs on the railroad. In one study of these

[13] M. Haire and J. S. Gottsdanker, "Factors Influencing Industrial Morale," *Personnel Journal*, 27 (1951), 445–454.

[14] *Findings from the Employee Questionnaire*, University of Michigan, Survey Research Center Report, April, 1949.

workers, it was found that they preferred their railroad jobs to factory work, even though the factory wage rates were considerably higher. The major reason was that they liked outdoor work and hated to be cooped up within the walls of a factory. These men lived in small towns and in rural areas. During the hunting and fishing seasons they took long week ends to pursue these activities. Their way of life, which was rural and outdoors and working in the open, even in bad weather, fitted in more with their pattern of living than did working in a mill.

That many workers compartmentalize their life off the job from their existence in the plant is shown in a wartime study of morale in five shipyards.[15] The yards investigated in this study included new plants where workers came into crowded communities and had to live under very difficult conditions of housing, of transportation, and even of community acceptance. Though these conditions affected morale and productivity, they were not nearly so important as were the factors in the shipyard itself. If the men had satisfactory wages, if supervision and management treated them fairly, and if the facilities for production were there, they not only produced well but liked their work. But if in-plant conditions were unsatisfactory, then favorable living conditions on the outside did not increase productivity or worker satisfaction. These findings indicate incidentally that we sometimes make too much of out-plant conditions as a factor in worker adjustment to the job. There can be no objection to therapy for the worker who has problems with his family and with his friends, but the first place to look in meeting problems of worker dissatisfaction is in the plant itself.

The Plant Life of the Worker

One reason why the workers in some shipyards were not too affected by unfavorable living conditions had to do with the many satisfactions in the plant which were not solely a function of job performance. Increasingly, industrial sociology is giving consideration to the plant life, or the social system, which the worker enters when he passes the factory gates every morning. It is this area which has much greater possibilities of improvement than the content of the work itself. This point has been well made by William F. Whyte [16] in the following comment:

> It is evident that the craftsman of old who made the whole product himself, who gained the satisfactions of developing his initiative and exercising his imagination in creating something new, is hardly to be found on the industrial scene today. These satisfactions of craftsmanship are gone, and we can never call them back. If these were the only satisfactions men could get out of their immediate work, then work would certainly be a barren experience today.
>
> There are other important satisfactions today: the satisfactions of human associations and the satisfactions of solving the technical and human problems of work.

[15] D. Katz and H. Hyman, "Morale in War Industry," in T. Newcomb and E. Hartley (eds.), *Readings in Social Psychology,* New York, Holt, 1947, pp. 437–447.
[16] W. F. Whyte, "Work and Human Values in Industrial Civilization," in Eugene Staley (ed.), *Creating an Industrial Civilization* (Corning Glass Company Conference), New York, Harper, 1952.

Industry itself has devoted time and thought to making plant life more attractive. Under pressure from unions and workers, there has been a marked improvement in conditions of work. Companies themselves have taken on the goal of modern functional buildings, with a maximum of light and air, with adequate shower and locker rooms, and with excellent safety equipment. In addition to physical conditions of work, many companies have given attention to the social and psychological atmosphere of the plant. They have instituted recreational facilities, plant magazines, and indoctrination and information programs. These reforms are generally within the frame of reference of management values, but they are designed to develop a plant life which gives the worker more to occupy his interests than the job itself. In addition, the social relations which affect the work process have received considerable attention. Training programs for foremen in human relations are fairly common. Now the plant life of the worker is affected by these measures of management, but it is also affected in other ways. The amount and type of interaction with his fellow workers and the friendship patterns in his immediate work group are especially significant. So, too, are the functions performed by the union in the shop, the social organization of the union in the plant, the relationships between stewards and foremen, and the organization of the work process. Even the size of the work group, of the department, and of the plant helps determine the character of the social life of the worker on the job.

Proper utilization of the many factors in the work situation other than the content of the job can make plant life so attractive that it could compete in desirability with life outside the factory. But the major developments in enhancing the attractiveness of the social system surrounding the job need to be examined critically because they are frequently paternalistic, bureaucratic, and overinstitutionalized. They seem to stem from the same basic institutional theory which has set the pattern for the organization of the work process and the production line. This theory has been aptly called the "machine theory of organization" by J. Worthy,[17] who has analyzed some of its assumptions in actual operation. It takes a machine as its model and applies the same logic of the mechanized assembly line to the human relations of production and to the community life of the plant. It ignores almost all factors of human motivation and is designed to remove human sources of error and to eliminate all human variability, save that which can be codified and fitted into specialized job assignments. Its postulates have been described as unity of command, centralization of decision making at the top of the hierarchy, specialization of function, and the standardization and routinization of all operations.[18] Uniformity and efficiency of the model are the central values of the system. This machine theory, applied to the production of material things, has unquestionably yielded bountiful returns. On the other hand, it is responsible for the very deprivations and frustrations in the work process which we are attempting to compensate for through a more interesting

[17] J. C. Worthy, "Factors Influencing Employee Morale," *Harvard Business Review*, Vol. 28, No. 1 (1950).

[18] D. Katz and R. L. Kahn, "Human Organization and Worker Motivation," pp. 146–171 of *Industrial Productivity*, Industrial Relations Research Association Publication 7, December, 1951.

and desirable plant life. Similarly, when applied to personal relations and social activities, this type of institutionalization, though it has advantages, can further contribute to the same type of frustration.

In application, the company following the machine theory proceeds as follows: It calls in experts in various fields to recommend the proper programs for the types of improvement desired for the workers. Directives go down the line, new responsibilities lead to new officers, and some accounting back to top management is required. For example, the decision may be to improve the two-way communication system in the company. Workers do not seem to know very much about how their work ties in to the organization as a whole, nor are they well informed about company earnings and company policies. The supervisory and line officers likewise seem to be poorly informed of what their workers really think. But instead of a thorough analysis of the fundamental causes of this lack of two-way communication, experts are called in to prescribe gadgets that fit into the machine way of thinking. The house organ is turned into a slick magazine with copious use of pictorial materials and rigid adherence to the Flesch formula (but the workers continue to read the *United Automobile Worker* or its counterpart). To take care of upward communication, suggestion boxes are installed so that workers can get their ideas to higher management. The foreman, the one natural link in the communication chain, is thereby bypassed. Since suggestions are not coming in fast enough, a competition is announced and a campaign is put on among divisions to win a company plaque for the most suggestions. There has been a problem of communication, the company has done something about it and is ready for the next problem. But no one has attempted to analyze the problem and to see that for adequate communication there must first be motivation to communicate and then some natural day-to-day basis for communication.

In general, in instituting programs designed to enrich the social system of the company, two important sources of motivation for the workers are overlooked. For one thing, the vitalizing effects of genuine participation by the workers is neglected. If new recreation rooms are planned, the architects and interior decorators are consulted. The workers who are going to use these rooms are not given the chance to develop designs or plans for the type of room or equipment they would like to have. Since one of the major needs of employees is the opportunity to make decisions and to become personally involved, it is often more important to satisfy this want than to satisfy the aesthetic standards of the expert consultant. Moreover, the best improvements and procedures are those which are acceptable to people and which will therefore be utilized, as N. R. F. Maier has demonstrated in using group decisions.[19] And people who have worked out a project and regard it as their own will find it eminently acceptable. The second reason for enlisting participation is not for the sake of participation but for the purpose of obtaining the most effective way of meeting worker needs. Because the workers themselves are intimately acquainted with the details of the situation, they may be in a better position to develop the means for solving the problem. To the extent that their solution is more effective in meeting the real needs of the situation, it contributes that much more to worker gratification. Many new buildings are well designed for public

[19] N. R. F. Maier, *Principles of Human Relations*, New York, Wiley, 1952.

display, for aesthetic consideration, or even for the ease of top administrators both during and after the process of construction, but they are poorly designed for the great majority of people who will be using them.

In one of the first companies studied by the Survey Research Center, the most common and bitter complaint was directed at the retirement system. This system was instituted before fringe benefits were as common for workers as they are now and constituted a real advance for the employees from an objective point of view. The employees had not been consulted, however, and this lack of consultation had the two disadvantages just referred to. The employees felt this was a company plan in which neither rank-and-file workers nor the union had anything to say. In addition, certain specific needs of the workers were not taken into account. Years of service before the age of thirty were not counted. Moreover, the amount of retirement pension was not large and employees would have preferred a system in which they could have increased their pensions through their own contributions—a sound principle. The company felt that this could be worked out through an annuity plan, already in existence, to which workers could make voluntary contributions. This, however, was too much of a jump for workers to grasp readily. The company, through failing to involve the workers in the planning of the retirement system, had turned a potential morale builder into a source of dissatisfaction.

Many real gains, however, have been registered for the life of the worker in the plant by improvements in working conditions, recreational facilities, and social climate, even though they have been introduced under the philosophy of machine theory. It is better to have showers and locker rooms and bowling alleys, even if paternalistically introduced, than not to have them at all. At their best, these attempts to create a more satisfactory plant life for the workers increase worker satisfaction with the company, as a system, but not with their jobs. There is increased motivation to stay within the company and enjoy its programs and benefits, but little of this effect is transferred to the work itself. And this is logical since the addition of benefits bears no relation to the productive process and to the energy required in keeping the process going. These rewards are grafted onto the work situation, and even when they improve the lot of the worker, they do not tie into his job in a meaningful manner.

Evidence for the separation between the two types of motivation, the desire to stay within the system or company and the involvement in the work process, is cited by D. Katz and R. Kahn from studies of four companies: a tractor factory, a railroad, a public utility, and an insurance company.[20] The high producers, those most involved in the work process, were no more satisfied with the many aspects of plant life than the low producers. These groups did not differ significantly in their satisfaction with most aspects of company policy and company programs, and when there were differences, they were contrary to the notion that increasing satisfaction with the plant increased satisfaction with the job. In fact, in one company the people most appreciative of the recreational facilities were found more among the low producers than

---

[20] D. Katz and R. L. Kahn, "Some Recent Findings in Human Relations Research," in G. E. Swanson, T. Newcomb, and E. Hartley (eds.), *Readings in Social Psychology*, rev. ed., New York, Holt, 1952, pp. 650–665.

among the high producers. And the people more involved in their jobs tended to be more critical of some company policies on placement and rating of workers. However, making plant life attractive increases worker motivation to stay within the system or company, even though it does not increase job satisfaction. Among male clerical workers in the public utility, the workers who found company programs more satisfactory had a significantly lower absence rate than workers less appreciative of these programs.

Under the most favorable circumstances, then, the attempts to create a more attractive plant life within the framework of machine theory still leave the basic conflict between the undesirable, uninteresting job and the sugar-coating of the circumstances surrounding it. Under less favorable circumstances, the reform of overinstitutionalization through more institutionalization can create even greater frustration.

The social satisfactions which workers derive from congenial associates and from group belongingness are deserving of more attention than research has accorded them. Even in large communities and large plants, the friendships formed in the immediate work group carry over to life outside the plant. For example, in one large tractor company employing some 20,000 people, 41 per cent of the employees said that they got together socially outside the plant with employees from their own work groups, *i.e.,* from the small segment of the plant constituting a section under a single supervisor.[21] In the same company, when asked, "If you had a chance to do the same kind of work, for the same pay, in another work group, how would you feel about moving?" the workers responded as follows:

Would rather stay where I am	63%
Would make no difference	22%
Would rather move	13%

Moreover, most of the workers felt that they were really part of their work groups and were included in its activities. In addition, when asked about such group characteristics as how well the men stick together, how congenial the group is, how much the men help one another out, and how good a group of workers it is, many more men rated their own group as superior than rated their group as inferior.

Satisfaction in identifying with one's own work group results both from congenial companions and from group responsibility in carrying out a common task. Fractionating and standardizing jobs can affect group responsibility and can decrease worker satisfaction through destroying the meaning of the work and minimizing the social satisfactions of team effort. The study of Trist and Bamforth of British coal-mining methods is very suggestive in this respect.[22] The British years ago adapted the mass-production methods of the assembly line to increase the efficiency of the old hand-got system of coal mining and in so doing replaced the small autonomous teams with seven new, different, specialized types of workers. The men undertaking these specialized roles are organized into three shifts: the cutting shift, which has the tasks of

---

[21] *Attitudes and Opinions of Hourly Employees,* Survey Research Center Report.
[22] E. L. Trist and K. W. Bamforth, "Some Social and Psychological Consequences of the Longwall Method of Coal-getting," *Human Relations,* 4 (1951), 3–38.

boring holes for the shot firer, of cutting into the coal face, and of cleaning out the undercut; the ripping shift, which rips the dirt out of the main and side gates and builds up the roof into a durable structure and also reassembles the conveyer on the new track; and, finally, the filling shift, which clears the coal from the passage and throws it on the conveyer belt. Though this longwall method of getting coal, employing machines, is an improvement over the old hand system, it has shown grave weaknesses. Productivity is low, cycle stoppages are not uncommon, absenteeism is high, and morale and worker satisfaction very low. Nor did the nationalization of the coal mines in itself improve the situation.

One problem is that most of the separate tasks are functionally interdependent, so that, if the borers on the first shift do a poor job, it affects the task of the men who follow. Since the conditions of mining vary from day to day, it is not easy to tell whether the difficulties at various stages of the process are due to poor work by someone along the line or to the nature of the pocket under attack. There is reciprocal scapegoating and interpersonal tension which carries over into life off the job. The fractionation of jobs has reduced both the variety and skill levels of the job and also the responsibility for the total task. Another weakness is that the effective basis for a cohesive work group has been destroyed. In the older system, the small work groups of two or more friends had group responsibility for their own small coal face. As Trist and Bamforth have summarized it, "The wholeness of the work task, the multiplicity of skills of the individual, and the self-selection of the group were congruent attributes of a pattern of responsible autonomy that characterized the pair-based face teams of hand-got mining."

A reorganization of the work process has been attempted in one coal field on an experimental basis, in which mechanization is retained but in which a small group will be given responsibility for carrying out all the specialized functions of the three shifts. The worker now has a greater variety of tasks, and he and his mates are responsible, as a group, for working a given section of a coal face. Under this new plan productivity has increased, absenteeism has decreased, feelings of fatigue are less frequently reported, and worker satisfaction has improved.

The use of group responsibility, though it runs counter to the principle of man-to-man accounting of machine theory, has rich possibilities for adding to worker satisfaction as it relates to job performance. Since the group as a whole is responsible, they can identify more fully with the product they turn out. They can cooperate with one another by helping the man who, for a given period, is too heavily overloaded. Moreover, they can interchange jobs and add variety to their monotonous work existence. Then, too, the usual social satisfactions from interaction with members of the same work unit can be integrated with stronger feelings of group identification. As the group grows more unified, it has greater attractiveness for its members. The limits imposed by the routine character of the work can be further stretched by giving the group responsibility for decisions which go beyond the work process and cover the personnel matters of who works overtime, when the group will recess for coffee, etc.

The work of Mayo and his followers has demonstrated the importance of the informal interpersonal relations which develop in every organization and which often contradict the pattern of the formal organization chart. The "Group Dynamics" movement has rediscovered the primary group and has shown how significant its functioning is to its members. The work of both these schools is in agreement on the essential point that human beings derive basic gratifications and essential meanings from their face-to-face associations with their fellow men. Mayo [23] reports:

> In industry and in other human situations the administrator is dealing with well-knit human groups and not with a horde of individuals. Wherever it is characteristic, as in the California of 1943, that by reason of external circumstance these groups have little opportunity to form, the immediate symptom is labor turnover, absenteeism, and the like. Man's desire to be continuously associated in work with his fellows is a strong, if not the strongest, human characteristic.

The use of group responsibility facilitates the natural tendencies of people to find satisfaction in interpersonal communication, in cooperative effort, and in group cohesion. Moreover, it can integrate these satisfactions with the work process and with group performance.

One caution—and it is an all-important one—should be taken with respect to the line of thinking which glorifies the primary group. The content of primary-group life in our culture is determined by the larger social structures in which it is imbedded. People are involved in, and dependent upon, organizations and systems which transcend the primary group. It is not enough, therefore, to accept the principle of group responsibility without some structural changes in the hierarchical organizations in which these groups operate. If all that is attempted is to give the group responsibility for work quotas without giving them power to make important decisions about the quotas and the means for achieving them, we are dealing with a manipulative device for getting more out of the workers without giving more. Such attempts are like the pseudo democracy in which students are given "self-government" with only the responsibility for policing and disciplining their own members on policies determined by the university administration. The notion of group responsibility must include the concept of *group autonomy*.

An example of high worker satisfaction is to be found in the Studebaker company, which has an enviable record with respect to overt conflict. This is possible in part because this company is not a pace setter in the industry but follows the wage pattern set in Detroit. But not all companies who are in a position similar to that of Studebaker have the same type of management-labor relations nor the same level of worker morale. It is of interest that at the Studebaker company the union contract gives the union stewards and the workers a real measure of the control and power which the factory manager, the personnel manager, and the top foremen have in other plants. The company in a certain sense subcontracts to the union the responsibility for keeping the assembly line running for a group piece rate. The number of men on the line and their earnings involve a union decision, and the stewards help allocate jobs

[23] E. Mayo, *The Social Problems of an Industrial Civilization,* Boston, Harvard Business School, Division of Research, 1945, p. 111.

through their interpretation of the seniority rules. Yet this small company continues to compete successfully in the market with the giants of the automobile industry, and its workers are probably more involved and identified with the company than is true of most industrial organizations.

A direct research attack upon the problem of group autonomy and group responsibility in relation to productivity and worker satisfaction has been made in a field experiment among clerical workers in a large insurance company by the Survey Research Center.[24] The underlying assumption in this experiment was that group process and group responsibility cannot function effectively at the local level unless the hierarchical structure of the company is changed sufficiently to increase the power and control of the people down the line. The department chosen for the experiment contained four parallel divisions, each of which was further subdivided into six sections, or work groups. Two of the divisions were assigned to *Experimental Group I,* where there was a downward delegation of authority. The department head assumed liaison responsibilities and permitted the division managers to take over many of his duties. The first-line supervisors, ordinarily responsible for the sections, moved into the task of managing their divisions. The rank-and-file employees took over the management of their sections. Hence, to implement their responsibility as a group, the workers had not only power formerly vested in the supervisor but control over some of the decisions regarding personnel matters and work process previously made fairly high in the supervisory line. They did not, however, have complete autonomy and were subject to some of the same company rules and regulations as other employees. The two other divisions were assigned to *Experimental Group II,* and here the experimental manipulation was in the direction dictated by machine theory. Controls from above were tightened and external pressures and regimentation were increased.

The analysis of the results of this experiment is still in process. Some suggestive findings, however, are available in advance of the complete report being prepared by the Michigan Survey Research Center. A year from the start of the experiment, both experimental groups had increased their own productivity significantly. Moreover, other groups in the company not included in the experiment had not changed significantly in this same period. Experimental Group II had increased its productivity more than Experimental Group I. But whereas the workers in Group II had increased their productivity under compulsion (staff was reduced without reducing the total work load), the workers in Group I were producing more because they wanted to. The effects upon worker morale and worker gratification were in the expected direction. Employees in the freer situation found their jobs more rewarding and were significantly higher on a self-actualization index based upon such questions as "Is your job a real challenge to what you can do?" and "How much does your job give you a chance to do the things you're best at?" The employees in Group I also showed greater liking for supervisors and managers as the experiment progressed, whereas the opposite was true in Group II. Furthermore, satisfaction with the company decreased in Group II. A finding very similar to the British experience in the coal mines, namely, that the regimented work groups showed

24 N. Morse, E. Reimer, and A. Tannenbaum, *The Experimental Change of a Major Organizational Variable* (to be published).

greater interpersonal hostility, also appeared in Group II. There were more reports of tension, friction, disagreeableness, and "fighting jumpiness" in interpersonal relations between workers in Group II as a result of the increased pressure, whereas more cooperation and friendliness were in evidence in Group I.

This field experiment demonstrates that worker satisfaction can be increased if workers are given greater freedom, as a group, to make decisions and take responsibility for a task. The downward delegation of power did not wreck the organization but actually raised the productivity level by 10 per cent at the same time that it increased morale. In short, it may well be that worker satisfaction will increase to the extent that partnership in production becomes a social reality rather than a slogan.

2

b · ORGANIZATION AND LEADERSHIP
OF GROUPS IN CONFLICT

IN THE preceding section of this volume attention has been centered mainly upon the individual and his motivations. We will now shift our focus to the groups and group contexts that are significant in industrial conflict.

Chapters 7 through 10 deal with important aspects of the union organization. The central question with which all these chapters are concerned is this: What are the institutional imperatives of the union, as an organization, that affect the union's role in industrial conflict? We want to know what happens to the aspirations and goals of individuals when they join together in organized groups for the pursuit of common objectives. We want further to examine the kinds of goals and objectives that are primarily a product of the union as an organized group. In terms of these questions attention is directed to structural and leadership features of unions as being particularly relevant to industrial conflict.

In Chap. 7 we secure a broad picture of the major features of the union as an organization. Chapter 8 focuses particular attention upon the issue of how the shift from craft to industrial unionism has been accompanied by a shift in program from demands for worker rights to a particular job to the goals of protecting the rights of workers to earn a livelihood at some point in the economy. This chapter represents a major modification of the Commons-Perlman interpretation of the "job-conscious" orientation of union goals. Chapter 9 deals with a little-understood aspect of internal union operations. In this chapter we can see how the union organization can be periodically stirred by internal competition for office and yet maintain a basic unity vis-à-vis the employer in collective-bargaining relationships. This chapter helps document the self-sustaining character of the union organization. The union does not act as a concerted group only in the face of conflict with an employer; there is a rich internal life exhibiting strife and drama, schism and reconciliation, which is almost independent of the collective-bargaining relationship.

Chapter 10 is particularly relevant as a basic criticism of the Commons-Perlman theory of the labor movement. In this chapter primary emphasis is given to the concept of social power, of which the Commons-Perlman view is singularly innocent. Mills shows how the powerful labor unions of our society come to achieve one aspect of their articulation with the social structure, through their national leaders. These leaders become a part of the national power elite. In this position they come to identify the national goals and the ideology of the elite with union goals and philosophy. This, in turn, reduces some of the elements of conflict in industrial relations.

Chapters 11, 12, and 13 deal with significant aspects of management organizations that have important bearings on labor relations. Chamberlain focuses his attention specifically upon decision making in the corporation as it deals with the area of employee policy. For the purposes of this volume, this restricted viewpoint is particularly essential. What collective bargaining succeeds in doing to the operations of the corporation is to change the basis and mode of enacting the policies that govern work behavior in the organization. It is therefore most pertinent to confine the analysis of the corporation to the areas in which collective bargaining has its largest impact upon corporate operations. At another level of analysis, when we examine the impact of the union upon corporation officers charged with executing the enacted labor policy, we encounter still a different set of problems. These are set forth in detail by Dalton in his examination of the role of supervision in collective bargaining.

The chapter by Bendix on bureaucratization in industry lays greatest stress upon the relations between business structure and organization and the self-image or moral outlook of the businessman. This chapter gives us the managerial counterpart of the union officers' view of their own goals and activities as developed both by Barkin and by Mills in Chaps. 8 and 10.

The general conclusion that flows from the essays of this section of the book is that the institutional imperatives of the union and the corporation, as well as their modes of articulation with the larger society, contribute both to industrial conflict and to industrial cooperation. The arguments and evidence marshaled in their support in these seven chapters suggest that the institutional setting of union-management relations contains important factors making for cooperative interaction, within which, however, conflict continues to have a significant place. The interaction, therefore, has displayed a preponderance of "antagonistic-cooperation" elements. This conclusion makes sense, for both unions and corporations are successful operating organizations that are woven into the broad social fabric. So long as that social fabric remains relatively intact, the position and activities of all its components will be so articulated as to sustain the larger social equilibrium.

CHAPTER 7 THE LABOR UNION AS AN ORGANIZATION

Joel Seidman   *University of Chicago*

A DISCUSSION of union goals and union structure, in so far as these have a bearing on industrial conflict, must center primarily on the national union, since the effective power to determine union objectives and to control union activities is lodged there. The goals that are decided upon and the tactics employed in order to attain them represent the response of the union, and especially of the union's top leadership, to the complex social situation in which it functions—a combination of the collective-bargaining relationship with employers, the threat of rival unions, the factional alignment within the union, and the views and expectations of the union membership and of unorganized workers employed within the union's jurisdiction. All this, in turn, must be placed against a broad background of legal rights and obligations and community pressure to which union leaders and members are subject. In the case of some leaders, the goals may be long-run ones, well thought out in advance; more typically, however, they represent the reaction to the problems and pressures of the moment.

Social Environment of the Union

The attitude of American employers to present-day unionism ranges from deep-seated hostility through grudging acceptance to appreciation of unionism as a constructive force, with a blend of contrary attitudes often found within the management group of a single business enterprise. The view adopted by a single management representative, in turn, is the product of his personality and value judgments, modified by the economic condition of his enterprise, his position in the management hierarchy, and the character and philosophy of the union leadership with which he must deal. Most of the powerful business enterprises in this country have recognized unions and now bargain with them because the nation's basic labor law requires such action; at the same time, they typically hold the union at arm's length and jealously restrict its sphere of influence. Smaller and weaker business units, concerned more with business survival than with ideological considerations, seek to avoid quarrels with powerful unions and sometimes welcome their help in solving mutual problems. At the other extreme, there are some firms, many of them found in the South, which still show the bitter enmity toward unionism that was so prevalent in management circles until a decade and a half ago.

Many management representatives who have been forced against their will to deal with unions now credit them with playing an important role in drawing attention to, and eliminating, sources of dissatisfaction which were bound to lower employee morale; others, conceding no proper role to union- ism where management is alert and well intentioned, see only interference with production, breakdown of work discipline, and less efficiency as the fruits of unionism. Where such attitudes exist, union leaders understandably may sense a hope on the part of the employer to undermine the loyalty of the member- ship and an ever-constant threat to the continued existence of the union.

While union leaders deal with employers who hold these various views, they see about them a number of other unions willing, often eager, to capitalize on their mistakes. Some of these other unions, more conservative in their social philosophy, depend to varying degrees on the good will of management and welcome assurances of management support in efforts to supplant the present bargaining agency. Other unions, more militant in their approach, seek to convince workers that they could hammer out greater gains in the bargaining process than the union now representing them. In some instances ideological considerations—as anti-Communist versus Party-line followers—embitter the conflict; in other cases rival unions chartered by the AFL and the CIO dispute a jurisdiction, either in full or with regard to selected workers; and in still other cases union groups, such as District 50 of the United Mine Workers, stand ready to enter almost any situation in which members may be gained. Even between sister unions in the same federation a borderland area often exists in which guerilla warfare is carried on. It is a rare union that enters into conflict with employers with full confidence that its flanks are secure against raids by rival labor groups.

More than this, the union leader must be on guard lest a rival within his own organization, profiting from his mistakes or unpopular actions, bring about his defeat at the next convention.[1] A union is enough of a fighting organi- zation to justify the use of a military analogy; yet it possesses, at least formally, a democratic structure that makes leaders dependent on the con- tinued approval of the membership and subject to replacement if policies prove too unpopular. A number of national union heads, to be sure, are so strongly entrenched that they can disregard the niceties of democratic pro- cedure and retain office as long as they produce some benefits for their member- ship. In some extreme cases democratic forms have been simply eliminated, as in the election of Joseph P. Ryan as president for life of the International Longshoremen's Association. In the more characteristic union situation, however, ambitious and capable men may arise within the organization who may aspire to the national presidency because of the great power and prestige associated with that position; and democratic forms may provide at least some opportunity to them. How to combine such natural leaders into a political machine that can control the union, giving each figure in the machine a post that satisfies his ambitions without letting him gain such a following that he can contest control of the union—such is the problem that confronts the national union head.

In his desire to retain office the leader is aided unwittingly by the very

[1] In this connection see Chap. 9.

large proportion of union members who do not participate actively in union affairs. A steelworkers' local that the author has helped to study has approximately 13,000 members, of whom only 50 to 75, or approximately half of 1 per cent, are in attendance at a typical biweekly membership meeting. Even during the heat of a strike the number present may not rise above 2 per cent, while 3 per cent represents an extraordinary turnout. This small attendance, typical of many large locals, permits organized groups of very small numbers of activists to dominate meetings and determine policy. Such factional control at the local level has its counterpart in the organization of a political machine, typically dominated by the national union president, which enters candidates in the national election and usually elects its slate without difficulty. In building such a machine the national president is aided by the international representatives or other pay-rollers, scattered among the locals, who function as a cohesive group in order to retain their jobs, by the union's publication, which becomes the political organ of the dominant group, and by the difficulty, in the light of membership inactivity, of the disciplinary powers of the administration, and of the lack of funds, in building a rival political organization.[2] In many unions, moreover, especially where a Communist group has functioned, political opposition may have become virtually synonymous, to the membership as well as to the leaders, with subversion; only in the International Typographical Union (ITU) has a two-party system, with its connotation of a loyal opposition, developed.

Whether the present union leader remains or is replaced by an ambitious rival, in the long run the security of the union depends on the state of mind of the union's membership. Will they reject the union's program in exchange for the benevolent dictatorship of the employer or for the blandishments of a rival union? Are they in favor of the union but not sufficiently loyal to keep their membership dues paid up in the absence of legal duty or social pressure? To what extent are unwilling members found within the organization, persons forced in by a union-shop clause or by the pressure of coworkers and remaining members of the union without ever acquiring a union point of view? The attitudes of the members are a reflection of many factors, including their family background, experiences in their present plants or in earlier jobs, and their assessment of unionism in general and of their present union in particular. For those who favor the union, in turn, attitudes may range from a belief that union membership is desirable insurance against the unlikely prospect that they will get in trouble with management to a strong conviction that unionism can profoundly improve their conditions of employment and raise the status that they enjoy as employees.

In the research project to which reference has been made the views of members of a steelworkers' local were sought as to the probable consequences of the union's disappearance, and overwhelmingly those interviewed asserted that this would make a great difference, not only to themselves but to most other workers. Most of the leaders believed that they would soon be discharged or that conditions would deteriorate so rapidly that they would quit. While the

[2] See suggestive article by Will Herberg, "Bureaucracy and Democracy in Labor Unions," *The Antioch Review*, 3 (Fall, 1943), 405–417.

inactive members did not expect that this would happen to them, they did believe that there would be a return to oppressive treatment by foremen, which they would be powerless to prevent.

"Management would do what they wanted to do," said one. "If you made one little mistake, you would be out, if they wanted you out."

In a typical response another inactive member said, "You'd lose everything. The company would really throw you around and put the pressure on. They'd be demanding, and high-pressuring everybody. They'd demote people any time they wanted. There wouldn't be any seniority."

In the words of an inactive foreign-born worker, the result of the union's disappearance would be that "we gotta be slave again. I don't want union to disappear. Might as well go to jail, that's all. Used to be, if foreman want to fire, he do it. Not any more."

If the membership of this local is at all typical of the labor movement, the conclusion is inescapable that even inactive members feel a continuing need for the union's protection, even though many of them may look upon union dues as rather like insurance premiums and on the union as a sort of policeman whose very presence may keep the company "honest" in its relations with them. This, in turn, suggests that the end of union security clauses, while it would increase the work load of union leaders and weaken the union's treasury, could not endanger the existence of unionism or materially weaken its ability to strike or to bargain effectively.

Nevertheless, union leadership has typically put its faith to a far greater extent in control devices, such as the union security clause, than in educational programs designed to build better understanding and thereby inspire greater loyalty. Experience in collective bargaining and in strikes and knowledge of the economic problems of an industry tend to make leaders impatient with the proposals offered by less experienced and more poorly informed union members. The leaders of any union, understandably enough, think themselves most competent to determine strategy and believe that the membership will progress most rapidly by accepting the leaders' advice and responding to their orders in disciplined fashion. To this must be added the fear, seldom admitted but nevertheless very real, that, as the membership becomes more informed, the number of potential rivals for union office is increased.

Bulking equally large in the thinking of union leaders are the unorganized workers within their union's jurisdiction, found either as a nonunion minority within units in which the union enjoys bargaining rights or in plants that the union is unable to organize. In either case they pose a threat, actual or potential, to the success, perhaps even to the continued existence, of the union. The presence of a nonunion group in an organized plant suggests either that some individuals remain opposed to unionism, despite its many opportunities to aid them, or that they are enjoying the benefits of unionism without sharing in the obligations of members. If the nonmembers are few in number, they may perhaps be ignored; there is always the chance, however, that they may grow in number and undermine the union's effectiveness. The unorganized percentage of the union's jurisdiction, in turn, weakens the union's effectiveness in bargaining and limits the improvements that can be obtained for its members, if these add to production costs, since each such improvement, unless voluntarily matched, may increase the competitive advantage enjoyed by the nonunion section of the industry over unionized competitors.

Difficult as all these problems may appear to be, the union does not have a free hand in its attempts to solve them. The law of the land grants certain legal rights to unions and imposes upon them certain legal restraints and liabilities. While state laws and local regulations have their influence, since the validation of the National Labor Relations Act in 1937, the Federal law has been decisive for most unions. Consequently, it has become part of the strategy of unions functioning within the Federal jurisdiction to qualify for bargaining rights under the Taft-Hartley law, to win elections and be awarded bargaining rights, and to avoid charges of unfair labor practices and damage suits under that law. At the same time, unions are exposed to other community pressures, including the pressures against strikes during wars or other periods of national emergency.

Institutional Goals of the Union

It is within this entire network of relationships that the union must determine its goals and strive to reach them. Some of these goals are institutional, seeking to ensure the survival of the organization, to safeguard its security against external or internal enemies, and to provide the basis for growth in membership, influence, and power. Other goals relate to the wages and working conditions of the membership, the original problems that brought the union into existence, and seek to win as much improvement as possible without harm to employment possibilities. Still other goals involve the wider community in which the union operates: here the union seeks political influence, the power to affect legislation and the behavior of political officials, and a wider stage on which its leaders may perform and gain prestige.

Inevitably, once the union has come into being, institutional goals directed toward survival and continued growth play a large part in its activities. The workers who participate in early struggles acquire a strong feeling of identification with the organization in whose name the struggles are carried on. To the emerging leaders, however, the union means vastly more: their success or failure in life and their position and their prestige, in their own eyes as well as in the eyes of others, are bound up with the success of the organization, whereas its failure means a return to the obscurity of the workshop, if indeed jobs are still available for them. Once the union is established, every growth in membership or influence increases the power and enhances the prestige of the leaders. Small wonder that the men in best position to determine the union's objectives give high priority to those that, while phrased in institutional terms, contribute so substantially to their own power and prestige.

The most controversial of these institutional goals is the union security clause, which from an early stage in the development of American unionism has ranked high among its objectives. Unions found themselves functioning in an insecure world, in which employers frequently sought the first opportunity to undermine the union and in which workers typically lacked the class consciousness that in industrialized European countries formed the psychological base on which unionism was erected. If the "free riders" could be forced to join and remain in the union, a constant source of irritation would be removed, the flow of funds into the union treasury safeguarded, and the time and energy of officers and active members freed for other tasks. In addition, the security clause served as the instrument of union discipline by compelling the discharge from his job of a worker who violated union rules and as a result lost his union membership. With the passage of the Wagner Act, bringing protection to the union against efforts by the employer to undermine it, one of the chief reasons for the union security clause ceased to exist. To some extent, union leaders continued to press for security clauses because these had become traditional and were associated in their minds with strong unionism; behind this, however, was the fact that one of the chief functions of the union security clause had been profoundly altered from protection against the employer to security against the threat of rival unionism.

While the union security clause seemed vital to the union leadership for all these reasons, from the point of view of the rank-and-file membership it served still another function, that of spreading the cost of union membership among all those who received its benefits. In the study of the steelworkers' local already referred to, virtually all the leaders, three-fourths of the active members, and a little over half of the inactives who were interviewed agreed that nonmembers should be forced to join the union on the ground either that the majority should rule or that all who shared in union benefits should help pay the cost.[3]

Another device that serves to protect the union as an institution is the grant of recognition or of exclusive bargaining rights. Prior to the validation of the Wagner Act the question of bargaining rights was one of the thorniest in American industrial relations. Many employers insisted that individual bargaining was superior from the point of view of the employee and of the community as well as from that of the employer; collective bargaining was condemned by them on moral as well as on economic grounds. Unions won recognition by strike action, and whether they won recognition only on behalf of members or obtained exclusive bargaining rights depended typically on the power they were able to develop. The Wagner Act, and more recently the Taft-Hartley Act, have removed this issue from the arena of labor-management conflict by the grant of exclusive bargaining rights, under appropriate conditions, to a union that demonstrates the support of a majority of workers in the unit and by protecting that right from challenge by a rival union for a minimum period of a year.

The labor movement has also sought from time to time to set up its own machinery for the solution of jurisdictional problems. From its beginning the AFL, with its concept of exclusive jurisdictional rights to national unions, found its units embroiled in bitter conflict as unions organized on the disputed boundaries of their jurisdictional grants or as established skills were broken down by the invention of new machinery or the development of new processes. In some instances the fight was over the control of a disputed group of workers, and in other cases it was over the right to perform a disputed operation. A

---

[3] Joel Seidman, Jack London, and Bernard Karsh, "Why Workers Join Unions," *The Annals of the American Academy of Political and Social Science,* 274 (March, 1951), 75–84.

decision of an AFL convention in one of these jurisdictional quarrels gave a measure of security to the victorious union, provided that the losing union accepted the decision in preference to risking loss of membership in the AFL. During and since World War II machinery for the settlement of jurisdictional quarrels has functioned within the building-trades department of the AFL, and at the present time comparable machinery is being established within the CIO.

Other institutional devices are planned to increase the loyalty of the membership. Such devices include sickness or death benefits, unemployment compensation, pensions for retired members, strike benefits, medical and hospitalization plans, educational and recreational programs, and a variety of similar benefits or activities. Social-insurance plans, once of great significance in many unions, became of much less consequence with the passage of social-security legislation in the 1930's, but they revived in importance with the recent popularity of health and welfare programs under joint agreement with employers.

The Union Organization and Collective Bargaining

Another set of union goals has to do with problems within the plant growing directly out of the employer-employee relationship. Wages are prominent among these, as are hours, working conditions, job security, seniority, grievance procedures, fringe wage benefits, and treatment by supervisors. Unions seek to increase the proceeds from work, improve the conditions under which work is carried on, determine the rights of each individual worker, and establish a mechanism by which these rights may be protected. The objective, broadly stated, is to establish a united front of employees in dealing with the employer so as to obtain the maximum concessions from him and to bring the united power of the group to bear when any one of them suffers a wrong. Since this wrong, as in a layoff out of order of seniority, may involve a corresponding benefit to another worker, an elaborate system of rules to determine one worker's rights against another's may need to be constructed before differences within the group can be merged and a united front presented to the employer.

With regard to wages, the union's objective is the twofold one of limiting competition within the work force and raising the level of wages as high as bargaining power and the competitive situation of the employer and the industry permit. Unions seek to limit competition among workers as to wage rates and output, either by agreement on a single standard to which all will adhere or by establishing a minimum below which none will go. Just as a local union will seek these objectives within a single plant or community, so a district organization or the national union will attempt to equalize wages over the wider area of competition. At the same time local union leaders are aware or soon learn that if, following a bargaining advantage, they force wages in their plant too far above the remainder of the industry, they will place their employer at a competitive disadvantage and reduce the volume of work available to their membership. National leaders, similarly, recognize that there are limits beyond which wages cannot be raised without a shift of work from the unionized to the nonunion section of their industry or a reduction in the volume of the product that consumers will purchase from their industry as a whole.

Union leaders are not free to consider the problem of wages purely as an exercise in economics. They are leaders of a mass movement, subject to a variety of pressures and cross pressures, who must meet the needs of their membership or risk replacement at the next election. If wage pressures are mounting, then an increase must be sought, even though the leaders are more fearful than the membership that a lower volume of employment might result. Similarly, in dividing the gains that can be won at any particular time, the leaders must balance somehow the rival claims of workers at different levels of skill. The less skilled workers in an industrial union may keep the gains equal to all because of their numbers and voting strength, or the skilled minority may obtain a larger share by a threat to bolt the union and join a rival craft group. A factional conflict within the union may compel the officers to seek wage gains at an inauspicious time, lest the failure to act vigorously become a source of attack during an impending election campaign. Similarly, a union that fails to match the gains won by a rival union runs the risk of inviting a raid when the contract or certification nears its expiration date.[4]

Although wages are important, workers may be more disturbed over a nonwage matter that directly affects them and makes life in the plant unpleasant. Sometimes working conditions are at fault, sometimes the lack of lockers or the condition of the rest room is the issue, sometimes it is the way in which supervisors address workers, sometimes it is the laying off or promotion of workers by favoritism rather than by seniority or ability. Members of minority racial or national groups, similarly, are alert to any evidence of discrimination, not only against themselves but against any members of their minority. These are immediate issues that all workers understand and to which many react emotionally, and they are all factors that management obviously has the power to correct. People don't like to be pushed around, and under nonunion conditions many of them believe that they have been pushed around far too frequently. Often issues such as these contribute far more heavily than do wage improvements to the building of union loyalties. Likewise, where they strongly influence union members' reactions, they will bulk large in the union's goals if the leaders are at all responsive to membership sentiments.

In seeking thus to advance the interests of their members, unions challenge more and more of management's acts and push farther and farther into the areas that management feels should belong exclusively to itself. How far unions penetrate into the area of management rights depends partly on the social philosophy of union leaders; a crusading type of union leadership, such as that represented by Walter P. Reuther of the UAW-CIO, interested in solving broad social problems, will challenge more decisions of management than will conservative leadership, such as that of Philip Murray in the steel industry. Where the industry is in a sick and depressed state, unions, in an effort to protect their members, will seek to influence more decisions than they will in a healthy, prosperous industry. Where large and powerful unions confront

---

[4] For a good discussion of the factors that influence wage demands, see Arthur M. Ross, *Trade Union Wage Policy*, Berkeley, University of California Press, 1948.

small and weak employers, they can impose their will more readily, whatever the nature of the issues in dispute. A marginal employer struggling to survive is in no position to fight a strong union and may willingly grant it a voice in areas usually reserved to management if the union's aid may increase the chances of survival.

The pursuit of these various collective-bargaining goals cannot be understood apart from the power relationship between the union and the company. In a compulsory arbitration system, such as in effect operated during World War II, a government agency, in this case the National War Labor Board (NWLB), serves as a court of last resort. Where no such court is available, the relative power of the two parties—the ability of each to inflict or withstand economic loss—profoundly influences the decisions that are reached. Often the issue involved in a strike seems minor, if not trivial, to an outsider, who sees both sides sustaining losses far out of proportion to the difference that caused the strike. Yet each party may be seeking to show the other that it cannot be pushed around; success may be measured not in terms of cents per hour but in terms of the lesson taught as to toughness and ability to withstand a long strike. Disputes grow more bitter as each party conceives the other to be a threat to it and reach an extreme where the union believes that management is out to destroy it. Where this is believed to be the case, strikes in violation of contract or slowdowns, perhaps otherwise condemned bitterly by the national union officers, will probably be sanctioned. In other cases the national officers may agree to a strike they think unwise or even illegal if they are convinced that the membership is so aroused over the issue that a failure to give support would cost heavily in loyalty and perhaps invite a raid by a rival union. With an eye on political pressures within the union, local union leaders, similarly, must make their decisions as to when to advocate a strike and when to advise settlement.

The decision to call or to settle a strike is one over which the leaders of the great labor federations, the AFL and the CIO, typically have little or no influence. Within the AFL the traditional autonomous rights of the affiliated national or international unions preserve to each of them control over strike policy as over collective-bargaining goals and internal organizational matters. In the case of the directly affiliated federal locals, however, which belong to no national union, the AFL may exercise control over strike policy. The AFL likewise has influence over strike policy where it sponsors an organizing drive in a nonunion industry or area; in the more typical cases its affiliated unions perform such functions, turning to the AFL only where they want its intercession with government officials or its help in channeling requests for funds or organizers to the other affiliated unions. Even in the somewhat more highly centralized CIO control over strike policy is similarly reserved to the affiliated national unions, though the organizing committees that laid the foundation for some of the national unions were directly appointed by the CIO head and subject to more influence from the CIO national office.

Within each national union the situation as to national or local control over strikes varies sharply, in accordance with the scope of collective bargaining, economic conditions within the industry, and the traditions of the union. In some cases, as in steel or coal the decision to strike is made at the national level, and the entire union or broad sections of it strike at once, with the local union retaining no control over the decision, except perhaps in a very limited and formal sense. At the other extreme, in localized, decentralized industries, the local unions make their own strike decisions, in some cases without even notifying the national office of their actions. All sorts of gradations between these extremes are to be found in the American labor movement. Sometimes the constitution of the national union requires approval of the national officers or executive board before a local may engage in a strike; sometimes approval is required for a strike shutting down all plants organized by the union in an area but not for one against a single shop; sometimes approval is required where strike benefits are sought from a national fund but not where the local or its members bear the financial burden themselves. If the local strikes in violation of the national union rules, its charter may be revoked or its officers replaced with appointees of the national office; often splits result from such actions, with the rival groups fighting for control of the local's name and assets, for the loyalty of the members, for recognition by the employer, and for the right to administer the contract. Usually the group that wins control over the jobs is the victor, with the workers having no choice but to register in that organization if they wish to continue working in the plant.

Workers differ sharply in their appraisal of the strike, depending on their degree of identification with unionism. Union leaders, on the local as well as the national level, tend to hold that strikes are justified without qualification, on the ground that only by strikes or the threat of strike action are concessions won; even where strikes are apparently lost, many of them argue, the workers nevertheless benefit in the long run because they have shown their strength, thereby making management more willing to make concessions in the future. This general point of view was held by most leaders of the steelworkers' local union to which reference has been made and, likewise, by about half the rank-and-file active members. Among the inactives, however, the response to strikes was far more conditional; as a group, they were in favor of strikes only when they felt sufficient cause existed and when the prospects for success seemed great enough. The inactives showed a far greater tendency than the leaders to weigh in pragmatic fashion the cost of a strike in lost wages against the gains won. Other factors are also important in determining workers' attitudes toward strikes; among such factors are the history of their own union, the strikes in which they have participated, their estimate of the employers' intentions, the size of their savings, the volume of unemployment, and their fear of replacement. All of this suggests that the decision of leaders to advocate the calling of a strike (or, in an autocratically controlled union, to call one) is influenced by their estimate of the psychology of the workers as an important factor affecting the power relationship between the parties.

The Union Organization and Community Goals

Union goals outside the area of collective bargaining, involving the larger community, are strongly influenced by the immediate needs of the union and the ideology accepted by the leaders. Where trades are taught in city schools, unions representing those trades will seek to influence the selection of teachers;

where craftsmen are licensed by a public body, the unions will seek representation on the body of examiners; where contracts may be awarded to either union or nonunion establishments, unions will seek to influence their flow to unionized firms. Where strikes are contemplated, unions will want the police neutralized so that effective picketing may be carried on without police interference. To achieve these objectives, unions must be active in politics and preferably must have an established position within the political machine dominant in their locality.

These are all short-run considerations, to be sure, but local union officials, unless their jobs are unusually secure, respond to short-run demands. To launch a labor party or to support any minority party requires a union officer who has unusually strong political convictions or who feels secure enough in his job to sacrifice immediate gains for the sake of long-run benefits. Antiunion behavior by Congress, such as passage of the Taft-Hartley Act, may arouse virtually all union leaders and activists against the men who voted for that legislation; yet this is also a short-run objective, one that they hope may be achieved without sacrificing the other immediate advantages to be gained by cooperation with the dominant local political machine, whatever its party affiliation.

How far union leaders go beyond this, in an effort to increase the union's influence in the community, depends upon the conception that they and the members hold of the union's function and, likewise, upon the extent of the government's activity in labor-management affairs. If union leaders believe that the union is exclusively a collective-bargaining agency, they will engage in community activities as a union only when they see a community threat to collective bargaining such as that posed by unfriendly police action on a picket line. If, on the other hand, they conceive of the union as an agency through which workers can and should extend their influence in society, they will seek to become active in community affairs to the greatest extent possible. Much depends on whether the leaders and members look to the union or to other agencies through which to function as citizens; and much depends, similarly, on whether they accept a conservative political philosophy or one that seeks to alter the established balance of society in favor of higher standards or greater rights for workers. At certain times, however, the government intervenes in the area of labor-management relations to such an extent that union leaders, whatever their social philosophy, must devote much of their time and energy to attempts to influence government action. This occurs during time of war or national emergency when strikes may be outlawed and wages controlled, and during peacetime whenever legislation affecting labor relations is under consideration.

These union goals—institutional, collective-bargaining, and community—result from the interaction of union leaders and union members in the complex social environment that has been sketched. The strong emphasis on institutional protection reflects the relative newness of the union, the opposition of employers, the indifference of a number of workers, and the hostility of the community at large. Union leaders, at the same time that they face these problems, have to be responsive to the shifting pressures within their own ranks in order to retain their positions and their influence. The union traditionally has been an insecure agency operating in an insecure world, dependent upon its fighting strength for survival; its leaders, at the local as well as the national level, have overwhelmingly thought in terms of current issues, of solutions for problems that immediately confronted them. Their long-run goals, needless to say, influence their decisions, but primarily they are men pragmatic in their philosophy and flexible in their methods, determining their objectives in the light of shifting considerations: the economic conditions of their industry, the polices of the government, the state of public opinion, the existence of rival unionism, the fighting power of the employer, and the loyalty and discipline of the union membership.

CHAPTER 8 LABOR UNIONS AND WORKERS' RIGHTS IN JOBS

Solomon Barkin　　　　　*Textile Workers Union of America*

R EFORMERS and trade-unionists over the years have been challenged by the highly protected position of property owners. How could workers secure an equal set of rights? The historical battle for political liberty resulted in freeing property from the restraints and the controls of the state. The rights of man became the immunities of property. After their release, legislation and the judiciary combined to protect property and erected a system of common law that effectively guarded property owners.

Such freedom was of no benefit to the mass of persons without property. For them a new system of rights has been sought. One was to establish a structure of inalienable personal rights in jobs and rights to income. These would balance the rights of property. But this course proved difficult and the results were inadequate.

The alternative course, a more fruitful program, has been to secure, through economic struggle and legislation, limitations upon the employer's exercise of his managerial powers and to prescribe conditions for the use of property which would create security for workers, regularize the claims of classes of workers to employment, and provide employment opportunities for all. These claims have not become common-law rights; they are concessions and claims wrested through, and protected only by, economic and political power.

We have evolved no general system of personal or collective property right in jobs. But trade-unions and reform groups have fought for, and secured, much legislation and many administrative policies which increase the worker's personal and economic security, assure national governmental responsibility for the maintenance of full employment, and prescribe terms of employment. The individual business organization is required to conform to these rules. Conditions favorable to economic security and full employment are thereby being created.

The right of individuals to a social system which produces economic security, expanding opportunities, and advancing living standards has been reflected in a number of the more recent national constitutions. It has reached its fullest expression in the Universal Declaration of Human Rights proclaimed by the United Nations, which declares that "all of us have the right to work and the right to choose the kind of work we may desire . . . [and] are entitled to just and favorable wages ensuring for ourselves and our families an existence worthy of human dignity—supplemented, if necessary, by other means of social protection."

Craft Unions—A System of Collective Property Rights in Jobs

Workers first sought a system of property rights in jobs under union control that would be equivalent to the system of legally recognized personal rights in property. The individual worker could not effectively secure personal rights in jobs. In seeking to promote his interests he had to band together with others into a union. It became evident, therefore, that the rights in the job would have to be lodged with the union, particularly as many union leaders in the early days of the British trade-union movement mistakenly identified these unions with the medieval guilds.

The advent of the commercial and industrial revolutions demolished the systems of legal rights to jobs and conditions of employment. The medieval guilds and laws of apprenticeship disappeared or were repealed. The cruel forces of early industrialism uprooted all forms of protection for the laborer and left the employer free to hire and secure his workers at his own terms. Revolts were many. Organizations of workers appeared but were demolished by the overwhelming strength of the employer with the conspiring aid of the law and the courts. Little experience was developed with collective bargaining.

Out of this struggle emerged the organization of craft workers. Their labors were prized; and their bargaining powers were at times considerable. Their unions were the first to survive. They became the base for the modern trade-union organization. For procedure and techniques they turned to the experience of the medieval guild. While unlike them in character, the craft unions could borrow and adopt many of their methods and approaches.

The craft union's goals are the protection and improvement of its members' position. Through economic power the craft union has sought to provide the defense previously furnished by customs and law. The union has pressed for policies which would give it, as a collective body, a property right in the job. It hopes to have a power akin to that of owning the jobs and to restrict them solely to its membership. While in some instances local unions have approximated this goal, they have never successfully challenged the basic right of the property and job owner to discontinue the total enterprise. They have never succeeded in establishing a worker's right in individual jobs on a par with the owner's freedom to make use of his property in his own interest. This failure basically distinguishes the strong and powerful craft union from the medieval guild, which controlled the number of enterprises.

The trade-union movement had to turn to approaches other than collective bargaining to provide the ultimate guarantee of employment opportunities for the great mass of its members. The craft union evolved a number of techniques to realize its goals of providing rights in jobs. These techniques include complete unionization of the craft, the closed shop, and the closed union. Some have been questioned as giving the collective group too much power and leaving the individual without outside protection against the union's decisions. But they are essential in providing the organized group of workers with an approximation of job security comparable to that enjoyed by property owners.

To secure this position the union had to drive for complete unionization of the labor market of the craft or labor group. Without such organization its power was constantly in jeopardy. This degree of unionization has usually been attained only through long and costly struggle. Where it has not been realized, it is because of employers' opposition and the support accorded them by legislation, courts, and the administration.

Having approximated or attained this goal, the craft union has usually striven to obtain the closed shop. Through the closed shop the union truly established its control or claims over jobs. Only union members can be employed therein. Usually the closed shop is associated with the practice of requiring employers to recruit workers only through the union. The union hiring hall or register becomes a significant vehicle to maintain job control. Only union members in good standing are allowed to remain on the job.

To maintain this position the supply of jobs must also be carefully husbanded. Rules on apprenticeship and the ratio of helpers to journeymen are set to prevent dilution of work and to maintain the number of jobs for craftsmen. Job duties are similarly defined to ensure the maximum number of jobs. The owner's or the foreman's right to work is precisely circumscribed. Mechanical or job innovations are eyed suspiciously lest the output increase and reduce the required number of workers or completely eliminate or reduce the need for the particular skills or experience. Minimum complements of workers are prescribed for operations and plants. As new processes develop, the unions eagerly seek to widen their jurisdiction to provide new employment opportunities for their members. The result may be jurisdictional conflict. Collective job control necessarily produces a keen interest in the supply of jobs. It has also prompted unions to use union labels and boycotts of nonunion products or of users of nonunion supplies to protect union jobs.

The third technique for realizing the control is the closed union, which ensures greater security for the organized worker. Through it the union can regulate the inflow of workers to correspond to the supply of jobs and establish an advantageous position for bargaining on the terms of employment. Entry into these craft unions is carefully scrutinized. In periods of unemployment the rolls are usually closed. After prolonged experiences with unemployment, the union is not likely to be liberal in accepting new members. Many craft unions have used a temporary work-permit system for recruitment of labor during periods of abnormal or seasonal expansion of jobs. Such permits allow new workers to be employed in union shops but usually limit their period of employment. The membership rights are usually limited to a single local union, and transfers from one local to another in the same international union must be specifically arranged and permission obtained. The work-permit system has produced problems of its own, since the persons employed on such work permits have frequently become the core for opposition union groups or the basis for antiunion employer campaigns. But it has produced the desired control over the labor supply.[1] The influx of workers has also been constricted

---

[1] H. J. Lahne, "The Union Work Permit," *Political Science Quarterly*, 66 (September, 1951), 366–399.

in some areas with the assistance of state or local licensing provisions which prescribe high-quality standards for performance and regulate the supply of such licensed craftsmen. The professional organizations have tended to follow these very same approaches.

Craft unions, to maintain the service and high quality of service performed by their membership, have sponsored instruction, examinations, and other similar educational projects. Such practices reinforce other programs designed to control the labor supply.

Within the structure of the closed-shop and closed-union system of control of jobs, there are two different bases for defining the individual's rights in jobs. In some areas the employer has been completely free to make selections. In others the union has operated the entire placement system according to its rules and procedures, possibly modified through negotiations with the employers. In the latter instances unions have set rules defining the individual's claims. Some have prescribed seniority provisions to regulate the expansion or contraction of the work force. Others have followed the principle of work sharing. Still others have other rules differentiating between permanent and temporary workers. The work-sharing arrangement has been most common among the older craft unions. The rights of the unemployed have also been defined by local procedures regulating the listing of the unemployed and their assignment to individual plants. Usually the principle of first come, first served is observed.

This craft-union program was the dominant approach in the first sweep of unionism following the organization of the AFL. The inability of craft unions to entrench themselves beyond a restricted employment area limited the opportunities for pressing this system. Besides antiunionism this program also faced resistance from employers and the courts and became less practical with the rise of modern large-scale and mass-production industries.

Legal and Judicial Restrictions on the Growth of Workers' Property Rights in the Job

Employers and our legal system have strongly resisted the rise of the system of collective property rights in jobs sought by craft unions. Even the more elementary worker rights to strike, unionize, picket, enjoy free speech, and bargain collectively have been realized only after long struggles. No sooner were they gained than the courts restrained them through new interpretations. The courts have spurned attempts to provide the worker with equity in jobs and thereby raise him to a position more nearly on a par with that of the property owner. Our legal system rests on the belief that personal freedom can be realized only through the exercise of a large measure of liberty in the use of property. It will not destroy that right, though it has abridged it at times. More likely than not, the courts in the name of freedom will seek to protect the individual worker from the decisions and the acts of the organized group of workers through their unions.

Restrictions on the Growth of Union Control

This country's judicial and legislative systems have operated to restrict the development of techniques of collective job control such as the closed or union shop and the rights to strike and picket for such control. The closed shop has been opposed through the years. The courts and legislation, particularly the former, have disapproved of it and restrained action designed to realize the closed shop. Only after years of battle was a legal position accorded it.

The Wagner Act specifically allowed for agreements providing for the closed shop. The courts in some states later recognized them as valid, even when they applied to an entire industry.[2] But this era of tolerance ended with the Labor-Management Relations Act of 1947 (Taft-Hartley law), which outlawed the closed shop and prescribed that union membership shall not be required until after 30 days following the beginning of a person's employment or the signing of a contract. Moreover, the closed union was required by the law to liberalize its entry policies to allow for the admission of new employees, for otherwise the employers could not be permitted to enforce the union shop. The union's ability to discipline its membership was also substantially weakened, since employers would be freed of their responsibility to enforce union membership where the union denied workers membership for reasons other than the failure to pay dues and initiation fees. The individual state legislatures and courts have adopted even more restrictive rules under the encouragement of the Labor-Management Relations Act of 1947. These state laws prevail over the Federal law.

Some individual unions have continued to maintain their controls over their labor markets and the supply of labor, but they are the exception. The economic strength they amassed over the years has preserved their controls. However, their hold is insecure. The Federal courts have already announced their intent to support the NLRB's efforts to prevent the enforcement of a union shop by strike action.[3] The maintenance of the closed shop is now truly at the employer's mercy. If he seeks to balk it, he can count on the NLRB and the courts to help him destroy it.

Essential to the realization of the controls contemplated by the craft union have been the rights to strike and to picket. Both were necessary to establish unions and wrest the recognition vital to their growth. Neither of these rights was easily obtained. Unions faced unsympathetic courts suspicious of strikes as violating property rights. Only after many years of bitter controversy have many states sanctioned primary strikes for legal purposes. The strike for the closed shop has been tolerated in an increasing number of jurisdictions. But even then some courts have insisted that the strike cannot be designed to achieve monopolies and that the union be open to all employees.[4] These advances were halted by the Labor-Management Relations Act of 1947

[2] Williams v. Quill, 277 N.Y. 1, 303 U.S. 621 (1938).
[3] NLRB v. Newspaper and Mail Deliverers' Union, 192 F. 2d 654 (C.A. 2, 1951).
[4] L. Teller, *The Law Governing Labor Disputes and Collective Bargaining*, New York, Baber Voorhes & Company, 1940, pp 276–282.

which declared illegal the strike for the closed shop or for the enforcement of jurisdictional claims.

The right to picket is vital to the success of a strike. But some courts branded picketing as "organized espionage." They identified picketing with the tendency to violence and damage to property and the intimidation of people. One court went so far as to observe that picketing "conspired to and did injure plaintiff's business and property rights to the extent that [the pickets'] acts constituted a nuisance to the plaintiff and the public . . . [and must be considered] an interference with an owner's business and deprive him of property rights, would not be the due process or equal protection of the law and would be a violation of the 14th Amendment of the Federal Constitution." [5]

It was only in 1940 that the Supreme Court declared peaceful picketing to be a normal exercise of the right of free speech. But hardly had this right been defined than the courts opened the opportunity for new restrictions by allowing injunctions to be issued whenever the state, either through the legislature or the court, declared "union objectives contrary to public policy." [6] The Labor-Management Relations Act of 1947 made peaceful picketing to aid a secondary boycott an unfair labor practice. Without legal sanctions for the closed shop and without the rights to picket and strike for the closed shop and union, collective property rights in jobs are difficult to realize.

Rejection of Legal Rights in a Job

Besides discouraging the development of the techniques of union control, the legal system has rejected every effort to affirm the individual worker's or the union's claims in the job. Two illustrations will highlight the difficulties in securing such legal sanctions.

The first relates to efforts to limit the employer's right to move the site of employment through relocation, establishment of branch plants, contracting out of work, or shutting down of plants. There is currently no legal base to prevent such moves, as they are usually considered exercises of ordinary business judgment, except where a collective-bargaining contract specifically prohibits them. Actual removal can then be enjoined, if it is obviously motivated by the desire to disregard the agreement. But the establishment of proof of such bad faith is difficult and involved.[7] The NLRB has placed restraints on threats to migrate or on actual migration intended to intimidate or discriminate against workers. In such cases decisions have awarded back pay and reinstatement of employees to jobs in existing or new plants to which the business had been removed. But the Board has not ordered reinstatement where jobs were not available or where new employees have not been hired to replace the persons discriminated against.[8]

The Labor-Management Relations Act of 1947 diluted even these protec-

  [5] Bull v. International Alliance, 119 Kan. 713, 241 Pac. 459 (1925).
  [6] S. K. Fraenkel, "Peaceful Picketing Constitutionally Protected?" *University of Pennsylvania Law Review,* 99 (October, 1950), 1–12.
  [7] 36 Col. L. Rev. 776 (1936).
  [8] 41 Col. L. Rev. 329 (1941).

tions by its free-speech provisions and limitations on closed and union shops. Since the only types of plant removals proscribed by the Board were those designed to impede organization, discourage participation in unions, and interfere with collective bargaining, the free-speech provision and the consequent limited usefulness of the employer's own words as evidence of intent have made for increased difficulty in proving these motives.[9]

More outright efforts to establish such job rights occurred in connection with the sit-down strikes of 1936–1937. The workers claimed a right to stay in the plant during the course of an industrial dispute. The right to picket peacefully and strike, it was argued, could be exercised in the plant as well as outside it. A union's desire to discourage plant operations could be more effectively realized by having workers stay in the plant. The result would be less violence if the employer would not initiate it. Had not the worker a "normal right to continue on his job unless some definite misconduct justifies his discharge?"[10]

Certain legal theorists supported this position.[11] But the courts would not support the strikers. The United States Supreme Court branded the sitdown as unlawful entry into property rather than as merely an unjustified claim to a job. It was an "illegal seizure of the buildings in order to prevent their use by the employer in a lawful manner, and thus by acts of force and violence to compel the employer to submit." The court added that "it is not essentially different from an assault upon the officers of an employing company, or the seizure and conversion of its goods, or the despoiling of its property or other unlawful acts in order to force compliance with demands."[12] The most important recent attempt to establish worker rights in jobs therefore ran afoul of the courts.

Industrial Unions—A System of Negotiated Personal Claims to Jobs

The craft-union system of collective property rights to jobs through unions did not make much progress in the face of the resistance from employers and the law, as described above. Both combatted workers' attempts to organize and resisted more particularly the craft-union technique of effective job control. The effort to build a trade-union movement on job control was further dashed by the newly evolving industrial system in which constant technical change was the dominant note.

These job controls rested on the existence of a stable technology. If jobs are recurrently being altered or eliminated and if older skills are being regularly supplanted by new ones, it is hardly possible to maintain such controls. The trade-union movement, if it was to protect the worker in this new industrial environment, had to redefine its procedures. Workers' security

---

[9] 50 Col. L. Rev. 1123 (1950).

[10] Statement by W. Mortimer, vice-president of UAW–CIO, in J. Seidman, *Sit-down,* Chicago, Socialist Party, 1937, p. 30.

[11] Leon Greene, "Sit-down Strikers Are Legal," *New Republic,* 90 (Mar. 24, 1937), 199–201.

[12] NLRB v. Fansteel Metallurgical Co., 306 U.S. 240 (1939).

could not be realized through control of specific jobs. Their security had to be assured through new methods. This new program for worker protection was associated with the Roosevelt era and the appearance of industrial unionism.

The trade-union in the newer industries cannot control a specific technology or job. The plant includes a vast range of jobs at which workers of the most diverse skills, experience, attitudes, and personalities may be employed. Workers band together into one industrial union for the same basic reasons. The union must reflect all their needs. It must obtain protection for all of them in face of technical changes which modify older tasks, supplant older jobs by new ones, substitute new production techniques and procedures for older ones, eliminate old products and create new ones, or level one plant to provide the base for new ones. Neither the jobs nor the supply of workers can be regulated. Since special skills and experience are not crucial on most jobs, large numbers of workers can qualify for employment in the plant. The union cannot realistically seek a closed shop in this environment. In fact, it usually asks only for the union shop, which permits employers to hire new persons irrespective of prior union affiliation as long as they become members of the union after a probationary period. The open union becomes prevalent, since union strength is dependent upon enrolling all who work in the plant.

In this setting the union does not seek collective property rights in jobs. Even when it protests an employer's effort to contract out specific types of work normally performed by his own crew, such as new construction or cafeterias, it is not seeking them for its own control. Its purpose, primarily, is to prevent a reduction of its following, for its strength may thereby be undermined as the size of the work force is reduced or other unions may challenge its claims for representation.

Another major union purpose is to maintain the job priorities and available employment opportunities for the present work force. The union's basic goal in negotiations is to define the rules regulating the rights of classes of individuals to different employment opportunities.

The union contract in an industrial establishment negotiated by this industrial union usually consists of extensive regulations concerning minimum terms of employment. Central to these contracts is the section relating to the procedures to be followed when the work force is curtailed or expanded and people are transferred. The union seeks to fix seniority as the governing factor regulating the flow of workers. Seniority is easy to define and it minimizes discrimination. Length of prior service is insisted upon as the principal guide in rehiring furloughed employees. Former employees should be given preference over new applicants in rehiring. Many other rules also systematize the procedures for distributing work in slack periods. Temporary employees are frequently treated more drastically than the permanent staff. Such regulations may also provide that employees eliminated by reason of technical product or operational changes within a plant shall be given preference to other jobs. Arrangements for retraining are outlined as are provisions for helping to maintain the employee's former earnings. As collective bargaining broadens its coverage, the union also seeks to secure rules for the transference of employees among plants within the same company.

The union's emphasis is upon getting rules which automatically define the claims of specific classes of employees. This is reflected not only in the protective provisions but also in the differentiated benefits for employees of varying periods of service. Higher vacation benefits are universally granted to longer-service employees. Even more significant for our purposes and discussion is the provision for severance-pay allowances, graduated by length of service, for employees displaced by technological or business changes. Some persons have interpreted such benefits as evidence of worker property rights in the job. They do not, however, originate from any such concept. They stem from the recognition of the employers' responsibility to facilitate the personal adjustment of long-service employees. In the case of aged or permanently injured persons, special arrangements are increasingly provided for pension payments which will allow such persons to retire from active industrial service.

A more recent demand in collective bargaining is for an annual wage. Unions are insisting that employers must operate their establishments so as to assure a full year's work or income to their employees. The constant drive in collective bargaining is to extend the minimum terms for the conduct of business to assure greater security to the workers. The specific form in which the demand for an annual wage will be realized is at present uncertain. Workers may be guaranteed full weekly earnings for specific weeks of unemployment or for a specified number of weeks per year; or a minimum annual income; or, as a minimum, a full week's pay for each week employed in the same manner in which minimum daily earnings are now guaranteed for each day the employee reports for work. All of these will prescribe minimum terms for the operation of a business and greater security of employment and income for incumbent employees.

Another restriction frequently imposed on the employer's unilateral action is that on his rights to introduce changes in products, technology, or jobs. Seldom is a limitation placed on the employer's right to make innovations of a technical nature. However, contracts do tend to restrict his powers to change worker effort levels or alter job patterns unrelated to specific technical changes. Many contracts require employers to follow a prescribed procedure for informing, and discussing planned changes with, the union prior to the introduction of changes. Unions are allowed to challenge, through the grievance procedure, the effects of the changes upon the worker.[13]

Another area in which employers' rights have been severely limited is that relating to the discharge of employees. It is commonly provided in union contracts that capricious and unjustified dismissals may be questioned. The burden of proof in these cases generally rests with the employer. Invariably they can be referred to arbitrators for review; the latter tend to be most exacting in their analysis, so that the evidence must be overwhelming to sustain a discharge.

The Federal labor-relations acts have provided workers with protection against interference, restraint, or coercion in their attempts to organize, to form and maintain trade-unions, or to bargain collectively through their own

[13] S. Barkin, "Human and Social Impact of Technical Changes," *Proceedings of the Third Annual Meeting of the Industrial Relations Research Association,* December, 1950, pp. 112–127.

representatives. A whole body of law has been developed which limits the employer's right to hire, discharge, or refuse to rehire employees with the purpose of discriminating against their union activities or membership. The NLRB has held that strikers must be reinstated where the strike itself was the result of an unfair labor practice committed by the employer or where he refused to bargain collectively with the properly designated collective-bargaining agent. In fact, the employer is obliged in such instances to discharge employees hired to take the place of the strikers. The courts have also sustained the NLRB in prohibiting discrimination against the union in the use of a meeting place in a company town.[14] Similar prohibitions against discrimination in the hiring and discharge of workers because of their race, religion, or color exist in a number of states. These laws contribute to personal security.

No system of property rights in jobs has been created by present procedures of collective bargaining. The trade-unions do not have a property right in a specific group of jobs or a right to limit the supply of labor to assure them the right to these jobs. Rather, the emphasis has been on making contractual agreements on minimum terms for the employment of the workers. Rules have been agreed upon defining the procedures to be followed when jobs are changed or eliminated. The rightful claims of different classes of employees are prescribed, and their relative position and benefits are set forth. Limits are set on the employer's freedom. Security for the individual worker is increased; his terms of employment have been advanced. But he has gained no vested rights in any particular job.

Full-employment Economy—The New Union Job Policy

The basic drive of the trade-union movement is to promote an expanding and prosperous economy in which full employment prevails and prices are relatively stable and in which a minimum satisfactory level of security is provided to everyone through a national system of insurance and services. Within such a society it can best promote workers' claims to a job and to satisfactory terms of employment.

Recognizing full well the limitations of the bargaining process, in an era of changing technology, in assuring employment to its members and to the working population as a whole, trade-unions have supported the general reform movements designed to place the responsibility for maintaining full employment upon the government. No other agency appears immediately available for adopting general policies to promote conditions favorable to full employment or for providing the projects necessary for supplementing jobs available in private industry. Trade-unions have therefore favored legislation empowering the government to maintain full employment, as witness their support of the Employment Act of 1946. The trade-unions have also endorsed regional development activities, both because they fill specific needs and because they extend the opportunities for employment and tap new resources. Backward industrial areas within the country and abroad must be aided in their development. Government contracts must be assigned to distressed areas to relieve unemployment and stabilize civilian industries.

[14] NLRB v. Stowe Spinning Co., 336 U.S. 226 (1949).

Unions have also favored policies which facilitate the workers' movements within an economy. They have supported employment exchanges which aid workers in their movements between jobs and social-insurance schemes which provide the necessary underpinning for general security and aid in the re-habilitation of individuals into effective self-supporting persons.

While trade-unions have hitherto relied primarily on the government for the development of such policies, there is an underlying hope among trade-unionists that a system of national collective bargaining will be evolved both on an industry and on a national basis. Through this mechanism each economic interest, such as workers, farmers, and industry, will bind itself for a designated period to follow specific policies and to observe rules of conduct. The guide-posts for the operation of an economy of full employment will be the result of governmentally supervised but privately negotiated economic policies. With an economy guided by policies assuring full employment, the issue of job property rights will loom less important. Workers will enjoy claims to, rather than in, jobs.[15]

Conclusion

The workers' fight for security has, by and large, except for areas in which craft unionism is strongly entrenched, been converted into a battle for an economic society which will assure an abundance of employment opportuni-ties for all. The right to employment, rather than a property right in a job, is the dominant aim. The courses followed to progress along this road have been both political and economic. The government has limited property rights and prescribed terms for their use which coincide with the goals of full em-ployment, advancing conditions of employment, higher standards of living, and self-organization of workers. Specific policies have been promoted to en-courage full employment. The rights of groups of workers to jobs and to specific terms of employment have been evolving through collective bargaining. Indi-vidual security and opportunity are being advanced in an era where govern-ment is determining, and trade-unions are negotiating, terms for the use of private property.

[15] S. Barkin, "National Collective Bargaining," *Personnel Journal,* 25 (November, 1946), 150–160.

CHAPTER 9 INTERNAL CONFLICT AND LABOR-UNION SOLIDARITY

Lloyd H. Fisher ° *and Grant McConnell*
University of California (Berkeley)

ONE of the most critical tests which we can apply to an organization, be it a state, a society, a club, or a trade-union, is the manner in which it deals with conflict and disagreement within its own boundaries. If we are able to characterize the attitude which is adopted toward conflict, we have done much to characterize the entire organization. This is most obvious if the object of inquiry is a state. It would be possible to include much that is essential to the understanding of Nazi Germany, for example, in a discussion of just this one point. When the test is applied to a private association, however, there is less agreement that the test is equally meaningful or, indeed, relevant at all. There is, in fact, a widespread assumption of unity inside private associations. This assumption appears to rest on the belief that, since most such associations are "voluntary" in the sense that membership or nonmembership is presumed to be a matter of individual choice, the basis for conflict is absent.

Internal Conflict in Private Organizations

In a trade-union it is usual to hear appeals for unity and emphasis on the common purpose of all the members. Such appeals are strongest and most effective when the organization is engaged in struggle with external forces, as in a strike or an organizing campaign. Indeed, the common hypothesis that the surest way to secure internal harmony and unity in a state is to engage in war has its analogy in the trade-union. The appeal to and for unity has generally been associated with the symbols of war, militance, the common defense, and the class struggle, in however dilute a form, and has been supported by the image of an enemy unified and strong. But these must be viewed as more or less consciously manipulated leadership appeals. The history of the American trade-union movement would strongly suggest that it was precisely in the periods in which the trade-union struggles were most bitter that the tolerance of internal division has been greatest and that it is the unions with least to fear from a counterattack by employers that have insisted upon basing their statecraft upon the model of a unitary state.

The actual lines of conflict which exist in a union are many. There are differences of interest between groups of different seniority, between groups of different ages, between groups in different plants, different localities, and

* Deceased 1953.

different crafts, and at times between employed and unemployed. There are perennial differences of interest between leadership and membership. This is not to suggest that all these differences are important, that they are equally important, or even that all represent conflicts. However, where difference of interest does exist at all in any degree, there is a potential of conflict. This conflict, which takes the form of factionalism, is, to paraphrase the words of James Madison in his famous discussion of faction, rooted in the nature of organization (if not in the nature of man).

This problem of internal conflict, of faction, must be solved if an organization is to survive. Some consensus must exist if the organization is to be capable of action. There are various ways in which this necessary consensus may be achieved. These may be summarized under three headings: (1) devices to secure a homogeneous membership, (2) suppression of dissent, and (3) the institutionalization of conflict.

The first of these methods is perhaps the most characteristic of private associations. The primary device here is the selective effect of the requirement that the member himself chooses to enter the association. Although in many instances there is a large element of fiction in this aspect of the "voluntary" association, the fiction is yet highly useful in the achievement of unity.[1] This selection by individual choice is regulated by the usual methods of membership qualifications: age, skill, religon, belief, compatiblity with other members, and so on. This is far from the end of the devices which are available and which operate to some degree in every voluntary association. The very policies followed in the substantial affairs of the organization will exert a continuing selective effect. Those members whose interests, beliefs, or tastes are grossly offended by the policies of the organization will tend to remove themselves by resignation, lapse of interest, or mere inaction. There is thus a tendency for growing homogeneity among the membership as the organization continues in existence. This factor in itself, if not countered by other influences, will result in a narrowed basis of the organization's constituency. The advantages of these and other devices having the same effect of developing homogeneity of membership are considerable. To the extent that members do have the same economic interests, for example, one of the primary causes of factional conflict has been reduced. In the labor movement this advantage may be seen in the long period of organization-by-craft ascendancy.

The second method is the most forthright and at times the most appealing to the leadership of an organization in which that leadership is convinced of its own rightness or is ruthlessly committed to enhancement of its power and is in a position to exercise drastic methods. This is outright suppression of dissent. It may range from arbitrary exercise of the common executive power to penalize those members who speak ill of their officers or who behave in a manner "unbecoming to a union man" to expulsion by the vote of a convention. These methods need little explanation and are sufficiently common to need little documentation.

---

[1] Here it is well to recall the effectiveness, in maintaining high "morale" in the Marine Corps, of the use of the reminder that its members had not been drafted, even where it was a transparent fact in many cases that the alternative to volunteering for the service was involuntary membership in another service.

The third method, the institutionalization of conflict, encompasses the devices which are usually regarded as democratic procedures. They include such techniques as a separation of powers, regular elections, referendums, freedom of speech, and so on. They all have this in common: they imply a recognition of the existence of conflict. In some way they all also imply toleration of conflict. In so far as they deal with conflict as a problem, they are means of channeling conflict within prescribed limits.

It should be clear that no actual organization solves its problems of internal conflict by any one of these methods. Even the most dictatorial organization finds it convenient to seek a homogeneity of membership, if in no other way than by simple ejection of dissidents. Even the most democratic tradeunions have drawn their lines of membership with an eye for homogeneity. All organizations must secure some minimum basis of consent. In practice, then, we should not expect to find any organization devoted purely to any one of these solutions.

It nevertheless remains true that the degree to which an organization has been able to institutionalize conflict is one of the crucial tests of the organization's character. The agitation for reform in the internal practices of trade-unions, from those over which the courts have taken jurisdiction to those urged by the American Civil Liberties Union,[2] are commonly designed to make the expression of dissent both possible and safe. Provisions in trade-union constitutions designed to secure regular and honest elections, freedom of speech, and nondiscrimination against union members for reasons of race, creed, sex, or citizenship are important, to be sure. But they stand without implementation and without the power to be made effective against the oligarchic tendencies of modern organization unless they are associated with political institutions which are themselves effective against the executive leadership.

There is only one device with which we have substantial experience which has proved capable of making conflict within institutional limits meaningful. This is a competitive party system. We as yet have no effective way of checking the antidemocratic tendencies delineated by Michels[3] other than by the regularized competition of parties. This competition is impossible, it is true, unless many of the standard devices of democracy, free elections, freedom of speech, and freedom of assembly are well secured. Yet it is increasingly true that the effectiveness of these devices is badly impaired without the additional feature of a competitive party system.

As we turn to the private or voluntary association, however, we are faced with the question of whether a competitive party system is possible. Thus, although, as indicated earlier, there are always latent conflicts within any group or any organization, the lines of conflict have been minimized by the drive for homogeneous membership, and there can accordingly—so it may be argued—be no prospect of developing a regularized and institutionalized party system. There can thus be no development of lines of internal suborganization along which opposition parties may form. Since the membership of a

---

[2] *Democracy in Trade Unions,* New York, American Civil Liberties Union, 1943; also this organization's more recent report and statement of policy, *Democracy in Labor Unions,* New York, 1952.

[3] Robert Michels, *Political Parties,* Glencoe, Ill., The Free Press, 1949.

voluntary organization shares the same fundamental interests and beliefs, there can only be a scattering of isolated and irregular factional opposition groups which will not provide the basis for a party structure. Lacking these differences of principle and interest, the voluntary organization will be abandoned to the iron law of oligarchy. Voluntary organizations are necessarily undemocratic.

How good is this argument? Is the voluntary association inevitably given over to oligarchy? Is it necessarily a one-party system? If it can be shown that a competitive party system is possible within a private association without damage to the primary object for which the association is formed and without impairment to the strength of the association in pursuing these objectives, then the argument is disproved. Empirically it may be true that the overwhelming majority of private associations exemplify the iron law of oligarchy. Nevertheless, if the law is not in fact inevitable, then it may not be necessary no matter how adverse the statistics may appear.

Two-party System in the ITU

The International Typographical Union (ITU) has a fully developed two-party system. This union, the oldest of the national unions, has a record of strength and success that is surpassed by few labor organizations in the world. This is true by almost any test which we may wish to apply. The rates of pay and hours of work which its members enjoy are among the most favorable to be found anywhere. Some years ago the leading historians of the American labor movement [4] singled out this organization as the union having the most complete job control of any union in the world. This statement is substantially true today. The union has firmly established systems of friendly benefits derived from its own efforts: pensions, mortuary benefits, and a well-supported home for the aged and the ill among its membership. Despite several periods of rapid technological change in the industry, periods which have seen the rapid obsolescence of its members' basic skills, the union has demonstrated a capacity for steady and consistent growth. It has emerged from the trying difficulties of transition from industrial to craft unionism. The ITU has provided leadership and impetus to the transformation of the American labor movement which came out of the rise of industrial unionism in the thirties, although in its own development it has moved in the opposite direction.[5]

This record has not been achieved through any policy of collusion with employers. On the whole, the ITU has enjoyed generally peaceful relations with employers. Nevertheless, the history of the union has been marked by major struggles. The most important of these include strikes for the 8-hour day and for the 44-hour week, campaigns in which the ITU took general leadership of the labor movement. More recently, the ITU has been in the position of leading organizational opponent to the Taft-Hartley Act. Lesser

---

[4] Selig Perlman and Philip Taft, *History of Labor in the United States,* New York, Macmillan, 1935, p. 51.

[5] C. P. Howard, president of the ITU, was the first secretary of the CIO. The union, however, was never in the CIO. In fact, while Howard was secretary of the CIO, another ITU official was secretary of the AFL.

battles have been fought with the *Los Angeles Times,* the Knight chain of papers, and, more recently, the organized newspaper publishers of Chicago. The union has been aggressive, resourceful, and effective.

The real achievement of the ITU, however, is the practical demonstration of democratic method which it offers to private organizations. There are many special features in the governmental structure of the union, and most of them are important to the democratic character of the organization. Here it is possible only to list some of the more significant. Elections to national office are regularly held every 2 years, with vote by the general membership, not by convention delegates. There are carefully drawn provisions to insure honesty in elections. Freedom of speech and expression is not only permitted but made effective by the guarantee of space in the official journal for dissent and criticism of the leadership. This is supplemented by a time-honored (although sometimes deplored) practice of printing irregular publications about union affairs by various groups in the union. The union has a system of law which has developed out of long experience. This is contained in its constitution, by-laws, and general laws. Conventions are annual by law. There is an effective system for regular and detailed accounting of union funds. There are provisions for initiative and referendum.

It is inconceivable that ITU democracy would have the same meaning without these provisions. However, these devices do occur in the governmental systems of other unions but without the same results. What gives them real effect in the ITU is the union's unique two-party system. As it stands today, the system consists of two formal parties, the Independent and the Progressive. These parties carry on organized campaigns in the biennial elections for international office and in the elections of the larger locals. Candidates and slates are presented to the union membership. The party campaigns are carefully prepared and energetically pursued by methods which are familiar to all who follow the presidential campaigns in national politics. Pronouncements, which are platforms in effect, are made by each party. In the issues of the *Typographical Journal* of April and May preceding each election, formal statements of each candidate's platform appear over his name. Since in the cases of the Independent and Progressive candidates, the only candidates having any prospect of success in the election, a process of formal endorsement by the parties has already taken place, these platforms are, in effect, the party platforms. The points of the respective platforms are repeated somewhat more uninhibitedly (although, considering some election material appearing in the *Journal,* this might seem difficult) in letters and leaflets sent through the mails to the membership from the party organizations. Meetings are held throughout the country by the parties in preparation for the election. The election is taken seriously and the contest is always real.

The other times at which the party conflict is visible are the annual conventions and the periods of divided control in the Executive Council. There have been protracted divisions in the Council, the most serious of which have occurred when one party carried the post of president and the other the post of secretary-treasurer. When this condition prevailed, there was intense conflict between the parties. On several occasions this has impaired the efficiency of the union itself. In each case where this has happened, however, the degree of impairment has not been serious, and the solution has come through the success of one party's slate either in whole or in large part at the next election. At times the bitterness of the conflict has become so intense that mudslinging occurs and personalities are besmirched.[6] Occasionally similar conflicts occur in the largest local unions.

It is only slightly less important to appreciate that this conflict, bitter as it sometimes grows, is conducted within definite limits. Success for either party does not result in mass expulsion or suppression of the vanquished. Ejection from the union does not occur on grounds of dissent or political activity within the union. Toleration of campaign excesses in practice goes considerably beyond what is formally required by the law of the organization.

Political Issues in the ITU

The question now arises, What is the basis for this party system? What is the conflict about? There follows an outline summary of the issues which have provided the grounds of battle in the campaigns since the party system first became fully visible. It may be said that the party system is considerably older than the period considered here. Its origins lie in the late 19th century. However, the point at which the system may be said to have become institutionalized was the convention of 1913. At this time the union had just passed through one of its most bitter periods of factional strife. The leadership and many of the members had actively deplored the strife. Efforts to do away with it had proved unsuccessful, however, and the circulation of factional leaflets, often of a scurrilous nature, continued at an undiminished pace. In this situation, the president of the union [7] wrote the following statement conspicuously in his annual report:

> Opposition in a trade union, when conducted along decent and manly lines, when based on principles and not on viciousness, when exercised in the desire to develop and strengthen the organization and not on the determination to discredit and pull it down is a good thing for the International Typographical Union. In an organization like ours there can and should be no unanimity of opinion. Criticism and clash of ideas bring forth, ultimately, the application of principles that are wholly beneficial in their effect. . . . Government is a compromise, but that compromise should embrace with it the well-digested thoughts and theories that are sure to advance, and not retard our onward march. There can be no criticism and there should be no criticism of opposition of this kind.

In the convention to which this report was presented, the Executive Council put forward a proposition to provide an outlet in the official journal of the union for the electioneering material which was appearing surreptitiously. The proposal carried, and very shortly the hitherto frowned-on political parties came out into the open with formal names, slates, and so on. This was the point at which the existing system became institutionalized.[8]

---

[6] Thus, through the years 1940 to 1944, the presidential candidates were exchanging epithets ("Doctor Goebbels") and accusations of Communism, selling out to employers, and so on. The union survived.

[7] James M. Lynch, *Annual Report of the President,* ITU, Annual Reports, 1913, p. 8.

[8] For action of the convention, see *Typographical Journal, Proceedings Supplement,* 43 (1913), 103. S. M. Lipset places the point of institutionalization of the party system some-

Table 9.1 covers the nineteen regular international elections which have taken place since the convention of 1913. In order to provide consistency of method, the issues have been taken from the "Political Section" of the official journal. They have been the issues which the presidential candidates have chosen to discuss. In one instance, the uncontested presidential election of 1914, it was necessary to draw the issues from the contested election for secretary-treasurer held concurrently (same ballot). The very lively elections of 1942 and 1944 could not be handled by use of the Political Section since during these years the section was greatly reduced in size and was useless for the present purpose. For these periods the source has been the strong controversy carried on in the pages signed by president and secretary-treasurer, the leading party opponents. The entire discussion is based upon a detailed examination of the history of the union's political life. However, in the table an attempt has been made to generalize and simplify the issues and the controversies to manageable proportions. Inevitably this procedure opens the door to bias. Any simplification of political conflict as extensive as exists here is in some degree a falsification.

What will be evident from the table is that the parties are not necessarily faithful to positions once adopted, nor are the issues in conflict necessarily deducible from the cloak of principle in which they are garbed. In any given election, the charge of oligarchy may be made by each side. The shift from support of local autonomy to support of centralization may be more affected by the results of the previous election and the prospects for the next than by any philosophy of government. Yet the election campaigns are hard fought, the party structure durable.

In the table a distinction has been drawn between the concentration of power within the Executive Council in the hands of the president and the concentration of power in the international at the expense of the locals. "Centralization" has been used to indicate charges of too great presidential power, and "autonomy" charges of too great international power. "Bread and butter" is used to indicate a demand that the union leadership pay more attention to narrow economic issues affecting the membership and less to "altruistic" causes. The "priority" law is perhaps the basic law of the union. It is in the main the rule of seniority, but it has been refined and adjusted so as to have become a complex code in itself.

It is now possible to return to the questions asked earlier. We already have the answer to the question of whether the voluntary association is *inevitably* a one-party state: It is not. We can also answer the question of whether a competitive party system in the voluntary association is possible: It is.

The answer to a question with which the paper opened is also apparent: There are a multitude of issues in a voluntary association on which the membership may divide. The mere fact of the voluntary feature in an organization

---

what later. Although the point is not developed, the reason appears to be that the present system began with the first successful challenge of Administration Party rule. Cf. S. M. Lipset, "Democracy in Private Government," *British Journal of Sociology,* 3 (March, 1952), 55. Although this may be a convenient point to take for certain analytical purposes, the party system was in lively operation from 1913 onward.

Table 9.1 **Issues in ITU Presidential Elections**

	Ins			Outs	
Year	Party	Issues	Party	Issues	
1914	I	The record	P	Oligarchy (centralization)	
1916	I	The record	P	Unaggressive economic policy, wasteful and inefficient administration	
1918	I	The record, IWWism	P	Economy	
1920	I	The record	P	Local autonomy, 44-hour issue, strikebreaking against New York local	
1922	P	Local autonomy for aggressive economic policy	I	Long-term record, experience, attempts to establish autocracy (centralization)	

(In this period, Progressive president was in minority in Executive Council.)

1924	P	The record, 44-hour strike, bread and butter	I	Waste and inefficiency, antagonized employers	
1926	I	The record, moderate policy	P	Centralization, economy, lower assessments	
1928	P	Obstructionism, oligarchy	I	Centralization, long-term experience, organization	

(Another period of divided Executive Council.)

1930	P	The record	I	Against autonomy, loss of locals	
1932	P	For centralization	I	For autonomy	

(Third party, Unionist Party, made something of an issue of unemployment.)

1934	P	The record	I	Share the work, more aggressive policy, pensions	
1936	P	The record	I	Share the work, lost strikes, work, more aggressive policy, centralization, CIO, mailers	
1938	P	The record, experience	I	Share the work, CIO, centralization, help locals	
1940	I	The record, CIO, subversion	P	AFL assessment, organization, autonomy	
1942	I	The record, *Journal*	P	AFL assessment, more aggressive policy, mailers	
1944	I	*Journal* censorship, AFL reaffiliation	P	More aggressive policy, NWLB, surrender of laws	

(Divided Executive Council.)

1946	P	The record (aggressive stand to NWLB, defense policy)	I	The home, priority law	
1948	P	The record (Taft-Hartley, defense policy)	I	Costly strikes, defiance of Congress, illegal transfer of funds	
1950	P	The record, experience	I	Organization, centralization, improve employer relations and public good will, sign non-Communist affidavit, officer's pensions	

P—Progressive Party.
I—Independent Party (formerly known as Administration Party).

does not eradicate conflict. As the early discussion indicated, this was to be expected. Although conflict is tolerated and institutionalized in the ITU, the issues are both real and numerous. Absence of conflict in an organization is prima-facie evidence that suppression of one kind or another has been practiced. It may not be said, moreover, that the quality of homogeneity of membership, which in one degree or another characterizes the voluntary association, is ever an adequate explanation for the absence of conflict. The ITU is a remarkably homogeneous organization, far more so than most unions. With minor exceptions, this is a craft union of typesetters. It has a well-established and well-defined tradition. Its members have all passed through an extended period of selection. Yet here we have the evidence of abundant conflict.

It remains to be asked what the lines of division actually are on which party organization may form. As we have seen, the issues in an organization are exceedingly numerous where their expression is permitted. In this condition, what is the rationale of party formation? The first theory which must be considered here has already been touched upon by implication. It is that parties must be formed about lines of divergent interest. This theory is notably unsatisfactory in explaining the ITU party system. This is a homogeneous organization from the standpoint of economic class. There are divergent groups, it is true. The most striking group is that of the mailers. This group became involved in controversy after 1926 and played a part in the presidential elections. However, this is too small a group to be significant as a class group. Moreover, the group became involved in politics well after the party system was established. Another group which has been moderately conspicuous at times is the unemployed. The interests of this group became the source of controversy. However, if the controversy is examined in detail, it is found that it played a relatively small part in the party battles. The explanation is that the parties were in large agreement on the policy to be followed: Work should be spread. The question was strictly one of degree. It is not altogether wrong to suggest that this was a "manufactured" issue.

There are two very real lines of potential division in the union. The most important is that between the "situation holders," those having regular jobs, and the substitutes. The regulation of the relationship between these two groups is the topic of much in the book of laws. Some Progressives claim that this issue was the source of their party's origin. However, it is abundantly clear that this issue has been taken out of conflict. This is now, in a very real sense, subject to law. The parties have an impressive record of agreement here. It is a remarkable fact that the priority law and the general topic appears only once in the tabulation of issues in presidential elections. There have been sharp disagreements in conventions on the details of this system. However, these have been over details. Wherever the charge of opposition to the priority law has been raised, it has been questionable and is to be likened to attempts by Republicans to label Democrats as traitors. This law is actually the foundation of the union and the parties; their leadership and the membership at large appreciate it. This is perhaps the principal explanation for the adamant stand of the ITU before the NWLB and the NLRB. If the book of laws was to be subjected to bargaining, priority was to be put in question and thus the entire constitutional structure of the union endangered.

The other line of division in the union is that between workers in newspapers and those in book-and-job plants. Different scales have always prevailed. This has never appeared as a national issue of politics. The difference is accepted.

The second theory which must be considered is that the parties diverge, in Burkean terms, on the lines of some principle. The first point to be noted is that very few issues are the exclusive possession of one party. The outstanding difference seems to be that at several times the Independents have argued for moderation while the Progressives have more frequently argued for militancy. This appears to be a real difference, and it would be possible to formulate a line of principle divergence on a conservative-progressive basis. This is the theory advanced by some Progressive partisans. But here it is interesting to observe that *both* parties have used the argument of experience where it has been possible for them to do so. This is a characteristically conservative argument for continuity and the use of time-sanctioned personalized authority. This argument was used by the Progressives in the 1950 election. Moreover, in so far as unemployment has appeared as an issue, it has been argued by the Independents, although unemployment might be assumed to be a characteristically Progressive issue. Lest it be assumed that there has been a divergence on the theory of the labor movement held by either party, it should be pointed out that, while the Progressives provided leadership for the CIO and have led campaigns against offensive governmental acts, they have also argued strenuously for bread-and-butter unionism. Although the Independents made much of the issue of AFL reaffiliation, the Progressives were the ones to return the ITU to the AFL fold. Thus we may conclude that, although there is some difference between the parties on the score of militancy, this difference is not great and is probably in part the result of fortuitous circumstance.[9]

It is clear that the usual explanations of a competitive party system are inadequate here. We must accordingly return to a more fundamental examination of the basis of party conflict.

Basis for Stable Party Organization

What, then, is the basis upon which permanent party organization might develop within private associations? There are, we think, good reasons for supposing that the answer is exceedingly simple and becomes difficult only if one accepts the conventional myths of the organizations themselves. Men differ, their situations differ, and so do their interests. Loyalty is always proportionate to the threat. An "American" is a nearly meaningless abstraction unless the country is at war; a "union man" is most identifiable when the plant is on strike; a Catholic, a Protestant, or a Jew is most recognizable at the critical moments of birth, marriage, and death. During the long interludes in which the questions do not involve ultimate loyalties, the interior differences within the membership are numerous and real. It is precisely because conflict is imminent and difference pervasive that the organizational loyalty myth is so

[9] S. M. Lipset emphasizes the divergence between the parties on this score. He describes (*ibid.,* p. 50) the split between them as being based on greater or less militancy of program. A detailed reading of the union's political history, however, will show that this divergence is easily exaggerated.

important in the politics of private groups. The function served by the loyalty myth is to announce and reiterate that no internal difference upon which factionalism might develop is so important as the closing of ranks against the common foe. Intolerance of political opposition within private associations testifies to the efficacy of the loyalty myth.

The simple fact is that, in the absence of the carefully cultivated unity myths, in the absence of leadership interests in noncompetition, and in the absence of the disciplinary weapons provided for the punishment of organized dissent, party organization within private associations would be much more common. We do not suggest that even so it would be widespread. There are complex sociological reasons for the development of bureaucracies which inhibit political expression, and these are at least as effective in private associations as elsewhere. However, it is quite certain that party organization would be much more general.

But the really important question remains to be answered. If a party system can exist without division along lines either of class or of principle, what is the basis for party organization? An examination of the table will disclose that there is a highly consistent pattern of division between the ins and the outs. This phenomenon has often been commented upon in national politics. It has been the basis for no little cynicism regarding parties. The inference is drawn that, since there is as much, or greater, consistency based upon the distinction between in and out as there is upon the distinction between programmatic parties, party contests are meaningless and of no importance. This is grossly in error.

If we examine the pattern of consistency evident in the table, a number of points are clear. The issues raised by the outs are more numerous, more concrete, and more important than those raised by the ins. There are typical in issues and typical out issues. The ins almost always run on their record. The outs usually make charges of centralization and defend local autonomy; they demand economy and efficiency; they seek greater organizational activity and a more militant leadership.

Each party is indeed in a position of inconsistency as it alternates between the role of government and opposition. Yet in terms of the issues which the party conflict raises before the membership, the correct and important issues are raised. The party in power ordinarily has some justification for taking pride in its accomplishments. Equally, each party out of power has always been correct in pointing to abuses, inertia, and necessary reforms. The vague stand on the record is an issue of substance. So is the attack upon it. It would doubtless be tidier if there were better prospects that a party platform had greater consistency from term to term. The collapse of the Socialist influence within the American trade-union movement virtually ended the political debate over principle and very much diminished the prospect of the development of any trade-union party of principle.[10] But the provision of an effective choice at each election is not a political gift to be despised.

This effective choice may represent no more than the continuous requirement that the membership review the transfer of power to the leadership. But the charge of oligarchy made by the opposition party is no idle charge. Who

[10] The Communist influence in trade-unions seldom offers an open and proclaimed political alternative and therefore stands on different grounds.

says organization *does* say oligarchy. It is one of the prime conditions of internal democracy that this issue be constantly reviewed.

It may indeed be true that the opposition is no less oligarchic in tendency and that its administration would inevitably develop the same autocratic tendencies as the leadership it attacks. Even if this were so—and it may be so—the inevitable attack upon the concentration of power, which accompanies each interparty contest for power, serves to dramatize the problem and to preserve it as a political issue for the membership rather than to merge it with the various other issues incidental to an efficient bureaucracy in a one-party political society.

A political party will not have a mass membership in union politics any more than it will in American national politics. The contemporary American party is characteristically a leadership party which must make its appeal to the voter at each election. Increasingly, all elections become votes of confidence or lack of confidence, and this is more true of a union election than of one for public office. Given the multiplicity of substantive issues and their complexity and the inevitable ignorance of the electorate, there seems no escape from this tendency. Under these circumstances the function of parties is to provide alternative leaders for the whole organization. Party contests within the ITU, even in form, are scarcely contests over policies. They are contests over the choice of leaders. Under circumstances in which the critical decision remaining to the voter is a statement of confidence or nonconfidence, the rival leader is the indispensable agent by which that decision can be given effect.

It must not be supposed that specific issues of substance such as mismanagement or the conduct of strikes or wage scales do not enter party contests. They do, and they are important. But almost all issues of substance are bound to be ephemeral. They get settled and cannot serve as the enduring basis for permanent political parties. The basis of any competitive party system must lie in the fact that one party or the other is a challenger of the existing organizational leadership. This is the single thread of consistency in any competitive party system.

The one really important feature of a competitive party system is that it is an institutionalization of conflict. We need not be concerned as to whether or not there are any grounds for the formation of parties. Every organization, every group of human beings, is rich in conflicts. There are always abundant issues—and real ones. Underlying all of them in an organization is the fundamental issue of leadership power. Organization cannot exist without leadership. Where leadership exists, there is an issue of power. Where adequate constitutional checks exist to place ultimate limits on the power of leadership, the inevitable differences of interest, desire, and belief can be relied upon to provide the basis for a competitive party system. Reciprocally, a competitive party system can be relied upon to give expression and meaning to the differences with which any group of men is endowed. The very oligarchic tendencies which have alarmed Michels and so many others paradoxically can themselves become the basis for the conflicts in which so much that is of value in civilization is embedded. Conflict under these conditions may well result in a more genuine consensus than any which relies on sheer homogeneity. The precondition for such consensus, however, it is that dissent shall not be suppressed and that conflict itself be tolerated.

CHAPTER **10** THE LABOR LEADERS
AND THE POWER ELITE

C. Wright Mills   *Columbia University*

Viewed from one special angle, the labor unions have become organizations that select and form leaders who, upon becoming successful, take their places alongside businessmen in and out of government and politicians in both major parties among the national power elite, for one function of labor unions—like social movements and political parties—is to contribute to the formation of this national power elite.

As new men of power, the labor leaders have come only lately to the national arena. Samuel Gompers was perhaps the first labor man to join, even though temporarily and quite uneasily, the national power elite. His self-conscious attempt to establish his place within this elite and, thus, to secure the labor interest as integral to national interests has made him a prototype and model for the national labor career. Sidney Hillman was not, of course, the only labor man to take up this course during the forties, but his lead during the early war years, his awareness of himself as a member of the national elite, and the real and imagined recognition he achieved as a member ("Clear it with Sidney") signaled the larger entrance, after the great expansion of the unions and after the New Deal, of labor leaders into the power elite.

Labor and the National Power Elite

We need not now become too fancy or too precise with the term "national power elite." By using it, I only mean to refer to the circles and individuals who as a collectivity share decisions having national consequences. In so far as events are decided, the power elite as a collectivity makes the decisions. No one, I believe, wants to argue that the chief of a roadside fruit stand has as much, or more, power in various social areas of life as the head of a multi-million-dollar corporation or that a lieutenant on the line in Korea is as powerful as the Chief of Staff in the Pentagon or that a deputy sheriff carries as much authority as the President of the United States. Well then, the power elite is a relative term; it refers to those who have the most say-so about those events that are decided. The definitive problem is at what level you wish to draw the line—you could by enlargement define the elite out of existence—and this varies with what you are interested in studying.

No one has made a systematic study of the most powerful actors in the political, economic, and military spheres of the United States social structure. We have partial studies, dating mainly from the muckraker era and from the thirties, which, by the way, are often more imaginative than systematic and more ideological than empirical. None of them includes labor leaders. Certainly today, however, no such study could be adequate, much less complete, if it did not include the top leaders of the major unions. There is, of course, much disagreement over how much power and what kind of power the men of labor now have; but this very fact points to them as a factor that must be reckoned with by those who would understand the main drift and the ostensibly powerful actors within it.

In this essay I will not be able to answer the very complicated question of "how much power" labor leaders now have, for no one could do so without also answering the same question for business executives, government officials, admirals and generals, major politicians, and other top national types. To state the question in answerable terms requires that we compare labor leaders with other members of the power elite as a total bracket, for the power of one can only be measured against the power of another.

There is, in addition, the question of just what role this entire elite plays in the shaping of our historic era. It may be best to conceive of history as not in any way the realization of the will of social actors. History may "just move along by itself," even though powerful actors attempt to move and shape it, and so things go on behind men's backs. There is an extreme view that by their schemes a relatively small group make history. And, of course, there are many intermediate views, some of them quite intricate. I shall not examine this range of issues here except toward the end of these remarks, and then only casually.

What I will attempt to do in this preliminary statement,[1] is to discuss in general terms the national roles of the key men of American labor and raise several questions about the functions of labor unions and of their top personnel.

Contexts of Union Functions

For a long time now it has been traditional to contrast business or market unionism with ideological or political unionism, as if these were types of unions or, at least, of ideologies. But it is probably more useful to think of these terms as simply indicators of two *contexts* in which unions operate. Unions may shift their attention to one or the other and may employ different tactics in one or the other at the same time, as well as at different times. This shifting is one meaning of such assertions as that the market is political and that politics has relevance for the market and that labor must now operate in a political economy. Yet we always have to remember that "labor" also operates in more local contexts and serves more local interests.

In fact, as we all know, there have been three major areas in which labor leaders have traditionally sought to share power with businessmen in economic roles and, now, with businessmen in political roles. *First,* in the plant or the local labor market, which at present does not seem to me to be the center of attention or struggle. *Second,* in the enterprise and in industry-wide sets of enterprises. Since the later thirties it is in this area that the sharpest disagreements have been raised, for this is the territory par excellence of managerial

[1] Preliminary, that is, to *The American Elite: A Study of the High and Mighty* (to be published by the Oxford University Press), on which I am now at work.

prerogative, upon which labor leaders have, of course, encroached. The notions of guaranteed annual wages, of profit sharing, of stabilized production schedules, of a controlled ratio of prices, profits, and wages, of industrial councils, or of "codetermination"—all lie here, although they, of course, may spill over into the third area. *Third,* in the national political economy, where big power blocs jockey with one another for a share in national decisions. For the sake of analysis this area should include, I believe, the international functions labor people have recently assumed in ECA and the Department of State.

I have reminded the reader of these contexts in which unions and their leaders operate in order to make this simple but often overlooked point: much controversy over the "nature" and function of labor organizations and of their leaders could be avoided if the disputants would continually specify to which context they have reference.

For example, in the first context a union may very well have as its major function the control of a job empire, yet, at the same time, in the third context it can be operating as a pressure group for power accumulation, a power to be used for broad as well as narrow purposes. It seems to me metaphysical, in the bad (*i.e.,* the uncontrolled) sense, to argue that the first function is the "real" one and the other not, or vice versa.

I shall return to this contextual principle of locating and interpreting union functions. Here I need only remark that in this general essay I am mainly concerned with labor leaders as members of the power elite in the national context of the political economy.

Labor Leadership and Status

Not all national labor leaders—although certainly more of them now than 25 years ago—have taken up the posture of the elite before themselves and before the nation. Much of the often curious behavior and maneuvering of labor chieftains over the last decade is explainable by their search for status within the national power elite, for in this context they have displayed extreme sensitivity to prestige slights. They feel that they have arrived, and so they want in. They want, "just like other big shots," to share the key decisions. The accouterments they have gained are on local, national, and international levels. In middle- and small-sized cities labor leaders now sit with Chamber of Commerce officials on civic enterprises. They receive honorary academic degrees. On the national level they expect and they get seats on production boards and desks in price-control agencies. On the international scene labor men have served with ECA missions, and as labor attachés they are now in American embassies all over the globe.

Their claim for status and power rests on their already increased power, not on property, income, or birth; and power in such situations as theirs is a source of uneasiness as well as a base of operations. It is not yet a solid and continuous base having the force of use and law. Their touchiness about prestige matters, especially on the national scene, is due (1) to their self-made character; [2] it is also due (2) to the well-known fact that their self-making

[2] See facts and figures in C. Wright Mills, *The New Men of Power,* New York, Harcourt Brace, 1948, esp. Chap. 5, "The Self-made Men."

was helped no end by government and the atmosphere it created in the decade after 1935; they are government-made men, fearing that they can be unmade by government. Their uneasy status is also a reflection (3) of the fact that they are simply new to the power elite and its ways. Finally, is it too much to suggest that (4) they feel a tension between their publics: their union members, before whom they cannot be too big a shot or too closely associated with inherited enemies, and their newly found companions and routines of life?

In the meantime in Washington, as well as in Europe, these men feel themselves to be members of a national elite, and they act that way and talk that way. They jockey for better positions and more say-so, which some of them understand now often entails greater prestige recognition, within this elite in which group they seldom or never acknowledge membership before the members of their union.

Many observers mistake the newer status accouterments of labor leaders for *evidence* of labor's power. In a way they are, but in a way they are not. They *are* when they are bottomed on and lead to power. They *are not* when they become status traps for leaders, without resulting power. In such matters it is well to remember that this is no chicken-and-egg issue. The chicken is power and comes first, the egg is status and comes out of this chicken.

Labor Leaders as a Bloc

Like business executives and large owners, labor leaders as a group are not wholly unified. Yet the often noted tendency of "the other side" to regard any move by any unit of one side as having significance in terms of the whole indicates clearly that, in the views, expectations, and demands of these men, they do form blocs, even if unwillingly. They see one another as members of blocs, and in fact they are interknit in various and quite intricate ways. But labor's men do not seem to have any continuous general staff, just as business does not center in Morgan's office. It is more complicated than that.

Individual unions may lobby for particularistic interests, which is the key to such lack of unity as labor as a bracket displays. But increasingly the issues they face and the contexts in which they must face them are national in scope and in effect; and so they must coordinate labor's line with reference to a national context, on pain of loss of power.

It is known informally and has been demonstrated statistically that the personal characteristics of these leaders, as well as their view of their organizational interests, differ according to the organizational bloc to which their unions belong. Both are self-made men of power, running—if the reader will forgive me—patrimonial bureaucracies.

The leaders of the AFL and of the CIO operate in two different kinds of hierarchies. And the differences are not merely organizational; the two houses of labor are inhabited by different types of men, related within each organization in different ways. At the top of the AFL's gerontocracy are older, relatively uneducated men who have authority over much younger, better-educated men. Age and education cause some tension within the AFL. At the top of the more professional bureaucracy of the CIO are slightly older men who are quite well educated, and these better educated leaders exercise authority over slightly younger and less well-educated men. Age and education are graded according to organizational structure. The facts of age, education, and types of hierarchy make for further differences in character, as well as outlook, between AFL and CIO leaders, which I shall not here examine.

Labor Leaders and Organizational Power

The corporate executive, like the labor leader, is a practical man and an opportunist, but for him enduring means, developed for other purposes, are available for the conduct of his political as well as of his business-labor affairs. The corporation is now a very stable basis of operation; in fact, I believe that it is more stable and more important for the continuance of the American arrangement than the lifetime family. The big corporations as a group give the executives a stable base for durable expectations; so the business member of the power elite can rely upon them in the pursuit of his short-term goals and opportunistic maneuvering.

But the union, unlike the corporation, is often in a state of protest; it is on the defensive in a sometimes actually, and always potentially, hostile society. It does not provide such enduring means, which are ready-made and at the labor elite's disposal. If the labor leader wants such means, even for his little goals, he must himself build and maintain them.

In the context of his union the labor leader is an elected official, dependent ("in the last analysis," which is not always made by history) upon the loyalty of fellow leaders and upon the rank and file of his organization. The great organizing upsurge of the thirties showed that officers who were not sufficiently responsive to the demands of industrial workers could lose power. The corporation manager, on the other hand, in the context of his corporation is not an elected official in the same sense. His power does not depend upon the loyalty of the men who work for him, and he does not usually lose his job if a union successfully invades his plants. The upsurges of the thirties did not oust the managers, whose responsibilities are not to the workers whom they employ but to themselves and to their scattered stockholders.

This difference in power situation means that the power of the business leader is likely to be more continuous and more assured than that of the labor leader; the labor leader is more likely to be insecure in his job if he fails to "deliver the goods."

Adventure, or what Max Weber called "booty," capitalism produces robber barons; in a somewhat delayed fashion and on a much smaller scale, labor unionism produces its labor racketeers. There is a Commodore Vanderbilt, and there is a Robert Brindell. At one point in its career industrial capitalism produces the sober, bourgeois entrepreneur, afraid of the encroachments of government upon his liberty. Correspondingly, labor unionism produces its sober labor leader, believing in voluntarism, afraid of government encroachments, not interested in labor solidarity, but working for independent and sovereign craft unions. There is the early Henry Ford, and there is Samuel Gompers.

Many American unions are still in the Gompers or Ford stage, and there are still spotty areas in the local union world which call to mind Brindell and

Vanderbilt. Yet if the old unionists have at times become *condottieri* leading roughneck bands for local robber barons, the new unionists may in time become administrators of disciplined and contented workers for large bureaucratized corporations, for now there is a new type of correspondence between business and labor and new types of leaders on each side within the power elite. It is not a mechanical or an exact corresponding, but it is coming about. The mass industries have produced in the world of giant corporations the engineering, managerial type of leader, and the unionization of these mass industries by the new business unionism is slowly beginning to produce an engineering, managerial type of labor leader. In a similar way both corporations and unions have come increasingly to operate in the context of the political economy; and so in a similar way the types of leaders they select and form become shaped for survival and efficiency in this larger context.

Labor Leaders and Expediency

However it may be with the business and political elite, there's nothing, it seems to me, in the make-up of the *current* labor leaders, as individuals and as a group, to lead us to believe that they can or will transcend the strategy of maximum adaptation. By this I mean that they react more than they lead and that they do so to retain and to expand their position in the constellation of power and advantage. Certain things could happen that would cause the downfall of the present labor leadership or sections of it, and other types of leaders might then rise to union power; but the current crop of labor leaders is pretty well set up as a dependent variable in the main drift.

Everyone seems agreed that United States unions, with minor exceptions, have eschewed "ideologies" and "programs" and have been "pragmatic" to an extreme degree.[3] This, however, is not saying as much as those who keep reiterating it seem to feel. One could substitute "corporations" or "political parties" for unions in the same sentence and have just as true a proposition. The problem of analysis for all these practical social creatures is not the earnest search for their outlook and programs and certainly not the search for new ways of moaning when no program is found other than the classic aim of "more." To analyze the national role of unions we should ignore what their leaders say, except strictly as strategical rhetoric, and examine two other problems:

First, just what major functions do these organizations fulfill (for whom and how) in the main drift?

Second, what is the main drift, the most likely outcome of the interplay between these power blocs for the changing shape of the political economy as a whole?

By the main drift, or master trend, I mean the general direction, if any, of the jockeying and compromises and struggles of organizations and of elites under present-day conditions. If they are strictly pragmatic and out to maximize their security of power and gain greater pay-offs, then what happens to them depends as much upon the whole context and their strength in it as upon any intentions they might have. So, given the several contexts in which

[3] See *ibid.*, Chap. 9, "Programs and Expediencies," esp. pp. 239–240.

these organizations and leaders *are* expedient, what main line, what direction are these organizations assuming?

If these are our questions, then, it seems to me, "the field of labor" as it is now instituted is not entirely an intelligible unit of study. It is clear that we cannot understand labor leaders without understanding labor unions; it should also be clear that we cannot understand these unions without understanding the business corporation and the modern state; and we cannot understand any of these structures today except as they interact with one another to form the going concern of the political economy.

This is not merely an affirmation of the important, although often mushy, principle that phenomena must be understood contextually. I mean more than that: I mean that I have come to the assumption that neither labor leaders nor labor unions are at the present juncture likely to be "independent variables" in the national context and that therefore most of their aspects and responses in which we are interested are more easily and more adequately explained as functions of other factors and contexts than of scholarly or gossipy details about their nature and doings.

Of course, this *is* in part a matter of the perspective which we assume. If we were interested in some administrative detail of unionism or some narrowed sequence of the history of a given union or were writing to inform businessmen what "labor" may do, then we might confine ourselves. But the perspective we choose to take up is set by the type of question of which I have given two examples.

Labor Leaders and the Labor Movement

There cannot very well be an interpretation of the labor leader without a theory of the labor organization and of such "movement" as it displays. The labor leader is a social actor, playing one of his major roles within a labor union and using that role as the base for all other public roles. The leader must adapt to whatever this union becomes; only within the limits it sets can he lead. Although these limits sometimes seem quite broad, he is, in the first instance, a union-made product.

If the labor union is an army, the labor leader is a generalissimo.

If the union is a democratic town meeting, the leader is a parliamentary debater.

If the union is a political machine, the leader is a political boss.

If the union is a business enterprise, supplying and withholding for a price a labor force, the labor leader is an entrepreneur, a contractor of labor.

If the union is a pressure group, the leader is busily at the hub of national pressure, in the halls of the invisible government.

If the labor union is a regulator of the workingman's industrial animosity, the labor leader is a salaried technician of animosity, gearing men at work into this organization and then easing the organization through the fluctuations of American society.

There is little question but that, at some point in the history of one or another union, we can find each of these functions predominating and the leaders spending most of their time, attention, and energy in fulfilling the role indicated. Even in cross section today one can find solid examples of each of them. These several functions vary in their mixture according to the economic and political times, according to the phase and position of particular unions, and according to the context in reference to which we raise our question. Two questions in fact, are presented.

First, under what conditions does one or another function come to predominate so as to be typical of, and central to, "the unions" at a given time?

Second, is there any tendency, because of the structural drift and the phases of contemporary unions, for unions as a whole to be more readily understood primarily in terms of one of these functions?

In this essay I have to skip consideration of the first question. If our answer to the second question is yes, then we must elaborate the function, especially in terms of further-running consequences when they interplay with the tendencies of corporations and of the state. Today, when all the major unions are in rather well-consolidated phases, no large organizational move is under foot, and all unions are the beneficiaries of a perilous boom based on war preparation; today, the unions operate as pressure groups in a manner quite like the Farm Bureau and the Trade Associations. My answer to the second question, then, is Yes, the central function of labor organizations in the national political economy today is that of a mass-organization pressure group. And what this means is that it is in terms of this image that most of what labor leaders do and fail to do can most readily be understood.

But the labor leader is a union-made product, I've said, *in the first instance*. For successful, top leaders there is a second instance. For such a leader is also made (selected and formed) by his membership in the national power elite and by what happens to him there. All that I have suggested here and briefly illustrated is that we must see and try to understand the leader as a man moving in the overlap of these contexts, the union world and the world of the national power elite. He is a man acting and thinking at the point of their intersection, and the social mechanics as well as the context of his thinking and acting involve the coincidences and collisions of both spheres.

Labor Leaders and Industrial Conflict

As members of the national power elite, labor leaders, by means of machines, run national pressure groups of mass organizations recruited from intermediate skill and income levels in urban areas. As procapitalist, hardheaded, pressure-group captains and as members or would-be members of the national elite, in so far as labor men talk seriously of programs, they will invariably conceive of them as realizable alongside the present corporations and within the present state framework. The leadership should gain more decision within the power elite; the organizations should accumulate more power and be integrated more firmly within the corporation; the membership should get a heavier, steadier cut within the present framework of the political economy.

These unions are less levers for change of that general framework than they are instruments for more advantageous integration with it. The drift their actions implement, in terms of the largest projections, is a kind of "procapitalist syndicalism from the top." They seek, in the first instance, greater integration at the upper levels of the corporate economy rather than greater power at the lower levels of the work hierarchy, for, in brief, it is the unexpressed desire of American labor leaders to join with owners and managers in running the corporate enterprise system and influencing decisively the political economy as a whole.

Their basis of operation is the mass organization, whereas that of business managers is the massed property they control or manage, and that of the politicians, the electorate, encased as well as may be in the political machine. Those who think of labor in political terms should not overlook the fact that pressure groups may be as powerful as political parties (or more so). Moreover their power tends to be less responsible. They are "private"; and so their leaders need not make any pretense at doctrinal justification or public accountability. All of which, in a situation like ours, no doubt increases their effectiveness. For the businessman, the politician, and the labor leader—each in curiously different ways—the more apathetic the members of their mass organizations (as long as they don't get restless and as long as they back up their leaders in "crises"), the more operating power the leaders have as members of the national power elite.

CHAPTER 11 THE CORPORATION
AS AN ORGANIZATION

Neil W. Chamberlain   *Yale University*

I<small>N THIS</small> chapter we are interested in how the institutional characteristics of the corporate business affect its making decisions concerning relations with its employees. The interesting feature of this topic is that in the representative case many important personnel decisions can be made by the company only with the joint action of an organization whose interests must in part be conflicting—the union of its employees.

Corporation as an Organization

Let us consider briefly the nature of the corporation. The name is given quite generally to institutions which have been formed and are carried on by numbers of individuals for their common advantage. The corporation is thus to be found in almost all walks of life, wherever individuals wish to pursue common interests within some formal institutional framework. Schools, churches, fraternal organizations, public works, social clubs, and occasionally labor unions, as well as business enterprises, have operated under corporate charters. These charters are issued by some government body, usually one of the states in this country, and set forth the purposes, privileges, and limitations on the corporators. Any textbook on business organization summarizes the chief characteristics of the customary corporate charter. For our purposes one aspect should be singled out, however. The incorporated activity is generally given the privilege of perpetuity. The life of the organization is not limited to the natural lives of those who originate it; it becomes almost a creature in itself. However dependent for its continuity on the lives of the individuals who compose it any one time, it is dependent on no specific individuals. Persons come and persons go, but the corporation may go on forever. In the law this separation of the life of the corporation from the lives of those who perform the corporate activity at any one time has been recognized by treating the corporation as a separate person, unreal in fact but real in law, fictitious, since the corporation *is* the people who compose it, but existent for many "practical" purposes.

Although the corporate form is to be found in a variety of social fields, as we have seen, in the United States its principal prominence has been in the field of business. Although there are many more unincorporated than incorporated enterprises (single proprietorships and partnerships are more common, for example), the corporate form is responsible for the greatest share of American economic activity. So much has the corporation come to be regarded as a business form that we are likely to consider the two almost as synonymous. Anyone who speaks about "corporations" is understood as speaking of business activity. This chapter is written about corporations, yet its discussion is confined to business units, though the analysis presented is more generally applicable.

In the business corporation we are used to dealing with three sets of participants: the stockholders, those who actually own and who legally hold ultimate control over the enterprise and for whose benefit it is presumably conducted; the board of directors, which acts as the direct elected representative of the stockholders, empowered by the latter to act on their behalf and wielding, with few limitations, the full legal authority of the stockholders as long as its actions are reasonably intended to prosper the stockholders' interests; and, finally, the group commonly designated as the management, chosen by the board of directors to carry on the continuing business of the enterprise and free to use their discretion within broad limitations, though required to obtain board approval for more important actions. Actually in the small enterprise these three sets of individuals may be merged into one. A small number of persons—perhaps the immediate present members of a family—may be stockholders, directors, and management combined. In the large enterprise some overlap is still to be found. Most commonly some of the directors—in a few instances all of them—are also members of the operating management.

In the typical large corporation, however, there has come to be a stockholding group so numerous and so scattered that it ceases to exercise any controlling authority. Through the proxy machinery operating management is usually enabled to secure a "rubber-stamping" of their nominees for the directorship. A great deal of criticism has been made of this management self-perpetuation by a kind of cooption, but it is difficult to see how any other system could have evolved within the existing legal framework. If the continuity of the corporation was to be assured, some group other than the sprawling, unorganized body of owners, unaware of others' very identities and incapable of assembling in any significant proportion in any location, had to preempt the legal power which had been vested in the stockholders. That need has been achieved by reconstituting the board of directors not in law but in fact; instead of a group governed by the stockholders and governing management, they have become a group governed by management and, by virtue of their legal position, permitting management to govern the stockholders. These relationships have created fascinating legal problems and a vast scope for social reformers. From the viewpoint of the social scientist, however, they raise problems of conceptualizing the corporation and, in particular, of conceptualizing the decision-making process within the corporation.

Despite this tangle and complexity of relationships within the corporation, there has been some historic tendency in the social sciences to treat the corporate decision-making process as though it were the cerebrations of a single individual. Economists in particular have tended to personify the entrepreneur and to build a price analysis in terms of the reactions of an individual to a changing structure of market prices. Perhaps the legal fiction of corporate personality has also contributed to the personalizing of the process of making of decisions in the business corporation. Even from the legal structuring of the corporation into stockholders, directors, and management it is evident, however, that the decisions which are made are not the products of a single mind. But the social scientist is not confined by the law in his study, and if he discerns other groups as constituent elements of the corporation, then these too —as well as those groups legally recognized—must be brought into the analysis.

From the social scientist's point of view, the decision itself provides a convenient point of departure. What is the "decision," who entered into its making, and in what capacities? These are questions we shall examine in this chapter. As we do so, we shall discover that some groups not normally considered to be part of the corporate structure actually enter into its decisions. The wage structure of a firm is an important corporate decision, for example, yet today that decision is as much influenced by the representative union as by the legal management. The union and the collective-bargaining process which accompanies it must then, somehow, be incorporated into our conception of the decision-making process in the business firm. Collective bargaining may indeed be viewed as one method of making managerial decisions, one form of the business decision-making process. Our concept of corporate decision making must therefore comprehend the bargaining process.

Corporate Decision Making

We can now turn to the concept of decision making itself. Just as in the behavioristic school of psychology decisions are revealed by actions (however verbally disguised), so is the corporate decision defined by actual conduct. Indeed, the decision-making process may be regarded as the process determining action. We treat the action itself as, evidently, the decision reached, whether verbalized or not, whether contradicting or confirming the verbalized form. In this sense the decision-making process is continuous with action. The daily resumption of the production program by the 8-o'clock shift is one instance of the making of a business decision, just as the directors' appropriation of a million dollars for plant expansion is another.

In an organization such as the business corporation, where actions are subdivided by specialization, decision making is necessarily a joint affair. If we raise our view above the actions of each particular individual and consider the *corporate* activity, we observe work flows, streams of activity eventuating in some result such as the marketing at a given price and time of a product or service of given specification. The actions of each individual are interconnected with the actions of others in some work flow contributing to such an outcome. Each work flow is an instance of a continuous decision-making process, of which everyone who is capable of affecting the outcome must be considered a part. At some point, to be sure, the effects of certain individuals on an outcome may be negligible, and we are justified in ignoring them as part of a particular stream of activity. We overlook the operations of the janitor in discussing production decisions, or we may view the manufacturing department in abstraction from the sales or accounting departments for certain purposes. Such arbitrary lines of demarcation do not vitiate the conception, however, since they must be drawn around any problem of knowledge. It is only what the economist does when he decides not to concern himself with chemistry or what the physicist does when he excludes sociology from his field of investigation, even though these are not completely discrete subjects.

Although every individual capable of significantly affecting an outcome must be included in the decision-making process, each does not play the same role. The placement of authority must obviously influence the impact which each of the interlocked individuals has on the result. Thus we may reasonably enough conceive of the production manager and the shop worker as part of the same decision-making process, for given decisions, but we would not consider that their relation to the process was the same. Each would have his effect on the production program: the manager who may have initiated and authorized the basic operations and the worker whose actions determine whether the manager's direction is executed as planned. If the worker's action is, in fact, something different from that directed by the works manager, the *corporate* decision becomes something other than that intended; the shop worker is thus inescapably tied into the corporate decision-making process but in a different manner from that of his superior. It is not necessary for us to develop the nature of the participants' roles for our present purposes, however.

Organization Characteristics and Decision Making

This conception of the decision-making process as a joint product is applicable to any business corporation, but the form or mechanics of the process is not so easy to generalize. Variations in the characteristics of the enterprise or of the industry to which it belongs are likely to introduce variations in the way its individuals are interconnected in the streams of activity which reveal the *corporate* decisions. It will be impossible in the scope of this chapter to do more than suggest some of the variations which are encountered.

1. The degree of separation between ownership and control of the corporation determines the extent to which these two interests, which may diverge, *significantly* affect business operations. Some students of industrial relations have, for example, suspected that owner-directed enterprises are more likely to accept the inescapable reality of rank-and-file participation in the conduct of a business, while a management divorced from ownership and dependent for its position upon control over the politics of the corporation (as, typically, in the large corporation) is more jealous of its power and less willing to admit that it is shared with others.

2. The size of the business has an enormous impact on the character of decision making. As a business expands, more and more of its formal efforts at coordination must channel through committees, composed of individuals who customarily are *representative* of the interests of some functional group, such as a department or a level of supervision. The introduction of staff functions is primarily a resultant of size: the large-scale enterprise faces problems requiring specialized analysis frequently enough to warrant hiring professional advisers, who must somehow be fitted into the streams of activity within the company even though denied the "right" to initiate action themselves.

3. The nature of a product, the diversity of production, and the rate of

change of a product are factors which are likely to affect in some manner the mechanics of the decision-making process. These will determine, among other things, the size of primary work groups, the degree of importance attached to integration of individuals in the work flow, the extent to which speed and flexibility of decision are required, and perhaps also the character of the individuals in the process. (It has been argued,[1] for example, that the very nature of, say, the coal or meat-packing or steel industry will have its molding influence on those who are associated with it.)

4. The degree of competition facing the firm is an important determinant of the form of the decision-making process. A sheltered enterprise can better afford to muddle along on an outdated routine or, alternatively, to indulge in experimentation, such as with junior boards of directors, multiple management, union-management cooperation, and so on. On the other hand, the firm which is confronted by a more merciless competition, from rivals in the same industry or innovations in another industry, is likely to develop a more nervous, high-strung and responsive integration of those in its decision-making streams.

Other influences, such as rate of growth and plant dispersion, likewise have their effects on the mechanics of decision making in the business corporation. In their totality the contrasts between two firms—let us say between the American Telephone and Telegraph Company and some local producer of men's shirts or between Standard Oil of New Jersey and a department store or between General Motors and a real-estate firm—may be so great as to suggest different genera of decision making rather than simply different species of the same process. Yet despite these diversities the same fundamental conception of the decision-making process as one integrating the activities of individuals in some stream of corporate activity, participated in by all who are in a position to affect the outcome, remains good.

Influences on Decision Making

In analyzing corporate decision making, it is important to maintain a distinction between two types of influences bearing on decisions. One influence is introduced by those who are actually party to the work process, in the sense that they are in a position directly to affect its outcome. It is in this sense that both managers and workers have been characterized here as participants in the corporate decision-making streams. But in other instances those who influence the outcome may not actually be party to the work flow; their influence derives from some contact with the corporation, as that of a government official, a customer, or a supplier of the firm. These latter influences, coming from contacts with the corporation rather than from direct participation in corporate activity, provide data which must be taken into account by those responsible for corporate decisions. Customer preferences, supplier offerings, and government regulations may in general be viewed as matters affecting the decisions of those who make up the corporation, having an influence on their actions similar to technological developments, market shifts, general business conditions, and so on.

Although influences on corporate decision making of those inside the

[1] In this connection, see Chap. 14, by Clark Kerr and Abraham Siegel.

firm and of those outside it may appear reasonably distinct on first encounter, they are not always easy to separate. Indeed, they require the same kind of arbitrary drawing of lines of demarcation which was remarked in identifying those who "significantly" affect a given corporate activity. This need for individual judgment, involving ultimately arbitrary classification, is inescapable in even the most scientific of investigations, however, and is in itself not condemnatory of the conception being presented.

Perhaps the clearest way of suggesting the difference between influences of contact and those of participation, in the decision-making process, is by reference to the influence on the single enterprise of other enterprises in the same industry, with respect to matters of collective bargaining. First, let us assume that the individual firm negotiates an agreement with the union, the terms of which are locally determined, free from any pressure of an "industry pattern." The terms which have been agreed upon by other employers in that industry will be influences entering the decision-making process as data. What wage increase other employers have granted will be information which will affect the decision made in the X company, but the other employers whose terms are being considered are not themselves party to the X company's decision. Their actions provide relevant facts which will enter the determinations made at X company, but their actions do not directly affect the outcome there. They may, indeed, be ignored.

Now consider the X company as one of a number of employers who have agreed to bargain on an industry-wide basis with the union. The firms choose a joint negotiating committee. Each company is represented on that committee and directly influences through its participation the actions of the committee. No longer can it be said that the other companies provide only data for the X company's decision; they are parties to that decision. On the subject matter involved A, B, and C companies have become an integral part of the decision-making process of X company.

Between these two cases, which are not actually polar cases, there is a broad middle ground of less easily classified instances, the best analysis of which has been provided by Prof. William Fellner of the University of California in his book *Competition among the Few*. Companies may be interdependent without being integrated. What he calls "conjectural interdependence" arises when the actions of one company are so significant to another as to influence directly and consciously the course of the latter's actions. It does not lower the price of its product because, if it does so, the other—a chief rival —will lower its price, and the initiating firm will be no better off than before. It engages extensively in product research because, if it fails to do so, its rival may get the jump on it in pioneering a new product. In such cases the members of one corporation do not actually *participate* in the decisions of another company, but their actions are so relevant as to have an almost predictable influence on the decisions of that other company. In the field of industrial relations such conjectural interdependence is evidenced in pattern setting and pattern following, where an almost predictable relationship of terms exists between certain firms, without the actual joint participation that characterizes multiemployer or industry-wide bargaining.

There are, then, industry influences—of data, of conjectural interdependence, of joint participation—which enter into any corporate decision-making process with respect to matters of industrial relations. Similarly, there are influences emanating from other employers in the geographical area or local labor market, whether or not companies are members of the same industry. Where a number of employers are using the same sources of labor supply, the decision of any one is likely to have some bearing on the decisions of others. This may take the form of information which must be taken into account. It may be the basis for a quasi agreement (such as an informal understanding that one company will not hire any worker already employed by another company or a community wage pattern that ranks one company relative to certain others). The influence of other firms on any one firm may come by actual joint agreement, bringing people from other enterprises directly into the decision-making process of the given company (firms may agree that no one will initiate a wage increase without prior consultation with the others).

The great variety of influences acting upon a corporation—from the industry, from other employers in the local labor market, and from customers, suppliers, distributors, the government, and so on—may all be considered relevant to the decision-making process in that corporation in one of the ways just pictured. This aspect of the analysis is important for establishing the general conception of decision making which is here adopted. In the remaining pages of the chapter, however, we shall not be concerned with the influences of data or conjectural interdependence on industrial-relations decisions of the firm but shall concentrate our attention upon direct, joint participation in the corporate decision-making process.

Primary Business Organizational Goals

Corporate decision making, as here conceived, involves the interrelated activities of individuals who significantly determine a given outcome. Though managerial position affects the role played in the decision-making process, it has no exclusive claim to participation in that process. Rank-and-file workers are party to it, too. When people whose respective positions may be counted upon to place them in different interest groupings are *part of the same process*, can we expect that their respective actions will come in conflict, in some degree nullifying or diluting the effort or intent of the other, producing a corporate decision which none really seek? Or is there something which we may call an organizational goal, which, no less than personal goals, motivates all participants similarly in a decision-making stream and serves to integrate their efforts? If an organizational goal exists, it could then be attributable to the worker as well as to the manager. It would supply a common bond of interest uniting their efforts and helping to overcome the divisive interests which otherwise might disintegrate or weaken their joint activities.

It is, of course, true that organizational goals and personal goals cannot be distinguished, in the sense that organizational goals can only be made real by becoming personal goals. But there is a sense in which the two can be differentiated. Organizational goals may be construed as objectives which are imposed on, or accepted by, individuals simply by virtue of their being part of the organization. Thus for the individual who identifies his future with the organization, there always exists the primary organizational goal of continuity. That such a purpose has some reality in the case of the business corporation has been attested to by a number of recent studies which reveal the lack of interest which the average worker has in employment with another company, once he has shopped around enough to feel reasonably well satisfied with his present job. As Prof. Lloyd Reynolds of Yale has shown in his study of the New Haven area, *The Structure of Labor Markets,* the price economist's construct of a worker who continually assesses the wage advantage to be derived from a change of employment is not supported by actual investigation. The increasing significance of seniority in the allocation of jobs is not alone responsible for such an attitude. There are underlying influences of social attachment to a particular work community which are equally strong.

It is not necessary that every worker feel this identification of his own and the company's future in order for continuity to become a significant organizational goal, serving as a common interest binding together all those in the decision-making processes of a given company. If some undefined but substantial proportion of the work group, including its key leaders, feels such an attachment, the presence of a smaller number of "floaters"—who may be in the course of finding their own long-run niches—may be tolerated without invalidating the organizational goal of continuity. It is probably a supportable hypothesis that, in businesses characterized by low turnover rates, the researcher would find a high degree of identification of a worker's *future* with the company's future. The time horizon may, of course, vary with the circumstances. In time of depression and mass unemployment one might find companies with negligible turnover rates whose workers would only be awaiting the return of good times to make a change. Nevertheless, it would remain true that, under the existing circumstances, such workers would be most upset over the present loss of their jobs and for an indefinite future would feel their own personal goals manifestly dependent upon realizing the organizational goal of continuity.

Nor need it be argued that this objective is held equally strongly by all those who are part of the enterprise. For some individuals severance of their connection with the company would carry greater loss than for others. The degree of a worker's attachment to an enterprise is a function of the total complex of his social relationships—something which goes beyond the present discussion.

Once we admit the reality of the primary organizational goal of continuity, a secondary goal of the corporation can be added: profitability. On its achievement depends the perpetuation of the business firm. We are perhaps accustomed to believe that many workers are unconcerned about the profit position of their company as long as they continue to receive their own pay checks. On the strength of such a belief we may question whether profitability can be considered as a common tie among all those party to the business decision-making processes. The reality of this secondary organizational goal is best demonstrated, however, by the sacrifices which workers have frequently volunteered to keep alive some firm which threatens to close its doors. It is true that, *as long as they continue to receive their regular pay checks,* they are likely to be uninterested in the company's profit position or interested only to the extent of criticizing the amount of retained earnings or the distribution of corporate receipts, but the threat of interruption of the flow of their earnings is enough to revive their interest in the company's profitability. It is an interest which exists, however, principally because, in the present institutional context, profitability is essential to continuity. It has, therefore, been labeled here as a secondary goal, existent largely because of its relationship to the primary goal of continuity and recognized in most instances only when that primary goal is threatened.

Collective Bargaining

So far, nothing has been said about the union, and it is now time to introduce it into the picture. The union too has its decision-making streams of activity, embracing all those who significantly affect its courses of conduct. Like the corporation, it too is subjected to a similar, if not parallel, set of influences bearing on its decisions. Parenthetically, the management of an enterprise is only one of these influences and not necessarily a determining influence on any given union decision, thus revealing the inherent fallacy of the old saw that "management gets the kind of union leadership it deserves." The union enters into the corporation as the direct representative of the latter's employees, and in so far as the employees themselves must be regarded as part of the corporate decision-making process, so too must their union which represents them. As long as a union is representative of its members, it cannot escape from affecting by its actions the outcome of corporate activities in certain areas of operation. The instigation of a slowdown, for example, is as much a part of the *corporate* decision with respect to rates of operation as is the schedule promulgated by the general manager. A union's attitude toward promotions may influence the foremen's recommendations as much as a personnel supervisor's written instructions, as a number of management members have testified. If one follows the conception of corporate decision making here presented, one cannot escape the conclusion that a union—not in any remotely abstract sense but in that of a given functioning group of individuals who are representative of the employees—is a part of the corporate decision-making process, for certain kinds of decisions, just as is management. Their roles need not be "equal" or similar, but both constitute direct influences on the corporate conduct. The corporation thus appears as a more complex social form than a legal study of its aspects would indicate.

If, then, we maintain that workers, as part of the corporate organization, are subject to the organizational goals of continuity and profitability, we should reasonably expect that unions likewise recognize these objectives. And indeed, in the present societal setting, a representative union cannot escape acknowledging them. It does so, however, for its own interests and not because of any sense of justice or fairness or kinship to management or owners. It is concerned with the continuity of the business organization because its members are concerned and because its own existence depends upon a continuing membership. It is concerned with a company's profitability only because that is essential to continuity and because the profit position of a company is the only basis for improving its members' economic status, an accomplishment on which its own perpetuation depends. Local 600 of the UAW is inescapably concerned that the Ford Motor Company continue its operations. John L. Lewis is vitally interested that the steel companies maintain their captive mines in production. For all their attacks upon management miserliness, both recognize that corporate profitability is essential to this result and to any improvement of union members' economic position. When the automobile and mine workers' unions survey the income statements of their respective companies, we may be sure that both rejoice to find a handsome total there (it improves the likelihood of good pickings), while a negative figure is cause for pessimism. The leaders of both are compelled, in the achievement of their own and the members' personal goals, by virtue of the institutional setting in which those personal goals must be achieved, to recognize these *organizational* objectives.

Conflict and Cooperation in Collective Bargaining

The special interest which a union has in the continuity and profitability of the business firm with which it is associated is a basis for both conflict and cooperation with management. Cooperation, in its most fundamental sense of working together, is essential to the satisfaction of the elemental organizational goals which both recognize. Yet this simple fact, which has often been stated, does not eliminate conflict over the apportionment of the benefits and disadvantages derived from this corporative functioning, benefits and disadvantages which flow from the character of participation in the functional process as well as from money receipts. Each group is interested in the continuity and profitability of the business for its own interests and seeks to satisfy its own interests at the other's expense. Such conflict cannot be pushed to the point of dissolving permanently the joint relationship, however, without sacrificing the interests of both. There is thus a strong incentive to the ultimate compromise of stalemated negotiations over the terms of cooperation. The relatively few instances in which some joint agreement is not forthcoming out of union-management negotiations, however bitter the conflict and however strong the resentment over the outcome, are evidence of the present strength of the compulsion to compromise. This commonplace fact is most eloquent as to the institutional bonds now linking together management and union. If we sometimes assert that strikes are broken when the staying power of the workers has collapsed, this is only another way of stating the worker's fundamental dependence upon his company, which provides the basis for his and his union's concern for organizational continuity.

Because of this inescapable cooperative bond, in the framework of our present institutions, the recently revived interest in union-management cooperation is well placed, providing it is concerned with improving the mechanics of the joint decision-making processes which bind the two groups together. The procedures for most effectively integrating numbers of individuals into work flows where all participants are agreed on the desired outcome are a subject for research and analysis, dissemination, and mastery. But any suggestion that cooperation can somehow ultimately push conflict off the stage is of course highly fallacious. Where the fruits of corporate activity are necessarily limited, there is bound to be competition among the parties in their apportionment.

Where alternative courses of action reward or penalize individuals differently, there is an inescapable clash in the act of choosing among them. The process of decision making is one of cooperation, but the decision itself is frequently a resolution of conflicts of interest.

It is true that the joint decision-making process may be used for administrative purposes in which conflicts of interest are largely absent, but this use is conditional upon some prior resolution of conflicts. If the competition over distribution of corporate returns and over the power to initiate action is resolved by agreement, then both parties may turn their attention to problems of production from which the competitive element has been largely removed. Union and management may both seek the same improvement in corporate performance, since each feels sure that the result will redound to its benefit. The programs of union-management cooperation now so widely discussed are of this administrative type. How successfully they function depends to a large extent upon how successfully the major conflicts of interest have been resolved to provide a firm platform for cooperation. If all participants are satisfied with the terms of cooperation, then cooperation, via the prescribed administrative procedures, will be more readily forthcoming. But cooperation will never replace conflict. The terms of cooperation must be renegotiated from time to time, and the causes for conflict can never be fully anticipated or resolved.

If, then, we recognize the inescapable bond of cooperation between union and management in the business corporation today, we may seek to strengthen the effectiveness of the procedures contributing to that cooperation. But conflict is no less inevitable, and our concern should be no less with the channels and effects of union-management conflict. We may reasonably seek to direct conflict into forms which do not seriously interfere with the rights which outsiders—third parties, nonparticipants—have some reason to expect.

CHAPTER 12 BUREAUCRATIZATION IN INDUSTRY

Reinhard Bendix   *University of California (Berkeley)*

Tʜᴇ bureaucratization of modern industry has increased over the last half century. At the same time the changes of industrial organization which have accompanied this development have contributed to industrial peace. The following essay is designed to explore some background factors which tend to support these two propositions. It seeks to establish that industrial entrepreneurs considered as a class have undergone major changes since the beginning of the 19th century. These changes have culminated in the development of an industrial bureaucracy. The consequences of this bureaucratization may be observed in the changing system of supervision as well as in the transformation of the prevailing ideology of industrial managers.

Introduction

Webster's Collegiate Dictionary defines "bureaucracy" as routine procedure in administration, as a system of carrying on the business of government by means of bureaus, each controlled by a chief. This definition reflects the fact that it has not been customary to speak of bureaucracy in industry. Traditionally, the term has been applied to the activities of government; it has been broadened to include large-scale organizations generally only in recent years.[1]

The polemic implications of the term bureaucracy obscure its use in a descriptive sense, and yet it is important to use it in that sense. "A system of carrying on the business of industry and government by means of bureaus" is a definition of "administration" as well as of bureaucracy. Yet the two terms are not synonymous. Bureaucracy suggests in addition that the number of bureaus has increased, that their functions have become specialized as well as routinized, and that increasing use is made of technical apparatus in the performance of these specialized functions, which is in turn related to the

---

[1] Bureaucracy in government has been analyzed in great detail, frequently with the implication that waste and indolence were widespread. Many of these studies received their impetus from the scientific-management movement. Cf. Dwight Waldo, *The Administrative State*, New York, Ronald, 1948, pp. 47–61. The conventional term for industrial bureaucracy is "business administration." The implication of this terminology is obviously that waste and indolence are absent from business, that productivity is synonymous with efficiency, and that business administration involves technical know-how which the businessman has to keep secret in order to retain his competitive advantage. The semantics of this controversy have not been analyzed to my knowledge.

increasing use of expert, technical knowledge. The use of technical knowledge in the administration of industry implies the employment of specialists, whose work presupposes the completion of a course of professional training. The work of these specialists entails the subdivision and consequent elaboration of the managerial functions of planning, production organization, personnel selection, and supervision.

These developments have many ramifications. They depend, on the one side, on the growth of training facilities in many fields of applied science. They make possible a centralization of authority in industrial management, which can be made effective only by a simultaneous delegation of circumscribed authority to specialized bureaus or departments. This encourages the substitution of deliberately planned methods of procedure for rule-of-thumb "methods," and this in turn promotes the utilization of mechanical devices. But the adoption of rational procedures achieves greater operating efficiency than is possible in less elaborated organizational structures at the constant risk of more bureaucracy, in the negative sense.

These remarks give an idea of the complexity of the process called "bureaucratization." Little is gained, however, by adopting a concise definition of this term. It is rather intended as the common denominator of many related tendencies of administrative procedure which have characterized government and industry in recent decades. But while the term itself remains vague, its component elements do not.

The following aspects of bureaucratization will be considered in this essay. In the first section it is shown that industrial entrepreneurs as a group have been transformed since the inception of modern industry at the beginning of the 19th century. This has resulted in the elaboration of managerial functions in industry. In the second section an attempt is made to sketch the changes of managerial ideology which have accompanied bureaucratization. The first section characterizes the development of industrial bureaucracy. In the second section certain ideological consequences are analyzed which are especially relevant for an understanding of peace and conflict in industrial relations.

Changes in Managerial Functions

The growing bureaucratization of industry may be analyzed in a variety of ways. The role of the employer has changed fundamentally since the rise of modern industry. The manager or owner of old, who knew and directed every detail of his enterprise, has become the modern industrialist who is above all else a specialist in business administration. Evidence for this transformation of the entrepreneur may be reviewed briefly.

In a report for 1792 Robert Owen states that it took him 6 weeks of careful observation to become thoroughly familiar with every detail of an enterprise employing 500 men.[2] An enterprise employing 500 men could be comprehended and managed at one time by a man of talent and experience. It is improbable that the same could be done today. A manager of a plant with 500 employees cannot be in daily touch with the details of the manufacturing process as Owen was. He will have various subordinates to supervise this

---

[2] G. D. H. Cole, *The Life of Robert Owen*, London, Macmillan & Co., 1930, p. 70.

process for him; also, this manager has lost most or all of his personal contacts with the workers in the plant. And although labor may be as efficient as it had been before this depersonalization of the employment relationship, this same efficiency is now obtained "at an increased cost in supervisory staff, complicated accounting methods, precise wage systems, liberal welfare provisions, checks and balances, scheduling and routine." [3] The point to emphasize is that bureaucratization of industry is not simply synonymous with the increasing size of the enterprise but with the growing complexity of its operation.

The bureaucratization of industry is, therefore, not simply the outcome of a recent development. In his analysis of the Boulton and Watt factory in 1775–1805 Erich Roll has described an elaborate system of keeping records, which was used as a basis of wage-determination, of cost-calculation, and of planning new methods of production. It is probable that this system was introduced when the firm passed from the original founders, who were in close contact with every operation of their enterprise, into the hands of the younger generation, who were not in touch with every operation and who, therefore, needed such a system of control.[4] At that time few firms were organized as efficiently as Boulton and Watt, but the case illustrates the fact that the bureaucratization of industry is not synonymous with the recent growth in the size of the large enterprises.

Corroborative evidence on this point is also contained in a study of American business leaders in the railroads and in the steel and textile industries, in the decade 1901–1910. The careers of 185 prominent industrialists were classified in terms of whether they had made their way in business by their own efforts exclusively, whether they had made their way in a family-owned enterprise, or whether they had risen through the ranks of an industrial bureaucracy; the results of the classification are shown in Table 12.1. These data make it apparent that prominent industrialists have had a bureaucratic career pattern at a relatively early time.[5]

Occupational statistics reflect this decline of the independent enterpriser and the increase of the "industrial bureaucrat," especially in the heavy industries. In the period 1910–1940 the number of independent industrial enterprisers declined from about 425,000 in 1910 to 390,000 in 1930 and 257,000 in 1940, in manufacturing, construction, and mining. In the same industries the number of managerial employees increased from 375,976 in 1910 to 769,749 in 1930 and 802,734 in 1940.[6]

The bureaucratization of industry has also profoundly altered the job environment of the lowest rung on the managerial ladder.[7] Until about a

[3] P. Sargant Florence, *The Logic of Industrial Organization*, London, Kegan Paul, Trench, Trubner & Co., 1933, pp. 159–160.

[4] Erich Roll, *An Early Experiment in Industrial Organization, Being a History of the Firm of Boulton and Watt, 1775–1805*, New York, Longmans, 1930, pp. 250–251.

[5] See William Miller, "The Business Elite in Business Bureaucracies," in William Miller (ed.), *Men in Business*, Cambridge, Mass., Harvard University Press, 1952, pp. 286–305.

[6] See Lewis Corey, "The Middle Class," *Antioch Review*, Spring, 1945, pp. 73, 77.

[7] See Chap. 13, by Melville Dalton, for a detailed discussion of the foreman's modern role in industry.

Table 12.1 American Business Leaders, by Type of Career and Date of Birth °

Type of career	Before 1841 %	1841–1850 %	1851–1860 %	After 1860 %
Independent	26	19	11	8
Family	22	24	42	36
Bureaucratic	52	57	47	56
Total cases (= 100%)	23	59	55	25

* William Miller, "The Business Elite in Business Bureaucracies," in William Miller (ed.), *Men in Business*, Cambridge, Mass., Harvard University Press, 1952, p. 291.

generation or two ago the foreman occupied a position of real importance in industry, especially with regard to the management of labor. In the majority of cases the foreman would recruit workers, he would train them on the job, he would supervise and discipline them, which included such handling of grievances as was permitted, and he would pay their wages on a time basis.[8]

Today the foreman performs the functions of the immediate supervisor of the workers, who is in effect the executive agent of various supervisory departments. And it is increasingly a matter of discretion for these departments whether or not they decide to consult the foreman. The following summary, based on a study of 100 companies which were sampled for the purpose of analyzing the *best* practices in American industry, illustrates this point clearly:

> *Hiring.* In two-thirds of the companies replying, the personnel department interviews and selects new employees, while the foreman has final say; but in one-third the foreman has no voice in hiring.
>
> *Discharge.* Foremen have some say in discharge, but only in one-tenth of all cases can they discharge without any consultation.
>
> *Pay Increases and Promotion.* These must almost always be approved by other authorities.
>
> *Discipline.* In only one-tenth of all cases do foremen have complete charge of discipline.
>
> *Grievances.* Discussion with the foreman is generally the first step in the grievance procedure, but the extent to which he settles grievances is not clear. A small sample in the automotive-aircraft industries shows that this may range from 45 to 80%.
>
> *Policy-making.* Only 20% of the companies replying held policy meetings with foremen.[9]

These findings make it apparent that the "average" foreman's responsibilities have remained, while his authority has been parceled out among the various supervisory departments. It is not surprising that this bureaucratization of

[8] See the detailed analysis of the rights and duties of subcontractors and foremen in England during the 19th century in William T. Delaney, "The Spirit and Structure of Labor Management in England, 1840–1940," Master's thesis, University of California (Berkeley), Chap. 3.

[9] Ernest Dale, *The Development of Foremen in Management,* American Management Association Research Report 7, 1945, p. 9.

supervisory functions has entailed inescapable tensions between the various departments performing these functions as well as tensions between these departments and the foremen. The latter have had to surrender their authority to the supervisory departments, but their responsibility for the execution of decisions has remained.

The changes in managerial functions which have grown out of the increasing division of labor within the plant and which are evident in the changing activities and career patterns of business executives and foremen are reflected also in the rise of "administrative overhead." A recent study of the rise of administrative personnel in American manufacturing industries since 1899 makes it clear that this rise has occurred throughout the economy (Table 12.2).

Table 12.2 **All Manufacturing Industries: Composition of Work Force in Administration and Production Categories, 1899–1947** [*]
(In Thousands)

Personnel	1899	1909	1923	1929	1937	1947
Administration	457	886	1,345	1,562	1,567	2,672
Production	4,605	6,392	8,261	8,427	8,602	12,010
Administration personnel, as per cent of production personnel	9.9%	13.9%	16.3%	18.5%	18.2%	22.2%

[*] Seymour Melman, "The Rise of Administrative Overhead in the Manufacturing Industries of the United States 1899–1947," *Oxford Economic Papers*, Vol. 3, No. 1 (January, 1951), p. 66.

A detailed examination reveals that this over-all increase in the ratio of administrative and production personnel is *not* systematically related to any one factor except size. Melman finds, somewhat paradoxically, that administrative cost as a proportion of production cost is lower in large than in small firms, despite the general upward trend in administrative personnel. His explanation is that all firms have shown an absolute increase in administrative overhead but that at any one time large firms as a group have a proportionately lower administrative overhead than small firms. This relative advantage of the larger firms is attributed to skill in organization. In the long run, however, all firms must anticipate an increase in administrative cost.

It should be added that a comparative study of administrative personnel in the manufacturing industries of other countries reveals similar trends, though it is noteworthy that the ratio of administrative as compared with productive personnel has increased more in the United States than in France, Germany, or England.[10] Melman's summary figures for a nationwide sample of manufacturing industries do not reveal the striking differences between industries,

[10] This comparative study cannot be reported here for reasons of space. But it should be mentioned that the economic meaning of this ratio depends in large part on the rate of capital investment. Industries which have a rate of increase in administrative overhead similar to that of the industries of the United States without, however, a similar increase in capial investment are obviously suffering from industrial bureaucratization far more than this country.

and it may therefore be helpful to cite a few sample figures from his data (Table 12.3).

Table 12.3 Sampled Manufacturing Industries: Administration and Production Personnel, 1899–1937 °

	Administration personnel as per cent of production personnel				
Industry	*1899*	*1909*	*1923*	*1929*	*1937*
Agricultural implements	22.1	18.6	19.8	18.3	20.6
Boots and shoes	6.2	8.1	10.8	11.0	8.5
Boxes, paper	6.3	9.1	13.6	14.4	16.1
Cash registers and business machines	15.9	23.8	23.2	36.9	37.7
Drugs and medicines	45.7	69.2	51.3	61.5	58.1
Electrical machinery	12.5	20.7	31.4	24.6	26.7
Explosives	17.3	12.3	33.6	38.2	44.4
Glass	4.5	5.3	8.6	9.7	11.5
Lighting equipment	12.8	20.1	22.9	20.6	19.2
Locomotives, not built in railroad shops	3.9	13.6	9.5	20.9	29.8
Meat packing, wholesale	15.3	20.1	24.8	22.8	29.2
Motor vehicles	13.1	13.3	11.5	14.8	16.9
Petroleum refining	10.0	19.3	24.1	35.6	45.3

* Seymour Melman, "The Rise of Administrative Overhead in the Manufacturing Industries of the United States 1899–1947," *Oxford Economic Papers*, 3 (January, 1951), p. 66.

These figures make it apparent that the over-all upward trend of administrative overhead covers a great diversity of particular developments. Although it is true that the average proportion of administration to production personnel has increased, there are significant differences between industries, and important fluctuations of this ratio have also occurred within an industry over time.

It may be useful to enumerate, in addition, some of the factors which are relevant for the interpretation of these statistics. Economically, it makes a great difference whether administrative personnel in industry increases together with a rapidly or a slowly expanding work force. That is to say, increasing administrative expenditures can be easily sustained in a rapidly expanding industry. Also, the increases of personnel in administration are accompanied by capital investments. Today, a given number of clerks can do a great deal more work than formerly, with the aid of various computing and multigraphing machines. As a group they also do a greater variety of work, owing to specialization and partial mechanization. However, neither the greater complexity of administrative work nor the various efforts at standardization and routinization can be measured by the number of clerks employed. The increase of administrative personnel is, therefore, only a proximate measure of bureaucratization.

Managerial Ideology and Bureaucracy

The general trend is in the direction of an increase in the complexity of managerial tasks. To assess the problems created by this trend, it is not sufficient, for example, to describe how the functions of hiring and discharge, of administering an equitable wage structure, and of processing grievances and disciplining workers have become the special tasks of separate departments. In order to understand the modern problems of management, we must realize that this separation of functions has created for all ranks of management an ambiguity which is in many respects similar to, though it is not so intense as, that of the foreman. The over-all managerial problem has become more complex because each group of management specialists will tend to view the "interests of the enterprise" in terms which are compatible with the survival and the increase of its special function. That is, each group will have a trained capacity for its own function and a "trained incapacity" to see its relation to the whole.

The problem of industrial management is to subdivide, as well as to coordinate, the tasks of administration and production and then to maximize the efficiency of each operation. In so doing it employs specialists, and each group of specialists must exercise considerable discretion in order to get the work done. That is to say, with each step toward specialization the centrifugal tendencies and, hence, the coordinating tasks of central management increase. Bureaucratization has accompanied the whole development of industry, but it has increased more rapidly since the inception of scientific management in the 1890's. The major development of trade-unions has occurred during the same period. If we consider these parallel changes it becomes apparent that the greater complexity of the managerial task has consisted in the need for intramanagerial coordination at a time when managerial leadership was challenged by the organizing drives of trade-unions as well as by the ideological attacks of the muckrakers. Hence the ideology of business leaders, their justification of the authority they exercise and of the power they hold, has gradually assumed a double function: (1) to demonstrate that the authority and power of the industrial leader is legitimate and (2) to aid the specific job of managerial coordination.

Until recently the ideologies of the industrial leaders did not serve this double function. In the past their leadership was justified by a reiteration of time-tested shibboleths which would make clear what was already self-evident to all but the most die-hard radicals. Success is virtue, poverty is sin, and both result from the effort or indolence of the individual. Together with this belief went the idea that every use made of property was beneficial to the social welfare, as long as it resulted in an increase of wealth. These ideas, which justified the authority and power of the industrial leaders, established a goal in life for everyone. The tacit assumption was that in the prevailing economic order the chances of each "to get to the top" were the same. Hence the success of the industrial leader was itself the token of his proved superiority in a struggle between equals. To question this was to bar the way of those who would succeed after him.

These ideas have never really died; there is much contemporary evidence to show that the beliefs of industrial leaders have remained essentially the same. Successful industrialists as a group have always tended to express views which ranged from the belief that their virtue had been proved by their works and that their responsibilities were commensurate with their wealth to the assertion that their eminence was self-evident and that their privileges could not be questioned. They would speak with Andrew Carnegie of the "trusteeship of wealth" and point to their benevolent relations to their employees, their philanthropic activities, and their great contributions to the nation's wealth as evidence of their worth. Others would think of themselves as "Christian men to whom God in his infinite wisdom has given the control of the property interests of the country." Nor can we dismiss the possibility that some of these industrial giants would say the first and think the second.

Fifty years later the same opinions are expressed, albeit in modern dress. Alfred P. Sloan [11] writes:

> . . . those charged with great industrial responsibility must become industrial statesmen. . . . Industrial management must expand its horizon of responsibility. It must recognize that it can no longer confine its activities to the mere production of goods and services. It must consider the impact of its operations on the economy as a whole in relation to the social and economic welfare of the entire community.

On the other hand, Tom Girdler [12] has written of his role in the company town which he had helped to develop:

> In fact I suppose I was a sort of political boss. Certainly I had considerable power in politics without responsibility to "the people." But who were the people in question? An overwhelming majority of them were the men for whom the company aspired to make Woodlawn the best steel town in the world . . . What did it matter if the taxes were soundly spent? What did it matter if Woodlawn had just about the best school system in Pennsylvania? What did it matter if there were no slums, no graft, no patronage, no gambling houses, no brothels? What did it matter if it was a clean town?

If all these wonderful things were done by the company for the people of Woodlawn, what did it matter that the company and its managers were not responsible to the people? As an Episcopalian vestry man, Girdler could also speak of Christian men who, by the grace of God, controlled the property interests of the community on behalf of the people.

Businessmen express themselves with the intention of demonstrating statesmanship and intransigence, then as now.[13] Yet even the celebration of the industrial leader has had to accommodate, albeit tardily, the Puritan

---

[11] Alfred P. Sloan, *Adventures of a White-collar Man,* New York, Doubleday, 1941, p. 145.

[12] Tom Girdler, *Boot Straps,* New York, Scribner, 1943, p. 177.

[13] The belief in progress and individual success through effort has not changed basically for the last century and a half, though it is possible to note a gradual secularization. There is little evidence of God in the praise of "work and still more work [by which] we capitalize our unlimited opportunities . . ." (Alfred P. Sloan). This secularization of the Puritan ideology of individual success has been traced by A. W. Griswold, "The American Gospel of Success," Doctor's dissertation, Yale University, 1933.

virtues of hard work, frugality, and unremitting effort to the qualities useful in a bureaucratic career. As the size and bureaucratization of business increased, this ideological accommodation could no longer be accomplished on the model of the Horatio Alger story. Of course, the idea of success as a reward of virtue is as much in evidence today as it was 100 years ago. But the celebration of the industrial leader can no longer suffice; it is accompanied today by a celebration of the organization and of the opportunities it has to offer. When A. P. Sloan writes that "the corporation [is] a pyramid of opportunities from the bottom to the top with thousands of chances for advancement" he refers to the promise of a bureaucratic career not to the earlier image of the individual enterpriser. And when he adds that "only capacity limited any worker's chance to improve his own position," [14] he simply ignores the fact that the methods of promotion themselves are bureaucratized, that they are regarded as a legitimate object of collective-bargaining strategies between union and management, and that under these circumstances minimum rather than maximum capacity is very often a sufficient basis for promotion. At any rate, the idea of thousands of chances for promotion is different from the idea of individual success. Outstanding industrial leaders of today will reflect this difference in their attempts to define the image of success in an era of bureaucratization.

It is important to recognize that today managerial ideology performs a second function. While it is still designed to inspire confidence in the leaders of industry, it should also aid modern managers to achieve effective coordination within their enterprises, which is today a far more difficult task than it was formerly. There is a literature of advice to the ambitious young man which has accompanied the development of industry. In this literature the hero cult of the industrial leader has been abandoned gradually, and advice well suited to the industrial bureaucrat has taken its place.[15] Hero cult and advice to the industrial bureaucrat involve partly imcompatible themes. The qualities of ruthlessness and competitive drive, while appropriate for the "tycoon," are ill suited for his managerial employees. This does not mean that these qualities are no longer useful but that they no longer provide a workable rationale for the majority of industrial managers.[16]

[14] Sloan, *op. cit.*, p. 153.

[15] We speak here of intellectual trends and do not imply that such trends occur by design. On the other hand, the problems of large-scale industry are real problems, and any intellectualized concern with them will have meaning in the context of these problems, even if they are deliberately ignored. If, for example, industrial leaders are praised today in the same manner as they were in the 1870's, it would indicate an ideological distortion of the present situation, when the opportunities for social mobility consist, for the most part, in climbing the bureaucratic ladder in industry.

[16] And it is possible that the ideology of the industrial bureaucrats, which was well summed up in Dale Carnegie's title *How to Win Friends and Influence People,* has affected the tycoon to the extent of changing his manners. See the suggestive comments on this point in David Riesman, *The Lonely Crowd,* New Haven, Conn., Yale University Press, 1950, esp. pp. 166–174, 236–239. Riesman posits a major change in character from the "inner-directed" personality of the "captains of industry" to the "other-directed" personality of the industrial bureaucrat, but I question whether one is warranted in inferring changes in "social character" from ideological and institutional trends. I question in particular whether white-collar workers of 1870 were inner-directed or whether industrial leaders of today are other-directed compared with their respective opposite numbers.

It may be useful to put formulations of these two themes side by side. The classic text of the individual enterpriser is *Self-help with Illustrations of Character, Conduct and Perseverance,* written by Samuel Smiles in 1859 and copied interminably ever since. Its purpose was,

> . . . to re-inculcate these old-fashioned but wholesome lessons . . . that youth must work in order to enjoy—that nothing creditable can be accomplished without application and diligence—that the student must not be daunted by difficulties, but conquer them by patience and perseverance—and that, above all, he must seek elevation of character, without which capacity is worthless and worldly success is naught.[17]

The classic text of the industrial bureaucrat is *Public Speaking and Influencing Men in Business,* written by Dale Carnegie in 1926 and used as the "official text" by such organizations as the New York Telephone Company, the American Institute of Banking, the YMCA schools, the National Institute of Credit, and others.[18] Though there is no single statement of purpose which can be cited, the following summary statement will suffice: "We have only four contacts with people. We are evaluated and classified by four things: by what we do, by how we look, by what we say, and how we say it." [19] In his foreword to this book Lowell Thomas [20] has written a testimonial to Dale Carnegie which gives the gist of this and many similar books with admirable clarity:

> Carnegie started at first to conduct merely a course in public speaking: but the students who came were businessmen. Many of them hadn't seen the inside of a class room in thirty years. Most of them were paying their tuition on the installment plan. They wanted results; and they wanted them quick— results that they could use the next day in business interviews and in speaking before groups.
> So he was forced to be swift and practical. Consequently, he has developed a system of training that is unique—a striking combination of Public Speaking, Salesmanship, Human Relationship, Personality Development and Applied Psychology. . . . Dale Carnegie . . . has created one of the most significant movements in adult education.

[17] Samuel Smiles, *Self-help* . . . , Chicago, Belford, Clarke and Co., 1881, p. vii (from the preface to the second edition, in which Smiles restated his major purpose, as he saw it, in response to the criticism which the book had received).

[18] A new version of this book was published in 1936 under the title *How to Win Friends and Influence People.* It has sold a total of 4 million copies.

[19] Dale Carnegie, *Public Speaking and Influencing Men in Business,* New York, Association Press, 1938, p. 509. Carnegie writes as follows: "I once asked a group of American businessmen in Paris to talk on *How to Succeed.* Most of them praised the homely virtues, preached at, lectured to, and bored their hearers. . . . So I halted this class and said something like this: 'We don't want to be lectured to. No one enjoys that. Remember you must be entertaining or we will pay no attention whatever to what you are saying. Also remember that one of the most interesting things in the world is sublimated, glorified gossip. So tell us the stories of two men you have known. Tell why one succeeded and why the other failed. We will gladly listen to that, remember it and possibly profit by it.' " *Ibid.,* p. 429. The shift from the praise of virtue to the description of "how to succeed" is well illustrated here, and if this passage is taken together with the one quoted in the text, it becomes clear that the techniques of "human relations" have superseded the idea of an emulation of virtues.

[20] Lowell Thomas, "Introduction," in Carnegie, *op. cit.,* p. x.

This new ideology of personality salesmanship appeared to put within reach of the average person the means by which to climb the ladder to success. No doubt this accounts for its popularity. But it should be added that its public acceptance implied a prior disillusion with the more old-fashioned methods of achieving success. The bureaucratization of modern industry has obviously increased the number of steps from the bottom to the top at the same time that it has made the Puritan virtues largely obsolete. It is probable, then, that the techniques of personality salesmanship became popular when the ideal of individual entrepreneurship ceased to be synonymous with success, while the image of a career of promotions from lower to higher positions became of greater significance. From the standpoint of the individual these techniques became a means of career advancement; from the standpoint of management they seemed to facilitate the coordination of a growing and increasingly specialized staff. In the context of American society this new ideology reflected the increasing importance of the service trades as well as the growing demand for skill in personnel relations.[21]

These considerations place the human-relations approach to the problems of labor management in a historical perspective. Attention to human relations has arisen out of the managerial problems incident to the bureaucratization of industry. It has also arisen out of the discrepancy between a people's continued desire for success and the increasing disutility of the Puritan virtues or of the tenets of Darwinian morality. But whatever their origins, the "personality cult" as well as the more sophisticated philosophies of personnel management have helped to make more ambiguous the position of the industrial manager. In giving orders to his subordinates in the past, the manager could claim to derive his authority from the rights of ownership conferred on him. For a long time the managerial employee had represented the "heroic entrepreneur," and he had justified his own actions by the right which success had bestowed upon him. But with the dispersion of ownership this justification became increasingly tenuous. Strictly speaking, the old ideology of success no longer applied to the managers since theirs was a bureaucratic, not an entrepreneurial, success. As the human-relations approach is extended downward from the office staff to the work force, managers come to attenuate their tough-minded conception of authority. But in so doing they are never single-minded. Their careers are often inspired by the older belief in the self-made man, though this belief is more and more at variance with their own experience in industry. In asserting their authority over subordinates as if they were the successful entrepreneurs of old, they come into conflict with the bureaucratic reality of their own careers. Yet if they adjust their beliefs to that reality, then they are faced with the dilemma of exercising authority while they deny the traditional claims which had hitherto justified this authority.[22]

[21] In this context it would appear as if the "New Thought" movement, which Griswold has analyzed, is *not* the lineal descendant of the "gospel of success," which may be identified with the Puritan tradition and the Darwinian creed of the Gilded Age. The outstanding difference between New Thought and "self-improvement" as well as the personality cult is that the first remained a cultist belief, while the second called for action and promised success if the lessons had been learned well.

[22] This ideological ambiguity is not confined to the managers of industry. In so far as salaried employees continue to believe in the free-enterprise system, they will tend to

It is at this point that managers are divided today in their attitudes toward their employees and toward their own exercise of authority. Many continue to believe in the heroic entrepreneur whose success is justification in itself, and they consequently resist the "tender-minded" approach to human relations in industry. They also resist recognition of the fact that the industrial environment has changed. Others have begun to reformulate the older statements of "business statesmanship" and "business responsibility" in keeping with the realities of industry in an era of bureaucratization. But in their attempts to do so they have had to demonstrate the self-evident truths once more that the economy provides ample opportunities, given drive and talent, and that those who succeed deserve to do so and provide a model to be followed. To develop an ideology along these lines by advertising the techniques of personality salesmanship and by celebrating the career opportunities of an industrial bureaucracy implies an interest in industrial peace, for these techniques and opportunities are beside the point under conditions of conflict. The new ideology is less combative than the old; but it is also insufficient because its appeals are more readily applicable to the salaried employee than to the industrial worker. The idea that all employees are members of "one big happy family" is a case in point, for the efforts to make this idea meaningful to the workers frequently take the form of personalizing an impersonal employment relationship. Perhaps this is appropriate for the managerial and ideological coordination of the salaried employees. It is, moreover, not surprising that the idea of the "family of employers and employees" often becomes the fighting creed of hard-pressed executives who seek to solidify their enterprises against the competing appeals of the trade-unions. But there is an element of cant in this approach which does not make it a promising foundation for a new ideology as long as democratic institutions prevail. Perhaps Horatio Alger is so reluctant to pass into limbo because his image implied an idealistic message. Perhaps it is the absence of such a message which makes the appeal to employees as members of a family so questionable. The ideological rationale of an economic order should have a positive meaning for everyone. The fact is that in this era of bureaucratization the industrialist does not have a fighting creed.

---

ignore their own dependent status and bureaucratic careers, which are the reverse of both freedom and enterprise (in the conventional economic meaning of these terms). Ideas are not abandoned readily under the pressure of circumstances. Indeed, there is some evidence to show that modifications of the ideal of individual success survive today among groups whose chances of individual success are minimal. Cf. Reinhard Bendix, "A Study of Managerial Ideologies, as It Bears on Drucker's Thesis," paper read before the American Sociological Society, Atlantic City, N.J., Sept. 3, 1952.

CHAPTER 13 THE ROLE OF SUPERVISION

Melville Dalton   *University of California (Los Angeles)*

THE great variation in size, character of product, and nature of technology in American industry is matched by the diverse structure of its supervisory forces. Industrial plants may range in size from the small owner-manager shop with one supervisor and a half-dozen employees to plants with from 1,500 to 3,000 supervisors over from 20,000 to 40,000 employees. In the small plant there may be only one or two strata of supervisors as against five to ten in larger plants. And in giant corporations consisting of numerous units under a central office the strata of supervisors may run to fifteen or more from the top officer to the lowest foreman.

Structure and Function

There is also much variation in the number and kinds of specialized organizations inside the ranks of management. In all supervisory hierarchies, however, the function of officials is presumed to contribute in some way to the productive and economic goals of the organization, whether the object of responsibility be care and control of material equipment, productive processes, or employees. Each officer has a specific status, a defined authority, and a delimited function that is important for production and that is presumably relevant to his special abilities.

Adding to the difficulty of realistically describing the functions of supervision is (1) the lack of standardization of titles, (2) the frequent variations in function of positions with similar titles because of differences peculiar to the technology or the industry, and (3) the fact that functions may change without change in title, as when officers may move (for uncertain periods) about the plant with long delays in title change and because change in title may mean embarrassing salary revisions.

In general those supervisors directly in charge of production workers are called "foremen." In the larger plants foremen have immediate superiors usually called "general foremen" or "general supervisors." Where a number of large departments exist in a single plant, each may be headed by a departmental superintendent. And when a number of departments have closely interlocking functions, the departments may be grouped to form a division, with the superintendents under the authority of a divisional superintendent. These superintendents usually report to the "general superintendent," "general manager," or "plant manager." All these officers may have assistants with varying functions and amounts of official authority.

The Foreman

Since in both larger and smaller organizations the mediating link between supervisory and production employees is the first-line foreman, the focus here will be chiefly on this officer and the conflict surrounding him in his various roles. The aim is to depict him as he seeks to reconcile the claims made on him from above and from below and as he attempts to win certain ends for himself. Any analysis of his role in industrial conflict must consider at least his behavior (1) as a communicator and interpreter of company policy, (2) as an agent in collective bargaining, and (3) as an individual working out his career. These points will be discussed in order and followed by an analysis.

The Foreman as Communicator and Interpreter. Officially the foreman carries out the wishes of his superiors and seeks to expedite production. Procedures vary with the plant and industry, but oral and written orders are passed to him to be translated into action. In some plants he is equipped with a loose-leaf manual which contains official policy as a guide for his conduct and which often interprets the labor agreement item by item. He also receives periodically revised booklets on general plant and safety rules, the contents of which he conveys to employees.

However, the character of work relations is often such that interpretation must perforce be extremely loose. This can be shown by brief descriptions of common practices in the areas of work scheduling, safety rules, and accident reporting.

In scheduling orders production-planning staffs are guided mainly by deadlines agreed on with the customer rather than by the convenience of production employees and their foremen. When a sequence of orders is submitted to the foreman, he and his men are expected to follow it.

But the foreman is frequently coerced by his subordinates into altering the production schedule. The writer has repeatedly seen this done as a means of adjusting the conflicting interests of a supervisor and his employees.[1] In one case some of the orders on a production line paid more than others because amount of pay varied with the properties of the product. Under pressures from the work group, which could restrict as a unit without any individual's receiving blame, the foreman of the unit allowed the higher-paying orders to be processed first. This naturally leads to a backlog of lower-paying orders (though *total* production is increased) and snarls the order schedule, which brings criticism on the foreman. However, it should be noted that his return from the concession usually reduces maintenance costs, for when breakdowns occur, the foreman lays a counterclaim on production workers to "pitch in and help" maintenance employees (forbidden by rules) get the equipment running again as soon as possible.

[1] Where sources are not given, data are drawn from the author's experience in industry, some aspects of which have been reported elsewhere. See "Conflicts between Managerial Staff and Line Officers," *American Sociological Review,* June, 1950, pp. 342–351; "Unofficial Union-Management Relations," *ibid.,* October, 1950, pp. 611–619; "Informal Factors in Career Achievement," *American Journal of Sociology,* March, 1951, pp. 407–415; and "The Industrial 'Rate-buster': A Characterization," *Applied Anthropology,* Winter, 1948, pp. 5–18.

Reverberations of this working adjustment may also bring conflict between production and maintenance supervisors (as well as among shifts of workers) when production foremen, eager to make a good showing and responsive to pressures of workmen running a series of higher-paying orders, insist on only a "patch-up" repair of broken equipment that may not last longer than the end of the current turn.

Motivated in part by a wish to reward individual workers who have helped him in the past (and on whom he may need to rely again), the foreman may, for example, also contradict company policy by moving a job to a less efficient and more costly position than where it is usually done.[2]

Most industrial concerns have strict policies concerning safety. Safety officials analyze each accident with respect to persons and situations "at fault" and to rules that may have been broken. Written descriptions of the accident are prepared and copies passed to all departments for foremen to discuss with workmen. In some cases workmen must read the descriptions and sign forms to that effect, which usually becomes only a ritual. Interdepartmental rivalry to have perfect safety records is encouraged. Safety meetings are held regularly. Precautions are taken against accidents by supplying workmen with safety equipment and making failure to use it a cause for "disciplining." Warning signs are posted throughout the plant, and safety inspectors make periodic visits and reports on conditions in the various departments. Often, in more than one language, rules prohibit behavior regarded as physically dangerous to oneself or others. Often statements in the foreman's manual imply that a relation exists between his safety record and his success in the organization.

Yet the pressure from higher officers for increased production is so great that often the only shutdown is a breakdown. Hence maintenance workers are frequently required to do repair work on machinery containing moving parts, which is forbidden. Again, rather than wait for an electrician, pipe fitter, or other maintenance specialist to arrive, as required by rules, the production workman may voluntarily with the foreman's knowledge—or involuntarily at his request—make the repair. In case of injury the foreman is responsible. Sometimes his immediate superior knows and accepts his expedient evasion of rules but officially censures him only in case of accident or detection by higher management. And in some cases even higher managers may give silent approval.

Space prevents discussion of cases, but in a similar way safety rules covering the handling of chemicals in lines and containers and of steam, air, and gas under pressure are also evaded. Production demands, discrepancies between theory and plant conditions, outdated rules, indifference, strict and loose interpretation of rules by different supervisors in the line department, inconvenience in following the rule, etc., may all be important factors in overstepping regulations. But the foreman usually has knowledge of conditions, and the situation frequently forces him to participate.

From what has been said about safety policy, it is obvious that the foreman will seek to avoid accidents and certainly will wish to escape the condemnation of a "lost-time" case. This last concern is so great in some instances

---

[2] See "Unofficial Union-Management Relations," p. 617; "The Industrial 'Rate-buster': A Characterization," p. 16.

that the foreman will suffer monetary loss and risk dismissal to conceal an accident.

When an accident cannot be hidden, in writing his report the foreman will seek to reduce his own involvement to the minimum. He cannot hope to escape all blame, for years of rule refinement, growing out of hundreds of accidents and many lawsuits, have made infinitesimal the number of mishaps that a higher manager could not show "as due to not following the rules." Furthermore, middle managers who fear the criticism of higher officers may refuse to accept logical proof that an accident was unavoidable. The foreman who gets on well with his superiors understands that he must become lightheartedly inured to absorbing blame from higher managers that is not necessarily motivated by malice.

The Foreman in Collective Bargaining. Practice varies, but labor contracts usually provide that the first step of the grievance procedure shall be at the level of the foreman. Failing of settlement there, the grievance moves to the departmental superintendent and then to higher levels until solved. For many reasons, such as foreman ignorance of management policy,[3] the wish of the union to bypass the foreman, the foreman's anger at having his decisions revoked by higher supervision, etc., the first step of the grievance procedure in practice often omits the foreman.

The last point will be discussed later in another connection, but here it should be noted that higher reversal of the foreman's decisions often induces behavior important for grievance procedure. At least two reactions of the foreman are noteworthy. One is the refusal to have anything to do with official grievances and to pass them up the line for higher officers to handle. Another is to initiate informal activities with the shop steward or grievance committeeman that will tend to make formal grievances unnecessary.

In the first of these actions the foremen typically seeks to magnify his shrinking authority. Under the guise of devotion to plant rules, he will interpret safety regulations strictly, especially where "troublesome" workmen are concerned. He will enforce the rule (customarily evaded) that workmen with minor lacerations or colds go to the hospital at once. And he will check to see that they report for daily dressings until officially released by the hospital. Workmen in large plants dislike waiting in line at the hospital, and they charge that wounds are dressed "till the scars disappear." Workmen with colds dislike going to the hospital, for there is always danger of being discovered with above normal temperature and thus of losing time by being sent home. After lost-time illness workmen must also report to the hospital for final checkup and permission to return to work, which may mean additional loss of time if they are still running a temperature. In some cases an understanding physician will advise a workman to sip a glass of cold milk just before leaving home to report for a temperature reading so that his temperature will appear normal.

Seeking to restore his waning influence, this same foreman will hold workmen on the job to the last minute and will tolerate no departures from card-punching rules, no tardiness, etc. He will withhold favors from workmen who trouble him and will seek to make job-skill tests (for promotion) as difficult

[3] J. Carl Cabe, *Foreman's Unions,* University of Illinois Bureau of Economic and Business Research Bulletin 65, 1947, pp. 11–13.

as possible and to postpone giving them as long as he can. Where some foremen are known to be relatively lax, it is obvious that this contrary use of rules to bolster status will stimulate conflict.

The second type of foreman, who is usually younger and has risen in the atmosphere of unionism, is prepared to bargain privately and without benefit of contractual provisions. He may have ambivalent feelings toward the union, but to some extent he accepts and apes the behavior of his superiors. That is, he does what is needed to survive and to ease conflict situations with minimum surrender of his psychological integrity.

For example, when demands are made on him by a grievance officer or shop steward, the granting of which would jeopardize him with higher management, he may reply with counterclaims rather than accede to, or refuse, the requests made. This puts the union officer in the position of having to consider the effects of commitments that may leak out to other departments,[4] and it frequently draws him to the foreman as one, like himself, who is "on the spot" and must "make a deal." Arrangements may cover schedules, steps in job reclassification, work distribution, unique favors, etc. The effect is to relieve current pressures and tensions and to develop skill in moving in areas uncharted by rules. Skill in sizing up developing situations and in seizing what is appropriate for his interest and protection is characteristic of this foreman. However, there are usually individuals (supervisory and/or nonsupervisory) involved in this bargaining who become uneasy and object to pragmatic arrangements, which tends to aggravate existing conflict. When leaks occur, friction may result inside the union, between strata of management, and, of course, between some members of the union and management since each, needing a defense, will name the other as the "cause" of the problem. In many cases "wildcat" strikes are due to situations too dynamic to be encompassed either by the intentionally ambiguous phrases of the contract or by attempts at covert adjustments.

Factors in Compromise of Foreman Leadership. The preceding sketch of the tensions and accommodations in which the foreman is caught will indicate some of the influences on his leadership and upward orientation. The nature of this leadership comes to be a reflection of his personal characteristics rather than a complex of behavior that is similar from one foreman to another.

Officially, his functions as a leader will at the minimum consist of (1) maintaining harmony in the work group, which includes getting along with the union, (2) keeping production at a high level with low cost of operation, (3) setting a good safety record, (4) cooperating with other departments, (5) keeping superiors informed, and (6) in general carrying out changing policies as they are given to him from day to day. Higher management will of course check his grievance, cost, and safety records and will learn how well he cooperates with production-planning and maintenance officers.

In trying to meet these expectations while working out his career and seeking to please those with power to promote him, the foreman, as was shown, often feels obliged to engage in behavior that interferes with his function as a leader and to depart from official procedures.

In terms of opportunity to advance to higher positions in his organization, by means of some fixed and official procedure, there seems to be justification

---

[4] See "Unofficial Union-Management Relations."

for the foreman's anxiety about his future.[5] Foremen may not have access to promotional statistics in the organization, but they are aware of who is selected and promoted. In seeking to explain their own slowness or failure in advancing, they fantasy a great deal concerning personal factors that may aid them in winning recognition. Hiding unacceptable incidents has been referred to as a negative means of impressing superiors. Falsification of reports is another. The common positive device is to copy the social characteristics of higher management. Foremen are not unique in sensing that attitudes and social attributes which their superiors find attractive outside the plant may also be appealing in the plant. Hence, despite ambivalences, many foremen seemingly adopt the attitudes of superiors and show verbal enthusiasm for favored political views, candidates, etc. This mask of congeniality is variously reflected. Only approved newspapers are carried into the plant. Rejected surnames are often changed. And in some cases radical changes in religious affiliation occur. Efforts are made to enter secret societies and other organizations to which higher managers belong. The successful display their insignia and badges of membership. Possession of these symbols and limited extraplant association with higher managers compensate to some extent for lack of status in the plant and *may* assist in winning status.

On the job, as noted, the foreman is often unable to coordinate production by official means and is reduced to bargaining with the union and covertly rewarding [6] those of the work group who will aid him in his dilemma. Where the foreman is unable to achieve satisfactory acceptance or to meet expectations passably, he is likely to revile his immediate superior and seek to cause him trouble. Lower supervisors are prone to feel that the officer just above them is responsible for their frustration and to regard managers two and three times removed (with whom they have few contacts) incapable of the blameworthy conduct they attribute to close superiors. Among foremen remarks are common that "if the big bosses knew what was going on, there would be a lot of people on the way out." Inability to alter the situation and fear of hidden reprisals sometimes prompt foremen to write anonymous letters to higher supervisors giving details of work relations, etc., that in the usual communication may be screened by intervening officers. And in some plants, of course, foremen turn to unionism.

Thus the foreman becomes preoccupied with much more than official procedures. A great deal of his time and thought is given to things quite apart from the goals of the organization. His function as a leader frequently becomes subordinate to his struggle for security and status. As has often been said, he becomes a "man in the middle" or a "marginal man." His status dilemma reaches the ultimate (1) where he is on hourly pay and punches a time card, (2) where minor personnel reorganization may drop him to the work level, and (3) where he stands to lose his seniority in the union and has alienated the work

---

[5] The literature is rich with comment on the foreman's insecurity. For example, see F. J. Roethlisberger, "The Foreman: Master and Victim of Double Talk," *Harvard Business Review,* 23 (1944–1945), 283–298; Cabe, *op. cit.;* and Donald E. Wray, "Marginal Men of Industry: The Foremen," *American Journal of Sociology,* 54 (January, 1949), 298–301.

[6] Cf. "Unofficial Union-Management Relations," p. 617.

group he supervises. Having to share blame for failures in the productive process, he must urge the policy of management on subordinates who are aware of his impotence. He must check situations that will trouble his superiors but report problems before they become too large for him to control.

Analysis

The role of staff organizations and the union in diminishing the foreman's status is well known.[7] However, his continuing place on the fringe of management is more difficult to analyze.

One explanation of his personal conflict is that he is expected to share the responsibility for decisions which he had no part in making.[8] Certainly he resents his trifling control over plant affairs. And thus, consciously or not, he often initiates conflict that may affect the total organization. A related view is that he lacks the prerogatives of management and suffers from pressures "to make him a salesman of management ideas." [9] Another view is that the foreman has been so shackled by formal rules that he no longer has the initiative or freedom to make any significant judgments of his own and consequently is unable to participate in the free and easy relationships with his employees and superiors that is regarded as essential for cooperative effort. He is caught between management's wish for greater efficiency and the work group's resistance and must "cooperate" with both.[10]

These views deal in the main with the foreman's condition and its effect on managerial structure. However, there is little recognition of the fact that other members of management are also involved in contradictory situations. This aspect of managerial conflict can be treated only superficially here. But the milieu of contradictions in which departmental superintendents often function in the larger plants may be noted as an example. This officer must repeatedly content himself with only *appearing* to meet the complex of official expectations. Then, too, he finds himself competing with other department heads to get increased operating allowances and favored consideration for his department. If he expects their cooperation, he must constantly give ear to the personal and career claims of supervisory subordinates. Since top management is disposed to regard the union somewhat as an ally in keeping him "on his toes," he must work out accommodations with the union that offer the least threat to his other goals. He must be alert to avoid setting precedents in his relations with staff organizations that can bring him trouble with top management. In plants that are but units subject to distant central offices, the departmental superintendent absorbs much of the vague fear that filters down through uneasy top local managers. And not least, he, like the higher officers of many organizations, is concerned about his career, which usually involves maintaining a larger place in the community than the first-line foreman holds.

----

[7] For example, see Delbert C. Miller and William H. Form, *Industrial Sociology,* New York, Harper, 1950, p. 211.

[8] Wray, *op. cit.*

[9] Miller and Form, *op. cit.,* p. 212.

[10] Roethlisberger, *op. cit.,* pp. 290–293. Cabe (*op. cit.,* pp. 15–16) implies that foremen want *more* training and guidance in the form of specified duties, responsibilities, etc.

The differences in kind and degree of tension in which foremen and higher officers move must be ignored here. The significant difference for conflict in supervision is that foremen and higher managers seem to have a differing capacity to make accommodations and to deal pragmatically with situations, which results in a different orientation to the problems of supervision. The attitudinal dissimilarity between first-line and higher supervisors is suggested by their verbal attacks on each other and by their opposing interpretations of formal rules. Excepting those cases in which individuals may climb chiefly by means of personal relations, the indications are that foremen who rise to higher positions either have or develop a code similar to that of their superiors.

Significance of Formal Rules. In their operation of a plant higher managers must of necessity consider many variables and contradictory factors, such as (1) the market and new techniques in relation to the economic and production goals of the firm, (2) public relations and the activities of competitors, (3) union-management problems in relation to ideal efficiency, and (4) the selection and advancement of new personnel. Hence they frequently have to make promises and give directives which they judge and hope will, but may not, work.[11] They lay down rules as general guides, usually with the tacit understanding that rules may be departed from [12] in achieving plant goals, but deviation resulting in hindrance of goals is unacceptable.

Caught between the plant goals and the demands of the situation, the executive almost of necessity equates justice with pragmatic action. His decisions are made in terms of settling those issues he feels are most significant and urgent. Consequently he resents the inability of foremen to "understand," and this is why he stresses "flexibility." Such phrases as "departing from principle but returning later in clearing up problems," and "two and two sometimes add up to five, but that's close enough" are common among executives.

But the older foreman, especially, feels that simple, unvarying principles should govern the relations between him and his superiors. If his services are valued, he expects that protection of his interests and the flow of rewards to him will be constant and unambiguous. The case of an aging foreman who sent a workman home for repeated tardiness reveals the typical barrier between lower and upper supervision. As was customary with him, the workman filed a grievance (which bypassed the foreman) with the superintendent, who sent the man back to his job. According to the foreman,

> I went over to O'Brien's [the superintendent's] office to find out why he had overruled me. He handed me a line of salve about "having to do it." Said it "was a small item, after all" and that he "might want a big favor from the union sometime in the future." He said, "We have to trade back and forth. Sometimes we give in; sometimes they give in. That's why we never have any big

[11] Peter F. Drucker comments on the problem in management of balancing adherence to principles with adjustment to changing conditions. See his *Concept of the Corporation,* New York, John Day, 1946.

[12] In the context of executive responsibility C. I. Barnard notes (1) that responsibility and "moral complexity" correlate, (2) that executives must "create moral codes" for others in the organization, and (3) that all leaders caught between purpose and environment are likely in time to become insincere. See his *Functions of the Executive,* Cambridge, Mass., Harvard University Press, 1945, pp. 272–284.

trouble!" Then he said he might have to reverse some of my decisions again sometime, but if he did, not to get sore about it, because he wouldn't mean no offense by it. Well, damn that noise! If O'Brien wants to make me look like a fool every time I make a decision, why, by God, he can make all the decisions. You know, two can play that game. I can give the boys [workers] every damn thing he can give them. Then when they come up with a big one that I know damn well he can't give them, I'll tell 'em to take it up to him.

These sentiments indicate why some executives regard the foreman as unsophisticated. Without clearly verbalizing it, they feel that his ideas of propriety in managerial behavior fail to cover the practical needs of administration, and they resent his failure to be flexible.

The executive, too, suffers in varying degrees from indications of disapproval that reach him, but apparently such factors as greater education, wider social experience, and a larger place in the plant and community assist in raising his potential for accommodation beyond that of the foreman with his narrower perspective. In the dynamic organizations of today successful administration—with minimum personal distress—probably correlates with ability to view unavoidable conflict situations pragmatically.[13] Though possibly camouflaged and cemented with fictions, those decisions will best fit the organization's functional code—and hence have truth and merit—which aid the firm's growth and continuance in competition with others.

Since fictions are an essential nucleus of their organizations, higher managers do not want departures pointed out and denounced. Hence, given the situations that prevail, the ideal foreman will be able to conform to organizational fictions and will also (1) be able to sense, without being told, when deviation from the fictions must be made, (2) have understanding of what problems can be taken to a superior for discussion and which ones must be settled expediently without reference to superiors, (3) have ability to detect developing trouble spots and protect superiors without action that would have repercussions, and (4) see that his superiors want loyalty, which will frequently mean silent bearing of blame for the undesirable effects of action unavoidably taken by superiors.

Supervision and Industrial Relations

As indicated in the above discussion, management can hardly be regarded as a closely knit unitary group. Too often the size and functional complexity of the managerial hierarchy increase the difficulty of communication, allow hard-pressed officers to evade expectations, and in some cases even offer opportunity for achieving officially unacceptable personal aims.

Since numerous officers of the union are perforce engaged in accommodative relations with members of management, they readily learn of conflicts inside management and (especially when their own commitments allow it and

---

[13] This behavior is apparently widespread. Cabe (*op. cit.*, p. 15) does not elucidate, but his statement that many of the foremen "in 8 major industries" objected that the formal organizational charts of their companies were not followed in practice suggests the nature of imagery among the foremen as well as the place of fictions in the plants.

pressures of the rank and file demand it) utilize these conflicts for the benefit of the union.

Inability of middle and lower managerial officers to protect themselves against this aggression exerts an upward pressure to centralize industrial relations in the organization. This does not necessarily guarantee that procedures and policies coming from the top levels will be any more adequate as operating codes. Since career-conscious lower and middle officers fear to report frequent failure to settle differences with the union by use of official procedures, they resort to whatever unofficial devices and practices will meet the demands of the situation without dangerous repercussions.

Resulting *sub rosa* agreements frequently leak out and come to the knowledge of dominant officers of both union and management. Those practices that are repeatedly found to be helpful in escaping conflicts come to assume somewhat the status of "common law," except that decisions reached are chiefly covert. However this body of common law, or informal and tacit understandings, infuses more realism into the official procedures from above. Most union and managerial officers who had been displeased with previous arrangements are then inclined to feel that passable efforts have been made to incorporate measures for reducing the "impositions" on them and are disposed to accept the official directives in good faith. But when the changing character of relations between union and management again outgrows the official restraints, recourse is had to the more fluid unofficial methods which may lead to new spearheads of behavior, subject, in turn, to new official controls—and so on in continuing interplay. Variations naturally occur, with inflexible adherents to either official or unofficial methods becoming focuses of conflict.

Because of his relationships at the base of the hierarchy, the foreman is confronted with the alternatives earlier noted. He feels pressures mounting on him to lessen the conflict in which he is caught, particularly in dealing with the union. To the extent that he learns to function flexibly and work out accommodations in response to imperatives playing on him, he becomes one of the major influences for reducing conflict within the organization and with the union in matters of daily contract administration.

2

C · SOCIAL AND ECONOMIC INFLUENCES

IT HAS often been observed that there are three groups of active participants in industrial relations: workers, unions, and employers. Our analysis of the roots of industrial conflict has dealt with all three of these groups. We have noted the psychological mechanisms involved in worker satisfaction and discontent and the particular sources of dissatisfaction in modern industrial life. We have examined the structure of unions and the relations between union leaders and members, as they relate to the functioning of labor organizations in the collective-bargaining sphere. Likewise we have described the goals and characteristics of business firms as well as the outlook and beliefs of business leaders.

Industrial relations are conducted not in a vacuum but in a specific economic and social context which exerts a powerful influence—some would say compelling influence—on the results. The chapters in this section are addressed to various features of this conditioning economic and social environment.

We asked Kerr and Siegel: Why has industrial conflict been prevalent in some industries and virtually absent in others? Why, for example, are strikes so frequent in the coal industry in every part of the world? Why has the longshore industry been marked by left-wing unions, intransigent employers, and bitter conflicts in many countries? How is the persistence of harmonious relations in clothing, paper and pulp, and certain other industries to be explained? Previous analyses of industrial conflict or peace have generally run in terms of labor-market and product-market differences, policies and attitudes of unions and employers, "human relations" at the work level, procedures for adjusting disputes, and influence of dominant personalities. Kerr and Siegel show that these factors, while perhaps useful in explaining differences in the degree of conflict between particular firms, cannot explain why some industries are chronically conflict ridden in many parts of the world while others are persistently peaceful. They find the central explanation in the location of the worker in society, with the nature of jobs serving as a secondary influence. An "isolated mass" of workers, insulated from society at large as "a race apart," will revolt frequently and bitterly, particularly when employed at unpleasant tasks, whereas individuals and groups who are integrated into the general community, through a multiplicity of associations, are less likely to strike. It follows, Kerr and Siegel state, that the way to reduce the intensity of conflict is to "integrate the worker and his associations, and the employer, as fully as possible into the general society without coercion." This proposition clearly has much wider significance than for industrial conflict only.

In Chap. 15, Rees deals with the influence of general business conditions on industrial conflict. The relationship between strikes and the business cycle has been dealt with by previous writers (Hansen, Yoder, and Griffen, among others) but without conclusive results. Rees finds a pronounced positive correlation, with strikes increasing in frequency during periods of prosperity and diminishing during depressions. The timing of the relationship is also of interest: strikes typically turn down before business activity reaches a peak and turn up some time after recovery has begun. Rees's explanation is based on the assumption that the strike has become a strategic weapon of business unions and is no longer an emotional or spontaneous protest of workers. "Grievances can be stored up for long periods," he states. "They are most likely to boil over into strikes or to be utilized by union leaders as strike issues when business conditions promise that strikes may be successful. The same provocation which causes a strike when employment opportunities are rising might cause only grumbling during a depression."

The impact of technology upon the structure of industrial organizations and upon the division of labor among the people who operate the machines and fill the jobs in production processes is the major concern of Moore in Chap. 16. Technology is perhaps the one aspect of the industrial complex that is most sensitive to change—where change is not only eagerly sought but highly rewarded. The fundamental priority of the technical apparatus of industry in ordering the division of labor in industrial establishments can hardly be overemphasized. It follows that much of the orderly conduct of affairs in business firms is tied to the underlying technology and the rate at which it changes. Moore calls our attention to some of the personnel consequences of technological change and development. In particular, he emphasizes that the social consequences of technological developments give rise to some of the central problems of the industrial-relations field. Technology has been destructive of solidarity within the ranks of management as well as of workers. An examination of these consequences leads Moore to some suggestive hypotheses.

Social power, a phrase common in the vocabulary of most observers of society, in spite of its vogue, is lacking in usefulness for want of adequate definition and analysis. In an incisive treatment of power, Blumer distinguishes it as a fundamental social process and illustrates the utility of the concept as an analytical tool for understanding industrial relations. His analysis is particularly illuminating when he contrasts power relations with "codified relations" and "sympathetic relations." The interaction between union and management requires the concept of power relations for its understanding. In Part 3b of this volume, where attention is focused upon efforts to remove sources of conflict, the concepts of codified and sympathetic relations may be usefully applied. Either through the institution of commonly accepted rules or codes of behavior or by securing sympathetic participation, management attempts to influence worker behavior through the social processes of codified and sympathetic relations. In the larger sense, we can suggest that labor relations become institutionalized when they are codified or sympathetic in character. However, the union-management relation is only partially institutionalized; episodically and periodically, it takes on the character of a power relationship.

The chapter by Daniel Bell deals, in historical perspective, with the effects which public opinion and the dominant values held by the public have on industrial relations. He particularly stresses the transformation in attitudes and laws pertaining to labor unions and the struggles that have attended these changes. While public opinion is characterized by diversity, by inner contradictions, and frequently by ignorance and misinformation, nevertheless, as Bell points out, it does have important impact on labor legislation and governmental action in industrial disputes. This influence is illustrated as it operated during the New Deal period and the years since World War II. As labor and business grow more conscious of public opinion, they turn increasingly to the use of propaganda weapons. In this psychological warfare, labor's alliance with New Deal political forces and with opinion-forming intellectuals leaves considerable doubt, Bell suggests, whether industry's intensive campaign to rewin the allegiance of working people is succeeding. He believes that the public, including workers and businessmen themselves, accepts widely divergent and opposed images of organized labor at present and that the general public has no clear idea about the distribution of power in our society. Yet the future of industrial conflict will depend in great degree on the direction that opinion takes on these questions, particularly in regard to labor's place in the political life of the country.

Taft deals with one further element in the context of industrial relations in his chapter "Ideologies and Industrial Conflict." Noting that various political movements have endeavored to extend their influence by penetrating labor organizations, Taft examines the consequences of this fact. Since most workers are not possessed by deep ideological convictions, Taft argues that radicals cannot enlist them directly in a fight for revolutionary objectives but only for ostensible "bread-and-butter" aims. Social-democratic ideology in Germany, England, and the United States as well as syndicalist ideology in France have not been permitted to dominate policy, he states, but instead have been adjusted to "reality." With respect to the Communists, Taft observes that the effect on industrial conflict will depend on whether they win control of the union administration. As a minority faction, "those imbued with a class-war ideology can . . . organize . . . smoldering discontent [against vested officials] into active revolt . . ." Once in control of a union, Communists are not necessarily more militant than non-Communists and do not engage in strikes unless some political purpose can be gained. Taft notes further that an aggressive antiunion ideology on the part of employers can be a potent cause of industrial warfare.

CHAPTER 14 THE INTERINDUSTRY PROPENSITY TO STRIKE— AN INTERNATIONAL COMPARISON

Clark Kerr and Abraham Siegel

University of California (Berkeley)

ARE certain industries in democratic industrialized nations consistently strike prone, while others are consistently strike free? [1] If the facts give an affirmative answer to this question, then how can this social phenomenon be explained? How do several of the standard theories of industrial peace and industrial conflict fare in the light of these facts? Finally, if it were desired either to encourage or to discourage the propensity to strike in an industry, how best should it be attempted? These are the four questions to which this chapter is addressed.

The Similarity of Behavior

Table 14.1 gives a generalized grouping of industries from the information set forth in more detail in Table 14.2 (see the Technical Supplement). This generalized grouping is possible because of the uniformity of behavior of certain industries in the eleven countries studied [2] (Australia, Czechoslovakia, Germany, Italy, the Netherlands, New Zealand, Norway, Sweden, Switzerland, the United Kingdom, and the United States).

The assignment of industries from Table 14.2 to a box in Table 14.1 is admittedly determined on a somewhat impressionistic basis. Only those industries which show a generally discernible uniformity of behavior in Table 14.2 are located in Table 14.1. Many industries in Table 14.2 do not appear in Table 14.1 because there are too few observations of them (as rubber) or because, while they are referred to several times (as paper), they are often in a paired grouping with some dissimilar industry (paper and printing) and there are too few separate rankings. The combination of distinct industries

[1] Man-days lost due to strikes and lockouts are used as the measure of the propensity to strike. Thus an industry may have frequent small strikes of short duration and yet be shown with a lower propensity to strike than one with a few big strikes of substantial length. We are more concerned here with the significance of strikes than with their numerical occurrence.

[2] While the data disclose a substantial consistency of behavior, it should be kept in mind that they reflect the experience of only eleven countries over a limited period of time and that the industrial breakdowns are not so numerous nor so comparable from one country to another, or even from one time period to another in the same country, as would be ideally desirable for the purposes of this analysis.

into the same statistical grouping is particularly vexatious (clothing and textile and land and water transportation,[3] for example) when each of them separately is an interesting case. The evidence for the placement of one industry (railroad) is partly from general knowledge, since it is not often clearly shown by itself. On the basis of general knowledge alone, several other groups might confidently be placed in this table—domestic servants, government employees, and white-collar workers in the "Low Propensity to Strike" box—and some reference will be made to them in the discussion.

Manufacturing (general) is, of course, an omnibus description, and the grouping may turn up in the "Medium" box only because quite divergent patterns cancel each other out. However, it seems more likely that general manufacturing (which includes, perhaps most importantly, metal working) is the significant standard case, and the question then becomes: Why are some industries more strike prone and others less than general manufacturing?

The industries in the "Medium" box may be divided into two types: those which are quite consistently medium strike prone (general manufacturing, leather, and construction) and those which vary considerably from "High" or "Medium high" to "Medium low" or "Low" (printing, chemical, and food and kindred products). Industries in the "Medium" category are likely to be either under balanced environmental pressures toward both conflict and peace or under such little pressure in either direction that forces arising from other sources than the industrial environment are predominant.

Table 14.1   **General Pattern of Strike Propensities** *

Propensity to strike	Industry
High	Mining Maritime and longshore
Medium high	Lumber Textile
Medium	Chemical Printing Leather Manufacturing (general) Construction Food and kindred products
Medium low	Clothing Gas, water, and electricity Services (hotels, restaurants, etc.)
Low	Railroad Agriculture Trade

* For the detail on which this table is based, see Table 14.2 in the Technical Supplement to this chapter.

[3] A particularly disturbing combination is transportation and navigation in Norway. Do railroads pull down the rank, or do both railroads and shipping rank low? If shipping ranks low, why is the Norwegian experience different from that in the other countries?

While the concern here is exclusively with industries, it is to be expected that individual firms in industries in the "medium" category should vary more widely one from another than firms in industries in the high-propensity or low-propensity categories. A medium-propensity industry is likely to give wide latitude for individual firm variations, while a high- or a low-propensity one is more likely to demand individual conformity; [4] and general observation attests that there is more uniformity in behavior among coal mines or government bureaus than among general-manufacturing plants.

Before turning to the question of whether there are any reasonable hypotheses to explain the apparently great impact of certain industrial environments on the propensity to strike, five exceptions (see Table 14.2) to the uniformity of behavior should be noted:

Trade in Sweden (higher than usual).
Mining in Germany in the second period and in the Netherlands during the second period (lower than usual).
Machinery in Germany (higher than usual).
Automobiles in the United States in the second period (higher than usual).
Agriculture in Italy, in Australia during the second period, and in New Zealand in the first (higher than usual).

For the first two exceptions we have no explanation to offer; but comments on the last three will be made later on.

The Explanations

Hypothesis 1. *The Location of the Worker in Society.* Is there any single theory which will largely explain the facts which we have found? Can we, at one and the same time, explain the high propensity to strike of miners, longshoremen, sailors, and loggers and the low propensity of government employees, grocery clerks, railroad employees, and garment workers? The first hypothesis is that the location of the worker in society determines his propensity to strike and that this location is heavily influenced by the industrial environment.

1. THE ISOLATED MASS. The miners, the sailors, the longshoremen, the loggers, and, to a much lesser extent, the textile workers form isolated masses, almost a "race apart." They live in their own separate communities: the coal patch, the ship, the waterfront district, the logging camp, the textile town.[5] These communities have their own codes, myths, heroes, and social standards.[6] There are few neutrals in them to mediate the conflicts and dilute the mass. All people have grievances, but what is important is that all the members of

---

[4] This is not to suggest that a single firm cannot make a record for peace in a war-like industry or a record for conflict in a quiescent industry but only that it is unlikely to do so.

[5] Some of these communities, such as the coal towns, are geographically isolated, while others, such as waterfront districts, are socially isolated within metropolitan communities.

[6] Hobsbawm notes that "the habit of solidarity suggests itself naturally" more in some industries, such as coal mining, than in others. See E. J. Hobsbawm, "The Machine Breakers," *Past and Present*, Vol. 1, No. 1 (February, 1952). See also comments by Seymour M. Lipset and Reinhard Bendix, "Social Status and Social Structure," *British Journal of Sociology*, Vol. 2, No. 3 (September, 1951).

each of these groups have the same grievances: industrial hazards or severe depression unemployment or bad living conditions (which seem additionally evil because they are supplied by the employer), or low wages or intermittent work. And here is a case where the totality of common grievances,[6a] after they have been verbally shared, may be greater than the sum of the individual parts. The employees form a largely homogeneous, undifferentiated mass—they all do about the same work and have about the same experiences. Here you do not have the occupational stratification of the metal or building crafts, of the hotel or restaurant, or of the government bureau.[7]

It is hard to get out of this mass. The jobs are specialized, and the workers come to be also. Skills are not transferable as they are for stenographers or electricians. Protest is less likely to take the form of moving to another industry and more the character of the mass walkout. Just as it is hard for these workers to move out, so also is it difficult for them to move up. To what higher occupational strata can the longshoreman or the coal miner or the logger rise in the natural course of events? Nor is he likely to be pulled from the mass in other ways. In these communities there are not the myriad of voluntary associations with mixed memberships which characterize the multi-industry town. The force of public opinion must seem rather weak to the logger in the camp or to the miner in the coal patch who never sees "the public"; and it is no more possible to cut trees than to mine coal with bayonets. The employer throws out few lines to these workers. He is usually an absentee owner who "cuts out and gets out" in the logging business or exhausts a mine and moves on or hires longshoremen on a casual basis or gets his views of personnel relations from the law on mutiny.[8] The worker is as detached from the employer as from the community at large.

[6a] The members of these groups not only have the same grievances, but they have them at the same time, at the same place, and against the same people. In the more peaceful industries their inevitable grievances are dispersed—by stratification of the workers (as in steel), by scattering of the employees (as in agriculture), by absorption of the workers into a mixed community (as in trade), by scattering of the targets (the employer, the landlord, the grocer, and the policemen being quite different people). The "mass grievance," not the individual grievance, is the source of the greater social difficulty. It may arise in the environment we are describing here, or may have a cross-industry content—for example, it may result from widespread unemployment, rapid inflation, general wage cuts. It is the mass grievance which leads to "class" action. The individual grievance can be more readily absorbed and managed by society. Industrial tranquillity depends on keeping grievances dispersed so that they may be handled one at a time. Proponents of social unrest are most successful in those places where, and at those times when, grievances are highly concentrated.

[7] Occupational stratification may be an unusually important aspect of the industrial environment, affecting the location of the worker in society and his propensity to strike. The iron and steel industry is often located in geographically isolated one-industry towns, and much of the work in it is arduous (see hypothesis 2), yet it is not particularly famous as a center of strike activity. Only three separate observations of this industry appear in our data (see Table 14.2), and they are too few for a confident generalization. The industry, however, seems to rank somewhat above the average ("High" in Germany in the second period and "Medium" in the United States in the first period and "Medium high" in the second). It might rank somewhat higher, nevertheless, were it not for the high degree of job differentiation which marks the industry and which both separates one worker from another and creates a ladder for each worker to climb.

[8] The industrial environment creates "bad" employers (just as it does strike-prone workers) who disregard the welfare of their employees because of the casual nature of

The union becomes a kind of working-class party or even government for these employees, rather than just another association among many. Union meetings are more adequately attended and union affairs more vigorously discussed; and, as one consequence, personal and ideological factionalism and rival unionism are more likely. Strife within and between unions is a sign that the union is important.

The strike for this isolated mass is a kind of colonial revolt against far-removed authority, an outlet for accumulated tensions, and a substitute for occupational and social mobility. The industrial environment places these workers in the role of members of separate classes distinct from the community at large, classes with their share of grievances. These individuals are not members of the ubiquitous middle class but of their own class of miners or longshoremen; and they do not aim to be more considerate of the general community than they think the general community is of them. Thus the isolated mass in a classless society may become something like the isolated class in a class society, more or less permanently at odds with the community at large.[9]

2. THE INTEGRATED INDIVIDUAL AND THE INTEGRATED GROUP. The opposite of the isolated mass is the integrated individual or the integrated group. "Integrated" is used here not in the psychological but in the sociological sense: absorbed in and unified with society at large. The workers in the industries at the other end of our scale—those in the industries where the propensity to strike is low or medium low (railroad; trade; agriculture; clothing; gas, water, and electricity; the services; and, we might add, government, domestic services, and clerical)—are given an industrial role to play which integrates them better into the general community. They are more likely (with the exception of farm hands) to live in multi-industry communities, to associate with people with quite different working experiences than their own, and to belong to associations with heterogeneous memberships. In these communities their individual griev-

their connection with them or who undertake to dominate their employees unduly, as landlord and policeman as well as employer, because they are the preponderant power in a one-industry community, or who do both.

[9] A third condition is necessary, in addition to the existence of a relatively homogeneous group of workers which is isolated from the general community, for an industry to be especially strike prone; but this condition is almost universally present when the other two are. This condition is the capacity of the group for cohesion. The existence of an identifiable group (such as the clothing workers) is not sufficient by itself nor is the fact of isolation (note the general lack of strikes by fishermen and oil-field workers) nor the two together, if cohesion is difficult for the isolated mass. The great hordes of agricultural harvest hands in the San Joaquin Valley of California have struck, but only with great difficulty, for they are such an inconstant, fluctuating, amorphous group. The capacity for cohesion is dependent on the fairly steady contact of the members of the group, which in turn creates the basis for permanent organization. Thus the itinerant but occupationally specialized sheepshearers in the western United States have long been organized, since they form a group of constant composition whose members have repetitive contacts with each other, while less specialized agricultural workers have not. An isolated mass can be kept from internal solidarity not only by the turnover of its membership but also by racial, religious, and nationality barriers—a social law on which certain American employers, particularly in earlier times, have founded their recruiting practices. Hawaiian sugar-plantation workers did not become effectively organized until they were "Americanized." See Mark Perlman, "Organized Labor in Hawaii," *Labor Law Journal,* Vol. 3 (April, 1952). Even agricultural workers strike when they move from a state of individual isolation in an isolated mass to the state of a cohesive isolated mass.

ances are less likely to coalesce into a mass grievance which is expressed at the job level. There are many neutrals in any dispute, and this helps to assure the impartiality of public officials.

In most of these cases the worker either can change his industry fairly readily without losing the value of his skill or has access to higher skilled jobs or managerial or even employer status. Generally, also, the employer is either not so remote or not so callous if remote. The industry has small-scale employing units, or the employer-worker relationship is normally a continuing one. And the community can bring pressure to bear to encourage peaceful conduct. The workers see and feel the general community; in at least three cases (railroads, public utilities, and government) the government asserts the supremacy of the public interest in continuity of service; [10] and in at least one other (clothing) the market for the products makes steady production the *sine qua non* for both investment and jobs. The union, except in the garment trades, where it runs the industry, and the railroads, where it administers seniority, is not so wound into the lives of the workers, and in no instance is it so much the chosen instrument for protest, if it exists at all.

The workers in these industries are generally more dispersed in the general community, more stratified in the hierarchy of jobs in each industry, more attached to their individual employers, more restrained by social pressures, and more able to escape job dissatisfactions without striking than are the workers in the high-propensity industries. The strike is against a known employer and affects a community of which the workers are a part. These workers are contained in society rather than maintained on its periphery.[11]

Several further notes are needed on the hypothesis that the location of the worker in society is the basic determinant of the interindustry propensity to strike. Agriculture in New Zealand, Australia, and Italy is, during certain periods, an exception to the rule of rural tranquility. Agriculture has also been an exception to this rule in California and Hawaii. These areas have in common large-scale agriculture. When agriculture moves from employing the single hired hand to large groups of socially isolated workers, it also moves from peace toward conflict. It is also instructive that the automobile and rubber industries, which rank so high in the second period in the United States, are

[10] Few man-days lost because of strikes do not necessarily indicate an absence of worker unrest, as the experience of the railroad industry in the United States attests.

[11] The industries ranked "Low" or "Medium low" may be divided into two distinct groups: (*a*) those in which the workers are relatively well integrated individually into the community (agriculture, trade, services), and (*b*) those in which the workers constitute collectively a recognizable group but where the group is under intense social pressure to settle its grievances peacefully (clothing, railroad, public utilities). In the two categories, the industries in the latter have demonstrated the greater inclination toward strikes. In either case, community integration, in contrast to mass segregation, is the key to the explanation of peaceful behavior. The farm hand living in his employer's family, however, is integrated into the community in quite a different fashion from the railroad workers whose union finds strikes socially unacceptable. The farm hands have no group cohesion while the railroad workers have a great deal, but the pressure of society is against their making effective use of it through the strike. A third situation exists where strikes are rare or nonexistent, but it does not show in our data. This is where the workers are not integrated into the community as individuals or through their groups but are so dispersed (lighthouse keepers, hunters, forest-fire lookouts and the like) that no group action is likely. These are the isolated individuals in society.

predominantly localized in the special communities of Detroit and Akron, which were also the two homes of the sit-down strike. The experience of two additional industries, while the data on them is by no means conclusive, seems to support this hypothesis. Man-days lost due to strikes have been much above the average in the toy-manufacturing industry in Germany and in quarrying (stone, clay, and sand) and the fabricating activities associated with it wherever they are separately identifiable, and both these industries isolate groups of workers from the larger society.[12]

The location of industries in the "Medium" box is not so readily elucidated by this hypothesis, although the occasional adventures into the conflict category of the printing and chemical industries might be laid to the well-developed sense of a common community which characterizes some printing trades and the frequent geographical isolation of chemical plants; and the consistently "Medium" behavior of the general manufacturing, construction, and leather industries, to the balance of pulls toward both group and societal identification. The employees of these industries often form cohesive groups, but these groups are neither isolated from society, on the one hand, nor under strong social pressure to avoid strikes, on the other; and these employees, while they belong to unions, frequently have strong attachments in other directions as well.

In summary, this hypothesis may be stated as follows: (*a*) industries will be highly strike prone when the workers (*i*) form a relatively homogeneous group which (*ii*) is unusually isolated from the general community and which (*iii*) is capable of cohesion; and (*b*) industries will be comparatively strike free when their workers (*i*) are individually integrated into the larger society, (*ii*) are members of trade groups which are coerced by government or the market to avoid strikes, or (*iii*) are so individually isolated that strike action is impossible.

Hypothesis 2. The Character of the Job and the Worker. The second hypothesis is that the inherent nature of the job determines, by selection and conditioning, the kinds of workers employed and their attitudes, and these workers, in turn, cause conflict or peace. If the job is physically difficult and unpleasant, unskilled or semiskilled, and casual or seasonal, and fosters an independent spirit (as in the logger in the woods), it will draw tough, inconstant, combative, and virile workers, and they will be inclined to strike. If the job is physically easy and performed in pleasant surroundings, skilled and responsible, steady, and subject to set rules and close supervision, it will attract women or the more submissive type of man who will abhor strikes. Certainly the bull of the woods and the mousy bank clerk are different types of people and can be expected to act differently. Certainly, also, the community is more sympathetic with striking miners coming out of the ground than with school teachers abandoning their desks.

This hypothesis explains a good many of the facts but not quite so neatly as the first. Sailors, longshoremen, miners, and lumberjacks are popularly accepted as being more vigorous and combative types than garment workers,

---

[12] A further illustration, not drawn, however, from the statistical data, is also instructive. Sailors working on oil tankers in the coastal trade of the United States, who are employed steadily by the same employer and have a more regularized family and community life than other seamen, are also less strike prone.

grocery clerks, railway conductors, hotel maids, or cannery employees; they seem to strike more often, and their strikes are also more violent. But textile workers and printing craftsmen, who also strike with some frequency, are not classed as so forceful. Teamsters, farm hands, steelworkers, and construction tradesmen, who are not usually delicate individuals, do not strike with unusual frequency.

Several other elements of the industrial environment were examined, but they did not seem to lead to a general theory of the interindustry propensity to strike. They may, however, be important factors behind the behavior of individual industries, or they may explain the different records of the several plants within an industry. These factors are the following:

1. The sensitivity of the industry to the business cycle.
2. The structure of the product market.
3. The elasticity of demand for the product.
4. Labor as a percentage of total cost.
5. The profitability of the industry.
6. The average size of plant.
7. The state of technological change.
8. The rate of expansion or contraction of the industry.

Reference to any or all of these elements, as a careful examination of the characteristics of the industries ranked in Table 14.1 will make evident, is insufficient to explain the bulk of the facts.

We are left, then, with the two general hypotheses set forth above, of which the former seems the more consistent with the known facts. The two theories, however, have a uniting thread. Both of them are consistent with the thesis that strikes occur where they can occur, that is, where the working-class community is closely knit and the workers forceful and not where the workers are dispersed and subdued. This is not the same thing, however, as saying that strikes take place where strikes pay, for grocery clerks are probably in a better position to benefit from strikes, if they could develop them, than are textile workers; and railroad workers, than sailors.

The two hypotheses can be combined to state that strikes occur most severely in industries which (1) segregate large numbers of persons who (2) have relatively unpleasant jobs. Mass segregation by itself is not enough, for members of the "lower gentility" (telephone operators, bank clerks, and the like) would probably not strike frequently, in deference to their lower-middle-class psychology, even if they were put off by themselves in large groups; nor is unpleasant work enough by itself, for scavengers, sand blasters, divers, and chimney sweeps have disagreeable jobs but are so scattered that joint action is almost impossible. The polar cases then may be described as follows: (1) an isolated mass of persons doing unpleasant work and (2) dispersed individuals doing pleasant work.

Certain Theories Examined

Two explanations of the ranking of industries by the propensity of the workers to strike have been offered: the location of the workers in society and the character of the jobs and the workers, both of which explanations relate to what may be called the industrial environment; but there are many other theories which can be applied to these data, although not specifically devised to explain them. How adequate are these theories in explaining these particular data? [13]

1. *The economic environment,* which for these purposes we shall define as the market aspects of the larger industrial environment which was discussed above, makes a contribution to an understanding of these data but by itself is an inadequate explanation. The industries located at each extreme have quite various product- and labor-market structures. An elastic demand in the product market may encourage peace,[14] particularly where business may be lost to

---

[13] There are other tests of the validity of these theories for the explanation of industrial conflict and peace than those of how well they elucidate these data. If the theories fail this test, this does not mean they will not pass other tests or explain other phenomena.

[14] An elastic demand for the products of a firm or a group of firms and an elastic demand for labor have been advanced on occasion as a basic cause of labor-management cooperation. The employer faces stiff competition, and the union does not wish to injure his competitive position. The union, however, may not be so considerate if (a) any job reduction for this firm is matched by an increase in jobs somewhere else for members of the same union organization and perhaps even for the same workers (as may often happen in local trade and service industries) or if (b) the union or its leaders, for the sake of survival, must make certain wage gains regardless of the potential effects (which may be much delayed) on job opportunities. Union-management cooperation is most likely to result when disturbing actions by the union would cause a loss of jobs to areas outside its job territory *and* where its leaders are in a position to consider this effect as the dominant influence. An inelastic demand for the products is probably more generally conducive to peace since it gives the employer greater leeway in accommodating himself to the union. Then a gap is more likely to exist between the maximum which the employer can readily afford to pay and the minimum which the union can reasonably accept. Richard A. Lester, however, states: "Practically without exception . . . labor-capital cooperation has been adopted by individual firms with a fairly elastic demand for labor either because of competition within the industry or because of the practice of contracting out for work. . . ." (*Economics of Labor,* New York, Macmillan, 1946, p. 697); and "union-employer cooperation to regulate competition has occurred, for instance in [several industries are enumerated]. . . . In such industries price-cutting and wage-cutting are likely to occur to an extreme degree because there is a large number of small employers in the industry, it is so easy to enter the business, and wages are such an important item in total costs." See *ibid.,* p. 145. Hence the need for the "stabilizing" effect of the union. Shister, in his analysis of union-management cooperation, also emphasizes the influence of the economic environment in working for cooperation: "union-management cooperation has appeared mainly, although not exclusively, when the bargaining unit was in an adverse economic situation." See Joseph Shister, "Union-Management Cooperation: An Analysis," in Richard A. Lester and Joseph Shister (eds.), *Insights into Labor Issues,* New York, Macmillan, 1948, p. 90. Shister states that, if the cost reductions resulting from union-management cooperation involve hourly wage reductions, "then it is necessary that the employer's demand for labor be elastic over the relevant range. A union would not be likely to agree to reduce wage rates, under union-management cooperation, if it did not see a possibility of gaining more than proportionately in employment and/or income from the wage reduction." See *ibid.,* pp. 90–91. Further illustration of arguments stressing the economic environment's influence in affecting industrial peace or conflict may be found in Frederick H. Harbison, Robert K. Burns, and Robert Dubin, "Toward a Theory of Labor-Management Relations," in *Lester and Shister* (eds.), *op. cit.,* pp. 8–14; and in John Dunlop's contribution to "Framework for the Analysis of Industrial Relations: Two Views," *Industrial and Labor Relations Review,* Vol. 3, No. 3 (April, 1950), where he states: "the

nonunion employers, and an inelastic labor-supply situation may lead workers to strike, since it reflects the fact that it is difficult for them to move out; but an elastic demand for the product may also cause trouble where a union is competing in a wage war with a rival union or is under pressure to match a pattern wage settlement and where the employer is handicapped in translating higher wage costs into higher prices for fear of losing volume, and an inelastic labor supply may encourage peace if it helps give rise to higher wage rates. Product-market and labor-market forces are, perhaps, more suited to explain variations among firms or between periods in the life of an industry than they are between industries over a span of time.

2. *The political environment,* particularly of the unions, has been persuasively adduced as the cause of industrial warfare or peace: the more secure the union and its leaders, the fewer the strikes; the less secure, the more numerous. The unions of grocery clerks, government employees, and agriculture workers, however, have generally less institutional security than those of coal miners, printers, and longshoremen, yet they strike less. More jurisdictional and organizational rivalries usually face the construction and railroad unions than the unions of miners, yet they are more peaceful. In the United States the leader of the mine workers is popularly conceived to have a more secure position than the chief of the airline pilots' association, yet his union strikes more; and peace descended on the West Coast waterfront when the established union leaders became less secure. Certainly the political environment of the union and its leaders is useful, even indispensable, in explaining certain situations at certain times,[15] but it does not provide a generally valid explanation of the interindustry propensity to strike.

Among the industries with a high propensity to strike, while unionism is usually most secure, union leaders and specific institutions may on the average be somewhat less secure than usual. This is consistent with the hypothesis that the "isolated mass" builds a strong union movement and that active memberships give rise to factionalism. Among the industries with a low propensity to strike, unionism finds its greatest uncertainty and factionalism its least assured market.

Employer associations are particularly strong where the industrial environment is coercive toward conflict (coal mining, logging, longshore, and maritime). While, by increasing the ability to pay of the individual employers, by increasing interemployer uniformity of terms and conditions of employment, and by lowering the level of the union's ultimate demands by raising the cost of strikes, multiemployer bargaining may encourage peace, it finds its origins, in part, in war.

---

conditions in the labor market in which the labor services are purchased by the management, and the conditions in the product market in which the output or service is sold" constitute an important aspect of the total environment impinging on the prospects for peace or conflict.

[15] Ross and Irwin conclude that "differences in the frequency of strikes between one country and another can best be explained by differences in the position of the union and the union leader" and that "internal factionalism, like external competition, encourages the development and prosecution of grievances." See Arthur M. Ross and Donald Irwin, "Strike Experience in Five Countries, 1927–1947: An Interpretation," *Industrial and Labor Relations Review,* Vol. 4, No. 3 (April, 1951).

Strikes may better be explained by looking not so much at the organization as at the membership. They occur most frequently not only in places where the membership is restless because of its industrial environment, as we have seen above, but also at times of membership unrest.[16] It is to the reactions of the workers and not to the tactics of the leaders that we must turn for the more basic explanations.

3. *Human relations* at the face-to-face level are said by some to explain not only industrial but even international relations. Misunderstandings are not inherent in a situation but result from faulty communications.[17] It may be true that face-to-face relations are worse between longshoremen and coal miners and their employers than between grocery clerks and theirs and that, if face-to-face relations were better between coal miners and their employers, there would be less conflict. But why are face-to-face relations often so unsatisfactory between coal miners and their employers? Is it because they always know less about semantics than construction workers and their employers, and is it only faulty communication systems which stand between them and ultimate harmony? And how are face-to-face relations to be improved? Can it be done by giving courses in group dynamics and introducing social engineers into the mines?

It seems more likely that some situations are structured against good face-to-face relations and that this structure is the more basic cause and the source of the more basic changes. The climate of face-to-face relations may be one way of testing and of describing the degree of conflict or cooperation in an industry, and there may be occasions when manipulation of these relations alone will bring great changes,[18] but it seems unlikely that the peace in gov-

[16] "Frequent disputes are mainly caused by dissatisfaction among the workers; strikes for improvements are frequent when rising prices are not adequately met by rising wages, strikes against a worsening of conditions when the workers are menaced by cuts and especially by wage cuts not justified by a proportional fall in prices." K. Forschheimer, *Some International Aspects of the Strike Movement,* Oxford Institute of Statistics Bulletin 10, January, 1948.

[17] "According to this approach [*i.e.,* the "human-relations" approach], actions and sentiments are the items to be explained: Why do workers increase (or decrease) their productivity? Why do they stay on the job—or go out on strike? Why do they express hostile (or favorable) sentiments toward management? And the analysis of patterns of interaction [where "interaction" refers to all personal contacts between two individuals or among three or more individuals] seems to me the most effective means of explaining actions and sentiments." See William Foote Whyte's contribution to "Framework for the Analysis of Industrial Relations: Two Views." The economic, social, and political environments are determinants in this schema only in so far as their influences are manifested in specific items of behavior of the people observed within the "social system" which the plant constitutes. The determining influence in shaping "sentiments" is the nature of the human relations which prevail: "The trouble is that people's sentiments cannot be changed by simply telling them that it is a good idea to change their sentiments. In this case [the Chicago plant of the Inland Steel Container Co.], union and management people began with hatred and distrust, while now mutual good will prevails. But the good will was a late arrival on the scene. It only developed *following* far-reaching changes in human relations. This is the sequence of change we see, as a rule: first a change in human relations, then a change in sentiments." See William Foote Whyte, *Pattern for Industrial Peace,* New York, Harper, 1951, p. 228.

[18] For example, by changing the structure of the work group. See E. L. Trist and K. W. Bamforth, "Some Social and Psychological Consequences of the Longwall Method of Coal-getting," *Human Relations,* Vol. 4, No. 1 (1951).

ernment agencies and the warfare on the waterfront are due primarily to the universal superiority in human-relations techniques of government bureaucrats over stevedoring contractors. Even if this were the case, it would still need to be explained why government draws to it a more skillful elite than the longshore industry. Labor relations may be a mirror in which the employer sees his own reflection—the decent employer may see decent relationships reflected back at him [19]—but why then are employers more decent in one industry than another? At this point some reference needs to be made to the industrial environment. *Causa causae est causa causati.*

4. *The trend of historical developments* varies considerably from one collective-bargaining system to another. In industries with a high propensity to strike, the origins have frequently been more violent and time has had less of a subduing effect. The printing trades tend to be among the earliest organized, as are the coal mines, but they both continue to be disposed toward conflict long after other industries have learned to tread a more peaceful path. The garment trades in the United States were organized in bitter struggles but, given an environment which was persuasive toward peace, soon established the standard for tranquil conduct. Both the nature of the birth and the trend of development must be explained by some common causes, for both have been quite uniform for the same industry from one country to another. More than historical accident is at work. The nature of the birth appears to be not purely accidental; so it is necessary to say more than that a bad start leads to poorer continuing relations than does a good one. Since time works fewer wonders with some industries than others, it is necessary to state more than that time smooths the wrinkles in the relationship.[20]

5. *Dominant personalities* certainly leave an imprint on relations in an industry;[21] but why do the coal and longshore industries bring a John L.

---

[19] Clinton S. Golden and Harold J. Ruttenberg, *The Dynamics of Industrial Democracy,* New York, Harper, 1942. "Management as a general principle, gets the kind of union leadership it deserves. A tough management begets tough union leaders, while a patient, friendly, cooperative management begets a like type of union leadership. . . ." (p. 58).

[20] See Robert R. R. Brooks, *As Steel Goes,* New Haven, Conn., Yale University Press, 1940. "There are three stages in the development of successful collective bargaining. The first is the signing of a contract by a company giving a union the right to bargain for its members only. Such a contract often amounts to no more than a letter of introduction. It may be followed by a period of intense conflict between union and management representatives during which the union fights for a permanent status, and the management fights for the *status quo ante.* In the second stage, individual companies concede a stable position to the union and cooperate with it in the adjustment of personal grievances, but the use of the word 'grievance' clearly suggests that union-management relationships remain essentially negative. In the third stage, collective bargaining becomes a cooperative relationship directed toward increasing the productive efficiency of the industry. Positive action toward this objective must ultimately lead to industry-wide union-management cooperation by organized workers and associated employers. . . ." (p. 190).

[21] Several of the case studies in the National Planning Association series "Causes of Industrial Peace" emphasize the importance of dominant personalities in the shaping of peaceful relations. For example, "Perhaps the most important factor [determining the course of the relationship] is the president of the company. His philosophy and his personality have had a great deal to do with the ultimate development of health. . . ." (Douglas McGregor and Joseph N. Scanlon, *The Dewey and Almy Chemical Company and the International Chemical Workers Union,* Washington, National Planning Association, 1948, pp. 63–64); or "A long and successful evolution has brought about these conditions, but what

Lewis [22] and a Harry Bridges to the fore, and clothing, a Sidney Hillman, and why do coal and longshore and clothing industries perform about the same way in other countries without Lewis, Bridges, and Hillman?

6. *Adherence to ideological views* or merely to certain specific attitudes toward the other party profoundly affects bargaining relationships and the propensity to strike.[23] Communist-led unions probably cause more trouble and tough-minded employers invite more than do non-Communist-led unions and softhearted employers. Belligerent unions and reactionary employers seem, however, to be more effect than cause, for the citadels of union radicalism and the hotbeds of employer reaction are found in about the same industries from country to country.[24]

7. It is suggested, particularly by certain economists, that the *selection of good bargaining techniques* can prevent conflict, since strikes never pay and peace does; [25] but all the parties, regardless of industry, have access to the same storehouse and can draw from it the sword or the green table as they wish. Better bargaining techniques can improve some situations, but it is not for lack of bargaining skill that so many strikes have occurred in the coal mines and on the waterfronts of the world.

8. *"Key" bargains* are thought to lead to more conflict than "satellite"

---

was the genesis of this evolution? Why did collective bargaining get off to a good start in this industry? The personality of Sidney Hillman played a dominant role. His constructive and honest approach was often an effective substitute for the picket line. . . ." (Donald B. Straus, *Hickey-Freeman Company and Amalgamated Clothing Workers,* Washington, National Planning Association, 1949, pp. 70–71).

[22] John L. Lewis may very well have made a greater contribution to industrial tranquillity than Sidney Hillman, for he has channeled the ineluctable unrest of the miners into mass strikes called (usually) at a time of year (in the spring) when they cost the nation the very least. Hillman headed a union which has made a record for industrial peace in an industry which is almost always peaceful.

[23] See Benjamin M. Selekman, "Varieties of Labor Relations," *Harvard Business Review,* Vol. 27, No. 2 (March, 1949). "Beyond any short-term changes in the bargaining program, accordingly, the ideological structure does constitute the most undeviating and ineradicable conflict pattern in present-day industrial relations. For the party-line leaders accept neither the system of free collective bargaining nor the American democracy of which it is a part. Manifestly, such an undivided focus on external goals means that the ideological structure of relationship possesses no innate potentialities for evolution toward a more accommodative structure of joint dealings. Consequently, the reliance on time and experience, which may prove helpful in other structures, in this one can become a source of actual danger. Only by ousting party-line leaders from positions of union leadership, whether by legislation or by employer resistance or by intra-union action, may this source of conflict be minimized."

[24] Not to be neglected is Communist selection of certain strategic industries for infiltration, including coal mining and water transportation. These industries, however, were the locale of many strikes before the Communists became active, but their efforts certainly have served to intensify the conflict in these already favorable environments.

[25] See J. R. Hicks, *The Theory of Wages,* New York, Peter Smith, 1948. "Under a system of collective bargaining . . . the majority of actual strikes are doubtless the result of faulty negotiation. . . . The danger lies in ignorance by one side of the other's dispositions, and in hasty breaking-off of negotiations. . . ." (pp. 146–147). For discussions of the importance of bargaining skill and techniques, see also Sumner H. Slichter, *The Challenge of Industrial Relations,* Ithaca, N.Y., Cornell University Press, 1947, pp. 138–145; and *Massachusetts Proposals for Better Industrial Relations,* Boston, New England Council, 1947, pp. 11–15.

bargains.[26] This thesis cannot be examined very adequately at the interindustry level, since, particularly in the United States, key bargains are made at the company level. However, the key nature of the bargains may explain the comparatively high ranking of the automobile industry in the United States during the second period and of the machinery industry in Germany, where the metalworkers' union is the largest and most powerful union and the normal pattern setter. Again, however, this theory is better at explaining individual situations than at explaining the propensity to strike industry by industry. The steel industry sets patterns in the United States but is not particularly strike prone, and the longshore industry sets no pattern but is strike inclined.

Theories of the Trade-union Movement

The trade-union movement is variously analyzed as moving toward "monopoly," "job control," "status" in its own trade-union society, "bureaucracy," "power accumulation," and "class consciousness." These are either the ascribed goals or contemplated ends, and it might be thought that, as individual unions reach the culmination of their development, some effect on their proneness to strike would be noticed—more peace in the first five cases and more conflict in the last one. What do the facts on the interindustry propensity to strike show? Generally the industries at the conflict end of the ranking have unions with a greater monopoly in the labor market than have those at the other end of the range. Once job control is obtained by the teamsters peace overwhelms the industry, but longshoremen continue their conflict after job control is seized. The garment workers have achieved a degree of status in a partially self-contained society of their own creation and seldom strike; typographical workers have also and are much less quiescent. The "iron law of oligarchy" has been confirmed by the coal miners' union in the United States without the dove of peace alighting on the coal tipple. Power has been accumulated by the unions of mine workers sufficient to make governments shake in the face of it, but the unions have not been satiated; but then the process of striving for power never comes to an end. The class-consciousness theory says that (1) workers are becoming more class minded and that (2), when they do, they are more inclined to violence against the surrounding so-

---

[26] Harbison and Dubin, Dunlop, and others emphasize the key-bargain hypothesis. Harbison and Dubin point to the difficulties in achieving good union-management relations where labor patterns are set rather than followed, and Dunlop points to the overall difficulties in establishing workable relations for the economy where a few key bargains set the pace for the followers. See Frederick H. Harbison and Robert Dubin, *Patterns of Union-Management Relations,* Chicago, Science Research Associates, 1947. "The question of corporation survival and maintenance of employment is not so likely to be a determining factor in negotiations between organizations such as General Motors and the GM Department of the UAW. Negotiations between such giants do not conform solely to our economic environment; indeed they actually tend to create much of the economic environment for the mass production industries. As we have indicated, the forces influencing collective bargaining in the power centers make the development of constructive union-management relations difficult. Here lies the most crucial problem in present-day labor relations. . . ." (p. 221). See also John T. Dunlop, "American Wage Determination: The Trend and Its Significance," in *Wage Determination and the Economics of Liberalism,* Washington, U.S. Chamber of Commerce, 1947, pp. 41–43.

ciety. While the first part of this theory is of doubtful truth, at least for the United States, the data seem to bear out the second part: workers strike most often and most violently when they are in an isolated mass with a strong sense of group, if not class, consciousness.

This suggests that some strikes have elements of a small-scale revolt against society rather than of bargaining tactics alone. There is a sense of a mass grievance against society and little sense of a community responsibility. The cost of striking is lowered, for there is more group support for the strike and less felt public pressure against it; and the gain in prospect is not alone a better contract but the release of accumulated tensions. The single equation of prospective economic cost against prospective economic gain (which will seldom show a positive surplus) is particularly inappropriate here, for cost and gain are calculated in more than the economic dimension. The revolt element is certainly not present in all strikes or even in many, but the industries where it may be present account for a substantial proportion of the man-days lost. In New Zealand, during the first period, over 80 per cent of all man-days lost were in mining and water transport alone; in Germany, during the second period, mining alone accounted for over 40 per cent of the total man-days lost; and in the United Kingdom, mining and quarrying accounted for almost 50 per cent of the total man-days lost in industrial disputes during the three decades covered (exclusive of the 1926 losses). It was out of the isolated masses of coal miners in Great Britain and of longshoremen in San Francisco that two of the greatest general strikes developed.[27]

Summary

The most general explanation of the interindustry propensity to strike is the nature of the industrial environment and, particularly, its tendency to direct workers into isolated masses or to integrate them into the general community. This hypothesis elucidates the behavior of most of the industries surveyed for most of the time periods covered and does so better than alternative theories. However, it does not explain the ranking of all industries for all the time and is less effective in analyzing why industries are medium strike prone than why they are high or low; and thus other explanations are necessary too. We are dealing with complex phenomena and must resort to multiple causation; and, as we have seen, other theories are helpful or essential in explaining certain situations.

The hypothesis of the location of the worker in society is useful for the one task of explaining the interindustry propensity to strike. It has little to

[27] A perusal of Wilfred Harris Crook, *The General Strike,* Chapel Hill, The University of North Carolina Press, 1931, indicates that many of the general strikes evolved from disputes in coal, lumber, textiles, and the waterfront: for example, the 1842 general strike in Britain developed out of a dispute in the collieries as did the 1902 strike in France; the 1904 strike in France began with a lockout of the harbor workmen in Marseilles, and the 1903 strike in Holland also grew out of a dispute which involved the dockers' union; the 1904 strike in Italy developed when troops were sent in to maintain order in a strike of miners; and the 1909 strike in Sweden involved a lockout of sawmill and textile workers (pp. 18–20, 38–39, 115 ff., 185, 283).

say about the behavior of individual firms, except that firms in industries located at the two extremes of the range are more likely to conform to the pattern of their industry than are firms in industries located in the middle of the range. At the level of the firm, many more factors than the industrial environment must be examined, particularly if the industrial environment is "neutral," as it appears to be for the bulk of manufacturing. The only explanation this hypothesis offers for the variation of the propensity to strike from one period of time to another is that the propensity will rise or fall in an industry or society as the workers become more isolated in masses or more integrated into society; and the only clues to the causes of international differences in the inclination to strike are that the industry mix of each nation is important, as is also the general integration of workers and their institutions into society.

The Greater Strategy

"Good" and "evil" in the industrial-relations field are not subject to discovery by any purely technical explorations but must be defined by the exercise of value judgments. It is generally, although by no means universally, accepted that the apparently endemic warfare in the coal industry is as undesirable as the coerced peace in the railroad industry; yet the first may be as environmentally inescapable as the second is socially inevitable. If we wish, nevertheless, to reduce the intensity of conflict in the industries characterized by a high or medium-high propensity to strike, without resorting to a social strategy of divide *or* conquer in an effort to create environments such as those surrounding the workers in some of the "Low" or "Medium-low" industries, what is the most general principle to be followed? It is not making the demand for all products elastic to encourage union-management cooperation, or giving the union a closed shop and an administration safe from the whims of the rank and file for the sake of institutional and leadership security, or training the managerial elite to manipulate the workers the right way, or waiting for time, which solves all problems, to solve this one also, or psychoanalyzing the leaders and turning them into more benevolent despots, or suppressing or encouraging certain ideologies or attitudes, or nailing a list of approved bargaining techniques on every conference table, or designating one industry (preferably one with no useful product) to mark the course for the lambs to follow (although all these devices contain some merit), but it is integrating the worker and his associations, and the employer, as fully as possible into the general society without coercion.[28]

[28] This is, of course, a prescription which is difficult, but not impossible, to apply to the coal mining or lumber or maritime industries. Actually integration is growing with the introduction of the automobile, the radio, and television, the decasualization of work on the waterfront and in the logging camp, the increasing acceptance of trade-unions by employers, by government, and by the community at large, and the spread of popular education. The "homeless, voteless, womanless" worker is now the rare exception, and workers and their institutions share more in the operation of society. With these fundamental changes the industries of high propensity to strike are presumably becoming less conflict inclined, although they may always rank high comparatively. If, instead of reducing conflict through a policy of individual and group assimilation, it were wished to intensify it,

The effort should be to increase vertical and horizontal mobility, to encourage a wide variety of mixed associations, to break down barriers between groups and between individuals, to create the mixed community instead of the "Gold Coast" or the "back of the yards," which alike inspire ideological thinking. The opposite road is toward the all-absorbing party of the Communists, the all-absorbing corporation of Mayo,[29] and the all-absorbing union of Tannenbaum.[30] Of the isolated group and the isolated groupless individual, it is the former which is the greater threat to democracy. Rather than either of these, however, we should encourage the limited-function party, the limited-function corporation, the limited-function union,[31] and the unlimited individual. The extreme left and the extreme right alike seek the answer in the monolithic organization. The democratic approach is for the individual to be many things, but most of all a citizen, and to find his protection from domination from any source in the multiplicity of organizations.

---

then the appropriate social program would be to isolate the workers and immerse them in a segregated organization.

[29] "Mayo gives us instances where industrial administrators have succeeded in making factory groups so stable in their attitudes of group cooperation that men in the groups explicitly recognized that the factory had become for them the stabilizing force around which they developed satisfying lives. . . . Thus Mayo shows us for the first time in the form of specific instances that it is within the power of industrial administrators to create within industry itself a partially effective substitute for the old stabilizing effect of the neighborhood. Given stable employment, it might make of industry (as of the small town during most of our national life) a socially satisfying way of life as well as a way of making a living." See Wallace B. Donham, "Foreword," in Elton Mayo, *The Social Problems of an Industrial Civilization*, Cambridge, Mass., Harvard University Press, 1945, pp. viii–ix.

[30] Frank Tannenbaum, *A Philosophy of Labor*, New York, Knopf, 1951. "In terms of the individual, the union returns to the worker his 'society.' It gives him a fellowship, a part in a drama that he can understand, and life takes on meaning once again because he shares a value system common to others. Institutionally the trade-union movement is an unconscious effort to harness the drift of our time and reorganize it around the cohesive identity that men working together always achieve. . . ." (p. 10). "The trade-union is the real alternative to the authoritarian state. The trade-union is our modern 'society,' the only true society that industrialism has fostered. As a true society it is concerned with the whole man, and embodies the possibilities of both the freedom and the security essential to human dignity. The corporation and the union will ultimately merge in common ownership and cease to be a house divided. It is only thus that a common identity may once again come to rule the lives of men and endow each one with rights and duties recognized by all. . . ." (pp. 198–199).

[31] See Will Herberg, "For 'Limited' as against 'Total' Unionism," *Labor and Nation*, Vol. 1, No. 5 (April–May, 1946). "Each kind of organization has its own proper function in the pluralistic scheme of a democratic society and for its own good as well as for the good of society as a whole, each should confine itself primarily to the sphere determined by that function. There are undoubtedly other purposes and interests of deep concern to workers, who, it must be remembered, are not merely workers, but men and citizens as well. For the furtherance of these purposes and interests there exist a wide variety of organizations—and where none exist new ones may be formed—in which trade unionists may naturally take part, though not as trade unionists but in one or another of the many capacities in which citizens function in a free pluralistic society."

Technical Supplement

Usable data were found for eleven countries, and the rankings prepared from these data are set forth in Table 14.2. Data were examined for six additional countries but in each case were inadequate:

<table>
<tr><td>Belgium</td><td>Man-days lost in industrial disputes, by industry, were not published until very recently.</td></tr>
<tr><td>Canada</td><td>No employment figures are available to match against man-days lost.</td></tr>
<tr><td>Denmark</td><td>Man-days lost are shown by occupation instead of by industry.</td></tr>
<tr><td>Finland</td><td>Data on man-days lost are given by occupation and by industry, but no comparable employment data are available.</td></tr>
<tr><td>France</td><td>Man-days lost are published in aggregate but are not broken down by industry.</td></tr>
<tr><td>Union of South Africa</td><td>No employment data are available to match against the data on man-days lost given by industry and occupation.</td></tr>
</table>

The essential facts on the data for the eleven countries follow:

<table>
<tr><td>Australia</td><td>Man-days lost and trade-union membership data are available for fourteen industry groups for approximately three decades, which have been divided into three periods in Table 14.2.</td></tr>
<tr><td>Czechoslovakia</td><td>Data on man-days lost are available for the same twenty industry groupings for the period 1921–1936 (except for 1926–1928 and 1931). Employment data for the same industry groupings are from the 1921 and 1930 censuses.</td></tr>
<tr><td>Germany</td><td>Data on man-days lost are available for twenty-one industry groupings for the period 1915–1924 and for twenty-four industry groupings for 1925–1932; and employment data, for the same groupings for 1907 and 1925. It has been assumed that employment ranking in those 2 years was representative for the two periods respectively.</td></tr>
<tr><td>Italy</td><td>Data on man-days lost are available for seventeen industry groupings only for the 8 years 1916–1923. Trade-union membership data for the same groupings are available for 1921.</td></tr>
<tr><td>Netherlands</td><td>Data on man-days lost are available for twenty-one industry groupings for the period 1918–1940 (except for 1919 and 1927). Comparable employment data are taken from the 1920 and 1930 censuses of industry. The data are divided into two periods in Table 14.2.</td></tr>
<tr><td>New Zealand</td><td>Data on man-days lost are available for approximately three decades (except for 1944 and 1945) for fifteen industry groupings; and trade-union membership statistics, for the same</td></tr>
</table>

groupings for 1924–1948. The periods set forth in Table 14.2 were selected for the consistency of behavior in each period.

Norway Statistics on man-days lost and workers covered by collective agreement are available for nineteen industry groupings for 1925–1949, but Table 14.2 is based only on the period to 1939 since strikes were banned during the war.

Sweden Man-days lost and workers covered by collective agreement are available for the same fourteen industry groups for 1920–1937.

Switzerland Data on man-days lost are available for the period 1927–1949 for ten industry groupings and are divided in Table 14.2 into two periods, 1927–1939 and 1940–1949, with employment data for 1930 and 1941 taken as representative for the two periods respectively.

United Kingdom Data on man-days lost are available for only six industry groupings. The ranking in Table 14.2 is based on the calculations of K. C. G. Knowles of man-days lost per worker in employment for the period 1911–1945.

United States Man-days lost and employment estimates are available for twenty-one industry groupings for the period 1927–1941 and for twenty-eight groupings for 1942–1948.

The industries for each period in each country (except the United Kingdom) were ranked, first, by number of man-days lost and, second, by volume of employment (or by union members or by workers covered by contract, as the case might be),[32] and then the relation of the one rank to the other was noted. Table 14.2 shows the industries in their resultant ranking. They have been arbitrarily divided into five categories as follows:

High   Man-days lost rank substantially above employment rank
Medium high   Man-days lost rank significantly above employment rank
Medium   About the same ranking for both
Medium low   Man-days lost rank significantly below employment rank
Low   Man-days lost rank substantially below employment rank

Man-days lost, in each case, are the total of man-days idle because of both strikes and lockouts. "Masked strikes" and "slowdowns" are not included.

---

[32] In the first instance (employment), the propensity to organize and then to strike is shown; and in the second and third (union members and workers covered), to strike after being organized. The difference is not so great, however, as might at first appear, since in four countries where employment data were not used (Australia, New Zealand, Norway, and Sweden), unionization is very widespread. We should have preferred to use employment data throughout since we are concerned with the propensity of the workers in an industry to strike or, since organization is normally a prerequisite to striking, to organize and then to strike. Generally, workers who are not easily organized are also the ones who do not readily strike once they have been organized.

Table 14.2 Interindustry Propensity to Strike

	High	Medium high	Medium	Medium low	Low
Australia 1919–1929	Mining Shipping, wharf labor, etc.	Wood, furniture, sawmills, etc. Books, printing, etc.	Other manufacturing industries Other land transport Engineering, metal works, etc. Building	Domestic, hotel, etc. Miscellaneous Food, drink, etc. Railway and tramway services	Pastoral and agriculture Clothing, textiles, boots, etc.
1930–1939	Mining Shipping, wharf labor, etc.	Pastoral and agriculture Other land transport	Engineering, metal works, etc. Food, drink, etc. Other manufacturing industries Wood, furniture, sawmills, etc. Books, printing, etc.	Domestic, hotel, etc. Clothing, textiles, boots, etc. Building Miscellaneous	Railway and tramway services
1940–1946	Mining Shipping, wharf labor, etc.	Books, printing, etc. Food, drink, etc. Other manufacturing industries	Building Other land transport Wood, furniture, sawmills, etc. Engineering, metal works, etc.	Domestic, hotel, etc. Pastoral and agriculture Clothing, textiles, boots, etc.	Railway and tramway services Miscellaneous
Czechoslovakia 1921–1936	Mining and metallurgy Quarrying and stoneware	Pottery and glassware Skins, leather, etc. Textile industry Chemical industry Paper industry	Building Wood Gas, water, and electricity Rubber Machines Printing Metals Clothing	Banks, etc. Food and drink	Hotels and restaurants Agriculture Commerce and auxiliary branches
Germany 1915–1924	Machinery Mining (coal, salt, etc.) Chemicals	Wood and wood products Printing and publishing Quarrying	Metals Forestry and allied products Fishing and animal husbandry Textiles Transportation and communication Leather Paper Gardening Arts and crafts	Construction Hotels, inns, etc. Health and sanitation Food, drink, tobacco, etc.	Clothing Trade

SOURCES: Australia—*Official Yearbook of the Commonwealth of Australia*; Czechoslovakia—*Manuel statistique de la république tchécoslovaque* and *Annuaire statistique de la république tchécoslovaque*; Germany—*Statistisches Jahrbuch für das deutsche Reich* and *Statistik der deutschen Reichs*; Italy—*Annuario statistico italiano*; Netherlands—*Jaarcijfers voor Nederland*; New Zealand—*New Zealand Official Yearbook*; Norway—*Statistisk Arbok for Norge*; Sweden—

	High	Medium high	Medium	Medium low	Low
Germany (*Continued*)					
1925–1932	Musical instruments and toys Iron-, steel-, and metal-works Quarrying Iron and metal extraction	Machinery (including vehicles) Electrical machinery, precision instruments, and optical industries Rubber and asbestos Fishing Textile Wood and wood products Paper and printing	Chemicals Construction Mining Theater, music, sports, etc.	Clothing Gardening and animal husbandry Leather and linoleum Transporta-tion and com-munication Water, gas, and electricity Food, drink, tobacco, etc.	Hotels, restaurants, etc. Health and sanitation Trade
Italy 1916–1923	Mining (extraction industries)	Food and drink Stone, clay, and sand Textiles	Skins and leather Buttons, etc. Paper and printing Metallurgy and machines Precision instruments and precious metals Clothing Transportation and communication Wood, straw, and allied industries Construction	Agriculture	Chemical industries Production and distri-bution of power, light, heat, and water Commerce and public services
Netherlands 1918–1929	Manufacture of goods of wood, cork, and straw Mining and peat cutting Manufacture of earthen-ware, glass, lime, and stoneware	Building and related industries Applied art Chemical industries Paper industry	Metal industry Diamonds and other precious stones Printing industry Fishing and hunting Transport Food, drink, and tobacco Textile industry Insurance	Leather, oilcloth, and rubber industries Gas, water, and electricity Clothing and cleaning	Agriculture Credit and banking Commerce

Arbetsinstallelser och Kollektivavtal samt Forlikningsmannens Verksamhet; Switzerland—*Statis-tisches Jahrbuch der Schweiz;* United Kingdom—K. C. G. Knowles, "Strikes and Their Changing Economic Context," *Bulletin of the Oxford University Institute of Statistics,* September, 1947; United States—*Handbook of Labor Statistics,* 1947 ed., *Statistical Abstract of the United States,* and *Strikes in the United States 1880–1936,* U.S. Bureau of Labor Statistics (Bulletin 651); and *Yearbook of Labor Statistics,* General-international Labor Office.

Table 14.2 Interindustry Propensity to Strike (Continued)

	High	Medium high	Medium	Medium low	Low
Netherlands (*Continued*) 1930–1940	Fishing and hunting Paper industry	Textiles Manufacture of earthen- ware, glass, lime, and stoneware Manufacture of goods of wood, cork, and straw Building and related industries Clothing and cleaning	Metal industry Mining, peat cutting Diamonds and other precious stones Applied art Food, drink, and tobacco Printing Chemicals Gas, water, and electricity Insurance Transport	Credit and banking Leather, oilcloth, and rubber industries	Agriculture Commerce
New Zealand 1920–1934	Mines and quarries Transport by water	Wood, etc.	The land (farming) Food, drink, etc. Power, heat, and light Metal Accommodations, meals, and personal services Skins, leather, etc.	Stone, clay, glass, and chemicals Miscellaneous Paper, printing, etc.	Clothing, footwear, and textiles Transport by land Building and construc- tion
1935–1939	Mines and quarries Stone, clay, glass, and chemicals Transport by water Wood, etc.	Power, heat, and light	Paper, printing, etc. Food, drink, etc. Metal Skins, leather, etc. Building and construction		Miscellaneous Transport by land Clothing, footwear, and textiles Accommoda- tions, meals, and personal services The land
1940–1948	Mines and quarries Transport by water	Wood, etc. Stone, clay, glass, and chemicals Power, heat, and light Accommoda- tions, meals, and personal services	Skins, leather, etc. Food, drink, etc. Paper, printing, etc. Building and construction Metal	Clothing, footwear, and textiles Transport by land	The land Miscellane- ous
Norway 1925–1939	Textiles Mining and quarrying Extraction of metals	Paper Leather and rubber Publishing and printing Metal industries	Food and tobacco Clothing Forestry Wood Gas and electricity Construction Hotels and restaurants Oils and lubricants	Chemical industries	Trade Transporta- tion and navigation Miscellane- ous

210

	High	Medium high	Medium	Medium low	Low
Sweden 1920–1937	Mining and quarrying	Leather, skins, and rubber	Forestry and wood Construction Paper and printing Chemicals Textiles and clothing Agriculture and fishing Food Other industries Commerce and trade	Metallurgy and construction of machines Land and water transport Public institutions and enterprises	
Switzerland 1927–1939		Leather and rubber Mining Wood and pottery Textile industry	Construction Clocks and jewelry Chemicals Metals and machines		Clothing Transport
1940–1949	Mining Wood and pottery		Chemicals Leather and rubber Construction Textiles Metals and machines Clocks and jewelry		Clothing Transport
United Kingdom 1911–1945	Mining and quarrying	Textiles	Metal and engineering industries Transport and communication Building and construction industries	Clothing	
United States 1927–1941	Anthracite-coal mining Bituminous-coal mining	Lumber, timber, basic products, furniture, and finished lumber products Textiles and apparel Leather and leather products Transportation equipment (including autos and auto equipment) Miscellaneous manufacturing industries	Construction Transportation, communication, etc. Stone, clay, and glass products Nonferrous metals and their products Tobacco manufacturing Iron and steel and their products Machinery (including electrical)	Services, personal, business, and others Food and kindred products Paper and allied products, printing, publishing, and allied industries Chemicals and allied products, products of petroleum and coal	Trade Other nonmanufacturing industries Agriculture, forestry, and fishing

211

Table 14.2 Interindustry Propensity to Strike (Continued)

	High	Medium high	Medium	Medium low	Low
United States (Continued) 1942–1948	Bituminous-coal mining Anthracite-coal mining Stone, clay, and glass products Automobiles and automobile equipment Rubber and rubber products	Leather and leather products Textile-mill products Lumber and timber basic products Nonferrous metals and their products Iron and steel and their products	Food and kindred products Products of petroleum and coal Transportation equipment (except autos) Machinery (except electrical) Paper and allied products Tobacco manufacturing Transportation, communication, etc. Construction Furniture and finished lumber products Electrical machinery	Printing, publishing, and allied trades Chemicals and allied products Miscellaneous manufacturing industries	Trade Apparel and other finished products Other nonmanufacturing industries Services, personal, business, etc. Agriculture, forestry, and fishing Finance, insurance, and real estate

CHAPTER 15 INDUSTRIAL CONFLICT AND BUSINESS FLUCTUATIONS

Albert Rees [1]   *University of Chicago*

It has long been recognized that there are cycles of strikes and that they are probably related to the business cycle. If the forces which tend to create a pattern of regularity in strike fluctuations can be identified, it is important to do so. Unless we learn to understand this pattern, cyclical changes in the level of strikes may be mistaken for permanent changes in the economic, social, or psychological determinants of the amount of industrial conflict. Since strikes are often the subject of legislation or other government action, such mistakes in the diagnosis of strike fluctuations might contribute to errors in public policy.

Nature of the Problem

Without examining any evidence, one might expect either a positive or an inverse correlation between strikes and the business cycle. The expectation of an inverse correlation could result from the view that strikes are essentially a protest of workers against intolerable conditions and that the conditions which provoke strikes are most common during depressions. This view is deeply rooted in Marxist thought, although the original statement of it does not mention strikes as such:

> The growing competition among the bourgeois, and the resulting commercial crises, make the wages of the workers ever more fluctuating. The unceasing improvement of machinery, ever more rapidly developing, makes their livelihood more and more precarious; the collisions between individual workmen and individual bourgeois take more and more the character of collisions between two classes. Thereupon the workers begin to form combinations (trade unions) against the bourgeois; they club together in order to keep up the rate of wages; they found permanent associations in order to make provision beforehand for these occasional revolts. Here and there the contest breaks out into riots.[2]

More explicit references to strikes as a protest in time of depression can be found in later communist literature. Thus a leader [3] of the Red International of Labour Unions said in 1931:

---

[1] The author is indebted to Profs. Milton Friedman, Joel Seidman, and Harold L. Wilensky for valuable suggestions. This chapter is based on an article in *Journal of Political Economy*, October, 1952, which presents in detail the statistical analysis the conclusions of which are summarized here.

[2] Karl Marx, *Manifesto of the Communist Party*, New York, International Publishers, 1932, p. 18.

[3] A. Lozovsky (S. A. Dridzo), *The World Economic Crisis, Strike Struggles and the*

213

The sharper a crisis becomes, the more it undermines the already tottering capitalist stabilisation, the more rapid the succession of political crises, the more they will be accompanied by an ever-increasing number of economic and political strikes. Even now the wave of discontent and workers' protests is rising. Even now hundreds of thousands of workers are demonstrating their discontent and despair by mass demonstrations and strikes.

The expectation of a positive correlation between strikes and the business cycle could result from either of two views. The first retains the notion of the strike as a protest but argues that protest does not occur when objective conditions are worst. Such a position has often been expressed in connection with the analysis of revolution. A good recent statement is that of Eric Hoffer: [4]

> Discontent is likely to be highest when misery is bearable; when conditions have so improved that an ideal state seems almost within reach. A grievance is most poignant when almost redressed. . . . It is not actual suffering but the taste of better things which excites people to revolt.

Alternatively, a positive correlation might be expected from the view that the modern strike is no longer essentially a protest but rather a strategic weapon of "business unions" in their continual quest for gains for their members. This weapon will be used when business conditions promise the most success. The following example of this position is taken from the report of the president of an international union to his members:

> We should always be prepared, ready and willing to strike, but never do so unless it is absolutely necessary as well as advisable, and after the chances of success and defeat have been studiously calculated. . . . Our condition, strength, locality, and resources, coupled with the strength and resources of the employer and trade conditions, should never be overlooked. . . . Strikes under any circumstances should not be countenanced until all honorable means, including conferences, conciliation, and arbitration to avoid them have been supplied. This expression of conviction goes double in times of industrial and commercial stagnation. [5]

Data on the relation between strikes and business fluctuations for any country should help to create an understanding of the basic nature of its strikes. Unfortunately, various students of this relation in the United States have not been in agreement. Hansen, analyzing strike data from 1881 to 1919, concluded that "strikes correlate inversely with the business cycle in periods of long-run falling prices, while they correspond directly with the business cycle in periods of long-run rising prices." [6] Griffen, analyzing strike data for 1881 to 1937, concluded that the troughs of his strike cycles corresponded generally with the years of depressions and that ten of the fifteen peaks of strike cycles

---

Tasks of the Revolutionary Trade Union Movement, Fifth World Congress of the Red International of Labour Unions, Moscow and Leningrad, State Publishers, 1931, p. 51.

[4] Eric Hoffer, *The True Believer,* New York, Harper, 1951, pp. 27–28.

[5] George W. Perkins, "Report of the President," *Proceedings of the Cigarmakers' International Union,* September, 1912. Reproduced in David J. Saposs, *Readings in Trade Unionism,* New York, Doran, 1926, pp. 181–182.

[6] Alvin H. Hansen, "Cycles of Strikes," *American Economic Review,* 11 (1921), 620.

corresponded with what he considered to be years of recession or depression.[7] Yoder, analyzing the same period as Griffen, concluded that sharp increases in strikes were associated with increases in business activity, while sharp decreases in strikes were associated with decreases in business activity. However, he cautions us that "no simple covariation such as might be measured by linear correlation is observable. For the forty-nine years for which numbers of strikes are available, the linear measure of correlation between annual measures of strikes and indexes of business activity is $r = 0.11$ (1 per cent limit: 1.36)." [8] A recent study by Jurkat and Jurkat shows a high positive conformity of strikes to the business cycle.[9]

The conflicting and somewhat inconclusive nature of the findings of previous studies indicated the need for further work. The author has recently completed a new study of the relation between strikes and the business cycle, the results of which are summarized in the following section.

Correlation between Strikes and the Business Cycle

The study which is summarized here is based on an analysis of the number of strikes beginning in each month for the period 1915–1950, as published by the Bureau of Labor Statistics. The method of analysis used was that of the National Bureau of Economic Research. The principal findings are as follows:

1. It is possible to identify, from deseasonalized data on the number of strikes, recurring cycles of very great amplitude.

2. During the period 1915–1938, there was a high correspondence between strike cycles and the business cycle. The conformity of strikes to the cycle during this period is greater than that of the average of 147 series on prices analyzed by the National Bureau and greater than that of any subgroup of prices, except prices of durable goods. This is noteworthy because price movements are generally considered an essential part of the business cycle, while strikes generally are not. However, the strike series does not conform to the cycle as well as do the averages of all series in each of these areas: construction contracts, production, payrolls and other income payments, and employment.

3. There was very little correspondence between strikes and the business cycle during the war and postwar years, 1939–1950. The lack of correspondence during this period occurs for three reasons: (a) There was a sharp drop in strikes from September, 1941, to November, 1942, associated with America's entry into the war and not corresponding to any contraction in business activity. (b) The mild contraction in business activity from February to October, 1945, was accompanied by an increase in strikes. The usual effect of a contraction in reducing the number of strikes was apparently outweighed by the re-

[7] John I. Griffen, *Strikes: A Study in Quantitative Economics*, New York, Columbia University Press, 1939, p. 49.

[8] Dale Yoder, "Economic Changes and Industrial Unrest in the United States," *Journal of Political Economy*, 48 (1940), 222–237.

[9] Ernest H. Jurkat and Dorothy B. Jurkat, "Economic Function of Strikes," *Industrial and Labor Relations Review*, 2 (July, 1949), 527–545.

moval of restraints on striking at the end of the war. (*c*) There was a sharp drop in strikes from April to November, 1947, associated with the passage of the Taft-Hartley Act and not corresponding to any contraction in business activity.[10]

4. It was possible to compare the timing of strike cycles and business cycles at six peaks and six troughs of business activity. The number of strikes generally began to decline before business activity did and generally started to rise after business activity did. In no case did strikes lag at the peak; they led in five cases and coincided in one. At the troughs, strikes lagged four times, coincided once, and led once (in 1932). The average lead at the peaks was five months; the average lag at the troughs was six months.

The study also analyzed the data published by the Bureau of Labor Statistics on the major issues involved in strikes and on the outcome of strikes. The issues involved are classified into three major groups: wages and hours, organization, and miscellaneous. Strikes involving both organization and wage issues are included under "organization," as are strikes over union security issues. The proportion of strikes in the category "wages and hours" rose during the depression of 1921 and rose sharply after 1929. However, the proportion of strikes involving wages fell slightly in the "recessions" of 1938 and 1949. The proportion of strikes involving organization fell in 1921, from 1929 to 1932, in 1938, and again in 1949. Strikes involving union recognition follow a pattern similar to that of all strikes involving organization.

Strikes involving wage decreases can be separated from all wage-and-hour strikes. As a fraction of all wage-and-hour strikes, strikes involving wage decreases show an extraordinary sensitivity to the business cycle. They rise very sharply in depressions and fall in the cyclical peaks. In only one case does the series fail to correspond to a cyclical peak or trough: it does not fall in the peak of 1919. In 1935 it has a pronounced rise not associated with a cyclical trough; this was probably a result of the invalidation of the National Industrial Recovery Act.

The results of strikes are classified into the categories substantially won, compromised, lost, and others. The "substantially won" category and the "lost" category respond to the major swings of the business cycle. Strikes won fall sharply in 1921 and fall in 1930 and 1938. Somewhat surprisingly, they rise from 1930 to 1932. Strikes lost rise sharply in 1921, rise from 1929 to 1932, and rise somewhat in 1938.

Data on the average duration of strikes are available annually since 1927 but show no relation to the business cycle.

Interpretation of the Findings

What is the meaning of the positive correlation of strikes and the business cycle? One approach suggested by the lead of strikes at the peaks would be to regard the relation as one in which strikes are a causal force and changes

---

[10] The Taft-Hartley Act was passed close to the middle of this period. The decline in strikes before its passage may have reflected an attempt by unions to influence Congress; that following its passage probably reflected caution on the part of union leaders while they were becoming familiar with the new law.

in business conditions, at least in part, a result of strike fluctuations. Griffen advances such a theory, although with some hesitancy. He argues [11] that a strike peak, by adversely affecting the expectations of businessmen, would cause a downturn in economic activity. The Jurkats also argue that strikes are a determinant of general business conditions, but in a different way. They hold [12] that strikes, by increasing wages, provide purchasing power and thus help to expand production during the upswing. Both views seem to overestimate the importance of strikes, and the second has the additional fault of over-looking the depressing effects of strikes and of wage increases through increases in costs and the creation of pessimistic expectations.

The Bureau of Labor Statistics has estimated the time lost in strikes as a per cent of total time worked for each year since 1927. The highest prewar figure was 0.43 per cent in 1937; the lowest was 0.05 per cent in 1930. The all-time high of 1.43 per cent occurred in 1946. These figures may somewhat understate the real loss, since strikes also cause idleness for many nonstrikers. On the other hand, some strike losses are recovered after the strike is over by increasing employment or hours to levels that they would not have reached if the strike had not occurred. The small magnitude of the strike loss indicates that we should abandon the notion that strikes are a cause of the business cycle.

The correlation can be much better explained in the opposite direction. Such an explanation does not need to assume that the timing of all strikes is determined by the business cycle. There will, of course, be many strikes whose timing is unrelated to business conditions. It is sufficient that the timing of a considerable proportion of strikes is determined by the cycle.

A cyclical fluctuation in the number of strikes could occur for any of three reasons: (1) The propensity to strike of workers in a given organized unit (department, plant, or company) could vary with the cycle. (2) The number of such units organized by unions could fluctuate with the cycle; since the great majority of all strikes are conducted by unions,[13] this could cause the number of strikes to fluctuate even though the propensity to strike in each organized unit remained constant. (3) The scope of strikes could change during the cycle, so that during the expansion strikes took place in small units (departments or plants), while during the contraction they took place in large units (companies or industries). This would cause cyclical variation in the number of separate strikes reported without any variation in the propensity of given workers to strike.[14]

Rough statistical checks can be made on the last two possibilities. No data are available on the number of organized units, but the number of union members serves as a crude substitute. The fluctuation in actual union membership is probably somewhat greater than that of the reported membership, since unions are reluctant to admit membership losses. Union-membership figures

[11] *Op. cit.*, pp. 51, 204. Griffen ascribes this view to A. C. Pigou. However, he clearly seems to have misinterpreted him. See A. C. Pigou, *Industrial Fluctuations*, London, Macmillan & Co., 1927, pp. 45–47.

[12] *Op. cit.*, p. 540.

[13] From 1927 to 1936 strikes which did not involve unions varied between 6 and 19 per cent of all strikes. In recent years the corresponding figure has been much lower, usually below 2 per cent.

[14] The author is indebted to Prof. H. Gregg Lewis for suggesting possibilities 2 and 3.

show declines in the depressions of 1921 and 1929–1932 which may help to explain declines in the number of strikes. At other times, however, union membership moves counter to the strike series; this is especially true in the expansion of 1922–1923 and the contraction of 1938. Even when the movements are in the same direction, the strike movements are much larger. Thus cyclical fluctuation in union membership is at best a minor contributing cause of the cyclical fluctuation in strikes.

Data on the number of strikes involving one, two to five, and more than five establishments is available annually since 1917. These series show no cyclical fluctuation. Cyclical variation in the scope of strikes does not seem to be a cause of the fluctuation in their number. Changes in the propensity to strike thus seem to be the principal cause of cyclical strike fluctuations. Why should these conform to the business cycle?

The finding that strikes are positively correlated with the cycle discredits the view that most strikes in the United States represent a protest against the worsening of conditions, although the data on strikes involving wage decreases show that there are some strikes of this nature. The statistical findings do not aid a choice between the view that strikes are usually a protest over grievances which have almost been redressed and the view that they are usually a strategic weapon rather than a spontaneous protest. The explanation which follows will adhere to the latter view. This seems consistent with the fact that most strikes are conducted by unions and with the predominant characteristics of trade-unionism in this country.

The principal economic factor affecting union behavior is the state of the labor market—the amount of employment available. Employment is very highly correlated with the business cycle. Strikes occur during periods of rising employment to secure wage increases and other benefits in unionized plants and also to organize the unorganized.[15] Rising employment and improving business conditions offer the unions a variety of strategic advantages. The employer's reluctance to lose his share of the expanding market and his observation of rising wages elsewhere lower his resistance to union demands. His ability to replace strikers with nonstrikers diminishes as employment rises, and the strikers have an increased chance of obtaining employment elsewhere if the employer succeeds in replacing them. If the expansion produces a rising cost of living, workers will protest in firms whose wages lag behind this rise.

An additional factor which may lead to an increase in strikes during periods of expansion is the increased willingness of workers to strike after a long period of steady work. At such times a short strike may be a welcomed vacation rather than a hardship. This factor was probably more important before paid vacations for wage earners became common.

In periods of falling employment there is a sharp drop in organizational strikes. Employees in nonunion establishments become afraid to form unions for fear that they can easily be discharged and replaced by others. Employees

---

[15] There are still a substantial number of strikes for union recognition, despite the Wagner and Taft-Hartley Acts. Some of these are in firms in intrastate commerce in states without comparable state laws; others represent a desire to avoid the delays and complications of representation elections.

already organized will also be afraid to strike when they see the bargaining power of the employer rise relative to theirs. The employer's hand may be strengthened by his ability to fill orders out of inventory or to make up lost production after the strike is over. The union may fear that a strike or the granting of economic concessions by the employer would damage his competitive position and thus imperil the jobs of some union members. This will be especially true where the employer faces competition from nonunionized employers. Moreover, workers who keep full-time jobs during the early stages of a depression usually get real wage increases without striking. These are produced, on the one hand, by the general tendency of wages to be sticky downward, reinforced by fixed-term union contracts, and on the other hand, by the fall in consumer prices. As the downswing progresses, a rising proportion of the diminishing number of strikes represents protests against wage reductions made or proposed by employers.

The explanation above assumes that the timing of strikes is largely in the hands of the union. It is true that "it takes two to make a quarrel" and that employers also have a strike strategy. By making or refusing to make concessions, employers can often determine whether or not a strike will take place. The employer is most anxious to avoid strikes when demand is brisk and business is profitable; he has less need to make concessions when times are bad. Hence, if employer strategy dominated the timing of strikes, we would expect an inverse correlation with the cycle. The finding of a positive correlation thus indicates that union strategy dominates the over-all picture, although this is probably not true in all sections of the economy.

While so far an attempt has been made to explain the general correlation between strikes and the cycle, the timing at the peaks and troughs has not been explained. Why does the strike peak consistently precede the peak in business activity? The strike peak probably represents a maximum in the divergence of expectations between employers and unions. Unions pay close attention to employment, which generally does not lead at the peak.[16] They will also be influenced by previous wage increases received by other unions and by increases in the cost of living. The attention of employers is likely to be focused on some of the activities which do lead at the peak, and they will thus resist demands for which the unions are still willing to fight. Of special interest to employers among the changes which generally precede the cyclical peak are the rise in the number and probabilities of business failures and the fall in investment, security issues, contracts, and orders.[17] Most of these changes reflect changed expectations on the part of businessmen. As the cyclical peak is reached, the more pessimistic expectations may be shared by some union leaders, and strikes fall off.

The prevailing lag of the strike series at the troughs is more simply explained. It seems to represent a "wait-and-see" attitude of union leaders, who want assurance that the revival is genuine before risking the jobs of their

---

[16] See Daniel Creamer, *Behavior of Wage Rates during Business Cycles,* National Bureau of Economic Research Occasional Paper 34, 1950, Charts 1 and 4.

[17] Wesley C. Mitchell, *What Happens during Business Cycles,* New York, National Bureau of Economic Research. 1951, p. 71.

members. The exceptional upturn in strikes of November, 1932, seems to be related to the election of President Roosevelt, which raised the hopes of unionists before his policies began to affect business conditions.

Political events, government policies, and the climate of public opinion all have an important influence on the timing of strikes and will account for many deviations from the normal cyclical pattern. The sharp impact of Pearl Harbor and the Taft-Hartley Act on the number of strikes is evidence of this. It could be argued that the conformity of strikes to the business cycle was a phenomenon of the interwar period and that primarily political determination of the timing of strikes, such as that of the past 10 years, can be expected to continue. However, disturbances in labor relations of the magnitude of Pearl Harbor and Taft-Hartley are rare, and it seems more likely that the timing of strikes will continue to respond to the business cycle, unless the amplitude of changes in business activity is much smaller in the future than it has been in the past.

Strikes may follow a pattern of response to recurrent political events, such as elections, superimposed on the pattern of response to business cycles. However, it is outside the scope of this paper to investigate this possibility.

If the business cycle is not the sole determinant of the timing of strikes, still less is it their cause. Most industrial disputes are caused by social and psychological forces or by economic forces which are noncyclical in nature. Many result from problems peculiar to labor-management relations in particular plants and firms. However, the cyclical pattern of strikes resembles the pattern of production of durable, rather than of nondurable, consumer goods. This suggests that many of the grievances of industrial workers are "durable" or at least "semidurable." Grievances can be stored up for long periods. They are most likely to boil over into strikes or to be utilized by union leaders as strike issues when business conditions promise that strikes may be successful. The same provocation which causes a strike when employment opportunities are rising might cause only grumbling during a depression.

It follows that the elimination of the business cycle would not necessarily reduce the number of strikes but might merely space them more evenly over time or alter the issues which occasion them. Changes in the cost of living would become less important as a cause of disputes, whereas the issue of wage increases to keep pace with rising productivity, now often a part of other adjustments to cyclical changes, would become more important in its own right. However, some strikes seem to serve useful social and psychological functions, and therefore the elimination of all strikes is not necessarily a desirable objective. The stabilization of the general level of prices and greater stability in employment are desperately needed for many other reasons. They will continue to be sought eagerly despite their failure to promise the elimination of industrial conflict.

CHAPTER 16 OCCUPATIONAL STRUCTURE AND INDUSTRIAL CONFLICT

Wilbert E. Moore   *Princeton University*

Occupational specialization, or the division of labor, has long been recognized as a variable closely linked to the industrial system of production. No society is or could be completely homogeneous in occupational roles. But it is especially in societies utilizing inanimate sources of power and inanimate mechanisms for multiplying the effect of human effort that the division of labor is most marked.

The functional connections between these aspects of industrial systems cannot be set out in detail here. It is perhaps sufficient to note that extensive occupational specialization is both a source and a consequence of the marked productive superiority of industrial as compared with nonindustrial economies. The productive efficiencies of specialization have been commented on since the classical writers in economics. Less frequently noted is the circumstance that the remarkable volume and efficiency of physical production, together with the extensive system of exchange inherent in the industrial system, have made possible and even necessary an elaborate specialization in the production of various "services." Some of these services which have been "moved into the market" through occupational specialization, for example, various aspects of the provision of economic security, are essential functions in any society. Other services are peculiar or peculiarly important in industrial economies, for example, distribution of commodities, technical education, and the keeping of elaborate records. The quantitative importance of still other services would appear to be in some measure simply the consequence of productive efficiencies and of the attendant possibilities of a mass market for nonmaterial products, for example, commercial entertainment and recreation.

The importance of the division of labor in industrial systems is not confined to its consequences for production and distribution. At least since the time of Marx,[1] the relations among various occupational positions have been recognized as having major implications for the structure and stability of society as a whole. And since the work of Durkheim on division of labor,[2] at least some social scientists have explored the proposition that occupational interdependence does not assure social solidarity.

The present essay is primarily concerned with the significance of *changes*

[1] For example, see Karl Marx, *A Contribution to the Critique of Political Economy,* New York, International Library Publishing Co., 1904, esp. "Author's Preface" and "Appendix."

[2] See Emile Durkheim, *On the Division of Labor in Society,* trans. George Simpson, New York, Macmillan, 1933, esp. "Preface to the Second Edition."

in occupational structure for the occurrence and pattern of industrial conflict. Its two major sections deal respectively with a review of the dynamic characteristics of industrialism and their occupational consequences and with the implications of those changes for industrial conflict.

Dynamic Characteristics of Industrialism

No industrial system is static in its economic or sociological features, and indeed it may be argued that in every industrial system change is institutionalized. Whether or not this is an essential feature of industrialism is not of immediate concern. The important facts are that change occurs and that in a broad sense the source and pattern of changes have common features through time and space.

In the following pages attention is first directed to changes in the organization of physical production, that is, of industry, in the narrow sense of manufacturing. The discussion then puts these changes into a somewhat broader setting by attending to long-term alterations in the importance of major categories of production. In combination these considerations will provide a basis for what may be a somewhat novel perspective on industrial conflict, discussed in the concluding section.

Productive Technology and Occupational Structure. Industrial economies are characterized by a more or less rapid rate of change in productive processes. Although various aspects of this change may be important for different purposes of analysis, it is common to refer to it as "technological." For the sake of simplification, the proximate sources or functions of technological change, in this sense, may be reduced to two: (1) changes in the total range of products available to "consumers" and shifts in the composition of the product structure of the economy and (2) savings and shifts in the use of the various "factors of production," for example, the substitution of capital for labor.

Regardless of the impact of technological change on the total volume of employment,[3] it is quite clear that the modification of productive processes has implications for occupational structure. These implications may be summarized as (1) the obsolescence of skills, (2) the dilution of skills, and (3) the demand for new skills.

1. One of the more obvious results of technological change is the decline or disappearance of the demand for certain types of skill. This consequence may arise either from the declining demand for particular products or simply from changes in productive processes. Major shifts of product structure are of course most evident in periods of change from civilian to military production or vice versa. Slower changes such as the displacement of horse-drawn vehicles by automobiles also account for obsolescence of skills. The result in the displacement of skilled workers is not markedly different where the source of the change is in the mechanization of operations. For example, production of a major part of the output of cigars by machine processes displaced a considerable portion of skilled cigar makers.

2. The dilution of skills through technological change has been com-

---

[3] For a review of this mooted point, see Wilbert E. Moore, *Industrial Relations and the Social Order*, rev. ed., New York, Macmillan, 1951, pp. 245–249.

mented on by many observers, with varying degrees of passion. The industrialization of handicraft production has been accompanied in general by tearing apart various processes formerly performed by one person and by either mechanizing the separate components or assigning the tasks to relatively unskilled workers. *Division* of labor as discussed in the literature usually has this connotation. It is particularly this feature of technological change that has led many writers to comment adversely on the effect of modern industry on routine and monotony and on pride of workmanship. The extent to which the judgment of the worker, to say nothing of his control of the tempo of work, has been radically reduced through direct servitude to the machine is well known. Continuous assembly operations, often taken as typifying the most technically advanced productive processes, serve to illustrate the dilution of skills attendant on technical change.

3. A much less commonly recognized feature of changes in productive processes is the demand for new skills. Again, this demand arises both from new products and from new processes for existing products. A few illustrations may serve to establish the point. The great industrial shifts represented by the use of the internal-combustion engine for transportation and by that of electronics for communication account for countless *new* occupations. Nor are these occupations exclusively, or even primarily, "unskilled." Similarly, the very fact that processes are subject to constant review and innovation implies a demand for engineers, draftsmen, and toolmakers. The growing importance of the machine-tool industry has both the immediate consequence of requiring an increasing number of highly skilled workers and the secondary consequence that installation of these machines in other industries may displace skilled workers.

One further comment on the occupational impact of technological change is of some importance because of the usually dismal view of the plight of industrial man. The specialization of tasks and the mechanization of certain operations substitute "semiskilled" machine tenders for the independent artisan. But once the worker's tasks have been routinized to the point sometimes portrayed as typical of industrial labor, there is considerable opportunity and likelihood of further mechanization. This means an even further decrease of labor required for each product unit but also means that a few workers once more become "masters" of the machine. The machine tender who supervises an extensive process by means of dials, gauges, and buttons is perhaps the true representative of mechanical production.

With reference solely to the changing technology of physical production, then, the following changes in occupational structure may be noted: a marked increase in the total number of distinct occupations because of specialization and the expansion of the range of products; a reduction of the proportion of unskilled workers through the increased demand for the semiskilled and skilled; and major changes in the occupational composition of various skill categories, particularly at the higher levels of skills.

Organizational Technology and Occupational Structure. The changing character of industrial production is usually discussed mainly or solely in terms of productive technology, that is, the utilization of knowledge and experience concerning the nonhuman world. Indeed it may be argued, on somewhat doubtful evidence, that this kind of technology is generally primary and in some sense a determinant of other productive changes. However, with any given state of engineering knowledge, in the narrow sense, there is a considerable range of variation in the techniques of organization. In fact, the usual argument may be reversed by maintaining that a considerable portion of technical innovation is itself the product of certain kinds of social organization, notably, the explicit creation of research and engineering departments in the manufacturing enterprise. The argument need not be settled for present purposes as long as some independent variability of organization technology is allowed.

The term "organizational technology" may elicit surprise from social scientists painfully aware of the shortcomings of organizational theory, but it appears that in certain respects the practitioners are ahead of the theorists and proceed upon the basis of the accumulated and communicated experience of "practical men" without benefit of precise and orderly knowledge. Comparable circumstances have, in fact, prevailed with reference to the knowledge of mechanics useful for industrial processes. And it is certainly clear that managers and specialized technicians in industrial plants experiment with organization and also utilize accumulated experience.

The outstanding change in industrial organization in the present context is the growing importance of large-scale enterprise. Stemming in part from the social invention of the corporation and in part from a variety of economic and technical circumstances, the large enterprise is characteristic of major sectors of industrial systems. This organizational change has had several consequences for occupational structure, and these are discussed in the following paragraphs.

1. The elaborate specialization of productive tasks discussed above with reference to mechanical technology is in large degree possible only within a single organization and, indeed, in a single plant. Although very considerable specialization between plants and companies occurs, this is much more in the nature of transfer of raw materials and component parts than of semifinished goods as such. Part of the reason is also social: the greater ease of regulating specialized activities through supervision and the authority of the employer than through the mechanism of the market for goods. In other words, a great deal of specialization is actually internal to large productive enterprise and is likely to be somewhat proportional to the size of the enterprise. In many instances the economic advantages of specialization do not exist except as the volume of product and number of employees allow further subdivision of tasks. Thus the very enterprises in which relationships are most likely to be formal and impersonal because of sheer size and attenuated lines of communication are also likely to exhibit the greatest heterogeneity of specific occupational roles.

2. The occupational specialization that is characteristic of large-scale enterprise entails an increasing proportion of supervisory and managerial positions in the total labor force. Specialization necessarily involves coordination in order to achieve a unified product. It is true that routinization of tasks may decrease the ratio of supervisors to persons supervised, but there is no evidence that this trend is the dominant one in contemporary industry. Even in this case, moreover, routinization by elaborate subdivision simply puts additional

demands on the second level of supervision, where coordination is made more problematical in view of the subdivision.

3. A development in industrial organization closely related to those already noted is the great expansion of "staff" services. These services may be loosely classified as those relating primarily to the internal operation, including changes in operation, of the enterprise, as a social and productive system, and those concerned primarily with the relations between the enterprise and important features of its environment. The principle that increasing size of organization tends to require disproportionate increases in formality and complexity is well known, if quantitatively imprecise. On this basis it might be theoretically argued that the "economies of scale" are somewhat overrated, but the fact remains that staff specialization accounts for important changes in the total occupational structure. The crude empirical evidence is provided in any giant corporation.

4. Since in the single enterprise the organization itself is one of the variables partially subject to managerial control, it is not surprising that attempts are made to control the supply of, and demand for, particular skills. Thus training programs at various levels in the industrial hierarchy require substantial numbers of corporate employees essentially as teachers. Such programs are designed in part to supply job qualifications that are somewhat peculiar to the industry or company. Of greater significance for the subject of this essay is the extent to which a corporation may meet a shortage of particular skills in the labor market by reorganization of tasks and job specifications. Whether the shortages are the result of deliberate restrictive practices on the part of skilled trades and professions or the unintended consequence of other forces, the counteraction of the employer may have important consequences for the occupational structure of the enterprise.

5. One further aspect of occupational change associated with the size and complexity of corporate enterprise follows from the developments just noted. This change is the increasing importance of college education, whether liberal or technical, for supervisory and staff positions. The possibility in business enterprise of direct ascent from the lowest ranks to the highest was certainly greater in the past, but it was probably overstated for even the period around the early part of the century. The line of ascent for the ordinary workman tends to have its ceiling at the first or second supervisory level, with junior managers and technicians recruited directly from the colleges. It cannot be argued from this that total mobility by merit is decreasing, in view of steadily increasing educational opportunities, but its pattern is certainly changing. First-line supervisors in particular are often "bouncing their heads against the ceiling," because experience alone is not, or is not thought to be, adequate basis for positions of greater responsibility.

Thus, in addition to changes in occupational structure more or less directly traceable to modifications in mechanical techniques and physical products, other changes are due in large measure to the increased size and complexity of productive enterprise, with attendant specialization at all levels of income and authority.

Broad Occupational Shifts. If attention is shifted from the occupational structure of the manufacturing enterprise to that of the industrial economy as a whole, even more marked changes are evident: the process of industrialization exhibits a substantial occupational shift from primary production (especially foodstuffs and minerals) to secondary production (manufacturing).[4] It is especially this transformation that represents a radical break in the worker's orientations and style of life and in the normal size of the productive unit in which he works. It is far more difficult in manufacturing than in either agriculture or mining to maintain traditional social ties and responsibilities, including relations with the directors of productive operations.[5] The factory system, with all its attendant social features, is the outstanding mark of the Industrial Revolution, as it is ordinarily understood and as the process is repeated in Asia, Africa, and South America.

In early stages of industrialization workers are in general relatively unskilled. Moreover, managers and men tend to be drawn from quite different sectors of the social structure. Contrary to common opinion this was markedly true of the early factory system, and the pattern is obviously being repeated in undeveloped areas. This circumstance throws a somewhat new light on the supposed rigidifying of class structure in industrial economies. For the sector of the population engaged in manufacturing the cleavage between bosses and workers, in terms of skill, wealth, authority, or position in the community, is generally sharpest at early stages of industrial development. The implications of this particular phase of the industrialization process for the incidence and form of industrial conflict are discussed in the following section.

For the oldest industrial countries a further occupational shift is of even greater significance: the increasing proportion of the total labor force involved in tertiary production (a wide variety of services).[6] This development is so marked that it accounts for not only the increase in the proportion of persons engaged in nonmanufacturing business enterprises of all sorts and in professional and governmental activities but also the increase of essentially service functions within the manufacturing enterprise. The white-collar worker simply does not fit neatly into the traditional molds of management and labor, either in theory or in fact.[7]

Specialization has also taken place in this broad occupational category, probably to a greater degree than in primary and secondary production. Thus older professional categories such as physician, lawyer, or engineer cover an ever-widening range of particular specialties, and new professional and other occupational specialists are constantly appearing. Although there has been very little analysis of these aspects of occupational structure, it may be specu-

---

[4] See Colin Clark, *The Conditions of Economic Progress,* London, Macmillan & Co., 1940; Queensland (Australia) Bureau of Industry, "The Distribution of Labour Between Industries, I–IV," *Review of Economic Progress,* Vol. 2, Nos. 4–7 (April–July, 1950).

[5] See Wilbert E. Moore, *Industrialization and Labor,* Ithaca, N.Y., Cornell University Press, 1951.

[6] See references in note 4. According to estimates summarized in *Review of Economic Progress,* Vol. 2, No. 4 (April, 1950), tertiary production accounted for some 15 per cent of the United States occupied population in 1820, 25 per cent in 1870, and 49 per cent in 1940. These proportions do *not* include clerical and staff services in agriculture, forestry, fishing, mining, construction, and manufacturing. The proportions engaged in construction and manufacturing have remained very stable at approximately 30 per cent since 1910, prior to which they were of course lower.

[7] See C. Wright Mills, *White Collar,* New York, Oxford, 1951.

lated that tertiary production lends itself to job diversification because the possible range of demand for services is intrinsically broader than that for physical commodities.

Despite the impressive range of professional and white-collar occupations, this segment of the working population has also not been immune to routinization and standardization of jobs. As service functions get to be marketed by large business enterprises, the specialist also turns out to be working for an employer other than the ultimate client, who thus becomes a customer. These changes in the occupational structure present many new problems for analysis, in terms of employment relations, but in general social scientists have thoughtlessly continued to accept the notion that industrial relations are most properly studied in "basic" or "mass-production" industries. The consequence is a grossly incomplete and distorted view of the tensions and strains and of the forms and incidence of conflict in the economy.

Implications for Industrial Conflict

Changes in the occupational structure, reviewed in the preceding section, provide at the very least a modification in the "environment" or circumstances of industrial relations. This minimal inference is likely to satisfy only those addicted to the Marxian or neo-Marxian view that there is *one* basic cleavage in the industrial system about which all actual or potential conflict is oriented. On other premises industrial relations comprise many interoccupational patterns, to which the changing occupational structure is of central rather than conditional significance. The shifting occupational structure of industry significantly modifies the environment of wage and salary workers. Employees are not a homogeneous single class, and it is no longer useful to picture them as such. The complex occupational structure which derives from modern technology and economic organization contains the roots of significant problems of industrial conflict. This view will encompass more of the observable characteristics of industrial systems than will the Marxian. It is the one adopted here as a basis for a brief and tentative discussion of the implications of occupational structure for industrial conflict.

Destruction of the Solidarity of "Labor." At the risk of considerable oversimplification, changes in the occupational structure previously summarized may be reduced to two general trends. Those trends are specialization, with its consequences for changes in demand for particular skills, and the movement of major portions of the working population away from direct participation in physical production. These processes are interrelated and in combination have resulted in an increasing heterogeneity of any industrial category corresponding to the rubric "labor." It is this consequence that partially justifies the somewhat tendentious reference to the destruction of the solidarity of labor. Several components of this process may serve to place the generalization in perspective.

1. The changing demand for skills in industry often upsets the more "normal" expectation of increasing skill and responsibility with age. Both public and industrial training facilities are primarily geared to the supply of new skills by youthful entrants to the labor force rather than by adult re-

training.[8] Thus several "skill generations" may be represented in the same manufacturing unit, with a negative correlation between age and seniority on the one hand and technical competence on the other. Even without such troublesome issues as pensions to divide laboring groups on age lines, considerable tension and conflict may thus appear because of technical changes in the organization of work and assignment of positions.

2. There is some evidence of the alienation and apathy of the lowest-paid sectors of the industrial labor force. This phenomenon may be due to past frustration of ambition [9] or simply to differing social backgrounds not conducive to the mobility aspirations expected in the labor force at large.[10] In either case the existence of such a segment of the work force inevitably introduces a cleavage in the ranks of labor. Even if it be argued that these workers are anachronistic, the implications of the skill generations discussed above would seem to point to their replacement by other frustrated and apathetic or embittered workers.

3. Since decision on technical and organizational changes is in large degree under the control of management, these changes may be used to reduce the power of workers or to foster cleavage among employees. One notable consequence of rapid technical innovation has been the destruction of the special bargaining power of particular groups of skilled workers. And it is not likely that this consequence has been entirely unintended.

4. The assumption that mechanical and organizational changes have been used as deliberate weapons is further supported by the fact that the occupational shifts involved tend to transfer operations from labor to management. Both the increasing importance of supervision where coordination of specialized activities is problematical and the increased role of research men, designers, and engineers lend credence to this view. Although recognition of this process may enhance the "solidarity" of the restructured rank-and-file labor force, there is no assurance that it will do so. In any event the question as to what is labor and what is management becomes increasingly arbitrary in these circumstances, with diversification and splitting of functions blurring lines. Where the line is drawn is itself a source of conflict between managers and unions, with competing jurisdictional claims. Foremen, guards, clerks, and technicians have collective interests at variance with other groups but generally provide a part of management's constituency when a dichotomy is forced on the structure of the enterprise.

5. The claim to represent labor in collective dealings, including conflict, with management is itself often disputed. In view of the kinds of cleavages in the ranks of labor that are intrinsic to the industrial system, plus added cleavages on ethnic, religious, and ideological grounds, rival unionism and intraunion factionalism are not surprising. What is surprising is the common failure to regard these circumstances as part of "industrial conflict." The cir-

---

[8] See Wilbert E. Moore, "The Aged in Industrial Societies," in *The Aged and Society,* Industrial Relations Research Association, Champaign, Ill., 1950, pp. 24–39.

[9] See Allison Davis, "The Motivation of the Underprivileged Worker," in William Foote Whyte (ed.), *Industry and Society,* New York, McGraw-Hill, 1946, Chap. 5.

[10] See Melville Dalton, "Worker Response and Social Background," *Journal of Political Economy,* 55 (August, 1947), 323–332.

cumstances are well known to policy-forming levels in management, and use of union factionalism and rivalry constitutes part of the modernized arsenal of employers in dealing with organized labor.[11]

6. Finally, the whole trend in industrial economies is such as to increase the proportion of persons who deal with symbols and with persons as compared with those who deal with physical products. The insistent believer in the common interests of all those who do not own or control capital will maintain that white-collar workers are still only workers. The analytical problem then becomes one of explaining the persistent stubbornness of these workers in refusing to accept the doctrine. To the analyst not committed to a single cleavage as more fundamental than others, in some metaphysical sense, the vast, growing, and highly diversified ranks of white-collar workers are further confirmation of the complexity of occupational structure in industrial systems. The weight of evidence points both to the lack of common orientations between manual and clerical workers and to the high degree of tension and lack of common focus in the latter group. Where routinization and impersonality are highly developed, that is, where the business structure fosters collective dealing, something approximating traditional modes of industrial conflict may occur. More commonly, the lack of a clearly institutionalized pattern of conflict has resulted in collective bargaining that is not so called and in sporadic dissidence and relatively unstructured conflict.

Destruction of the Solidarity of "Management." As already implied, that sector of the occupied population loosely classified as management has not been immune to the same pressures that have tended to splinter the ranks of labor. Here, too, specialization and the absorption of new functions have tended to introduce sources of tension and strain between managerial groups. Again, several aspects of this process may be identified.

1. As noted elsewhere,

> The potentialities for "collective bargaining" between formally constituted units and between informally organized factions and cliques have been persistently obscured by the preoccupation of managers and scholars alike with management-labor relations. The industrial hierarchy is not simply divisible at one level in the hierarchy; it is fissionable.[12]

Competition for the scarce resources of the enterprise (particularly power and budget), rank-oriented frictions, and line-staff tensions are common in industrial enterprises. The normative expectations of graded authority serve to hide such conflicts from public view and to limit the forms of their internal manifestation; they do not prevent them.

2. Managerial factionalism may even lie behind collective relations with "external" groups, such as stockholders, customers, or unions. The officially authoritarian structure of management, as compared with the officially democratic structure of unions, for example, reduces the likelihood that this factionalism can be used as a weapon in collective dealing with management. The industrial-relations implications of the general process of corporate decision making are only beginning to come under scrutiny of social scientists.

[11] See Moore, *op. cit.,* Chap. 14.
[12] *Ibid.,* p. 97.

3. As a result of the radical and rapid restructuring of the occupational cross section of management and of the legally sanctioned appearance of independent unions and collective bargaining, the policy-forming managers have shown increasing concern for the "loyalty" of all workers and especially of the "management team." Often with considerable reluctance, based in part on considerable ignorance of social phenomena, top managers have tended to admit that production workers exhibit loyalty to union organizations. But the absence of complete uniformity of doctrine and policy within management, particularly if the differences represent collective interests, is regarded with grave apprehension. Part of the apprehension may be well taken, for organizational survival under conditions of extreme specialization is by no means assured. But it seems improbable that elaborate attention to communications, to the airing of grievances, and to indoctrination and loyalty tests will eliminate the sources of tension and conflict. Purposive effort may regulate the incidence of hostilities and partially prevent the rigidification of conflict patterns through time. In this respect the constant change of the managerial structure, largely the result of other pressures, may be quite functional for survival of the organization.

Some General Hypotheses. Several highly tentative but possibly provocative hypotheses about the changing character of industrial conflict may be drawn from the foregoing discussion:

1. Although the subject needs much further exploration through time and space, the broad changes in the occupational structure in the process of industrialization suggest that *industrial conflict, in its traditional sense, primarily fits a particular "stage" in industrial development.* That stage may be represented by the shift from primary to secondary production, prior to the elaborate specialization that tends to make the line between management and labor blurred and shifting and prior to the extensive development of tertiary production.

2. Conflict is, by definition, two-sided. However, under conditions of fractionated interests and rapidly changing circumstances, it is still possible that *industrial conflicts will be sporadic and* ad hoc *and that on successive issues the sides may line up differently.* If the survival of industrial societies depends upon the absence of internal conflict, they may well be doomed. It is, however, arguable that a fairly extensive tolerated conflict, under circumstances where no single issue is persistently overriding and definitive of all other loyalties, will permit a viable social system.

3. Even in the absence of overt conflict, it seems probable that *there will be considerable sources of tension and pull-hauling, with consequent possibilities for coalitions and manipulation.* Despite nostalgic reformers of industry as a social system, the industrial way of life is not a simple one. It seems improbable that any amount of tinkering with the industrial organization will allow it to serve the broader functions of voluntary associations and of the community and at the same time to maintain its advantages in productive efficiency. As it is impossible for the individual or the society to survive solely on the basis of rational production of goods and services, participants in the process must necessarily subscribe to other values and also serve other interests. For a productive system as intrinsically changeful as modern industry,

the balancing of interests must always be somewhat problematical. No industrial society has solved these problems, and some of the attempted solutions through totalitarian controls are neither demonstrated for the long run nor acceptable in terms of liberal institutions. A proper understanding of the problems, including a persistent refusal to indulge in oversimplified and stereotyped notions about the nature of industrial organization, may possibly aid in living with tension and change.

CHAPTER 17 SOCIAL STRUCTURE AND POWER CONFLICT

Herbert Blumer   *University of California (Berkeley)*

It is fitting in a symposium dealing with our industrial scene to view and discuss labor-management relations in terms of power conflict. Such a treatment is needed to portray our industrial life in one of its important dimensions and thus to complement the picture yielded by the bulk of studies being made by psychologists and social scientists. For reasons that need not be considered here these latter studies favor the premise that industrial relations are naturally cooperative and based on mutuality of interest. Opposition, strife, and conflict in industrial relations are regarded as unfortunate deficiencies that can and will give way before enlightened attitude, technical knowledge, and the application of scientific method. There is grave danger that studies and interpretations based on a premise which ignores or misconstrues power relations may yield a distorted and fictitious picture of contemporary industrial relations and thus may lead to unwise policy and to unfruitful methods of control.

Introduction

Several lines of consideration suggest not only the advisability but the necessity of viewing the industrial sector of our society in terms of power struggle. First, it should be noted that our society itself is clearly caught up in the play of power. The picture is one of innumerable groups and organizations relying on the exercise of power at innumerable points in seeking to maintain position, to achieve goals, and to ward off threats. To show this we need only refer to the operation of interest groups in our society.

Our American life invites, fosters, and sustains interest groups essentially everywhere: geographically from small villages at one extreme to our widespread national domain at the other and institutionally through the gamut of business, politics, education, science, religion, art, health, and recreation. Many people are erroneously inclined to think of interest groups as confined only to a few huge national organizations exerting pressure on governmental agencies or on public opinion. Actually, an interest group arises whenever individuals become organized or united in pursuit of some actual or imagined common interest and seek to forge in a recalcitrant world a line of action on behalf of that interest. Our democratic society gives extensive freedom to people everywhere to organize and act in response to a shared interest. Our national life, in one of its major dimensions, consists of the acts of such groups —local clubs, cliques in a church, chambers of commerce, businessmen groups, teachers' organizations, lodges, political clubs, trade associations, medical associations, veterans associations, church organizations, political parties, labor unions, educational societies, industrial corporations, and a variety of other organizations seeking to realize the special interests for which they exist.

This proliferation of interest groups imparts a vital power dimension to our national life. As these groups, ranging from small and loosely organized cliques to large tightly knit national federations, seek to further, sustain, or protect their respective interests, they are thrown at innumerable points into opposition and conflict with one another. It is at these points that power relations emerge and develop as a result of efforts to use strategic position, strength, influence, and skill to achieve or protect interests that are threatened, hindered, or blocked by opposing interests. It should be apparent that a large national society whose social and legal codes allow and indeed encourage people to act collectively on behalf of their group interests would inevitably be marked by extensive areas of power action. This must be recognized as true of our American society.

It would indeed be strange if our industrial arena did not show power situations comparable to those in other areas of our American life. The most careful observation of American industry reveals clearly the presence of power play and power conflict. Power actions are to be noted in the competitive struggles between business organizations, in the conflicts between different business interests, in the internal politics of large corporations, and in the half-hidden struggles between administrative units of production in factories and plants; in the factional strivings within labor unions and in the rivalries and disputes between labor unions; and in the relations between managements and labor unions. Power action in the industrial field varies greatly in intensity and persistency from place to place. It is likely to be casual, episodic, and minor on local levels and to be sustained and vigorous in the case of large national organizations. Whatever its variation in occurrence and degree from one point to another, its widespread existence suggests that it is an indigenous factor in our contemporary industrial organization.

Indeed the conditions in our industrial life are peculiarly conducive to the emergence of power relations. The sanctioning of success in business competition encourages vigorous action which may infringe on the acts of others; the extension and integration of the economic market bring in a larger number of economic-interests groups and increase the chances of opposition between their lines of interest; the dynamic changes in our economy open new areas for exploitation and thus for increased encroachment of groups on groups; the growth of huge organizations lays the stage for inner conflict and struggle for control; and the increasing unionization of industrial workers introduces a greater amount of union pressures. As a result of conditions and influences such as these, our industrial society becomes subject at innumerable points to power actions between trade associations, between business corporations, between units and echelons of management, between groups of stockholders, between occupational groups, between factions in unions, between labor unions, between unions and managements, and between aggregations of labor unions and aggregations of managements.

These casual observations are sufficient to invite a consideration of industrial relations from the standpoint of power effort. Further, they should be a signal of warning to the many of us who study the industrial arena with a disregard for the presence of power struggle and with a misconstruction of its play. They point particularly to the need for caution in recommending ways of handling industrial problems which are based on studies ignoring the factor of power action.

Analysis of Power

It is advisable to make a brief analysis of power action. Power relations seem to be one of the basic forms of relationship between human beings and of human groups. The other important kinds of social relation are what may be termed "codified" relations and "sympathetic" relations. The distinctions between these three forms of social relation seem to be of crucial importance.

The drawing of the distinction can begin with codified relations. By such relations I have in mind those governed by rules, understandings, and expectations which are shared and followed by the parties to the relationship. How the parties stand with regard to rights, privileges, prestige, authority, and deference is laid out by a defining code; accordingly, the line of behavior of each in regard to the other is already established. Under such regulating social codes there is minimum occasion for conflict between the parties. Where such conflict arises or threatens to arise, the controls which are indigenous to the code are invoked as corrective devices for forcing the relations and the lines of behavior back into conformity with the code. Such codified relations are to be found wherever stable group relations exist. Concern for them has been particularly the stock in trade of sociologists and anthropologists in their pre-occupation with custom, tradition, group norms, role relations, and culture.

It is important to see that these codified relations between groups and between individuals may involve significant differences in prestige, authority, and dominance between the participants. To take a few stray examples, we need merely think of master and slave, parent and child, feudal nobles and serfs, high and low castes, and military officers and private soldiers. It is a serious mistake, in my judgment, to regard such instances of codified relations as power relations because of the exercise of authority, prestige, and dominance by one party over the other. Where such dominance and directing control is prescribed and channelized and hence accepted and followed as the natural course, there is no power relation nor power action. In such a codified situation, there is no freedom of action, no pursuit of conflicting interest, no clash of lines of action, no jostling and maneuvering for advantageous position, and no test of strength.

A second major type of social relations I have termed sympathetic relations. In them the participants show sympathetic regard for each other's position and are guided by such appreciation. Such relations are marked by the presence of, and guidance by, personal sentiments and understanding—as in the case of sympathetic concern and care. While this kind of social relation and action is to be found particularly in friendly or intimate relations, it may occur between detached, remote, and even alien groups and individuals—as in the case of generosity of the victor, expressions of aid to the struggling, and sympathetic concern for those caught in a plightful condition.

Again, it should be noted that in sympathetic relations there may be very obvious differences in positions of dominance. This does not establish the relation as a power relation. In sympathetic relations dominance, strength, and advantageous position, while present, do not set the goals of action; instead, action is formed and directed by appreciation and regard for the other party. Hence there is no struggle and hence no resolution of the relation in terms of respective strength.

In contrast to codified relations and sympathetic relations power relations are set and guided by respective positions of effective strength. This redundant statement points to a number of crucial features of power relations. First, a power relation is marked by an opposition of interests, intentions, and goals. In the pursuit of their respective objectives the parties are thrown into conflict with each other, and a contest of intention and will occurs. Second, in pursuing its objective each party uses and relies on its sources of strength instead of being confined to a codified channel of action or guided by sympathetic regard for the other. Third, because of freedom of action thus provided, there is elbow room for scheming, maneuvering, the devising of strategy and tactics, and the marshaling and manipulation of resources. Since action is neither held to an application of a code nor guided by a consideration for the other's welfare, a premium is placed on the successful pursuit of *one's own goal,* thus inevitably introducing egotism and possibilities of ruthlessness that have always made power action morally suspect. Where people in pursuit of goals are thrown into opposition to one another, with sanctioned or allowable leeway in the forging of actions to achieve success in the face of such opposition, and where the pursuit is not made subservient to considerations of each other's welfare, the stage is set for power action.

From this brief sketch of the generic nature of the power relationship it should be evident that power relations in our modern world are common and widespread. Conditions of our modern society are continuously at work to set and reset the stage for power action. The emergence of new groups or organizations, the development of new interests, the redirection of old interests under the dynamic play of events, the emergence of new uncodified areas, the crumbling away of old codifications, the increasing throwing together of groups who have little or no sense of common loyalty, and the absence of concern for the welfare of groups standing in opposition to one's own objective—all these factors, which are so pronounced in modern society, make power action widespread.

Most power relations in our society are localized and restricted, and the preponderant portion of them scarcely affects the welfare of the community life that embodies them. Power relations become a matter of concern in proportion to the size of power groups and to the extent of the ramified effect of their action. Thus it is "big power" that today awakens alarm and stimulates the interests of students—power relations as they appear in the strivings of nations on the international front and in the struggle of large interest groups in the domestic arena.

While power relations in the case of big power fit the generic pattern spoken of above, they show more pronouncedly certain features that should be noted. In the case of big-power groups power action comes to be more a matter of persistent policy and its pursuit more of a sophisticated art. Because a big-power group is subject recurrently to opposition and thwarting of its interests and aims over a lengthy span of time, it comes to be organized and girded in terms of a career of continuous power play. The big-power group is directed by an executive set of "full-time" individuals entrusted with the needs of understanding the developing world in which the power group operates, of coping with the immediate situation, of planning for the future, of developing policy, and of devising strategy and tactics to implement that policy. Power action thus tends to become a matter of studied group policy. Power policy and power action, one may say, become professionalized in the hands of experts. Power tends to be exercised calculatingly and rationally, *i.e.*, with constant and paramount regard to the advancement or protection of the interests of the power groups. There is likely to be more adroit and effective use of the power possibilities in the power situation and less restraint in the willingness to use such possibilities. Finally, it should be noted that the directorship of the big-power group, by virtue of its size and complexity of organization, is likely to be removed significantly from the direct and continuous participation of the membership or of the bulk of followers of the power group. All these mentioned considerations are equivalent to saying that power action comes to its "purest form" in the case of big-power groups.

This brief analysis of power action may be ended with a few words on controlling the power process. Oddly, the most effective restraint on the exercise of power is the calculation of the losses that might be sustained through its use in given situations. Power action, by definition, encounters resistance and is subject to assessment by opposing groups who seek in their own interest to locate its points of weakness and vulnerability. Thus its use and extension are subject to the limitations of possible failure, of exceeding its potential, of encountering the risks of unsustainable loss. This self-limitation inherent in the power process is far more effective than is realized. Without this self-correction, power struggle would attain the unrestrained viciousness which is usually and unwarrantedly ascribed to it. Yet this self-limitation clearly does not operate where there is a preponderance of power lodged in one of the parties to the power struggle or where there is a miscalculation of the costs and effects of a given line of power action.

Reliance on moral injunction or on exhortation to good will, while recognizably one of the conceivable methods of controlling power struggle, is essentially weak and nonenduring. Moral imperatives are not congenial to the power process; such imperatives tend to becloud that process, as each party proclaims and believes that its position and action are righteous.

Public opinion as a control of power struggle has greater influence; yet it is episodic, merely limiting at certain points, and susceptible at other points to direction by the parties to the struggle.

Control by law, if backed by effective punitive sanctions, has proved to be a more effective control of power action.

Finally, as reflecting such effectiveness of law, the state by virtue of its greater strength has the possibility of curbing power action, although at the expense, it must be seen, of becoming thereby the arena itself of the power process.

Labor-Management Relations as Power Relations

Labor-management relations may now be considered in the light of the foregoing analysis of power.

The generic conditions of the power process clearly exist in labor-management relations. First, with the organizing of workers a genuine opposition arises between the interests of labor unions and of management. Such opposition in interest should not be regarded as an alien occurrence, as an imported deficiency, or as a breakdown of a natural harmony. Instead, it stems from the natural functions of management and of labor unions. The function of management is to operate the business enterprise efficiently; its paramount interests are to manage profitably and to have the right to exercise that management. The labor union has as its paramount interests (1) the protection and advancement of the industrial welfare of the workers and (2) the survival and growth of the union as an organization. That these respective sets of interests come naturally into opposition is evident. Actions on behalf of the welfare interests of workers and of the institutional interests of the union run athwart the actions stemming from the interests of management in the profitable operation of the business enterprise and in the right to manage. Any reader who is inclined to question the truth of this assertion needs only to reflect on the meaning of collective bargaining. Collective bargaining is a device for achieving the accommodation of opposed demands and positions, demands and positions that stem from, and reflect, the respective interests of organized workers and management. The very existence of collective bargaining (which in our industrial society is the law of the land and is recognized as the chief mediating agency of labor-management relations) bespeaks underlying opposition in interest between labor unions and managements.

We need to note further that, in the pursuit of their respective interests vis-à-vis each other, managements and unions are not under the dominance of codified relations. Each is granted a relative freedom of action in place of being compelled to abide by sanctioned regulations. Thus the parties may choose what to propose, what to reject, and what line of action to follow. This condition sets the stage for the use of available strength in pursuing interests—a practice which reaches its apogee in the test of power in the labor strike.

Finally, labor-management relations are marked by the remaining salient feature of power action: flexibility in maneuvering, in scheming, in marshaling resources, in grasping advantages in passing events, or in general exploiting whatever the situation seems to afford for the advancement or protection of interests, as immediately defined by each party.

Power action is usually not conspicuous nor striking in the relations of unions and managements on the local level, particularly when local unions enjoy a high degree of autonomy. It comes to be pronounced, however, in the case of large international unions which have to function *as single entities* vis-à-vis large corporations, trade associations, and employer organizations.

My remaining remarks are devoted to a consideration of the power process in the case of big-power groups in labor-management relations in our society.

We should note, first, that the large union and the large management are steadily forced in their relations with each other to act as single entities. This creates in each the need for effective organization, effective inner control, and expert direction. The hierarchic structure of management readily allows, in its case, for meeting these needs. For its part the union in meeting these needs is increasingly forced to lodge the making of policies and of decisions in a top leadership and thus to strip away autonomy from the rank-and-file member and from the local union. The effort to achieve unitary direction on the part of a heterogeneous composition introduces an inner power process into the union—a condition which, in itself, is met in time by a concentration of control in a directing leadership. Just as a large army engaged in military campaign cannot allow autonomous policy and decision making to its units but must act concertedly, so similarly the large union and the large management are each under compulsion to act as single entities.

We should note in the case of large unions and large managements the fact that each organization has a career yielding memories of the past, giving a peculiar meaning to the needs of the immediate present, and requiring a girding for the proximate future. In an arena of opposing groups seeking to advance or protect their respective interests, this need on the part of professional leadership to preserve and further an *enduring* organization induces a working psychology of power orientation and power action.

What are the earmarks of such a power psychology? One of the essential features is a lively scrutiny of the operating situation to ascertain what threats it holds, what obstacles it sets, what advantages it contains, and what exploitable facilities it yields. The companion feature is an alertness in marshaling and in directing available sources of strength. The interaction of these two on behalf of sought objectives provides the working rationale of power action. Too much space would be required to trace out these features in practice amid the relations of big labor unions and big managements. However, a few general characteristics of their power action should be noted.

First, the fact that the arena in which big unions and big managements operate is subject to high dynamic play introduces a conspicuous fluidity into their relations. Such happenings as shifts in the economy, changes in the cost and the standard of living, political developments, new legislation and prospective legislation, judicial interpretation, stirring up of membership, and inner shifts of power are a few of the many factors at work in our modern society which impart a fluid and rather unpredictable character to big-power relations between labor and management.

Next, this dynamic setting leads conspicuously to rational expediency in the direction of power action. Policies in this shifting and uncertain setting become increasingly subject to compromise, tempering, and redirection under the impact of the passing array of newly developing situations.

Third, the relations between the parties become tenuous, shifting, and tentative as each views the other and awaits developing action on the part of the other.

Finally, because of this tenuous and shifting nature of the relations between prodigious power groups operating in a dynamic arena, there is an increasing tendency for the power struggle to move over into the political arena. There is increased readiness to use the powers of the state through legislation, executive decision, and administrative action as the means of fortifying the security of one's own interests. The need of countering such efforts brings the other party into the political field. Further, a recurring inability to accommodate successfully their immediate opposed aims leads to intercession by the state on behalf of its own interests. This transferring of the power struggle between organized labor and management from the industrial arena to the political arena marks a major transformation in their relations, with consequences which, while only dimly foreseen, will be momentous.

The foregoing observations on the power process in labor-management relations are sketchy. However inadequate, they underline the need of recognizing that relations between managements and labor unions are set by each party acting faithfully on behalf of its respective interests and that these interests typically run counter to each other. This fundamental fact should not be veiled by a contention that, since management and workers are dependent on each other in the carrying on of the business enterprise, their interests are mutual. Such a contention is belied by the evident need of managements and labor unions to bargain and reach temporary agreements—to accommodate their respective wishes and demands in a workable adjustment. These conditions induce and sustain the use of power, a use which becomes pronounced in the alignment of large unions and large managements. Students of industrial relations will distort their subject matter and emerge with unrealistic results if they ignore the play of power or confuse codified and sympathetic relations with power relations.

CHAPTER 18 INDUSTRIAL CONFLICT AND PUBLIC OPINION

Daniel Bell   *Editorial Department*, Fortune

Invent the printing press, said Carlyle, and democracy is inevitable. But in a democratic society, composed of multiple individuals and diverse groups, who is the "public" and what is the "community" interest? [1] The utilitarians, the first to give politics a calculus and thus attempt an experimental science, utilized the distinction between a social decision (the common good) and the sum total of individual (egoistic) decisions. While older moralists assumed a natural harmony of the two, Jeremy Bentham knew that such identity was artificial. He felt, however, that they could be reconciled by the legislator through "a well-regulated application of punishments." [2] In our own time we know how difficult such a process can be.

Public Opinion in the Mass Society

The distinction might be reworded in the modern idiom as one between "ideological" and "market" decisions. For example, a poll seeking to gauge the degree of voluntary cooperation regarding rationing might ask: "Should manufacturers stop making civilian suits and use the limited amount of cloth for Army uniforms?" Every patriot—and in this instance each American is one, of course—will say yes. But each individual, fingering his own threadbare coat, might say, "I need a suit," and go out and buy one. Thus the public, through a poll, has endorsed a social decision, yet the sum total of individual decisions, registered by the market, is very different. [3]

The clash between market behavior and ideology is a conflict not only within individuals but also within groups and between groups. The labor move-

---

[1] "Unless there are methods for detecting the energies which are at work and tracing them through an intricate network of interactions to their consequences, what passes as public opinion will be 'opinion' in its derogatory sense rather than truly public, no matter how widespread the opinion is." See John Dewey, *The Public and Its Problems*, Chicago, Gateway Publishers, 1946, p. 177.

[2] Jeremy Bentham, *Principles of Morals and Legislation*, London, Oxford, 1907, pp. 2–3. See also Elie Halevy, *Growth of Philosophical Radicalism*, New York, Macmillan, 1928, pp. 14–18.

[3] The distinction is much more than one between opinion and behavior. Quite often the ideological decision will have much more weight and meaning for an individual than his own immediate self-interest, seen in rational market terms, and he will *behave* on the basis of ideology rather than of market considerations. The task of a social psychology is to identify under what conditions the ideological or market considerations will be followed.

ment, for example, has strongly favored lower tariffs and international trade. Yet the seamen's unions, while generally supporting these goals, also urged legislation which restricted the amount of Marshall Plan aid that could be shipped in foreign bottoms, while the textile unions fought vigorously for quotas on foreign imports. Such illustrations of the general proposition that groups which are parts of larger movements with broad ideological goals are often forced by self-interest to negate those objectives can be multiplied in every functional grouping in American life. A public opinion which claims to reflect a public interest is inherently, therefore, an unstable compound of ideological and market decisions. The question whether such opinions can lead to action, and of what kind, depends upon the degree of tension between the two types of motive and upon the degree of identification with one or the other.

If the effort to ascertain public opinion is compounded by the complexities of the public's interests, the very nature of opinion itself adds complications to an analysis of its meaning and impact.[4] Classical learning always made the distinction between knowledge and opinion. It is a relevant distinction in seeking to assess a public's opinion regarding a problem. The Taft-Hartley Act, for example, runs to thirty close pages. What is the meaning of an opinion on *the* act? Some sections of the act deal with broad values (*e.g.* the prohibition on a closed shop); others, however, deal with complicated technical problems that may have equal consequences for the nature and administration of power (*e.g.* the limitations of the general powers of the NLRB by making the general counsel an independent office).

In what way can broad opinion deal with these problems? What interpretative facilities are available to make public opinion "knowledgeable?" Certainly the newspapers of the country are ill equipped to do the job. One can leave as moot the question of whether the concentration of ownership of newspapers and other media influences the presentation of news. But the very definition of news, as employed by the nation's press, precludes any serious attempt to educate a public on complicated issues. News is defined in terms of scoop, sensation, tension, and conflict. Personalities make news, trends do not. Hence the difficulty of obtaining solid information from the flow of news across the pages of the press.[5]

The very torrent of news and the multiplicity of diverse events create a rip tide which decisively shapes a fundamental "set" to opinion expressing. Daily a man is called on to understand, and pass judgment on, the problems of the dollar gap, Yalta, South African *apartheid,* and the moral dilemmas of using Tito, aid to Franco, defense of Formosa, and the like. There is instilled in the individual a growing sense of helplessness and bewilderment; out of it emerges a powerful undertow of generalized hostility—what Kris and Leites

[4] For Lord Bryce, for example, public opinion "is a congeries of all sorts of discrepant notions, beliefs, fancies, prejudices, aspirations. It is confused, incoherent, amorphous, varying from day-to-day and week-to-week."

[5] The Commission on the Freedom of the Press, an inquiry chaired by Robert M. Hutchins, concluded: "Our society needs an accurate and truthful account of the day's events. . . . These needs are not being met." See *A Free and Responsible Press,* Chicago, University of Chicago Press, 1947, p. 59. For an analysis of the concentration of ownership and lack of competition among the daily press, see Herbert Brucker, *Freedom of Information,* New York, Macmillan, 1949, 67 ff.

call "projective distrust." [6] And in the growth of suspicion, there arise the fear of being used and the feeling that, behind all these events, someone is pulling the strings. It takes a high degree of sophistication, Freud wrote, to believe in chance; primitive fears are allayed more easily by a devil theory of politics. In our time, the conspiracy theory of events has gained ground. Along with these suspicions, there is an accompanying decline of moral temper. The instances of a Dreyfus case and the execution of a Nurse Cavell are swamped in the mass terror of concentration camps, purge trials, and forced labor. Numbers produce stupefaction, not indignation.

Despite the increasing striations in American society and the stretching of divisive tensions, there are, paradoxically, the increasing compulsion to fashion a unifying ideology and a necessity to assert the overriding claims of the public on all issues. This is a need imposed, in part, by the pressure to achieve a national consensus on foreign policy and, in part, by the effort of disparate power groups to claim a general sanction for their partial policies. However synthetic the origin of these impulses, more and more a public is "created," and, in the self-consciousness of a role, it creates itself in the effort to achieve a cohesive identity.

And yet may not this identity be a "false consciousness" in that the mask of consensus hides the conflicts of interests underneath or assumes that these can be reconciled through some facile process of semantic or emotional interpersonal discourse? Industrial conflict may be taken as a case study of this proposition.

Opinions and Values

Opinions are framed by the dominant values of a society and by the way these are refracted through the interests of particular groups. In this context, why have the demands of labor provoked so much emotion and resistance? Over the past two decades, the farmers have successfully claimed a measure of financial support and security from the United States government: they have obtained farm support prices, crop insurance, rural-electrification co-ops, a county-agent system, etc. If anything smacks of "creeping socialism," this is it. Nowhere is there any outcry against these "encroachments"; in fact, each party vies to promise the farmer more. Yet trade-unionism, which has asked for little more than the farmer has obtained, finds its claims violently denigrated.

The reason for this paradox lies perhaps in the nature of property and in the values that have clustered about it. The farmer is an independent yeoman who exists in a trading relationship to the dominant power groups in the society. Symbolically, his demand for security is a defense of property rights. The worker exists in a subordinate position to the property owners, and his demands involve an inherent challenge to the nature and justifications of the property system itself.

In its own image, American trade-unionism has *not* been revolutionary.

[6] Ernst Kris and Nathan Leites, "Trends in Twentieth Century Propaganda," in Geza Roheim (ed.), *Psychoanalysis and the Social Sciences,* New York, International Universities Press, 1947. Yet if the authority is too powerful, this projective distrust may turn into abject dependence.

The early 19th-century unions were "escapist." They sought to avoid facing the problems of factory life by espousing free land, producer cooperatives, political action, and the like. The formation of the AFL in 1886, with its emphasis on craft organization and trade agreements, signalized an acceptance of capitalist society. For that reason, Gompers, the totem of American labor, was sharply attacked by the Socialists.

Yet what the Socialists, who thought only of winning full power, did not see and what the capitalists, who sought to retain all power, did was that unionism, in a fashion, is a revolutionary force. While it does not aim at overthrowing power, it means, by curbing the arbitrary and unilateral right of an employer to hire, fire, promote, and set the pace and conditions of work, a distinct sharing of power. And, more important, it challenged the older justifications of unilateral power which gave a moral and psychological strength and unity to the business class. The dominant creed of 19th-century American capitalism, fashioned largely by the Supreme Court philosophy of Justice Field, saw in economic freedom a natural right. Any state attempt to regulate the conditions of work, interfere with the liberty of private contract, or curb private property was rejected out of hand. "Throughout the period, indeed, the presumption of immorality rested on those who would detract from the rewards of capital," writes an historian [7] of the period. The social Darwinism which underlay this doctrine sanctioned industry's resistance to unionism. In fact, beginning with the railroad strikes of 1877, which arose at the end of the longest depression in United States history, almost every major strike for the following 40 years was attended by an outbreak of violence. By threatening the integrated philosophical value system of the business community, unionism provoked anxiety regarding the correctness of a style of life, in all its dimensions.

Until the 1930's, trade-unionism in the United States existed only at the periphery of American capitalism.[8] In a few areas, such as the garment and typographical trades, both typically small entrepreneur in structure, a genuine industrial government had been achieved. In the building trades, unionism existed, but largely as part of a collusive web with employers to mulct the public. The railroad workers, by legislative pressure and because of their strategic position, had won the right to organize but exchanged for it, in the Railway Labor Act of 1926, a complicated obstacle course which hindered their use of the strike. Coal unionism had to struggle against the fury of the state police, while the copper-mining, lumbering, and other frontier-type unions had been fractured by vigilante action. Industry was able, by and large, to resist unionism because of government protection—often through the use of state militia to protect strikebreakers—and by appeals to middle-class morality, which often culminated in private vigilante actions.

The early campaign against unions was initiated by the National Asso-

[7] Robert Green McCloskey, *American Conservation in the Age of Enterprise,* Cambridge, Mass., Harvard University Press, 1951, p. 17.

[8] By 1910 only the brewery workers were more than 50 per cent organized; by 1920 only clothing, coal-mining, and railroad workers were more than half organized; no union had organized more than 60 per cent of its industry. See Leo Wolman, *The Growth of American Trade Unions, 1880–1923,* New York, National Bureau of Economic Research, 1924, Tables 6 and 7 and pp. 137–155.

ciation of Manufacturers (NAM) as a result of labor's partial victory in a 6-month-long coal strike in 1902, which ended when President Theodore Roosevelt recognized labor and created an arbitration commission. (J. P Morgan refused to sit with a union man on the board; so the latter was designated as a sociologist.) The NAM fostered the growth of local employers' organizations and citizens' groups across the country. In some places, as in Cripple Creek, Colo., the Citizen's Protective League, led by the bank president and the city attorney, organized a vigilante posse which rode the strikers out of town. In the press and at public meetings, citizens' associations waged a vigorous propaganda campaign against labor. Charles W. Eliot, president of Harvard, glorified the strikebreaker as an "American hero" and pleaded that the employer should allow "no sacrifice of the independent American worker to the labor union." [9]

This pattern of events was repeated in the years following World War I. President Wilson, seeking to avert the rapidly spreading industrial conflict, in October, 1919, called an industrial conference. The AFL urged labor's right "to be represented by representatives of their own choosing." The employers refused, and the wartime labor truce was shattered. Throughout the country, a crop of new employer groups were formed to press for the "American Plan," *i.e.*, the open shop. In 2 years, every state in the union was blanketed with American Plan groups. The theme stressed the traditional American morality: a union interfered with a man's right to work where and how he saw fit; it destroyed the inalienable right of an employer to run his business as he saw fit. The campaign was a success. By the end of the twenties, unionism was at its nadir.

Two singular factors introduced by the New Deal changed the entire picture. One was the crucial fact that government, for the first time, effectively backed labor's right to organize. But equally important was the fact that the NLRB, exercising an administrative discretion far beyond its charter, extended the right to organize, to a voice on a range of issues on which the Wagner Act had never trenched. "There was not a word in the hearings, in the committee reports or in the debates to suggest that the [Wagner] Act could define the subjects for collective bargaining and give the Board power to resolve the issue in disputed cases," write two Harvard scholars.[10] In effect, what the NLRB did was to force that sharing of power which labor had demanded. By defining and extending the scope of compulsory bargaining issues, the Board successively brought into union purview not only wages and hours but holiday and vacation pay, discharges, bonuses, profit sharing, work loads and work standards, subcontracting shop rules, work schedules, rest periods, merit increases, and, finally, in the historic *Inland Steel* case of 1948, the area of welfare benefits and pensions.

Behind these governmental actions lay a revolution in law as well as in established American values. In giving unions these powers, the law was recognizing a set of *group* rights over and above any individual rights. As

[9] Cited in Selig Perlman and Philip Taft, *History of Labor in the United States*, Vol. 4, New York, Macmillan, 1935, p. 136.

[10] Archibald Cox and John T. Dunlop, "Regulation of Collective Bargaining by the National Labor Relations Board," *Harvard Law Review*, 63 (1950), 395.

the Supreme Court declared in upholding the National Labor Relations Act, these statutes empower the majority of any employees in any unit to "collectivize the employment bargain." [11]

This assertion of "group rights" provides a forceful commentary on the relation of law and the mores. The Depression had given a severe jolt to the old notions of individual reliance and risk, yet the whole weight of tradition and the dominant ideology of the country were still behind this belief. In this instance, the law following the political revolution of the day acted as a lever against the mores. And yet a paradox occurred. While public opinion by and large has favored unionism in general, on many of the specific functions which violate older beliefs of individualism, the same public opinion has been hostile. Yet, in this generally favorable disposition to unionism, the social affirmation has overridden many of the specific condemnations.[12]

Employers did not accept this social revolution without a struggle. From 1936 to 1939, when the CIO began its assaults on the great redoubts of steel, automobiles, and rubber, the country got a strong whiff of class warfare. In the Ohio River manufacturing centers, flying squadrons, sit-downs, mass walkouts, and similar new techniques of guerrilla unionism were employed to keep a factory shut tight and to prevent the entry of scabs. Alarmed by the threat to traditional property rights, many employers struck back. In the small towns of "industrial valley," employers sought to enlist middle-class opinion behind them. The most publicized and, for a while, most successful method was the so-called Mohawk Valley formula, utilized by Remington-Rand. In various parts of the country, the formula was repeated. Citizens' committees were launched in a dozen cities. Attempts were made to coordinate them into a national organization. At points, sporadic violence flared again. In Hershey, Pa., irate farmers, barred from selling their milk to the chocolate company, stormed the plant and scattered the strikers.[13] Yet the counteroffensive failed.

---

[11] So new is the collective-bargaining contract, compared to the body of opinion on the common law of contracts, that the courts have so far failed to develop an adequate legal theory to rationalize the enforcement of an *individual's* right against an employer, growing out of a *collective* contract. So far, three contradictory theories have been evolved: the usage, or custom, theory, the "agency" theory, and the "third-party beneficiary" theory. Some persons, despairing of squaring common-law principles with a collective-bargaining contract, see the latter, as Justice Jackson did in the *J. I. Case Co.* case, as a trade agreement; some regard it even as a treaty rather than conventional contract law. As Prof. Gregory remarks, "social change has been too rapid and violent in this field to allow for the slow process of judicial adaptation." See Charles O. Gregory, *Labor and the Law,* New York, Norton, 1946, p. 384.

[12] For a theoretical discussion of the relation between law and opinion, see A. V. Dicey, *Law and Opinion in England,* 2d ed., London, Macmillan & Co., pp. 1–16. For an appraisal of the conflicting sociological views, see the methodological appendixes in Gunnar Myrdal, *An American Dilemma,* New York, Harper, 1944, pp. 1027–1064. For a relevant study on the role of law affecting discrimination in employment, see Morroe Berger, *Equality by Statute,* New York, Columbia University Press, 1952.

[13] For a comprehensive account of these groups, see Louis G. Silverberg, "Citizen's Committees, Their Role in Industrial Conflict," *Public Opinion Quarterly,* 5 (1941), 17–37. The NLRB description of the Mohawk Valley formula can be found in V. O. Key, *Politics, Parties and Pressure Groups,* New York, Knopf, 1942; and in Selden C. Menefee, "Propaganda and Symbols Manipulation," in *Industrial Conflict,* First Yearbook of the Society for the Psychological Study of Social Issues, New York, Cordon, 1939.

New Deal governors, such as Murphy in Michigan and Earle in Pennsylvania, kept the state militias neutral. A spotlight on antiunion methods and exposés of company unions by the NLRB put the corporations on the defensive. Perhaps most effective was the La Follette Civil Liberties Committee, which, over a 2-year period, documented a black record of labor spies, tear-gas purchases, and employment of professional thugs and strikebreakers by the blue-ribbon corporations of United States industry, among them General Motors, Bethlehem Steel, RCA, and others.

By 1940, the period of violence was over and unionism had won acceptance. There were several reasons: most immediate, perhaps, was the need for uninterrupted production as war orders from Europe mounted; secondly, the large size of the corporations and the new degree of union strength made it difficult to recruit the many thousands of strikebreakers for full-scale industrial warfare; third, government pressures put the corporations on the defensive; and, finally, the entry of the United States into the war created a need for national unity.

In the short space of 7 years, from 1935 to 1942, the character of the economy had been significantly changed. Union membership had more than tripled, and 10 million workers, one out of four in the nonagricultural labor force, were organized. Once at the periphery, unionism was now solidly established in the core of the economy—in steel, automobiles, rubber, glass, meat packing, shipping, and transportation. The unionization of these mass-production industries meant not only a measure of democracy in large monopolistic sectors but a new and significant impact on the wage-price structure. The large AFL unions, teamsters, building trades, garment workers, etc., bargain principally in local labor markets, and the impact of their wage bargains is limited to those areas. (Thus the wage rate of a bricklayer in New York has no direct effect on the rate of a bricklayer in Minneapolis or upon the construction costs in that area.) The large CIO unions, however, bargain in a manner that affects entire industries, and the impact of a key wage negotiation is felt on a national scale, both in the linked wage bargains with related industries and in the local labor markets in which different plants of the industry are located. Moreover, a strike in any of these industries assumes a "national" character in both its scope and its economic impacts, a factor which later gave rise to the "national emergency provisions" of the Taft-Hartley law. This new economic power plus the political ties and influence of the labor movement with the New Deal and Fair Deal administrations gave rise to the new image of "Big Labor" as a powerful force which, in turn, like "Big Business," also had to be curbed.

The Pattern of Opinion

The only consistent measure we have, rough as it is, of public opinion toward labor consists of poll data.[14]

From 1936 to 1942, the Gallup poll (American Institute of Public Opin-

---

[14] Most of the questions reported here are drawn from the following compendium: Hadley Cantril and Mildred Strunk (eds.), *Public Opinion, 1935–1946,* Princeton, N.J., Princeton University Press, 1951. In some cases, the polls discussed are taken from the Gallup sheets released to the press.

ion, or AIPO) repeatedly asked the question "Are you in favor of labor unions?" Admittedly a buckshot question, its repetition for 6 years nevertheless provides an interesting trend line.[15] The results are shown in Table 18.1.

Table 18.1   Attitudes toward Labor Unions, 1936–1942

Date	Favor, %	Oppose, %
August, 1936	76	24
August, 1937	76	24
June, 1939	70	30
December, 1939	74	26
May, 1940	74	26
June, 1941	67	33
November, 1941	67	33
May, 1942	67	33

Consistently, more than two-thirds of the sample accepted unionism as a legitimate institution in American life. Yet on many specific problems, one finds a startling reversal of attitudes. During some of this same period, Gallup asked (March, 1938): "If an employer has labor trouble in this community, do you think he is justified in moving his plant to another community?" Forty-seven per cent said yes, forty-one per cent said no, twelve per cent were of no opinion.[16] In February, 1937, 44 per cent of a sample sympathized with General Motors workers then on strike, while 56 per cent favored the employers. In November, 1937, 73 per cent felt that state and local authorities should use force in removing sit-down strikers. In July and August, 1937, 57 per cent said yes to the question "Should the militia be called out whenever strike trouble threatens?" while 43 per cent said no.[17]

In these instances, responses to *specific* questions tended to follow older norms and traditional values, although the public had made an ideological commitment, in general, to the legitimacy of labor.

Since polls themselves play a role in proving to the public what public opinion is, the problems of poll analysis, as well as the substantive results, merit discussion.

What the polls mean, in the first instance, depend upon its phrasing. Paul Studenski [18] of New York University asked some students:

Should every worker be forced to join a union?
    9.3% said yes
    88.9% said no
    1.8% don't know

A week later, the question was reformulated and presented to the same group:

[15] Reported in C. Wright Mills and Hazel Gaudet, "What the People Think," *Labor and Nation*, Vol. 2, No. 1 (November–December, 1946).

[16] Cantril and Strunk (eds.), *op. cit.*, p. 329.

[17] All these questions are from Gallup polls reported in *ibid.*, pp. 816–817.

[18] Paul Studenski, "Polls Can Mislead," *Harper's Magazine*, December, 1939, cited in Lindsay Rogers, *The Pollsters*, New York, Knopf, 1949, p. 111. For a detailed analysis of a more subtle change resulting from a rewording of polls, see the analysis of the January and February, 1946, *Fortune* polls by C. Wright Mills and Hazel Gaudet Erskine, "What the People Think: Anti-labor Legislation," *Labor and Nation*, Vol. 3, No. 2 (March–April, 1947).

Is it proper for a union to require all working employees in an industrial enterprise to join a union

Under any circumstances?	7.4%
When the union controls a minority of the employees?	2.6%
When the union controls a majority of the employees?	37.6%
Or is it improper under any circumstances?	45.0%
Don't know	7.4%

The shift, as a result of the change in phrasing, speaks for itself. Not only wording but the selection of issues themselves raise the question of bias. Arthur Kornhauser, in a study of 155 questions asked by the different polling organizations, found that only 8 dealt with the positive or favorable features of unionism, that 81 were concerned with union faults or proposed restrictions on unions, and that 66 were neutral or doubtful.[19] Kornhauser raised other pertinent questions. When *Fortune* in February, 1941, asked: "How many labor leaders in your community do you think do a good job in representing labor; are fair in dealing with employers; are honest in handling union funds?" how can the public answer this except in terms of general prejudice; how many persons have genuine knowledge as a basis for specific value judgments?

Since the polls often serve as a pressure on the legislator to act on a specific issue, the question of the public's knowledge is paramount. In February, 1947, Gallup asked: "Do you think Congress should or should not forbid jurisdictional strikes?" Some 68 per cent said yes, 25 per cent said no, and only 7 per cent said they didn't know. When asked however to define "jurisdictional strike," only 12 per cent were able to give an approximately correct definition, 78 per cent could not.[20]

In the last 5 years, the Taft-Hartley Act has been the touchstone of labor controversy. In repeated Gallup polls, a large plurality of the voters, as shown in the table below, indicated dissatisfaction with the Wagner Act.[21]

Do you think the Wagner Labor Act should be left as it is, changed or done away with?

	May, 1938	November, 1938	March, 1939	January, 1947
Left as it is	38%	30%	34%	36%
Changed	43	52	48	53
Done away with	19	18	18	11

[19] Arthur Kornhauser, "Are Public Opinion Polls Fair to Organized Labor?" *Public Opinion Quarterly*, 10 (Winter, 1946), 484–500. Says Kornhauser, "Doubtless some justification can be found for this preponderantly anti-union emphasis by reference to 'popular interest and news value.' It is none the less important to recognize the one-sidedness. . . ."

That polls can reinforce such biases is also true. In March, 1941, Gallup asked: "Westbrook Pegler, the newspaper writer, claims that many labor union leaders are racketeers. Do you agree or disagree with him?" Seventy-two per cent agreed, fourteen per cent disagreed, fourteen per cent had no opinion (in Cantril and Strunk (eds.), *op. cit.*, p. 396). The question is one of context. Americans tend to believe that "it's all a racket," that politicians are crooks and businessmen are cheats. So it is "natural" that, where the image is one of a "racket society," labor leaders might be included. But why is the question asked, then, about labor leaders alone? And in the phrasing of the question what does "many" mean?

[20] Hazel Gaudet Erskine, J. Bernard Phillips, and Ruth Harper-Mills, "Polling Opinion or Planned Confusion," *Labor and Nation*, Vol. 3, No. 6 (November–December, 1947).

[21] *Ibid.*

The astounding fact, however, was that, in May, 1938, 56 per cent of the electorate did not know what the Wagner Act was or did not care whether or not it was revised. Two years later, despite the volume of public debate, the proportion of uninformed and no opinion had risen to 58 per cent. Most startling of all, in January, 1947, when a hostile Congress was primed to pass a new labor law, the figures had risen to 69 per cent.[22] After Congress, in June, 1947, had passed the Taft-Hartley Act and after the issue had been debated by President Truman and Senator Taft over a nationwide hookup and the Congress had overridden the Presidential veto, 39 per cent of respondents told a Roper poll that they hadn't even heard or read about the law. Of those who had, 75 per cent could not pick out a provision they considered particularly good, and 85 per cent could not pick out a provision they considered particularly bad.[23]

The confusion over the meanings is best illustrated in one of the most widely quoted labor polls in recent years: a study by the Opinion Research Corporation to sound out "the ordinary worker's real opinion of the Taft-Hartley law."[24] On the act as a whole, 54 per cent disapproved, 31 per cent approved, 15 per cent had no opinion. Yet on individual provisions of the act there was a sharp reversal of form. Seventy per cent favored a provision requiring 60-day strike notice; seventy per cent approved of the right of a company to sue a union for violation of contract; fifty-eight per cent wanted to bar a union from contributing to political funds; forty-eight per cent were for outlawing the closed shop.

When "averaged up," concluded Robinson, the vote shows 72 per cent of the workers approving Taft-Hartley provisions. Explaining the initial disapproval of Taft-Hartley and the approval of individual provisions, the study pointed out that 54 per cent of the sample were unable to name any specific provision of the bill correctly. Despite this, "it seems clear," Robinson argues, "that the American worker favors what is in the Taft-Hartley law—but doesn't know it."

Yet was it so clear? That 54 per cent could not identify any provision could indicate that actually there was no formed opinion but that answers were given only because of the asking. What is an opinion, the don't know or the answer expressed when pressed to make a yes or no choice? Equally misleading is the question of averaging. How can one average together percentages on different items without knowing how strongly persons feel about the different items? [25] Nor does an accounting of what a worker feels about ten different

[22] Figures cited in Rogers, *op. cit.,* p. 146; and in Elmo Roper, "Where the People Stand," *Labor and Nation,* Vol. 5, No. 3 (May–June, 1949). Both Rogers and Roper cite many instances of public ignorance, such as the following items: Four years after Philip Murray had become president of the CIO, only one-third of the public knew that he held that post. In 1944, 45 per cent of a poll did not know what the Little Steel Formula, the government's yardstick on wage increases, was. Almost as many thought it was a means of helping small steel producers compete with larger companies as could identify it correctly. In 1946, 31 per cent of a poll had never heard of the Bill of Rights; 36 per cent had heard of it but could not identify it; and 12 per cent gave confused or contradictory answers.

[23] Reported in a summary of polls, *Public Opinion Quarterly,* Summer, 1947.

[24] Claude Robinson, "The Strange Case of the Taft-Hartley Law," *Reader's Digest,* January, 1948, condensed from *Look,* Sept. 30, 1947.

[25] As three critics pointed out in a caustic appraisal of the methodology of the poll,

items tell us how he might feel about the use of the ten in one package as a law regulating labor. The ideological commitment to the symbol is often much greater than the sum of the responses to the individual items.

And yet, despite the passage of the Taft-Hartley law and much of the hostility expressed against specific union operations, the Gallup poll, in August, 1947, repeating its earlier question "In general, do you approve or disapprove of labor unions?" found 64 per cent voicing approval, 25 per cent disapproving, 11 per cent undecided. The percentages were unchanged since 1939! [26]

The Power of the Public

Public opinion, however muddled, was the force which backed the new curbs on unions enacted in the postwar years. The wartime strike actions of John L. Lewis had fanned wide indignation, and in 1943, Congress passed the Smith-Connally law, which outlawed strikes in government-operated plants, set a 30-day cooling off period for strikes in private plants, and gave the President seizure powers for the duration of the war. Congress expressed the feeling that, in the postwar period, the Wagner Act would have to be revised. It had not dealt with emergency disputes, secondary boycotts, and jurisdictional strikes. Meanwhile, the internal operations of the unions and the powers of union leaders to create abuses were subjects of many newspaper inquiries. On V-J Day, as Clark Kerr [27] points out, management "was clearly in the key position." It had come out of the war with a new prestige. "Now the initiative was with it and it had to decide in which direction or directions to exercise it."

Labor, like the New Deal generally, was clearly on the defensive. It had no program to offer, and it sought largely to maintain the *status quo*. One wing of business took some tentative steps to maintain the wartime harmony. At the initiative of Eric Johnston, of the U.S. Chamber of Commerce, a labor-management conference in March, 1945, promulgated a charter which recognized labor's right to bargain. Both Roosevelt and Dewey hailed the document; seemingly, the shades of Wilson and Gompers had become refulgent. If the project had spirit, however, it lacked body. The NAM abstained. The AFL refused to ratify the charter because of the presence of the rival CIO.

Organizational jealousies apart, such a pollyanna structure would have collapsed just as soon under the pressures of other events, for some test of strength between unions and business was inevitable. Wage rates during the war had been tethered by the Little Steel Formula, although income had risen because of extra overtime work. Now, as the work week fell, labor opened a drive to maintain take-home pay. Industry, in the midst of reconversion, decided to sit tight. The result was the greatest strike year in American history. In 1946, a staggering total of 110,000,000 man-days were lost through strikes,

it is difficult to tell how many persons might favor all ten of the items or even five or six of the provisions, since we do not know "whether it is always the same people who are for the law and the same people against it on each provision." Erskine, Phillips, and Harper-Mills, *op. cit.*

[26] From a newspaper release by Public Opinion News Service, Aug. 1, 1947.

[27] Clark Kerr, "Employer Policies in Industrial Relations," in E. Wight Bakke and Clark Kerr (eds.), *Unions, Management and the Public*, New York, Harcourt Brace, 1948, pp. 306–307.

as against a prewar high of 28,424,000 in 1937. It was not only the number on strike but their rapid succession that created public tension. A winter-long auto workers' strike, which shut down General Motors, was followed by one in steel. Shortly after, the railroad workers threatened to strike and were halted only by Truman's threat to draft them into the Army. The ubiquitous John L. Lewis came on stage, and when negotiations collapsed, the government seized the mines. In Pittsburgh, a utility strike almost paralyzed the city.

In none of these instances, however, did industry attempt the violence and back-to-work measures of the late thirties. The counteraction came through the legislator. The symbol of the struggle was the "national-emergency strike." The fact that labor was powerful enough to shut down a whole industry lent color to middle-class fears that Big Labor was running the country. Each national strike of long duration, with the attendant publicity about the economic effects, had given rise to outcries for action. In December, 1945, President Truman, in an effort to head off Congress, proposed a plan for 30-day cooling-off periods and the appointment of fact-finding boards to submit reports on national-emergency disputes.[28] These proposals, however, were weak tea for the Congress. In February, 1946, the Congress passed the Case Bill, whose provisions were later repeated in Taft-Hartley. Truman's veto was sustained by only five votes.

The failure of the administration to act on labor problems was one of the chief political issues of the 1946 campaign. The GOP cry was that the "public's rights" had to be protected by legislation. On this issue plus the hue and cry over controls, the Republicans won control of Congress. Shortly after, the NAM formulated the provisions of a new labor law.[29] Except for a ban on industry-wide bargaining, the Taft-Hartley Act passed by the 80th Congress embodied those policies completely. The act, frankly, was political. A number of lawyers for large corporations participated in its formulation; the technical drafting of the law was paid for directly by the Republican National Committee.[30]

The debate over Taft-Hartley was one of the most intense in legislative history. The AFL pledged a million and a half dollars in advertising for radio and newspaper statements. The CIO held rallies in a dozen cities. A meeting in New York's Madison Square Garden heard Mayor O'Dwyer blast the act. But the Republican party rolled up resounding majorities of 320 to 79 in the House and 69 to 24 in the Senate. Labor sought to flood the White

[28] In the light of later industry charges that fact finding was a means of imposing labor's demands, labor's reaction is interesting. The day after Truman spoke, Philip Murray charged the administration with yielding "in abject cowardice" to industry and laying the groundwork of a legislative design "to weaken and ultimately destroy labor union organizations."

[29] Reprinted in Bakke and Kerr (eds.), *op. cit.*, pp. 207–208.

[30] The lawyers were Theodore Iserman, whose law firm represented Chrysler, and William Ingels, of Allis-Chalmers. The technical drafting was done by a former House Labor Committee employee named Jerry Morgan. Said congressman Samuel McConnell, in defending the mode of payment, ". . . the committee's funds were earmarked for other purposes . . . and we thought that [payment by the Republican National Committee] was proper because we regarded enactment of a new labor law as a party responsibility." *Hearings before Committee on Education and Labor on H.R. 2032*, 81st Cong., 1st Sess., Part II, 1196 ff.

House with messages. By June 18, the Capitol had received 157,000 letters, 460,000 cards, and 23,000 telegrams, "more," claim Bailey and Samuel, "than ever before in history on a single issue." [31] But these were of no avail. Congress overrode Truman's veto by almost the exact majorities.

In the political arena, Taft-Hartley became like the goal-posts after a football game, to be torn down or defended at any cost. It was one of the chief issues in three subsequent political campaigns. In the steel strike of 1952, when the Supreme Court struck down President Truman's seizure order, following the industry's refusal to accept the Wage Stabilization Board's recommendations (because, said U.S. Steel, it would force the industry to accept the union shop), Congress immediately began to chant that Truman invoke the 80-day injunctive procedure of Taft-Hartley rather than permit the strike, and they even went so far as to pass a memorial telling the President that this was the will of the Congress.

By polarizing the labor issue, Taft-Hartley had the effect of catapulting labor more squarely into politics than ever before. It intensified the efforts of both labor and industry to win over that ambiguous animal known as public opinion.

The Propaganda War

In a country as opinion conscious as the United States, it was inevitable that public relations become a highly self-conscious instrument of labor and business groups. In the early days of the AFL, Sam Gompers, keenly aware of labor's pariah status, sought to distinguish the Federation from the radical labor groups by "supping" with the powerful tycoons of the country. Together with the mine workers' leader John Mitchell, Gompers joined, and became vice-president of, the National Civic Federation, an organization headed by Republican kingmaker Mark Hanna. If Gompers overestimated the gains to be achieved through this hat-in-hand approach, other unions were able, in specific situations, to mobilize the sympathy of society elements and turn it to the union's advantage. The most effective, in this respect, was the International Ladies' Garment Workers' Union. In 1909, when 15,000 women dressmakers went out on strike in New York, only to meet the brutality of the police and the violence of "gorillas" hired by employers, a wave of sympathy swept the city. A meeting at the Hippodrome was arranged by Mrs. O. H. P. Belmont, a society leader of the day. A committee of women headed by Mrs. Belmont and Anne Morgan, the sister of the financier, raised money for the strike fund. These women were suffragettes, and in this instance and many others, female solidarity was more important than class consciousness.

In general, those unions which have had a socialist or progressive leadership have been, because of their alliance with middle-class intellectuals and with the various reform movements of the day, such as child labor, women's suffrage, housing co-ops, etc., most mindful of the impact of their policies on the public and most interested in swaying public opinion. This is particularly

[31] Stephen Bailey and Howard Samuel, *Congress at Work*, New York, Holt, 1952, p. 152.

true of a union like the ILGWU, whose own activities in providing a "way of life" for its members through summer camps, health centers, cultural activities, and the like, have provided attractive and natural copy for the press. In 1949, the ILGWU set up a number of FM radio stations across the country, in New York, Chattanooga, and Los Angeles, as community stations. When FM failed to make headway as a broadcasting medium, the stations were disbanded.[32]

While a union like the ILGWU has received a favorable press as an institution, an individual like Walter Reuther has, by imaginative and articulate comment on social issues, symbolized the "new labor leader" created by the New Deal. Like the ILGWU, the auto workers have been cognizant of the need to enlist community support of their work. During the winter-long General Motors strike in 1945–1946, the union invited various community persons, under the leadership of Rev. Henry Hitt Crane, to set up a national citizens' committee and hold hearings on the strike issues. But publicizing a complex economic argument on wage rates and make-up pay is a far different endeavor than calling attention to instances of stark brutality.

In recent years, the trade-unions have sought to formalize their public-relations programs. Some union leaders like Petrillo and Dave Beck have hired regular public relations firms to "humanize" them. The AFL has expanded its budget, and one of its chief activities, at a cost of $750,000 a year, is sponsoring news commentator Frank Edwards on 160 stations across the country.

In these efforts, there is little direct effort, organizational or otherwise, to work with middle-class groups. During the war years and shortly after, the CIO made such an effort. Under Sidney Hillman, it formed the National Citizen's Political Action Committee, which, together with the Independent Citizen's Committee of the Arts, Sciences and Professions, formed the Progressive Citizens of America. Despite its auspicious start, the organization was taken over by the Communists in 1947 and became the nucleus of the Henry Wallace campaign in 1948. Since that time, the CIO's PAC has quietly steered away from middle-class groups, and its relations with even the liberal, non-Communist, Americans for Democratic Action have been distinctly formal.

Apart from having fingers burned by the Communists, the labor movement has failed to create a bridge to middle-class liberal groups for a variety of internal reasons: in the last 7 years, it has been preoccupied with consolidating its own forces, for it has had, it should be remembered, few years, apart from organizing strikes and government regulation, to weld its own power; the decline of the New Deal intellectual periphery has corresponded to a decline in the intellectuals in the labor movement; at the same time, for a variety of market and structural reasons, the trade-union movement is still distinctly a specific interest group concerned with its own needs first, rather than a broad social-reform movement seeking wholesale change in the nature of the society.[33]

Yet if labor has a root strength in the American community today, it is

[32] Perhaps the most important source of good will created by the ILGWU is its disbursement each year of hundreds of thousands of dollars to community organizations such as the Boy Scouts or the National Multiple Sclerosis Society.

[33] For an elaboration of this theme, see Daniel Bell, "Labor's Coming of Middle Age," *Fortune,* October, 1951.

because it is one of the constituents of the New Deal revolution which, breaking the crust of older privilege, afforded not only workers but also farmers, ethnic and national minority groups, and the *déclassé* intellectuals a middle-class stake in the country. By its historic identification with Franklin D. Roosevelt and with the assumption by "Big Government" of a responsibility for welfare measures for the people when needed, labor stands and falls with the concept of the "welfare state." In this ideological, if not organizational, alliance, lies labor's basic strength and limitation in relation to public opinion in the United States.[34]

It has been industry's prime concern, in the postwar years, to change the climate of opinion ushered in by the thunderstorm of the depression. This "free-enterprise" campaign has two essential aims: to rewin the loyalty of the worker which now goes to the union and to halt creeping socialism, with its high tax structure and quasi regulation of industry. In short, the campaign has had the definite aim of seeking to shift the Democratic majority of the last 20 years into the Republican camp.

The apparatus itself is prodigious: 1,600 business periodicals, 577 commercial and financial digests, 2,500 advertising agencies, 500 public-relations counselors, 4,000 corporate public-relations departments, and more than 6,500 "house organs" with a combined circulation of more than 70 million.[35]

The output is staggering. The Advertising Council alone, in 1950, inspired 7 million lines of newspaper advertising stressing free enterprise, 400,000 car cards, 2,500,000 radio "impressions," and countless statements and speeches at trade and community conclaves by thousands of corporation presidents and officials. Some companies, like Allis-Chalmers, provide lectures on the economic system to their workers on company time (leading to the charge of creating a "captive audience"). General Motors has subsidized a full-length movie on the profit system. Many companies are making wide distribution of free-enterprise comic books—in one of which, *The Fight for Freedom,* employees learn what really caused the Revolution of 1776: Over in London, it seems, there were those government planners. . . .

By all odds, it adds up to the most intensive "sales" campaign in the history of industry. And yet, as *Fortune* remarked in an explosive article in September, 1950, the whole campaign "is not worth a damn." Said William H. Whyte, the *Fortune* writer, "The Free Enterprise Campaign is psychologically unsound, it is abstract, it is defensive and it is negative. Most important,

---

[34] For an elaboration of this argument, see Samuel Lubell, *The Future of American Politics,* New York, Harper, 1952, Chap. 4.

[35] The figures are estimates supplied *Fortune*'s advertising department. For a discussion of corporate house organs, see "How to Play the House Organ," *Fortune,* October, 1952. To see the magnitude of some expenditures, General Motors publishes fourteen "external" periodicals to 4 million customers, stockholders, and interested persons and thirty-seven "internal" periodicals, including the *Executive Bulletin* for 90,000 salaried personnel and *Folks* for 500,000 employees and suppliers. There are about 800 labor papers in the United States with a total circulation of "twenty to thirty million." Labor papers are of two kinds: the *union* periodicals, the house organs of particular unions, and the local or community labor papers, which are issued by the state or city central labor body or "endorsed" by some local union bodies. Since many of the latter have inflated circulation for advertising purposes, no accurate count is possible. Few of the labor papers, however, compare with the slick, profusely illustrated, company house organs.

in a great many of its aspects it represents a shocking lack of faith in the American people and in some cases, downright contempt." [36]

Industry is not only defensive but also curiously uncomfortable about the opposition. An editorial in the *Saturday Evening Post* some years ago asked, "Must Propaganda be the Monopoly of our Leftists?" Arthur Krock stated in a column,[37] "it is from what is currently the 'left' in the United States that the greatest volume of this literary product comes with greater subtlety. . . ." Most labor publicists and editors of liberal publications would rub their eyes at such statements. Yet they contain a warped kernel of truth. In so far as the set or context of public opinion is still liberal or, at the minimum, while "Herbert Hoover" remains a fear symbol and the scar tissue of the Depression still shows, proliberal statements tend to have a greater "resonance" than business statements, no matter how mechanically amplified the latter may be. Secondly, a significant section of the intellectual class of the country, in the faculties of the large universities, in the publishing and literary world, and in government, remains New Deal (one has only to see how quickly the Keynesian revolution triumphed in economics). And these articulate individuals form the greater part of the opinion-forming elite of the country.

Some Contrast Conceptions and Reality

One of the striking aspects of opinion formation in the United States today is the bewildering "contrast images" that emerge when labor and business are confronted with each other. Businessmen have argued, before Eisenhower, that this is a "laboristic society" which is creeping toward socialism or toward "statism." Labor claimed that Big Business was dominating the mobilization program and running the country.[38] The fact that few people seem to have had a clear idea of where power actually lay in the country or had some intellectual apparatus to identify the locus of power itself speaks much about the changing structure of American society.[39]

Apart from the question of how much power it actually has, labor today is firmly rooted in American life. In the plant, a measure of industrial democracy and union security has been achieved. General Motors' C. E. Wilson, who swore in 1947 that he would "go back to the farm" rather than agree to any form of the closed shop, 3 years later signed a union-shop agreement with

[36] William H. Whyte, Jr., *Is Anybody Listening,* New York, Simon and Schuster, 1952, p. 8 (a collection of the *Fortune* communications series). For an earlier analysis of the themes of business and labor propaganda, see Menefee, *op. cit.*

[37] *The New York Times,* July 14, 1949.

[38] Some interesting evidence of opinion on a local scale can be seen in Detroit, where, according to a recent study, the better-educated groups were more likely to think that "rich people" and "businessmen" run the town. However, higher economic status was more significantly related to the belief that labor unions run the city. See Arthur Kornhauser, *Detroit as the People See It,* Detroit, Mich., Wayne University Press, 1952, pp. 50–52. A survey by the Survey Research Center of the University of Michigan on attitudes toward business showed that 55 per cent of the persons interviewed thought labor unions had more power than Big Business and 41 per cent thought the converse.

[39] One attempt to explain this confusion is made by David Riesman, *The Lonely Crowd,* New Haven, Conn., Yale University Press, 1950, Chap. 11. This writer has made an extended analysis in the forthcoming volume of essays in honor of R. M. MacIver.

the UAW-CIO. Mary Heaton Vorse, who witnessed the violence of the 1919 and 1937 steel strikes, marvels at the fact that in Charleroi, Pa., the mayor's and other city officials' cars led a parade of steelworkers during the 1949 pension strike.[40] Despite its giant strides, labor still looks on itself as a cowering minority often at the mercy of a marauding business class which is still intent on wiping out all its gains. In its rhetoric and in its propaganda, these images still stand paramount.[41]

On the other side of the coin, businessmen have a distorted image of a coherent trade-union movement powerfully allied with the "intellectuals" in an effort to change the social character of the society. This image has even less reality than the labor cliché about Big Business.

The result, however, of both these stereotypes has been to create confusion and to deepen suspicion regarding each of them in the "public mind." In this polarization, one can find the source of much of the tension and frustration of middle-class opinion, particularly of the "small-town mind," which tries to locate its own place in an increasingly amorphous society.

In the America of the 1950's, the large corporation has accepted the trade-union as a permanent fact of economic life. It is still a question whether the businessman and, particularly, the small-town individual will accept labor as a permanent part of the political life of the country. It is in that area, the heart of middle-class opinion, that social peace in the United States stands in the balance.

[40] Mary Heaton Vorse, "An Altogether Different Strike," *Harper's Magazine,* February, 1950, pp. 50–57.

[41] For an analysis of labor rhetoric, see Benjamin M. Selekman, *Labor Relations and Human Relations,* New York, McGraw-Hill, 1947, Chap. 8; also Daniel Bell, "The Language of Labor," *Fortune,* September, 1951. For a discussion of the cohesiveness of the business community, see David Truman, *The Governmental Process,* New York, Knopf, Chap. 8, esp. pp. 253 ff.

CHAPTER 19 IDEOLOGIES AND INDUSTRIAL CONFLICT

Philip Taft   *Brown University*

THE concept of ideology, although invented in France, was first systematically developed by Marx and Engels. They interpreted the term "ideology" as a system of ideas based upon the material conditions of production and expressing the interests of a class upon the plane of thought. An ideology expresses "man's attitude to the surrounding world and explanation of the purpose of the world as a whole," [1] and it frequently comprises a complete system of interpretation of social and political phenomena. Ideologies not only serve as explanations of the world but inspire the attitudes and conduct of individuals and groups who seek to fashion the world in accordance with their ideological predilections. Political ideologies such as communism, socialism, and anarchism are elaborate and detailed social philosophies. They are in a large sense a "complete, harmonious and consistent system of explanation of the purpose of society and of the surrounding social, economic and political phenomena." In addition, the above political ideologies set forth long- and short-run practical objectives; "to influence future social and political developments, they try—with a most ambitious design—to decide mankind's destiny." [2]

Marxist Doctrines on Industrial Conflict

Right at the beginning Marx, the founder of "modern socialism," recognized the importance of trade-unionism in heightening class struggle. The importance of the trade-unions was "not in the immediate result," the raising of wages, "but in the ever expanding union of the workers." The existence of railways and other improved means of transport meant for Marx that local struggles could be transmuted "into one national struggle between classes." [3] Marx's views on the role of trade-unions were expressed in more detail in a resolution penned by Marx and adopted by the Geneva congress of the International Workingmen's Association (First International). Not only must the trade-unions concentrate upon improving the wages and working conditions of labor but must "learn how to act consciously as focal points for organizing the

[1] Feliks Gross, "The Mechanics of European Politics," in Feliks Gross (ed.), *European Ideologies,* New York, Philosophical Library, 1948, p. 5.

[2] *Ibid.*

[3] Karl Marx and Frederick Engels, *Manifesto of the Communist Party,* Chicago, Charles H. Kerr & Company, n.d., pp. 26–27.

working class in the greater interests of its complete emancipation." [4] At the same congress a statement was issued that "in the actual situation of a struggle between labor and capital, the *strike is a necessity*." [5] The congress recommended that its affiliates set up defense funds so that, on behalf of their just demands, strikers would be aided in resisting their employers.

The First International was not an organization dominated completely by Marx and his followers. On the contrary, every branch of nascent and developed radicalism was represented there, and the sentiments expressed at conventions often represented compromises that were acceptable to the representatives of different radical doctrines. It can therefore be accepted that, in the gestating period of modern radical doctrines, the proponents of the various and, on some points, conflicting radical ideologies regarded the labor union and the strike as necessary means for carrying on their activity and achieving their aims. The development of militant ideologies which emphasized the class struggle and the irreconcilable conflict between labor and capital inevitably stimulated industrial strife, but it is extremely difficult to isolate the effect of ideologies, as labor difficulties are usually a response to several factors.

Yet indirect evidence indicates that ideology can be a factor in promoting or restraining industrial conflict. It must, however, be noted at this point that it is not only the ideology of revolutionary groups seeking to reorganize society but also the ideology of employers who may believe that they should be absolute masters "in their house" which may lead to industrial conflict. The various groups of social revolutionaries regarded the formation of trade-unions as essential to the promotion of revolutionary aims. Unions were held to be weapons for marshaling workers into serried ranks capable of resisting the claims of the capitalist and for the training of workers for unified and militant action. Unions were also regarded as a means for the achieving of immediate concessions.

Adjustment of Ideology to Reality

As workers seldom engage in strikes for purely ideological purposes, it becomes difficult to isolate the effect of ideology upon labor strife. But the notion of irreconcilable conflict between employer and worker and the insistence upon the pursuance of more militant policies by the proponents of revolutionary ideologies undoubtedly make compromise more difficult and may thereby accentuate and encourage labor disputes. There is, however, not much evidence to show any correlation between the ideology of a union which is well established and the number, frequency, or length of labor disputes. The German free trade-unions, in the pre-Hitler period, accepted the doctrines of socialism, although their socialism was a mild, reformist variety, and the number of labor disputes cannot be said to have been much greater than the number in countries where the unions did not accept socialist doctrines. Moreover, as in the United States, German unions sought to regularize their relations with employers through the

---

[4] Quoted in A. Lozovsky, *Marx and the Trade Unions*, New York, International Publishers, 1942, p. 18. See also G. M. Stekloff, *History of the First International*, London, Martin Lawrence Ltd., 1928, pp. 83–84.

[5] Oscar Testut, *L'Internationale*, Paris, E. Lachaud, 1871, p. 63 (italics in original).

collective contract.[6] The agreements, prior to World War I, covered mainly small- and medium-sized industries. The heavy, monopoly industries refused to deal with unions and fought them by the use of strikebreakers, company unions, and refusal to bargain. There was some opposition to collective contracts among the more militant members of the trade-unions, but this program was defended on the ground that collective agreements were proof of equality between employer and employee. It is clear, at least in this instance, that the ideology was adjusted to the realities of the situation rather than the reverse. The collective contract which regularized the relations between employer and employee might meet the objections of those who believed in the existence of irreconcilable class conflict, but unions as going concerns found it easier and more desirable to adjust their ideological principles than to allow their ideology to determine the policies of their union.

The English experience is not unlike that of Germany. Established unions whose official view may be socialistic are not more prone to engage in industrial warfare than are unions whose socialist ideology is more muted. Strikes, as election to office, tend to be based upon reasons other than ideology. In present-day England most officials of trade-unions, whether "appointed or elected, are chosen for administrative ability and less for their exploits than formerly, although even now, in some unions, many secure appointments or election because their political views happen to coincide with those of a vocal minority." [7] The ideological influence in the unions of England as well as elsewhere is likely to manifest itself through this "vocal minority," and the "outlaw" strikes that have been the more typical kind of strike in England during its government by the Labor Party are influenced by the radical ideology of the leaders, although the dissatisfactions of the mass of workers with the terms of employment or with the decisions of a tribunal are perhaps the decisive reasons for these walkouts. "The active branch membership criticises the national leaders for conservatism and gradualism and for not pushing wage claims hard enough." However, "it is significant that in spite of all the criticism of executives, when they come up for re-election they are almost invariably voted back to office, apparently by the very section which has been most critical of their official activities." [8]

It is clear that ideology may be a factor in industrial disputes when the membership is dissatisfied and angry at the conduct of the officials of the union, for those imbued with a class-war ideology can at such times act as leaders and organize the smoldering discontent into active revolt against officers and employers.

Syndicalism as an ideology emphasized not only the class war but a militant and uncompromising struggle against the employer at the plant level. Syndicalism was not only a protest against capitalism; it also found the hesitant, compromising, parliamentary tactics of the socialists distasteful. Revolutionary syndicalism dominated, in the period of 1892–1909, the French trade-union

---

[6] Nathan Reich, *Labour Relations in Republican Germany: An Experiment in Industrial Democracy 1918–1933,* New York, Oxford, 1938, pp. 63–65.

[7] *British Trade Unionism,* London, PEP (Political and Economic Planning), 1948, p. 22.

[8] *Ibid.,* p. 24.

movement. It was uncompromising in philosophy and advocated direct action, sabotage, the general strike, and avoidance of political action by labor groups, but the "heroic" period of French syndicalism was only a passing phase.[9] Writing during the first flush of French syndicalism, Prof. Charles Rist explained that strikers were more largely influenced by conditions in the labor and product markets than by ideological considerations.[10]

Even the militant doctrines of syndicalism were softened by time, although there is no conclusive evidence that the ideology of syndicalism was responsible for the increase in labor disputes which took place in France between 1891 and 1910 and 1911. The strikes mainly involved wages and the hours of labor, and while one may assume the militant leadership stimulated rather than restrained the tendency to strike, it is doubtful whether strikes would have risen as sharply if real grievances had not existed.

Ideological Influences in American Unions

Ideological influences also played a role in many phases of the history of American trade-unionism, but the influence of these ideologies upon labor disputes has not been very great under normal circumstances. In times of tension, excitement, or discontent, ideological influences may be more important. In the United States, the proponents of several kinds of revolutionary ideology played an important role in the founding of many unions and also of the AFL. Marxist and Lassallean socialists and anarchists all played a role in the fashioning of modern American trade-unionism, but their significance, especially that of the Marxist ideology, was in immunizing the trade-union movement against the influence of "trust busters" and monetary reformers and in developing a job-conscious type of trade-unionism. As shown by Prof. Perlman, in the "strife and turmoil of factional struggle, the small group of Americanised Internationalists in the East withdrew to build up a potent trade union movement upon the basis of wage-consciousness but non-socialistic philosophy." [11] Many of the unions in the 1880's were under socialist influence, but as the leaders became absorbed in the day-to-day problems of their organizations, "their original philosophy kept receding farther and farther into the background until they arrived at pure trade unionism." [12] Their knowledge of socialism and the doctrine of the class struggle led them away from having faith in the reform panaceas popular with post-Civil War middle-class reformers. "The philosophy which these new leaders developed might be termed a philosophy of pure wage consciousness." [13] In the case of the United States, the revolutionary ideologies brought or imported from abroad by leaders of trade-unionism were transformed in the American environment into a trade-

---

[9] Édouard Dolléans, *Histoire du mouvement ouvrier*, Vol. 1, Paris, Armand Colin, 1939, pp. 117–148; Jean Montreuil, *Histoire du mouvement ouvrier en France*, Paris, Editions Montaigne, n.d., pp. 194–195.

[10] Quoted in Montreuil, *op. cit.*, pp. 237–238.

[11] John R. Commons *et al.*, *History of Labor in the United States*, Vol. 2, New York, Macmillan, 1918, p. 354.

[12] *Ibid.*, p. 308.

[13] *Ibid.*, p. 308.

unionism emphasizing limited gains, collective contracts, mutuality of interest, and peaceful settlement of industrial disputes.

The change in ideology undergone by many of the early leaders did not put an end to the effort of those who espoused a more militant labor philosophy to influence and direct the American trade-unions. The socialists sought to win the labor organizations to their views, but they sought to redirect the political activities of organized labor more than to determine the relations of workers to employers. There is no evidence either that American unions led by socialists were more militant or that they experienced more strikes than did those officered by nonsocialists. As a matter of fact, when a group of militants launched the dual movement of the IWW, the great majority of socialist trade-unionists abstained from joining that enterprise. The IWW espoused a revolutionary philosophy resembling at many points French revolutionary syndicalism.[14] The IWW was not a "pure" trade-union movement but a combination of revolutionary propaganda league and embryonic industrial union. The latter feature was usually subordinate to the former, but it is difficult to attempt to assess the importance of ideology in the strikes of this organization because the workers involved were usually among the more severely exploited and were among those who suffered from the most grievances. The IWW usually entered these controversies at the request of a number of participants, sometimes because regular unions usually showed a reluctance to assume leadership of a spontaneous strike. The expenditure of money and energy in guiding and supporting unorganized workers engaged in a spontaneous labor dispute has not usually been regarded as a good investment by many unions. Because of its class ideology and its emphasis upon the solidarity of all labor, the IWW was willing to assume leadership, and its guidance may have prolonged or extended specific labor disputes. Only in this respect could it be argued that ideology had an effect upon industrial strife.

Communism in American Unions

The IWW were not the only group that sought to determine the policies of the trade-unions and thereby to influence the attitudes of labor organization toward strikes and collective bargaining. There were always individuals and groups who favored a more militant policy toward the employer, but they were, in the main, scattered and unorganized. The Russian Revolution of October, which brought the Bolsheviks (now called Communists) to power, introduced a new element into the labor movements of all countries. While the organizational forms of strict Party discipline devised by Lenin—operation through minority caucuses and subordination of the interests of the union to the Party—can be regarded as the result of peculiar Russian historical conditions and as a Russian phenomenon, by a process of diffusion these attitudes and institutions were transmitted to other countries. The policies aimed to capture and control trade-unionism in order to infuse it with a more militant philosophy and a more aggressive program. In contrast to the earlier efforts

[14] The IWW was largely an American phenomenon, but many of its views were close to those of the *Confédération Générale du Travail*.

the plan worked out was based upon a centralized and unified attempt to win over the entire labor movement and its affiliated divisions through the planned campaigns of organized minorities.

The initial attempt was made by the Trade Union Educational League, established in 1920 by the present chief of the Communist Party of the United States. While at the beginning the League disguised its objectives, it soon became apparent that it aspired to gain control of various trade-unions for the purpose of conducting a more aggressive policy against the employer. The League did not succeed in permanently attaining its objectives in many unions, but its influence was directed wherever possible toward greater militancy by the organized workers. In the ladies' garment industry a long strike seems to have been needlessly brought about in the New York market in 1926, after League adherents had won control over the local unions.[15] The strike might be attributed to the influence of the militant ideology espoused by the League, but perhaps more accurately the strike was due to a struggle for power between League adherents and the more conservative officials. The furriers' unions, which at the time came under the complete domination of a Communist group, have not engaged in more frequent strikes than have the other unions in the garment trades. It might, however, be argued that ideology is perhaps a more potent cause of strikes when its exponents are a minority within a union. Then their attacks and criticisms of the union's policies and officers may make it more difficult to work out the adjustments and compromises frequently made necessary by economic realities.

Up to 1936 and 1937 those espousing a revolutionary ideology either were outside the general labor movement or occupied an insignificant place within the regular unions. The Trade Union Educational League had, by 1928, transformed itself into the Trade Union Unity League, an admission that the attempt to capture the trade-unions by infiltration had failed. Its failure to gain influence was in part due to its Communist views. The Unity League sought to build an organization under its colors and slogans, and its efforts were scarcely crowned with success. The onset of the Great Depression did not increase the following of the Trade Union Unity League, but the developments and tensions undergone by the labor movement, beginning in 1933, created a favorable soil in which its adherents, although not its organization, could function. However, the change was not primarily due to the changed attitude of the worker but to the changed conditions within the labor movement.

The Great Depression undermined the industrial workers' confidence in the benevolence of big business, and when the first New Deal administration broke down the barriers erected by industrial enterprises against the unions, employees in many plants rushed to affiliate with organized labor. In many firms little or no organization existed, and the absence of any established group of officers enabled the exponents of radical ideologies to gain office and influence. The situation was, in this respect, accentuated by the split within the labor movement which began in 1934 and culminated in the creation of the CIO. The new unions established by the organizing campaigns launched by the CIO required a whole group of officers from top to bottom. In some in-

[15] Selig Perlman and Philip Taft, *History of Labor in the United States, 1896–1932*, Vol. 4, New York, Macmillan, 1935, pp. 544–545.

stances these positions were acquired by workers with ordinary trade-union outlooks, but in other instances individuals and organized groups were able to gain place and power who were exponents of radical doctrine. The success the latter achieved was in the main due to the alternative leadership that existed in the ranks and to the reaction of the workers in the industry. Nevertheless, for the first time in the history of trade-unionism, many individuals who believed in a revolutionary ideology headed, or were in a significant minority in, important labor unions in the United States.

Although radical ideas played some role in the strikes that followed World War I, the influence of the radical minority was not of long duration. The turn toward more conservative policies, the failure of militants to crack the citadels of the open shop, and the preemption of radical agitation by the Communists shifted organized labor toward more moderate opinions. Nevertheless, the new organizations were open to the influence and dominance of aggressive and talented men and women, who could avoid the slow and often painful process of fighting their way up the official escalator. Labor journalists, parliamentarians, speakers, and organizers were needed, and this offered an unequaled opportunity for the exponents of revolutionary doctrine. Many gained leadership in growing local unions, and some achieved prominent positions in the new international unions.

The effect upon industrial strife of the ascendancy of these groups in the union depends upon whether they win control of the administration or not. If they are an influential opposition, radical ideologists are likely to make more difficult the arranging of wage bargains and other conditions of employment. To some extent, this is true of any kind of opposition to the union organization, but a group with an ideological base is likely to be more tenacious, resourceful, and ruthless than a group merely intent upon capturing office in order to introduce modest changes in policy. However, once in control of a union, Communist officers or their fellow travelers are not necessarily more militant in pursuing their aims, nor do Communist-officered unions engage in more strikes than do those officered by non- or anti-Communists. If one were to compare the strike record of the independent United Electrical and Machinery Workers, a union that severed its affiliation with the CIO to avoid being kicked out for following the political line of the Communist Party, with the strike record of the UAW-CIO, it is likely that, if there were differences in the ratio of strikes to membership, the percentage of the independent group would be lower. Communist officers are as cognizant as others that strikes are both risky and expensive to the union, and they will not engage in them unless some political purpose can be gained.

This raises the question of why the Communists would seek to win control over the trade-union movement. The theory of organization developed by Lenin [16] requires that Communists should seek to dominate all forms of labor activity by moving into positions where they can influence and determine policy. Trade-unions are regarded as transmission belts between the Party and the worker, the means by which he can be influenced. Also union funds can be drained for supporting ostensible labor causes which are, in fact, Party causes. In critical times strikes can be called in strategic industries over pre-

[16] See *What Is to Be Done?*, New York, International Publishers, 1929.

sumed economic grievances but actually in pursuit of Party policy. Such strikes were called, during the Communist-Nazi honeymoon period, in the Milwaukee plant of the Allis-Chalmers Manufacturing Co. and at North American Aviation, Inc. In places, as in France and Italy, where the Party is more confident of its position and where its followers are more numerous, control over the unions enabled the Party to call political strikes which debilitated the economy. However, when a change in worker sentiment took place, the Party followed a more cautious trade-union policy.

Employer Ideology

The ideology of employers on labor matters has always been more simple than the complex philosophies evolved by revolutionaries. For a long period in American industrial history, a large and influential body of employers refused to recognize and negotiate with their employees over the conditions of employment. Control over wages and conditions of employment was regarded as the exclusive prerogative of the employer. The refusal to recognize or deal with the union had been, in the years prior to 1937, a significant cause of labor strife, and some of the most violent and bitter clashes between labor and management have been over the question of recognition of the union. One need only mention the open-shop drives in the early part of the century and after World War I and the refusal of the great industries to tolerate union members in their plants to visualize the effect that employer ideology had on labor strife. It is obvious that a militant employer antiunion ideology can have a much more severe effect upon labor strife than can a revolutionary ideology espoused by radical groups. This follows from the manner in which the various ideologies impinge upon industrial relations. The worker is not an "ideologue." He usually wishes to improve his standard of living through his union, and he is only mildly, if at all, interested in revolutionary change. Therefore the exponents of radical ideologies cannot directly enlist the worker in a fight for a revolutionary objective. Workers can be marshaled only to serve an ostensible economic end, and it is normally only by duplicity that the worker can be led out on strike to serve a radical cause. Consequently, if the Communist wants to retain his position and influence in the union, he must be careful to shield his aims, and consequently, he cannot risk the union in many "profitless" industrial skirmishes. The radical ideologist can, however, give voice and leadership to dissatisfaction against the officers and the economic bargains they reach. Under some circumstances, irregular or outlaw strikes can be fomented, but usually the ideology will not play an important role on the labor side. In contrast, an aggressive antiunion ideology by the employer is likely to cause many industrial disputes, as many workers are likely to desire organization and collective bargaining.

Such organizations as the League for Industrial Rights, the "citizens' alliances," and the National Erectors' Association were once militant opponents of unionization, as were the National Metal Trades' Associations, the National Founders' Association, and even the NAM. Several of these associations went beyond ideological support of the open shop and also pursued a policy of active support, by financial and physical means, of employers engaged in a dispute with a union over recognition. The drive against unionism in the steel industry, in the first decade of the century, and the refusal of the head of the giant United States Steel Corporation to grant any kind of recognition to outside unions are manifestations of an employer ideology which has caused an infinitely greater number of strikes than all the revolutionary doctrines that have been propounded since Plato's *Republic*. This is inevitable, for the worker is seldom influenced in his decisions to strike or not to strike by questions other than those affecting wages and conditions of employment. Radical ideologists can influence labor disputes under very limited circumstances. The employer's ideology, in contrast, is a direct and immediate influence in determining labor disputes, for if he is opposed in dealing with a union, his attitude is likely to provoke not only the occasional strike but often the most bitter type of strike. It seems therefore a reasonable conclusion that labor ideologies are usually an insignificant factor in industrial disputes and that certain employer ideologies have been of great importance.

3 DEALING WITH INDUSTRIAL CONFLICT

a •ACCOMMODATING TO CONFLICT

As THE reader will have gathered, opinions differ as to whether industrial conflict is a serious problem in the United States. These differences are partly the result of divergent concepts and definitions: economists tend to think of industrial conflict as denoting overt belligerency, usually in the form of the strike, while psychologists understand it as referring to antagonistic desires and interests, on the part of individuals and groups in society, which may or may not lead to open struggle. The differences also depend on one's belief as to the legitimacy of contention: some sociologists regard the labor-management dispute as evidence of breakdown and disorder, while others view it as a sign of industrial democracy at work. Finally there are important disagreements as to the facts, for example, whether strikes are an insignificant or major source of economic loss.

Whether or not industrial conflict in general is deemed a serious social problem, it is clearly a practical problem for the parties immediately involved in labor-management relations, who must live with each other, despite some division of interest, as a matter of necessity. And certain particular conflicts—those disputes which threaten to create an emergency or which interfere with work of national importance during a war—constitute a problem with which the government must contend.

Regardless of divergent theories and interpretations, therefore, industrial conflict must be dealt with, or "handled." Efforts to deal with it have taken three forms: First is a set of procedures for reconciling, compromising, or adjudicating controversies between unions and employers. Second are various attempts to eliminate the underlying sources of controversy. Some have evolved as new phases of personnel administration, such as programs to improve relations between supervisors and rank-and-file employees at the work level. Others have been largely created in the collective-bargaining process, such as the provision of systematic job priorities. Still others are the product of legislation, such as the responsibility for the level of employment which Congress assumed in the Employment Act of 1946. Third is a series of social controls imposed by the state and Federal governments. These again are of various types. Some are designed to restrict the allowable area of conflict by prohibiting or policing various methods of conducting it. Others provide a peaceful alternative to belligerent trials of strength, such as the certification procedure under the Wagner and Taft-Hartley Acts. Still others attempt to maintain production and facilitate settlements in "emergency disputes" of one kind or another.

The four primary procedures for accommodating differences between unions and management are contract negotiation, grievance negotiation, mediation, and arbitration. These procedures are analyzed and evaluated in the successive chapters by Harbison, Kennedy, Warren, and Bernstein. They make up the collective-bargaining system which is in effect throughout large sectors of the American economy—particularly in basic industries, manufacturing, construction, transportation, and public utilities—and which strongly influences industrial relations elsewhere.

The collective-bargaining system rests on several implicit assumptions, one of which is that society can tolerate the cost and inconvenience of most of the work stoppages which occur when the right to strike is preserved. As Gustav Peck [1] noted in a recent report to the U.S. Senate,

> Under collective bargaining, disagreements of the parties which appear to be final are tested by work stoppages before the parties are willing to make further compromises and adjustments in order to settle the dispute. . . . Since the product or the service which is the end result of the enterprise is needed by its customers, many will be inconvenienced or will suffer losses or hardship when the supplies or services are cut off. This is a price paid for the function of the joint determination of the terms and conditions of employment by the parties most at interest. . . . That there could be such stoppage of production is the risk of every effort at collective bargaining. . . . It is the known cost of a strike to the parties which generally results in the avoidance of the stoppage by acceptable compromises. Even when a strike occurs, its cost to the parties remains the most effective deterrent against its prolongation.

Another assumption of the collective-bargaining system is that systematic procedures can minimize, although they cannot entirely eliminate, the incidence of overt conflict. Kennedy states in Chap. 21 that a principal value of the grievance procedure is "the existence of system, of formal arrangements, and of a device for introducing order and due process into what otherwise remains a confusion of relationships and easily becomes a clamor of voices." This characterization applies equally to other bargaining processes. One cannot but be impressed by the widespread consensus concerning effective procedures of negotiation, mediation, and arbitration which has developed in the past two decades and by the rapid adoption of such procedures. Today there is basic controversy only with respect to "emergency-dispute" procedures.

Collective bargaining, as Harbison observes in Chap. 20, not merely "provides a partial means for resolving the conflicting economic interests of management and labor" but also "greatly enhances the rights, dignity, and worth of workers as industrial citizens" and further "provides one of the more important bulwarks for the preservation of the private-enterprise system." Collective bargaining has the last-named result, says Harbison, for several reasons:

[1] "Emergency Dispute Settlement," staff report to the U.S. Senate Subcommittee on Labor and Labor-Management Relations, 1952, p. 3.

First, it provides a drainage channel for specific dissatisfactions and frustrations which workers experience on the job; second, it helps to "humanize" the operation of an essentially impersonal price system by making it more generally palatable to workers as a group; and, third, it absorbs the energies and interests of the leaders of labor who might be inclined to work for the overthrow of capitalism if this avenue of activity were lacking.

CHAPTER 20 COLLECTIVE BARGAINING AND AMERICAN CAPITALISM

Frederick H. Harbison   *University of Chicago*

COLLECTIVE bargaining is now firmly rooted in our industrial society, and unionism is generally accepted as one of the hallmarks of the American way of life. An increasing number of employers today are joining with the nation's labor leaders in proclaiming that collective bargaining is not only compatible with our private-enterprise economy but probably essential for its very survival. The NAM and the Chamber of Commerce are both "for" collective bargaining (although they may voice disagreement with organized labor on its appropriate scope), and few candidates for political office would dare to attack the basic idea of freedom for workers to organize for the purpose of dealing with their employers. Indeed, as a nation we believe so firmly in our system of collective bargaining that we are sending company and union leaders abroad to "sell" it to our friends and allies in foreign countries.

What then are the essential characteristics of this institution which is now so widely defended by the American people? What are the objectives of the parties who participate in it? What functions does it perform in our economy, and what is its future role most likely to be? These are the questions which we shall attempt to answer in this chapter.

Essential Characteristics of Collective Bargaining

First, collective bargaining is strictly *a relationship between organizations*. Contrary to a mistaken belief in many quarters, collective bargaining is not a relationship between management and workers. Management-employee relations encompass direct dealings between company officials and workers as individuals, whereas collective bargaining is confined to dealings between company spokesmen and the *representatives* of the union which is the bargaining agency of the employees.

Second, collective bargaining is *a power relationship between organizations*. Bona fide collective bargaining does not exist unless the union has the ultimate right to resort to force, in the form of a strike, and unless the representatives of management also have the ultimate right to refuse workers employment if they are unwilling to acquiesce to the demands of the union. Stated more bluntly, collective bargaining does not exist unless each party is free to negotiate with a club which is within handy reach in case of necessity.

Third, collective bargaining is essentially *a treaty-making and treaty-enforcing process between companies and unions*. The end objective of collective bargaining is to arrive at a mutually satisfactory contract setting forth, for a period of time, agreements on such things as wages, hours, and other conditions of employment. During the period when the contract is in force, the principal activity of the parties is the administration and interpretation of its provisions. In well-established collective relations this treaty-administering function is customarily performed in a very orderly manner.

Finally, collective bargaining is in practice *a process of accommodation between companies and unions.* Although open conflict and guerrilla warfare may be characteristic of some relationships at particular points of time, the vast majority of collective relationships provide an avenue for orderly and peaceful resolution of differences through compromise, agreement, and cooperation. Thus, despite the fact that collective bargaining has its roots in a conflict of interests between capital and labor and cannot exist without the right of both parties ultimately to back up their respective interests with force, it is really an instrument for furthering industrial peace. It is a way of organizing divergent interests in such a way as to resolve rather than to extend open conflict.

Driving Forces in Collective Bargaining

The union as an organization attempts to effect a proprietorship over the discontents, aspirations, and special interests of workers in the factory, mine, or office.[1] Though American unions are sometimes interested in community relations and are becoming increasingly active in national and world affairs, their core function is still collective bargaining with employers. This is their main business and consumes their major energies.

The objectives of union leadership in the process of collective bargaining fall perhaps into five broad categories: [2]

The first set of objectives is concerned with the preservation and the strengthening of the union as an organization. In this area labor leaders press for such things as the recognition of the union's functionaries in the plant, the checkoff of dues, and the union shop. The objectives are 100 per cent membership in the union and full-fledged recognition of the organization in the shop. These are the essential goals of all unions.

The second group of objectives centers upon getting "more" for the membership. Here we have the familiar demands for higher wages, shorter hours, holidays, vacations, sickness allowances, pensions, and a host of other material benefits which workers want. When economic conditions make the attainment of additional concessions impossible, then the job of the union is to preserve the benefits which have already been won. A union which cannot deliver in this area will not survive for very long.

Third, the union is constantly striving to acquire a greater measure of control over jobs. It must act as a watchdog on management. In order to

---

[1] For this particular concept, which is expanded somewhat at the end of this article, I am indebted to the late Prof. Lloyd Fisher.

[2] The concept of the objectives of unions and companies developed in this section is borrowed from Frederick H. Harbison and John R. Coleman, *Goals and Strategy in Collective Bargaining,* New York, Harper, 1951, Chap. 1.

build the prestige of the organization and to protect the members' interests, union leaders naturally feel that they have to protest company actions, police them, or actually participate with management in making important decisions which will affect individual jobs and employment opportunities as a whole. Inevitably, therefore, unions encroach upon the domain of managerial authority.

Fourth, union leaders are usually concerned with broad social and economic goals. They look upon collective bargaining as an instrument for placing human welfare before profits and human rights before property rights. Yet, as a practical matter, the modern unionist openly or tacitly admits that these goals must be advanced within the context of the private-enterprise system. In the final analysis, therefore, the objective of most American unions is to make the existing enterprise system more responsive to human needs.

Finally, the actions and policies of union leaders are also explained in part by personal goals and ambitions. They naturally strive for personal status and power, and they are anxious to build reputations as "good fighters for labor" and as "competent bargainers." These goals may be advanced in a variety of ways, ranging all the way from attacking the employer to playing the role of "labor statesman."

The common denominator of all these union objectives is *to put pressure on the employer*. In so far as the core activity of organized labor is collective bargaining, the central purpose of a union is, therefore, to generate pressure on management to achieve the objectives described above.

It follows, then, that management's objectives in collective bargaining are primarily concerned with developing a strategy for making adjustments to union-generated pressure. The core function of a business enterprise, however, is not collective bargaining. Most of management's energies are directed to other activities, such as procurement of materials, production planning, financing, and sales promotion. Management is under pressure to keep its stockholders happy and to satisfy its customers. The union merely brings into play a third pressure, the pressure to satisfy the workers and the institution which bargains for them. In collective relations, therefore, the employer is usually on the defensive. The company has an interest in preserving the *status quo,* whereas the union is usually anxious to press for changes. Within this context management's objectives in collective bargaining probably fall into these general categories·

First, management is interested in the preservation and strengthening of the business enterprise. It is concerned with both its economic and its organizational welfare. It needs to keep costs down to make profits; it needs to set aside reserves to finance new equipment and plant; and it needs to build teamwork and to develop morale in the working force. The union may threaten the enterprise in several ways. It may press demands which would impair the financial health of the firm, or it may frustrate management's efforts to build a loyal organization. In response to such pressure the company may try to hold the union at arm's length, or it may attempt to use the union as a means of helping build a better organization and to enlist its support in increasing output and improving efficiency.

Second, management is nearly always concerned with retaining control over the business and preserving its freedom to exercise its central managerial functions. Obviously, management's concern with its prerogatives is likely to clash with the union's quest for control over jobs. Here again the company may choose different means to achieve the same ends. It may attempt to minimize union interference with its prerogatives, or it may look upon the union as an instrument for implementing its policies and actions.

Third, management strives for "businesslike" relations with "responsible unionism." It wants union leaders to guarantee performance under the contract. It seeks assurance against work stoppages during the life of the agreement. In short, it strives for stability and predictability in its collective-bargaining relationships.

Fourth, management is usually deeply concerned with the preservation of the enterprise system of which it is a part. Consequently, in the minds of many company executives, collective-bargaining relationships must be consistent with the broad goals of preservation of individual initiative, freedom to venture, and the theory of the competitive market, which are conceived to be the cornerstones of economic progress. In broad terms, management is anxious to promote the kind of relation with unions which will protect and bolster free enterprise.

Finally, as in the case of union leaders, company officials have personal goals and ambitions which they may seek to advance in their capacity as business leaders. In management-union relations, as well as in other phases of business management, they seek to build reputations as men who can be "firm but fair" or executives who can "combine sympathy for human needs with practical business judgment."

At the bargaining table and during the day-to-day administration of the contract, company and union officials are continually dealing with issues arising out of the pursuit of the broad objectives outlined above. Some relationships appear to be fraught with conflict, whereas others appear to be quite harmonious. The determinants of the conflict-cooperation pattern in various relationships lie beyond the scope of this article. They stem primarily from *the varying means employed by the parties to achieve their ends* rather than from differences in the basic objectives themselves.[3] Nevertheless, whether the process is arduous or relatively painless, collective bargaining in most cases provides an orderly means of accommodation of the objectives of the parties. Company and union leaders, in their capacity as statesmen, diplomats, or just plain horse traders, usually manage to find some way of compromising in areas of basic disagreement and of cooperating where they have common interests. Collective-bargaining relationships often break down; sometimes the government is forced to intervene to bring pressure for a settlement; and all long and costly strikes are not completely eliminated. Yet industrial conflict is really not a major problem in the United States today. In 1947, for example, 24 out of 25 of the 100,000 collective-bargaining contracts in effect were negotiated without work stoppages. The few strikes which do occur, moreover, are usually the result of honest differences in opinion and occur within the frame-

[3] For a detailed analysis of this concept, see *ibid.*, Chaps. 2–4.

work of collective bargaining rather than as a manifestation of militant class conflict.[4] In the steel strike of 1949, for instance, it was not uncommon to find companies supplying coffee and doughnuts to pickets and negotiating with unions on "ground rules" for the orderly walkout of strikers, the categories of persons who would be allowed to go into the mill, and the procedures for resumption of operations at the termination of "hostilities." Indeed one might say that "peaceful" strikes are becoming more and more accepted as a normal and legitimate part of the process of modern collective relations. The remarkable thing is really not that we have strikes but that we have so few of them in a country where unionism is so firmly entrenched.

Functions of Collective Bargaining in the United States

What, then, can be said regarding the consequences of collective bargaining? What tasks can it be expected to perform under modern American capitalism? I would argue that collective bargaining, where it operates with reasonable success, fulfills three major functions: first, it provides a partial means for resolving the conflicting economic interests of management and labor; second, it greatly enhances the rights, dignity, and worth of workers as industrial citizens; and, third, as a consequence of the first two functions, it provides one of the more important bulwarks for the preservation of the private-enterprise system.

On behalf of its members, the union demands wage increases, vacations with pay, pensions, sickness benefits, and many other things which workers want. In practically all collective-bargaining treaties, agreement on these matters is reached, the final settlement usually being somewhere between what the union asks for and what the employer at the outset says he is willing to give. When the contract is finally signed, the union leadership usually takes pains to point out that the new terms and conditions of employment represent a victory for the workers. Thus most workers in organized plants probably feel that the union has pushed the employer about as far as he will go. Management customarily indicates that, although the concessions have been perhaps too costly, it will try to get along somehow. For all practical purposes, then, these economic issues are resolved for periods varying from perhaps 6 months to as much as 5 years. Provision is made, furthermore, for the orderly settlement of individual grievances over wage rates and employment rights during the life of the contract. From the standpoint of the workers, this method of getting *commitments* from management on wages and working conditions is much more satisfying than being forced to rely on managerial discretion on such matters. Management can also breathe more easily knowing that these issues are more or less settled for the time being. On the part of both parties, therefore, there is usually a sense of satisfaction in concluding by mutual agreement a treaty which gives each a feeling of security, if not a sense of achievement.

The economic impact of these bargains on individual firms and on the economy as a whole, however, is an entirely separate question. Economists as

[4] Clinton S. Golden, "A Positive Approach to Peace," in *The Causes of Industrial Peace*, National Planning Association Case Study 5, 1949, pp. 53–57.

yet have not been able to resolve their differences—either in theory or in fact— on the impact of the union. For example, the late Henry Simons and his followers would argue that unions possess almost unlimited monopoly power and succeed in benefiting their members only at the expense of the unorganized groups in society. They would also contend that collective bargaining, in exerting an upward pressure on wages, must inevitably result either in price inflation or in general unemployment.[5] Yet other economists tend to discount the effect of unions on wages, on allocation of resources, and on general levels of prices and employment. Milton Friedman, for example, has stated that the long-run effect of unions on the structure and level of wage rates and, thereby, on the allocation of economic resources is of minor magnitude in comparison with other economic forces.[6] He is joined by Prof. W. A. Morton who tends to attribute the recent inflation to monetary factors rather than to union pressure generated through collective bargaining.[7] The empirical evidence in this area is quite scanty and as yet does not provide sufficient evidence to prove either of these contentions. Thus the "jury of economists" weighing the economic impact of the union is hung.

Obviously, then, we cannot claim that collective bargaining has any effect on the redistribution of income; nor can we rely on it as a means of altering the share of labor and capital in the fruits of economic progress. Indeed it is quite possible that the standard of living of unionized workers is not really raised at all as a direct result of collective bargaining, despite the fact that there may be a widely held belief among the leaders and members crediting the union as the primary cause of economic gains. However, we can be reasonably certain that, when a worker gets a wage increase through the process of collective bargaining, he naturally tends to give the union credit for it, for he has no way of knowing whether he would have gotten it in the absence of collective bargaining.

The second function of collective bargaining is the protection and advancement of workers' rights and freedoms on the job. In the unionized plants the collective agreement establishes the framework of a system of industrial jurisprudence. It defines the rights of individuals and groups, and it provides machinery for the adjudication of grievances. At every turn, moreover, collective bargaining forces management to take cognizance of the effect of its decisions on the rights and interests of workers. If management decides to introduce new methods and machinery, for example, it must carefully weigh the impact of such changes on the workers involved. Or, if it wants to promote an employee to a higher position out of line of seniority, it must be absolutely certain that the individual involved has superior ability and competence. In short, the mere existence of a collective-bargaining relationship, quite apart from the specific clauses in the contract, puts continuous pressure on the employer to eliminate causes of employee discontent and to think in terms of

[5] See, in particular, Henry C. Simons, "Some Reflections on Syndicalism," *Journal of Political Economy*, March, 1944; and Charles E. Lindblom, *Unions and Capitalism*, New Haven, Conn., Yale University Press, 1949.

[6] Milton Friedman, "Some Comments on the Significance of Labor Unions for Economic Policy," in *The Impact of the Union*, New York, Harcourt Brace, 1951, Chap. 10.

[7] See Walter A. Morton, "Trade Unionism, Full Employment, and Inflation," *American Economic Review*, March, 1950.

human values in the management of people. One of the most striking features of American industrial relations, moreover, is the energetic response of employers to actual or potential union pressure. This pressure often leads to programs for better selection and placement of employees, improved foreman-training programs, better systems of wage and salary administration, and more effective two-way communication between management and workers. Such positive responses may be even more prevalent in the unorganized establishments than in unionized plants, for in such cases management often bends over backward to treat employees decently if for no other reason than to prevent them from bringing a union into the plant.

Thus the collective-bargaining contract establishes the body of law, and the union provides the police force for protection and extension of employees' rights on the job. To be sure, this system is not without its defects and drawbacks. First, some labor leaders, as they become securely entrenched in their unions, tend to lose touch with the rank and file and to become insensitive to the complaints and desires of the people they are supposed to represent. Second, some types of rigid working rules and regulations prescribed by contract may be as distasteful to some workers as unilateral managerial authority. Third, in rare instances, management and labor bureaucrats may conclude "sweetheart agreements" which completely ignore the fundamental interests of workers. Yet few persons would deny that, on the whole, the direct and indirect consequence of collective bargaining is to bring about more consideration for the freedom, dignity, and worth of the workingmen and workingwomen in modern industrial society.

To the extent that collective bargaining operates successfully as an orderly means of resolving the conflicting economic interests of management and labor and to the extent that it enhances the dignity and worth of laborers in their role as factors of production, it provides some very substantial support for our system of democratic capitalism. It does this in three ways: first, it provides a drainage channel for the specific dissatisfactions and frustrations which workers experience on the job; second, it helps to "humanize" the operation of an essentially impersonal price system by making it more generally palatable to workers as a group; and, third, it absorbs the energies and interests of the leaders of labor who might be inclined to work for the overthrow of capitalism if this avenue of activity were lacking.

The operation of collective bargaining as a drainage channel for worker dissatisfactions is so obvious as hardly to warrant further elaboration. In this country day-to-day union-management relationships center on problems arising at the bench. The average local union leader spends most of his time listening to complaints and settling grievances which arise out of specific conditions on the job. Management likewise devotes a great deal of time and energy not only to adjustment of grievances but to elimination of causes of worker dissatisfactions as well. In other words, collective bargaining usually provides a strong incentive for the company to "clean up its backyard and keep it as tidy as possible." The "winning of concessions" by the union in each new contract, moreover, tends to create the impression among workers that they are doing a pretty good job of periodically and systematically "shaking down the boss" for their share of the fruits of economic progress. Every time a wage increase is won through the collective-bargaining process, the worker probably feels more satisfied with collective bargaining and a little more happy about living under the private-enterprise system. Although very few workers participate actively in the affairs of their union, they appear to have confidence in the ability of union leaders (acting as their "Philadelphia lawyers") to keep an eye on management and to effectively voice their interests. Thus the leader of a radical movement who would overthrow or in any way alter this very satisfying and successful method of getting "more" from the employers finds little support among modern rank-and-file workers. Even the so-called Communist-oriented union leaders are forced to become expert practitioners of the art of collective bargaining in order to acquire and hold the reins of power in their organizations.

The humanizing influence of collective bargaining on modern capitalism, though perhaps not so obvious, is nonetheless of profound importance. Many of our outstanding economists have postulated the idea that the optimum allocation of economic resources stems from the mechanistic operation of blind and impersonal forces. They are also likely to refer to labor as a "commodity" or as "another factor of production" in an economic system which works best when each participant uses it as a vending machine. This kind of intellectual rationale, of course, is repugnant to American workers who are convinced that labor has values distinguishing it from, and placing it above, other factors of production. An American is conditioned by his parents, by his teachers, and by all the media of mass communication to believe that he is born free and equal, is endowed with the right to seek redress of grievances wherever they arise, and is heir to an economic system guaranteeing him the right to work and to earn a good living. The emphasis which collective bargaining places on human values, therefore, provides him with a rationale for believing in the existing enterprise system. The very process of establishing wages through bargaining, even if income levels of workers may not be substantially influenced thereby, gives workers a feeling that blind economic forces are being properly tempered by human forces.

The process of collective bargaining also absorbs the energies and interests of many leaders of the working masses who might otherwise direct their energies to the overthrow of the existing economic order. Most students of labor movements would agree, I think, that the more a union leader concentrates on collective bargaining, the more conservative he is likely to become. American labor leaders, almost without exception, have moved from left to right as they have gained experience with, and become absorbed by, the process of negotiating and administering treaties with employers. To the extent that collective bargaining appears to bring results and to command the support of the rank and file, the labor leader devotes more time and energy to it; and, to the extent that he concentrates on bargaining, the chances are that he may make it more successful. This is, of course, one of the reasons why the American labor movement is so job centered rather than politically oriented. Labor leaders in this country can effectively command the support of their constituents and rise to positions of fame and power without bothering very much about political objectives.

For all these reasons collective bargaining is an institution which bolsters the existing economic order in our country. It flourishes and survives only in the climate of private enterprise. It both creates the machinery and provides the rationale for endorsement of capitalism by employers, labor leaders, and workers.

Conclusion

In any type of society the industrial worker, for the most part, works harder than he likes at tasks which are frequently arduous, usually monotonous, and sometimes dangerous. On the job he is nearly always subject to the direction of higher authority. His income is seldom sufficient to cover what he thinks his needs demand. The natural state of the industrial worker, therefore, is one of discontent. In a prosperous country, such as the United States, this feeling of discontent may not be so acute as it is in countries where the worker barely earns subsistence for himself and his family. But even where living standards are comparatively high, workers always want more. Indeed they may be more vociferous in their demands for more in an economy of abundance, rather than in one of scarcity, as they become accustomed to frequent and continuous rises in their standard of living. The industrial worker thinks that others minimize the importance of the work he performs, and he is usually fearful and often suspicious of "the boss" whose authority he must respect if he is to keep his job. As we have already mentioned, a labor union seeks proprietorship over these dissatisfactions, fears, and suspicions. It gives organization to these discontents, mobilizes them, and directs them to the attainment of particular ends.[8]

Union activity may direct the organized discontent of workers into (1) somewhat uncoordinated mass demonstrations of protest, (2) organized political activity, and (3) collective bargaining. Though in all countries unions may channel activity simultaneously in all these directions, labor movements of particular countries are characterized from a functional standpoint by *the emphasis* placed on one or the other of these means. The core function of the labor movements of France and Italy, for example, is political action. In England and Sweden unions emphasize both political action and collective bargaining. In the United States collective bargaining is the dominant function of trade-unionism, though political action is looked upon as an auxiliary activity.

If the analysis set forth in this paper is correct, therefore, a union movement which emphasizes collective bargaining is inevitably a conservative movement, for collective bargaining is inseparable from private enterprise. Thus, through the process of collective bargaining, American unions organize and direct the discontents of labor in such a way as to bolster rather than to upset our system of democratic capitalism.

The widespread acceptance of collective bargaining in our economy, then, is not hard to explain. For workers it provides a feeling of reaping tangible benefits, and it greatly enhances their status, dignity, and importance as members of the labor force. For employers, who might be fearful of open revolt by the working masses, collective bargaining is a lightning rod which effectively

[8] Here, again, I am indebted to Prof. Lloyd Fisher for some of these ideas.

grounds any organized efforts to overthrow the existing order. To leaders of labor collective bargaining offers creative opportunities to build socially acceptable organizations and to gain respect and power in the community. To the public at large collective bargaining gives promise of providing an orderly means of resolving conflict between capital and labor and of insuring a measure of industrial peace.

Some economists condemn unions as formidable labor monopolies and collective bargaining as an economic evil, yet, except in isolated cases, they are unable to give factual substantiation to their charges. Some labor leaders decry the attempts of particular employers to bust unions and short-circuit genuine collective bargaining, yet labor organizations are becoming stronger and more firmly entrenched each day. Many managements claim that unions are demanding and getting too much, yet business firms continue to make record profits. Some people say that unions are undermining industrial efficiency, but there appears to be no general slackening in the rate of increase in the productivity of labor. The public gets concerned over certain kinds of strikes but seems to forget about them shortly after the workers return to their jobs. With all this grumbling and complaining, however, collective bargaining is constantly and inevitably being woven into the fabric of our society. It is part of the American culture.

It is important to remember, nevertheless, that the widespread acceptance of collective bargaining in this country has taken place during a sustained period of full or nearly full employment. To be sure, unions in our basic industries were born during the Depression; but they grew to mature stature in the upswing of the business cycle, followed by a period of war mobilization, and then an era of postwar full employment. If business were to be drastically curtailed again in a severe depression, there is no assurance that organized labor would continue to rely primarily on collective bargaining to achieve its ends, for the failure of private enterprise to provide jobs would probably be accompanied by the failure of collective bargaining to cope successfully with labor's discontent. In such a period organized labor might well concentrate its energies on political objectives. The dominance of collective bargaining as a method for resolving conflict is logically, if not exclusively, associated with a society which is capable of sustaining economic prosperity and maintaining quite high levels of employment. As Americans we would do well to keep this in mind when we try to export our system of collective bargaining to countries where economic conditions may be substantially at variance with those prevailing in our homeland. The United States has the most vital and dynamic private enterprise in the world; it is not by mere accident that it also has one of the most conservative and job-centered labor movements in the world.

CHAPTER 21 GRIEVANCE NEGOTIATION

Van D. Kennedy   *University of California (Berkeley)*

THE negotiation of grievances is an integral part of the total collective-bargaining process. It is generally held to embrace both the procedures and the human relationships which are central to union-management relations *between* contract negotiations. Given this central role, grievance negotiation obviously has serious import for the problem of industrial conflict. It is the theme of this chapter that grievance negotiation, like any other form of union-management interchange, can be the means of creating, aggravating, or prolonging conflict but that it is on the whole a process and a set of relationships which contain inherent elements making for the reduction of conflict.

Relation of Grievance Negotiation to Contract Negotiation

Contract negotiation is the process by which unions and managements adjust their relations and differences as operating organizations and block out the broad lines of legislation which are to govern the entire bargaining unit for a stipulated period into the future. By contrast, the province of grievance negotiation is each local work place, and the process involves primarily the daily adjustment of individual rights.

Viewed as a process for accommodating conflict, grievance negotiation must be sharply differentiated from contract negotiation. It is at one and the same time less fateful and more complex: less fateful, because the stakes are smaller in grievance adjustment; more complex, because the ranges, intricacies, and sheer number and detail of the problems and human relationships covered in grievance negotiations ordinarily greatly exceed those of contract negotiations. In this discussion it will be assumed that the grievance process may be defined to include every interchange, however informal, between workers, union representatives, and management which arises out of some form of employee dissatisfaction in the work relationship and which arises in a bargaining unit covered by an existing union contract. Grievance negotiation is therefore a continuous process. Conflict is rarely so constant; it is much more likely to erupt in the periodic climaxes associated with contract negotiations. Besides, grievance issues are seldom so important as contract issues. Most commonly, a grievance represents the complaint of an individual or of a small group of workers in a single shop. It may test the meaning of an agreement clause, or it may raise a question of equity. No matter how important such issues are to the aggrieved individuals, the consequence of deadlock or loss of the grievance is normally not a strike. In contract negotiations the typical issue is one which involves the bargaining unit as a whole, and the outcome will determine important rights for a definite period to come. Moreover, contract issues must be disposed of by indivisible groups. The significance which attaches to a negotiation is measured by the sum of the issues which must be settled before a contract is signed. The constant process of grievance settlement, on the other hand, does not build up the pressure which comes from the cumulative weight of interdependent issues.

Another difference between the two processes is that each has its own peculiar institutional involvements. Grievance negotiation is preeminently a local affair. As industrial relations become increasingly centralized at the contract-negotiating level among top executives of large multiplant corporations, employers' associations, and national unions, the adjustment of grievances remains one of the few functions left to many local unions. Grievance negotiation involves a whole range of personalities and functionaries, such as members of the rank and file, shop stewards, business agents, grievance committeemen, local union officers, foremen, departmental supervisors, and local management officials, who in a great many cases never participate in contract bargaining. Furthermore, much grievance adjustment takes place without becoming involved in the organizational relationships between local plant management and local union and without engaging top representatives of these local organizations. It is to a large extent a relationship which is initiated and completed, in the form of personal and informal adjustments between workers, their immediate union representatives, and foremen, without institutional overtones.

These differences are all important from the point of view of industrial conflict. What they show is that, as a system of accommodating industrial conflict, grievance negotiation works in a very different sphere of the total union-management relationship and in a very different way. By contrast with contract negotiation, grievance adjustment is a continuous process which operates at the work level; it deals with the complaints of individuals or of small groups of workers; its participants are the lowest levels of union and management representation; and it operates in an atmosphere in which tensions are more personal than institutional, the stakes are not critical, and the ultimate sanction is not the use of force.

The Subject Matter of Grievance Negotiation

For a proper understanding of the potentialities of the grievance process for adjusting conflict, it is necessary to review the issues or sources of conflict which come within the reach of this process. Because of the endless variety of problems which can arise in shop relationships, because of the informality of the process at the first step, and because of the large number of different individuals within an establishment who can become involved in grievances, the process is adaptable to several kinds of purpose. For this reason grievance negotiation has a variable relation to conflict.

The most orthodox and most frequent purpose of grievance systems is the interpretation and administration of union agreements. This is essentially a matter of implementing and enforcing compliance with the broad decisions reached in contract negotiations. A closely related purpose is the correcting of injuries and wrongs allegedly suffered by individuals and groups. This may be accomplished in the form of agreement interpretation or may occur without any very clear basis in an agreement clause. The point is that the animus behind such proceedings is a strong sense of personal wrong, which seeks expression and relief regardless of the agreement. A third purpose which is worth noting, although it is closely related to the purpose of agreement interpretation, is agreement making in the sense of amplifying and extending the terms of an agreement. Many observers have testified not only that unions sometimes process grievances with this intent but that the effect of a line of grievance settlements is, frequently, to add to the agreement or to give an agreement provision a meaning and definitiveness not found in the original negotiation. Candid unionists acknowledge the same facts. The UAW-CIO, for example, has given its stewards the following practical advice: [1]

> Your troubles come from grievances which aren't clearly covered by the contract. Many complaints are apparently justified, but seem to have been overlooked when the contract was drawn up.
> When this happens, you have to go through the agreement with a fine-toothed comb for the nearest approach to the case. Sometimes it will take some pulling and hauling, but after all, the U. S. Constitution has been used for 155 years and still covers everything Congress does pretty well. A good union contract should cover most conditions in the plant for 12 months.

In all these situations the grievance process serves the general purpose of adjusting disagreements, individual dissatisfactions, and conflict without recourse to strike threats and use of force.

Quite a different kind of purpose can be seen at work in some grievance relationships. In these cases the grievance process is not used to settle problems between worker and supervisor or union and management but to promote the interests of either or both parties in connection with a future test of strength. In the nature of the union-management relation the union is more often in a position to make this use of grievance activity. One typical union objective is to build up pressures on certain issues, within the membership and the union hierarchy, looking toward the next contract negotiation. In unusually incompatible relationships the grievance process may operate as a sort of guerrilla warfare during which the parties keep sniping at each other and endeavor to keep their forces at a martial pitch in preparation for the open conflict which will follow expiration of the contract. In these situations grievance negotiation is not primarily a means of resolving conflict.

Still another purpose is discernible in some grievance handling. This purpose does not pertain to the union-management relationship but to the internal politics of the union organization within a plant. Where a plant is large enough to permit the shop-steward or committeeman form of organization and these representatives are subject to elections, the active and successful prosecution of grievances can be a principal means of gaining political merit. Where grievance adjustment becomes a vehicle for active union politics or factionalism,

---

[1] *How to Win for the Union,* 7th ed., UAW-CIO Handbook for Stewards and Committeemen, 1945, p. 48.

the net result in terms of conflict is not certain. There may be an increase of friction in shop relations. The total number of grievances handled is almost certainly higher than would otherwise be the case. But this is not the same as an increase in conflict, except by a very limited interpretation of the term.

Regardless of the several general purposes for which grievances may be prosecuted, certain specific issues recur most frequently as the subject of grievances, and we may now turn to an examination of these issues. Given the broad definition of grievances being employed in this discussion, it is obvious that the possible diversity of issues is limitless. Nevertheless, actual practice demonstrates that the bulk of grievances is associated with a reasonably limited number of problem categories. Each major category tends to correspond with one of the major subject areas covered by most union agreements. Several of these principal categories of grievance issues may be mentioned without attempting to indicate their order of frequency.

The problem of discipline, as meted out by management in the form of reprimanding, penalizing, and discharging individual workers and groups of workers, is a universal source of grievances. Most acts of managerial discipline are occasioned by individual infractions of shop rules, such as intoxication on the job, pilfering on company premises, brawling with fellow workers; by individual acts of insubordination, such as refusal to comply with instructions from supervisors; by incompetent work; and by job action, slowdowns, or stoppages. As a rule, it is only when discipline has arisen from the last set of circumstances that grievances prompted by discipline may be said to reflect a conflict situation involving tension between union and management.

Another common-agreement subject which produces grievances in many industries is seniority. The application of this rule in all its various forms to such important changes in employment status as layoff, rehiring, transfer, and promotion leads inevitably to many challenges. The disputes arise most frequently over the meaning of agreement clauses, over the assessing of ability when the agreement requires that it be weighed along with length of service, and over the charge that management has been guilty of discrimination in administering seniority provisions.

The application of job classifications and descriptions to individual jobs and to individual employees makes up a third important category of grievance issues. The possibilities for disagreement under this heading are too numerous to list in detail. The problem of when to upgrade an employee who is in an occupation which is subdivided into two or more classes on the basis of skill, responsibility, and experience and the problem of how to classify, and what rate to pay for, a new job or a job some of whose elements have changed may be cited as typical examples.

A related but distinct source of grievances is the problem of production standards or work loads. The essential question which continually arises here is How much work can rightfully be required of a worker on any given job in an hour's time or in the course of an 8-hour day? But the question reappears in a thousand variations and is constantly revived by new methods, new products, changing machine speeds, changing manning requirements, and the pressure of competition in a dynamic industrial environment.

In the many industries which employ incentive systems of wage payment the operation and administration of these systems lead to frequent grievances. The most common problems are associated with the setting of rates on new or changed jobs and with the demand by workers for protection against loss of expected earnings, which may result from a large number of unforeseen contingencies.

In those industries, such as the railroad, maritime, hotel and restaurant, local-transit, and other service industries, which are characterized by numerous special job conditions, these conditions and the work rules which are customarily found in the union agreements are a major source of grievance activity.

This review of the most common categories of grievance subject matter suggests another important fact, namely, that there is little uniformity in the character of grievance issues throughout American industry. The nature of the most common grievance subject matter varies greatly by industry, by individual establishment, and over time. One of the most basic variables is the nature of the jobs and conditions of employment. In the hotel and restaurant industries the practice of tipping, the matter of free meals, uniforms, and laundry, the handling of special occasions, the necessity for split shifts and part-time work, and the enforcement of job classifications throughout a group of highly diverse and competing establishments are regular subjects of grievance negotiation. In the railroad and local-transit industries the assignment of runs, the handling of, and accountability for, money, shift arrangements, and the regulation of such matters as reporting in, layover, turnarounds, and terminal time are typical work rules which are the subjects of grievance adjustment. In longshoring the constitution of work gangs, the administration of safety rules, the regulation of sling loads, and the application of penalty rates for certain types of cargoes are important items in grievance adjustment.

By contrast with these industries where special working conditions and the work rules governing them show up frequently in the grievance process, the conditions of work in most plants of the heavy manufacturing industries do not call for a complex structure of work rules. In an auto plant, for example, the large number of employees within a single establishment, the extreme specialization of job content, the large number of employees usually required on each job classification and within easily interchangeable groups of jobs, and the constant process of technological change and managerial improvement all mean that the handling of individual wage-rate and classification problems and the application of seniority rules are likely to be important sources of grievances. On the other hand, in the hotel and restaurant industries, in building service, and in the building trades, the dispersion of the work force among many employers, so that there may be only one or a few workers on each classification in an establishment, and the irregularity of employment or the rapid turnover among both employers and employees mean that length of service has little meaning in governing job tenure. In a like manner a differentiation can be made between those industries and plants where some measure of control over hiring by the unions is customary and those where it is not. In the first type of situation the hiring function is almost certain to give rise to grievances, whereas in other industries such grievances are rare.

The relative importance of various grievance subjects may change over time. During World War II the tight labor-market conditions in many industries resulted in a marked falling off of grievances involving such subjects as discipline, hiring control, and seniority. Layoffs were unnecessary, new workers were welcome whatever the means of recruitment, and the enforcement of shop rules was greatly relaxed. During the wholesale layoffs and employment shifts which accompanied the postwar reconversion, there was a heavy spate of seniority grievances in many industries. When an employer installs a new incentive plan, inaugurates a job-evaluation program, or introduces major technological changes, a period of intensified grievance activity associated with the new problems created at the work level is almost sure to follow. In recent years the change in general economic outlook from a "sellers' market" to a "buyers' market" which has overtaken a number of industries has been accompanied by a perceptible increase in grievances involving such issues as discipline and production standards, reflecting the efforts of employers in these industries to reduce costs and improve competitive positions.

Needless to say, quite apart from the environmental variables discussed above, the quality of over-all union-management relationships in each bargaining unit has a good deal to do with the kinds of issue which predominate in the grievance process. If there is conflict in the general bargaining relationship, it will probably show up in grievance negotiations as well. If the higher-level conflict is intense and is marked by disagreement over such power-sharing matters as union security and management's prerogatives, it will usually be reflected in an abnormally high proportion of grievances growing out of management's attempt to control work stoppages and insubordination by discipline and out of the union's efforts to exercise job control by challenging management decisions on hiring, promotions, production standards, job classification, and the like. Robert Dubin made a study of the operation of the grievance process in three union-management relationships which were selected as representing respectively conflict, arm's-length relations, and cooperation. One of his findings [2] was that in the cooperative relationship a significantly higher proportion of the grievances dealt with working conditions and with questions of agreement interpretation which least involved power-status questions. On the other hand, in the conflict and arm's-length relationships a significantly higher proportion of the grievances had to do with bargaining issues and charges of discrimination which reflected tensions in the over-all organizational relationships. Dubin also found that a substantially higher proportion of all grievances were carried beyond the first step, before being settled, in the arm's-length and conflict relationships than in the cooperative example.

The evidence of the Dubin study is corroborated by the results of an intensive investigation of all grievances which were carried beyond the first step during a 3-year period at a large automotive plant. It revealed [3] that the largest proportion of appealed grievances related to matters which the agree-

[2] Robert Dubin, "The Grievance Process—A Study of Union-Management Relations," Doctor's dissertation, Department of Sociology, University of Chicago, 1947, p. 157.

[3] Bernard Karsh, "The Grievance Process in Union-Management Relations," Master's thesis, Department of Sociology, University of Chicago, 1950, pp. 134–138.

ment could not spell out in definite terms. They were also matters requiring the application of criteria on which the parties were not likely to agree or on which they were likely to have different objectives.

Another aspect of top-level union-management relations which can affect the grievance process is the extent to which management holds to a strict construction and tight administration of the agreement. Liberal policies may tend to encourage a larger number of grievances than otherwise, grievances which a more legalistically minded management would find illegitimate, and to encourage the settlement of an abnormally large proportion of grievances at higher levels of the grievance procedure. The differences in the operation of the grievance process at the Ford Motor Co. and General Motors Corp. are well known. Several factors are responsible, but one of the reasons is the difference in underlying attitude toward contract administration which has existed between the two managements.[4]

Grievance Negotiation as a Means of Resolving Conflict

While the purpose of this section is to discuss the ways in which grievance procedures can reduce conflict, we must not overlook the fact mentioned above that the grievance process can also be used to sustain and feed conflict. This application of grievance procedure is most likely to occur under several special circumstances. If contract-bargaining relationships between a union and an employer are marked by such conflict that many issues are not really settled by the agreement, the conflict may well carry over into shop relationships and the grievance machinery easily becomes the means of continuing the struggle. William F. Whyte, in his recent study of labor relations in a steel plant,[5] makes very clear the extent to which a grievance procedure can be devoted to the purposes of conflict.

Sid Lens is even more explicit on this point.[6] He does not see grievance procedure as essentially an instrument for the resolution of conflict which, on occasion, may be diverted to contrary ends. Rather he sees the grievance process as simply one means by which the general union-management relationship is manifested. Since he seems to conceive of conflict or "class warfare" as almost inevitable in American industrial relations, he views the grievance process in the same light:

> Grievance machinery, then, is not a deterrent to class war. It is merely an attempt to *organize* the conflicts between unions and employers and to *contain* them within certain specified bounds. . . . Each side lays aside its most potent weapons for more important days. But the grievance procedure offers an opportunity for a realignment of forces, for fencing and minor skirmishing, for strengthening of positions.[7]

[4] Fred H. Harbison and Robert Dubin, *Patterns of Union-Management Relations,* Chicago, Science Research Associates, 1947.

[5] William F. Whyte, *Pattern For Industrial Peace,* New York, Harper, 1951, esp. pp. 25–27, 37–45, 62.

[6] Sid Lens, "Meaning of the Grievance Procedure," *Harvard Business Review,* Vol. 26 (November, 1948).

[7] *Ibid.,* pp. 720–722.

We need not accept Lens's particular slant on union-management relations in order to appreciate the value of his contention that the quality and character of the general union-management relationship in a bargaining unit are basic and that, if conflict is pervasive in that relationship, the grievance process is not capable of effecting any deep changes in it.

In plants where the union is torn by factionalism, there is a natural tendency for each faction to use the grievance machinery as an apparatus for gaining advantage over its rival. Even where there is no particular factionalism but active political competition marks the elections to shop-steward positions and other union offices, the results may be somewhat similar. In both situations the absolute number of grievances processed at all levels will tend to be higher than usual, and they may well be prosecuted with abnormal vigor and aggressiveness. These conditions do not necessarily add up to an increase of conflict, but they can. It is not that conflict as an initial cause of grievances has increased but that the militant ferreting out and processing of complaints by zealous union representatives may well produce increased tensions.

In bargaining situations not set apart from these special circumstances, the evidence is overwhelming that the grievance-negotiating mechanism is, on the whole, a means for accommodating conflict. The remainder of this section is devoted to a review of the principal ways in which the grievance process achieves this result. The very words "procedure," "process," and "mechanism" suggest one of the basic explanations: it is the existence of system, of formal arrangements, and of a device for introducing order and due process into what otherwise remains a confusion of relationships and easily becomes a clamor of voices. The virtues of this aspect of grievance procedure are most apparent in large plants where the number of employees and of plant representatives, both union and management, is large and where several levels of authority intervene between worker and foreman and the top officials who have final participation in grievance settlement. There is an abundance of literature on the procedures of grievance negotiation. This literature deals with the variations in, and pros and cons of, such matters as the following: the number of steps at which grievances are considered between the point of origin and final appeal to arbitration; the manner in which, and the extent to which, grievance handling is reduced to writing; the time limits at various steps; the organization of union and management for grievance administration; financing the grievance process; and the distribution of authority between the grievance steps.

Procedural details can affect the functioning of a grievance system, but they do not justify detailed discussion here. The procedures actually used in practice vary greatly and depend upon the nature of bargaining units, past experience between the parties, and the policies of individual employers and unions. Some of the most persistent and characteristic procedural differences occur between what may be termed factory-type plants and industries and non-factory-type situations. The basis for the differences lies in the number of employees represented in each establishment. Where the number per establishment is small, as is true generally in house building, restaurants, retail stores, trucking, entertainment and music, building service, job shops, etc., formal union representation in each establishment may be nil and managerial organization extremely limited. As a result, the full-time, salaried business agent typically supplants the working shop steward or committeeman as principal grievance representative for the union, and the owner, manager, or superintendent takes the place of the foreman in shop-level grievance settlement for management. And this is typically the only grievance step at the shop level. Contract bargaining in these industries is customarily multiemployer in character. Thus the next level of grievance negotiation is usually the last step of the procedure short of arbitration. Ordinarily it involves full-time officials of the local union and officers or a committee of an employers' association. A further characteristic of grievance procedure in these situations is a high degree of informality, in the sense that a sequence of three or four well-defined steps rarely exists and grievance handling is seldom reduced to writing. It is in the large factory-type plants common to major manufacturing industries, therefore, that one finds the carefully defined and regulated systems of several appeal steps (to appropriate authority levels in large union and management organizations) which are the prime concern of the grievance-procedure literature.

Despite the great diversity of procedural detail found in practice, there is a large measure of agreement on the importance of a few procedural principles. Expeditious processing is universally recognized to be desirable, whether or not it is implemented by formal time limits. One concrete piece of evidence of this recognition is the extent to which unions and employers arrange for special treatment—by taking out of turn, skipping appeal steps, or reducing time limits—such crucial issues as discharges and other disciplinary action, rates on new jobs, and other matters involving back pay or a large part of a bargaining unit.[8]

The maintenance of some written record or evidence of grievance settlements to forestall later misinterpretations and for future reference is a widely recognized procedural principle. However, this practice is not so generally observed, and there is considerable disagreement as to the stage in proceedings when a written record becomes necessary. A third precept of good grievance procedure which has achieved very general acceptance is the necessity of a terminal point to any grievance system in the form of third-party arbitration. It provides an alternative to the use of force in the settlement of certain types of disputes. In a sense, also, the mere existence of final and binding third-party decision as the certain and predictable destination of all unsettled grievances is the fact which makes a viable procedure of grievance negotiation. Like any due-process arrangement, much of the effectiveness of grievance procedure is reflected in the extent to which questions are settled without its full exercise. It is pertinent to note in this connection that in most shop relationships the great bulk of grievances is settled at the first step of consideration without formalization in writing or appeal to higher steps.[9]

[8] A recent survey of contract provisions by the U.S. Bureau of Labor Statistics revealed that special handling arrangements of one kind or another were made for certain issues in 55 per cent of the agreements surveyed, covering 70 per cent of the workers. See "Grievance Procedures in Union Agreements, 1950–1951," *Monthly Labor Review*, Vol. 73 (July, 1951).

[9] Harold Davey sets the proportion of first-step settlements "in a smoothly operating" procedure at 95 per cent. See his *Contemporary Collective Bargaining*, New York, Prentice-

Another feature of the grievance process which contributes to dispute settlement is the possibility it offers in involving higher levels of authority in adjustment of work-level grievances. It is this fact which gives meaning to the right of appeal in the large number of grievances which arise from the conviction of individual workers that they are the victims of discrimination, favoritism, and capricious treatment by their immediate supervisors. In addition to the advantage of superior authority the higher levels of union and management representation who may be called into grievance negotiation have other advantages in reaching settlements. The higher the level of the appeal, the more detached, presumably, are the negotiators from the emotions and partisanship of the original incident. The higher levels may also be assumed to be more conversant with the agreement, more familiar with union-management policies and practice, and able to judge the single issues in a context of total plant relationships. Finally, the higher-level negotiators are in a better position to command full information about a grievance. As mentioned earlier, the identity of the higher levels of authority who become involved in grievance negotiation varies greatly. In large, national, multiplant bargaining units there are typically three or four levels of appeal above the first step, and the top levels customarily involve central-office representatives of the corporation and national union officials.[10] In local market and non-factory-type bargaining units the number of grievance steps is usually smaller, and representation is ordinarily confined to officials of the local union or joint board and to local management or an employers' association.

A third element which makes for melioration in grievance negotiations is the presence of at least a minimum degree of the reasoning process. As a system of adjustment which proceeds by a sequence of appeals to different persons at higher levels of authority and which terminates, in most cases, in a third-party decision rather than in a test of strength, grievance procedure makes relentless demands on the participants. The aggrieved and his supporters must make a case, and the employer's representatives must refute it. This requires argument, investigation, and evidence. These do not guarantee agreement, but even less are they effective means by which to sustain conflict. The several practices of putting grievances and grievance answers in writing, keeping minutes of grievance meetings, and maintaining files of arbitration decisions, where they are observed, are all designed to further this purpose.

Closely related to the above aspect of the grievance process is the notion that over a period of time grievance negotiation builds up a system of law to govern shop relationships. This law consists of a body of precedents in the

---

Hall, 1951, p. 283. In the automotive plant studied by him, Bernard Karsh estimated that, even during a wartime period of somewhat tense relations, five times as many grievances were settled at the first step as were appealed to the second step and beyond. See Karsh, op. cit., p. 65. Melville Dalton has noted that in another large manufacturing plant the most successful committeemen each year settled a large proportion of grievances without formal processing. See his "Unofficial Union-Management Relations," *American Sociological Review*, 15 (October, 1950), 614.

[10] The U.S. Bureau of Labor Statistics found that participation by representatives of the national union at some stage of the grievance process was provided for in 39 per cent of the agreements surveyed, covering over three-fifths of the workers. See "Grievance Procedures in Union Agreements, 1950–1951," p. 37.

form of accumulated agreement interpretations and of commonly held criteria to be applied in the settlement of new problems. Some degree of common law development is inescapable under almost any regime which provides a fairly systematic basis for handling agreement-interpretation problems. The development is most apparent in situations where detailed grievance records are maintained and arbitration decisions are carefully indexed, are supplied to union grievance representatives, and are looked upon as binding precedents.

Two important qualifying observations need to be made about the three conflict-solving aspects of grievance procedure which have just been discussed. The involvement of higher-level authority, the substitution of argument, investigation, and evidence for force, and the development of a body of accepted standards and precedents for meeting dispute situations are all elements in the grievance process which, unquestionably, facilitate dispute settlement when they come into play. The first qualification to be noted, then, is that these three elements have their greatest impact on grievance settlement above the first step. It is at the secondary levels of grievance negotiation that higher authority and the legalistic approach begin to take hold. These are features of the process which become important in the adjustment of the small proportion of grievances which get past the first step. At the same time, it is the appealed grievances which are usually the most difficult issues and most symptomatic of conflict.

The second qualification has to do with the values of informality in grievance adjustment. The three features which have been under discussion all tend to add some formality to the grievance process, and as indicated, formality can be of utility in accommodating conflict, especially in large, strife-torn plants. But it is equally important to note the uses of informality and its prevalence in the grievance process. Informality is helpful in dealing with the large proportion of grievances which are peculiarly personal and emotional in quality. Informality may also be useful in accommodating the grievance process to the dynamic character of shop relationships. Benjamin M. Selekman is one of the most persuasive analysts of this phase of shop relations. "They cannot be regarded at any time as something finished once and for all—complete, final, and unchanging in form. Instead, sheerly because they are relationships, they remain fluid, evolving, continuously affected by changes in any of the variable constituents that at any time determine their quality." [11]

There can be little question that grievance settlement at the first step is a highly informal process in most plants and shops. It occurs in a face-to-face contact between people who ordinarily know each other fairly well and who must continue to work in close association in the future; the results go unrecorded; the higher levels of union and management authority have little disposition to review step-one settlements as long as they cause no trouble; and workers, foremen, stewards, and business agents in American industry are pretty solidly committed to the principle that what their superiors do not know about deals made at the work level will not hurt them. Informality means, among other things, a minimum of preoccupation with legalism and with con-

[11] Benjamin M. Selekman, *Labor Relations and Human Relations*, New York, McGraw-Hill, 1947, pp. 77–78.

sistent interpretation of agreements. As Sid Lens [12] points out, grievance settlement at the first step is "amenable to many 'bootleg' and extra-legal tactics and pressures" and for this reason is often regarded as "the most advantageous from the union standpoint." Melville Dalton [13] reports as his observation in a big plant not only that the most successful shop stewards were those who obtained informal settlements of most grievances but that rule and contract evasion was common and was cooperated in by workers and stewards. If this is the picture in big plants, there is no reason to expect greater formality in step-one grievance adjustment in non-factory-type industries, where the work force is widely scattered among numerous individually small establishments and where the grievance process occurs largely without benefit of shop-steward structure.

The above discussion has emphasized the advantages of the informality which is an inherent quality of grievance adjustment at the first step. There is a sense in which informality, or the conscious rejection of formalism, at the top administrative levels of grievance procedure may also help reduce conflict. Selekman makes an eloquent case for the possibilities which lie in a conscious and imaginative use of the grievance procedure by both management and union officials for gauging and improving shop relationships. He argues for a clinical approach to grievances.[14] The cardinal principle of this approach is that the purpose of the grievance process is to solve the problems of human relations in the constantly changing context of the shop community. This implies a great deal more than the approaches which look upon grievance procedures as primarily an orderly system for determining employee rights under the rules of the contract. The clinical approach rejects the distinctions which are frequently made between legitimate and illegitimate, real and imaginary grievances. It is interested in getting at the sources of friction in shop relations before these break out in the form of specific disputes. This approach calls upon both management and union, therefore, to make the grievance process the occasion for exercising to the full the best human-relations techniques.

There is one other function inherent in the grievance process which may be important to the problem of conflict. This is leadership training. For the labor movement of today, which is no longer in an era of organization and rapid growth and which is particularly deficient in facilities for recruiting and training new leadership, grievance activity in local plants and bargaining units is one of the chief training and proving grounds for future union leaders. We have no good evidence yet as to the quality of leadership material which is being turned out. However, the foregoing discussion gives reason to hope that participation in grievance negotiation may prove an effective school in which to train new union and management leadership in the arts of wise industrial relations.

[12] Lens, *op. cit.*, p. 718.
[13] Dalton, *loc. cit.*
[14] Selekman, *op. cit.*, pp. 87–110.

CHAPTER **22** MEDIATION AND FACT FINDING
___

Edgar L. Warren   *University of California (Los Angeles)*

Mediation may be broadly defined as any noncoercive third-party intervention for the settlement of labor-management disputes. One's attitude about such a process is shaped and colored by his feeling toward industrial conflict. Where work stoppages cannot be tolerated, mediation is of little value. Procedures for dispute settlement short of compulsory arbitration presuppose the pressures of industrial conflict, including withdrawal of employment and job action by workers, as elements for producing agreement. These procedures cannot, therefore, be relied on for assurance against strikes, boycotts, and the other manifestations of industrial conflict. However, if one holds the opinion, expressed elsewhere in this volume, that conflict may be constructive, mediation may be viewed as a process for restraining the clashes which are an important part of collective bargaining. The discussion in this chapter is based on the idea that mediation is not a method for suppressing industrial conflict. It is, rather, a means for minimizing the conflict that is inherent in modern labor-management relations.

Mediation—A Pressure Method

A great variety of procedures used to minimize industrial conflict may be classified under the heading of "mediation." These range from the mildest form of "conciliation," for example, by a phone call from an interested third person to one of the disputants, to "fact finding," where a Presidential board makes public recommendations on the terms of a proposed settlement. As the term is used here, mediation is not limited to either statutory or customary procedures; it includes every step short of final and binding arbitration which might be taken by an agency of government, or by some other third party, to settle a labor dispute. It is the thesis of this chapter that, whatever the form of mediation, the essence of the procedure is the exertion or channeling of pressure on one or both of two parties in dispute to obtain the necessary concessions for the settlement of their differences.

Mediation is a method of persuasion, using pressures some of which are intrinsic in labor disputes and some of which are created by the mediator. In any instance there is apt to be a multiple interaction of different pressures, some of which are working in opposite directions. All these may be classified into three forms: personal, social and political, and economic. It is the function of mediation to exert, channel, and control these pressures in their different forms.

Personal Pressure. Most people think of mediation as a personal-relations or selling process. They see the mediator as a personable fellow who is an expert in the art of influencing people. Personal relationships and pressures—the use of argument, logical persuasion, and cajolery—are generally considered the root of mediation efforts. "Human relations" plays an important part in the settlement of many disputes. John R. Steelman and William H. Davis, among others, achieved notable reputations in the use of personal pressure, although it may be noted that this is not the only technique of which they are masters. It is also not the principal element in most mediation efforts.

The overemphasis on the personal factor in mediation stems at least partially from the dramatic appeal of personal achievements. It also has its origin in an exaggerated opinion of the importance of the personalities in leadership positions. A labor dispute is frequently viewed as a disagreement between opposing leaders. The union and employer principals, their views and their personalities, often delay a meeting of minds, and in isolated instances are responsible for the disagreement. The substantive issues separating the parties are, however, more basic to a settlement of the average dispute.

Social and Political Pressure. The opinion of outsiders—the citizenry as a whole or particular groups of people whose views are important—may have a significant bearing on the reaching of an agreement. These opinions exert social or political pressure on the disputants. Thus, for example, the employer may be influenced by the views of other employers, and the decisions of the union will be colored by the attitude of other unions and union leaders. The competition between union leaders—the desire of one official to obtain for political reasons a settlement better than those previously achieved—has been long recognized. Similar forces are at work in shaping the decisions of employers. When C. E. Wilson of the General Motors Corp. signed an agreement in 1948 with the UAW-CIO which called for annual wage increases based on increased productivity and for increases to compensate for the rising cost of living, he was roundly criticized by many businessmen. A person of lesser stature than Mr. Wilson might have found it impossible to disregard views widely held throughout the business community. To a varying extent such outside pressures will modify the personal effort of the mediator, just as he may seek to modify them.

Public opinion, as represented by the attitudes of the general public and the press regarding the merit of the positions of the two parties, also affects what one side will give and the other accept. Usually the force of public opinion is dependent on the extent to which large segments of the population are vitally affected by an actual or potential cessation of work. For this reason local transit companies or other public utilities may find it difficult to resist proposals that outside experts be permitted to arbitrate the issues in dispute. The success of the NWLB during World War II was also related to this factor. One of the unusual aspects of coal miners' strikes in recent years has been Mr. Lewis's apparent lack of concern about the public's reaction to work stoppages. Even in these instances, however, the strikes have normally not been allowed to disrupt seriously the supply of coal available for ultimate consumers, and Mr. Lewis has been quick to indicate that his miners will not tolerate real suffering.

The marshaling of these political and social pressures is an important aspect of mediation. Often the mediator will seek the assistance of particularly influential outsiders. He points out to the disputants how public opinion is developing. In some instances this type of pressure may take the form of a press release, designed to channel public pressures. Most frequently public statements are designed to be impartial, as with Roosevelt's "a plague on both their houses." In rare instances of national importance highly placed mediators have publicly assessed blame for a continued work stoppage. President Truman was not averse to this procedure. More often the mediator confines his public-pressure activities to urging that the parties consider outside attitudes and opinions.

Economic Pressure. While both personal and social pressures may be important, the economic forces at work in every labor dispute are the primary determining factors making for a settlement. Hence it is these forces which establish the effectiveness of particular mediation efforts. Workers on strike can live for a while on their savings and on contributions from their union's strike fund, but these sources are not inexhaustible. Employers also can "live on their fat," but at some point, if they are to continue in business, they must resume production. Each day the likelihood of a work stoppage approaches if no settlement is reached; and each day a stoppage, once begun, continues, this pressure on both the employer and the union is increased. The factors which make for the relative economic strength of the two parties thus set the framework within which mediation efforts are carried on and against which they must be measured.

A number of the elements comprising this economic strength may be isolated. In the first place, the extent of the grievance felt by rank-and-file members of the union will determine its ability to carry on a successful strike. If, to use a simple example, the wage rates paid in the particular plant are substantially below rates paid in comparable plants, the workers' incentive to strike will be sufficiently strong to offset many other economic handicaps. Under such circumstances, many strikes have been carried on to a successful conclusion with only limited financial support. The actual degree of the inequity may not be so important as the imagined disparity, but attitudes which are persistently held by large groups of workers usually have some basis in fact. The same is true with respect to wages in relation to increases in the cost of living and, probably to a lesser extent, in relation to the employer's ability to pay a wage increase.

Secondly, the approaching deadline set for strike (or lockout) action will have an important bearing on the economic positions of the parties. Strikes which have been only tentatively authorized produce little pressure on either party. Mediation is difficult at such times. The reality of the strike—the potential loss of pay by employees and of production by the employer—begins to take shape at the "eleventh hour." For this reason a large part of the actual mediation operation takes place late at night. There is a gradual build-up of pressures, finally including the last-moment preparations for plant maintenance and for picket-line duty, until the exact hour for strike action is reached. Once work has stopped the pressures for settlement are relaxed. The parties' efforts are then concentrated on making the strike successful or on keeping the plant operating. From this low point pressures again build up as production and pay are not forthcoming.

The greatest economic pressure working on the union for a settlement is the actual loss of pay by employees, just as the greatest pressure on the employer is the loss of production. Each day the strike continues or seems likely to continue, this pressure becomes greater. The first week of a strike is kind of a holiday, but the ninth or tenth week may bring real hardship and, eventually, catastrophe.

Several factors may partially relieve the pressure of production and pay losses. In a tight labor market a large proportion of the workers are able to secure other jobs and thus feel under no urgency to end a strike. Mediation is, therefore, often more difficult in periods of full employment. Similarly, employee savings or a large union "war chest" may mitigate the full impact of economic pressure on the strikers. In the same manner the economic position of the employer—his reserves, his tax position, the extent to which losses will be borne by the government, etc.—will modify the normal effect of pressure through loss of production. When stockpiles are excessive, employers may welcome strike action.

The mediator has, of course, little direct control over these economic pressures. He can, however, measure their impact and make certain that the parties understand the extent to which these forces will shape a final settlement. We can also, as will be shown below, channel pressures to produce agreement.

Exertion and Channeling of Pressure in Mediation

As we have said, the mediator's job is essentially one of exerting pressure or of channeling existing pressure in a way that will produce the earliest possible settlement. Unlike the parties, the mediator is not concerned with the content of the settlement. This fact is his greatest strength. It permits him to make an objective analysis of strengths and weaknesses in the positions of each party. It also enables him to see that pressures are exerted, ruthlessly if necessary, where they will be most effective.

Mediation is a process in which the particular type of effort to be utilized must be determined to meet the requirements of the particular dispute. The degree as well as the kinds of pressure which will influence the attitudes and decisions of the disputants vary. The personalities of the management and union leadership may be all that is preventing a settlement. More frequently, basic economic differences are present. In some instances the differences are wide, in others narrow. The mediation process at work may be illustrated by some of the factors which influence the kinds and degree of pressures that may be used.

The Issues in Controversy. The kind of mediation required will, of course, depend significantly on the issues in dispute. Mediation is most difficult where matters of principle, such as an employer's resistance to a union-shop provision, are involved. A grievance over the discharge of a union officer may be less amenable to mediation than a dispute over basic contract terms. Mediation is easiest where there is no important element of principle and where there are a variety of possible solutions. Where only the matter of a wage increase is at issue, for example, there will be many pressures making for a compromise settlement. It is an issue concerning which there are an infinite variety of potential settlements. It is also an issue where the factual situation—the amount of increase in the cost of living since wages were last adjusted, increases granted by comparable employers, the level of prevailing rates paid by competitors, etc.—in itself exerts pressure for a particular settlement. Further, there is usually a flexibility in the bargaining positions of both parties and at least a possibility of "give and take" by the negotiators. Presumably the employer can compare the cost of a larger increase to the loss from curtailed production, and the union can calculate the disadvantages of a strike as compared with the acceptance of a lesser wage. Under these circumstances the mediator's power of persuasion has a fertile field for expression. A cold-blooded analysis of the economic forces which will have an almost inevitable effect on the terms of the agreement to be reached cannot be ignored. As the deadline draws near, both sides will tend to appraise their relative positions realistically.

The Economic and Social Importance of the Operation. Obviously, mediation efforts will vary with the economic and social importance of the goods or services produced. Just as a Presidential fact-finding board would not be appropriate in a dispute of a local clothing manufacturer, so the use of a regular staff conciliator would not be considered feasible where the United Mine Workers of America and the Bituminous Coal Operators are concerned. Generally speaking, the greater the national importance of the case, the more important the use of political and social pressures as distinguished from personal or even economic pressures. This forms the basis for almost all fact-finding procedures. Techniques based on personal pressures, such as keeping the negotiators in session all night, might be quite effective in a dispute involving a small foundry but would be meaningless if used as a tactic in a strike against the United States Steel Corporation.

Time Stages of the Controversy. The length of time a dispute has continued and the particular stage it has reached will also have an important bearing on the kind and degree of pressure which will be most effective. Postponement of the date for strike action is at the heart of many mediation efforts. The strike deadline as an important pressure working on both the union and employer has already been mentioned. Not only have the procedures under the Railway Labor Act and the Labor Management Relations Act of 1947 been specifically designed to produce postponements, but every mediator seeks delay in many types of situations. When the union agrees to a postponement, the pressure for concessions on the employer is immediately relaxed and the total balance of pressures making for settlement is drastically altered. This factor is, of course, modified by the extent of grievance felt by the employees. It is conceivable that a strike which has been repeatedly delayed and postponed will have more solid rank-and-file support than one called according to an original time schedule. The 1952 strike in basic steel may be a case in point. In any event, one of the union's greatest economic strengths is its control over the date when a strike will take place. When this control is voluntarily released by the union or is taken over by the government, the union has little choice but to accept the best possible terms the employer will voluntarily offer.

When a strike is in effect, the time element also plays an important part in mediation efforts. The longer the stoppage continues, the greater the pressure on both sides for settlement. This frequently gives rise to the mediation tactic of "sitting the parties out." Unless production is needed for such purposes as national defense, the mediator can often play his most effective role by allowing the economic forces created by the strike to operate. At this stage, the union and possibly also the employer may seek more active intervention by the mediator.

The Economic Strength of Each Party. Perhaps the most potent factor determining the pressures which may be exerted in mediation is the comparative economic strength of the two parties. If the union is particularly weak because of a loose labor market and a deficient union treasury, for example, there is slight pressure on the employer to make concessions. Under these circumstances the mediator's only recourse for settlement may be to convince the union that it will not be able to carry on a successful strike. Similarly, in a tight labor market and where a loss of production is costly to the employer, a small show of strength by the union may result in major gains. If, however, the strength of the two parties is in approximate balance, the mediator may be able to channel pressures for the most effective results. Thus the mediator may get an employer's customers to insist on the importance of an early settlement so that they will not be deprived of their source of supplies. In the case of a union where a substantial degree of public interest is involved, the mediator may point out that postponement of the strike is the only way to avoid a government injunction. He might also secure a postponement to allow the parties to determine what kind of a settlement will be reached in a particular pattern-setting collective-bargaining situation. A good deal of the mediator's effectiveness in dealing with economic pressures will be based on his ability to make a realistic appraisal of possible future trends and the comparative economic positions of the parties.

The Political Atmosphere. The political atmosphere within which the dispute is carried on—in the plant community, the local area, or the nation—will also influence the kinds and degrees of pressure which may be exerted to obtain agreement. For example, many unions have contended that "the cards are stacked" against them in conducting an organizing strike under the Taft-Hartley Act. In time of war the coercive powers of government will be utilized more freely against strike action than in peacetime. In some instances these powers may be used to the union's advantage, as in the 1952 steel dispute involving the union-shop issue. Local plant politics may be no less important than the national scene; the existence and strength of rival unions, defections within the union, the employer's attitude about unions in general, and the particular union or its leaders are all examples of influences which will have a bearing on the kind of mediation required. Similarly, the attitude of the public and the press in the community within which the strike takes place will affect the degree and kinds of pressure which will make for effective mediation. Sometimes these forces are such that a mediator will issue public statements about the progress of negotiations or even about the attitudes of the parties. By both private and public statements he may seek to control and channel these social pressures to ensure a settlement of the dispute.

The Personality of the Negotiators. The most effective kinds and degrees of pressure will also be determined by the personal characteristics of the persons making decisions on both sides of the bargaining table. These may be the formal negotiators or they may be others who are functioning entirely behind the scene. Not infrequently the mediator finds it necessary to bypass the negotiators and make private contact with the president of the company or with a particular international union representative. Pressure exerted on those not empowered to make decisions is futile, and mediators initially endeavor to determine whose views will have a decisive influence in the particular dispute. Sometimes personalities and attitudes will be crucial in the final settlement, particularly where a dispute of principle, such as over the union shop, is involved. The effective mediator will do everything he can to understand and to influence the decision makers.

The Personal Characteristics of the Mediator. A final factor bearing on the pressure utilized in particular disputes is the personality and ability of the mediator. At least one mediator achieved a national reputation for success by a flair for publicity, a congenial personality, and a willingness to outsit the negotiators. His typical method of operation was to arrive in town with front-page pictures and headlines announcing that he had come to settle the dispute. The parties couldn't refuse to meet with him or, once in session, couldn't afford the adverse publicity that might result if they walked out. After getting the negotiators in a room and exchanging pleasantries, he might lean back in his chair and go to sleep, but the parties were forced to keep talking. This process of wearing the bargainers down to the point where they begin to make concessions has been attempted with many variations by many mediators. Other mediators rely on statistical data and a cold appraisal of economic realities; some, on a clever maneuvering of the parties into untenable positions; and others, on their personalities. Varying amounts of personal, social, or economic pressure will be used according to the needs of the particular dispute and also according to the mediator's own habits and methods of operation.

The discussion to this point has dealt primarily with professional mediators—persons who carry on the work as government employees. However, the professionals represent only part of the story. Literally thousands of labor disputes have been settled with the assistance of persons who have been called on to intervene in particular situations because of their knowledge and the prestige of their persons or positions. Men of the cloth, college professors, judges, and other public officials have made great contributions in reconciling differences between employers and unions. The views of these "outsiders" are often thought of as representing the public interest. Their opinions on the terms of a proper settlement may be more persuasive, therefore, than the opinions of even more skilled mediators.

The ranks of mediators include many business executives and union officials, who also are frequently asked to assist in the settlement of difficult disputes. Their understanding of the special problems involved and their ability to "speak the language" of the disputants give added weight to their views. Professional mediators are often chosen because of their unique knowledge and experience in the handling of labor problems, but the outsider may have even a greater understanding of these problems. The nonprofessionals, whether experts or merely persons with great human understanding, intervene successfully in labor disputes to the extent that they can bring added pressures for achieving accord on one or both of the parties.

Fact Finding—The Use of Pressure in Major Disputes

Where the pressures available to normal conciliation and mediation are not sufficient to bring about a settlement of strikes vitally affecting the public interest, it may become necessary to use extraordinary devices to assure supplies of necessary goods and services. Compulsory arbitration would be one such technique. Other less coercive procedures may also be utilized. These include a variety of forms of fact finding, recommended settlements issued by a governmental agency in the form of orders, court injunctions against striking unions or their leaders, government seizure of struck facilities, and Presidential messages urging the enactment of special legislation by Congress. Governmental fact finding, also referred to as compulsory investigation or as the use of boards of public inquiry, is a pressure device which has been widely used in recent years.

Fact finding is normally used only in those situations where settlement of the dispute has not been achieved by normal mediation efforts. It is actually only a strong form of mediation, and essentially, it is not a method so much for finding facts as for exerting added pressure. When this procedure is resorted to, it is assumed that it is necessary for purposes of public policy to exert the greatest possible amount of pressure, short of compulsion, to assure settlement of the issues in dispute.

Fact finding involves the investigation of disputed issues by an *ad hoc* panel or board appointed by the President or some other governmental agency. The boards may consist of several persons, all without special-interest connections, or they may be tripartite in nature. Usually the members are recognized national authorities. The power and responsibilities of the board vary in accordance with the terms of its appointment. Hearings are held to establish pertinent facts on each issue, and reports are published relating these facts to the positions held by each party. The process rests on a theory of sweet reasonableness: that the facts impartially assessed will themselves dictate a fair and acceptable settlement. It is now widely recognized, however, that the assessment of facts in itself provides little of the pressure necessary to produce agreement.

For fact finding to be effective, some device is necessary to place pressure on recalcitrant parties to yield or make concessions. Adjuncts to the procedure are therefore used to increase its pressure value. These adjuncts include public recommendations by the board for a settlement and governmental sanctions to force acceptance of terms related to these recommendations.

The Taft-Hartley Act prohibits boards appointed under its procedures from making public recommendations on the terms of a proposed settlement. Under the Railway Labor Act, on the other hand, reliance is placed on the effectiveness of such recommendations. During World War II it was found necessary to utilize the prestige of government "orders" to make public recommendations effective.

It is usually believed to be the function of fact finding to create pressure on one or both of the parties to get them to accept what the board considers to be reasonable terms. The parties cannot ignore the conclusions arrived at by a disinterested panel of experts for a fair and equitable settlement. The extreme weight of social and political pressure tends to support the findings of the experts and force an agreement consistent with their recommendations. The real pressure a fact-finding board can exert is based, therefore, on the power to make explicit public proposals. With this power the board can win the respect of the parties, obtain public support for its proposals, and either hammer out a settlement or lay the groundwork for one. Without it labor and management may disregard the board except for presenting their respective positions for the record, and the function of the board is reduced to insignificant reporting. Without recommendations detailed reports are seldom read, and they can have little influence on public opinion. If public opinion is to be utilized, it must have specific recommendations about which to crystallize.

Two objections are customarily voiced to giving fact-finding boards authority to make public recommendations. One is that there is no assurance that the fact finders will be either impartial or expert. This is true, but the objection does not touch on the merits of the procedure. The other objection is that the procedure is closely akin to compulsory arbitration and that it is difficult to withstand the pressure for acceptance of the recommendations. This claim has not always been borne out in practice, as witness the recommendations of the Wage Stabilization Board in the 1952 steel dispute. It is evident, however, that the value of the procedure rests on the fact that the parties usually cannot ignore public recommendations.

On the basis of the preceding analysis it may be stated that labor disputes which have a vital effect on the public welfare require that special pressure techniques be available for their settlement. The range of pressures which may be exerted in such major disputes must be broader than those used in normal mediation. Fact finding, with authority given to the boards for the issuance of public recommendations, may be sufficient to force the parties into agreement. When agreement is not reached, other procedures may be required if the public health and safety would be impaired by a work stoppage. These would include the potential use of sanctions, such as seizure and injunctions, to be applied against either or both parties.

Since the existence of "cut-and-dried" procedures tends to prevent the success of normal mediation efforts, it is important that the use of extraordinary procedures be clothed in uncertainty. Neither the employer nor the union should know in advance what form governmental intervention will take. When one party becomes aware that it is in its interest to do nothing, the basis for a voluntary settlement of the dispute is removed. Each disputant is placed under the strongest form of pressure if it fears what might happen if agreement is not reached. These extraordinary procedures also need to be characterized by their infrequent use. The mere availability of stated procedures releases pressure on the weaker of two parties for settlement. The more special pressure methods are used, the less uncertainty there is and the more ineffective the methods become.

CHAPTER 23 ARBITRATION

Irving Bernstein   *University of California (Los Angeles)*

THE theme of this chapter is that arbitration must be viewed as a facet of the collective-bargaining process, reinforcing it, supplementing it, but, in any case, subordinate to bargaining. Among the three participants in arbitration— management, union, and arbitrator—there can be no debate over which is least important: the arbitrator.

Before turning to the major discussion, an explanation is in order about a subject that will be ignored, namely, compulsory arbitration. This decision has been made for two reasons: first, because all contemporary American experience is with voluntary systems, except for a few states that legally require the arbitration of public-utility disputes; and, second, because almost all experts view dimly the practicality of imposing compulsory arbitration generally in this country. Hence our exclusive concern is with voluntary arbitration systems.

Arbitration Systems

Classifiers may divide the practice of arbitration into the following categories: first, the relationship to the collective-bargaining agreement; second, the status of the arbitrator; and, third, the arbitral structure.

1. *Relationship to Agreement.* From the standpoint of the contract, there are two arbitration systems: those designed to write agreements for the parties and those intended to administer contracts already executed. For purposes of clarity—usage is loose—the former type shall here be called contract arbitration and the latter grievance arbitration. The two differ sharply. It is important that the reader distinguish clearly between them in each phase of the discussion that follows.

Contract arbitration is typically a "one-shot" affair, set up to deal with a particular dispute and dismembered with its settlement. The arbitrator, rather than the parties, decides the terms of their agreement, substituting his judgment for theirs in the bargaining process. Changes in an agreement affect all the employees in the unit. Hence contract arbitrations are of great importance.

EXAMPLE. The contract between the local transit company and the street-railway employees' union has expired, and they have deadlocked in a wage dispute. Rather than permit a strike to occur, they agree to submit the controversy to a leading arbitrator in the community and to be bound by his award. This document of agreement is not part of their collectively bargained contract.

Grievance arbitration, on the other hand, is a continuing function, with a lifetime coinciding with that of the agreement itself. It gets its name from the fact that it serves as the terminal point in the grievance procedure, requiring the final disposition of disputes which the parties were unable to resolve at prior steps. Its subject matter invariably includes interpretations and applications of the contract and alleged violations of it. In some relationships, it extends to any controversy that arises during the contract's term, including matters not covered by the specifications in the last sentence. Rather than a substitute for, grievance arbitration is a supplement to, collective bargaining. Typically, a grievance case affects only one employee or a handful of employees. The impact of the individual case, therefore, is normally not so great as in a contract arbitration. Some grievance arbitrations, however, are very significant.

EXAMPLES. The local rubber-hose plant with 150 employees and the rubber workers' union have a contract which requires arbitration as the final step in their grievance machinery; they find it necessary to arbitrate approximately twice each year. The company fires an employee for excessive absenteeism, citing that clause of the agreement that permits discharge for "just cause." The union contests the action, arguing that mitigating family circumstances undermine the justness of the cause. Unable to agree, the parties call in a local professor, whom they have never employed before, to decide the dispute. Or a great automobile company with many plants throughout the nation and the auto workers' union have a national contract, with arbitration as the terminal point in their grievance procedure. Since they average 200 cases annually, they have chosen a permanent umpire, to whom all these cases go.

The incidence of contract arbitration differs markedly from that of grievance arbitration, that is, the former is used sparingly, the latter almost universally.

The great majority of contract changes are made by unions and management either in direct negotiations or with the limited assistance of mediation. Contract arbitration, therefore, plays a minor role in collective bargaining as practiced in this country. A study by this writer of the incidence of wage arbitration (a large majority of contract cases involve wages) has led to the conclusion that no more than 2 per cent of general wage changes in peacetime are arrived at by this machinery.

The industry distribution of this minor fraction is significant with respect to both those industries that use it and those that do not. The former consist primarily of three groupings: public utilities, nonutility industries directly affecting the public (trade, services, etc.), and industries which have historically engaged in contract arbitration (textiles and printing, in particular). The study revealed that, for wage cases in the 1945–1950 period, utilities constituted just under half (urban transit was much the most important, with heat, light, power, and water, as well as water transportation, being of moderate significance), nonutilities affecting the public comprised one-eighth, and the traditional group provided one-sixth of the total. These three together supplied three-fourths of all wage cases. It is worth noting that three out of five occurred in industries where a work stoppage would have had an immediate impact upon consumers.

Since the categories cited comprise together no more than a small segment of the American economy, it follows that many industries either do not practice contract arbitration at all or use it very rarely. This is the case with the mining group, with manufacturing (excepting a few light industries), and with finance and insurance. Further, the great majority of large enterprises (excluding some utilities) never arbitrate contract changes.

High incidence in the public utilities stems from a recognition by both management and unions that contract arbitration, despite inherent limitations, is preferable to the stoppage of a vital service. In many cases, both accept the concept that the public health and safety or, at least, its convenience cannot long be jeopardized. As a consequence, unions hesitate to strike for fear of losing public sympathy. Further, government—Federal, state, or local—cannot tolerate a stoppage beyond the point where general suffering begins and usually acts before that condition prevails. Hence the "right" of a public-utility union to strike is circumscribed, as compared with organizations in less essential fields, and the union can often get "more" by arbitration.

By the same token, utility management is less willing to permit a stoppage to take place and thereby incur public wrath. Consumers, particularly within the business community, urge the utility to concede. Finally, and perhaps most important, a petition for an increase in rates based on higher wage costs resulting from an award is more readily justified before a regulatory body than is one stemming from a joint agreement.

In turning to grievance arbitration, we find an entirely different situation. In 1949, for example, the Bureau of Labor Statistics found that 83 per cent of a sample of almost 1,500 agreements provided for arbitration as the terminal point in the grievance procedure. Only one of twenty-seven industry groupings revealed fewer than 50 per cent of the firms without such provisions. There is no reason to attach significance to deviations between industries. Much the same result was obtained in a more comprehensive survey of California agreements. Among 1,707 contracts for 1950 analyzed, 1,309 (77 per cent) provided for arbitration. There were no important derelict industries.[1] The conclusion is clear: grievance arbitration is an integral part of the structure of collective bargaining in the United States.

This widespread acceptance of grievance arbitration stems from two considerations: first, the inherent value of an effective grievance procedure and, second, the fact that unions and management yield relatively little power by inviting outside intervention in this area.

Since this type of arbitration is an indispensable cog in a grievance machinery, its popularity mirrors the general acceptance of such systems. The merits of grievance procedure are clear: First, it serves as an orderly substitute for the strike during the term of the agreement. Second, it administers the con-

[1] "Arbitration Provisions in Union Agreements in 1949," *Monthly Labor Review*, 70 (February, 1950), 161; *Arbitration Provisions in California Union Agreements*, San Francisco, California Department of Industrial Relations, Division of Labor Statistics and Research, 1951, pp. 6–7.

tract by resolving differences over interpretation. Third, it provides an outlet for employee "beefs." Finally, it improves the efficiency of the firm by keeping the working force more content. Viewed from the vantage point of the public interest, in fact, there are no valid objections to such machinery.

The acceptance of grievance arbitration by unions and management is also based on the fact that they retain a large measure of control over the system. The risks, in other words, are of a far lower order of magnitude than those that lurk in a contract arbitration. Their agreement specifies the authority of the arbitrator, thereby reserving to them the basic decision over how far he may go. In practice, a grievance arbitrator whose awards constitute contract violations will not survive. The tenure of many permanent arbitrators is terminable at any time by either side. Further, the matters submitted to arbitration are of relatively secondary importance. Putting the point another way, grievances submitted to arbitration are seldom worth a strike to the union or a lockout to the employer.

2. *Status of the Arbitrator.* There are two forms of tenure that the arbitrator can enjoy: *ad hoc* (temporary) and permanent.

The *ad hoc* arbitrator is chosen by the parties to decide one case or, sometimes, a small group of cases heard at the same session. His selection follows the emergence of the dispute. The parties are under no obligation to employ him again. Contract arbitrations are virtually always conducted on an *ad hoc* basis. The great majority of agreements provide for grievance arbitration of this sort.[2]

A permanent arbitrator is selected for a period of time rather than for a case or block of cases. Normally, the duration of his service coincides with the life of the contract. His selection precedes the occurrence of specific disputes. He need not be and usually is not employed on a full-time basis by the parties to one agreement. An individual arbitrator may, therefore, serve as permanent umpire under several contracts at the same time. His duties and terms of employment may be set forth in the collective-bargaining agreement or in a separate document. Permanent arbitration is limited to grievance matters. Permanent arrangements are common in the large, multiplant, mass-production firms and under multiemployer-association master agreements, especially in the needle trades.

This suggests the two terms commonly used for permanent arbitrators, namely, "umpire" and "impartial chairman." The former is widely employed in the heavy industries, for example, automobiles, steel, farm equipment, and rubber. The term impartial chairman is particularly associated with the needle trades and industries related to them, such as hosiery. The titles are associated with quite different conceptions of arbitration. Umpireships tend to be narrower in outlook than impartial chairmanships. That is, the latter more frequently permit a wider scope of authority for the arbitrator, a lesser emphasis

---

[2] In the U.S. Bureau of Labor Statistics study of 1949 agreements, 1,237 were found to contain arbitration clauses. Of these, 79 per cent provided for temporary machinery; only 14 per cent, permanent. In California, the disparity was even sharper. Of a total of 1,309 agreements with arbitration provisions, 93 per cent were temporary, and only 3 per cent permanent. "Arbitration Provisions in Union Agreements . . . ," p. 163; *Arbitration Provisions in California Union Agreements*, p. 11.

on the language of the contract, and more frequent resort to mediated settlements. In part, this stems from the fact that the chairman is usually a member of a tripartite board.

3. *Arbitral Structures.* There are, at bottom, two structural types that may be used in arbitration: an all-neutral arrangement or a tripartite board with voting representation from both union and management in addition to the neutral(s). There are numerous variations. The all-neutral type normally consists of one arbitrator. In important cases, however, there may be two or even three neutrals. Tripartite boards most commonly comprise one representative from each of the three sides. Variations are one-two-two and two-two-two set-ups. With these boards, of course, it is necesary to have a majority in order to arrive at a decision, sometimes a difficult accomplishment. An in-between form is a tripartite machinery with voting power reserved exclusively to the neutral(s). Tripartite structures are more common than single arbitrators in collective-bargaining agreements.[3] In practice, however, the parties often agree to waive the tripartite requirement, particularly in *ad hoc* grievance cases where the magnitude of the dispute does not justify the bother and expense.

Approaches to Arbitration

It has become commonplace to contrast the "judicial" and "collective-bargaining" philosophies of arbitration. Some argue that arbitrators are blood brothers of judges and should behave accordingly, that the procedure in which they participate should be patterned after rigorous court processes. Others claim that arbitration is related to collective bargaining and should be conducted with a cousinly disrespect for legalism. The debate may be considered on two levels, one of formal procedure and the other of substance. With respect to the former, the bargaining approach now prevails widely. Only rarely, for example, are the rules of evidence observed or are witnesses sworn. Further, many arbitrators dispense with the transcript.

With regard to substance, the situation is more complex, that is, differing structures and issues evoke varying degrees of judicialness. Under some circumstances, the arbitrator is more willing to expand the scope of his authority, to consider more daring standards of decision making, and to engage in mediation than he is in others. Speaking very generally, the bargaining approach is more prevalent in contract than it is in grievance systems, with permanent rather than with *ad hoc* arbitrators (especially in the needle-trades impartial chairmanships—there are notable exceptions among the umpireships) and under tripartite boards rather than under single arbitrators. That is, one might expect a more legalistic approach from an arbitrator sitting alone in an *ad hoc* grievance case than from a tripartite board in a contract case.

In any case, the great impact of collective bargaining upon arbitration is worth sketching. Arbitrators with a penchant for turning a well-worn phrase enjoy noting that arbitration is an "extension" of, or "substitute" for, collec-

---

[3] In the U.S. Bureau of Labor Statistics study noted above, 56 per cent were tripartite, as compared with 37 per cent single. For California, the corresponding figures were 67 and 29 per cent. "Arbitration Provisions in Union Agreements . . . ," p. 163; *Arbitration Provisions in California Union Agreements,* p. 11.

tive bargaining. The awards and the literature are heavy with restatements of this notion. An old coin, nevertheless, has the same value as a new one. In this discussion, once again, it is important to distinguish between contract and grievance arbitration.

Emerging as it does out of collective bargaining, contract arbitration rests on the same bases and is bounded by the same limitations. The first is that bargaining rests ultimately upon the right of union or management to withdraw labor or jobs. The collective agreement is a sign that they have elected peace rather than war, for its term. If they choose to arbitrate or, in Soule's phrase, take "the peaceful uncertainty of an arbitral settlement," they have implicitly agreed that it is preferable to the costs and risks of a strike or lockout. They expect, and properly so, that the third party's decision will approximate what they would voluntarily have agreed upon themselves. Hence he is often obliged to consider not only the equities shaping the issues but also the parties' relative bargaining power. If he fails to do so, he may undermine his basic function—keeping the peace.

This leads directly to a second basic relationship of contract arbitration to bargaining, namely, acceptability. A rejected decision is no decision at all. Hence the arbitrator must recognize that the capacity of the parties to effectuate his award is an integral part of it. Again, he will have betrayed his purpose if his decision produces a work stoppage.

As a consequence—the third consideration—there is pressure upon the contract arbitrator to give weight to those criteria which the parties would have emphasized in bargaining and to disregard those that they would have ignored. His award, therefore, is a product of mixed considerations: the economic and the political, the measurable and the immeasurable, and the rational and the irrational. Contract arbitration, like bargaining, often defies logic.

Grievance arbitration, too, rests upon a collective-bargaining foundation. This is apparent in its conventional justification as the alternative to a work stoppage during the life of the agreement. Historically, it emerged in essentially its present form in the needle trades because they were bedeviled with strikes over piece rates. To eliminate these stoppages during the term of the contract, the parties concluded upon grievance arbitration. It served as a direct substitute for the strike. In fact, in labor-contract theory, the no-strike and arbitration clauses are interlocked. Unions seldom permit the exclusion of an agreement provision from arbitration without reserving at the same time the right to strike on that matter during the term.

The bargaining nature of grievance arbitration is frequently reflected in its procedures as well. As already noted, it is often practiced with the informality of negotiations rather than under the strictures of the courtroom. Further, in impartial-chairman systems, grievances are sometimes settled rather than determined. That is, the parties trade off one against another rather than obtain a ruling from their chairman. More rarely, the same occurs under umpireships and in *ad hoc* systems.

On the contrary, however, grievance arbitration departs from the flexibility of bargaining as a function of the signally important role played by the contract. This document creates the grievance system, defines the authority of the arbitrator, and (where his jurisdiction is limited to its interpretation or application) fixes substantive limits to the range of his decision making. In relation to the agreement, there are three types of grievance matters that reach the arbitrator: first, those involving conduct explicitly permitted or denied by the contract; second, those evoked by vague or ambiguous language or which uncover a conflict between several of the contract clauses; and, finally, those with which the contract fails to deal. With the first, the clarity of the contract reduces his function to that of fact finder. The facts fall either within or outside the limits of the agreement. He has no choice but to comply with its language. With the second (probably the source of most grievance arbitrations), he can exercise a considerable judgment. With the last, he must depend upon the source of his authority. If the parties limit his jurisdiction to the interpretation or application of the agreement, he obviously cannot rule on something beyond its scope. If they impose no such restriction, he is free to consider the equities much like a contract arbitrator.

The Arbitrator

There is in many of us a yearning to play judge. This may spring from a wish to pry into other people's troubles. Or, since some of us are convinced that we can handle our neighbors' affairs better than they, meddlesomeness may be compounded with the desire to be socially useful by resolving the difficulties of others. Both factors may be—and probably are—irrelevant to, if not actually in conflict with, effectiveness as an arbitrator. Nevertheless, they help to create a large pool of aspirants for the field of arbitration. The number of practitioners, however, is quite small. The National Academy of Arbitrators, for example, had only 176 members in 1952.

This discrepancy between the wish and the fact calls for explanation. In the first place, there is no great need for arbitrators because there is so little work to go around. Since arbitrators are called in only when their services are required there can be no make-work. Second, entrance into the trade is difficult. One must be known and accepted both by key union and management people in one's locality and by the agencies that assist in the appointment of arbitrators, such as the Federal Mediation and Conciliation Service and the American Arbitration Association. It is hard for the newcomer to gain this acceptance on his own. In fact, most arbitrators have broken in through experience with a government labor agency, notably the NWLB. Finally, and probably most important, it is virtually impossible to make a living out of arbitration. A few succeed in doing so for a year or two in a major umpireship, and a handful do nothing else. The great majority of arbitrators, however, practice on a part-time basis, deriving their principal income from some other source.

Good arbitrators are hard to come by because the qualifications are specialized and, hence, rarely met. Perhaps most important is expertness in the labor field. This includes a broad range of knowledge in such areas as the economics of the industry, union structure and policies, contract provisions (many quite esoteric), and the potentialities and limitations of the arbitration process. Also important is a feel for collective bargaining, embracing such factors as the capacity to give and take with negotiators, the ability to separate bluff from insistence, and the perception to determine the limits of acceptability. A second qualification is good judgment. The arbitrator is called upon to make decisions not only in his award but in the procedural steps en route to it. At many points, he flirts with disaster and must have his wits about him. Third, he should be fair-minded. This means that he owns a mind open to the reception and weighing of evidence and that he can limit his motivating considerations to the case before him. It does not imply that he is without opinions, but rather that he can distinguish between his own views and the merits of the dispute facing him.

In the light of these qualifications, it is clear that no one profession supplies the best training. Competent arbitrators are drawn from the universities, particularly those with labor specialties, from the bar, from government service, from the bench, from business, and from the ministry. Obviously, incompetents come from the same sources. Speaking very generally, management, with an interest in narrowing the scope of arbitral discretion, tends to favor men with legal backgrounds, in the hope that they will construe strictly. For reverse reasons, unions are inclined to prefer professors and ministers.

The preceding discussion should leave no doubt that arbitration is far from being professionalized. It cannot, for example, be compared in status with medicine, architecture, or the law. This is because of the hazards of income and survival, the relative newness of the field, and the dearth of schools for training. The National Academy represents a first step in the direction of professionalization.

Some Controversial Issues

The development of arbitration in the United States in the past half generation has been striking. There is little doubt that management and unions agree upon more aspects of the process than those they dispute over. The few areas of disagreement, however, are challenging, and they supply the burden of this section.

1. *Arbitrability*. Sharp differences in viewpoint exist over the subject matter appropriate for arbitration. This issue of scope is related primarily to grievance arbitration. Before turning to it, however, a few comments are in order in the contract area.

From what has been said of the incidence of contract arbitration, it is clear that the majority of managements and/or unions feel that the writing of agreements as a whole is an inappropriate subject of this process. For the minority who are prepared to arbitrate their contracts, a further limitation is evident. They are more willing to submit monetary matters than nonmonetary. This viewpoint is more prevalent among employers than among labor organizations. The reason is clear: contract arbitration is more useful for issues that can be compromised than for those that cannot. A difference over 10 cents per hour can be adjusted; a dispute over the union shop is very difficult to compromise.

In the grievance area there is a significant disagreement between labor and management. The former is eager to broaden the scope of arbitration, while the latter is anxious to impose limits. Speaking generally, unions want the grievance arbitrator to have jurisdiction over all disputes that arise during the life of the contract. Since they lack the right to strike in this period, they want a recourse beyond the employer.

Management, by contrast, seeks to limit the arbitrator's authority to the interpretation and application of the contract. Some employers, notably in the automobile industry, go further and exclude some provisions of the agreement itself from his jurisdiction. Management is particularly anxious to prevent a whittling away of its prerogatives and to avoid giving the union a second chance to obtain a concession which it failed to win in the negotiation of the agreement.

There is something to be said for both views. The liberal position has the advantages of providing a method of resolving unforeseen disputes during the term of the agreement and of giving workers an immediate outlet for pent-up grievances. At the same time, it carries within it seeds of abuse, for example, a systematic effort to undermine a contract provision jointly agreed upon after hard bargaining. Where both sides concur upon a broadening of the scope of arbitration, the risks evaporate. If, however, either side insists upon narrowing the arbitrator's jurisdiction, he has no alternative but to fall in line. Speaking very generally, a widening of the area of arbitrability that the parties agree to is a test of the maturity of their collective bargaining.

2. Ad hoc *versus Permanent Status.* This issue relates exclusively to grievance arbitration. As the collective-bargaining agreements testify, the majority of unions and managements prefer the *ad hoc* system. In part, this may represent the relationships in which there is so little arbitration that there can be no justification for a permanent arbitrator. The others, however, may reflect a misapprehension over how fully the permanent arbitrator's time must be employed. As already noted, he usually works part time and often is engaged only rarely. Hence the permanent arbitrator system is appropriate to moderate-sized as well as to large firms and associations.

The superiority of the permanent over the *ad hoc* machinery is readily shown. In the former, the arbitrator becomes expert in the particular contract, the method of wage payment, and the economics of the industry. Similarly, he becomes acquainted with key figures on each side. His decisions are consistent, avoiding the retrial before a new arbitrator of cases already decided. The time spent in selecting the arbitrator, in arranging for meetings, in conducting the hearing, and in writing the award is kept to a minimum. As a result, the cost per case to the parties is lower. On the other side the principal objection is tactical: the union or the employer may feel tied down with an arbitrator whom they have grown to dislike or who they think will award against them in a key case. Even here, however, they can protect themselves by reserving the right to discharge him at will. In light of the preponderance of advantages over disadvantages, it is probably safe to predict that the permanent-arbitration system will gradually expand its coverage in industry.

3. *Tripartite versus Single Structures.* There is no universally superior form; in some situations, a tripartite board is preferable, and in others, it is not. Broadly considered, such a system is better adapted to contract arbitration, particularly wage cases, and a single arbitrator is more effective in grievance matters. Exceptions, however, are legion. If, for example, the contract

dispute is over a nonmonetary issue, tripartitism probably has little to offer. In impartial chairmanships in the needle trades, where the scope of arbitration is unlimited and mediation is common, a three-way board has much to contribute.

In the arbitration of general wage changes in new contracts, tripartitism is normally preferable. The advantages are three—acceptability, information sharing, and mediation—and they are interwoven.

An essential of arbitration is compliance with the award. In the typical three-way setup, the neutral must win a majority to make a decision. Hence it is impossible to render an award repugnant to both sides. Further, participation in decision making by a representative of the minority tempers potential majority extremism. The neutral, in other words, learns the objections of the loser before issuance of the award, thereby defining the borderline of noncompliance in advance. Under the pressures of acceptability, tripartitism drives the award toward center.

The advantage stemming from information sharing works two ways: the neutral learns what the parties really want (and don't want), and they know what he intends to do. Obviously, it is of importance that the arbitrator discover how much in cents per hour each side will "take." It is entirely possible to endure a dozen days of formal hearing without acquiring this knowledge. Partisan board members make it a virtual certainty that the neutral will be told how far they are prepared to go. Further, the tripartite form is a means of making a green arbitrator more sophisticated about the industry and about the bargaining relationship. Finally, this system undercuts the element of surprise by informing the losing party in advance of an imminent unpleasantness. Bad news is more acceptable when received gradually.

The final advantage of tripartitism in wage cases is an enhanced prospect of mediating a settlement. Under the pressure of gaining a majority, the neutral is influenced to bring the case to a conclusion. In searching for what each side will take, he may discover that they are closer together than either believes. Everyone agrees that mediated settlements are preferable to those reached by arbitration. The presence of partisan representatives on the board offers many opportunities to explore an agreement. Gaining a majority is sometimes difficult. Both partisan spokesmen recognize that one of their votes is needed to make the decision. Hence they are tactically pressed to give ground gradually in order to keep the neutral as close to their real position as possible without losing him to the other side.

In the typical grievance system, tripartitism has little to offer affirmatively and may actually produce undesirable results. Here the focus is on the collective-bargaining agreement, whose language provides for standards of decision making absent in the contract case (unless the parties create them in a special submission agreement). The flexibility of tripartitism may simply be a device exploited by one side to divert the decision from the compulsions of the contract to a bargained settlement beyond its scope. That is, the arbitrator might be driven to a position unsupported by the agreement in order to gain a majority. Normally, that would be an undesirable result; it would have merit only if both parties favored it.

Further, the issues involved in grievance arbitration seldom justify the added burdens of expense and administrative inefficiency. Partisan representatives are usually paid for their time; hearings are extended; more copies of documents are required; and time schedules are drawn out. These factors defeat the basic purpose of grievance procedure: the orderly and rapid disposition of employee grievances under the contract.

Finally, even the advantage of the tripartite form in contract cases is limited by two conditions: first, that the partisan board members are of roughly equal competence and, second, that they behave responsibly. If either the labor or the management member much exceeds his counterpart in bargaining skill, experience, knowledge, and force of personality, he may be able to shape the award to a form not supported by the merits of the case. Similarly, if a partisan representative seeks to obstruct the board's operation (such an attitude is infectious), he will either produce a bad decision by forcing the neutral over to the other side in order to gain a majority or provoke the resignation of the neutral, with the consequent failure to issue an award at all.

4. *Mediation in Arbitration.* Perhaps the most controversial issue is that of whether it is appropriate for the arbitrator to seek to reconcile differences rather than to render an award. Those enamored of the narrow judicial viewpoint would bar any mediation in arbitration, but they are a dwindling minority. Clearly, this procedure has much to offer but, again, under tailored circumstances. The tailoring, it should be emphasized, is largely that of the parties themselves, in that the character of their relationship conditions the possibility for mediation.

Speaking generally, unions tend to be more favorable to mediation than is management. This is because they have more to gain from shaking the arbitrator loose from the contract, from a widening of the scope of arbitration. In a particular proceeding, however, either side may prefer a settlement. Here the propensity to mediate is a function of the regard each party has for its case. The one with a good case prefers an award; the one with a poor case hopes for a deal.

The prospect for mediation is obviously brighter in some circumstances than in others. It is sometimes desirable in contract cases, particularly in money disputes. Here the arbitration process is a direct substitute for bargaining and offers many of the characteristics of the negotiating table. Even in grievance arbitration, mediation is sometimes exploited to good effect. Here it is more appropriate for the impartial chairman than for the *ad hoc* arbitrator. The former is in a tactically sound position to mediate because he, presumably, has the confidence of the parties, is familiar with key figures on each side, and has a continuing interest in building the relationship. Under the impartial chairmanships in the needle trades, mediation is considered an integral part of the chairman's function. Occasionally it occurs under the umpireships in the mass-production industries. Where either side, however, insists on restricting the umpire to arbitration, he must go along. The temporary arbitrator is in an entirely different situation. Unless the parties agree to the contrary, he is under pressure to follow the language of the contract, to base his award solely on the evidence presented, and to avoid pragmatic solutions.

The prospect for mediation is also conditioned by the mediability of the issue. In a contract case, as already noted, a money matter is readily compromised, while union security presents greater difficulty. In a grievance case involving discharge, the employer's act under the contract is either supported or not. If reinstatement is involved, however, there might be room for bargaining over the amount of back pay. An unambiguous contract provision covering the point at issue is the strongest preventive to mediation in grievance arbitration.

No matter how compelling the logic of mediation, the arbitrator inevitably runs a risk in attempting it, namely, failure. Unsuccessful mediation complicates his ultimate responsibility of rendering a decision and takes time. He must tread warily, particularly to avoid commitments as to what he will decide if negotiations break down. Such commitments—the parties usually seek to extract them—weaken his effectiveness and can prove embarrassing. If mediation is attempted, the arbitrator must be careful lest he destroy his paramount function as arbitrator.

Conclusion

It is well to undertake these final remarks with a word of caution that has been noted at several points heretofore. Arbitration, as part of collective bargaining, is a complex, protean process, whose understanding is not necessarily forwarded by logic alone and whose use requires accommodation to the individual relationship and issue. Even the most valid generalizations do not apply in all cases. Nevertheless, there are meaningful patterns that do emerge.

Arbitration has become an important factor in the settlement of labor-management disputes in the United States. Unions and employers have embraced it as an integral part of their collective relationships. This acceptance approaches universality in grievance cases but is quite rare in contract disputes.

In mature relationships, where the bargained area has expanded furthest, there is often a tendency for arbitration to atrophy. This is the case in the needle trades, in the Pacific Coast pulp-and-paper industry, and, to a lesser extent, under the General Motors-UAW contract. Such disuse of arbitration with age reflects both the growing ability of the parties to resolve conflict without outside assistance and the disposition of issues through the establishment of precedent. Some argue with persuasiveness that the arbitrator attains full success when he works himself out of a job.

Arbitration is by nature a conservative process. In the grievance area, most arbitrators are confined by the contract, and this is the reason for the chafing evidenced by unions over the issue of scope. In contract cases, which are more important, arbitrators seldom are willing to initiate a new policy. Rather they tend to be influenced by comparisons with other groups. This is why militant unions are averse to submitting important departures in policy to arbitration.

Finally, and to return to the theme stated at the outset of this chapter, arbitration has limitations as a means of dispensing with industrial disputes. Conflict is inherent in the collective-bargaining process; the threat and calling of strikes and lockouts are required to produce agreement. Since arbitration is a part of collective bargaining, it cannot escape from the force of conflict. Arbitration, therefore, cannot eradicate conflict, but it can mitigate its effect and rechannel its incidence into areas in which it can serve useful purposes.

3

b · *EFFORTS TO REMOVE*
SOURCES OF CONFLICT

The content of this section is not separated in any basic sense from the preceding section. The parties to conflict constantly address themselves to the task of removing their disagreements, each striving, of course, to reduce the tensions on a basis satisfactory to his own group. Collective bargaining and other procedures discussed under "Accommodating to Conflict" are at the same time attempts to remove sources of conflict. What distinguishes the problems of the following chapters is their concern not with the settlement of specific issues that have already become bones of contention but with *potential* troubles, with underlying strains that may lead to, or aggravate, particular grievances.

Almost everyone wishes to see industrial conflict diminish. Even those who believe conflict necessary and desirable and who consider its complete elimination unthinkable still favor the "right" kinds of move to decrease the amount of conflict and to mitigate its occasional intensity and bitterness. Almost all would like to remove ill will and irritations as much as possible without sacrifice of other values held more precious. But this question of other values—of what price harmony—cannot be escaped. Efforts to remove the sources of conflict always occur within a framework of assumptions as to limiting conditions. Usually this means making those improvements that can be introduced without any essential change in the institutionalized power relations, without concessions that "go too far." A crucial question, accordingly, is how far actual and proposed efforts proceed and with what effectiveness.

The following chapters examine and assess some of the principal activities which aim both to minimize dissatisfactions conducive to conflict and to foster good will and a spirit of cooperation. Two kinds of activities are to be distinguished: those that introduce substantive changes such as improved wages, employment conditions, and work rules; and those that use educational and communication methods to change the way people perceive or interpret the objective relations. The contents of this section deal primarily with the former. While the communications processes are not singled out for separate treatment, however, aspects of these activities appear in almost every chapter here as well as in earlier sections (see Chaps. 13 and 18). Nevertheless, since the bearing of communications on industrial relations is not specifically discussed in any one chapter, we may appropriately comment on it here before turning to changes in objective conditions as ways of reducing conflict.

The communications approach has been strongly emphasized in management circles during recent years. There can be no question that many misunderstandings are prevented and needless fears and suspicions avoided through improved communication processes in industry. Transmission of clear instructions, reports, and explanations up and down the line serves to keep all parts of an organization effectively informed and interrelated. In addition to these indispensable communication functions, most large companies also expend considerable effort in attempts to improve employee attitudes. These activities seek to provide employees with "sound economic ideas" and to win their loyalty, understanding, and support. The methods include use of employee magazines, financial statements, pay-envelope messages and other printed materials, loud-speaker systems, bulletin boards, foremen's statements, talks by major executives, and whatever other procedures appear promising for circulating desired ideas. Likewise common are attempts to open better channels of communication "upward," from employees to management, by means of attitude surveys, personnel counselors, suggestion boxes, training foremen how to listen to their men, and numerous other methods, not excluding consultation with union representatives.

No blanket evaluation of these varied activities is possible. Exaggerated hopes that simply "telling" employees would solve labor-management difficulties have now been rather widely exploded.[1] But more sophisticated activities continue to constitute an important part of industry's program for removing sources of conflict and building a foundation of common understanding. Unfortunately, little is known as to whether and under what conditions genuine understanding results and whether more accurate understanding produces more amicable relationships. There is an easy oversimplification ordinarily voiced to the effect that, if labor and management only understand each other's aims and problems, they will adjust and get along peacefully together. This may or may not hold true in particular instances.

Educational messages and persuasive communications from management will obviously elicit quite different reactions, ranging from unquestioning belief to utter disbelief, depending in part on whether or not the views are met by telling counterclaims from unions or other sources. Whether one interpretation or another is accepted will also be determined by the worker's own experiences and existing attitudes—by what he is *prepared* to believe, by his emotional attitudes toward the source of the communication, and by the sentiments prevailing among his friends and fellow workers. Significant in this connection is the finding of opinion surveys showing that the vast majority of factory employees declare their conviction that union leaders are more interested in the workers' welfare than are the heads of the company.[2]

[1] For example, see William H. Whyte, Jr., *Is Anybody Listening?* New York, Simon and Schuster, 1952.

[2] For a recent survey on this point, see "What Factory Workers Think Now," *Factory Management and Maintenance,* 110 (September, 1952), 84–90.

Returning now to attempts to remove causes of conflict by changing substantive conditions, it should be noted, first of all, that most of the activities originate with the employer and deal with the individual enterprise. However, these efforts frequently involve the labor union too, rather than remaining unilateral; and in some instances the union initiates the changes. Whether the employer acts alone or jointly with the union, the programs usually aim to improve morale, to maintain a cooperative spirit between management and employees, and to create a climate of feeling conducive both to productive efficiency and to the ready, peaceful adjustment of specific conflicts as they arise.

Chapters 24 to 29 describe and assess some of these principal "morale-building" and "human-relations" activities. Myers first provides a broad view of the purposes and viewpoint of progressive personnel administration and then sketches ways in which it attempts to deal with several basic problems which lie at the center of much industrial conflict. The activities considered are company wage policies, efforts to stabilize employment, elimination of arbitrary management procedures, and improvement of employee status and recognition. In all these matters it is made clear that the labor union plays an important part. Myers concludes that significant progress has been made over recent years in reducing tensions in these areas and that additional advances are to be anticipated.

The problem of wages is dealt with in further detail by Livernash in Chap. 25. Here attention focuses on internal wage-administration procedures and on the great strides industry has taken toward establishing more systematic and equitable bases of payment according to job level and individual or group performance. The analysis points to the overwhelming importance of management and union *attitudes* in determining the success of any wage plan and to the need for labor's participation if the complex issues that arise are to be satisfactorily handled. Strong emphasis is placed on the fact that job evaluation and other techniques are secondary to agreement on fundamental objectives and policies. Wage-administration procedures can either increase or decrease conflict, depending on circumstances and on the broader setting of union-management relations.

It is becoming ever more fully recognized that wages and employment security are not the only sources of discontent and conflict. Interest in meeting the human problems of industry also leads to active concern about the physical and social conditions of work and about effecting better adjustments between workers and their jobs. Chapters 26 to 29 deal with these matters. In Chap. 26, Walker examines the impact of the technological environment on the factory worker. He points to desirable reconciliations of the contrasting viewpoints of the industrial engineer and of the social scientist or student of human relations and proceeds to illustrate some of the newly explored possibilities of reversing the work-simplification and specialization trend through "job enlargement." At least in special instances, results have been secured that are favorable both for production and for human satisfactions. Suggestions along these and related lines indicate encouraging possibilities for removing some of the negative human effects of machine work. It may well be that factory employment can be made to accord much better than it now does with the personal and social needs of men and women living in mid-20th-century America.

The theme of broadened participation by all those engaged in industry is central to the following two chapters, on union-management cooperation and on the "group-dynamics" approach. Both the accomplishments and the limitations of labor-management cooperation plans are outlined by Dale in Chap. 27. A suggestive analysis is made of features that characterize successful and unsuccessful programs, and Dale presents his thoughtful interpretations of what the underlying requirements are for effective, continuing cooperation. At a more abstract and psychological level, Haire in the next chapter summarizes significant portions of the thinking developed by Kurt Lewin, Moreno, and others in respect to the inner relationships and functioning of small groups. He describes illustrative applications to problems of training, communication, and decision forming within groups in industry. This chapter also contains a sketch of the famous Hawthorne-plant research and of later developments in the study of group processes, teamwork, and informal social relationships in the factory.

In Chap. 29, Raney considers personnel procedures having to do with training, selecting, and placing workers, from the standpoint of what these procedures do to increase employee interest and satisfaction and thus to reduce potential grievances and hostility. Since attempts fully to utilize workers' abilities encounter extremely serious difficulties, however, and since workers and unions often believe that qualifications are unfairly appraised and that employees are inequitably treated in these matters (whether or not this is objectively true in any given case), it appears that accomplishments along these lines are easily exaggerated as far as prevention of conflict is concerned. Nevertheless, there can be little question that systematic, competent, aboveboard personnel procedures for effecting better adjustment of individuals to work opportunities produce less friction than exists where little attention is paid to these needs. The prospect of favorable results is especially good if the views of employees are adequately represented in the planning and administration of the program.

In addition to the efforts of employers and unions to remove sources of conflict, large-scale moves by government have also grown more and more important. These governmental actions usually pertain to entire industries or to all industry—as seen in social-security legislation dealing with old age, sickness, and unemployment; wage-and-hour laws; regulation of factory health and safety conditions; and legislative measures for economic stabilization. Here, too, labor and management organizations play a part, if not in proposing the measures and either supporting or opposing them, at least as participants in their operation and enforcement. Haber's chapter summarizes and evaluates the principal ones of these governmental programs as they bear on industrial conflict. He cautiously concludes that it is too early to say whether these measures are likely to reduce conflict. Certainly the growth of social legislation has tended to bring up new issues for labor and management to deal with, and it has been one of the forces pushing industrial conflict farther into the political arena. At the same time, developments in the legislative field have been accompanied by increasing attention to these broader issues as sub-jects for collective bargaining as well. Finally, the chapter reminds us that, whether or not social legislation reduces conflict, it performs other important functions in helping to meet the serious economic problems of wage earners.

Difficult and disturbing questions can be asked and are asked from time to time—though remarkably rarely in the scholarly literature—as to whether the various industrial and governmental activities discussed in this section serve to reduce conflict. The authors of these chapters call attention to a number of these controversial questions. Other underlying questions were referred to in Parts 1 and 2a. For example, there is the most general issue of what goal is sought in respect to conflict: Is it desirable to eliminate all conflict? What types of industrial conflict, if any, should be preserved—under what conditions, expressed in what ways, subject to what kind of controls? Is industrial peace desirable if it is brought about by "softening up" the other side to achieve a unilateral reduction in fighting strength and in readiness to fight if it becomes necessary? One needs to examine every plan for removing sources of conflict to ascertain the extent to which it has this objective and to judge what long-run results are likely to flow from peace arrived at through one-sided "disarmament."

Another question is this: Removing particular sources of conflict, fore-seeing possible grievances and correcting the condition in advance, and meet-ing demands before they are made—do such procedures necessarily diminish conflict? The same question can be asked in reference to employer actions devoted to employee welfare, such as recreation, education, comfort, health, and personal adjustment. The answer to all these questions is often too readily assumed to be an affirmative one. Surely the improvements may be most com-mendable and in the true interests of employees. But managements are fre-quently gravely disappointed at the unimpressive morale consequences and the continuation of conflict. Clearly there is more to be weighed than the merits of the objective changes introduced. As was suggested in Part 2a, workers' wants and expectations are also basically involved. Particular concessions may fall short of satisfying whipped-up anticipations. Or the spirit of the concessions may be negatively interpreted; workers or union officials may feel ignored and may resent the fact that they were not consulted. Or the changes, while appreciated, may quickly stimulate desires for new and bigger concessions. No simple one-to-one relationship exists between specific, well-intentioned moves to reduce conflict and the actual achievement of the in-creased harmony that is sought.

Even the enlightened emphasis by management—and by social scientists —on increased individual and group participation in industry and on im-proved consultation and communication is open to parallel questions. It is too easily concluded that special cases of successful cooperation, group deci-sion making, "flattened" organizational structure, or human-relations pro-cedures are generalizable. Moreover, the criterion of "successful" is too often limited to short-run considerations and individual worker benefits, ignoring such questions as whether participation on small matters leads to demands for a voice in larger issues and whether management stands willing to extend the decision sharing to significant management functions, or the question of what happens to the strength and spirit of the labor union as it continues to cooperate.

The possible criticisms implied in questions such as these certainly do not undermine all the good work—practical and experimental—that has so encouragingly expanded over recent years. The chapters that follow provide ample evidence that important advances are being made. At the same time, we cannot let our hopes and enthusiasm deter us from asking the questions that tough-minded social scientists have special obligation to press.

CHAPTER 24 BASIC EMPLOYMENT RELATIONS

Charles A. Myers   *Massachusetts Institute of Technology*

THE employer-employee relationship is a focal point in the analysis of industrial conflict and in the examination of methods for reducing it. The terms on which the employee sells his services, the regularity of his employment, and the conditions under which he works are all basic employment relations which give rise to conflicts between employer and employee and between employers and the union representatives of their employees.

If the employer hopes to reduce the occasions for conflict, in his effort to achieve the objectives of the business enterprise, he must give attention to the following areas of actual or potential conflict: (1) "unfair" or "inadequate" levels of wages; (2) unstable and irregular employment; (3) arbitrary and capricious management action; and (4) inadequate employee status and recognition.

These sources of conflict and grievance spring from basic human wants and expectations and from the tendency for industrial societies in many instances to block or deny their realization. Whether "wages" or "human relations on the job" are more important for workers today is really irrelevant, and many attitude surveys and much management thinking have fallen into the error of contrasting the two. The goals and job satisfactions of industrial workers in America will differ in particular plants or industries, depending upon the degree to which certain ones have already been achieved or realized and upon the general social and economic environment at the time.[1] The significant point, however, is that, unless each of these employee goals or aspirations is met in some measure by the employment relationship, the occasion for tension and conflict remains.

Approach of Industrial Management

It is fair to say that industrial management in America has increasingly been concerned with these areas of conflict. There are, to be sure, still some management officials who think of production largely in technical terms, apart from the aspirations and behavior of the employees whose cooperative efforts make it possible for an organization to achieve high productive efficiency. But their number has been decreasing, and today many managers would agree that

[1] Cf. Charles A. Myers and George P. Shultz, *Dynamics of a Labor Market*, New York, Prentice-Hall, 1951, Chap. 6; Lloyd G. Reynolds, *The Structure of Labor Markets*, New York, Harper, 1951; and Ross Stagner, "Psychological Aspects of Industrial Conflict, Part II, Motivation," *Personnel Psychology*, 3 (Spring, 1950), 1–15.

the essential task of management is to get effective results through other people. As a consequence, personnel administration and industrial relations are now increasingly recognized as part of the basic responsibility of line management officers, advised and assisted by staff specialists.

Effective personnel administration seeks to provide those conditions of employment which enable employees to achieve as many as possible of their individual and group goals and aspirations at the same time that they are encouraged and motivated to give their best efforts to the organization in achieving its objectives.[2] Dissatisfied or aggrieved employees are not willing or enthusiastic workers. The areas of actual or potential conflict outlined above, therefore, are central problems for personnel administration. The ability of the firm to meet these problems successfully will depend, however, not only on the intiative and resourcefulness of its management but also on the product-market situation it faces and on the institutional framework, including the particular union, within which it must plan and operate. The union as an institution has objectives and pressures of its own, some of which are apart from, or even in conflict with, those of management.[3] Mature managers recognize that these institutional needs of the union and union leaders require certain approaches and methods of accommodation if conflict is to be reduced and if mutual as well as separate organizational goals are to be achieved.

Importance of the Union-Management Relationship

The growth of a strong American labor movement during the past two decades has tended to reduce the occasion for conflict in certain areas by providing workers with an instrument of protection, protest, and action. But it has also increased the possibility of conflict with management on the determination of basic employment conditions. The bitter struggles over union recognition and representation in the thirties are too well known to require documentation or elaboration; and the more recent postwar disputes over wages and "union security" are fresh in our memories.

As the labor movement has consolidated its strength in the United States and as American employers have learned to accept and bargain with unions,

[2] This statement is based on the assumption that the firm's profit goals will not be met *without* an effective work force which, in a democracy and under conditions of full employment, cannot be driven to tasks but must voluntarily want to do them in return for the fulfillment (at least partial) of its own goals. "Proof" of this proposition is found in the increasing number of successful firms which have devoted major attention to improving personnel administration and union-management relations. This is not scientific proof, for other factors are also at work to explain the success of the firm, and there are cases of profitable firms which appear to have very poor relationships with employees and unions. But these are becoming less frequent in American industry, especially as the strength of unions has increased. Further evidence of the correspondence between enterprise objectives and the reduction of conflict in employer-employee relations may be found in the work of the social psychologists on leadership. For one analysis applicable to industry, see Douglas McGregor, "Conditions of Effective Leadership in the Industrial Organization," *Journal of Consulting Psychology*, 8 (1944), 55–63.

[3] For a fuller discussion, see Solomon Barkin, "A Trade Unionist Appraises Management Personnel Philosophy," *Harvard Business Review*, Vol. 38, No. 5 (September, 1950); and Wight Bakke, *Mutual Survival: The Goal of Unions and Management*, New York, Harper, 1946.

the amount of open conflict has declined in many industries. Public policies protecting the right to organize and bargain collectively have certainly hastened the maturing process. This does not mean that employers and unions generally now accept each other's goals; but it does mean that the attempts of each to destroy the other are largely in the past.

The variety of union-management relationships in the United States is still great, however, ranging from periodic open and ill-disguised hostility to harmonious and cooperative relationships, sometimes with a tinge of collusion at the expense of the consumer.[4] Management's efforts to reduce conflict over basic employment relations are always within the context of the particular union-management relationship. Even nonunion firms approach these problems with an eye to their impact on possible unionization.

If management is seeking to avoid unionization or to weaken or contain an existing union in the plant, its approach toward wage determination or other aspects of the employment relationship will be different from the approach of the management which wholeheartedly accepts the union as an institution with problems and goals of its own. In the former case, management will generally attempt to use the personnel-administration program as a means of strengthening the ties of loyalty with individual employees, by-passing the union if possible. In the latter, management recognizes the importance of a strong, well-disciplined union as a communication channel to and from employees, and the personnel program is developed as a means of strengthening both the employer-employee relationship and the union-management relationship and not as a means of driving a wedge between employees and the union. A major effort is made by both parties here to accommodate conflicting interests and to work out mutually acceptable solutions to the problems of the employment relationship.[5]

Back of every union-management relationship is the power element. The union's ultimate right to strike may be the final factor which persuades management to reach an agreement, just as management's ultimate right to close the plant may force the union to make a proposal which is more acceptable to management. Power may not be equally distributed, however, and when a management possesses more strength than a weak union, the determination of employment conditions will be essentially unilateral on management's terms. Conversely, if the union is dominant, employment conditions established by union-management agreement elsewhere will be imposed on the weaker management. But the seeds of conflict are present in these situations; the weaker party is always looking for an opening to press an advantage, and discontent is just under the surface.

This background must be borne in mind in the following discussion of the ways in which American management has attempted to reduce and remove conflicts arising over unfair or inadequate levels of wages, unstable and ir-

---

[4] For fuller discussions of types of union-management relationships in the United States, see Frederick H. Harbison and John R. Coleman, *Goals and Strategies in Collective Bargaining,* New York, Harper, 1951; and Benjamin M. Selekman, "Varieties of Labor Relations," *Harvard Business Review,* 27 (March, 1949), 175–199.

[5] For detailed examples of this type of relationship, see the case studies, *The Causes of Industrial Peace under Collective Bargaining,* Washington, National Planning Association, 1948–1953.

regular employment, arbitrary and capricious management action, and inadequate employee status and recognition.

Company Wage Policies

Wages represent "costs" to business firms, and "incomes" as well as "status" to employees. The division of the product of industry between employees and other claimants, therefore, always involves actual or potential conflicts. Management, concerned with the profitability and survival of the firm, is faced with pressures which affect what it is willing to do in setting wage levels and in making changes in these levels. Employees and, in unionized firms, the union representatives also face pressures which affect their willingness to accept management's wage offers. Management's task in reducing conflict, therefore, has been to try to resolve these pressures and reach an accommodation of the wage objectives of managements, employees, and unions.[6]

Increasingly, with the spread of collective bargaining and strong national unions, employers have been concerned with "keeping in line" with other comparable employers on wage levels and wage changes.[7] Wages which are in line with those in other firms are more acceptable to employees and easier to defend. Thus they meet the minimum labor-supply objectives of employers: holding present workers and not discouraging new applicants. This is true of nonunion as well as unionized firms, although the former tend to relate their wage levels somewhat more to the local labor market as a means of attracting and retaining workers and also avoiding unionization.[8] Collective bargaining in industries like basic steel, major autos, "Big 4" rubber, "Big 4" meat packing, flat glass, and Class 1 railroads has resulted in industry-oriented rather than community-oriented wage policies. Normally, therefore, firms in these industries are more concerned with what their product-market competitors are paying labor than with what their labor-market competitors are doing. But even in these industries, local labor-market pressures become important when there are serious local manpower shortages and, conversely, when local unemployment is greater than in other communities.

While the pressure of what other firms are doing, either locally or in the industry, is probably the predominant one on management wage policy,

---

[6] Much of the following is based on recent research on company and union wage policies. Among these studies are the following: Richard A. Lester, *Company Wage Policies: A Survey of Patterns and Experience,* Princeton, N.J., Princeton University Press, 1948; Arthur M. Ross, *Trade Union Wage Policy,* Berkeley, University of California Press, 1948; Lloyd G. Reynolds, *The Structure of Labor Markets,* New York, Harper, 1951; George P. Shultz, *Pressures on Wage Decisions,* New York, Wiley and Technology Press, 1951; and Charles A. Myers and George P. Shultz, *The Dynamics of a Labor Market,* New York, Prentice-Hall, 1951.

[7] Earlier, some large firms were known as "wage leaders" and often consciously sought to pay above "prevailing rates" in order to attract better employees. Many of these have found that "unions have considerably increased the costs or disadvantages of wage leadership," since the unions tend to use a favorable settlement in one firm as the basis for demands on others. Consequently, some of the former wage leaders now try to stay in line with other large firms in the industry. For examples, see Lester, *op. cit.,* p. 43.

[8] Cf. Myers and Shultz, *op. cit.,* Chap. 8.

other pressures are intermingled with this. Product-market competition, a declining level of business activity in the industry, and the worsening financial condition of the firm force some managements to "get tough" in negotiating wage changes with unions. Faced with these conditions, which often mean some loss of employment, unions have frequently been less aggressive in making wage demands and more accommodating in reaching agreement with management.[9] Thus the pressure of what Ross has called "coercive comparison," which drives most unions and managements to agree on the "patterns" set by key bargains in periods of expanding or full employment, when profits are good, becomes relatively less important as economic conditions in the firm or industry become less favorable. In other words, "ability to pay" is inevitably an important consideration in wage policies, emphasized in good times by unions and in lean times by employers.

Still another pressure, usually an upward one in recent years, is the change in the "cost of living," or consumers' price index. Since changes in the index represent a definite quantity, both management and unions have a readily available fact to support their respective positions. The possibility of using cost-of-living-index changes as the basis for wage changes, in the effort to reduce conflict, is illustrated by the well-known General Motors-UAW agreements of 1948 and 1950, which have been widely followed in other industries since the start of the Korean war and adopted by the Wage Stabilization Board as a basis for approving wage changes under controls.

Another General Motors-UAW innovation in wage policy was the "annual improvement factor," providing a specific annual wage increase in recognition of the fact that "a continuing improvement in the standard of living of employees depends upon technological progress, better tools, methods, processes and equipment, and a cooperative attitude on the part of all parties in such progress." [10] Thus increased productivity, the factor which has accounted for the long-term rise in real wages in the United States, was specifically recognized in an important labor-management agreement.

It is obvious that these pressures vary over time and are often conflicting at the same time. In the absence of generally agreed-upon criteria for determining wage levels and changes,[11] managements—and unions—are inclined to use only those criteria or arguments which they believe will most convincingly support the position they have adopted in response to the pressures on them. The ability of management to resolve these pressures successfully depends, in part, on the skill and maturity brought to the problem of wage determination and, in part, on the relative importance of wage costs to the firm.

When wages are a small part of total costs, as in the oil industry, for

[9] The absence of many general wage changes following the 1948–1949 recession is a good example. For other illustrations, see George Seltzer, "Pattern Bargaining and the United Steel Workers," *Journal of Political Economy,* 59 (August, 1951), 319–331; and Myers and Shultz, *op. cit.* Chap. 9.

[10] Agreement of 1950 between General Motors and the UAW. It is worth noting that this improvement factor was not related to any measurement of increases in labor productivity in General Motors alone.

[11] Cf. John T. Dunlop, "The Economics of Wage-dispute Settlement," *Law and Contemporary Problems,* 12 (Spring, 1947), 281–296; and Sumner H. Slichter, *Basic Criteria Used in Wage Negotiations,* Chicago, Chicago Association of Commerce and Industry, 1947.

example, and when for various other reasons operations have been fairly profitable, wage determination has not generally been a great source of friction. Management in these situations is in a better position to meet the pressures of employees and of the union on wages without threatening the survival of the firm and its continued growth. The "economic compatibility" of the parties is easier to achieve.[12] When these favorable conditions are not present, however, management's only alternative to open conflict is the frank factual presentation of the situation facing the firm, its employees, and their union representatives.

American managements have increasingly adopted the approach that it is better to be candid about the pressures on wage policies at all times than to become "factual" only when the shoe pinches management's foot. There has been, therefore, an increasing use of the following in wage negotiations: wage surveys to find out what other comparable firms and industries are paying; factual presentations of the firm's production, inventory, sales, and earnings data for the current year or period and expected near-term trends, including capital requirements; and cost-of-living data. The effort to relate wage determination to these factual bases is not easily made, and a considerable experience of demonstrating management's honesty and good faith is required before mutual trust and respect is established. Even then there is no guarantee that conflict will be eliminated, but the chances of its being reduced are greater.

Within recent years, conflicts have also arisen over the "fringe" aspects of the wage bargain: paid vacation, paid holidays, pensions, and other benefits. Formerly, these were often unilaterally determined by management, but unions have shown increasing interest in improving these conditions as a supplement to, or in lieu of, basic wage increases. Detailed discussion of these fringe items is impossible here, but it is obvious that the same pressures have affected the parties as in the case of wage changes. Essentially, the same possibilities of agreement or of conflict are present.

One important and largely unsolved aspect of the wage question is the regularity with which wages are paid over the year. Organized labor's demand for a "guaranteed annual wage," recently revived by the UAW and the Steelworkers, is an indication of the importance attached by workers and unions to the total amount of wages received as income as well as to the hourly rate or earnings.

Management's Efforts to Stabilize Employment

The guaranteed annual wage makes sense only in terms of fairly stable annual employment. In a competitive, market economy is it possible for individual firms to achieve stable employment for most of their employees? The answer to this question will indicate the extent to which individual employers can provide guaranteed annual wages and the extent to which it may be necessary to rely on government fiscal and monetary policies as a means

---

[12] For a discussion of a specific case, see Clark Kerr and Roger Randall, "Crown Zellerbach Corporation and the Pacific Coast Pulp and Paper Industry," Case Study 1 in *Causes of Industrial Peace under Collective Bargaining,* Washington, National Planning Association, 1948, Chap. 5.

of assuring full employment and, hence, achieving regularity of wage incomes by another route.

There is a long history in America of company efforts to stabilize employment.[13] These have been most successful, however, with respect to seasonal and intermittent unemployment; cyclical unemployment is largely outside the control of individual firms. Among the methods used to regularize sales and, therefore, employment are the following: developing new uses and new markets for existing products, adding new products and diversifying the line of products generally, simplifying particular products to avoid small-lot orders, and changing consumers' buying habits by advertising and sales promotions in off seasons. When seasonal variations in sales persist, it is still possible to regularize employment by the following devices: manufacturing standard products for inventory during slack sales periods and standardizing products to permit this, developing a flexible schedule of hours to provide overtime work at straight time rates during busy seasons and work sharing at less-than-normal hours during slack seasons, and deferring maintenance and repair work for slack seasons. To facilitate these methods of regularizing employment, firms have also centralized the initial hiring and layoff procedure, trained workers for more than one job, and transferred them from job to job and from department to department as operations fluctuated.

How effective are these methods, and how general is their application? Certainly in the firms whose experience is most publicized, the results are striking. Such firms as Procter & Gamble Co., Nunn Bush Shoe Co., and Geo. A. Hormel & Co. have achieved greater stability of employment and of wage incomes, under plans which differ somewhat in their details. To be sure, these firms are in consumer, nondurable-goods industries which enjoy a relatively stable demand, and those who deprecate what employers can do individually to stabilize employment continually stress this point. But these firms had considerable seasonal unemployment before serious efforts were made to reduce it. Furthermore, there are examples in virtually every industry, including automobiles and machine tools,[14] of ingenious employer efforts to iron out some of the irregularities that occur when management is unconcerned about stability of employment and wages. Many executives still tend to make sudden decisions and to implement them immediately, unwilling to delay action so that the impact on workers can be cushioned. As one writer [15] has said of the most

[13] A full account is found in Herman Feldman, *Stabilizing Jobs and Wages*, New York, Harper, 1940.

[14] The change in the date of the annual model change-over helped to reduce some irregularity of employment in the automobile industry, and the UAW has claimed that more could be done along this line. For other examples in other industries, see Feldman, *op. cit.;* and *To Make Jobs More Steady and to Make More Steady Jobs*, St. Paul, Minnesota American Legion Foundation, 1944.

[15] A. D. H. Kaplan, *The Guarantee of Annual Wages*, Washington, Brookings, 1947, p. 76. Another study concludes: "Although the guarantee of work and wages has become an important management issue, the great majority of business managers have not given it the attention it deserves. Businessmen generally need to make a mental readjustment, involving a willingness to study the issue, and also to develop a conviction that they must do everything possible to increase the regularity of wages." Joseph L. Snider, *The Guarantee of Work and Wages*, Boston, Harvard Business School Division of Research, 1947, p. 169.

successful stabilization (and annual-wage) plans, "each of them was inaugurated by executives ardently devoted to the idea and willing to give the program the large amount of effort that its success entailed. . . . It was not only thought out in advance, but it was thoroughly gone over with the employees, and it received a high measure of acceptance from them before it was inaugurated."

It is true, however, that employment fluctuations are normally greater in the consumers' durable- and capital-goods industries than in the industries where the most striking stabilization efforts have taken place. The possibility of achieving the *same degree* of success is consequently less. This means that the prospect of a guaranteed annual wage for all present employees in consumers' durable- and capital-goods industries is more limited, in so far as the ability to pay such wages depends upon previously stabilized employment.

There is no experience with an industry-wide guaranteed annual wage, which is implicit in the union demands. Careful analyses of the consequences of imposing such a requirement on all firms in an industry indicate that business changes and expansion would be impeded and that, consequently, a rigid guarantee would conflict with the possibility of achieving and maintaining full employment.[16] In other words, a guarantee should not be imposed which will commit the firm to providing more than it can reasonably provide with careful management attention to stabilization of employment. Many managements can do more to provide regular work and wages than they are now doing, and the demand for a formal guarantee forces them to do more. But it must be a *limited* guarantee, as most of the present plans are, since it is impossible for any single employer to guarantee all present employees their present jobs for an indefinite period. Moreover, the guarantee should be integrated with the present unemployment-compensation system, and corporate tax laws should be amended to permit the accumulation of tax-free wage reserves.[17]

To summarize, irregular employment and wage incomes will continue to be a source of conflict between managements and labor until more attention is given by management to achieving what it is demonstrably possible to achieve in stabilizing employment. But continued high-level employment is a necessary and permissive condition for successful wage guarantees by individual employers.

Even though management may succeed in providing wage guarantees and adequate wage levels, however, the possibilities of conflict over other employment conditions remain. The principal remaining areas of actual or potential conflict involve arbitrary management action and inadequate employee status and recognition.

---

[16] Kaplan, *op. cit.*, Chap. 9; and Alvin H. Hansen and Paul A. Samuelson, "Economic Analysis of Guaranteed Wages," Appendix F in *Guaranteed Wages*, report to the President by the Office of War Mobilization and Reconversion Advisory Board, 1947. Hansen and Samuelson conclude (p. 453): "There are important limitations to the device [guaranteed wages] as an anti-depression measure—especially in comparison with other economic policies such as fiscal policy and other full employment programs. In view of these limitations, so long as our society suffers from rather wide fluctuations in business activity, Guaranteed Wage plans should be introduced only with proper safeguards."

[17] Similar proposals were made by Hansen and Samuelson, *op. cit.*, Chap. 6.

Reducing Arbitrary Management Action

The growth of trade-unionism in the United States was a challenge to the unilateral right of management to take action regarding conditions of employment. This, in itself, has reduced the possibility that arbitrary or capricious management decisions would continue to be the occasion for conflict that they were in the past. The union is now ready to question management when the "law of the shop"—the collective agreement—is not observed by management representatives, and the grievance procedure is the usual channel by which these complaints are resolved. All of this has been a positive gain for industrial peace during the last two decades.

There have been, of course, changing standards of what constitutes arbitrary management action. As unions have grown in power, actions which would have been ignored in earlier days are now challenged. Approaches which were commonly used by an earlier generation of management are now rejected by the newer group of managers which grew up with unions and which has been exposed to more enlightened management methods.

Management itself has sought to reduce the possibility of arbitrary action by its representatives. In part, the growth of strong unions forced management to do this in self-protection, in order to avoid work interruptions and time-consuming grievance negotiations. Also important, however, has been the growth of the management viewpoint discussed earlier. With or without unions, arbitrary and capricious management orders and actions are now often seen as disruptive of employee morale and inadequate for the achievement of management's goal of building effective work teams to accomplish the organization's objectives.

This is the real significance of the personnel-administration, or "human-relations," approach of modern industrial management; any other approach is simply poor management. Arbitrary management action has declined as a consequence of the emphasis on management and supervisory training in human relations, the general practice of advance explanation and consultation before taking action, and the development of consistent policies which are uniformly applied throughout the organization.

Improving Employee Status and Recognition

These same two concurrent developments—the growth of strong unionism and the change in management's personnel approach—have done much to restore the status and recognition which employees lost when they became members of large industrial organizations whose principal concern was for technical efficiency largely regardless of human costs. Job dilution, work simplification, and subdivision and specialization of labor were carried in some plants to the point where employee resistance to change and lowered morale and productivity were common.

The task for effective management was to provide job satisfactions from work which would result in high productivity. In part, management has tried to do this through well-rounded personnel programs which stressed the importance of treating workers as individuals with goals and problems on the job as well as outside the plant. More recently, there has been an effort by some managements to restore certain job satisfactions through "job enlargement," through giving each employee a job which he can see as more clearly related to the whole product or service of the enterprise.[18] This is not the "speed-up" or increased work assignments requiring greater effort; instead the objective is to restore some of the status workers possessed before the introduction of the worst practices of "scientific management."

Still another approach is to develop greater "participation" by employees in the solving of production problems, one by-product of which is increasing employee status and recognition. However, unions have more frequently pressed management into programs of this sort than management has been willing to initiate them. This is because some managements have feared sharing information and problem solving with employees and union representatives. Encouraging employee participation in meeting the problems of the firm is largely meaningless without real problems to work on and full sharing of information. The response, both in terms of productivity and in terms of employee status and recognition, from successful participation plans is evidence of their value in reducing employer-employee and union-management conflicts.[19]

Union membership itself has brought improved status and recognition to employees. When management has accepted the union and attempted to develop amicable relations, employees who are union officers enjoy a new type of industrial citizenship—participating in the joint determination of basic conditions of employment and in solving a multitude of day-to-day problems arising in the plant. Active union members, using the grievance procedure and participating in union meetings which involve decision making, also achieve a new position and new satisfactions. As unions grow larger and become more centralized, however, it may be questioned whether union membership always brings these benefits to the rank-and-file worker.[20]

Concluding Observations

We have seen in this chapter how the growth of a strong labor movement and the development of a new philosophy of management in America have served to reduce the possibilities of conflict over four principal, basic, employment relations: (1) unfair or inadequate levels of wages, (2) unstable and irregular employment, (3) arbitrary and capricious management action, and (4) inadequate employee status and recognition. Real progress has been made in the last 20 years in reducing the tensions arising in each of these areas.

It has been suggested, however, that the absence of conflict is itself an insufficient criterion for evaluating the quality of labor-management relations.[21]

[18] James C. Worthy, "Organizational Structure and Employee Morale," *American Sociological Review*, 15 (April, 1950), 169–179.

[19] See Russell Davenport, "Enterprise for Everyman," *Fortune*, January, 1950. For a fuller discussion of these programs, see Chap. 27 in this volume.

[20] For fuller discussions, see Chaps. 7, 9, and 21 in this volume; and George Strauss and Leonard Sayles, "The Unpaid Local Union Leader," *Harvard Business Review*, 30 (May–June, 1952), 91–104.

[21] Cf. Harbison and Coleman, *op. cit.*, Chap. 6.

In an "armed-truce" relationship, for example, the competition between the union and management for the loyalty of employees may result in better employment conditions. Management may pay higher wages, provide steadier employment, avoid arbitrary action, and do various things to improve employee status and recognition in order to develop loyalty to the company. Unions, on their part, may make continual demands for material improvements and more assiduously protect employee interests as a means of winning membership loyalty to the union. In harmonious situations, on the other hand, there is the possibility that the desire of both parties for good union-management relations may obscure what happens to the basic conditions of employment enjoyed by employees as union members.

While all of this can, and probably does, occur in some instances, the undercurrent of conflict which is always present in the armed-truce type of relationship is a constant threat to the ability of management and unions to achieve their respective (and, in part, common) goals. There is a positive gain in a democratic society when important institutional groups, such as managements and unions, are able to accommodate their interests to each other. The process of accommodation need not be at the expense of workers as employees and union members or at the expense of consumers, as case studies have shown. And the alternative to successful accommodation is conflict—latent or open. This is not an appealing alternative in a society which is built on increasingly interdependent economic units and which puts a high value on the freedom of economic interest groups to work out their own problems without government interference.

CHAPTER 25 WAGE ADMINISTRATION AND PRODUCTION STANDARDS

Edward R. Livernash   *Harvard University*

INDUSTRIAL conflict arising over a particular wage rate or over one of the many aspects of a particular wage-incentive plan is not necessarily attributable to an improper or inequitable wage rate or effort relationship. The more general causes of conflict may simply find an outlet in the form of a wage-rate or incentive grievance. Two specific points should be emphasized in this respect. The first is the importance of the basic attitudes of the parties plus the degree of mutual understanding between them. The second is the mingling of general wage-level considerations with internal wage-rate conflict. Each of these points will be discussed before turning to a brief analysis of internal rate relationships and to various wage-rate procedures and problems.

The Importance of Basic Attitudes

Union leaders almost unanimously take an extremely negative attitude toward all of the so-called scientific procedures employed in the administration of the internal wage-rate structure. At the same time there are many instances in which a particular union and a particular management are employing these techniques constructively and harmoniously. Why, in concept at least, are unions so critical, for example, of job evaluation?

Union authors have stated important specific objections to job evaluation which relate primarily to its lack of precise validity and to its failure to give consideration to relevant determinants outside the sphere of job content.[1] Giving weight to these objections and also admitting the difficulty and risk of the period of introduction, union arguments and objections appear only to qualify the usefulness of evaluation. They do not negate its value. They do not appear to be adequate reasons to account for the distrust and suspicion of evaluation as something to be avoided like the plague. They do not square with the instances of constructive and harmonious use.

In some instances management has been motivated to adopt job evaluation in order to control autocratically, or at least more autocratically, internal rate relationships. Job evaluation may thus be set up as a scientific procedure in which the word "scientific" may be read as "management prerogative." To

---

[1] See, for example, Solomon Barkin, "Wage Determination: Trick or Technique," *Labor and Nation,* June–July, 1946; and William Gomberg, "Union Attitudes on the Application of Industrial Engineering Techniques to Collective Bargaining," *Personnel,* May, 1948, p. 445.

the extent that job evaluation is employed as a device to narrow or avoid collective bargaining, it obviously creates distrust and suspicion and breeds conflict. The fact that it may be so used and the fear that it will be are certainly important phases of the explanation of the general negative union attitude.

As with so many personnel procedures and techniques, the manner of administration is of extreme importance. In one environment of attitude and policy a job-evaluation plan may be constructive, in another the identical plan may be the focus of irritation and conflict. Democratic and autocratic evaluation ought not to sail under the same flag. Moreover, students must recognize that administrative policy reflects, perhaps unconsciously, basic labor-relations attitudes.[2] Such attitudes do not exist in a vacuum, and there is a "latent" as well as a "manifest" base to specific administrative procedures, policies, and actions.

In a similar vein there is a claim to precise scientific determination of wage-incentive standards, which is in fact a reflection of basic management attitude. The feeling that any criticism of a wage-incentive standard is uncalled for because of the validity of the procedure for establishing standards is on a logical par with a union's refusal to accept any standard, other than "more," for the resolution of a controversy. While everyone pays lip service to the importance of basic attitudes and policies, the place to study this general topic is in day-to-day administrative decisions and actions.

Of course, the degree of bitterness and the extent of conflict over the internal rate structure will be influenced by basic attitudes regardless of the method of payment and whether or not one or more of the various technical procedures are used. Also the terms "autocratic" and "democratic" are in danger of misinterpretation. Their meaning is certainly not identical with that commonly understood in the field of political science. With reference to the internal rate structure, the distinction between a reasonably open-minded approach to the correctness of initial management decisions and a fairly closed-minded approach, while admittedly oversimplified, may be closer to the mark. Finally, there is a range of difference for union attitudes as well as for management attitudes. The reasonably constructive versus the highly belligerent attitude shown in different union situations will serve to illustrate.

The purpose of these remarks is to make it clear that merit rating, job evaluation, time study, effort rating, and other such procedures can never be divorced in discussion or application from basic union and management attitudes and their interaction. Procedures are not panaceas, as witnessed by the vivid recollection of a purple-faced executive whose opening gun was "that damned union has ruined *my* job-evaluation plan."

The General Wage Level and Internal Rates

Job evaluation in its purest form maintains a clear-cut distinction between the general level of wage rates and wage differentials. There is much to be said for keeping the pay for the particular man, for the particular job,

---

[2] Many phases of D. McGregor, I. Knickerbocker, M. Haire, and A. Bavelas, "The Consultant Role and Organizational Leadership: Improving Human Relationships in Industry," *The Journal of Social Issues*, Vol. 4, No. 3 (Summer, 1948), bear upon this point.

and for all jobs collectively in separate administrative boxes with separate standards for the validity of the changes involved. There is also a logic and meaning to the internal rate structure. Nevertheless, there is some danger of becoming too sophisticated in our analysis. Certainly the motivation for many individual wage-rate grievances is indistinguishable from the type of discontent leading to a demand for a general wage increase. In a period of rising cost of living with general wage movements and general discontent in the air, individual rate grievances appear to become more frequent.[3]

Sitting through several months of initial grievances accompanying the introduction of an evaluation plan for state employees reinforced this opinion of mixed motivation. Some employees had no complaint over their job description nor over their job rating nor over their pay in relation to other state jobs with which they were familiar. They simply were not getting enough money to keep up with the cost of living and relative to prevailing rates. Other employees who argued job rating appeared to do so insincerely and were expressing a general discontent. The point, of course, may also be reversed. Some who stated general discontent felt a keen sense of injustice in the distortion of customary rate relationships or in the fairness of a newly created alignment of rates. The point, however, is that perfection in internal rate alignment, if such could be defined and achieved, would not eliminate individual rate grievances.

It is likely that lower-paying highly competitive industries and lower-paying companies within an industry have more individual rate grievances than those industries and companies in which there is a relatively more satisfactory general level of wages. It is also likely that attitude studies assigning little importance to the general level of wages as a source of discontent have been conducted, for the most part, in companies in which the general level of rates is comparatively good.

Whatever may be the particularized motivation for various individual wage grievances, a negative working hypothesis may be repeated: they are not all attributable to the logic of internal rate relationships.[4]

The Organization of the Internal Wage-rate Structure

When we attempt a logical analysis of the internal rate structure, it must be admitted that defining a correct relationship is far from easy. Job evaluation never pinpoints the placement of a job, and neither does comparison with market rates. Market comparisons are rarely possible for a very high proportion of jobs and, where possible, usually yield a fairly wide range of rates frequently with no clear mode.

The lack of precision, by whatever standards are applied, to determine a correct rate for a particular job leads one to wonder why there are not more

[3] This is only an opinion from limited observation in particular companies and of petitions to the NWLB and the Wage Stabilization Board. Knowledge of the timing and frequency of individual rate grievances is in fact very limited.

[4] The interaction of general wage-level influences and grievances, with an analysis of various related considerations, is well demonstrated for a particular segment of an industry in George P. Shultz, *Pressures on Wage Decisions,* New York, Wiley and Technology Press, 1951.

wage grievances than there actually are. Why is there among employees such a high degree of acceptance of established wage differentials?

This may seem a strange question in that it is the reverse of the one usually asked, but there is hardly a rate for which a plausible case could not be made for at least a modest change. Because of the indefiniteness of wage standards, such a change in either direction would be approximately as logical as the existing rate. Still most workers on most jobs continue to accept existing differentials.

A partial explanation is that the rate becomes so closely associated with the job that, in one sense, it is the job. One job may be a "better" job than another simply because it pays more. The social structure in the work environment adjusts to, and builds upon, the rate structure as it has traditionally existed. Ambitions are centered upon working up the wage ladder, with complex seniority patterns woven into the promotional customs, and the social standing associated with the particular job is to a considerable degree dependent on the rate. A worker who might tear up the plant to correct a 10-cent accounting error in his week's pay might also work all his life without seriously questioning a rate for a job.

It is not easy to say to what degree and in what respects the logic of job content is unimportant. A number of specific examples come to mind: (1) In one company all the major maintenance crafts are in the same labor grade and rate range. This evaluated result follows a previous custom of equal payment. In a neighboring plant these same craft skills carry historical differentials. In each instance they are accepted as correct. (2) Within one industry several different skilled jobs are at the top of the pay ladder in different companies. Where job *A* is at the top it appears to be regarded as most skilled by management and employees alike. The same is true where job *B* is the most highly paid. (3) A recent discussion between several officials of a company (no grievance was involved) related to increasing a job some 40 cents per hour. The differential with an associated job had been constant for 25 years. The logic for change was good, but no serious consideration was given to such an unheard-of change in established relationships. These examples illustrate the strength and importance of custom.

On the other hand, where jobs are directly comparable through the specific type of skill involved, the lack of logical payment can readily become a grievance. Nurses on a disturbed ward feel logically entitled to more pay than nurses not on such wards; the multilith operator doing more difficult work wants more pay than the multilith operator doing less difficult work. Jobs within skill families are more closely knit on logical grounds than are job comparisons cutting across such families.

While logical comparisons are probably most significant within skill families, both logical and traditional relationships are also most meaningful (1) within work groups and (2) among key jobs. Neither the term "work group" nor "key job," however, can be easily defined.

Spatial and physical divisions help to define work groups, as do departmental and organizational distinctions. Skill families have already been mentioned, but there are also broader process divisions such as production, clerical supervisory, maintenance, etc., which mark off large areas of jobs. Female versus male jobs may create separate groups. Work flow and temporary interchange of employees create lines of comparison, as do promotional sequences. Large wage differentials are not typically the basis of individual grievances, as the top and bottom of the wage scale are too far removed for direct comparison (larger groups may, however, become involved in a broad skill-differential issue). The employee is most interested in "close" comparisons, though to some extent chain reactions may be set up by adjusting a particular rate. These chain reactions are limited or weakened by other group distinctions.

Just as some wage comparisons are more meaningful than others, so also some jobs are more important than others in knitting the internal wage structure together. The use of the term "key job" in this sense is not identical with its use in defining jobs which are most suited for labor-market comparisons nor with its use in the evaluation process of rating jobs. Nevertheless, most jobs which are important in market comparisons are also important in the internal rate structure. They do, in general, connect the internal rate structure with external wage forces.

The concept of a key job in the internal rate structure can be understood by considering the following questions as to various jobs: If the wage rate on this job is changed *how many* and *what other* wage grievances may well be created? In some cases almost no other jobs will be affected; in other cases a particular group of jobs, without any widespread reaction; in still other cases practically every other job, in a broad group or the entire organization.

In making the above statement, there must be qualifications as to the amount of the adjustment, the reasons for the change, the timing involved, and other surrounding circumstances. Knowledge is so limited that there is no point in attempting to generalize to any great extent on individual observation, but the loose hypothesis being suggested is that one or more key jobs dominate a group, that nonkey jobs can be changed with minor repercussions within the group, that the key jobs can only be changed by also adjusting most of the jobs within the group, and that a key-job change, depending upon the importance of the key job, may necessitate changes in other key jobs, approximating plant-wide repercussions in some cases.

The purpose in discussing the organization of the internal rate structure has not been to state a complete theory or explanation. Rather the purpose has been to clarify and emphasize certain points: (1) The lack of precision of the standards for determining wage differentials must mean, in relation to the number of grievances, that most workers most of the time accept the rate as a traditional and customary part of the job. It also means that individual grievances may be motivated by many psychological, sociological, and economic factors without conflicting drastically with available standards. Finally, no logical determination of wage differentials will eliminate completely all wage grievances, though in so far as such logical standards are agreed to and accepted, they can play an important role in reducing and settling grievances. (2) Both logical and traditional relationships among jobs are important. To some degree logical analysis may unconsciously accept existing relationships. The role of logic may also be of greatest importance in close comparisons rather than in broader relationships which express, with lags and distortions, labor-market forces. (3) Whatever general explanation of the internal rate structure may be evolved, it must recognize that not all wage-rate comparisons have equal meaning to employees and that not all jobs are of equal importance in the establishment and modification of the rate structure. There are many substructures within the administrative framework of wage determination for the company as a whole.

The Nature of Job Evaluation

Job evaluation involves the written description of job content, the analysis of this content in terms of job factors, and finally, the grouping of jobs into labor grades and the attaching of wage rates (single rates or rate ranges) to these labor grades.

The different systems of job evaluation are too diverse for description in this chapter. They vary from simple classification plans to ranking plans without point values and to various types of point plans. Most evaluation plans in use today are point plans. The National Metal Trades plan, with its predetermined scale associating points with defined degrees of each factor, is probably the most widely used single plan. There are now very few highly complex plans, and the differences among plans are not of great importance. This is particularly true since most plans have now gone through a considerable period of trial-and-error adjustment.

The job factors differ in number and in title and overlap within broad areas.[5] The factors may be grouped conveniently under the headings of skill, responsibility, working conditions, and effort. Skill and responsibility may even be combined as the more positive basis for payment and contrasted with working conditions and effort considered as the disutility aspect of payment.

The degree of skill is frequently rated directly under this heading, or a similar general title, and separately as (1) training and experience required and (2) knowledge required. The knowledge, education, or "know-how" phase of skill is quite distinct from the coordination and manual skill required in performing the job. Skill rated directly combines the above elements and may add a measure of the degree of complexity in something approaching a three-dimensional definition of the term. Training and experience required is the most easily understood measurement of skill, with its direct comparability to all types of work, though this last measurement is not so objective in application as might first be presumed.

Responsibility in nonsupervisory factory jobs is a difficult factor to analyze, understand, and apply. The definition frequently turns upon the possibility or probability and the amount of dollar damage to tools, equipment, material, and product. There appears to be a high correlation in the application of responsibility and skill factors to most factory jobs, though this statement is merely an opinion and might not be substantiated by thorough statistical analysis. The meaning of responsibility, however, is to a considerable degree an indirect measure of the skill required to avoid damage, and the correlation arises through this type of approach to responsibility.

[5] The high degree of overlap is made very clear in the series of studies by C. H. Lawshe, Jr., and associates, appearing in various issues of the *Journal of Applied Psychology*.

In so far as responsibility differentiates jobs from the norm established by skill, it appears to demand and pay for superior attention or diligence. Just how superior attention or diligence can in fact be expected or obtained on these special jobs is not altogether clear. Perhaps employee selection for, and retention on, certain jobs justifies differentiation as to responsibility, but again, it is not clear that market rates correlate with premium pay for responsibility apart from skill. Wherever the truth may lie, rating jobs on responsibility allows room for considerable difference of opinion.

The negative qualities of job content measured by more than normal physical effort and by undesirable working conditions are less important in total points than skill and responsibility. For this reason they do not appear to be too difficult to use, but from an abstract point of view they are not clear-cut concepts. Physical effort required on a job (being somewhat too critical) tends to degenerate into a weight-lifting contest, while the pillow stuffers are required to work the hardest. There is, however, a tradition and a reality in paying "heavy" work a premium. Hazard is difficult to evaluate, but there is also a very abstract judgment in measuring and equating noise, heat, fumes, and other undesirable features.

Opinions differ as to how precise and meaningful this process of factor analysis can be. Certainly, none of the factors are particularly objective, and attempts to narrow their scope to increase their objectivity come to grief, as they then no longer measure the required attribute. For example, one might try to use "tolerance required" to measure skill, but such a measure, while more objective, would not measure skill because of the various ways by which a given tolerance can be obtained. On the other hand, the factors do not bog down in a sea of confusion. A group of informed individuals rating jobs independently and through discussion typically reach substantial agreement.

The impression which it is intended to convey is that the factor-analysis process is a useful device to secure agreement as to the placement of jobs. Ratings do not employ measuring rods which can be validated to any meaningful degree apart from group judgment. No physiological measurement of fatigue would validate the physical effort ratings; statistical records of damaged product would not validate responsibility ratings; training time records would not distinguish between required, desired, and actual experience.

In considering job evaluation as a device to secure agreement on the placement of jobs, the weighting of the factors requires special consideration. Weights come from accepted wage differentials for key jobs. This is true in the over-all sense that, if working conditions were given a major weight and skill a minor weight, there would be no correlation with the realities of the market place. From this point of view, however, most plans in use today, through experience in prior applications, have arrived at satisfactory maximum weights.[6]

---

[6] This is not intended to rule out difference of opinion as to maximum weights, since increasing the weight of a given factor on all jobs may displace only a few jobs significantly and still preserve reasonable correlation with market rates. See the discussion of the weighting of responsibility and skill in Clark Kerr and Lloyd Fisher, "Effect of Environment and Administration on Job Evaluation," *Harvard Business Review*, May, 1950, p. 89.

Weighting is worked out in the process of placing key jobs on the skeleton scale. This must be done in such fashion that total points correspond with accepted wage differentials, and a certain amount of trial-and-error modification of placement of jobs to points may be considered as one phase of attaching wage rates to jobs. There is the assumption that, if the weights work out reasonably well for key jobs, they are therefore proper and adequate for all jobs.

The distribution of points in placing key jobs on the skeleton scale (with emphasis now upon key in an internal-rate-relationships sense) involves a kind of group judgment different from the process of rating skill among a family grouping of jobs. Consider maintenance job A and production job B. The scoring of only two jobs and on the basis of relative manual skills and job knowledge of diverse kinds seems to this writer to involve a large element of "how much should we pay these jobs" as the determinant of the scores. It must be added, however, that this rating judgment is made in an atmosphere of analysis which takes a fresh view of the worth of jobs apart from distortions of past technology, though never divorced completely from the conscious and unconscious influence of customs and tradition upon judgment.

Job evaluation must be tailored to fit the labor market in the placement of "external" key jobs on the skeleton scale and tailored to fit broad group judgments in placing the remaining "internal" key jobs on the scale. Points in the beginning of a plan are a complete abstraction and take on meaning as jobs are filled in to give specific content to broad definitions. Once the skeleton is formulated, other jobs are placed with a closer degree of direct comparison. Even in this latter process two different rating groups will have many variations of minor magnitude.

If the above view of the rating process and of the meaning of the factors is reasonably accurate, agreement is the essence of the detailed placement of jobs and of the formulation of the skeleton. Agreement is a process involving job analysts, an executive rating committee, supervisory opinions and criticism, and employee criticism and opinion. Employee criticism may be worked out through various forms of union participation either on a formal or informal basis. The degree to which agreement is achieved marks the degree of success of the initial application. Thus, if the evaluation process is viewed realistically, there is little meaning to a hard-and-fast contrast between a bargained and an evaluated scale except a more clear-cut recognition of objectives.

Before leaving the somewhat technical side of job evaluation, a reminder is in order that many of the wage improvements associated with evaluation come from administrative changes. The evaluation program may be associated with the centralization of wage-administration control. Going from more decentralized control to a higher degree of centralized control may create for the first time the opportunity to remove certain inequities. Day-to-day attention to wage differentials may be considerably strengthened, responsibility more clearly placed, and procedure more carefully worked out; and, in a broad sense, an organization may simply start carrying out a managerial function which had formerly been neglected.

Furthermore, job duties and responsibilities are more clearly established with attention to the distinguishing characteristics between closely associated jobs. Catchall titles are abolished or refined (many different jobs may have been paid under the title of clerk or common labor). Employees are more accurately allocated to job titles; rates are no longer personalized. Essentially identical jobs are paid under the same title or at least at the same rate, past technological and other changes are recognized in stating job content, and other common-sense grounds for equity of payment are recognized.

The rate structure may be improved by reducing the number of rates of pay to fit a simple system of labor grades, thus wiping out many meaningless rate differentials. The job-title structure is also usually simplified. The study of jobs may also clarify promotional sequences, improve hiring and training, and increase efficiency through process and organizational changes.

Job Evaluation as a Source of Conflict

The most important problem in the use of job evaluation has been discussed in the introduction to this chapter: the question of basic management and union attitudes. This can now, however, be clarified in some important respects. The first is the period of introduction of job evaluation.

If the management constructs the evaluation plan and brings the finished product to the union with an insistence upon accepting the placement of jobs virtually without criticism, the plan may well, if accepted, usher in a period of unrest and bitterness leading to its destruction.

Under the above circumstances the union may take a militant attitude toward the plan, bring grievances at every opportunity, and push each grievance with a get-all-we-can attitude; and the net result is that the grievance pot boils even more vigorously in the atmosphere of points and factors than it did in the absence of such refinements. This is likely to be especially true since the employees have not had an opportunity to digest and accept the changes. Any wage change in which some employees get more than others disturbs existing social relationships among jobs in a very fundamental way and can be neither rushed nor pushed.

On the other hand, if the management objective is to use evaluation as a basis for securing agreement upon a more equitable wage structure and the union accepts this basic goal, the period of introduction can be one in which employee morale is strengthened. This is not to say that every employee will be satisfied with the placement of his job nor that the management will be entirely satisfied with some of the revisions that have worked their way into the plan through union and employee criticism, but the true attitude of both parties will be that the wage structure has been improved. The majority of employees will share this opinion. Such a period of introduction provides a mutual basis for a future administrative approach which requires a reason for the modification of the accepted placement.

With tolerance on both sides the evaluation process at least narrows the range of bargaining and separates general discontent from reasoned changes. It cannot rule out meaningful considerations which are not strictly part of the job-content analysis, such as extra consideration for dead-end jobs, changes in particular market rates, craft rivalry, and other such influences, but it is not particularly a distortion of evaluation to recognize some element of outside considerations within the factor analysis. Nor is it out of the question to have some outright exceptions to the plan as long as the reason for their existence is clearly stated and recognized.

One particular policy consideration stands out, in addition to the fundamental goal implied above, and that is the acceptance of the effect of technological change upon wage rates. If technological change reduces the skill required to perform a job, the job must be reduced to its appropriate rating. This does not mean that individual employees need to be cut, but new employees must accept the appropriate rate of pay for the new job.

If a union is unwilling to accept this concept and to recognize that sharing the gains of technological progress should be through the avenue of a general increase in all rates, there is no point in attempting to introduce an evaluation program. Again minor compromise in application may be absorbed without destroying a plan, but the policy must be mutually acceptable to avoid continuous controversy of a major nature.

Over time, conflict between market rates and evaluated placement may develop. The significance of this problem will depend upon the labor market in which evaluation is being used. A plant with a relatively high general level of rates is in a much more favorable position to avoid such problems. So also is a plant geographically isolated from other firms in the same industry. A highly structured unionized market may make a lone-wolf approach to evaluation unwise. Again, however, if a policy of meeting market rates in general but not necessarily in particular is mutually acceptable, as it should be if evaluation is to be used as the major wage-differential criterion, conflict should not be particularly serious on this score. If major changes in wage differentials should occur, a basic revision in evaluation placement may be required to readjust the plan.

Job evaluation does not necessarily create nor alleviate conflict, but there is no issue in job evaluation that cannot be resolved to the mutual satisfaction of both labor and management. The most fundamental gain is in squarely facing broad policies involved in the administration of the rate structure such as technological change and the manner in which market rates will be met. A satisfactory frame of reference for the settlement of grievances can be evolved. In a common-sense way a more equitable rate structure can be created in good part through improved administrative machinery.

These gains do not come from the procedure as such. They come from improved understanding and improved administration. Lacking these fundamentals, evaluation can aggravate or at least perpetuate conflict over rates.

The Bargained Rate Structure

No hard-and-fast distinction can be made between a bargained and an evaluated scale. Consider, for example, two transitional situations. In one instance a company has worked out an evaluation plan which they use unilaterally as a general guide. The union accepts evaluation standards on an informal basis for most wage grievances. Policy issues have been faced with reasonable clarity and administration is good. The wage structure and wage policy are more satisfactory than in some instances of impressive formal plans.

In another instance a very informal classification plan with labor grades but no specific evaluation system is administered very harmoniously and constructively through a union-management wage committee. While this procedure might be judged inferior from a technical point of view, it is difficult to see how any improvement in labor-management relations could be obtained by a change in procedure.

Finally, many bargained structures are perfectly satisfactory to the management, the union, and the employees. The number of rate grievances is not excessive, and those that arise are settled in a reasonable, constructive way. In some wage structures the number of distortions may be sufficiently great that evaluation would be a meaningful gain, but it is easy to exaggerate the benefits, particularly as the period of introduction involves considerable time and effort with no guarantee as to the ultimate improvement of morale.

Wage Incentive Plans and Production Standards

Wage incentive plans build upon an evaluated or otherwise determined hourly rate structure. The most common system is probably one in which a base rate is set, equivalent to the minimum or midpoint of the hourly rate range, with the production standard set to yield about 25 or 30 per cent above base for the normal operator.

Piece-rate industries and companies very often have no clear-cut separation between the base rate and the production standard. The piece rate combines the wage rate for the job and the production standard into a single question of how much the job should pay. This frequently becomes equated with existing average earnings rather than with any already established norm. Some piece-rate firms observe an operational distinction between the wage rate and the production standard, but the custom and tradition of the piece-rate industries is a direct earnings approach.

Logically, a double approach is the superior one. With a distinction between the money rate and the production standard, a grievance can be investigated and handled as either a wage-rate or production-standard problem. Of course this distinction is inherent in all incentive plans, and the wage-rate aspect of incentive plans is no different among incentive jobs than among hourly paid jobs.

The production standard thus becomes the incentive problem. There are many ramifications to this subject, and they can be developed only to a modest extent.

The fundamental question of the accuracy of production standards can lead to a long and somewhat fruitless discussion or debate, to which the writer does not feel capable of making any meaningful contribution. Once a standard is set, we may find that actual earnings are 10 per cent below the agreed-upon expectancy level. Which is wrong, worker performance or the production standard? It is very doubtful whether there is a meaningful answer to this question. If worker performance is 40 per cent below expectancy with a carefully set standard, there can usually be no question that the workers have decided the standard should be revised before they go to work. In between these extremes there are certainly instances which are most difficult to decide. About all that can be concluded is that fine precision in setting standards is out of the question, but reasonably accurate standards can be set with worker cooperation.

New products and new methods add to the difficulty of setting standards because workers themselves are not sure of the degree to which familiarity will improve their performance. To this must be added the virtually irresistible desire to get new products or methods at a somewhat more favorable level than existing standards.

Rarely is production so simplified that the men on a given job can work as a group or as individuals on a single production standard or a single piece rate. A job involves a group of standards or piece rates, and equity among these standards introduces a new dimension to wage determination.

Equity among various tasks on a single job is of the most immediate and direct concern to the employees on the job. It involves no comparison with other jobs and no criticism that the men on one job are taking advantage of the men on other jobs. On the other hand, it offers a continuously open avenue to improve gradually the earnings potential of the job as a whole by upgrading the tighter standards to the earnings-effort level of the looser standards.

There is no way of avoiding this problem of equity. Loose standards cannot be cut without jeopardizing the entire incentive plan, and superior methods of setting standards can only, at best, narrow the problem.

Different work groups accommodate themselves in different ways to these differences. One group may develop a complex seniority pattern giving the "best" work to senior employees. Another group may share all work equally. A group may be dominated by a few employees who "hog" the best work. Another group may take the work as assigned by the foreman, who, depending upon his attitude and ability, may have any one of a number of methods for distributing work.

Related to the above question of distributing the best work is the problem of distributing the quantity of work. Without developing the problems of scheduling production and balancing lines to meet production, it is clear that the individual worker at any one time is not a completely free agent. His decision is not a simple one of how fast he should mow his own lawn. He is hemmed in "fore and aft" by the work flow and "sideways" by other employees on the same job. There is an element in any incentive plan, subject to adjustment over time, that, if one employee on the job earns more, someone else must take less.

The above paragraph may appear naïve, but it is equally in error to point out a work group dividing output equally and to shout "restriction of output." Five men dividing work on a job may be doing the same total output as a group of seven in which the fastest is doubling the pace of the slowest.

While there are the same kinds of problem in distributing work and balancing production lines to meet production schedules in a day-rate plant, the problem is more nearly a management responsibility. Too many men on a job will not cut the earnings of the group, workers will not gang up to get an employee off the line to increase individual earnings, and if one worker decides to work a little faster, another is willing to take it easier.

In addition to all the above problems, variations over time in all the factors which influence employee earnings give rise to additional inequalities. Variation in the flow of work, variation in the quality of materials, machine breakdown and machine efficiency, and other operating changes all influence employee earnings. In some cases there are guarantees for protection of earnings; in others there are not.

There are many more opportunities for grievances and complaints under an incentive system than under a day-rate method of payment. The wider range of problems and the dynamic and continuous influence of change create a more or less continuous turbulence. A statistical study of the quantity of grievances under incentive as compared with hourly rates would no doubt show a significant difference.

All incentive plans are not equally effective. Some managements are incapable of providing sufficient volume of work, except spasmodically, to create a smoothly functioning plant. Antagonisms may develop in which workers see the only opportunity for increased earnings in looser production standards rather than in increased output. If workers aggressively fight for high earnings through stints and restriction of output, the level of efficiency of the plant may approximate that of Old Sam making bassoons. So many inequities in standards may be present, accompanied by frequent guarantees and other special payment considerations, that a concept of voluntary incentive has lost most of its meaning.

In addition to this broad problem of efficiency, to some extent an incentive system pits one worker against another and may create a type of rugged individualism foreign to other methods of payment.

Another special type of incentive problem develops between a loosely operated incentive plan and the day work in a plant. Skill may become seriously underpaid for day workers as incentive earnings rise to unexpected levels.

There is no easy conclusion to a discussion of conflict under incentive methods of payment. Operational wage problems are obviously greater under incentive than under day work. New dimensions of conflict are introduced. However, increased efficiency and improved earnings may more than offset these difficulties. On the other hand, incentive payment may maintain competitive position with mediocre managerial efficiency and low earnings potential for employees. Incentives present no clear simple picture.

Plant-wide Incentive

A detailed discussion of plant-wide incentives is not possible in this chapter. The purpose of separation, however, is to indicate that these plans are fundamentally different from individual incentive plans. Also, plant-wide plans are relatively new, and some types may prove to be decidedly superior to others.

A standard for a plant-wide plan established through dollar sales or physical units is typically influenced by variables other than employee efficiency. Major changes in technology, changes in product mix, changes in wage levels and prices, and other basic factors introduce elements of uncertainty in many such plans. On the other hand, they are largely free from the individualistic, competitive aspects of the usual type of incentive plan and may work out to stimulate as high a level of plant efficiency as do the more traditional incentive plans. In fact, through cooperation in improving methods of production, they may, as a long-term trend, be a sounder basis for improved plant efficiency than a mere incentive to turn out more product under accepted methods of production and organization.

The results of plant-wide incentive plans introduced into the New England area during the war indicate that such plans fall into two categories: those that worked very well and those that did not work at all. There seemed to be almost no "mediocre" plant-wide plans. Clearly, on logical grounds the conditions which are necessary to make a plant-wide incentive plan work well are quite different from putting a carrot in front of the individual's nose. A cooperative type of attitude and of accomplishment is the basis of operation. This does not appear to come easily or automatically but, once achieved, gives hope for a sounder basis of union-management relations than exists in the average plant.[7]

Conclusion

Conflict arising out of the detailed operating problems of internal rate relationships is not, in and of itself, of a very fundamental nature. From a cost point of view many internal adjustments may be made without a drastic change in labor cost. An individual wage grievance can typically be settled upon its merits without raising a serious cost issue. Also, if basic policies have been agreed upon, no fundamental issue of "principle" will be at stake in a particular wage grievance.

Superior techniques, used with tolerance, assist in the constructive and harmonious settlement of these grievances. Their primary contribution can be, though not necessarily will be, assistance in facing the more important wage-administration policies in a direct fashion, with agreement as to basic objectives, within which the techniques will then supply more adequate administrative machinery. Superior techniques can narrow the range of case-by-case bargaining both by creating wage policies and by providing standards to assist in reaching detailed decisions.

Sometimes techniques are employed with no meeting of minds as to basic objectives and policies. Sometimes techniques are used as though they were a substitute for wage policies, when, in fact, they are almost empty shells if their purpose and major operating policies are not clearly stated and agreed upon. This was true with some wartime adoptions of job evaluation to avoid stabilization, and is true if basic union or management motivation is not sincerely in the true interest of the evaluation or incentive plan being considered.

Regardless of reasons, if wage administration plans are used without agreement as to basic policies and major operating procedures, they can easily become the focus of conflict and make no meaningful contribution to harmonious relationships.

[7] For a most interesting discussion, see George P. Shultz, "Worker Participation on Production Problems," *Personnel*, November, 1951. Also see Chap. 27 in this volume.

Internal wage administration exists in a broader setting of union-management relationship. It exists also in a broader external wage environment. These broader factors are of fundamental importance. Under unfavorable circumstances internal wage adminstration can be a hectic, serious, continuous source of conflict. Under favorable circumstances grievances are minor and not too frequent, and the internal structure can be adjusted to meet problems and changed conditions as they arise.

CHAPTER 26 WORK METHODS, WORKING CONDITIONS, AND MORALE

Charles R. Walker   *Yale University*

In 1936 and 1937, a wave of sit-down strikes swept through the rubber and automobile plants of the United States. The workers on strike wanted higher wages, union recognition, and an organized machinery for the handling of day-to-day grievances; but above all, they were striking against what they called the "speed-up" of work as governed by the assembly line. The causes of every major strike are complex and frequently so interwoven as to be inseparable, but somewhere among the causes—and frequently basic to the others, as in the case of the sit-downs—are work methods and working conditions. Two years before the first sit-down strike, the country experienced a nationwide walkout of textile workers. Here discrimination against union members, wages, and many other issues were involved, but the dynamic origin of disturbance, not only in 1934 but through the remaining thirties and after, was the introduction of new methods and new machinery, all of which were generally lumped by the workers and denounced as the "stretch-out." [1]

If particular work methods or undesirable working conditions may sometimes cause a national walkout, they are also the common origin of innumerable lesser conflicts in the world of industry. The net result of a minor conflict over a work method may be a day's slowdown or a grievance fought through the local plant's grievance machinery, or perhaps hostility is expressed in low-quality work or a high rate of absenteeism. This paper will concern itself with such day-to-day conflicts which stem from work methods and working conditions. When neglected or misunderstood, these "merely" local disturbances can with surprising rapidity grow into a national emergency.

The Industrial Engineer and the Behavioral Sciences

One of the functions of management in any given manufacturing plant is seeing to it that "each operation shall be done in the best manner, that is by the best possible procedure, and that it shall be done in the shortest possible time." [2] In order to achieve this objective, the works manager and the in-

---

[1] For a thorough study of the origin of conflict through changes in textile-manufacturing work methods, see Elliot Dunlap Smith and Richmond C. Nyman, *Technology and Labor,* New Haven, Conn., Yale University Press, 1939; and Richmond C. Nyman and Elliot Dunlap Smith, *Union-Management Cooperation in the "Stretch-out,"* New Haven, Conn., Yale University Press, 1934.

[2] Dexter S. Kimball and Dexter S. Kimball, Jr., *Principles of Industrial Organization,* New York, McGraw-Hill, 1947, p. 240.

dustrial engineer must combine men and machines; so, at once, problems of human motivation enter into their professional activities. Increased output and better quality at less cost may be their goals, but among the instruments for achieving them are human beings. For this reason, the skillful and intelligent industrial engineer, as most textbooks and all professors advise, must take "due account of the human element." Otherwise the activities of the engineering department may produce not greater efficiency but lowered morale and conflict. Precisely what does taking account of the human element mean? The textbooks never say he shall "take due account of the mechanical element." Why? Because it is understood that, so far as machines go, the industrial engineer can turn to a reliable body of facts and principles accumulated in the realm of the physical sciences. But to whom is he to turn for his knowledge of the human element? It will be the contention of this chapter that he should turn to the behavioral sciences and also that the behavioral sciences—and especially industrial psychology and industrial sociology—*should turn to him*. Between them, between the engineering and the social sciences, it should be possible to accumulate the relevant material and, through collaboration, to remove some of the sources of industrial conflict in the modern factory.

I am introducing the industrial engineer into this discussion at the beginning because he is in an obviously strategic position in relation to work methods, working conditions, and morale. To begin with, he provides management with a knowledge of machines and of their proper layout in the factory. Then, using techniques of time and motion study and the principles of work simplification, he strives to teach the easiest and most economical use of the workers' abilities in order to produce the most.

There have been many times when an improvement in working conditions removed a source of conflict and, at the same time, measurably increased efficiency. The achievement of the two goals at once, however, is *not always* possible, and both the industrial engineer and the social scientist should recognize this fact. In the early history of industrialism, one of the bitterest sources of industrial conflict was the unsafe and unhealthy working conditions which prevailed in many mines and mills, both in this country and abroad. Without doubt, the now general enforcement by industrial management of rigorous rules for health and safety is due—apart from union pressure—to the realization that safety is generally both a humane policy and an economical one. Nevertheless, it is accepted that the correction of an unhealthy condition need not be justified as "good business." It is common humanity and "in the public interest." Other examples might be cited. Many "conditions" in modern factories, such as excessive fatigue, physical or mental, can—and should—be changed not only because the industrial engineer feels the change will make the plant more efficient but, even if it won't, because it is in the public interest or should remove an obvious and justifiable complaint and source of conflict.

The social scientist—like the engineer—is interested in the improvement of methods and working conditions, but his emphasis is on motivational problems and on the social relationships inside the factory and out. Is it possible to bring together these different approaches? I believe that it is and that, unless this is done, we shall never solve some of the most pressing problems of industrial conflict in the modern factory.

Here are a few examples to illustrate some of the areas of potential collaboration between the two fields of knowledge. The examples frankly stress the weakness of a purely engineering approach. But it should be said at once that industrial engineers could also point out the weaknesses of the average social scientist's approach to factory problems, due to the latter's ignorance of engineering principles and practice. My hope is that both professions will waste no time in looking down their noses but will begin constructive collaboration.

Let's start with what both the social scientist and the progressive industrialist know and say about "communications" in the modern factory.

An alert management seeks to keep lines of communication open from top to bottom (and bottom to top) and to see to it that contacts are free and untrammeled both within and between the levels of the organization. One reason for all this is that there is a recognized correlation between frequent and friendly interaction of this kind and the absence of industrial conflict.

In the light of this emphasis, look at the typical activity of the industrial engineer. To the average worker—and supervisor—the industrial engineer or whoever determines "methods," when he comes into a particular department, be he staff member or consultant, is too often a stranger. He asks questions and makes notes. He doesn't talk like anybody else. Frequently he or his representative does not talk at all; he merely observes and jots down numbers on a large piece of paper. Surely he does not act or interact like other men. His behavior is calculated to arouse suspicion. And it does. The day when time-study experts never spoke to the worker at all but watched him from a concealed post of observation is long past. But unfortunately, in many plants, the day of a fully cooperative relationship based on normal interaction and mutual trust has not replaced it. Either a practical mill man, if given the chance, or a psychologist might help to rub out this occupational defect of many designers of methods and working conditions.

Let us assume, however, that the industrial engineer we are considering has the good sense to recognize these dangers and to compensate for them. By manner and personality—and by his reputation for fairness—he wins the good will of the department where he is making his engineering study. What then? It is common sense, but also the testimony of the behavioral sciences, that language which is not understood or is imperfectly understood can be one of the greatest sources of distrust and fear. From my own experience, I would estimate that half the resistance to the recommendations of industrial engineers arises from a failure by managers, supervisors, or workers to understand them. Now the need for specialized concepts and vocabulary in specialized branches of knowledge is taken for granted. But all men are laymen, except in their own specialties. It is of the first importance, then, that the industrial engineer find a way to communicate with the four strategic groups of "laymen" with whom he must deal daily: management, supervision, union leaders, and workers.

Again let us assume that our hypothetical engineer has overcome this difficulty. We'll say that he has recognized the problem and has reduced his findings to their simplest expression and, further, that he has taken ample time—with the permission and encouragement of management—to instruct both supervisors and workers in the meaning and scope of his recommendations. This is particularly important if an incentive plan is involved.

We come to the heart of this introductory discussion, a basic difference in approach to work methods and working conditions between the industrial engineer and the social scientist. I will argue not that one is right and the other wrong but rather that both need to see each other's viewpoint if problems in this field are to be solved. To illustrate:

The chief engineer of a large American corporation described to me one day a program which, when completed, would tell every worker in his company "exactly how to do his job down to the last detail." This would serve a psychological as well as a mechanical purpose, he added. "Not only will the operators not have to think any more, but they will be much happier on the job and more loyal to the company when we are able to show them that we know so much more about their jobs than they do."

From a psychological standpoint, how could he be more wrong? To begin with, nearly every worker who has been on his factory job a few months knows more about it than any outsider will ever know. But the important point for this discussion is a different one. It is the assumption by this chief industrial engineer that the way to make a man happy and loyal is to show your superior knowledge and tell him exactly how to do his work.

Peter Drucker [3] sums up the dilemma suggested by this conversation as follows: "The industrial engineer," he points out, "sees in the human being a tool and that means that, to him, the human being is the more productive, the more thoroughly his work has been set up and laid out *for* him. The social scientist lays stress on man's need to participate. He, therefore, concludes that the human being is the more productive and the more efficient, the more *he himself* designs and lays out his own work."

Toward a Common Ground

Now consider these two points of view. One can hardly argue with the industrial engineer as to the usefulness of applying the laws of physics and physiology to discovering the easiest and most economical ways of doing a job; nor can one argue with the social scientist that the average man is happier in his work—and less likely to be frustrated and hostile to management—the more he feels himself a participator in the doing of it and not a tool manipulated by someone else.

What is the solution of the dilemma?

Here is an example of at least one path *toward* a solution. A machining division in a large American company making calculating machines was organized in the conventional fashion. Highly trained men made setups on the lathes, grinders, screw machines, etc., with which the department was equipped. Workers, called "operators," operated the machines. Highly trained inspectors inspected the product. This arrangement had been agreed upon by the engineers as the most efficient.

A few years ago, the company decided to make a human-relations experi-

---

[3] Peter Drucker, "The Human Being in Industrial Production," p. 71 of *Proceedings, Fifth Annual Time Study and Methods Conference,* sponsored by Society for Advancement of Management and American Society of Mechanical Engineers, Management Division, New York, Apr. 20–21, 1950.

ment based upon the idea of giving workers greater participation in the process. They let the ordinary operator make his own setup and do his own inspection. After a year of trial the results of the experiment were impressive. The workers declared their definite preference for the new arrangement. Feelings of frustration and boredom, which had formerly existed in the shop, diminished or disappeared. At the same time, management was pleased because the rate of production was maintained and an improvement in quality was recorded. In addition, there were substantial savings through a reduction in the number of rejects.

The engineers continued to contribute their knowledge, which was now being used and applied by a different set of people and in a way different from the way the engineers, when they were acting as psychologists, thought effective.[4] We will return to this particular example again in another connection.

Now for one more illustration suggesting the need for greater attention to human motivation in dealing with methods and men. Many incentive plans designed by engineers have run into difficulties because they misinterpreted or overstressed economic motivations. Here is an example in somewhat simplified form. Ten men have been accustomed to work together as a crew and receive a group bonus. An industrial-engineering study shows that six of the men are on "direct" production, *i.e.,* their work can be directly measured in units of output and units of time. The other four are on "indirect" production. One of the latter is a crane man, another a setup man. The work of these four, however important for over-all efficiency, cannot be measured in units of time and units of production. The industrial-engineering department recommends that the six "productive" workers be put into a new incentive plan and that the four "nonproductive" workers henceforth be paid on day rate.

Is this recommendation made on engineering grounds alone? No. It is also based on certain assumptions about human behavior. These assumptions are sometimes implicit, but they are also sometimes made explicit in memoranda to management. They are these: the fewer there are in the bonus pool, the more each individual will make and, therefore, the six individuals whose direct efforts really control production will work a lot harder under the new bonus plan than under the old.

What happens is often quite different. To management's astonishment, the process is performed not more but less efficiently than before. Finally, the ten men walk out in protest against the plan. Management asks what is wrong.

If the men are questioned, the explanation emerges. Briefly, they have *not* acted according to the motivational assumptions of the industrial engineer. They have been more interested in seeing that the rest of the crew shared a bonus with them than in making more money as individuals. Doubtless this "explanation" can be further elaborated by pointing up "psychological drives" and "cultural conditioning." But enough has been said to make the single point that the plan was based on an assumption about human behavior which was false. Or it can be summed up by saying what (in my judgment) the industrial engineer making his recommendation to management might have said had he taken account of well-authenticated studies of human behavior in comparable conditions:

---

[4] For a full account of this experiment, see Charles R. Walker, "The Problem of the Repetitive Job," *Harvard Business Review,* Vol. 28, No. 3 (May, 1950).

The study of crew X by the Industrial Engineering Department shows that six workers perform direct work, four indirect. . . . Any new financial-incentive plan which uses the engineering data here presented should take account of at least two types of motivation common to crews of this kind: the desire of the individual to earn more money and the desire of the individual to remain part of, and loyal to, a primary human group of which he has long been a member. A plan which allows only a part of the crew to participate in bonus earnings naturally will pit one motivation against another. It is possible that the individualistic motivation may win out. On the other hand, it may not; and in that case, the new incentive plan, because it provokes conflicts and bitterness, may be less profitable to management than the old. A compromise solution of the problem is to provide a bonus for the indirect, or so-called nonproductive, workers based on a percentage of the total output of the crew. This will retain the purely economic motivation and will also take account of the crew's sentiments of mutual interdependence and social solidarity. One method for calculating the indirect bonus is . . .

All the problems of method or working conditions discussed above are of as great interest to the union as to management, and rarely are they successfully solved in the absence of a sound working relationship between company and union. Unions, of course, differ in their attitudes and policies toward changes in work methods, toward incentive plans, and toward the introduction of technological innovations, but the usual approach of the major national unions might be briefly summarized as follows: [5]

1. Most unions have come to accept some of the principles of "scientific management" in spite of its earlier identification with antiunionism. As a result, many, such as the unions in steel, textiles, and clothing, now employ technical engineering personnel.

2. Most unions have accepted the principle that changes of a technological and routine character should be approved if they help to establish competitive parity for the employers. They distrust or oppose changes which push levels of effort beyond prevailing standards in the industry.

3. On incentive systems, unions oppose high-task systems such as Bedaux and, in general, complex and rigid plans. They tend to favor simple and flexible ones.[6]

It is almost impossible to compress into brief compass the "principles" which should govern as complex an activity as union-management relations in the field of work methods and working conditions, but for one phase of these activities, that connected with incentives, William Foote Whyte has succeeded, in an article which combines case-history material with sound generalizations. The key emerges in Whyte's treatment of conflicts over rate setting at the Inland Steel Container Co.'s Chicago plant. After giving the "case," he writes: "What lesson can be drawn from this case? The particular procedures involved

[5] The problem of work methods in craft unions, with the special question of restrictive work practices and featherbedding, will not be surveyed in this chapter.

[6] I am indebted for guidance in making this summary statement to conferences with several trade-unionists but especially to those with Solomon Barkin. For an excellent summary of union opinion and policy in matters of work methods, see Solomon Barkin, "The Technical Engineering Service of an American Trade Union," *International Labor Review,* Vol. 61, No. 6 (June, 1950) (reprinted in pamphlet form by the International Labor Office, Washington).

here might not fit the needs of other situations, but the general conclusion is clear: only when the rate-setting activity is *effectively integrated* into the pattern of supervision and union-management relations will workers respond strongly to financial incentives. . . ." [7]

Technological Environment, Human Adjustments, and In-plant Society

So much for the need for the architect of methods and working conditions to know the principles of human behavior. What further have the behavioral sciences to say about the field of work methods and working conditions as related to efficiency and to the removal of frustration and conflict? Some of the earliest studies in this field were focused on fatigue and on the effects of work and working conditions on the health of the worker. Notable among these were the studies conducted under the auspices of the British Medical Council as early as World War I. As a result of their findings, hours of labor in British munitions factories were sharply reduced, and at the same time, *output increased.* Following these studies of physiological fatigue came the early monographs of Wyatt and Fraser on "mental fatigue" and on the psychological effects of "increased mechanization." By now, a very considerable literature has grown up both in the United States and abroad on the more specific problem of the repetitive and monotonous job. [8]

In recent years, the emphasis of industrialists and of social scientists has tended to acquire a more "positive" accent. The problem has been said to be less how to reduce mental fatigue than how to "appeal to ego motivations" in order to make jobs *more* satisfying or interesting or how to increase "pride in work."

However phrased, it is easy to see that exploration and interest in the field, whether theoretical or practical, have been closely tied to the development of modern technology and increasingly to the application in the modern factory of mass-production methods. For this reason, the author and his colleagues at Yale have found it useful to adopt in all such research the concept of a "technological environment." Just as the *natural* environment of mountain or valley, wind, rain, and temperature profoundly conditions living and *working* conditions for a rural population, so, in advanced industrial sectors, the technological milieu, an environment of machines, largely molds the daily work experience of modern man. As a rule, however, these terms are used in our research far more

---

[7] William Foote Whyte, "Economic Incentives and Human Relations," *Harvard Business Review,* 30 (March–April, 1952), 78.

[8] S. Wyatt and J. A. Fraser, *The Effects of Monotony in Work, A Preliminary Inquiry,* Industrial Fatigue Research Board Report 56, London, His Majesty's Stationery Office, 1929. Other relevant British reports issued by the Board are H. M. Vernon, S. Wyatt, and A. D. Ogden, *The Extent and Effects of Variety in Repetitive Work,* Report 26, 1929; S. Wyatt and J. A. Fraser, *The Comparative Effects of Variety and Uniformity in Work,* Report 52, 1928; S. Wyatt, *Incentives in Repetitive Work,* Report 69, 1934; S. Wyatt and J. N. Langdon, *Fatigue and Boredom in Repetitive Work,* Report 77, 1937; and S. Wyatt and J. N. Langdon, *The Machine and the Worker,* Report 82, 1938. Also see Elton Mayo, *The Human Problems of an Industrial Civilization,* New York, Macmillan, 1933, Chap. 2, "What Is Monotony?"; and Walker, *op. cit.*

specifically and refer to a particular technological environment of a particular industry or plant, for example, a chemical plant, an automobile assembly line, or an automatic textile mill.

The first thing that emerges from any sort of sociological study of such *specific* technological environments is their important effect on methods and working conditions and, through these, on the *character or quality of a man's work experience,* hour by hour and day by day on the job. Let me illustrate in a very rough way. The leading characteristic of many jobs in chemical plants, considered from the industrial worker's point of view, is that they make a great demand in terms of responsibility for expensive materials and for the safety, even the lives, of other men. Translated into daily work experience, that means careful attention to detail at certain moments, as turning a valve at a precise instant and to an exact point. But on the other hand, throughout much of the working day, there is little pressure to get out the work, nor is the job either nervously or physically fatiguing.

In contrast, take an automobile assembly line. In most of the jobs, no scrupulous care is required at particular moments to avoid loss of limb or property. But on the other hand, these same jobs are repetitive and are performed under constant pressure, especially if they are on the main conveyor line.

In contrast to both these technological environments, consider the wholly automatic departments, say, in certain modern textile plants. Here extreme mechanization has brought the character of the worker's technological work environment full cycle back toward that of a highly skilled craftsman. The semiskilled or unskilled machine tenders, "the proletariat," have been eliminated, and engineers and their maintenance crews composed of skilled mechanics are all that remain.

These examples suggest at once the importance of good methods of selection to see that the man who might make a good chemical operator, for example, but who hates assembly-line jobs gets into the right job for him. Techniques of selection and scientific methods of exploring and recording traits of personality are being improved and more widely applied, but unfortunately the practical task of relating such human traits to actual job characteristics in specific technological environments has made too little progress.

Such differing technological environments suggest another point besides the one of "matching men and jobs." There may be certain characteristics in the modern work environment to which the average normal person can never properly "adjust." If that be true, technological or other factors creating those particular characteristics ought to be changed so that particular jobs may be better adapted to human needs and limitations. Here is an illustration: There is considerable evidence that a minority of persons in the population prefer, or are indifferent to, a repetitive job. How large is that minority? Assume that it is around 10 per cent of the average work force in American manufacturing plants. If more than 10 per cent of the jobs in a given plant are repetitive, then in the interest of adjustment either something should be done to change the character of those repetitive jobs or else more people who like them should be found and hired by the factory. This is an oversimplified example. But it may serve to emphasize the point that there is more than "fitting the square peg into the square hole" to solving the problem of reasonable job satisfaction and efficiency in the modern factory. On the simple point of repetitiveness, I would hazard the guess that the average mass-production factory always has a substantial majority of its employees who are on repetitive work and who, because they dislike it, are at least potential sources of unrest and lowered morale.

Another significant point emerges if one studies the relation between particular technological environments and human behavior. A particular technology like that of an automobile assembly line not only affects the individual on the job in his daily work experience but also molds in good measure the character of what might be called in-plant society. For example, an automobile assembly line largely determines the kind of social relations that are possible among workers and between workers and supervision. Because of the character of the technology and work methods, there are, to begin with, few true team relationships possible. The typical work group is four or five men working at separate tasks on the line. They are near enough to one another to exchange a few words, but their jobs are not functionally related. In short, the tendency of the work method is to keep group morale at a "low temperature." The noise and the tension of the line also impose severe limitations on social intercourse. In contrast, take the process of making seamless tube in a steel mill. This is typical of many situations in the metalworking industries where men are knit together in small groups of two or three and the small groups into larger crews of twenty-five or thirty men.

Such close-knit work groups, in which the job of each member is functionally dependent on the job of all the others, frequently produce a vigorous team spirit which contributes both to efficiency and to the personal satisfaction of the teams' members. Where the technical requirements of a manufacturing process call for such team organization, this fact may be welcomed by an alert management as providing a favorable environment, so to speak, for industrial cooperation. Where the work method divides or isolates the working force, either geographically or functionally or both, it may be important to seek other means of creating a cooperative work climate. In stressing the frequent utility of crew organization in promoting such a climate, it is not implied that all crews are efficient or satisfactory to their members. This much, however, may be said: A well-knit team of, say, thirty men generally has a higher *potential* for morale making than a weak organizational group—or no group at all—of thirty men. But that potential can be used by the group to influence the group to act either for or against production. The direction chosen will, of course, depend on many variables inside and outside the group. Elton Mayo's studies of work groups in wartime industries are a valuable contribution to the question of relations between group organization, morale, and productivity.[9]

An interesting difference—from a motivational point of view—between the two particular technological environments which have been mentioned is this: On the assembly line, only a tiny fraction of the "product" is ever seen or handled by most workers. In the tube mill, the whole product, from a billet to the finished pipe, as it moves through a series of machines, is worked on

[9] Elton Mayo and George F. F. Lombard, *Teamwork and Labor Turnover in the Aircraft Industry of Southern California,* Harvard University Graduate School of Business Administration, Business Research Studies, No. 32, 1944.

by everyone and can be followed by the eyes of all members of the crew. Workers frequently go to the cooling and inspection tables to look over, for their own satisfaction, the job they have just done. My own studies in the steel and automobile industries [10] suggest that a close relation to the product (the whole product or a substantial part of it) is often a positive factor in producing personal satisfaction and high-quality performance. From the negative standpoint, the following comment [11] by an assembly worker makes a similar point:

> When the plant was running only a few cars through an hour I used to install the whole front and back seat assemblies. But when the cars speeded up, I was put on the job of installing the rack that the front seat slides back and forth on, and my job was *broken up and simplified. I'd like to do a whole fender myself from new material to the finished job.* It would be more interesting. [Emphasis supplied.]

An able summary of this point has been made by James C. Worthy,[12] of Sears, Roebuck:

> We have found that where jobs are broken down *too finely* we are more likely to have both low output and low morale. Conversely, the most sustained efforts are exerted by those groups of employees who perform the *more complete sets of tasks* (e.g., salesmen, supervisors, master machinists, etc.), and these likewise exhibit the highest levels of morale and esprit de corps. [Emphasis supplied.]

These, then, may serve to illustrate the impact of *different* technological environments on the jobs of individual workers and on the character of social relations and of in-plant society as a whole. Not all the unfavorable work environments can be turned into favorable ones. But some can be. And we shall not know how many or how until we study them in detail, tracing with the aid of both the social scientist and the engineer actual and particular relationships between methods and morale.

The relation of what we have called an "unfavorable work environment" to industrial conflict is frequently indirect. Unsafe, irritating, or unusually fatiguing working conditions tend to condition the work force toward controversy or conflict. The immediate cause of conflict might be a foreman disciplining a worker for coming in late or some other remote or trivial cause. Such an incident arising in a department with an unfavorable work environment might flare into a serious controversy. By the same token, if the environment was a favorable one, the probable chances of extinguishing the spark of controversy before it became a flame would be high.

[10] See Charles R. Walker, *Steeltown: An Industrial Case History of the Conflict between Progress and Security,* New York, Harper, 1950; Charles R. Walker and Robert H. Guest, *The Man on the Assembly Line,* Cambridge, Mass., Harvard University Press, 1952; and Walker, "The Problem of the Repetitive Job."

[11] Walker and Guest, *op. cit.,* p. 58.

[12] James C. Worthy, "Organizational Structure and Employee Morale," *American Sociological Review,* 15 (April, 1950), 174 (from a paper read before the Forty-fifth Annual Meeting of the American Sociological Society, New York, Dec. 29, 1949).

Constructive Steps

Now, in general, what do those who have studied in this field have to say about how to solve some of the psychological and social problems created or accented by modern technological environments? What can be done to eliminate the mental fatigue from repetitive jobs or the strain of highly paced ones where, as has often been said, fatigue comes because the rhythm of the machine is "substituted for the rhythm of the man?" Or what can be done to give mass-production workers the satisfaction and pride in work we associate with craftsmen? In short, what can be done to mitigate or reverse dissatisfactions arising from methods or working conditions that lead to conflict?

An absolute answer is, of course, total mechanization, the elimination of all direct-production workers. In many fields of manufacturing, however, this will not be a practical answer because of cost factors. In other fields, there will be increasing efforts to reduce manpower through "automatization." [13]

Nearly everyone is familiar with some of the commoner devices or techniques that have been adopted to answer some of these questions in a practical way. There is the rest pause, to begin with, whose practical and psychological effects were analyzed by Mayo in several of his earliest studies. [14]

There is the practice of "rotation" between jobs, a technique which is being more and more widely adopted, though it requires a skillful application by management if it is to be successful. In one company which adopted the technique several years ago, operators work as members of teams which are shifted from one set of jobs to another daily. Individuals learn specific operations in blocks of twelve and receive an increase of pay when they successfully master a new block. Management reports that job rotation has proved far more efficient than individual job assignment.

In order to give the overspecialized worker a sense of the *total* product, some manufacturing plants give talks, tours of the whole plant, and demonstrations on the use of the product. There is also the theory adopted by many managements that one of the purposes of fringe or welfare benefits is to compensate the worker for the more irritating or monotonous aspects of his work.

Another approach to the problem of satisfaction and morale has been through methods of organization which permit workers greater participation in the production problems of their work and sometimes participation in profits or in labor savings. A consideration of profit- or savings-sharing plans is beyond our scope, but it should be said that, where profit sharing is tied to direct participation in the solving of production problems, that touches on the subject of this chapter. It is not a simple matter to organize an efficient and en-

---

[13] For a brilliant discussion of this "answer" and the problems it presents, see Norbert Wiener, *The Human Use of Human Beings*, New York, Houghton Mifflin, 1950.

[14] Mayo, *loc. cit.* Also see *Fourth Annual Report*, Industrial Fatigue Research Board; H. M. Vernon, T. Bedford, and S. Wyatt, *Two Studies on Rest Pauses in Industry*, Industrial Fatigue Research Board Report 25; and Vernon, Wyatt, and Ogden, *On the Extent and Effects of Variety in Repetitive Work*, Report 26.

during system of participation by hourly wage earners in the solution of day-to-day production problems; however, examples are multiplying of managements which have done so with success.[15]

In this by no means exhaustive list of practical devices to meet the problem of morale or of satisfaction under modern working conditions, notice that, with the exception of job rotation, all of them attempt to balance or compensate for what is admittedly irritating or frustrating labor rather than to change the character of that labor. Such compensations are of undoubted value, but I would like to touch upon an effort only recently receiving recognition, namely, a direct attack on the problem through alterations in job content itself and thus in the individual's immediate work experience.

One example of such an approach has already been given: that in which the jobs of ordinary operators were "enlarged" through combining the skilled occupations of setup men and inspectors with the routine occupation of machine operator. Even in mass-production factories where there are assembly lines, the idea that a job can be "enlarged"—and, by the same token, made more significant and absorbing—is gaining ground. In the assembly of certain types of electric motors and other fairly elaborate products, successful experiments have recently been made which show that the job of the individual assembler can be very substantially enlarged without impairing efficiency.[16] It is not being suggested here that the production manager can or should return to the age of craftsmanship and have each individual workman build, for example, his own automobile! It *is* suggested, however, that the principle of extreme subdivision of labor in the modern factory is being shown to be subject to its own law of diminishing returns. The application of the mass-production method does not require that a worker perform as few motions as possible. Rather, he may have a whole series of different operations, just as long as he performs the basic motions of each one in the simplest and most efficient way. The trend of the past 100 years toward specialization cannot be reversed, but experiments are urgently needed to discover the psychological as well as the mechanical advantages and limitations of the mass-production method.

In recent years, objective evidence has been piling up rapidly to support the conclusion that the kind of work a man does is a crucial factor in his morale. For example, summarizing the findings of studies made on worker morale and motivation over the past few years, Daniel Katz,[17] of the University of Michigan, writes:

[15] The work of Joseph Scanlon, of the Massachusetts Institute of Technology, has been devoted to developing plans which combine profit- or savings-sharing features with participation by the workers in the solution of production problems. For a popular account, see Russell W. Davenport, "Enterprise for Everyman," *Fortune,* 41 (January, 1950), 55. See also G. P. Schutz, "Worker Participation on Production Problems: A Discussion of Experience with the 'Scanlon Plan,'" *Personnel,* 28 (November, 1951), 201–210; Lester Coch and John R. P. French, "Overcoming Resistance to Change," *Human Relations* (1948), 512–532; and James J. Gillespie, "Work Psychology and Time and Motion Study," *Advanced Management,* 16 (April, 1951), 4–6.

[16] A report of these experiments is now in preparation by the author of this chapter.

[17] Daniel Katz, "Morale and Motivation in Industry," in Wayne Dennis *et al., Current Trends in Industrial Psychology,* Pittsburgh, Pa., University of Pittsburgh Press, 1949, pp. 155–156.

The central fact about the outcome of the studies of worker morale is that they do not corroborate the general philosophy of management which emphasizes the importance of external rewards. Workers like jobs that give them a chance to display their skill and to show their worth, and they place considerable value upon being a member of a congenial work group.

In the swelling stream of current research on workers' attitudes, morale, and motivation, new light is certain to be thrown on the field of "methods and working conditions." [18] Of particular value for those who wish to reevaluate the influence of the intrinsic job experience on human behavior is the work, too little known in this country, of W. Baldamus, Research Fellow of the University of Birmingham, England.[19] Dr. Baldamus has developed a useful method for analyzing elements of work experience in terms of their psychological impact on the individual worker. He has also shown, through statistical studies, a neglected correlation between types of work and the rate of absenteeism.

Summary

To summarize briefly, then, the relations between method, working conditions, and morale:

1. Complaints over methods and working conditions are daily the cause of conflict in the shop and factory. Unless satisfactorily dealt with, such sources of local disturbance may develop into industrial conflicts of nationwide proportions.

2. The industrial engineer is today the architect of much of the technological environment and many of the work methods of modern industry. Collaboration between the industrial engineer and the social scientist, resulting in a combination of engineering methods and the principles of human behavior, is called for if many basic sources of conflict in the modern factory are to be removed.

3. One answer to the problem of human adjustment in the factory is automatization, where the engineer and maintenance men replace the "machine tender."

4. Some technological environments are more, some less, favorable to a cooperative work climate.

5. Techniques such as rest pauses, welfare activities, participation in problem solving, and others are useful in *compensating* for an unfavorable work environment.

6. But it is also partially possible to change the character of that environment through enlarging and enriching the content of the individual job.

7. More and more attention is being given by practical administrators in

[18] New work relating to questions raised in this chapter is in process in a number of universities, including Michigan, Chicago, Yale, Harvard, and the Massachusetts Institute of Technology.

[19] W. Baldamus, *Incentives and Work Analysis,* limited ed., Faculty of Commerce and Social Science, Research Board, The University, Birmingham, Eng.; and "Type of Work and Motivation," *Journal of Sociology,* 2 (March, 1951), 44–58.

industry and by research institutions to increasing men's satisfaction with their work and to removing sources of conflict connected with work methods and working conditions.

We are, I believe, only at the threshold of a scientific understanding of man's relation to work and especially of his relation to the new technological environments within which much of the work of the modern world is being performed. "Machines alone do not give us mass production," Henry Ford II, grandson of the "father of mass production," told the Society of Mechanical Engineers a few years ago. "Mass production is achieved by both machines and men. And while we have gone a long way toward perfecting our mechanical operations, we have not successfully written into our equations whatever complex factors represent Man, the human element."

CHAPTER 27 UNION-MANAGEMENT COOPERATION

Ernest Dale   *American Management Association*

U NION-MANAGEMENT cooperation, like politeness, means many things to many people. Among the interpretations we find that historically it has frequently been identified with a sentimental desire for "industrial democracy." But in this sense it has remained so vague and so broad that almost any aspect of good industrial relations could be fitted to it. Secondly, it may be a device for manipulating labor in a direction desired by management. It is this result that is sometimes accomplished by psychological techniques, applied in a Machiavellian manner to modern labor-management relations. Thirdly, it may be an instrument for unions to gain economic and political power, as expressed through "codetermination," that is, union participation on the board of directors and the joint appointment of personnel managers by unions and management. Finally, union-management cooperation may be considered as a technical concept referring to a process of mutual accommodation. It may be defined as an activity in which unions and management attempt to accomplish objectives of mutual interest. This conception is based on the assumption that each of the parties can achieve some of its objectives more effectively with the aid of the other party.

In this last sense, therefore, union-management cooperation is built on the recognition of mutual dependence. Unless each party is able to remove, or at least reduce, the objections of the other to its plans, policies, and actions, there may not be enough support from the other party to ensure successful accomplishment of its objectives. On the contrary, there may be a degree of open or tacit resistance which would defeat its efforts. Even if one of the parties held completely autocratic powers over the other, the individual members could withhold their reserve powers and contribute only enough to escape detection or punishment. The resistance to the other party's objectives is likely to be the greater, the greater the threat to its own basic values from the other party.

Union-management cooperation may take place in a formal or informal manner. We shall confine ourselves to the formal plans which provide for regular meetings between union and management representatives rather than deal with the informal relationships which have been more widely studied but can be less definitely analyzed. The cooperation need not be confined to particular subjects or programs, but usually it proceeds best if the parties focus on the solution of specific problems. This tends to improve understanding, relationships, and results. The process is ordinarily carried on with the aim of increasing productivity (unit-cost reduction) and, at the same time, in order to improve mutual regard for one another. The emphasis in cooperation is on matters of joint interest, which distinguishes it from collective bargaining. The latter tends to emphasize matters of divergent interest.

The conduct of cooperation may be classified into several levels, in terms of the type of behavior involved: there is, first, informational cooperation, in which unions and management jointly gather facts; second, advisory cooperation, in which either side consults the other before taking action; third, constructive cooperation, in which either side may make constructive suggestions for improvements to the other; and, finally, joint determination, in which both sides have an equal voice in the resolution of matters of joint interest, including the right of unilateral withdrawal.

The concept of union-management cooperation which has been described will be considered now in its historical developments and in its contribution and limitations with respect to the reduction of industrial conflict.

Experience with Union-Management Cooperation

The potentialities of cooperation between unions and management were recognized long ago by members of management and labor as well as by psychologists and sociologists. For example, Frederick W. Taylor [1] testified in 1912 before the House of Representatives Special Committee as follows:

> The great revolution that takes place in the mental attitude of the two parties under scientific management is that both sides take their eyes off the division of the surplus as the all-important matter, and together turn their attention toward increasing the size of the surplus until this surplus becomes so large that it is unnecessary to quarrel over how it should be divided. They come to see that when they stop pulling against one another, and instead both turn and push shoulder to shoulder in the same direction, the size of the surplus created by their joint efforts is truly astounding. They both realize that when they substitute friendly cooperation and mutual helpfulness for antagonism and strife they are together able to make this surplus so enormously greater than it was in the past that there is ample room for a large increase in wages for the workman and an equally large increase in profits for the manufacturer.

A few years later Samuel Gompers, president of the AFL, poured out his enthusiasm about the potentialities of union-management cooperation to Bernard Baruch at the Paris Peace Conference in 1919,[2] when he likened the labor movement to Niagara Falls, "whose tremendous power might be channeled for good—or ill." Subsequently the AFL frequently went on record in favor of union-management cooperation.[3] This came about as a result of a change in its wage philosophy, accepting marginal productivity as a factor limiting wage increases. It began to pay some attention to the cost as well as to the income aspect of wages. The AFL also changed its attitude toward scientific management from violent opposition to some degree of acceptance. Contributing to

---

[1] Testimony before the House of Representatives Special Investigating Committee, June, 1912, partly quoted in F. B. Copley, *Frederick W. Taylor*, New York, Harper, 1923, p. 11.

[2] As told to the author by Harold T. Clark, Cleveland attorney.

[3] Jean Trepp McKelvey, *AFL Attitudes toward Production, 1900–1932*, Ithaca, The New York State School of Industrial and Labor Relations, 1952.

these changes was the belief that the antiunion campaign of the employers might end in union recognition by management and in moves toward cooperation, for since the union was a repository of much valuable experience, cooperation with it would lead to an increase in profits. Another factor was the great personal influence of Gompers, who tried to cap his career by an acceptance of orthodoxy in a world to be made safe for democracy and free from strife.

There was also the influence of foreign experience such as the British reconstruction reports concerned with the reduction of industrial strife through cooperation.[4] This experience included the practical example of the Whitley Councils, a kind of congress of organized employers and unions in different industries, which considered common problems.[5] Finally, there was the example of the German works councils, which were established by law to bring about some union participation on boards of directors and in the factory.[6]

In the United States the first actual instance of union-management cooperation was probably that started by Capt. Otto S. Beyer, Jr., who introduced it in the government's Rock Island Arsenal during World War I. Its success led Beyer to recommend such a plan to the railroad unions while they were still working under government operation. But the return of the roads to private ownership and the depression postponed a practical start until 1923, when the Baltimore & Ohio Railroad adopted the plan. Two years later it was introduced on the Canadian National Railroads. These two experiments have survived in some fashion. Other plans of cooperation on some of the other railroads lasted for a few years until the Great Depression.[7] Union-management cooperation on the railroads covered about one-sixth of the mileage operating in the United States and Canada and took place chiefly in respect to the maintenance of equipment. It resulted in better relations between the men and the management, better knowledge of the operations of the railroads, and fewer grievances.

The AFL took a long time to put its declared intentions into practice. Not until 1930 were specific efforts made to offer to employers the practical advantages of union-management cooperation in return for recognition. But only three small plants made such a trial possible, and their impending bankruptcy foiled this effort in connection with the much vaunted Southern organizing campaign. While the AFL lacked the ability to translate its broad objectives of promoting efficiency into specific action, much of the responsibility for the failure of cooperation in the twenties must be placed on management's shoulders. Employers refused to assist the frail practical efforts and generous hopes of the unions. They never grasped their great chance of working out joint interests until the Great Depression swallowed up any remaining idealism and pushed the two parties more irreconcilably than ever into the struggle over divergent interests.

Two other plans—those of the Cleveland women's garment industry and

---

[4] John Hilton, *Memorandum on the Industrial Situation after the War,* London, Garton Foundation, 1918.

[5] J. B. Seymour, *The Whitley Councils Scheme,* London, King, 1932.

[6] Nathan Reich, *Labor Relations in Republican Germany: An Experiment in Industrial Democracy,* New York, Oxford, 1938.

[7] For detailed accounts, see Louis A. Wood, *Union-Management Cooperation on the Railroads,* New Haven, Conn., Yale University Press, 1931; and Sumner H. Slichter, *Union Policies and Industrial Management,* Washington, Brookings, 1941, Chaps. 15–16.

Naumkeag—failed under the adverse conditions of sections of the clothing and textile industries of the 1920's and 1930's, when the overwhelming burden of joint responsibilities brought a breakdown of peaceful labor-management relations.[8] However, in the secular decline of the men's clothing industry in the 1920's, the cooperation of the Amalgamated Clothing Workers of America helped that union to maintain its membership and its relations to management better than if there had been no such cooperation. The number of work stoppages showed a downward trend after 1935 in the men's clothing industry (except for 1937). This industry has been considerably more peaceful than industry as a whole, as evidenced, for example, in the decreased number of arbitration cases and awards.[9] A similar experience during the 1930's and 1940's in the millinery industry can be traced partly at least to the results of union-management cooperation.[10]

The period of the 1930's largely interrupted the activities of union-management cooperation. This was due partly to the difficulties of realizing gains through cooperative efforts and partly to the great organizational turmoil of the labor movement. Nevertheless, the mounting unemployment problem forced some of the newly organized unions to offer cooperation to employers in order to save their existence by saving the jobs of their members. This the steelworkers' union did quite successfully in some forty to sixty smaller plants.[11] A number of the steelworkers' plans have been carried forward to more comprehensive programs for reducing the proportion of labor costs to total costs (or sales) through cooperative efforts,[12] somewhat on the model of the flexible wage plan of the Nunn Bush Shoe Co. This gives management a temporary protection against a slump in sales and provides the union with more of a tangible share in cost reductions and a better insight into the business.

Under the impetus of wartime needs for increased production and better industrial relationships, some 5,000 labor-management committees with over

[8] Slichter, *op. cit.*, Chaps. 14, 18; Richmond C. Nyman and Elliot Dunlap Smith, *Union-Management Cooperation in the "Stretch-out,"* New Haven, Conn., Yale University Press, 1934; and Elliot Dunlap Smith and Richmond C. Nyman, *Technology and Labor,* New Haven, Conn., Yale University Press, 1939.

[9] Slichter, *op. cit.*, Chap. 17; and Kurt Braun, *Union-Management Cooperation: Experience of the Clothing Industry,* Washington, Brookings, 1947.

[10] Paul F. Brissenden and John N. Keating, "Union-Management Cooperation in Millinery Manufacturing Industry in the New York Metropolitan Area," *Industrial and Labor Relations Review,* 2 (October, 1948), 3–32.

[11] C. S. Golden and H. Ruttenberg, *The Dynamics of Industrial Democracy,* New York, Harper, 1942, Chaps. 8–9.

[12] Russell W. Davenport, "Enterprise for Everyman," *Fortune,* 41 (January, 1950), 55–59. See also "Union-Management Cooperation," *Monthly Labor Review,* 52 (June, 1941), 1351–1359; J. M. Scanlon, "Profit Sharing under Collective Bargaining: Three Case Studies," *Industrial and Labor Relations Review,* 2 (1948), 58–75; Ernest Dale, *Greater Productivity through Labor-Management Cooperation,* New York, American Management Association, 1949; R. Dubin, "Union-Management Cooperation and Productivity," *Industrial and Labor Relations Review,* 2 (1949), 195–209; *Partners in Production,* New York, Twentieth Century Fund, 1949; C. S. Golden, R. C. Tait, *et al.,* "Union-Management Cooperation," in *Proceedings of the Fourth Annual Meeting of the Industrial Relations Research Association,* Urbana, Ill., Industrial Relations Research Association, 1952, pp. 164–187; and George P. Shultz and Robert P. Crisara, *The Lapointe Machine Tool Company and United Steelworkers of America,* Washington, National Planning Association, 1952.

7 million workers were registered with the War Production Board from 1942 to 1945. Most of them handled certain war-related activities in their plants, but not more than 10 to 20 per cent concerned themselves with production activities. About 60 per cent of the committees were functioning in one capacity or another at the close of World War II, but by 1948 only 5 per cent of those originally existing still continued.[13] The author who gave these figures concerning wartime experience concluded that "one result, emphasized more than any other accomplishment, was the improvement in employer-labor relations. While committees did not solve basic economic issues, they promoted understanding and eased situations caused by long hours, concern over War Labor Board wage cases and union contract negotiations. . . ." [14]

Types of Cooperation and Their Contribution toward the Reduction of Conflict

The historical survey shows that specific efforts toward the solution of problems of joint interest through union-management cooperation may be helpful in reducing conflict. Hence it may be worthwhile to examine the types of cooperation in the order of their likelihood of success. An attempt to collect evidence for this purpose was made through a questionnaire sent by the author to 1,000 manufacturing companies believed to engage in some kind of cooperation. Of the 263 who replied, 226 stated that they had been practicing some form of cooperation.[15] They had attempted, through direct or indirect efforts, to increase productivity and to achieve some measure of mutual accommodation. Table 27.1 shows the types of problem on which some degree of agreement was reached in cooperation programs between unions and management and also in programs between employees and management in which unions did not participate.

The majority of these types of cooperation are reported to have resulted in tangible improvements in dealing with the problems considered. The industrial relations between the two parties frequently changed from hostility to "peaceful disagreement." The record also shows that cooperative plans have not, by any means, worked in all cases. Many unions and companies believe that alternative means are preferable. From the limited experience it cannot be said that union-management cooperation will necessarily provide a solution to any industrial-relations problem. But it can be stated that it offers at least one possible answer and that there has been enough success with it to make its consideration worthwhile. It may therefore be of interest to indicate briefly those types of cooperation which are so obviously to the advantage of both sides and with the disagreements so relatively rare that they offer a good chance of success; next, those which lie in the twilight zone between success and failure because the benefits are less obvious or the possibility of difference of opinion

---

[13] Dorothea de Schweinitz, *Labor and Management in a Common Enterprise,* Cambridge, Mass., Harvard University Press, 1949, pp. 36–37.

[14] *Ibid.,* p. 81. See also Carol Riegelman, *Labor-Management Cooperation in United States War Production,* Geneva, International Labor Office, 1948.

[15] This number is somewhat less than the number of companies still engaged in cooperation just after the end of World War II. *Ibid.,* p. 37.

Table 27.1   Types of Cooperation

Subjects	Employee-management cooperation	Union-management cooperation	Total
Safety	22	14	36
Waste	27	6	33
Understanding of company policies	25	7	32
Regular attendance	24	4	28
Employee insurance	20	7	27
Quality control	21	5	26
Tools	23	2	25
Employee health	18	6	24
Job evaluation	14	9	23
Lateness	20	2	22
Training and apprenticeship	16	5	21
Methods improvement	18	3	21
Incentive systems	15	4	19
Labor turnover	18	1	19
Working conditions	15	3	18
Discipline	14	2	16
Production planning	14	1	15
Technological changes	11	2	13
Setting output standards	11	2	13
Utilization of machinery	12	0	12
Employment stabilization	10	2	12
Promotional programs	8	3	11

is greater; finally, those aspects of cooperation which are at present more likely to end in failure than in success.

Types of Cooperation Likely to Be Successful. Almost all those types of cooperation are likely to be successful which engender relatively little difference of opinion or which are concerned with problems the solution of which is not subject to disagreement and the results of which are of great mutual benefit clearly visible to both parties. The subject most likely to succeed in union-management cooperation is accident prevention. Both sides have human, moral, and economic interests in the reduction of work injuries, interests which in the sum of their strength probably exceed any other matter of joint relations. Results in the field of accident prevention can be measured more accurately than in any other subject of cooperation because of the need to keep accurate data for insurance premiums and claims and because of the influence of the National Safety Council. Safety work is also one of the few areas in industrial relations where the variables of union-management cooperation can be fairly successfully separated from other influences. Significant savings in money and health resulting from cooperation in this area are reported by many companies. Joint efforts at reducing waste are another example of cooperation likely to be successful. The results can be easily measured, recognized, and distributed. Practically everyone can make a contribution. Joint collection of facts may clarify difficult situations, resolve disputes, and lead to better understanding of mutual problems.

Types of Cooperation with Uncertain Chances of Success. Subjects of cooperation falling in the twilight area between success and failure are job evaluation, improvement of working conditions, and absenteeism. On the one hand, there is mutual interest in bringing about greater equity in the distribution of the wages bill, in providing better surroundings, and in reducing wage losses through absences. Improvement in these areas cuts grievances and sources of mutual irritation. On the other hand, managements have at times been unwilling to pay the costs of the adjustments jointly arrived at, and they complain about the lack of competence of union members, the bypassing of the foremen, and the conservatism of the craft unions in regard to changing work methods. Unions, for their part, are sometimes seriously troubled by being held responsible for unadjusted complaints, unaccepted suggestions, and interference with the personal habits of their members (in the case of absenteeism).

Types of Cooperation Not Likely to Be Successful. Cooperation is likely to fail in those areas where it is most needed, namely, where there are the greatest differences of opinion between the two parties and considerable power to disagree. Management may feel a responsibility to let the unions have a voice in areas in which agreement is difficult, largely in order to facilitate consent, and the union may feel a responsibility to management for "a fair day's work" and to their members for "fair pay" (*e.g.* protesting higher standards which may offset increases in wage rates). Hence the unions may want their own time-study stewards to share in the responsibility and authority for setting standards. Usually, however, the joint responsibility is too much of a burden for union representatives. They may ask for it, but they may actually be unwilling to take it because it may associate them with failure or, in case of success, mark them as overly "management-minded."

A telling example of failure of cooperation is joint responsibility in time study. If the union engages in this joint activity, it may take on too much because of the great difficulties of accurate work measurement and the impossibility of satisfying all concerned. The union has to undergo the heavy expense of training time-study stewards and of paying them, in order to insure their independence. Similar problems may arise in joint administration of discipline. While it may be possible to overcome the difficulties, the union will often prefer to "walk the last mile" with a disciplined member or to utilize the grievance procedure to protest output rates which it considers too high rather than to accept responsibility for the actions. For its part, management is often reluctant to let go of a function in which the chance of agreement appears so slight.

Possibilities and Limitations of Union-Management Cooperation

What can be learned from the analysis of past and present union-management cooperation as a means of reducing industrial conflict or removing some of its sources? The conditions of possible success may be traced through the successive phases of the cooperative process: "good faith" as a precondition; establishing the framework; and the conduct of cooperation.

Good Faith. Good faith is required as a basis for cooperation. Each side must recognize that it can accomplish its objectives to some extent only through the other and must act on that assumption. This is obvious when one regards the close interdependence of the two parties for the achievement of their economic goals, status, equality of treatment, participation, etc. Good faith requires the recognition of potentially constructive contributions by both sides and a favorable attitude toward their utilization. This, in turn, assumes knowledge of one another's problems, aspirations, and difficulties, the possibility of accomplishing one's objectives with the aid of the other, a standard of conduct toward the other somewhat equivalent to that applied to personal friends, the contemplation of agreement, and the use of suasion toward that end.[16]

As evidence of labor's good faith, management frequently includes the stipulation of such basic conditions as these: First, labor's attitude should hold promise of "constructive possibilities" such as absence of strikes and violence, a well-administered contract, a smoothly working grievance procedure, a genuine interest in the well-being of the company. Second, management's right to manage must not be challenged—a position which may be defended on the grounds of the necessity for conserving management powers, safeguarding stockholders' rights, and fulfilling a responsibility to employees by safeguarding their individual freedom against invasion by organized groups. Management's right to manage is also stressed as a compensating activity in this age of declining pecuniary opportunities. Third, management commonly feels that the economic contributions of cooperation should outweigh its costs. There is doubt whether labor really has a strong desire for cooperation and, if it does, whether it can bring a broad enough point of view to the problems, whether it can overcome educational deficiencies and the ignorance of the techniques of cooperation, and whether it will avoid conflict with the organization "principle" that responsibility should be undivided and that authority should correspond to responsibility.

The success of many suggestion plans offers evidence, however, that rank-and-file labor frequently does exhibit the intelligence and the desire to make constructive contributions. After all, a proportion of present management were once ordinary workers themselves. The men on the job are more familiar with their own work than anyone else, and they may bring a fresh point of view to job problems, while the union representatives may supplement this by supplying larger, over-all views. Training and direction may greatly aid working people in presenting their ideas clearly. The problems of sharing responsibility are worked out successfully at the executive level, and presumably this can also be accomplished at the worker level, especially in respect to long-run problems.

If there is good faith on both sides, even the first two conditions of management will be less serious than they appear at first sight, for the very essence of good faith is the assurance of the constructive possibilities which management requires. This basis for cooperation is usually evident on a number of subjects, even in the case of radical and "unconstructive" unions. These unions

---

[16] This point is well analyzed in Neil W. Chamberlain, *Collective Bargaining*, New York, McGraw-Hill, 1951, Chaps. 18–19. The definition and nature of cooperation described in this chapter are based to some extent on discussions with Prof. Chamberlain.

recognize that they have to render service to their members in order to maintain themselves, and toward that end they need to secure some degree of cooperation from management. The problem of sharing managerial powers would seem to be a matter of alternatives. In the areas of management authority that are challenged by the unions, management either may share power in a constructive way through cooperation or may be forced to make concessions as a result of collective bargaining. If there is good faith (and admittedly there may not be, or it may be difficult to know whether there is), then the threat to managerial power would not arise, because cooperation would promote the very objectives which power reservation attempts to maintain.

On the union side the prerequisites of good faith include, first, the condition that cooperation should not threaten the organizational security of the union. When the union fears that the basic existence of its organization is threatened, all resources are mobilized to defend it. As Seebohm Rowntree once pointed out, "When union-management relations are in the fighting stage, the union sends its guerillas; only when relations are relatively peaceful, does the union send its ambassadors." If the guerrilla situation prevails, union members may be afraid to serve on union-management committees, or if they do serve, they may refuse to commit themselves to anything. Here again, if good faith exists in the sense in which it was defined, this would imply a genuine acceptance, on the part of management, of organized labor, a sincere demonstration that there is no thought of undermining the union through cooperation but rather that the mutual education in each other's motives may result in the betterment of labor relations generally. Similarly, it may be pointed out that good faith fulfills another requirement of labor: the recognition of labor as a constructive force. A third implication of good faith is a standard of conduct on the part of management that assures that the union representatives' security will be maintained. Rightly or wrongly, the members may suspect that their representatives who enter into cooperation may no longer retain their sense of union responsibility, for "feet under the same mahogany table don't kick." But here again, the existence of good faith would make it possible for management to aid the labor members in demonstrating their ability to increase the economic and noneconomic benefits of the members through cooperation. The union representatives may increase union membership by demonstrating to doubtful employees that they, as union officials, are capable of constructive and harmonious relationships with management. In some cases cooperation may even turn out to be the factor which saves the company from bankruptcy and hence may be the means of saving the members' jobs.

There is one final set of conditions which cannot easily be met by management. Either intra- or interunion disputes may make cooperation difficult, if not impossible. Several well-functioning committees have had to be abandoned because cooperation was not in accordance with the policy of the international union. While international officers may, on the one hand, welcome cooperation because it reduces their problems and shows them to be "labor statesmen," they may, on the other hand, fear to be considered collaborators, or they may decide that the local is losing its militancy. Some of the facets of the international's policy and conditions may be viewed as inconsistent with good faith; such inconsistencies may be a revolutionary philosophy, a policy of handling disputes on an industry-wide basis, the occurrence of intraunion disputes between cooperating and noncooperating units, the fear of rival unions (*e.g.* the absolute unwillingness of John L. Lewis's union to participate because it was Philip Murray's idea), and the absence of a competent staff.

This final set of conditions for cooperation also includes the basic attitude of the union leadership. A large section of the "old-line" leaders do not think in terms of cooperation. Those who have had long tenure of office (the average length of the international union president's term of office in ten "representative" unions is said to be 26 years) [17] have gained and held their power by being fighters, and they are not likely to change. Those who are subject to reelection at frequent intervals (often the officials of the local) at times consider reelection their most important objective, since otherwise they can accomplish nothing. They must "sell a package" annually and "deliver" higher wages, shorter hours, and better working conditions. The easiest way to achieve these things is to "let management find the means." If necessary, they may agree to the installation of an incentive plan, though many unions oppose this. However, successful cooperation might be a welcome package too.

The "new" union leaders, who may be well versed in economics and are often highly sophisticated in argument, tend to consider the scope of union-management cooperation inadequate. According to them it usually takes place within a framework of economic policy largely determined by management alone, and management's unwillingness to share its prerogatives makes little true cooperation possible—even though such sharing may increase total revenue. The new leaders may stand aloof because management does not run after them or because they fear that cooperation may undermine their ability to fight. They may consider the plans which management is willing to offer "so stripped of vitality and potentialities" as to be offensive. While they do not belittle the importance of the formal machinery of consultation, they say they will judge labor-management cooperation by the extent to which labor can be instrumental in determining policy and the extent to which its reasonable suggestions are given effect. If employees and union are to be placed in a totally subordinate position, if they are allowed to discuss matters of only minor importance, and if their suggestions can be referred to only advisory, not policy-making, bodies, then the new leaders believe the rank-and-file representatives will probably lose their enthusiasm for labor-management cooperation.

Establishing the Framework. Important disagreements may arise in setting up and carrying out cooperation. Such disagreements may be due to the nature of the formal organization, the composition and powers of the members of the group, the methods and procedures, the nature of the subjects and of the decision-making processes, the carrying out of the resolutions of the meetings, and the checking of the results. In view of the variety and divergence of the disagreements which may arise, it would seem appropriate that special machinery should exist to resolve them. The appropriate machinery would appear to be collective bargaining, which is devoted to the resolution of differences of interest. The cooperative machinery should not be burdened with problems which, in its very nature, it is not designed to handle (unless the differences are minor and temporary). The collective bargain should resolve the fundamental

[17] Eli Ginzberg, *The Labor Leader*. New York, Macmillan, 1948, p. 64.

differences so that the two parties can devote themselves to the pursuit of joint interests. Where differences are of a major nature and cannot be resolved by collective bargaining, it is not likely that union-management cooperation will be successful. There are two exceptions to this statement. First, some problems are of such great mutual interest that they can be solved regardless of the general relationship between the two parties. For instance, there are a number of important accident- and waste-reduction programs which succeeded even under such adverse conditions as were created by radical unionism and strong managerial antiunionism. Secondly, union-management cooperation may be the very instrument to overcome fundamental differences. As a famous sociologist put it: "There is no reason why . . . the labor of supplying society with all the material goods needed for its general comfort should not become both agreeable and attractive. There is no necessity of waiting for the slow action of evolution in transforming human character. The result can easily be brought about by the transformation of human institutions." [18] Thus the very organizational form of union-management cooperation and the successful collaboration on projects of great mutual interest may in the course of time lead to cooperation on matters of lesser mutual interest.

A second important factor in establishing the framework of cooperation is the company's position in the industry. This is particularly important in determining the objectives of the program, whether it should be aimed at better industrial relations or at cost reduction. For purposes of this analysis three major types of firms may be distinguished: dominant, semidominant, and subordinate. Dominant companies are those whose profits are high and continuous; in their major markets sales of their chief products account for from 20 to 90 per cent of the industry's sales. Often they have only a small number of competitors; patents and long-established good will may be factors. Under these circumstances possible savings of money and time through cooperation are less important than in the case of firms less favorably situated. In the large dominant company the objective of cooperation tends to be "good industrial relations" rather than cost reduction; and since such firms are often powerful enough to prevent unions from disturbing day-to-day efficiency, cooperation is designed mainly (1) to ward off major labor disturbances, since the cost of shutting down and starting up again is often high, if not prohibitive, and (2) to win the approval of the general public. But it should be noted that many companies in dominant positions feel strong enough economically to ignore the possibilities of cooperation altogether or to give it up soon after introducing it. Instead they are economically quite free to pursue courses which stress the maintenance of management rights and established relationships with labor, stricter supervision, and discipline; they rely on high wages and generous benefit plans, communication plans, and status recognition in order to prevent disturbances with their employees.

Where the company in the dominant position is small in terms of sales and number of employees, its views are somewhat different. Such a company hopes to keep costs so low that the entry of newcomers into the industry will be hazardous, and at the same time it hopes to establish or maintain a level of wages well above that of the local community; therefore, cost reduction

[18] Lester F. Ward, *Applied Sociology*, Boston, Ginn, 1906, p. 336.

tends to be more important. Emphasis on a high degree of labor participation is often found, principally with the aim of arousing the local union to higher productivity and of avoiding any hostile intervention by the international.

If the firm is subordinate, sales of its main product in its major market are only a small proportion of the total industry sales of that product, and profits are small (usually less than 5 per cent of invested capital after taxes). Such firms are naturally interested in reducing unit costs so as to maintain their existence. Usually they cannot increase revenue by influencing prices, and if the union is industry-wide, the bargaining powers of the subordinate company tend to be inferior; it has little or no power to change the wage or security policy of the union—it can merely complain and sign the contract. In so far as most other firms in the same industry have similar relationships, one way of getting a "competitive edge" is through union-management cooperation. Under keenly competitive conditions the union may cooperate in order to survive, since a reduction in the number of jobs or the failure of wages to rise sufficiently may lead to a loss of members. Thus the resources of national unions and the ability of local leaders (who in some cases are extremely competent) have occasionally been made available to the hard-pressed small firm, or at least there has been ready consent to the measures proposed by the companies in an effort to stay in business.

The firm in the semidominant position (a position between dominant and subordinate) is often more receptive to cooperation than either of the other two types of firm. While there may be no immediate and acute need to cut costs, such a firm is considerably more interested in cost reduction than the large firm, especially in the long run. Also it has to make up for certain lacks, for example, its personnel department is not likely to be so well staffed. It has less influence on the union than the dominant company. On the other hand, the union is less likely to be concerned with "policy" and the "record," especially if the semidominant firm is hard pressed by a few large competitors or has less than average ability to pay under conditions where multi-unit bargaining prevails. The companies are not averse to cooperation because they can thus promote both good labor relations and productivity. Hence cooperation tends to be most widespread for this type of company.

The final "framework" consideration is the stage of the business cycle in which programs of union-management cooperation are started. In the majority of cases, it appears to be easier to start in periods of prosperity than in a depression. For labor the risk of unemployment as a result of increased productivity is less, since those who are displaced can usually be absorbed in other departments of the company or by some other concern. The chance of fairly tangible and immediate gain is greater because the company can frequently afford to be liberal. Since the political and economic strength of the union is usually greater in times of prosperity than in a depression, it can afford to take a stronger position and to be less afraid of domination by management. Management can more easily afford to bear possible losses of cooperation in the early stages; since cost reduction may not be such an urgent problem, it can devote itself more to the less tangible aspects of cooperation. Increases of output resulting from cooperation are more likely to be sold profitably when product demand is expanding. Finally, both labor and management may win public approval if they consciously link higher wages to higher productivity in times of rising prices and thus provide a stabilizing influence.

On the other hand, a great obstacle to cooperation in prosperity is that both sides may see no need for it at a time when both profits and wages are rising. However, in a depression, the need for cooperation is apparent because of pure economic necessity. Then it is often born of fear: on the part of management, fear of further monetary and prestige losses; on the part of labor, fear of unemployment. When things get bad enough, both may be willing to clutch at any straw. Labor may also be forced to cooperate because, during the depression, its bargaining strength may be greatly reduced. On the other hand, it must be noted that, if cooperation in a depression is to be effective, labor may have to assume a high degree of responsibility. Since cost-reduction efforts may require reduction of jobs, labor representatives may be saddled with the blame, even though adverse results would have occurred without their participation and might have been worse. If, on the other hand, the union refuses to participate, it has little chance of making a real contribution or gaining any credit for successful efforts. Managements fear possible losses and waste of time from union cooperation. There may be too many other important problems, and the union's potential contribution may be of minimal importance.

Conduct of Cooperation. Even when considerations of good faith and the nature of the framework for cooperation are satisfactorily met, the problem of the successful conduct of cooperation remains. To some extent this refers to the successful selection of cooperating representatives and to the organization and procedure of committee meetings—considerations which space prohibits my discussing here. To some extent the conduct of cooperation depends on the support of the key persons in management and labor. An auspicious start can often be made through a top management or union official, and they need to convince other top officials in their organization. Even if top support cannot be obtained, it may still be possible to start minor types of cooperation at lower levels. For example, the personnel director or the union's safety committee can initiate safety meetings. Success on a small scale can then be used as an argument for the spread of the experiment. Finally, foremen and shop stewards need to be reassured and integrated into the program.

In setting up a particular type of committee, many managements will tend to argue for the exclusion of union participation on the grounds that the possibility of collective bargaining and, hence, the pressing of disagreements may be eliminated, that independent individuals should have a greater chance of participation, that many problems are departmental or employee-management problems, and that the line of managerial organization is strengthened if cooperation is built on the departmental unit. These arguments are likely to lose much force if the exclusion of union officials not only causes the loss of their contributions but brings about their active opposition. Furthermore, many subjects such as job evaluation and employment stabilization, training programs, and accident prevention are often discussed more effectively on a plant-wide basis, which parallels that of the local union organization in most instances. Then, too, cooperation at the departmental level encounters the difficulty that the foreman, who is a key management person in employee-management cooperation, may be quite incapable of directing the effort.

Finally, there is the problem of gain sharing. Both union and management may have to keep in mind the necessity of selling a larger output which results from cooperation and the consequent need for a wider diffusion of the gains through price reductions to maintain or increase sales. In addition, there is the problem of what part of the gains accruing from the increased productivity should go to labor and what part to management. Obviously, as things stand at present, there is no absolute and correct standard for fair distribution. About the most that can be said is that the more successful plans of cooperation tie the reward closely to the amount of effort involved and make the connection between the effort and the reward very plain. It must be remembered that a mere increase in the firm's revenue-paying capacity is not likely to be satisfactory to the union. Tests which they apply to cooperation—and sometimes find wanting—include the disadvantages which result along with the gains and the way in which the gains are shared. The memories of unemployment, speed-ups, downgrading, and rate cutting of past plans are still strong in many unions. An integrated plan like that of Geo. A. Hormel & Co., which includes cooperation, an incentive plan, and a guaranteed annual wage, all with union participation, is rare. The solution of this problem, as of so many others which arise in cooperation, is a rather specific preliminary analysis of what good faith implies and of a framework which limits the range of possible disagreements.

CHAPTER 28 GROUP DYNAMICS IN THE INDUSTRIAL SITUATION

Mason Haire   *University of California (Berkeley)*

Twenty years ago there was relatively little interest in the nature of the work group, in the social organization of the factory, or in problems connected with the internal dynamics of groups at work. The difference between management and workers was clearly seen, but chiefly in terms of their different responsibilities to the industrial organization. Management's view of its job and of the skills required of it was chiefly in terms of financial decisions, planning of production, work methods, wage-payment plans, and the like. Management efforts to deal with employees concentrated on the individual and gave little attention to groups or social relations in the plant. Today, in contrast, we have a great deal of interest in such things as the role of the leader in the group, the effect of group participation in making decisions, the motives and attitudes of workers. Within this relatively short time there has been a tremendous growth of interest in problems connected with the work group as such and a corresponding growth of ideas and experiments concerning the nature and importance of groups at work. This chapter is aimed at describing the history of this change and at identifying and analyzing the principal concepts that result from it.

By and large the interest in groups has not directly and specifically affected industrial conflict. It has not found its primary application at the points where industrial conflict erupts into acute symptoms: negotiation problems, threatened work stoppages, grievance procedures, and the like. Instead, the work centering in group dynamics has chiefly influenced thinking about underlying areas of labor-management contact: problems of leadership, training, productivity, and managerial personnel policies and practices.

Historically, the current interest in what has been called "the dynamics of the work group" and in "human relations in industry" dates from the famous research work of the Mayo group in the Hawthorne plant of the Western Electric Co. and, more specifically, from the publication, in 1939, by F. J. Roethlisberger and W. J. Dickson, of *Management and the Worker*.[1] They first dramatized the social organization of the work group; their statement of the problem initiated and gave shape to much of the current interest in employees' attitudes; and they were the first, as far as I know, to use the phrase "the human problems of management" and, consequently, to give rise to the host of implications that flow from this statement of the problem.

[1] Cambridge, Mass.. Harvard University Press, 1939.

Three other forces have accounted for a good deal of the direction that these interests have taken since then: In the late 1930's Lewin was becoming interested in the dynamics of groups, and the early work of Lippitt and White on the "climate" of groups and of Bavelas on leadership as a group problem mark the beginning of a line of work that has grown tremendously in this area. Moreno's work on sociometry and on sociodrama (role playing) instituted a second line, which has also contributed to shaping research and thinking in this area. Finally, during the war and immediately following, there was a rapid rise in the tendency for industry, and other institutions, to ask for help with various internal problems, and for social scientists to provide it. This had the combined effect of leading many sociologists, anthropologists, and psychologists out of laboratory problems and toward a realization of the problems of people at work, while at the same time the social scientists' way of phrasing problems led members of industry to see social and human factors among the important aspects of the work situation.

Starting with the Hawthorne experiments and shaped in its development chiefly by these three lines—the work of Lewin and his followers, the work of Moreno and that stimulated by his ideas, and the consultative role of the social scientist—there has arisen a large body of theoretical and experimental work on problems centered on the work group and, perhaps, an even larger popular interest in the subject.

History

The Hawthorne studies began in 1927, against a background of managerial interest in efficiency experts whose chief contributions were in terms of such things as incentive plans, work simplification, and speed-ups. The Harvard group began with the sober academic aim of finding "the relation between conditions of work and the incidence of fatigue and monotony among employees." [2] Their original plan was to segregate five employees from an operating department and, by varying such factors as temperature, humidity, and hours of sleep, to see the effect of these factors on output. It was conceived to be a year's project. Instead, they were led into a maze of human problems acting as determinants of productivity—into attitudes, motives, interpersonal relations in groups, and strong forces from the group itself. Instead of spending a year, they stayed 5 years, and the publications from their study are hardly finished now.

Their first experiment began with the introduction of unaccustomed rest pauses, asking the question Will the introduction of rest pauses reduce fatigue and monotony and, hence, increase output? At the conclusion, considerable rise in productivity was evident, but the experimenters felt that

> . . . it is clear that two essentially different sorts of changes occurred . . . those changes introduced by the investigators in the form of experimental conditions [*i.e.*, the rest pauses, etc.] . . . and a gradual change in social interrelations among the operators themselves . . . and between the operators and their supervisors. . . . From the attempt to set the proper conditions for the

[2] *Ibid.*, p. 5.

experiment, there arose indirectly a change in human relations which came to be of great significance. . . .[3]

The next variation consisted in shorter working days and weeks, and again an increase in output was evident. However,

> . . . a change in morale had been observed. No longer were the girls isolated individuals, working together only in the sense of an actual physical proximity. They had become participating members of a working group with all the psychological and social implications peculiar to such a group.[4]

A detailed analysis of the wage incentive as a determinant of increased output was made, leading the investigators to conclude that the wage itself was not adequate to account for the change and that, in fact,

> . . . only in connection with the interpersonal relations at work and the personal situations outside of work, to mention two important variables, could its [the wage's] effect on output be determined.[5]

At each step in the attempt to investigate the effects of external conditions, the research was forced back to a consideration of personal factors and group forces. This gradual elimination of mechanical peripheral explanations forced the investigators more and more into two kinds of interest: the first was an interest in the operators as individuals, with special reference to their attitudes—something which led eventually to the installation of the now famous counseling system at Western Electric and contributed greatly to the more recent interest in the attitudes and motives of workers. The second result of the experiment was to force the investigators to pay more and more attention to the role of the work group and to institute a detailed study of the social organization of the factory.

Not only the reality of the group but also the strength of the group became apparent. The group operated quickly and effectively both to protect itself from internal violations of its own patterns and to protect itself from the outside. The group effectively restricted the output of individuals. Acting in fear of real or fancied consequences of a high production rate, the group put social pressures (ridicule, ostracization, and the like) on those who exceeded the implicit "group rate." Indeed, the operation of this restriction was so careful that there was considerable evidence not only of restriction of output but of false production records which underestimated actual output in order to keep the reported production (and, hence, pay) in line with the group standard.

These factors and these findings led Roethlisberger and Dickson (as well as the others of the Harvard group—Mayo, Whitehead, Homans, *et al.*) to put increasing attention on the social organization of the work group, on the implied problem of the relation of a supervisor to his subordinates, on the communication patterns within the group, on the motives and attitudes of the workers, and in general, on the complex of problems under the heading of "human relations in industry."

[3] *Ibid.*, pp. 58–59.
[4] *Ibid.*, p. 86.
[5] *Ibid.*, p. 160.

After the publication of these researches, thinking about industrial problems was radically and irrevocably changed. It was no longer possible to see a decrement in productivity simply as a function of changes in illumination, physical fatigue, and the like. It was no longer possible to look for an explanation of turnover simply in terms of an economic man maximizing dollar income. The role of the leader began to shift from one who directed work to one who enlisted cooperation. The incentive to work was no longer seen as simple and unitary but rather infinitely varied, complex, and changing. The new view opened the way for, and demanded, more research and new conceptualizations to handle the problems.[6] Whyte's *Human Relations in the Restaurant Industry* is a classic in detail and insight, as an example of a study of the social organization of working groups and of the implications of these group forces for industrial problems.

The work of the Lewinians on group problems was also first published in 1939, as Lewin, Lippitt, and White reported on the studies of autocratic and democratic climates in groups and on their effect on the behavior of the group and the individuals.[7] In these experiments, several boys' clubs were formed and the leaders carefully cultivated various roles for themselves and the members: in one case, a democratic permissive leader; in another, an autocratic directive leader; and in another, a somewhat wishy-washy laissez-faire kind of leader. Detailed records of the behavior of the members of the various groups were taken, and an analysis was made of such things as the amount and direction of aggression as a function of kind of leadership, the productivity of the groups under different climates, their fixity of purpose, and the like. The experiments began both a methodology and a theoretical interest which has grown and contributed greatly to research on groups and group processes. At about the same time, Bavelas was working with a project of training group leaders in recreational centers, and his work [8] brought the interest in group processes down to the more specific problem of the way in which leaders function and of the role of the leader in the group.

At about this same time, two currents of thought introduced by J. L. Moreno were also influencing the thinking and research concerning groups in the industrial setting. In 1934, Moreno published his monograph *Who Shall Survive?* [9] in which he spells out his notions about sociometry and the analysis of intergroup relations. The other main concept—that of sociodrama, or role playing—is harder to date. Moreno's *Psychodrama* was not published until

[6] In general terms, the line of development indicated by the Hawthorne research has been carried on by Homans at Harvard and is represented in B. B. Gardner and D. G. Moore, *Human Relations in Industry,* Chicago, Irwin, 1950; and in B. B. Gardner and W. F. Whyte, "Methods for the Study of Human Relations in Industry," *American Sociological Review,* 11 (1946), 506–512.

[7] K. Lewin, R. K. White, and R. Lippitt, "Pattern of Aggressive Behavior in Experimentally Created 'Social Climates,'" *Journal of Social Psychology,* Vol. 10 (1939); R. Lippitt, "Theory and Experiment in Social Psychology: Autocratic and Democratic Group Atmosphere," *American Journal of Sociology,* Vol. 45 (1939); and R. Lippitt, "An Experimental Study of the Effect of Democratic and Authoritarian Group Atmosphere," *University of Iowa Studies in Child Welfare,* Vol. 16, No. 3 (February, 1940).

[8] K. Lewin and A. Bavelas, "Training in Democratic Leadership," *Journal of Abnormal and Social Psychology,* Vol. 37 (1942).

[9] New York, Beacon House, 1934.

1946,[10] but his interest in the technique and his work in the field date back much further. Indeed, Moreno himself suggests that his own play groups at the age of four and a half mark the beginning. However, the impact of the idea of role playing on industrial group problems began toward the end of World War II.

Moreno's sociometry is essentially an attempt to measure the network of relations between individuals within a group. Instead of taking a group as an entity or as representing a single force (as, for instance, the "democratic" climate in the Lippitt and White experiments above), he tries to get at the kinds of bond that exist between members, and his sociometric technique is to map these relationships quantitatively by having each member, for instance, list the persons in the group whom he likes most and least. By collecting these responses, it is possible to draw a structural map of the group in terms of the bonds holding the accepted members of the group in and those tending to expel the rejected members. The main influence of this idea seems to have been that it provided another technique for handling the problem indicated by Roethlisberger and Dickson when they spoke of the social organization of the factory, in that it allowed the investigator to specify the kind of relationships within the social organization, to quantify them to some extent, and to define them in such a way that one group could be compared with another. The second important contribution of sociometry is that it led the study of group processes back to an individual basis. Instead of viewing the group sociologically from the outside, as if it were a single entity, Moreno's technique led investigators to see the group from the point of view of the member of the group. The study of groups is, thus, the consideration of the way in which the individual sees the group and also, because the picture of the group is one of relationships between individuals, the study of roles in groups and of patterns of interaction between the members. All these things—the possibility of mapping group relations, the emphasis on the individual's view of the group, and the idea of roles in relationships and of an analysis of interaction patterns between group members—contributed greatly to the development of work in the field.

The idea behind Moreno's second major contribution—psychodrama or role playing—can best be illustrated by an example. Let us suppose an industrial trainer is working with a group of foremen to teach them, for instance, the importance of "getting the facts before you make a decision." He can tell the foremen that they must get the facts, but the foremen may not know how to; the principle may not have any specific directions for them in terms of actual behavior. Likewise, the instructor may tell the foremen that a subordinate will be resentful if action is taken without involving all the facts. Again, this is a somewhat isolated idea, and while the foremen may understand and even agree with it, they may miss its complete impact. Consequently, the instructor sets up a role-playing situation in which one foreman plays the role of a subordinate who has, for instance, missed work without calling in, while someone else plays the role of the foreman involved. The players are separated from the audience, and the play foreman rebukes the worker. The individual playing the worker may now feel, to some extent, the injustice of the rebuke without full information, and the group sees the foreman's technique somewhat

[10] New York, Beacon House, 1946.

more objectively. The scene is repeated with the play foreman trying to find out why the apparent infringement occurred. Now the possibility of getting information is not a verbal direction to him, but he can feel to some extent the possibility of actually doing it. The group may suggest other ways, and other members may try them out. The result is that the reason for the principle is felt in terms of the reactions of the person rebuked, and certain kinds of behavior in the relationship may now be seen as possible in action.

The essentials of the technique seem to be that the play situation provides an opportunity to do something in an environment protected from many of the pressures that are imposed upon action in real life. The situation makes it possible for the actor actually to feel the problem within himself, instead of hearing it described verbally, and he may learn entirely different things thereby.[11]

Concepts

The effect of these historical trends has been to shift the kinds of interest in research and conceptualization regarding the industrial situation. Within the plant these developments have led both labor and management—though, at present, the changes are most clearly seen in managerial thinking—to look again at the organization, the work situation, and the relation between people at work.

Paradoxically, one of the results of the new interest in the structure and characteristics of the work group has been that much more attention has been paid to the individual as the importance of his attitudes and motivation and of the roles he plays in the group becomes better recognized. A second general result has been a great increase in the attention paid to the problem of individual motivation at work and to the reanalysis of the question Why do men work? with a new emphasis on nonfinancial incentives. The recent stress on incentives other than pay seems directly linked to the tendency to analyze individual motivation (and the repeated finding that the implications of an "economic-man" theory of motivation are inadequate) and to the realization of the powerful effect of group pressures of the kind Roethlisberger and Dickson pointed out in discussing restriction of output. A third general psychological area which has been emphasized by the development of group theory is the field of perception. More and more attention is paid to the way the group member sees his group, sees himself, and sees his superiors and his job. A faint beginning of a phenomenological approach to the problems of interactions in industry seems discernible as a result of attention on the problems of groups.

In many ways, the most striking single change has been not the influence of Moreno, Lewin, or the Harvard Business School but the tremendous change that has come about because a large group of people with basic training in general psychology have become concerned with the problems of groups at

---

[11] In this sense, Moreno's notion has an interesting point of contact with the almost forgotten James-Lange theory of emotion, one of the earliest psychological theories. This theory maintained, in brief, that emotion follows, and is the result of, action. In Moreno's terms, one might say, similarly, that the learning needed is an emotional reorganization. Since this is so, an intellectual or verbal approach is not effective. Action produces the emotion, and the emotional learning must come through action.

work. The presence of this group of psychologists in the field has brought about a particular kind of analysis of causal factors. Without them, the interests in perception and motivation mentioned above would have no context into which to fit. Although it is relatively much more difficult to identify their specific points of influence, the psychologists who broadened thinking about industrial problems from the more traditional industrial psychologists' considerations of individual differences and aptitude measurements to include the concepts of learning, perception, adjustment, motivation, and the like, have done much to make possible the more specific developments mentioned here.

Within this general framework, a group of more specific concepts emerge as new and relevant:

1. *Participation*. The importance of participation—of participation of the individual in matters relevant to him, of participation of the individual as a representative of the group, and of participation of the individual in the group—has been one of the most striking results of the interest in group phenomena. Allport's paper [12] on participation presents a good general survey of the situation, but the true importance of the notion is perhaps better seen in the details of specific research.

Bavelas [13] provides a good example in an experiment with a group of production workers. The workers in Bavelas's situation were producing goods by methods and at rates which had been thoroughly explored by time-study industrial engineers. They were paid piece rates, on the basis of a standard 60 units per hour, and were working at about the standard rate. The plant psychologist held meetings with representatives of a group of the workers, in which he first created a permissive situation in which they could discuss the problems of their work and then led them to make a group decision about the rate at which they thought they could produce the same items. The decision was made in the security of the psychologist's assurance that their rate of production would not influence the piece rate nor would they be expected to maintain it if they decided subsequently not to. In spite of the fact that the supposed ceiling on the job had been 75 units per hour, the decision was first to produce 84 units, and this was subsequently raised to 95. In fact, the new production stabilized in the neighborhood of the high 80's and was maintained there for a matter of months. Meanwhile, the rest of the plant and other work groups who had the same attention from the psychologist but did not have the same kind of participation in the decision about production rates continued to produce at the old rates. It seems clear that much of the before-and-after difference in the experimental group is the difference between the situation where one works by methods and at rates that are set from without and to which one must conform, and the situation where one participates in deciding for himself at what rate he will work.[14]

[12] G. W. Allport, "The Psychology of Participation," *Psychological Review,* 53 (1945), 117–132.

[13] A. Bavelas cited in N. R. F. Maier, *Psychology in Industry,* Boston, Houghton Mifflin, 1946, pp. 264 ff.

[14] A similar effect of participation in group decision on behavior is shown in some very ingenious studies of food preferences conducted under Lewin's supervision during the war. K. Lewin, "Group Decision and Social Change," in T. M. Newcomb and E. Hartley (eds.), *Readings in Social Psychology,* New York, Holt, 1947.

In another experiment in the same area, Coch and French [15] worked with textile workers on the role of the group in restricting output. In the particular plant, it was frequently necessary to change work methods to meet competitive situations within the industry. Typically these changes in method involved an initial drop in productivity as the workers learned an unfamiliar task. Moreover, those who had previously met the standard on another job learned more slowly than new trainees, indicating some additional negative force in the retraining situation. The relearners also typically showed a lower final level of performance than their own old level or than new trainees did and typically showed more grievances and higher turnover. In all, the problem of new methods was a real and expensive one to the company. Hypothesizing that the resistance to change occurred because the workers were frustrated by their inability to do the new work at first and that the transferred workers developed a strong group with negative attitudes toward the job, Coch and French provided participation in the change for some of the workers and not for others. The participation group was told about the economic factors calling for new methods, and the problem was discussed by them. Suggestions as to changes came from them, and the group itself provided representatives to make experimental runs on the new methods on the basis of which time studies were set up. The control group was changed in a more conventional manner. The production department modified the job and set a new piece rate. The workers were called in and the new rate and method were explained, as well as the reason for the change. The essential difference seems to be between the change that is imposed from without and that which arises from within as a result of participation and in which the member of the group feels some involvement himself. In the case studies by Coch and French, the results indicated that the participation group learned faster than the control group, attained a higher final level, and showed less turnover and fewer grievances. In all these cases, the experimenters feel that the mechanism which makes the participation effective is the fact that the individual sees himself and the task differently, that the participation and consequent involvement change the motivation involved, and that the group-decision situation allows the pressures of the group to be directed toward action rather than toward hindering it.

It might also be suggested that these same characteristics of participation and of its effect on the individual's motivation and commitment to the change may well be playing a large part in the success of many of the so-called profit-sharing plans which have been in vogue in recent years. Although they are usually explicitly based on a simple economic theory of motivation in which increased productivity is achieved through offering the worker a share in the profits, the mechanism of such a plan, in fact, usually includes more involvement on the part of the hourly paid worker with the decisions about production and involves his having a share in many of the decisions himself. In view of the striking results indicated in these experiments on participation, it is possible that the chief causal agent in many of the profit-sharing plans is less in the economic incentive itself than in the altered role of the individual and his membership in the group as a function of the operation of the plan. In

[15] Lester Coch and John R. P. French, Jr., "Overcoming Resistance to Change," *Human Relations*, 1 (1948), 512–532.

Russell Davenport's article [16] on the Scanlon profit-sharing plan, such an interpretation of the phenomena seems to fit the situation well.

2. *Roles*. The concept of roles in relationships, which had previously been very largely confined to the sociologist, has assumed considerable importance in the study of groups. Here, as investigators probe into types of behavior patterns in groups, into the structure and organization of groups, into emerging leadership, and the like, a concept is needed to cover the integrated behavior pattern which characterizes a man's activity and defines the kinds of relationships he has with others. Previously, sociological definitions of role had tended to emphasize the institutional character of a role. Thus a father's role consisted in playing the part of (*i.e.*, doing what was appropriate to) a father in a given culture. It was thus defined largely in terms of a niche in an institutional organization and in terms of the way in which the person was seen by other members of the culture. Now, with increasing attention paid to the individual and to his activity in small groups, more emphasis has been put on the functional value of roles in determining interaction patterns and small-group structure and on the meaning and importance of particular roles to the individual.

Good operational definitions of roles in this sense are hard to find. For the most part, investigators seem to feel that the term points to something real and important in group phenomena, but the concept is left, for the moment, largely undefined. Benne and Sheats [17] have approached the definition of roles by example, in an attempt to classify kinds of roles in terms of their function in the group. Thus an attempt is made to separate "group task-oriented roles" from "group building-and-maintenance roles" and to relate these to some extent to the needs of the individual who plays them. Virtually everyone who works with group problems seems to feel the need of such a concept, and its further definition and refinement may well materially advance research in this area.

Much of the research on groups has implicitly utilized a concept of roles and, in so doing, has helped to show its importance. The early Lippitt and White experiments, mentioned above, on democratic and autocratic groups provided situations in which the leaders played very different roles, and much of the analysis is in terms of the consequent roles of the members and of the effect of these role possibilities on the group structure and productivity. Similarly, many of the attitude studies which followed from the general line of interest traced in this material have come to emphasize, for instance, the different modes in which the foreman or supervisor can carry out his function. These too constitute roles which are available to him as the leader, and the study of their differential effectiveness is a very promising area. It is also interesting to speculate on the possibilities of an analysis of the roles that are possible for labor and management in their relationships and on the relative fruitfulness of various role combinations; indeed, it seems possible that the best statement of the problem of industrial peace may be in terms of the mutual perception, by labor and management, of compatible roles. The notion of roles

[16] Russell W. Davenport, "Enterprise for Everyman," *Fortune*, 41 (January, 1950), 55–59.

[17] K. D. Benne and Paul Sheats, "Functional Roles of Group Members," *Journal of Social Issues*, Vol. 4 (Spring, 1948).

is clearly linked to the lines of development traced in the interest in the work group. The use of this concept represents an attempt to place the individual with respect to the group, an attempt to represent the meaning, for his motivation, of his position in the group, and an attempt to handle the integrated character of his behavior patterns. While the thinking and research in this area is still relatively incomplete and unfinished, it is an approach that holds considerable promise.

3. *Training Techniques and Leadership Concepts.* Growing out of the attention to roles and out of Moreno's interest in role playing come both a new view of the leader in terms of his relation to the group and its members and a set of techniques for training leadership skills. The use of role playing for leadership training has mushroomed until there is hardly a major company that has not tried it at some time nor a major personnel association or training director's group that has not held meetings on the subject. The essential character of the psychodramatic, or role-playing, technique has already been described. It provides an opportunity for the player to see his own role more clearly, to see the relation of specific actions of his own to the formation of his role in a group, and through the protected practice session, to modify his role by trying out other courses of action in play. A clearer picture of the use and values of role playing is best seen in the detail of the specific situation. Good examples of such situations are provided in virtually verbatim transcripts by French.[18]

In the same context, the emphasis on roles in relation to group members and the interest in the individual motivation of the member of the work group have led to real revision of the notions of leadership. An excellent example of the influence of these tendencies is seen in McGregor's article on the conditions of leadership.[19] McGregor approaches the problem of industrial leadership by an analysis of the motivations of the subordinate workers, identifying in detail the subordinate's dependency, his need for independence, his need for security of various sorts, and the social and egoistic need satisfactions which he may obtain at work. Then, seeing the leader's task as that of obtaining help from his subordinates and maintaining their willingness to work, McGregor goes on to define the role of the leader in terms of the kinds of behavior demanded by the situation and by the subordinate's needs. Such a view of leadership naturally fits the use of role-playing techniques in training leaders, since it places so much emphasis on the leader's behavior as it is seen by, and as it affects, the individual subordinate.

4. *Communication Patterns and Interaction Patterns.* Increased attention on the composition and structure of groups has focused research and thinking on two allied problems. One of them is the set of problems associated with communication within groups: problems of the patterns of communication within groups and the relation of communication to the structure of the group

---

[18] J. R. P. French, Jr., "Retraining an Autocratic Leader," *Journal of Abnormal and Social Psychology,* Vol. 39 (1944); and J. R. P. French, Jr., "Role-playing as a Method of Training Foremen," in S. D. Hoslett (ed.), *Human Factors in Management,* New York, Harper, 1946.

[19] D. McGregor, "Getting Effective Leadership in the Industrial Situation," *Journal of Consulting Psychology,* 8 (1944), 55–67.

and to the function and effectiveness of groups. In addition, there has been a great deal of activity in the development of theories of communication in general—outside the particular sphere of an interest in the group as such or of the industrial group specifically—and much of this work is contributing tangentially to an increased understanding of the nature and importance of communication in work groups. Bavelas [20] has made a first attempt to construct a theoretical model by means of which the problems of communication within groups can be handled, and there is no doubt that valuable research will flow from this. With industry facing bigger and bigger problems of communication both within and outside its own organizations, this field promises to be one of the most crucial in future development.

At the same time, and partly as a result of the same pressures, there has been an increasing development of methodology for studying interaction patterns within groups and for using these categories of interaction to help define the structure of the group and to diagnose the causes of its fruitfulness. Bales, particularly, has provided research workers with a method for observing the interaction between members of a group and for categorizing the types of behavior that occur, *e.g.*, dominance and submission, attack and defense, cohesion, disruption, etc. Such an approach provides another dimension to the study of groups. On the one hand, it gives a fuller picture than the bare structure of likes and dislikes that is the result of the conventional sociogram. The structural map of the group now has more detail and meaning as it is further defined in terms of the kinds of behavior that occur along the lines of organization. On the other hand, this technique provides a more detailed and more manipulable analysis of the social organization of the group than the primarily sociological description initiated by Roethlisberger and Dickson. The over-all characterization of the social organization of the work group often provides real insight into the nature of the group, but at such a general level that it is hard to handle either theoretically or experimentally. Techniques for recording interaction patterns promise to provide a means whereby the valuable contributions of the sociological analysis can be retained but described in a more manageable form—one that is more closely related to the role of the individual in the group and to his particular behavior.

In summary, we have a line of work which has very greatly changed thinking about the industrial work group, not only the thinking of research workers in the field but that of management and union groups within the industrial situation. It is a line which got its initial impetus from the Hawthorne studies and was shaped in its development by the Lewinians and by Moreno's ideas. It has given rise to a recognition of the social organization of the factory and to the role of group pressures and individual motivations at work. In its development, it has spotlighted the importance of roles in relationships and their function in the structure of groups, the tremendous resources tapped by the participation of group members, the detailed structure of groups and of interaction patterns between members of groups, and the effect of all these on the effectiveness of groups. It has led research back to an analysis of the motivation of the individual who is a member of a group, to his perceptions of himself and

[20] A. Bavelas, "A Mathematical Model for Group Structures," *Applied Anthropology,* 7 (Summer, 1948), 16–30.

his position in the group, and to his attitudes and feelings about work, the company, and himself. It has led to the restatement of the problem of industrial leadership, to the development of new training techniques, and to increased attention on the problems of communications within groups. As an experimental and theoretical field, it is new; in many ways it is advancing at very different rates in different areas; and many of its concepts lack the clarity of definition of more fully developed disciplines. In spite of these difficulties, it offers great promise for improved understanding of the problems of people at work. In this sense it is an attack on the problem of industrial conflict at its base in the nature of the labor-management relationship.

In connection with the scientific analysis of work groups, two issues are often raised which lead to sharp and important moral questions. In the first place, it is often said that the elaboration of leadership techniques and the so-called human-relations point of view primarily represent tools for management to use *against* labor. In the second place, even when the developments are not attacked as being one-sided in the labor-management relation, it may be felt that they involve a kind of "manipulation," a way to "trick people into doing things," and as such are morally wrong. Each of these points warrants attention on ethical grounds.

It is certainly true, historically, that the developments in group dynamics and the concepts discussed here have primarily been associated with a management point of view. This is partly because management has kept closer contact with academic research and partly because management has hired the consultants to work on their problems. While these facts may account for the historical development of the emphasis on management's problems, they do not amount to a moral sanction. The social scientist is still responsible for an ethical judgment regarding the community effects of his work. To date, it is impossible to say that research in this field has fully recognized its responsibility to the community or that it has impartially furthered its application equally among management and union groups. Social scientists in this respect seem to be in the position of the nuclear physicists who, concentrating on what they fondly believed to be an isolated laboratory problem, created a major social force. Many of them are beginning to wrestle with the moral implications of their research at this time. Similarly, it seems time for the workers in the field of group dynamics in industry to face clearly the societal implications of their work and to think out their responsibilities to the groups involved and to the community.

The second problem—the criticism of manipulation—seems to disappear as an ethical issue upon examination. The implicit argument seems to be that it is bad to use an understanding of the reasons people do things to get them to do things one wants them to do. It seems to violate the privacy and integrity of the individual for us to use our knowledge of his motives to direct his behavior. Certainly the idea of being so manipulated ourselves causes a sense of uneasiness in all of us. However, it hardly seems possible to live in an interdependent society without spending a good deal of time trying to get people to do things we want them to do. The issue that causes the uneasiness seems to be the rational and explicit use of knowledge to further our cause. Our culture is becoming more and more interdependent—in specialized production systems, at home, and in the community. In the face of these things, it becomes increasingly true that we must achieve our need satisfactions through other people. Since this is true, it means that we must work through people and that we must try to get them to do things we want them to do. To use a better understanding to achieve this end is only to accomplish it better.

The moral problem does not entirely disappear, however. Although manipulation, in this sense, seems inevitable in human organizations, two points still seem to remain for crucial value judgments in its accomplishment. Society has always outlawed certain techniques for getting people to do what one wants them to do. As our understanding of behavior becomes more and more refined, we will have to refine equally the moral judgment on the kinds of coercion—however subtle—that are approved and disapproved. Further, the manipulator who modifies another's behavior must always bear responsibility for the cost to the other—in whatever terms—of the modification. It is the responsibility of the behavior changer to anticipate the consequences of the change and to protect the other in so far as possible.

CHAPTER 29 RECOGNITION AND UTILIZATION OF EMPLOYEES' ABILITIES

Edward T. Raney   *Wayne University*

MANAGEMENT has become increasingly concerned with the problem of creating worker interest in job assignments as a basis for lessening industrial conflict. It is believed that self-motivated workers who are intrinsically interested in their jobs and who take pride in the accomplishment of their assigned tasks are likely to be both high-producing workers and ones who do not actively engage in various manifestations of industrial conflict as an outlet for dissatisfaction or lack of interest in their jobs.

Better Placement of Employees

An important aspect of the creation of worker interest in jobs is the consideration of the worker's potential skill and ability. Workers who have reason to believe that management is making an honest effort to find a place in the organization for them in keeping with their skills develop a sense of well-being and confidence in management which is reflected in their attitudes toward jobs and toward productivity. Characteristic of a modern business or industrial personnel program are the maintenance of personnel-skill inventories, job-transfer and promotion procedures to ensure better placement of workers, procedures for recruitment from within the organization, extensive programs of training employees as a primary aid in this recruitment, and various other procedures for locating, developing, and placing workers in terms of their potential ability and achievement.

Whenever such programs are successful in shifting at least a small percentage of workers into more appropriate jobs or whenever such programs lead workers to believe that management is concerned with, and will take steps to utilize, their potential skills, management gains a dividend in increased employee loyalty and productivity. Because this is true, these programs are being adopted by many companies and are being broadened by those companies which have had some experience in evaluating the programs.

These programs came into being for several reasons. It has become more and more difficult to recruit workers with specific skills in the open labor market. Management has been forced to recruit from within its own organization. Training programs to develop already recruited skills available within the organization produce not only a supply of labor otherwise not obtainable but also a supply of workers interested and motivated in their jobs. An extra dividend is derived from encouraging workers within the organization who have not yet been promoted to hope and work for a better and more interesting assignment. This situation has been confirmed by surveys of workers' opinions which indicate that lack of opportunity for promotion or transfer to jobs in keeping with workers' abilities and interests is a source of job dissatisfaction. Also, surveys of especially productive occupational groups indicate a high level of job interest and satisfaction in achievement brought about through the utilization of their abilities and skills. It has become evident to management that better placement of employees and utilization of their skills make an effective contribution to the prevention of industrial conflict.

Satisfaction in Placement Depends upon Workers' Attitudes

It should be recognized that reports by workers that their abilities are not fully utilized are expressions of feeling and attitude toward their jobs and not necessarily reports on actual job conditions. At the time of the interview the worker may have been influenced by any one of a number of feelings. He may have a rather generalized feeling that, given a proper chance by management, he could perform well on a job carrying a higher pay classification and more status. He may be remembering a job which he wanted, though another worker received the promotion or transfer. He may think that management fills most good jobs from outside the organization because the man hired for a particular job that he or his friend wanted was so recruited. He may realize he is in a dead-end job. He may think that he has not advanced in the organization as much as he should have. In his opinion his friends with other organizations may have advanced more rapidly.

These and similar feelings are not ordinarily arrived at by a careful analysis of such factors as what his own potential ability is, what management has done for him, and what the manpower requirements of the organization are. The attitudes represent rather the worker's reaction to the way he feels that he or fellow workers have been treated by management. In fact, dissatisfaction with management's use of his abilities may result from incidents or problems quite unrelated to his job. In his personal affairs financial problems may have developed which could be solved if he received higher wages. In such case his present job, which up to now was one in which he was well adjusted, becomes a job which fails to give him an opportunity to show what he can do. If he should fail now to get a promotion, i.e., a job paying more money, he now feels that his abilities are not fully utilized. To take another possibility, his wife may have become discontented because a friend's husband was promoted to a better job, or he may be criticized by his family because he didn't receive a promotion to a job which he personally didn't care for. Such pressures in family and social relationships may be reflected in the worker's opinion of management's use of his abilities.

Further, it is possible that any condition of employment, other than full use of ability, which tends to develop a feeling of unrest, insecurity, or job dissatisfaction may well be expressed overtly by the worker in terms of a definite attitude that he is in a job which does not fully utilize all of his abilities. For example, personality difficulties with supervisors and fellow workers may develop in the worker a distaste for a job and a desire for a different and better job, perhaps interpreted by the employee as a case of not having his abilities recognized.

On the other hand, it should certainly not be assumed that, whenever a worker reports that his ability is not being utilized, it is a case in which management has made every effort to train and place the worker properly but the worker has not recognized and appreciated it. Many reports are based on fact. Often management has not utilized the worker's skill, although management may feel, from its point of view, that the man's abilities are fully utilized.

Thus the problem of whether a worker's ability is fully utilized usually becomes a matter of opinion, an opinion dependent on a number of factors which may not be easily identified. Management, the unions, and the worker must all recognize that utilization of ability in industry is not an easily attained goal. The satisfactory achievement of the goal is determined not only by actual employment conditions but, in an important degree, also by existing attitudes—and both the conditions and the attitudes depend on a number of factors, not all of which are directly controlled by management, by the worker, or by the unions. A number of these factors are summarized in the following paragraphs.

Many Factors Influence Utilization of Ability

1. Difficulties in measuring a worker's ability in a reliable and valid manner may result in honest differences of opinion between worker and management. Most judgments of abilities are based on subjective opinions which may be easily influenced by prejudice, bias, or simply poor judgment. If such judgments are not so invalidated, it is difficult to prove that they are not. Objective measurements of samples of behavior, such as those used in various testing techniques, are not usually sufficiently valid to be substituted for subjective opinion, although test results are being used and accepted as complements to subjective opinions. The most acceptable approach is the accumulation of records over a period of time, including both subjective opinion and objective data from as many sources as possible. Here again, however, if the records are not made available to the employee and discussed with him as they are accumulated, the worker has cause for claiming possible prejudice.

2. Similar difficulties in the determination of what constitutes adequate performance on a job also result in honest differences of opinion between worker and management regarding the employee's competence to do the job. Many operations are set up in such a way that an individual's effort is not easily identified; for example, it is dependent upon the efforts of others. In some cases work standards may control more or less the kind of job a worker does; in other jobs work standards are so vague that success on the job is a matter of the supervisor's opinion. As a matter of fact, the development of better methods of measuring abilities has been seriously handicapped because adequate criteria of successful job performance have not been identified.

3. The fact that ability to do a job may depend almost entirely upon the worker's having an opportunity to learn a job, either through formal training or job experience, may seriously limit job opportunities for any given worker. Potential ability cannot be utilized in industry unless the potential is developed through training and experience.

4. Worker ability is a direct function of motivation. Individual motivation will necessarily change from time to time because of a variety of causes which may or may not be related to the job. A change in a worker's goal in itself may bring about dissatisfaction and a feeling of not being fully utilized in his present job.

5. Opportunities for utilization of ability are limited to the requirements of the industrial organization. This limitation becomes more pronounced as a worker advances in an organization, but it is also important at low levels in advancement from routine repetitive jobs to the more desirable skilled assignments.

6. Requirements for ability in an organization do not remain static. Conditions within and without the organization may eliminate or change the nature of job requirements before workers have developed the ability to do the job or before the workers get a chance at promotion.

7. Requirements of an organization usually cannot be met adequately when all promotions are given to personnel developed within the organization. New blood, new ideas, and new approaches are needed in order to keep the organization in an alert competitive position. Too much inbreeding tends to limit variation in management initiative.

8. Full utilization of ability does not necessarily bring promotion and increased status in an organization. Many jobs in industry are operations which require the development of specific skills. Possession of these skills may not lead to further advancement in the organization but may allow for full utilization of the employee's most valuable present ability.

9. It should be recognized that the worker, management, and the union may not define utilization of ability in a similar manner because their goals may differ. The worker looks at the problem of full utilization of ability in terms of the desirability of the assignments which he receives. The most desirable assignments are those which also carry a higher pay rate, although many workers are content with assignments which offer more status or social prestige or an opportunity to do what the worker likes to do. When an opportunity occurs for a worker to improve his status, his approach will tend to be in terms of a justification for his being the man for the job rather than in terms of an objective analysis of his real abilities. However, if he obtains the desired job, he will feel, at least for a while, that his abilities were recognized and utilized, whether or not the maximum of his assumed ability is required by the assignment. Thus, if an assignment offers more money, more prestige, and/or more desirability, the worker usually feels that management is recognizing and rewarding his ability in an appropriate manner.

10. Management looks at the problem of full utilization of ability in terms of its goals (efficiency and productivity) rather than in terms of an individual worker's goals (the achievement of job desirability). Management's goal is met and, from its point of view, abilities are being utilized when work standards, either formally expressed or unexpressed, are satisfactorily complied with —and when, in addition, a supply of workers is assured who can perform in a similar or better manner to meet replacement or expansion demands for manpower. Jobs in industry, whether hourly rated or salaried, are made up of a number of specific duties and responsibilities which must be performed at least up to

a certain degree of proficiency in order to maintain an even flow of operations throughout the organization. A worker, hourly rated or salaried, executive, technical, or professional, is meeting management's goals if he can perform a prescribed set of these duties and responsibilities in a manner efficient enough to contribute to the maintenance of the over-all operation. As a matter of fact, when a worker can perform his assigned duties in a more productive manner than anyone else, thus assuring an even more productive organization, that worker, in terms of management objectives, is likely to be thought of as fully utilized no matter what his actual or potential ability may be. Because this is true, workers who are outstanding in proficiency in any one job may find it difficult to obtain a transfer to another assignment of like responsibility and may have little or no chance at promotion. However, management is beginning to discover that, unless the worker's goals are met, management's objectives of efficiency and productivity cannot be achieved because the efficiency and productivity of workers is dependent upon feelings of satisfactory movement toward their own goals. To the extent that this relationship is recognized by management, to that extent management has developed personnel programs which seek to assist workers in meeting their goals.

11. Union policy concerning utilization of skill tends to emphasize a different goal: reward of workers for length of service with an organization (seniority). Full utilization of workers occurs, in effect, when all openings, except for entry jobs, are filled by training workers who have earned seniority rights. When workers with more ability and/or training but less seniority are available, such workers should wait their turn which will come through the accumulation of seniority rights. For the most part, when workers with seniority are promoted and cannot meet the work standards set up by management, there is a feeling on the part of the union that the fault lies with management for not having provided the worker with a better training program.

12. Since opportunities are not limitless and since any worker's goals are changeable, there may always be an area of disagreement between the worker and management on how well management has utilized abilities. Full utilization of workers' abilities may be impossible of attainment.

Management Needs to Recognize Workers' Goals

Management, by defining ability in terms of relative success in meeting work standards, may create a feeling on the part of their employees that management is interested only in production and not in the people who get out production. This conflict seems inevitable as long as management must have a primary interest in obtaining more production at less cost while the workers' primary interest tends to be in obtaining more pay, more status, and more self-expressive opportunity for utilizing their real or imagined abilities.

The most significant attempts to solve this conflict have been through the development of programs by management to ensure recognition and reward of potential abilities of workers by means of a regular and systematic program of pay raises and promotions. These programs generally include a more or less exhaustive inventory of workers' skills and abilities and a procedure for filling job openings as they occur from within the organization, since management has the responsibility not only for maintaining an adequate labor force for meeting work standards but also for providing an adequate supply of replacements. Through these programs management seeks to meet its organizational responsibilities at the same time as it provides workers with opportunities for better use of their potential abilities.

As indicated above, there is evidence that recruitment from within the company, in-service promotion programs, do pay dividends in terms of employee loyalty, job satisfaction, decreased turnover, and increased efficiency. This type of approach by management has certain limitations, however, which may not be recognized by workers. First, it may be inadvisable to fill all job openings with workers from within the organization. In-service training tends to inbreeding of ideas. A certain amount of inbreeding of ideas is very good because it tends to lend stability to an operation over a period of time. However, too much inbreeding tends also to limit the number of new ideas and new approaches introduced into an organization, which in turn may weaken the organization and its program over a period of time. In any organization some turnover is healthy; new blood may be necessary to keep the organization in a good competitive position. Each time an outsider is brought into the organization, however, there will be a feeling that management has digressed from its policy of fully utilizing the skills of its present employees. This will be true even though management has included in its statement of policy on promotion allowance for bringing in a certain percentage of employees from other organizations.

Second, in spite of an in-service promotional program, not all workers will be satisfied because there will not be sufficient opportunities for each worker to obtain the particular assignment that he considers in keeping with his abilities. It should not be forgotten that the function of management is to maintain a going organization, which means the continued provision of services or products, and not to arrange opportunities for all workers concerned to have an assignment which they desire. The nature of prescribed duties and responsibilities will be determined and limited by the operations in which the company is engaged. It is management's responsibility to assign these duties and responsibilities in such a manner as to conduct as efficient a business as possible. A worker's opportunities will be limited to the operations available within the organization, unless he is the very unusual worker who creates his own opportunities, and as he climbs the organizational levels, he will find fewer and fewer such opportunities. There can be only one president, only a few vice-presidents, a limited number of department heads, and only a few more section supervisors or foremen. Also, in a large organization (and frequently even in a small one), a surprisingly large number of jobs (perhaps 25 to 50 per cent) are more or less dead-end jobs which require very specific skills and abilities, which, having been learned, even for the sake of a promotion, tend to limit future promotions because of their very specialization. An in-service promotional program is not the over-all answer to job dissatisfaction due to malutilization of skill, because there are simply not enough opportunities to allow for full utilization of abilities.

Third, in-service promotional programs must be supported by in-service training programs; otherwise workers will not be ready for promotions when opportunities do arise. This statement implies that ability to do a job is a matter of training as well as of ability, that potential ability is not usable unless the worker has been trained or developed, and that the worker with potential ability has nothing to offer unless he trains himself or is trained by management. If this point of view is accepted, then management not only has the responsibility for utilizing a worker's ability fully but also has the responsibility for developing the worker's potential ability so that such ability can be utilized. Otherwise, workers will have to accept the responsibility for developing their potential ability in order that management may utilize it, or the worker must face the fact that his abilities will not be utilized. Unless employees have assurance from management that such potential will be utilized, they will hesitate to pay the costs involved in obtaining training. Also, the worker is usually not in too good a position to determine just what kind of training management can utilize. If management assumes the expense, management has no assurance that the workers will stay with the company after being trained. Job and market conditions change, so that workers may not get the jobs for which they were trained since the jobs may no longer exist at the end of the training program. Nevertheless, management is increasingly assuming responsibility for the development of workers in order that their potential ability may be fully utilized.

A program for developing workers places on management the further responsibility of determining, before training starts, what a worker's potential may be. It also creates another area of dissatisfaction for the workers who are not selected for training and who feel that they are thereby discriminated against. They will feel discriminated against because they believe that, if given a chance, they would have succeeded as well as those who received the training. As long as the primary criterion of selection is a supervisor's judgment, formally called merit rating in industry, the worker may have a justified cause for disputing the validity of the selection process. In fact, union policy has rejected merit rating in favor of seniority as a selection procedure, primarily because merit ratings are, in the last analysis, subjective and consequently open to possible favoritism, prejudice, and unreliability. As yet, methods have not been developed for assuring valid and honest subjective ratings of individuals. Perhaps the most reliable, but unfortunately the most expensive, selection technique is the job tryout, the method whereby an employee is given a trial on a job under normal conditions of supervision and training to discover whether he can perform satisfactorily. It is customary for unions to point out that this method is the only valid method available at present. It is difficult to refute these claims in the light of the experimental evidence of the possible unreliability of subjective judgments and of the limited validity of most so-called objective (testing) techniques.

Perhaps the answer is training for all who wish it, which appears to be implicit in the point of view most generally expressed by labor representatives, since union policy tends to advocate that seniority should be a primary, if not the sole factor, in determining promotions. Under this policy, advancement becomes, by definition, a reward for service. When a worker has completed more service than any other employee, he is the logical person to select for the next job in line. If the worker with longest seniority cannot do a job, it may not be because he lacks the ability to do the job but because management has not trained him. When this approach is followed to its logical conclusion, it implies that management does have the responsibility for training all workers and should not discriminate on the basis of estimated potential ability before training. Every worker should be given the right to train for any job. If he can learn it, the one with most seniority is rewarded by getting the job when an opening occurs. This procedure, of course, would entail considerable expenditure in training costs, which would be passed on to the consumer.

This union point of view, as well as the policies followed by management in its training programs and by the worker who believes that, given the chance, he could always do a job at a higher pay level, assumes that ability is something which is learned, that it is dependent on opportunity to learn, and that full utilization of ability carries with it the necessity for opportunities to develop potential skills. Personnel programs conducted in line with this philosophy have to become programs of personnel development. This implies personal counseling as well as personnel recruitment, employment, and adequate placement.

Conclusions

1. A factor in industrial conflict is the failure on the part of management to recognize the necessity for giving adequate consideration to worker goals of satisfaction and achievement in work through utilization of their abilities along with consideration to management's own goals of efficiency and productivity.

2. Utilization of worker ability involves not only selective placement on the job but also consideration of a worker's total personal adjustment both on and off the job.

3. Full utilization of worker ability may be impossible of attainment since it is dependent on many factors not under the direct control of management. The best approach to the problem available to management at present is probably a program of continuous personnel development and counseling.

CHAPTER 30 SOCIAL-SECURITY LEGISLATION AND INDUSTRIAL CONFLICT

William Haber   *University of Michigan*

THE causes of industrial unrest and conflict do not lend themselves to simple analysis and classification. The responsible factors are many and complex. Among these, insecurity—whether of job, income, health, life, old-age dependency, or status—has always occupied a prominent place.

Insecurity

Fear of joblessness is assigned a major role in explaining the working rules and job customs of industrial workers, whether organized or unorganized. Restrictive practices, jurisdictional rules, penalty overtime rates, seniority— these are but illustrative of the hundreds of job rules whose prevalence is largely the result of workers' experience with unemployment. Not infrequently specific labor conflicts revolve around the issues of economic security. In the postwar strikes in the automobile industry and the long steel strike of 1947, retirement pensions for employees were an important issue. And the literature of American unions makes a bold prediction that the annual wage may become an important issue in the "next round" of collective bargaining. Thus social security has achieved a high priority in the scale of demands of organized workers. The so-called fringe issues in collective-bargaining contracts, for example, are usually concerned with employee welfare programs, with wages during sickness or hospitalization, with group life insurance, and with retirement benefits.

This shift from individual to group responsibility for dealing with the problems of insecurity has affected industrial conflict in several important respects. In the first place, it has greatly enlarged the interests of workers in the role which legislation can play in furthering their social objectives. Traditionally, American labor unions relied primarily upon economic action through collective bargaining to achieve their program. In recent years, a legislative approach through political action has received increased emphasis. To some extent, the area of conflict has been transferred from the picket line and the collective-bargaining conference to the political arena and the legislative hall. At the same time, legislative programs and interests of the unions have been broadened in scope to include the whole range of government activity affecting both domestic and international issues—a far broader perspective than that of traditional unionism. As a result, the area of conflict is concerned with the central political issues of government, with tax policy, unemployment programs, wage and price controls, fiscal policies, and international affairs—all of which have a bearing on economic security.

Development of Social Legislation

Social legislation to deal with the problem of security has been developed in all modern industrial nations for many years. Germany in the 1880's and England after 1910 pioneered in several forms of social insurance designed to deal with income loss resulting from sickness and unemployment. In these and, subsequently, in most other lands, the method of social insurance through legislation has been relied upon to provide an underpinning of minimum income security for an ever-increasing proportion of the population. The German development at the end of the 19th century was inspired by a belief that industrial conflict would be reduced and that the rising wage-earning class would be less inclined to flirt with revolutionary ideas. The British movement after 1910 was in part a reaction to the widespread poverty of large sections of the British working-class population. It came also from the belief that the method of social insurance could be effectively employed to deal with the inevitable insecurities faced by the industrial population in modern society. And, as developed in the "cradle-to-the-grave" program of the Beveridge Plan, the idea was developed of national obligation to provide "freedom from want" through state action by underwriting a standard of minimum needs below which no one would be permitted to fall because of interruption to private earning power.

While social legislation as a method of dealing with economic security is of more recent origin in the United States, it has made rapid strides since 1935. Before that year, American social insurance was largely confined to state workmen's-compensation legislation for industrial injuries and, in some states, for occupational diseases. The movement for old-age pensions was under way in the 1920's, but before 1935, the state program for the aged was but little better than general relief with which we became acquainted on a mass scale during the Depression of the 1930's. The health-insurance movement, born in the enthusiasm following the passage of accident-compensation legislation, made no headway. And unemployment insurance, in spite of serious public concern with the problem of unemployment in 1914, 1920–1921, and after 1929, was enacted only in Wisconsin, in 1932. The public-assistance programs for dependent children, the blind, and the disabled were on a local or state basis with meager funds and only partial coverage in most states. And the voluntary group-insurance plans for hospitalization, surgery, and medical care were still to be developed. In brief, social-security legislation had hardly begun in the United States, the most industrialized nation.

The explanation for this tardy development is to be found largely in American political and economic institutions. The newness of the country and the relationship between population and resources spelled years of rapid economic growth and a steadily increasing number of jobs and opportunities. The adverse effects of industrialization were perhaps deferred longer in the United States than in England or in the continental nations. A large proportion of our people depended upon agriculture or self-employment for their income. Unemployment was looked upon as a personal problem, and even now many would characterize the unemployed as "some folks who won't work." Old-age dependency was a relatively minor problem on the farm and in the small rural town. Emphasis on thrift and self-reliance went hand in hand with a philosophy that the government had clearly limited powers. Such authority as government possessed to deal with the problems of the wage earner belonged to the forty-eight states under their "police powers," and not to the Federal government. This was a serious retarding factor to the enactment of social legislation. Most states hesitated to impose tax burdens upon their employers for social insurance in the fear that they would thus place their industry at a disadvantage in competing with other states.

An additional cause for the slow beginning of social-security legislation was found in the fact that the rural legislator, a controlling voice in most legislative bodies, was not overly sympathetic to the economic problems of the urban wage earner.

Social insurance in the United States took a bold leap forward with the passage of the Social Security Act of 1935. The facts in support of such legislation had long been known. Congressional committees, investigating the economic depression, dealt with the effects on family income of unemployment, sickness, disability, and the death of the breadwinner. These facts alone, however, were not sufficient to explain the adoption of such significant legislation. Two other developments account for the sharp reversal in the American attitude on social legislation as a method of dealing with the economic problems of the wage earner.

The first is the Depression of the early 1930's. That catastrophic period in our recent history made a deep impression on the minds of most Americans and influenced their thinking on economic and political issues for a long time.

Unemployment and economic insecurity reached into the homes of millions of families to a greater degree than ever before. Many millions, including white-collar workers and professional people, experienced for the first time the degradation of applying for public relief. The sense of security of millions of farmers and skilled workers, groups heretofore reasonably confident of their economic outlook, was severely shaken. The demands for public relief taxed the resources of the local and state governments. For the first time in the nation's history, the Federal government passed legislation providing funds to aid the states and localities in meeting the relief and emergency work needs of the unemployed population.

The second reason for legislative action grew out of increasing public awareness of the problem of the aged. The steady increase in the number of aged people and the proportion of older persons in the total population became a problem of national concern. By 1980, it was indicated, the number of persons over 65 would exceed 20 million. The disturbing aspect of this development grows out of the fact that only one-half of the men and only 1 out of 10 women in that age group are self-supporting. And since persons at 65 will, on the average, live another 13 years, the economic problems resulting from the gap between physical life expectancy and working life expectancy are staggering. These facts compelled consideration of some method, more formal and certain than public relief, to deal with the problem.

The passage of the Social Security Act launched the Federal government on a program of assuring minimum income for millions of insured persons. It set up a Federal system of old-age and survivors' insurance. Through the tax-offset methods of "inducement," it led to the adoption of a system of unemployment insurance by all the states. Relying on the grant-in-aid principle, there was established a public-assistance program for the aged, the blind, dependent children, and the disabled. Also provided was Federal aid for the expansion of our public-health and child welfare services.

Perhaps more significant than these specific provisions, the adoption of the Social Security Act established a pattern for government activity in dealing with the economic risks of the population. Once accepted, Congress and the states had to deal with proposals for increasing the coverage, extending the program to include additional risks and enlarging the benefits. The Federal Social Security Act has been amended in 1939 and in 1950 and again in 1952. The state unemployment-insurance acts and public-assistance legislation have been revised continuously in response to group pressures, changing concepts of adequacy, and the purchasing power of the weekly benefit.

Magnitude of Social Legislation

As a result of these factors, plus the widespread popular and political support which has been accorded to the social-security program, it has now become a major activity of the Federal and state governments. In terms of coverage, nearly 40 million workers are protected by workmen's-compensation legislation against industrial accidents and occupational diseases. More than 80 million living persons have accumulated wage credits under the Federal old-age- and survivors'-insurance program, and over 46 million are actually covered by this legislation. About 35 million workers are estimated to be protected against partial wage loss due to unemployment by the state unemployment-insurance laws. The coverage provisions have been steadily liberalized, both in the Federal legislation dealing with retirement and, at a slower pace, in the forty-eight state unemployment-insurance laws. The trend is to enlarge coverage further, and the proposals for universal coverage, particularly for retirement, have been made for some time by the Federal Security Agency.

At the end of 1951, nearly 4 million persons were receiving old-age- and survivors'-insurance benefits; nearly 3 million of them were persons over 65 years of age. More than 5 million persons were receiving public assistance from one or another of the Federal-State assistance programs. About one-third of all persons over 65 years of age in the population were receiving social-security benefits.

The total expenditure for social insurance in 1951 exceeded $5,500,000,000. This included retirement annuities under the Social Security Act and under the Railroad Retirement Act, pensions for civil servants and veterans, survivors' benefit, disability payments under the state and Federal workmen's-compensation laws, and unemployment insurance. These insurance payments increased steadily from slightly over $1,000,000,000 in 1940. Including public assistance payments in 1951, the total social security outlays in that year exceeded $7,500,000,000. These expenditures are bound to increase further as more people reach retirement age and qualify for benefits. While large, it is pertinent to note that these social-security payments represent less than 4 per cent of the total personal income in 1951.

The accumulated reserve held in trust accounts by the Federal government suggest the magnitude of the social-security operation. The total contributions under the old-age and survivors' insurance since the beginning of 1937 exceed $20,900,000,000, and the trust-account balance in March, 1952, was over $16,000,000,000. Together with the unemployment-insurance trust account, which was nearly $8,500,000,000 in March, 1952, the social-security reserves were nearly $25,000,000,000.

How Much Social Security Can We Afford?

In spite of widespread public support, social security is still a highly controversial subject in the United States. The major issues and problems raised by both critic and advocate are concerned with basic questions. It is not possible to consider all the major issues and problems in this brief chapter. We shall limit ourselves to a brief consideration of several basic issues.

The question of the cost of social security is uppermost in the mind of most of its critics. Since all social-security expenditures must come out of current production and income, it is quite pertinent to inquire what proportion of total production society is willing to distribute for the maintenance of the unproductive portions of the population. The question is also related to taxes and tax rates and to one's conception of the point beyond which high taxes discourage incentive and production.

However, to ask the question in terms of how much we can afford is to oversimplify a rather complex problem. To ask whether we can afford a certain expenditure is to assume that the outlay would not be made if it could not be afforded. This is hardly true of most social-welfare expenditures. Many of these costs have a high priority in our scale of values. In addition, social-security outlays do not necessarily represent net additions to costs. People in need, whether old, sick, or unemployed, are cared for somehow, and social-security expenditures, to a considerable degree, represent a method of social cost accounting and not a new drain on our national income and output. This is important to keep in mind in connection with our mounting costs for the aged. In the past, these costs have been met by others, and they are now, through social-security legislation, being socialized. Monthly annuities for the aged or unemployment insurance to the jobless may represent transfer payments, a shift in purchasing power from one group to another, and not additional claims upon the nation's product.

Basically, how much we can afford depends on the size of our national production. That sets the practical limit of our liberality with low-income groups, with needy people in general, and with the level of benefits we are able to establish. Equally significant, however, are the competing demands for a share of the national product which is subject to government control through taxation. In recent years, for instance, the cost of the national defense program claimed the largest share of the Federal budget. Relatively speaking, national defense needs have the highest priority, and all other proposals must be subordinate to this objective. In other words, given a national product, the amount we are willing to set aside for social security depends on the importance occupied by this program in the minds of the public or the legislature.

As we have seen, social security has had wide public support and is likely to continue to receive it. Therefore, whether we shall be able to bear the higher social-security costs in the future will depend primarily on whether our national income continues to increase. The rate of growth of our national product depends on many factors. Among these the rate of capital formation is especially important. Capital formation is, in turn, influenced by public policy, the rate of return on investment, and the volume of savings and taxes. One cannot say, on the basis of the known evidence, that we have reached the point where these factors are likely to retard capital growth and economic progress seriously. Unless this takes place, with the resulting decline in technological advancement and productivity, our social security costs can be met.

Compulsory Retirement and Old-age Insurance

Public opinion on compulsory retirement has been undergoing a radical change in recent years. During the depression years after 1930, retiring older people from the labor market was assumed to be necessary on the basis of the mistaken "lump-of-labor" conception about job opportunities. The Social Security Act retirement provisions were influenced by this idea, and retired persons were denied the monthly benefit if they returned to work. It was assumed that, by forcing older workers out of industry, jobs would be available for unemployed younger men with family responsibilities.

The private retirement plans, including those recently adopted through collective bargaining, with isolated exceptions, also contain compulsory retirement at a fixed age. The purpose is to create promotion opportunities for younger men, especially in executive positions. For manual workers, the effect is to remove the painful decisions which must be made if retirement is a matter of individual determination.

Medical evidence and experience with retirement suggest that the selection of any arbitrary age at which retirement would be required results in great injustice to large numbers of workers. The Social Security Act assumed that people would retire at age 65. As a matter of fact, the average of retirement under that act is 69. Large numbers of older workers continue to work beyond that age.

Apart from the question of inequity in forcing retirement, except for people unable to continue to work because of disability, the economic consequences of such action are of considerable importance. Such a policy compels us to support a substantial number of people in idleness and deprives the nation of the value of their contribution to the national income. In 1948, for example, it was estimated that workers over 65 contributed over 10 billion dollars to the national product. We can ill afford to lose this large amount of goods and services. In view of the increasing numbers who will reach age 65 in the next 25 years, it is all the more important that we revise our notions about retirement and change our legislation and other practices to avoid forcing older workers into idleness. More important than good legislation is the need for developing practical programs designed to increase employment opportunities for older workers in industry and the public service.

Level of Benefits

At what level of living do we wish to maintain those who receive benefits under the social legislation? In general, public-assistance benefits in the United States are based on need. Social-insurance benefits, whether in the form of old-age benefits, unemployment insurance, or industrial accident insurance, are supposed to be related to past earnings. Actually, however, neither of these criteria has been followed in practice. Inadequate appropriations or the setting of maximum amounts as an upper limit to assistance payments usually restrict the amount available to needy families considerably below the budgetary deficiency which may have been found to exist. The political and economic philosophy and the social attitudes of legislators and public officials are often translated into the allowable assistance grants. These attitudes as to the maximum amount of assistance that families in need ought to have, rather than differences in economic or tax resources, frequently explain the wide geographical differences in public-assistance payments in the United States.

In theory, at least, the economic philosophy of the legislator should be of relatively minor importance in determining the level of benefits in social insurance. Benefits are paid as a matter of right, and their amount is related to past earnings. In actual practice, however, this principle has never been applied without serious modification. To begin with, the social-insurance-benefit formula is invariably biased in favor of the low-income worker. Thus those who barely qualify as eligible to receive benefits are assured a minimum weekly or monthly payment usually considerably higher in proportion to their regular wages than that for higher-income persons. The introduction of dependents' benefits, now part of our old-age-insurance legislation and already made part of some state unemployment-insurance laws, also modifies the earnings principle as an exclusive basis for determining the level of benefits.

A different limitation (and one designed to reduce the benefit) is that set by legislative policy which determines the maximum weekly or monthly benefit payable to an insured person. When unemployment-insurance legislation was adopted in 1936, it was assumed that a weekly benefit which approximates 50 per cent of average wages should be adequate to meet the nondeferrable outlays of an unemployed worker and to see him through normal spells of unemployment without serious reduction in his standard of living. At that time, most states adopted a maximum weekly amount of $16. Since 1936, that maximum has been increased in all states and, in most states, by as much as 50 to nearly 100 per cent. The average weekly wage, however, has advanced more sharply. As a result, the level of benefits in unemployment insurance today represents a much smaller proportion of average wages than it did when the program was initiated.

What factors determine the limits in benefit amounts set by the Congress or the legislature? Unfortunately, there are no generally accepted criteria for determining the adequacy of a weekly or monthly benefit. At one extreme is the full wage; at the other, a subsistence level. Between these, a number of measures of adequacy may be employed. Thus one could compare (1) the level of benefits today with the level established when the program was adopted, or (2) the benefit levels in one state with those in another comparable state, or (3) the benefits under one program, such as unemployment insurance, with those prevailing in another program, such as accident compensation or old-age insurance, or (4) benefit levels as an arbitrary proportion of wage loss, or (5) some measure of workers' need during unemployment. Such objective measures may influence the economist or the social worker. The legislature is more concerned with the possible effect of the size of the benefit on incentives, availability for work, or active search for a job or on industrial discipline, personal thrift, and similar qualities exceedingly important in a private-enterprise economy. All forms of social insurance are surrounded with a moral hazard, although there is no way of determining how many of, and at what point, those in receipt of social-security payments will "settle down" and live on the lower standard until the benefit is exhausted. Levels of benefit which might induce such conduct are suspect, and such suspicions explain the slow progress made in increasing the benefit amounts beyond a certain proportion of wages, especially in unemployment insurance.

American benefit levels do not appear to have departed from the "floor-of-protection" concept. The volume of malingering which exists is related to poor administration more than to the adequacy of the benefit for near-normal standards of living. Nor is there any significant evidence that social-security benefits have adversely affected the incentive to save or to work.

Social Insurance and Universal Pensions

The present old-age-insurance program has been subjected to strong criticism from two sources. The advocates of the Townsend Plan and the General Welfare Program are opposed to an insurance scheme which relates benefits to past earnings and thus limits the monthly pension. More serious criticism has come from conservative sources, including the Brookings Institution, certain insurance-company executives, and some economists. They urge that in a social-insurance law it is not necessary to have premiums or "contributions" and reserves, that the law should be financed on a "pay-as-you-go" basis, and that the so-called reserve is really nonexistent since the funds have been "lent" to the government and spent. Under the present contribution schedule, the real costs of old-age insurance are hidden, and this leads to higher benefit levels than we would be willing to approve if each generation had to meet its own pension costs.

Three major revisions are proposed. The first is to pay flat benefits to all, discarding the present method of relating benefits to past earnings. The second is to extend coverage to the entire population and thus merge the old-age-assistance program with the old-age-insurance program. Finally, many would introduce a means test as a basis for the receipt of benefits, thus abolishing the present provision under which benefits are paid as a matter of right to those eligible to receive them.

The weakness of the present plan arises from the existence of two systems of old-age security. One is "earned": when qualified, the recipient is "entitled" to it. The other is free. The free pension may in fact be considerably higher than the earned pension, and this had led to some pressure to increase the insurance benefits. The solution, to be sure, is in extending coverage to provide retirement protection to the entire population. It does not follow, however, that a flat pension is more desirable or that the pension grant should depend upon a means test.

The uniform benefit for all may have considerable justification in foreign countries where the wage differentials are relatively small. American wage patterns have wide variations on an occupational and geographical basis. A flat pension would disregard such differences. The introduction of the means test would increase the cost of administration and weaken the psychological value of the retirement benefit. Such a test and the investigation which usually accompanies it have been found distasteful and degrading by most Americans who were subjected to it during the Depression. The contributory principle, with the benefit related, at least to a degree, to past earnings, "fits" the American free-enterprise scene and, in addition, maintains a relationship between benefits and contributions which can serve as a brake against irresponsible proposals to increase benefits. The goal of full coverage for the entire population is highly desirable and will no doubt be reached in the near future. There is a strong case, however, for awaiting more experience before discarding the reserve method or adopting the means test and the flat benefit.

Issue of Health Insurance

The controversy concerning health insurance has undergone a radical change in recent years. In the first place, the insurance principle has been more widely adopted in the field of medical care than anyone would have predicted only a decade ago. The report *Health Insurance Plans in the United States,* prepared in 1951 under the direction of Dr. Dean A. Clark for the Senate Health Subcommittee, points out that about 75 million people, nearly half of our population, already have insurance against some part of the cost of medical care. Other studies have estimated that some 77 million people have some type of hospital coverage, some 50 million have some type of surgical coverage, and more than 20 million have some insurance protection for other medical expenses. Included in the latter group are a growing number of comprehensive plans which cover the entire costs of the services of physicians and general hospitals. The insurance idea, once highly controversial, is now accepted and, as the figures above indicate, is already widely adopted.

The current controversy is, therefore, not about health insurance but about whether government action should be employed in extending such medical-care insurance to the entire population, that is, compulsory health insurance. Those who urge such action contend that the voluntary insurance movement is most common among people easily accessible to group insurance and less common among those difficult to reach by the group method. As a result, those who fall within the category of the poorer risks—rural residents, lower-income families, aged persons, and Negroes—are less likely to qualify or to have health insurance. To reach these groups and to overcome other limitations of private voluntary insurance plans, the advocates urge that insurance should be legally required of the entire population. Only thus will the advantages of such insurance become available economically to the majority. Such a program, through legislative action, "can be so designed to maintain medical efficiency and freedom and democratic methods of administration."

No social-insurance proposal in the United States has been opposed with as much vigor and success as government-sponsored health insurance. The opposition, directed by the American Medical Association, believes that widespread legal requirement of medical-care insurance is not necessary and that its adoption would lead to waste, a large bureaucracy, centralized administration, and a deterioration in the quality of medical care.

The health-insurance debate has, unfortunately, been carried on with a degree of emotionalism not likely to contribute to public understanding of the difficult problems which must be considered in any compulsory scheme. The discussion has been unnecessarily partisan and bitter. The alternatives do not always represent mutually exclusive choices. These choices are not always clear-cut, and some compromise between compulsory insurance and voluntary insurance will undoubtedly be formulated in the near future.

Public understanding will be better served if the discussion and the research are directed to the specific areas where public action is likely to take place. How, for example, are the advantages of health insurance to be extended to that half of the population not now protected? If a comprehensive plan is to be avoided, how can public action contribute best in dealing with the problem of prolonged, or, as it is more commonly called, "catastrophic," illness? How can a public plan maintain local administration? Should the role of the public agency be limited to meeting costs or requiring insurance, leaving service and administration to local or voluntary agencies? These are the types of problem on which more light is needed if legislation, whenever adopted, is to be practical.

Some Controversial Issues in Unemployment Insurance

Although the unemployment-insurance system has been in operation for nearly 15 years, the plan cannot be said to have been fully tested. Benefits became payable in 1938. The war in Europe began a year later, and in 1940, our own defense program was under way. Full employment prevailed during the war, and except for a short reconversion period, postwar employment has been at or near full-employment levels. How adequate are the reserves which have been built up? Can the system remain solvent in the face of a substantial recession or depression? Is unemployment insurance adequately financed?

The huge reserve, over 8.8 billion dollars, was created by fortuitous circumstances—a decade of nearly full employment. In national terms, a reserve of such size should be adequate to enable the insurance system to discharge its obligations. This reserve, however, does not represent a national pool. The funds are credited to specific states, and the excess in the trust account of one state cannot be transferred to meet a possible deficit in another state. Many states are decidedly overfinanced, that is, their trust-fund balance is larger than they will need under any conceivable circumstances. In a few states, adverse economic conditions could lead to insolvency, unless benefits were reduced or payroll taxes increased.

This condition has created the need for some reinsurance or equalization fund to assist temporarily those states whose reserve may become exhausted. Under one plan, the Federal government would establish a loan fund and temporarily advance non-interest-bearing funds to such states, to be repaid as economic conditions improve. The second plan would provide an outright grant to the financially embarrassed state, under certain conditions.

The states are opposed to any plan which is likely to give the Federal administration increased control over their operations. On the other hand, the Federal administration has thus far insisted that a grant of funds to the state in financial trouble or a loan of such funds cannot be made without imposing on the state certain requirements as to tax rates and perhaps other conditions.

Experience rating has been the most controversial issue in the financing of unemployment insurance. When originally adopted, its major objective was to encourage stabilization of employment by reducing the rates of employers with good employment experience. The possibility of lower tax rates also increases employer interest in the administration of the unemployment-insurance law, and such employer policing has been an important result of these provisions.

The major reason for the rapid adoption of experience rating, however, is not related to job stabilization or employer policing. Most state unemployment-insurance laws were overfinanced. The states, however, could reduce their taxes only through a system of experience rating. Uniform reductions in the employment tax were not permitted by the Social Security Act. As a result, all states have adopted some type of experience-rating plan.

The labor opposition to experience rating grows out of three developments. In the first place, the unions contend that the focus on a lower payroll tax leads employers to resist liberalization of the state law. Any increase in benefit amount or duration of payments would increase the claims on the employer's account, reduce his balance, and increase his tax. He is, therefore, more inclined to resist proposals for increasing the benefits than he would be under a financing system in which his individual tax would not be directly affected.

The second objection made by the labor unions to experience rating is that this scheme increases an employer's interest in contesting individual claims for unemployment insurance. Every claim denied maintains the balance in his account and may avoid an increase in his tax. However, employers are interested in resisting claims for benefits, by workers who may not be entitled to them, for reasons of personnel policy, quite apart from the effect of such payment on the tax rate.

The strongest objection to experience rating results from disqualification provisions in the state insurance laws. The critics of experience rating contend that the prospect of lower rates has led employers to insist on more stringent qualification as a condition for the payment of benefits. In recent years, a large number of states have increased the stringency of the disqualification provisions. Thus the laws in such states deny benefits in cases where the unemployment was not "attributable to the employer" or where the worker was not "actively seeking work." And in such cases, in some states, the benefits rights are completely canceled.

Such provisions are criticized as too severe and as a denial of benefits to thousands who left work for good personal cause, even though not attributable to the employer. The AFL and the CIO have opposed this trend in state legislation and urged Federal action to check it. Their objective is a national unemployment-insurance law and, failing that, some national standards which would limit the states' power to deny the payment of benefits. The states have successfully opposed the extension of Federal control, and under present employment conditions, there is little prospect for any Federal legislation in this area.

Social Security and Employment Stabilization

The Depression of the 1930's increased public interest in economic stabilization, and the passage of the Social Security Act was presumed by many to contribute to that objective. It was urged that the flow of benefits to the unemployed and of annuities to the retired aged would support mass purchasing power and check a business decline, while social-security taxes coupled with other fiscal policies of the government could avoid overexpansion. The experience-rating feature of the unemployment-insurance laws was specifically designed to stimulate employment regularization, particularly in seasonal industries.

There is little evidence that social-security taxes or benefits payments can make a substantial contribution to employment stabilization. Under present limitations as to coverage and benefits, unemployment-insurance payments, for example, seldom make up more than 15 to 20 per cent of the total wage loss due to unemployment, even under present conditions. While experience rating may, under certain circumstances, lead to seasonal regularization, it can contribute little or nothing to the control of other major causes of unemployment. Social-security measures can make only a meager contribution to economic or employment stabilization.

Such an objective can best be sought by more direct measures, with government fiscal policies coupled with public works and full-employment legislation. The Employment Act of 1946, originally introduced as a "full-employment act," declares it to be the government's policy "to promote maximum employment production and purchasing power." While it says nothing about guarantee of jobs, it does imply commitment to stimulate flagging business activity and to take up any employment slack.

Social Security and Industrial Conflict

How has the social-security movement in the United States affected industrial conflict? Has it tended to reduce the area of controversy between labor and management? Have significant issues been transferred from the economic to the legislative arena? Is there a likelihood of closer collaboration between labor and management in formulating practical legislative programs to deal with security problems?

Precise answers to these questions must await a longer experience. Developing problems and trends can, however, be recognized and stated in sum-- mary form.

The enlarged role of government in economic matters in general and in social security in particular has led to a more active contest between management and labor before Congress and the state legislatures in influencing legislation for social security. However, this contest in the legislative field has not removed these issues from the area of collective bargaining—quite the contrary. When unions failed to "sell" the legislature their concept of an adequate retirement or unemployment-insurance benefit, they tended to transfer the issue to the economic area. Thus collective-bargaining retirement pensions are largely the outgrowth of the unions' reaction to inadequate retirement benefits provided by the public program. And the proposal by the steel and auto unions for guaranteed annual wages is partly designed to increase the amount and duration of unemployment-insurance benefits. In brief, the development of social security has led to a broadening of the area of collective bargaining to include security issues heretofore not generally considered as falling within its scope. The "welfare-fund" strikes in the coal industry and the pension strikes in the steel and auto industry were a direct outgrowth of failure to agree on the formula to deal with these problems.

On the other hand, general recognition by management of the importance of social security has tended to create a more favorable attitude toward legislative proposals to liberalize the social-security program. Management realizes that an inadequate public program may lead to demands for meeting the security problem through collective bargaining. In addition, the experience in joint administration of the collective-bargaining social-security program leads to a better understanding of the problem by both management and labor.

It is too early to determine whether the increase in state responsibility for social security is likely to reduce conflict in the long run. Foreign experience is not applicable. Ours is an expanding economy, and experience in Britain and other countries would throw little light on this subject. In any event, social security plays an important part for wage earners in meeting serious economic problems in an orderly manner, even though it may not make a measurable contribution toward the reduction of conflict.

3

C · SOCIAL CONTROL

OF INDUSTRIAL CONFLICT

I<small>F</small> T<small>HE</small> institutionalization of collective relations between management and labor were complete and stable, there would be a minimum of concern by the organs of society about controlling these relationships. However, we live in a dynamic and changing society. Its stability is shifting, and its equilibrium is delicately balanced. The power struggles between management and labor spill out of the bargaining arena and into the sphere of government. Furthermore, there are many shadow spots even within the bargaining-centered areas in which either management or labor may find that its collective action impinges upon a larger social interest. The organs of government inevitably are called upon to exercise control and constraint over that behavior of the parties to industrial relations which affects the broader social structure.

One of the central problems involved in the control of groups within a society is the elaboration of a value system that defines the mode and direction of such control. The long-time historical perspective underlying governmental control of industrial relations is set forth by Wolfson in Chap. 31. It is clear that in the United States there have been different values, characteristic of different periods of our history, which have given their imprint to governmental control. It is also evident that the going values reflect contemporary themes of the dominant groups within the society.

While Wolfson searches for the underlying values that gave direction to the governmental control of industrial relations, Aaron draws attention more specifically to the actual legislative enactments and court rulings that embodied the contemporary labor-relations rules. Aaron's chapter points out how the legislators and jurists incorporated in their laws and decisions the value systems of their contemporaries. Taken together, these two chapters give us a correlated view of the landmarks in the development of governmental policy controlling industrial relations.

The challenging complexity of modern society is laid bare in Witte's analysis of governmental action to control industrial strife during periods of national emergency. There is neither a single philosophy nor a single method to guide the social control of conflict during national emergencies. What we can be certain of, however, is that the society will undertake direct action to minimize social disorganization during periods of stress. Such periods are also likely to be times of experimentation, for when a society is under stress, the maintenance of stability as an immediate social goal may justify drastic action for its achievement. Witte shows the variety of different approaches that the government has taken in experimenting with the control of potentially disorganizing industrial strife during periods of social emergency.

Any realistic view of an industrial democracy in action must take into consideration the fact that the contesting parties in the industrial sphere are certainly not passive groups. Indeed, as Eby points out in Chap. 34, organized management and labor deliberately seek to influence public opinion and governmental action for their own interests. Drawing particularly upon his own experience as a former labor-union functionary responsible for influencing favorably the climate of public opinion and action, Eby examines some of the goals and methods used in this field. His general conclusion is that knowledge and personal identification are more substantial influences upon the crosscurrents and eddies of public opinion than is propaganda. His observations and interpretations thus interestingly supplement Bell's material in Chap. 18.

In general, a vacuum of power can be threatening to a society only if it persists. The government as the ultimate power holder is quick to fill the power vacuums in industrial relations; it directs its actions toward defining the societal rules of the game and toward the use of sanctions for their enforcement.

CHAPTER 31 SOCIAL CONTROL OF INDUSTRIAL CONFLICT

Theresa Wolfson   *Brooklyn College*

Social control of industrial conflict can best be viewed in the context of the values that have guided legislative enactments and their judicial interpretation throughout the history of this country. Value systems underlying our legislation and judicial interpretation are in turn the product of social, economic, and political forces and reflect the interplay of power groups in our society. That we have but slowly accepted the responsibility of social control of industrial conflict is in part a reflection of the growth in the size of factory units of industrial organization and the power of organized labor. Human values stem from human choice, but it is certainly true that "moral value systems change more slowly than the social conditions which originate them." [1]

In almost every industry, improving on an original design is facilitated by practical trial on a small scale, but the experimental process in social organization is rarely feasible and has been accomplished piecemeal in the United States. Wesley Mitchell once declared that the process of initiating industrial improvement is far simpler than the process of initiating social improvement. "In all known societies decision-making gains direction from being pointed toward and guided by certain core values which for that society at least transcends all others." [2] In our country, we have tended to operate with a code of values which arises from an agricultural and mercantilistic economy. We have professed these values on the Sabbath and have been puzzled by the confusion that overwhelms people who, in their daily lives, are compelled to do one thing and believe another.

In the field of industrial relations, some of these value premises which have stemmed from our agricultural stage of development are the following: that a worker is "worthy of his hire"; that there is an inherent dignity of labor; that workers are entitled to a fair day's wage for a fair day's work; that the entrepreneur is entitled to a fair profit; that the harder one works, the easier it will be to accumulate enough capital to become an independent entrepreneur; that there is a fundamental harmony between capital and labor; and that temporary economic disturbances cause setbacks to the tide of increasing production and expanding prosperity. These values are not mutually consistent. Nor are they necessarily fundamental by virtue of being either self-evident or subject to proof. Neither our economists nor our political

[1] Franz Alexander, "Values and Science," *Journal of Social Issues,* 6 (1950), 30.

[2] Kenneth D. Benne and G. E. Swanson, "The Problem of Values and the Social Scientist," *Journal of Social Issues,* Vol. 6, No. 4 (1950).

scientists have ever been able to determine scientifically what a fair wage is, what a fair profit is, or what the dignity of labor really means. It may very well be that these decisions cannot be made by the social-science technician but only by the moral philosopher who clarifies the *value* basis of each concept, considers the social attitude toward such a concept, and then cooperates with the economist in considering the economic implications of such a new and revitalized value. Meanwhile we are in the dilemma of attempting to solve industrial conflicts pragmatically, without being oriented and "guided by certain core values."

History of Labor Legislation and Social Values

The history of the control of industrial conflict in the United States can very well be traced in the history of labor legislation. The attitude of the community toward the trade-union in the early stages of our economic life was revealed by its legal spokesmen. It was an attitude generally critical of any attempt on the part of workers to organize in order to "secure a fair day's wage." The very process of organization was interpreted as *a conspiracy in restraint of trade* and implied a denial of the right of the worker to increase his own wealth in his own way if that way necessitated *group action.* Between 1806 and 1842, the common-law doctrine of conspiracy was invoked against workers who combined in trade-unions. The legislative and judicial processes focused on creating and perpetuating the atomistic life of the worker.

The case of *Commonwealth v. Hunt* (1842) marked the end of the conspiracy doctrine as an obstacle to labor-union organization. This decision by Justice Shaw did not end the concern of the courts with industrial relations. It merely set up a *value:* worker organization in trade-unions was not necessarily a conspiracy in restraint of trade; workers could organize if their goals or the means used to achieve them were lawful, moral, and not oppressive. The right to organize, however, did not guarantee the opportunity to bargain collectively, and employers continued to use the courts in their opposition to organized labor.

The expansion of American industry, the continued development of resources, and the increasing proportion of manpower in industry were accompanied by an expanding trade-union movement. The growing concentration of industry into monopolistic patterns jolted the American lawmaker into a consciousness that the free-enterprise system of old was being left far behind. In 1890, the Sherman Antitrust Act was passed, ostensibly to break up "combinations of capital in restraint of trade." Under the Sherman Act, prosecutions of labor unions as carrying out actions in restraint of trade were initiated by employers through the agency of the courts. The *Danbury Hatters* case was the outstanding example of the working of the Sherman Antitrust Act. In addition, the use of injunctions against organized labor became an even more common device to prohibit union organization and activity. The Clayton Antitrust Act was passed in 1914 to provide relief from the Sherman law for the labor unions. Section 6 of the Clayton Act specifically enunciated a *value:* "the labor of a human being is not a commodity or an article of commerce."

The antitrust laws did not apply to trade-unions as such—but they did apply to union activities.

The passage of the Railway Labor Act in 1926 marked a change in public opinion as far as an essential industry was concerned. "Congress felt that industrial peace on the railroads could be achieved through the collective bargaining process." [3] Railroad employers were required to bargain collectively with the freely selected representatives of their workers. This eliminated the company-controlled union, although it was not specifically so stated in the law. The Supreme Court, in the 1930 *Texas and New Orleans* decision, "recognized the authority of government to provide a measure of protection to the right of workers to self-organization and collective bargaining." [4] In fact, the decision stated that promotion of the collective-bargaining process is of "the highest public interest." A new social value was being created.

The legal climate surrounding trade-unionism in the period between 1806 and 1932 has been described as "extremely cold and hostile." [5] A century is a long enough time in which to create a tradition—and the traditions surrounding industrial relations were those of conflict, either physical or legal. The governmental position in the control of industrial conflict was generally aligned with the interests of management. Yet the society had accepted the institution of trade-unionism as early as 1842, and a growing labor-union movement could hail the Clayton Act as labor's Magna Carta with a confident expectation that the power of government had finally legitimized unionism.

Modern Labor-relations Legislation

National emergencies frequently accelerate the tempo of social change. The Depression of 1929 culminated in the election of Franklin D. Roosevelt. The economic system was bitterly challenged, and 15 million workers found themselves out of work, not because of their own inadequacy nor because of ineptness on the part of the corporations which employed them, but because of economic processes over which no one individual or group of individuals had any control. There was an atmosphere of apology because the economic system had failed to function normally.

Edward Lindeman, the social philosopher, declared that science releases energies but does not provide direction. Science had been responsible for the development of a vast production machine which spewed forth goods and services that could not be distributed. The advisers of President Roosevelt searched desperately for solutions to the dilemma and came up with the New Deal program and, specifically, the National Industrial Recovery Act. The government was assumed to have the responsibility of providing effective steps to further economic recovery. In addition, Section 7A of the act established the right of employees to self-organization and collective bargaining. Section 7A represented the most affirmative stand yet taken in the direction of govern-

---

[3] Fred Witney, *Government and Collective Bargaining,* Philadelphia, Lippincott, 1951, p. 194.

[4] *Ibid.,* p. 196.

[5] *Ibid.,* p. 103.

ment support of union organization. The New Deal program reflected a changing governmental stand as far as industrial relations were concerned. Not everyone's point of view had changed, however. In fact, many employers and employers' associations, with the first flush of economic recovery, encouraged company unions as meeting the conditions of Section 7A, without the liabilities of bargaining with independent unions. A battle ensued between the growing trade-union movement allied with agencies dedicated to new social values and the employers concerned with maintaining their legal, economic, and social powers.

On May 27, 1935, the National Industrial Recovery Act was declared unconstitutional. On June 27, one month later, the Wagner Labor Relations Act was passed by Congress. "Public policy had come a long way since the labor conspiracy cases of 1806. Society now declares that collective bargaining is socially desirable." [6]

The Wagner Act was responsible for creating an atmosphere of acceptance of the labor union *and* of collective bargaining. This favored the growth of industrial unions in the CIO and accelerated the growth of industrial and craft unions in the AFL. The unprecedented development both in membership and in power of the two labor federations resulted in a division among employers. A large number of employers came to accept the trade-union as a sort of junior partner in the process of production and were learning to make the adjustments essential to industrial peace, even though such a peace was limited to the duration of the collective-bargaining contract. On the other hand, other employers viewed with suspicion and fear the growing strength of organized labor. They were determined to put every obstacle in the way of this movement.

The Wagner Act was denounced by its opponents as being discriminatory in favor of organized labor, which, to be sure, it was. In fact, the reason for passing the act was to create a more equitable balance between management and organized labor in the collective-bargaining process. This group further contended that since the government had helped labor to organize, it had the responsibility of restricting both the means and the ends to which labor was committed. They declared that, since the government regulated the degree of combination among industries in order to provide some measure of competition, the government had a similar responsibility with reference to the "monopolistic" trade-unions. Psychologically, it is understandable that organized labor's challenge to authority would be resented by those accustomed to a unilateral direction of business firms. The contest between the established group and the new arrival takes place in every phase of human activity.

The Wagner Act involved a limited form of government regulation. It forced the acceptance of a position which had hitherto been fought out on the industrial battlefield, namely, that workers could form their own unions and bargain with employers regardless of the quality of union leadership, the union's economic philosophy, or the strength of employers in the industry.

[6] *Ibid.,* p. 207.

World War II and After

The attempt on the part of the government to stabilize wages and prices during the war emergency resulted in the further injection of the government into the collective-bargaining process. The NWLB was created in January, 1942, as an agency to settle industrial disputes. Production was of the essence in the war program. The Board encouraged the usual procedures for union-management negotiation: collective bargaining came first. But if no basis for negotiation could be achieved, the mediation of the Federal Conciliation Service became the next step. If this agency failed, then the NWLB assumed jurisdiction. It could use mediation, voluntary arbitration, or compulsory arbitration. Finally Congress passed the War Labor Disputes Act which gave authority to the President of the United States to seize war facilities; made it a criminal offense to instigate, direct, or aid a strike in a government-seized plant; prohibited labor organizations from contributing funds for political purposes; and outlawed strikes in privately operated war plants until 30-day strike notices had been filed and a vote taken to indicate the strike desires of war workers.

The NWLB was soon engaged in dealing with the entire gamut of collective-bargaining problems. Perhaps the most important legacies of NWLB policy in institutionalizing collective bargaining were in the areas of union security, seniority, and grievance procedure. The Board developed the "maintenance-of-membership" principle that has continued, in its basic form, to provide union security. It stabilized the principle of seniority by tying wage increases to automatic progression through a rate range for a job. Finally, the Board placed great emphasis on establishing a grievance procedure as a standard feature of the bargaining contract, to have an established way for handling daily problems of contract administration and interpretation.

The regulation of wages, hours, and working conditions by the NWLB had its repercussions in the postwar period. Though many unions came out of the war numerically far larger than they were when the war began, the growth had been uneven in terms of inner strength and inner responsibility. Therefore, there evolved in the postwar period two group attitudes. On the part of labor leaders, there was a desperate need to recover status in the eyes of the union membership and to serve their members more effectively and more intelligently in a situation where government restraints and regulations had but recently been withdrawn. When a child has been told by its parents to do this and not to do that for many years, his ability to assume responsibility, to act with maturity, and to plan with intelligence is definitely undeveloped. To some extent, this happened to organized labor.

American industry, on the other hand, was deeply disturbed by the recognition of the growing strength of unions and by the aggressiveness that organized labor displayed within the plant and at the negotiating table. The threat to industry's authority seemed more dangerous and the idea of labor-management cooperation was once again pushed into "limbo." The emergency was over; old problems of rising prices remained, and new problems of increasing purchasing power in the face of withdrawn government regulations developed. The climate of opinion with respect to the scope and boundaries of collective bargaining had become murky.

The growing power of organized labor seemed to shift the pendulum. The Wagner Labor Relations Act of 1935 represented an effort on the part of the government to encourage union organization, to provide a basis for industrial peace, and to improve the status of workers. The role of the government during World War II had strengthened organized labor to the point where organized management began to fear for its own position.

The Taft-Hartley Act was passed on June 23, 1947, over the veto of the President and as a result of management pressures. The social climate which made the act possible was not a rational one. There was no scientific evaluation of the operation of the Wagner Labor Relations Act.

> The two laws approached the problems of employer-employee relations differently, and they went off in different directions to find solutions. The Wagner Act put its faith in collective bargaining; but while the Taft-Hartley Act paid lip service to the principle of collective bargaining, its insistence on "legal rights" encouraged individual bargaining and, to an even greater extent, government determination of the labor bargain.[7]

The basic rights and responsibilities established by the act emphasized specifically that the worker:

> . . . (1) may get a job without first having to join a union, (2) may be free from either company or union coercion in deciding whether he wants a union, (3) may engage in legitimate union activity without interference from either the company or union, (4) may get protection against coercion or intimidation if employee wishes to stay out of union organizing campaigns, (5) may make his own decision by written authorization if he wishes to have union dues deducted from pay, (6) may take up his grievance directly with company and get it settled, providing settlement is in line with union contract and union representative is given opportunity to be present, (7) may vote, by secret ballot, on whether he wants union shop (where all employees must join union after 30 days) if 30 per cent of employees want such election, (8) may ask for election to eliminate union shop if 30 per cent of employees want such election, (9) may hold his job in union shop so long as he pays dues and initiation fees, (10) may ask for election to disqualify union which has had bargaining rights in his company, if a substantial number of employees want such election, (11) may obtain annual financial reports from his union if union has complied with requirements of Taft-Hartley Act, (12) may be admitted to union membership without discrimination where there is a union shop, (13) may collect back pay if discharged because of company or union unfair labor practices, (14) may take legal action to recover losses in pay for time lost because of jurisdictional disputes and secondary boycotts. . . . [The employee] (1) may not strike during 60-day period when new contract is being negotiated, (2) may not vote in election for a union to represent him if he is on strike for economic benefits and he has been replaced."[8]

---

[7] William M. Leiserson, "For a New Labor Law—A Basic Analysis," *The New York Times Magazine*, Feb. 6, 1949.

[8] *The Taft-Hartley Law, What Does It Mean and How Does It Affect Employees, Unions, Employers?* Brooklyn, New York, Brooklyn Chamber of Commerce, Bureau of Employee Relations, 1947.

Seven years have elapsed since the passage of the Taft-Hartley Act. It is impossible to state that the act has created a sound national policy for industrial relations. The law does not encourage further unionization. The fact is that union membership has grown very little since 1947. The law does not encourage free collective bargaining on a mature basis. Government intervention has become an inevitable factor in industrial disputes. The law has not eliminated strikes or industrial tension. The tyranny of "labor bosses," which the law was to eliminate, still remains in a few unions. The strikes involving public interest and public welfare still continue. The antisocial acts within the union still remain. Trade-unions are social institutions reflecting all the weaknesses of human beings in our society. Like other social institutions, trade-unions suffer many inadequacies in terms of their own objectives.

Private versus Public Interest

Industrial relations, in the light of our earlier economic philosophy, has been considered to be primarily a *private matter* between the employer and the employee or between a group of employers and an organization of workers. As long as our economy was expanding but predominantly agricultural, this concept of the industrial conflict as a private affair involved little in the way of public concern for a social policy of control.

In the last half of the 19th century, when small entrepreneurs were absorbed into large corporate enterprises, the relationship between groups of workers and these corporate enterprises extended much more into the public domain. It was as though the family quarrel had reached out to include all the "in-laws" and their in-laws. The bitter strikes in the coal mines, on the railroads, and in the building trades which took place in this era of the 1870's and 1880's still seemed based on "personal conflict." The newspaper cartoons that described strikes and industrial disagreements between workers and employers made use of stereotypes. The employer was pictured as a fat man with a diamond stickpin in his tie and a cigar dangling out of the corner of his mouth. The worker was cartooned as a rather emaciated weakling or as a bewhiskered brute with a bomb in one hand and a stick of dynamite in the other. The use of violence in these industrial conflicts was hardly personal. However, some agitators felt that, if they could only get rid of Frick or Carnegie or even President Cleveland, who called out the Army to protect the property of the Pullman companies, the industrial conflict could be solved. Industrial conflicts became more and more a *social* concern as the protagonists became larger and more powerful and as their area of control reached out across the country. In fact, in spite of the strong feeling on the part of both management and unions that the collective-bargaining process concerns only the immediate groups involved and must therefore be taken out of the public domain, the history of social control of industrial conflict shows greater and greater *public* concern.

There is no universally accepted definition of "public interest," or of "the public." Is the public the uninterested bystander in an industrial dispute? Does the public include all those affected directly or indirectly by the dispute? Does the government represent the public? Why is "impartiality" so essential a characteristic for settling industrial disputes? Is there a different public for each labor dispute?

If we are really concerned with an integration of *value* and *action,* we must secure some clarification to these questions. Every industrial dispute is presented as having public significance. Since industry is concerned with the production of goods and services which add to our national wealth, the public interest has been focused upon those forces that tend to interrupt production. We have become aware, in the 20th century, of the need for some policy which will regulate the activities of the protagonists in industrial conflict and which will establish the power to call a truce for a specified period of time in order to facilitate the continuity of industrial production.

Since every trade-union recognizes that the welfare of the sum total of its membership is not necessarily synonymous with the general public welfare, there is an inevitable contradiction between the theory of the early classical economists and the practices of the 20th-century trade-union movement. The trade-union groups in the United States represent, at the present time, some 15 million of the 62 million gainfully employed. That is a large "public" in and of itself. Were it completely unified and disciplined, it could pack quite a wallop as an interest group! However, when the coal miners are on strike, the rest of organized labor is not too concerned except as they are consumers of a scarce commodity. Should coal become too scarce, the public through various governmental authorities may demand solutions which the trade-union movement may resent on principle—but which the trade-unionist as a coal consumer must accept!

In any one industrial conflict, the public may be described as the sisters and the cousins and the aunts of everyone outside the immediate group involved. The public may not actively understand the nature of the contest, may not even be intelligent about the factors involved, and may seem to have no particular concern in its outcome, but simply because the public is the great amorphous body outside the immediate participants in an industrial conflict, it has, perforce, an important role in the changing pattern of social control. It is no longer true that free collective bargaining is the concern solely of the participants in the process. In a democracy, when "we speak of the 'public interest' we have under discussion not a system of devices designed to protect one autonomous group of the population from attack by two others, equally independent, but a program that must be calculated to promote the interests of both workers and employers, for to one of these categories most citizens belong." [9]

The dilemma in which we find ourselves lies in the fact that we have accepted as assumptions of our society the free-enterprise system along with a minimum of government intervention. And yet the attempts we have made toward the solution of our economic problems depend upon either the use of force and power or the intervention of the government. The history of early labor relations in the United States is strewn with violence and force—weapons used by industry and workers alike. As we evolved out of this primitive stage, we adopted a policy of legislation and judicial interpretation which presumably

[9] Jesse Freidin, "The Public Interest in Labor Dispute Settlement," *Law and Contemporary Problems,* 12 (Spring, 1947), 367.

substituted civilized processes for the more primitive ones—but the advantages were still in favor of employers. As organized labor grew in strength, if not in stature, the need to protect the public interest became more and more articulate. The tendency to make the government the regulator, the decision maker, and the arbiter grew apace.

The collective-bargaining process represents a major step toward industrial democracy. Organized labor matured slowly, but perhaps no more slowly than other social groups in our society which have had *duties* but few *responsibilities* for decision making. We learn from the leaves of the educator's notebook that a child matures and becomes responsible in direct ratio to the trust parents place in him and the respect which they show him. Obviously this fact does not eliminate authority—but authority should stem from *know-how* and *ability* rather than from political and economic "connections." Collective bargaining has been responsible for more *industrial peace* than industrial conflict. That is a fact which we do not emphasize sufficiently.

In the opinion of the writer, the concern for *public interest* represents a social value of great significance. That the emphasis in settling industrial disputes is placed on how it affects the welfare of a community is extremely pertinent. What disturbs the writer is the fact that we have rarely defined the public interest in terms of goals and objectives and that we are all too frequently hypocritical about which public we are serving. In a democracy there are many publics; we should be mature enough to face that fact and not to try to cloak it in an all-enveloping cape of obfuscation.

A major dilemma with which our society is faced is to determine how the broad social interest can best be served in the control of industrial conflict. It is now clear that the potential impact of industrial conflict upon the productive stability of our society is so far-reaching that the government will always exercise direct control over collective bargaining and the conflict it may engender. We have seen how the values that underlie the legislative and judicial controls have reflected the existing climate of opinion and the strength of the groups wielding significant social power. Are we destined to have governmental power always expressive of a contemporary viewpoint of the dominant power groups? Or are we emerging into an era where more enduring ideas and values defining the general welfare will provide the criteria for the social control of industrial relations?

CHAPTER 32 CHANGING LEGAL CONCEPTS AND INDUSTRIAL CONFLICT

Benjamin Aaron   *University of California (Los Angeles)*

THE term "industrial conflict" immediately suggests strikes and lockouts and perhaps violence as well. Certainly the history of labor-management relations is replete with incidents of this kind, which are dealt with elsewhere in this volume. Underlying these outward and dramatic evidences of conflict, however, is a philosophy of industrial relations, a series of concepts with respect to the objectives of the conflicting parties and the means by which such objectives may be achieved. These concepts commonly find expression through the medium of legal institutions. An understanding of the methods by which we have sought to control industrial disputes in this country is dependent upon a knowledge of the economic, political, religious, and philosophical sources of our common and statutory law. This chapter will attempt, in barest outline, to indicate the principal mainsprings of American labor law as well as some of the more significant changes which have taken place in that body of law during the present century.

Individualism in American Labor Law

In his great essay on the common law Roscoe Pound noted that a peculiarity of Anglo-American and, more particularly, American legal thinking "is an ultra-individualism, an uncompromising insistence upon individual interests and individual property as a focal point of jurisprudence." [1] This spirit of individualism stems in part from 18th-century classical economic theory and political doctrine and from the 19th-century scientific writings of Darwin and Spencer. Its roots go back, however, to the end of the 16th century, which marked the rise of theories of natural rights concurrently with the growth of Protestantism and the emancipation of the middle class. Puritanism, based as it was on the doctrine of a "willing covenant of conscious faith" made by the individual, had a profound effect upon legal thinking and legal institutions in this country. [2] To it may be attributed, among other things, the conception of abstract liberty of contract, which preserved for so many years the validity and efficacy of such legal fictions as the "yellow-dog" contract, and also the hostile attitude of bench and bar to statutory law, an opposition which was finally overwhelmed, without ever having been won over, only by the New Deal tidal wave of legislation.

[1] Roscoe Pound, *The Spirit of the Common Law*, Boston, Marshall Jones, 1921, p. 37.
[2] *Ibid.*, pp. 42–59.

These various influences in our law tended over the years to blend with, or moderate, each other, to become quiescent for a time, and then to emerge once again in statutes or in judicial pronouncements. Some of the early concepts molded by these forces have stood the test of time better than others. Thus it will be observed in the discussion which follows that the principle of competition, though in somewhat modified form, has retained its position as a dominant influence on our system of labor relations, while the concepts of individualism and of natural rights, which formerly bulked so large in American labor-relations law, have been greatly moderated by the exigencies of our complex and closely interrelated industrial society.

By the middle of the 19th century the doctrine of criminal conspiracy had ceased to be used in this country as a judicial weapon against union activities; after the Civil War it was employed only occasionally to break up strikes. However, the law relating to peaceful union activities in pursuit of economic objectives did not develop along uniform lines in the various states.

Regulation of Ends and Means

In Massachusetts the "illegal-purpose" doctrine was enunciated by the Supreme Judicial Court in a series of cases involving an attempt of a business combination to establish a monopoly and attempts by labor unions to secure the closed shop and to prevent their work from being contracted out to non-members.[3] What the businessmen could do in the name of free competition the workmen were forbidden to do on the ground that their basic purpose was to injure others without justification. The most noteworthy aspect of the Massachusetts cases was decided in the decade commencing in 1896, however, in the series of prophetic dissents written by Justice Holmes, whose views were to become a dominant force in directing the path of our law. His philosophy is best expressed in his famous dissent in *Vegelahn v. Guntner*. Noting that "in numberless instances the law warrants the intentional infliction of temporal damage because it regards it as justified," Holmes declared that the true grounds for determining when justification exists are "considerations of policy and of social advantage" rather than "logic and the general propositions of law which nobody disputes." Free competition, he thought, is a social advantage since it "is worth more to society than it costs"; consequently, "on this ground the infliction of the damage is privileged."

But what kinds of conduct are embraced by the term "competition"? In response to the argument that the conflict between employers and employed is not free competition, Holmes suggested substituting the term "free struggle for life." He thought it "plain from the slightest consideration of practical affairs, or the most superficial reading of industrial history, that free competition means combination . . . in ever increasing might and scope. . . ." This combination, he observed, was "patent and powerful" on the side of capital, and he felt that combination on the side of labor "is the necessary and desir-

---

[3] Bowen v. Matheson, 96 Mass. 499 (1867); Carew v. Rutherford, 106 Mass. 1 (1870); Vegelahn v. Guntner, 167 Mass. 92, 44 N.E. 1077 (1896); Plant v. Woods, 176 Mass. 492, 57 N.E. 1011 (1900); Berry v. Donovan, 188 Mass. 353, 74 N.E. 603 (1905); Pickett v. Walsh, 192 Mass. 572, 78 N.E. 753 (1906).

able counterpart, if the battle is to be carried on in a fair and equal way." As we shall see, this philosophy provided one of the principal justifications for the National Labor Relations Act, adopted some 40 years later.

In New York the Court of Appeals also formulated the state's policy, with respect to permissible union activity, in several cases involving the closed shop.[4] The view which it adopted, sometimes referred to as the "civil-rights" doctrine, was simply that unions were free to pursue their economic objectives so long as the means which they employed were neither criminal nor tortious. The New York court thus reached the same conclusion as Holmes, but by a different route. It scrupulously refrained from evaluating a union's motives as long as the means which it employed were legal. Holmes, on the other hand, started with the proposition that the intentional infliction of harm was actionable, unless justified, and then found justification in the competitive struggle among workmen and between workmen and employers.

With few exceptions it was the Massachusetts illegal-purpose doctrine which was followed by other state courts in the succeeding years. While the right of employees to strike against their own employer for certain specific and limited objectives, such as increased wages or shorter hours, came to be universally recognized, strikes for the closed shop and for other "secondary" purposes were frequently condemned. Moreover, picketing, without which a strike could usually not be successfully maintained, was either prohibited or substantially restricted by court injunctions in most jurisdictions. Resort to this device in labor disputes was an American innovation. In England, where it originated, the injunction was utilized only to preserve physical property from irreparable damage. In the United States, however, the term "property" was expanded to include intangible business interests. Commencing about 1880, and particularly after the Supreme Court's decision in the *Debs* case [5] in 1895, the labor injunction became the chief weapon of employers in combating concerted union activities.

The Labor Injunction

In issuing injunctions in labor disputes the courts proceeded on either or both of two different theories. The first, as already mentioned, was that the union's objective was illegal. The other theory was that the act of picketing was itself a form of lawless intimidation and therefore not to be permitted. A classic expression of this view appears in a Federal court opinion written in 1905: "There is and can be no such thing as peaceful picketing, any more than there can be chaste vulgarity, or peaceful mobbing, or lawful lynching." [6] Thus between these two theories of illegal purpose and illegal means the unions were effectively hemmed in.

That the injunctive process was greatly abused during this period has long ceased to be a matter of debate; the indictment against the courts is too well

---

[4] National Protective Ass'n v. Cumming, 170 N.Y. 315, 63 N.E. 369 (1902); Jacobs v. Cohen, 183 N.Y. 207, 76 N.E. 5 (1905).

[5] *In re* Debs, 158 U.S. 564 (1895).

[6] Atchison, T. & S.F. Ry. v. Gee, 139 Fed. 582, 584 (C.C.S.D. Iowa 1905).

documented to be refuted.[7] As early as 1896 the Democratic National Convention went on record against "government by injunction" under which the Federal judges had become "at once legislators, judges and executioners."[8] A mounting agitation for reform culminated in the passage of the Clayton Act in 1914. Section 20 of this act purported to limit drastically the power of the Federal judiciary to issue restraining orders and injunctions in labor disputes. This proved not to be the case, however, for the Supreme Court subsequently ruled in the *American Steel Foundries* case [9] that the statute introduced no new principle into equity jurisprudence but was "merely declaratory of what was the best practice always." Nothing in Section 20 legitimized "that which bears the sinister name of 'picketing,' " said Chief Justice Taft, speaking for the majority of the Court. Only one union representative was allowed to be stationed at each entrance of the struck plant, the Court's purpose being "to prevent the inevitable intimidation of the presence of groups of pickets, but to allow missionaries."

State laws with provisions modeled after Section 20 of the Clayton Act, but interpreted by the state courts as effectively prohibiting the issuance of injunctions against peaceful picketing, fared no better. An Arizona statute so construed by the highest state court was held unconstitutional by the Supreme Court on the ground that it denied to employers the equal protection of the laws guaranteed by the 14th Amendment.[10] Thus organized labor was deprived of any real relief from government by injunction until 1932, when Congress passed the Norris-LaGuardia Anti-injunction Act.

Yellow-dog contracts were also successfully used against labor unions until 1932, when in Section 3 of the Norris-LaGuardia Act they were finally declared to be contrary to public policy and unenforceable. These contracts were simply pledges exacted from workmen, as a condition of employment, that they would not join a labor union. As between the parties, the pledge was legally meaningless; there is no record of a single action brought by an employer for its breach. The great value which it had for employers was that the courts treated it as a property right. Consequently, efforts by a union to organize workmen who had entered into such contracts with their employer were regarded as tortious attempts to destroy his property and were enjoined.

Early attempts by the Federal government to bar such contracts on interstate railroads and by the states to make them illegal within their borders were struck down by the Supreme Court as unconstitutional invasions of rights guaranteed by the 5th and 14th Amendments, respectively.[11] The majority opinions in the two leading cases are of particular interest, since they express in such pristine terms the theories of abstract freedom of contract and of individual rights which then prevailed. Thus in the *Adair* case we hear Justice Harlan stating with finality that in all particulars of the employment

---

[7] See Felix Frankfurter and Nathan Greene, *The Labor Injunction,* New York, Macmillan, 1930; and Charles O. Gregory, *Labor and the Law,* New York, Norton, 1946, pp. 95–104.

[8] Gregory, *op. cit.,* p. 83.

[9] American Steel Foundries v. Tri-City Central Trades Council, 257 U.S. 184 (1921).

[10] Truax v. Corrigan, 257 U.S. 312 (1921).

[11] Adair v. United States, 208 U.S. 161 (1903); Coppage v. Kansas, 236 U.S. 1 (1915).

relationship "the employer and the employe have equality of right, and any legislation that disturbs that equality is an arbitrary interference with the liberty of contract which no government can legally justify in a free land." To the protests that the employee's equality was a fiction and his liberty of contract therefore a mockery, Justice Pitney responded majestically in the *Coppage* case that, since it was self-evident from the nature of things that some persons must have more property than others, it was "impossible to uphold freedom of contract and the right of private property without at the same time recognizing as legitimate those inequalities of fortune that are the necessary result of the exercise of those rights."

Antitrust Legislation

The tremendous economic development which took place in this country after the Civil War, if it did not completely undermine the belief that unrestricted competition and the survival of the fittest produced the best of all possible worlds, did give rise to widespread misgivings about the future. The rapid increase in the number of industrial leviathans, or "trusts," caused people to question the means by which such great power was accumulated, and the injurious consequences to the public of "unfair" competition between businessmen became a major political issue. In 1890 Congress passed the Sherman Antitrust Act, which declared illegal "every contract, combination . . . or conspiracy, in restraint of trade or commerce. . . ."

Whether or not Congress intended to include the activities of organized labor within the scope of the Sherman Act is, of course, a matter of historical debate. For all practical purposes, however, that issue was settled by the Supreme Court in 1908, when it held in the *Danbury Hatters* case [12] that the act outlawed an interstate secondary boycott by the AFL against a Connecticut hat manufacturer. Since activities in violation of the act not only could be enjoined but also rendered the violators subject to heavy fines and imprisonment, the Supreme Court's decision was a shocking blow to organized labor. Consequently, when the Clayton Act was passed 6 years later, the rejoicing of unions and their supporters was understandable. Not only did Section 20 of that act give promise of relief from labor injunctions, but Section 6 declared that labor organizations and their members should not "be held or construed to be illegal combinations or conspiracies in restraint of trade, under the antitrust laws."

Subsequent developments, however, dashed even the most modest hopes of the labor leaders. The fate of Section 20 and of similar provisions in state statutes has already been reviewed. The application of Section 6 proved to be equally disappointing. In the *Duplex* case,[13] decided in 1921, the Supreme Court held that this provision did not exempt a labor union or its members from accountability "where it or they depart from its normal and legitimate objects and engage in an actual combination or conspiracy in restraint of trade."

[12] Loewe v. Lawlor, 208 U.S. 274 (1908).
[13] Duplex Printing Co. v. Deering, 254 U.S. 443 (1921).

National Labor Relations Act

In the foregoing discussion an attempt has been made to trace the main patterns of social control of industrial conflict from early in the 19th century down to the year 1932, which marked the beginning of a new era in this country. The history of the entire period demonstrates the success with which society, "disguised under the name of capital," as Holmes put it, was able to resist the concerted efforts of workmen to seek to improve their economic condition. Statutory regulation was at a minimum, and the courts, overwhelmingly hostile to the institution of unionism, were quick to hold, on the basis of concepts borrowed from other fields of law, that the concerted activities of unions were illegal. Hence it is all the more remarkable that in the brief period from 1932 to 1947 there could have taken place the tremendous revolution in the philosophy of industrial relations described below.

In 1935 Congress adopted the National Labor Relations (Wagner) Act, the first Federal statute of general application dealing with labor relations. The most noteworthy feature of this act was that it deprived employers within its scope of their established common-law right to refuse to recognize or bargain with labor unions and imposed upon them the duty of bargaining exclusively with the labor organizations chosen by a majority of their employees. Such a fundamental shift in policy could not have taken place overnight; the guiding principles of the Wagner Act had their roots in earlier experience, the immediate antecedents being Section 7A of the National Industrial Recovery Act of 1933 and the amended Railway Labor Act of 1934.

Of crucial importance is the fact that the Wagner Act was enacted in the depths of the Great Depression. It was designed to organize workers for collective bargaining, in the hope that by this means wages and working conditions within and between industries could be stabilized. The desperate plight of the country had forced a reevaluation of the basic tenet of our labor-relations law. In the opening section of the act Congress rejected the prevailing doctrine of the past century and accepted as a true and undesirable fact the thesis that the "inequality of bargaining power between employees who do not possess full freedom of association or actual liberty of contract, and employers who are organized . . . substantially burdens . . . the flow of commerce. . . ."

The Congress was concerned, however, more with the economic than with the ethical implications of this situation. It believed that inequality of bargaining power tended to aggravate recurrent business depressions by forcing down wage rates and the purchasing power of wage earners and that the refusal of employers to recognize unions led to industrial strife. Consequently the Wagner Act was intended to promote the organization of employees in order to equalize their bargaining power with that of their employers and to facilitate collective bargaining between the two groups.

The Wagner Act may thus be viewed as the embodiment of those ideas of competition expressed by Holmes 40 years earlier: in the struggle for life the competitors must have equal bargaining power if the contest is to be fair; and the role of government is to fix the ground rules and then stand aloof. It also represented a belief in the self-regulating characteristics of collective bargaining, a conviction that competitive forces of approximately equal strength will arrive at a *modus vivendi* satisfactory to themselves and beneficial to the public.

The Wagner Act was bitterly opposed by employers generally, and not until its constitutionality was upheld in the *Jones & Laughlin* case [14] in 1937 did it actually become effective. Almost immediately thereafter, however, its influence became felt. Not only did it make possible the successful drive by the newly formed CIO to organize millions of mass-production workers, but it changed the whole basis of the relationship between employers and employed. Majority rule became the guiding principle, and to the majority went the all-important right of exclusive representation. Once a union had been certified, individual bargaining was outlawed. So too were such familiar practices by which employers sought to forestall union organization as blacklists, discriminatory dismissals, surveillance of union members, establishment of company-dominated unions, and the like. Employers were no longer permitted even to tell their employees what they thought about the advisability or inadvisability of joining a union. All these activities were made employer unfair labor practices; on the other hand, the act contained no provisions regulating unions.

In addition, the governmental function of enforcing the rules was shifted largely from the courts to an administrative tribunal, the NLRB. The Board's discretion was almost unlimited, its rules were flexible, and its decisions, of necessity, favored the unions, which were the chief beneficiaries of the act. The historical positions of unions and employers were thus reversed within a few years; for the first time the latter found the enormous power of government aligned on the side of their opponents.

Court Decisions in the New Deal Period

This changing social climate was bound to produce important revisions in judicial doctrine. The Norris-LaGuardia Act had practically eliminated the possibility of Federal courts issuing injunctions in labor disputes, and some states enacted similar laws. There was still, however, a very large area of activity, untouched by statute, in which the common law prevailed; and it was in this area that the new judicial approach had its greatest effect. In a series of decisions beginning with the *Thornhill* case [15] in 1940, the Supreme Court completely altered the legal status of peaceful picketing. What the Court had, as late as 1921, described as a "contradiction in terms," became a constitutionally protected right, equated with freedom of speech. Where before the Court had struck down state laws designed to legitimize peaceful picketing, it now even proscribed state policies which denied that right to those who were not employed by the picketed employer.[16]

Even in the application of the antitrust laws the Supreme Court finally gave to organized labor an immunity which most people thought Congress had never given. In a truly remarkable decision handed down in the *Hutcheson*

---

[14] NLRB v. Jones & Laughlin Steel Corp., 301 U.S. 1 (1937).

[15] Thornhill v. Alabama, 310 U.S. 88 (1940).

[16] AFL v. Swing, 312 U.S. 321 (1941).

case [17] in 1941, the Court majority construed the Sherman, Clayton, and Norris-LaGuardia Acts in such a manner as to protect unions from prosecution for restraint of trade, except when they act in collusion with employers to achieve that purpose. Exit the illegal-purpose doctrine; in its place was substituted one more viable from the unions' point of view: the "inappropriate-ally" doctrine.

Whether or not these new relationships between labor, management, and the government would have adjusted into a satisfactory equilibrium without further legislation will never be known. World War II intervened shortly after collective bargaining became the national labor policy, and for 4 years the basic aspects of industrial relations were regulated by the government. It is worth noting, however, that within limits the governmental controls were shaped and administered by representatives of industry, labor, and the public, a fact which indicated the continuing strength of the belief that the government's role in this area should be primarily that of an umpire.

The Countermovement After World War II

Nevertheless, the counterrevolution in industrial relations was already under way. It began during the war with legislation in the states restricting union activities and culminated in the passage of the Taft-Hartley amendments to the National Labor Relations Act in 1947. The latter represented a new attitude toward unions, one which regarded them as equal or superior in power to employers and therefore subject to the same kinds of regulation. Another equally significant feature of this new attitude was its emphasis upon the rights of individual employees and the imputation of conflict between their interests and those of their collective-bargaining representatives. A number of concerted activities by unions and their members were declared to be unfair labor practices. More importantly, however, Congress regulated a number of substantive provisions in the collective agreement, such as union security, apparently in the belief that the parties could not be trusted to act in the public interest. In the name of the free-enterprise system Congress thus substituted terms prescribed by the government for provisions customarily negotiated by the parties.

A number of theories have been advanced to explain why the pendulum swung back so quickly. Professor Taylor has suggested the difficulty of formulating a single national labor policy adapted to various economic conditions. He concludes that it was the "conditions of a scarcity of labor, rising profits and wages, and an almost insatiable demand for the products of industry" which convinced Congress in 1947 that, from the national point of view, the continuation of the collective-bargaining system was not imperative.[18] To this basic reason may be added the wave of postwar strikes, which seriously alienated public opinion, however much their economic consequences may have been exaggerated, and the growing power of unions over certain segments of the economy and over the lives of individual workers.

[17] United States v. Hutcheson, 312 U.S. 219 (1941).
[18] George W. Taylor, *Government Regulation of Industrial Relations,* New York, Prentice-Hall, 1948, p. 253.

Once again, the changes in legislative policy were accompanied by a reorientation of judicial policy toward picketing. As early as 1942 the Supreme Court had begun to whittle away at the doctrine which placed peaceful picketing on a par with free speech. In the *Ritter* case [19] it upheld the right of a state to restrict peaceful picketing "to the area of the industry within which the labor dispute arises" and to forbid "the conscription of neutrals" in other industries. In more recent years the Court has gone still further. While it has never returned to the earlier notion that there can be no such thing as peaceful picketing, it has ruled that such picketing may be enjoined if its purpose is to violate valid Federal or state laws or policies.[20]

The postwar period has also been marked by a resurgence of individualism and the doctrine of natural rights. The growing concern in many quarters over the oppressive bigness of government, labor, and industry has been partially expressed in the form of "right-to-work" laws in various states, in the demands for the atomization of large collective-bargaining units, and in the agitation for more democracy within unions. At the same time there has been an increasing trend which seems to be in the opposite direction: an impatience with strikes and other forms of industrial unrest and an insistence upon more governmental intervention in the public interest. These apparent conflicts obviously cannot be explained in narrow terms and solely within the framework of industrial-relations policy; they are but reflections of the underlying and continuous problem within a democracy of reconciling individual rights with the broader interests of the group.

Future changes in our policies regarding the regulation of industrial conflict will necessarily be governed by the same forces which are shaping other phases of our domestic affairs. At present no well-defined pattern appears to be developing. Neither organized labor nor organized management has so far been able to exercise sufficient political power to control the direction of labor legislation or even to maintain consistency in the laws which are enacted. For the most part our labor laws have been adopted hurriedly and in an emotional atmosphere generated by popular dissatisfaction with a particular condition. At times they have benefited labor; at other times, management. In most cases these laws have been designed to correct a disequilibrium between the power of two contending forces.

If any trend is discernible, it is one away from the principle that free competition between labor and industry for larger shares of the national wealth is worth more to society as a whole than it costs. There is not only resentment over the economic plight of weaker groups, which may be caught helplessly in the struggle between the titans, but also fear that the nation may be dangerously weakened by such internal conflict in its crucial contest for world leadership with a powerful foreign foe. Viewed in this light, the resurgent individualism of recent years is something far removed from its Puritan origin. It is, in fact, not inspired so much by a rejection of governmental authoritarian-

---

[19] Carpenters & Joiners Union v. Ritter's Café, 315 U.S. 722 (1942).

[20] *E.g.*, Giboney v. Empire Storage & Ice Co., 336 U.S. 490 (1949); Int'l Brotherhood of Teamsters v. Hanke, 339 U.S. 470 (1950); Gazzam v. Building Service Employees, 339 U.S. 532 (1950); Int'l Brotherhood of Electrical Workers v. NLRB, 341 U.S. 694 (1951).

ism as by a belief that government should exercise more stringent controls over a few powerful groups in order to benefit the country as a whole.

So long as present world conditions continue, the outlook in this country would seem to be for increasing governmental regulation of industrial conflict by means of restrictive legislation and judicial intervention. The question of whether these interferences with the "free struggle for life" between industry and labor will be beneficial or harmful to our society in the long run awaits the judgment of history.

CHAPTER 33 INDUSTRIAL CONFLICT IN PERIODS OF NATIONAL EMERGENCY

Edwin E. Witte   *University of Wisconsin*

WHAT should be done about strikes producing national emergencies has been one of the most discussed subjects of the last few years. Many differing proposals have been made on the course of action which should be taken by the government. But there has been no legislation on the subject since Congress in the Taft-Hartley Act prescribed a procedure to be followed which few people think is adequate. So the question is a likely one for further legislation in the near future.

1952 Developments

A major reason for the great popular interest in this subject is that we have recently had several major industrial conflicts which it was feared would cripple the entire economy. Foremost among these was the steel dispute, which culminated in a nationwide strike in the summer of 1952 after having made front-page headlines for more than 6 months.

This dispute concerned the terms of new agreements to replace those which expired on December 31, 1951, between nearly all the major steel companies and the United Steelworkers of America. There was little or no bargaining preceding the expiration date of the old agreements. While leading company executives had indicated earlier that the steelworkers were entitled to a wage increase proportionate to the rise in the cost of living, the companies, acting jointly in negotiations, refused to consider any increase. On the other side, the union announced that it would not accept a settlement limited to the increase in the cost-of-living index. Similar adamant positions were taken by both sides on union security, management prerogatives, and all other issues in dispute.

Shortly before the scheduled beginning on January 1 of a nationwide strike called by the union, President Truman persuaded Philip Murray, the president of the United Steelworkers, to call off the strike on the promise that the dispute would be referred to the Wage Stabilization Board for investigation and recommendations. The WSB wrestled with the case until late in March, during which period the scheduled strike was further postponed. Then the WSB came up with recommendations for a large wage increase and a union shop, to serve as a basis for negotiations between the parties. These recommendations were made over the vigorous dissent of the industry members of the WSB. The steel companies announced their rejection of the recommendations but at the government request resumed negotiations with the union. Some progress seems to have been made in the negotiations, but no agreement had been reached by April 9, the last strike deadline. Aside from collective-bargaining issues, the question of ceiling price adjustments for the steel companies was importantly involved in the stalemate.

A few hours before this deadline, President Truman issued an executive order providing for government seizure of the steel mills, which was followed by the calling off of the strike. The President's seizure order was not based upon any statute but on implied executive powers under the Constitution. The seizure was promptly challenged in the courts by the steel companies. District Judge Pine held the President's action unconstitutional, but the Circuit Court of Appeals stayed his order pending appeal to the Supreme Court.[1] The Supreme Court, on June 2, in a 6 to 3 decision [2] held against the government, whereupon the steel mills were promptly returned to private operation and the steelworkers went out on strike.

The Justices who concurred in the decision did so in five separate opinions. Some of the Justices held that the President can never seize private property without express legislation giving him such power; others held that he can do so only in all-out war emergencies; while a third view stressed that Congress in the Taft-Hartley Act has prescribed the procedure to be followed in strikes producing national emergencies.

When he seized the steel mills, President Truman asked the Congress for statutory seizure authority. He renewed this recommendation after the Supreme Court's decision, calling attention to the fact that the steelworkers had postponed their strike at his request for a much longer period than they would have been required to do had the Taft-Hartley Act been invoked in December. Congress responded by overwhelmingly adopting a resolution that the President should obtain an injunction under the Taft-Hartley Act and by failing to enact any further legislation for dealing with labor disputes producing national emergencies. The President refused to invoke the Taft-Hartley Act, and the steel strike continued for nearly 2 months. Then, when steel stocks had reached such a low point that widespread layoffs were occurring in many fabricating plants, the steel companies and the union reached an agreement and the government allowed a considerably larger steel-price increase than it had previously indicated it was willing to grant. The labor settlement was strikingly similar to the recommendations of the WSB 4 months earlier, but with enough variations to enable both sides to claim a victory.

During the pendency of the steel case, before the Supreme Court, another major labor dispute of long standing in which the President had resorted to seizure was settled by agreement of the parties. This was the dispute over wages and working rules between all the railroads of the country and the railroad brotherhoods, which led to the government's seizure in August, 1950. During the entire 21 months of government "operation," the railroads were actually

---

[1] Judge Pine's decision has been reported in Youngstown Sheet & Tube Co. *et al.* v. Sawyer, 30 L.R.R.M. 2001 (April 29, 1952); the Circuit Court of Appeals' decision in Sawyer v. United States Steel Corporation *et al.*, 30 L.R.R.M. 2056 (May 2, 1952).

[2] Youngstown Sheet & Tube Co. *et al.* v. Sawyer; Sawyer v. Youngstown Sheet & Tube Co. *et al.* All decisions in this case are reproduced in *The New York Times*, June 3, 1952.

run by their own managements without interference, with the companies retaining and distributing all profits. Wage increases were granted classes of employees whose unions negotiated new agreements with the carriers, but all conditions of employment remained unchanged for the engineers, firemen, and conductors because their unions did not conclude new agreements until late in May, 1952, whereupon the President promptly ended government operation. Seizure was effective in preventing any nationwide strike, but several smaller strikes did occur. In each instance the government secured injunctions to end the strikes on the theory that a strike during a period of government operation is illegal.[3]

In 1952 also occurred several other strikes in which there was considerable demand for governmental action to treat these disputes as producing national emergencies. The most important of these was a strike of the Oil Workers which cut off 35 per cent of the gasoline supply of the country. In that strike the government limited the amount of gasoline the commercial airlines might use and restricted military aviation. But neither in that strike nor the others did the government either seize the properties or invoke the Taft-Hartley Act; and all were settled without great losses or inconvenience to the public.

History of Governmental Action in "National-emergency" Strikes

While these developments have brought the problem into greater prominence than ever before, there have been numerous earlier instances in which the government intervened drastically to prevent or end strikes endangering national security.[4] Several governors, as well as President Hayes, proclaimed the railroad strikes of 1877 to constitute emergencies and used the militia and

[3] In December, 1950, "wildcat" strikes were started at many terminals by yardmen belonging to the Brotherhood of Railroad Trainmen. The government at once secured injunctions from the United States District Courts at Chicago, Cleveland, and Washington, directing that these strikes be ended forthwith and no others undertaken while the railroads remained under government operation. When the strikes did not end at once, the government started contempt proceedings against the Brotherhood and its principal officers. The strikers then returned to work, but in January the switchmen at some terminals all simultaneously reported "sick." The government then proceeded with the contempt cases. The Brotherhood was found guilty and was fined in the courts at Chicago and Washington, but the cases against the officers were dismissed when the strikes ended largely through their efforts.

In March, 1952, the Locomotive Engineers and the Railway Conductors called strikes on the Western Division of the New York Central and at the St. Louis terminal and announced that they would later strike other lines unless their contract demands were met. The government secured an injunction against these strikes, which was promptly complied with, but the unions appealed to the Supreme Court. They also filed a brief, *amicus curiae*, in the steel case, supporting the position of the companies that the President lacked seizure powers.

[4] In addition to the more specialized articles cited in later notes, the following accounts of what has been done by the government in national emergency strikes are noteworthy: Edgar L. Warren, "Thirty-six Years of National Emergency Strikes," *Industrial and Labor Relations Review,* October, 1951; Edgar L. Warren, *The Settlement of Labor-Management Disputes,* Rio Piedras, P.R., University of Puerto Rico, 1951, pp. 60–75; Herbert R. Northrup, *Strike Controls in Essential Industries,* New York, National Industrial Conference Board, 1951; and Clinton L. Rossiter, "The President and Labor Disputes," *Journal of Politics,* 11 (1949), 93–120.

the Federal troops to try to keep the trains running. The militia and, less frequently, the troops have been utilized in many great strikes since, primarily to preserve law and order, but with pronounced effects upon their outcome. Quite often, also, Presidents and governors have more directly sought to bring about settlements, most commonly through public statements but, at times, also as direct negotiators.[5] Congress and the state legislatures, similarly, have intervened in many great labor disputes, principally through the exercise of their investigatory powers, but often with hopes of affecting a settlement which have seldom been realized.

Government seizure in strikes producing national emergencies is of more recent origin.[6] President Theodore Roosevelt forced the operators in 1902 to agree to the establishment of the Anthracite Coal Commission for the settlement of the long-drawn-out anthracite-coal strike, by threatening to seize and operate the mines. During World War I President Wilson made three seizures in connection with labor disputes, the largest of which involved the Western Union Telegraph Co.

In World War II the President seized the properties of three companies, to end or prevent strikes, while we were still in the defense stage of the war, prior to Pearl Harbor.[7] During the war proper the government made forty-six seizures in connection with labor disputes, some of which involved many companies. Included among them were three different seizures of all the bituminous-coal mines and one of the anthracite-coal mines, as well as the seizure of the

[5] Edward Berman's *Labor Disputes and the President* (New York, Columbia University Press, 1924) is an excellent account of Presidential intervention in labor disputes during the years 1894–1922. See also *Federal Aid in Domestic Disturbances, 1903–1922,* Sen. Doc. No. 263, 67th Cong., 2d Sess. (1922); and J. A. Dacus, *Annals of the Great Strikes,* Chicago, L. T. Palmer, 1877.

[6] On government seizures in labor disputes the following accounts are, perhaps, the best: Wayne Morse, "Congress Should Pass Legislation on Seizure Power," 98 Cong. Rec., 4164–4186 (Apr. 18, 1952); Harold S. Roberts, *Seizure in Labor Disputes,* Honolulu, T.H., University of Hawaii, 1949; Richard B. Johnson, "Government Seizure in Labor Disputes," Doctor's dissertation, University of Pennsylvania, 1948; Marie-Louise Paternoster, "Government Seizure in Labor Disputes," *Labor Law Journal,* 3 (May, 1952), 341–349, 369; Ludwig Teller, "Government Seizure in Labor Disputes," *Harvard Law Review,* 60 (September, 1947), 1017–1059; and Bertram F. Willcox and Elizabeth S. Landis, "Government Seizures in Labor Disputes," *Cornell Law Quarterly,* 34 (1948), 155–181. Supplementing the discussion of seizures as a method of settling emergency strikes, it should be noted that state statutes in Kansas, Massachusetts, Missouri, New Jersey, and Virginia authorize the governor to seize and operate public utilities in the event of interruptions through strikes, whether or not the strikes produce real emergencies. In Kansas, Missouri, and New Jersey seizure is incidental to compulsory arbitration; in Virginia, a substitute therefor. A North Dakota law (never used) authorizes the governor to seize any property to avert a strike threatening a calamity. Under a Hawaiian statute of 1949, enacted during a serious longshoremen's strike, the Territory took over the entire stevedoring industry. While an injunction sought by the union to enjoin the Territorial government from continuing the seizure was denied (Longshore Workers' Union v. Tsukiyma, 24 L.R.R.M. 2490), the strike continued for several months until a settlement was worked out by Federal mediators.

[7] The three instances of seizures prior to Pearl Harbor involved the Federal Shipbuilding Corporation, Air Associates, Incorporated, and North American Aviation, Inc. The seizures during the functioning of the NWLB are dealt with in *The Termination Report of the National War Labor Board,* Vol. 1, Washington, U.S. Department of Labor, 1948, Chap. 39 and Appendix J-39.

Montgomery Ward stores in many cities. Twenty-six of the seizures were directed against strikes, while twenty were made in cases of noncompliance by employers with recommendations of the NWLB for the settlement of labor disputes.

Since the close of World War II there have been eleven orders of seizure by the President. Nearly all have involved major industries, many companies, and thousands of employees. Under a Presidential order of seizure in 1946, all the bituminous-coal mines of the country were operated by the government for more than a year. There have been seizures on three different occasions of all the Class 1 railroads. Other major seizures in the postwar period have been those of most of the oil refineries in 1945, of the major meat-packing plants in 1946, and of the steel mills in 1952.

Injunctions taken out by the government to stop strikes producing national emergencies have been somewhat less frequent. The first such injunction was that taken out by Attorney General Olney in the Pullman strike of 1894. Another leading case was the injunction Attorney General Palmer directed against the United Mine Workers in 1919 to prevent a nationwide coal strike; and a third, the injunction issued by Judge Wilkerson in the railroad-shop-crafts strike of 1922.[8] Since World War II there have been fifteen injunctions at the instance of the United States government in emergency strike situations, eight of them premised upon the Taft-Hartley Act.[9]

A milder form of government intervention is the appointment of fact-finding boards to investigate and report on labor disputes in actual or pro-

[8] The cases referred to in this paragraph are: *In re* Debs, 158 U.S. 564 (1895), affirming 64 Fed. 724 (1894); United States v. Hayes (U.S. Dist. Ct., Dist. Ind., Oct. 31, 1919) (unreported); and United States v. Railway Employees' Department, AFL, 290 Fed. 978 (1922).

[9] Injunctions under the emergency provisions of the Taft-Hartley Act were issued in the following cases: United States v. Carbide & Chemical Corp., 21 L.R.R.M. 2525 (1948), in which there was no settlement until after the injunction expired; United States v. United Mine Workers, 21 L.R.R.M. 2570, 2721, 22 L.R.R.M. 2005, 24 L.R.R.M. 2111 (1948–1949), in which the union was fined $400,000 and its president, John L. Lewis, $20,000 for contempt by Judge Goldsborough; United States v. Longshoremen, CIO, 70 F. Supp. 2352 (1948), in which a long strike followed the expiration of the injunction; United States v. National Maritime Union, 22 L.R.R.M. 2275, 2306 (two cases at New York and Cleveland); United States v. Int. Longshoremen's Ass'n, AFL, 22 L.R.R.M. 2421 (1948), in which a strike followed expiration of the injunction; United States v. United Mine Workers, 25 L.R.R.M. 2381, 2447 (1950), in which charges of contempt were brought against the union and Lewis, of which they were acquitted by Judge Keech, after which the operators settled pretty much on the union's terms; United States v. Mine, Mill, & Smelter Workers (U.S. Dist. Ct., Dist. Colo., Sept. 5, 1951), in which a settlement was effected while the injunction was in effect without any participation by the board of inquiry.

The seven cases in which the Government resorted to injunctions to stop strikes, under authority other than the Taft-Hartley Act, were the four cases against railroad brotherhoods referred to in note 3 and the following cases: United States v. United Mine Workers, 19 L.R.R.M. 2059, 2076, 2079, 2086, 2121, 2346 (1946–1947), in which the union was fined $3,500,000 and Lewis $10,000 by Judge Goldsborough for contempt, convictions which the Supreme Court affirmed, with reduction in the penalty on the union to $700,000; United States v. Locomotive Engineers, 22 L.R.R.M. 2063, 2184, 2267, 335 U.S. 867 (1948); and United States v. Switchmen's Union, 97 F. Supp. 97 (W.D. N.Y. 1950), accompanying an order of seizure of the Rock Island Railroad.

claimed emergency situations. Most of these fact-finding boards have been appointed under either the Railway Labor Act or the Taft-Hartley Act, but some have been created without express statutory authority.

Under the Railway Labor Act, ninety-nine emergency boards have been appointed to date by the President. The appointment of such emergency boards is discretionary but is a regular procedure after all other methods for settlement have been exhausted. Strikes and changes in working conditions are prohibited until 30 days after the emergency boards make their recommendations for settlement. Under the terms of the law strikes and unilateral changes in conditions may occur legally thereafter, but in recent years seizures and injunctions have been utilized to prevent strikes even at that stage.

Under the Taft-Hartley Act the President may appoint a board of inquiry whenever he believes that an actual or threatened strike imperils the national health or safety. The board of inquiry investigates the dispute and reports to the President what the issues are but is forbidden to make any recommendations for settlement. After receipt of the board's report the President may instruct the Attorney General to seek an injunction to prohibit or end the strike. Such an injunction, if issued, runs for a maximum of 80 days. In the interim the President is to reconvene the board of inquiry for a further report, which also is not to include any recommendations. Thereafter the NLRB is to conduct an election among the employees on the acceptance of the employer's last offer for settlement. If they vote against acceptance, the workers are free to strike after the expiration of the injunction. At this stage the President has the further duty of making a report on the dispute to the Congress, with such recommendations as he deems appropriate. Under this act nine boards of inquiry have been appointed by the President—seven in 1948 and one each in 1950 and 1951.[10]

Ad hoc fact-finding boards appointed without express statutory authority were utilized by President Wilson on a number of occasions during World War I. At the close of World War II President Truman recommended legislation to authorize the President to appoint fact-finding boards to investigate and make recommendations for settlement in emergency strike situations, pending whose report strikes were to be illegal.[11] Congress failed to do so, but the President or the Secretary of Labor, nevertheless, appointed fact-finding boards in thirteen of the great strikes of 1945–1946, one more such board in 1949, and two in 1951.[12]

Finally, note needs to be taken of the machinery for the settlement of wartime labor disputes. In World War I many adjustment boards were established by executive orders for the settlement of labor disputes in specified war industries, and in March, 1918, the WLB was created with jurisdiction in all

---

[10] The 1948 cases are discussed at some length in Joint Labor-Management Committee, *Final Report,* Rep. No. 986, 80th Cong., 2d Sess. Part III, 16–22.

[11] Special Message, Dec. 3, 1945; and S. 1661, 79th Cong., 2d Sess., 1946.

[12] Complete information about these fact-finding boards prior to 1951 is given in *Federal Fact-finding Boards and Boards of Inquiry 1945–1951,* Washington, U.S. Bureau of Labor Statistics, Division of Industrial Relations, 1952. See also Bryce M. Stewart and Walter J. Couper, *Fact Finding in Industrial Disputes,* New York, Industrial Relations Counselors, 1946.

other disputes threatening interference with the war effort.[13] In the "defense" stage of World War II the National Defense Mediation Board was organized— almost a replica of the WLB of World War I and with the same jurisdiction.[14] This board functioned reasonably successfully from March to November, 1941, but distintegrated over the issue of the closed shop in the captive coal mines. This was followed by the hurried passage by the House of Representatives of the Smith bill forbidding all strikes in defense industries.[15]

Pearl Harbor occurred 2 days thereafter. In the resulting fervor of patriotism the leaders of labor and industry made public declarations which constituted the "no-strike pledge" of World War II. Thereupon the Smith bill was allowed to die, and the President created the NWLB for the settlement of all labor disputes endangering the war effort.[16]

The NWLB functioned from January, 1942, to December, 1945, and in that period dealt with nearly 21,000 labor-dispute cases. Until June, 1943, its authority stemmed from an executive order issued under the war powers of the President. In that month it was given statutory authority by the Smith-Connally Act,[17] which also weakened the no-strike pledge by implying that strikes interfering with the war effort might legally be undertaken after an affirmative vote of a majority of the workers. But throughout the war the Board took the position that every strike had potentialities of interfering with the war effort and violating the no-strike pledge.

When South Korea was invaded by the Communists in June, 1950, the nation realized that it again faced a dangerous emergency and began large-scale rearmament. Labor disputes, fortunately, did not loom large at that time, and there were divided counsels on the need for emergency adjustment machinery similar to that of World War II. In the Defense Production Act of 1950 Congress did not vest such powers in the WSB.[18] Instead it provided that the President might convene a high-level labor-management conference to try to arrive at agreed procedures for handling labor disputes in defense industries.

---

[13] On the adjustment of labor disputes in World War I, the most comprehensive accounts are Alexander M. Bing, *War-time Strikes and their Adjustment*, New York, Dutton, 1921; and Gordon S. Watkins, *Labor Problems and Labor Administration in the United States during the World War*, Urbana, University of Illinois Press, 1919.

[14] The activities of this agency are discussed in detail in *Report on the Work of the National Defense Mediation Board, March 19, 1941–January 12, 1942*, U.S. Bureau of Labor Statistics Bulletin 714, 1942.

[15] H.R. 4139, 77th Cong., 1st Sess., 1941.

[16] *The Termination Report of the National War Labor Board*, Washington, U.S. Department of Labor, 1948, is a detailed documentary account of the organization and activities of this Board. *Problems and Policies of Disputes Settlement and Wage Stabilization during World War II*, U.S. Bureau of Labor Statistics Bulletin 1009, 1951, is an appraisal of the Board's functioning prepared for the National Securities Resources Board by men who held top staff positions with the Board. "Wartime Handling of Labor Disputes," *Harvard Business Review*, 25 (September, 1947), 1017–1059, is an account of this subject by the author of this chapter.

[17] 57 Stat. 163.

[18] The WSB was created by Exec. Order No. 10161, 15 Fed. Reg. 6105 (1950), and reconstituted by Exec. Order No. 10233, 16 Fed. Reg. 3503 (1951). These Executive Orders were issued under the authority of the Emergency Price Control Act of 1950, Pub. L. No. 774, 81st Cong. This act was continued, with modifications (which did not affect the structure of the WSB) by the Emergency Price Control Act of 1951, Pub. L. No. 96, 82d Cong.

Such a conference was never convened, but when the WSB was reorganized by an executive order in May, 1951, it was vested with power to deal with two types of disputes cases: those submitted voluntarily by both parties and those which the President might refer to it as likely to result in a national emergency.

Under this authority the WSB during the next year dealt with some twenty labor disputes. Most of these were cases voluntarily submitted; only a few disputes were referred to the Board by the President. Among the latter was the steel case—which overshadowed everything else done by the Board. Although it handled all other cases successfully, its recommendations in the steel case spelled its doom. In the Defense Production Act of 1952 Congress once more reorganized the Board and expressly deprived its successor of all disputes-settlement powers.

Appraisal

None of the methods which have been employed by the government to cope with labor disputes producing national emergencies have proved wholly satisfactory. Strikes they were designed to prevent have occurred in numerous instances. All methods have at times produced injustices and have had undesirable results.

Probably most nearly satisfactory was the wartime adjustment machinery of World War II. The no-strike pledge and the NWLB did not prevent all strikes. There were a great many strikes, with a tendency toward an increase as the war approached a close. The man-days lost through strikes in the war period, however, totaled only 36,000,000, compared with 116,000,000 in the first year after the war.

Decisions of the NWLB were interpreted by the courts as having the legal effect of recommendations only, but in nearly all disputes cases they were accepted without much question by both parties. There were around 200 cases of noncompliance, in 46 of which the President seized the properties and in 4 other cases applied other sanctions. The government seizures were pretty effective in ending strikes, but less so in cases of noncompliance by employers. When Japan surrendered, the government was still operating the properties seized in sixteen cases in which it had never secured compliance.

Nobody was entirely satisfied with the government's labor policies in World War II. Labor felt that the wage-stabilization policies were unduly restrictive; management objected to recommendations for union maintenance of membership and "fringe" adjustments. Both sides complained that governmental determination of conditions of employment had replaced collective bargaining. The Conciliation Service, similarly, complained that the NWLB's decision-making power rendered efforts at mediation futile. Actually, far more collective agreements were concluded during the war than previously, most of them without intervention by the NWLB; but the Board decisions set the pattern for collective bargaining, and stabilization policies restricted the wage increases the parties might agree upon. The Conciliation Service was greatly enlarged during the war; but doubtless, the existence of the NWLB operated in many cases to induce one or both parties to gamble on its decision in preference to settling earlier. When Japan surrendered, all groups on the NWLB joined in suggesting to the President that the Board be directed to take no more new cases and to terminate its existence as soon as the pending cases were decided. The NWLB was probably terminated too soon, but it is clear that it could function effectively only so long as the no-strike pledge remained in effect, and neither side was willing to extend this pledge.

Of all methods which have been tried in dealing with labor disputes of an emergency character in peacetime, the one under which there has been the most extensive experience is the Railway Labor Act.[19] Until World War II this was acclaimed by everyone as a great success. Since then we have had several important railroad strikes. All these have been ended without serious damage only by resort to the more drastic methods of governmental intervention. Today scarcely anyone is satisfied with this legislation except the people who have been associated with its administration, who insist that the difficulties which have developed have resulted not from the law but by reason of departures from its procedures and intent. As there is no agreement on a substitute and both the carriers and the railroad unions want adjustment machinery applicable only to them, however, no basic changes seem likely.

Neither has the Taft-Hartley Act machinery for dealing with emergency disputes proved completely satisfactory. While in 1952 Congress asked the President to invoke the Taft-Hartley Act against the steelworkers, in 1949 the same anti-Administration bloc in the Senate passed the Taft substitute to the Administration bill to repeal the Taft-Hartley Act.[20] This added the presidential power of seizure to the provisions for boards of inquiry and injunctions in emergency disputes. It also made the boards of inquiry mediation agencies, authorized them to make recommendations, and repealed the provisions for a vote on the employer's final offer of settlement.

As has been noted, the present provisions have been utilized in nine cases. One was settled before the Board convened; another before the Board made its report; and in a third case the President did not apply for an injunction (wanted by the union) although a strike was in progress. In all other cases 80-day injunctions were secured. In two of these cases strikes occurred after the 80 days had elapsed. In another there was no settlement until after the expiration of the injunction, but also no strike. In all cases there ultimately were settlements—as is normal in all labor disputes—but in only one instance is there evidence that the Taft-Hartley Act machinery was helpful in bringing about the settlement.[21]

[19] Good presentations of diametrically opposite views on the value of the railway-labor-disputes legislation are the papers presented at the annual meetings of the Industrial Relations Research Association by H. R. Northrup (con), in 1948, and by I. L. Sharfman (pro), in 1951, published in the *Proceedings*. A good recital of the occurrences of recent years is David Levinson, "Railway Labor Act—The Record of a Decade," *Labor Law Journal*, 3 (January, 1952), 13–29.

[20] S. 249, 81st Cong., 1st Sess., as passed by the Senate.

[21] The cases in which injunctions were issued under the emergency strike provisions of the Taft-Hartley Act are enumerated and briefly discussed in note 9. The case in which the parties reached a settlement after the President had created a board of inquiry, but before it convened, was the American Telegraph & Telephone Co. long-lines case in 1948; the two in which a settlement was reached while the board of inquiry was functioning but, apparently, without its participation, were the bituminous-coal-miners case in June, 1948, and the Mine, Mill and Smelter Workers case in 1951; and the case in which the President

The most drastic methods of governmental intervention in emergency situations—injunctions and seizure—have generally proved effective in ending strikes, although this has not always been true. Seizure of the anthracite mines near the close of World War II did not get the miners back into the pits until a settlement was worked out. Seizure of the tugboats in New York harbor in November, 1945, did not end the wildcat strike of the small number of tugboatmen, and the great harbor remained idle until William H. Davis, appointed as a special mediator when the food supply of New York City ran low, conferred with the strikers and worked out an adjustment of their grievances. Injunctions directed against strikes have generally been observed, but the injunction secured by the government under the Taft-Hartley Act in the early winter of 1950 did not end the wildcat strikes of the coal miners until Judge Keech acquitted John L. Lewis of contempt charges for violating this injunction, which was followed by the complete surrender of the operators.

Seizure has often meant little beyond "running up the flag," leaving the old management in control and interfering little with its operations. Ultimate authority, however, rests with the government, and it sometimes has taken actions in seizures to which the management violently objected. In the Montgomery Ward seizure it replaced the company president and forcibly ejected him from the premises. In the Trans-Mississippi Trucking Lines seizure in 1944 it reduced the salaries of company executives. In World War II when the seizure was made because employers would not comply with decisions of the NWLB, the government generally put these decisions into effect once it assumed operation. On the other hand, when the government seized properties to end strikes, it always insisted that employees return to work before it would consider their grievances.

Both the policy of preserving the *status quo* during seizures and that of making changes in conditions of employment without the management's approval give rise to serious problems. Preserving the *status quo* in conditions of employment while the employers get all profits seems unjust to the employees; moreover, it affords no incentive to the employers to reach a settlement. Putting into effect, during seizures, conditions the management does not approve virtually compels it to accept these conditions when resuming control. The government is liable to the owners for fair compensation for the use of their property, but the principles governing the determination of such compensation are "a Pandora's box of unsettled questions." [22]

---

declined to seek an injunction (desired by the union), although a strike was in progress, was that of the CIO Packinghouse Workers, also in 1948. The one case in which the board of inquiry played a major role in bringing about a settlement was that of the bituminous-coal miners early in 1950.

A good discussion on the way the emergency provisions of the Taft-Hartley Act have worked out is Sylvester Garrett, "The Emergency Disputes Provisions of the Taft-Hartley Act as a Framework for Wartime Dispute Settlement," *Industrial Relations Research Association Proceedings, 1950,* pp. 25–33.

[22] United States v. Pewee Coal Co., 341 U.S. 114 (1951). In another case, the government has recently settled for $8,000,000 claims against it growing out of the seizure of the properties of the Trans-Mississippi trucking operators in World War II, following an adverse decision by the Court of Claims in the case of one of these operators. See 30 L.R.R., No. 3, May 12, 1952, p. 20.

Future Policies

The $64 question remains: What is to be done about strikes producing national emergencies? [23]

Strikes to improve conditions of employment have always been legal in the United States. The right to strike is closely associated with democratic concepts of freedom. Strikes are an outlet for pent-up emotions which, when suppressed, may find expression in much more destructive ways. Their possibility serves the useful purpose in collective bargaining of inducing the parties to compromise differences.

Some restrictions upon the right to strike, however, are not incompatible with the important functions which it serves. Nearly everyone recognizes that strikes may be forbidden by agreement during the life of contracts. Some strikes, also, have always been forbidden by law, as for instance, strikes for the purpose of extortion.

That there are also situations in which even strikes for the improvement of conditions of employment become intolerable cannot be gainsaid. A strike in the armed forces is revolution. A strike which deprives our troops in time of war of badly needed supplies amounts to giving aid and comfort to the enemy. In a highly interdependent society such as we have today, some strikes may operate to deny goods and services needed by large numbers of nonparticipants for their survival.

But past experience suggests that such serious emergencies are far less common than seems to be implied in much of the discussion of this problem in recent years. While we have had some strikes which have produced serious inconveniences, there has never been a strike in this country in peacetime which has resulted in extreme suffering to nonparticipants. Both workers and employers have usually realized that strikes must not be carried that far, however angry they may be with each other.

In wartime, strikes in the plants of suppliers of war materials may result in unnecessary loss of life in the armed forces and in defeat. As strikes are often contagious, even strikes in nonwar industries become matters of serious concern.

A two-sided no-strike pledge, such as we had in World War II, is the most effective device for coping with the problem of strikes in wartime. Such a pledge is not an absolute guarantee against all strikes, particularly unauthorized strikes. In World War II, however, it operated not only to prevent all AFL and CIO unions from calling or sanctioning any strikes but to lead the labor leaders to assume the major part of the difficult job of promptly getting wildcat strikers back to work.

But this pledge proved successful only because it also included the promise of both employers and unions to abide by decisions of the NWLB on issues in

[23] The policies here advocated are in general, although not complete, agreement with those set forth in *Strikes and Democratic Government*, New York, Twentieth Century Fund, 1947, and in numerous speeches and articles by William H. Davis, George W. Taylor, and Wayne Morse. For widely differing views, readers are referred to numerous articles on the subject by Sumner H. Slichter and Ludwig Teller, and to Congressional hearings and speeches on labor-relations legislation, which, ever since World War II, have devoted a large amount of attention to strikes producing national emergencies.

disputes which they did not resolve through collective bargaining. To prohibit strikes without at the same time affording an alternative method for settling disputes not only results in grave injustice but invites a complete breakdown of the no-strike policy.

The machinery for the settlement of labor disputes which the parties do not settle themselves or submit to binding, voluntary arbitration must needs be governmental. On the basis of experience on both all-public and tripartite boards, I strongly believe that tripartite boards are greatly superior for the settlement of disputes involving the terms of labor agreements.[24] True, many decisions of such boards will be by majority vote, with the public members casting the deciding votes. But under the tripartite system, with the employer and union members free to withdraw at any time, at least every important decision must be such that both parties are willing to live with it and to present a unanimous front when it comes to enforcement. Getting such a measure of agreement is not easy and the need for doing so slows up decisions. But it results in sounder decisions and is a method for preserving many of the advantages of collective bargaining at a time when unrestricted collective bargaining is impossible.

For the same reason, as much voluntarism as possible needs to be preserved in the settlement of labor disputes. Settlement of disputes by governmental fiat appears simple, but compulsion will break down unless it is acceptable. In the United States employers and unions do not want compulsory arbitration. Experience in World War II also suggests that there are advantages in broad but not definitely defined powers as to what the government can do to enforce its decisions. The parties should always be encouraged to settle disputes without governmental intervention and be left free to modify board decisions by mutual agreement where not clearly in contravention of established wage-stabilization policies.

In peacetime it is a part of the American way of life to encourage labor and management to settle differences through collective bargaining rather than by governmental compulsion. Collective bargaining implies and includes occasional interruptions in relations. Strikes are a price of liberty and are far less costly than attempts at suppression.

The possibility of very serious consequences from strikes undoubtedly exists, although true national emergencies are far less common than often pictured. The fact that they may occur renders legislative provisions desirable for dealing with such emergencies. This has become the more necessary because it has now been settled that the President lacks inherent power to deal with strike emergencies, except possibly in times of declared war.

[24] The favorable view of tripartism in the organization and functioning of emergency-disputes-settlement agencies here presented is based upon the author's observations and experiences as a member of the NWLB in World War II. This favorable view was held by nearly all the men who served on this Board and in its subordinate agencies in all three of the constituent groups—public, industry, and labor. It is believed to be shared also by most of the men who have served on the present WSB. One public member of the NWLB, Dexter M. Keezer, however, was very critical of tripartism in his "Observations on the Operation of the National War Labor Board," *American Economic Review,* 36 (1946), 233–257. A few industry members agreed with Keezer, and this view is the one now taken by the major business organizations.

Congressional leaders appear to be of the opinion that Congress is the branch of our government which should decide what should be done in each such critical situation when it arises. A legislative body of two houses, with 531 members between them, however, is not likely to deal effectively with such situations on a case-by-case basis. The function of the Congress is to make laws, prescribing the rules to be followed, not to execute these laws in particular situations. The Constitution wisely makes that the duty of the Executive.

The situations in which labor disputes may develop into genuine national emergencies are extremely varied and unpredictable. A strike when there is an acute shortage of badly needed goods is much more serious in its consequences than is a dispute involving many more workers when there are large surplus stocks. In time of all-out war any strike may endanger the national safety, which is not true of the great majority of strikes in more normal times. In circles extremely hostile to the unions there is at this writing strong support for restrictions on industry-wide bargaining; this proposal is often presented as the solution of strikes producing national emergencies. That there is little, if any, relation between the size of the bargaining unit or the number of workers involved and the critical effects produced by a strike is illustrated by the wildcat strike of the tugboatmen in New York harbor in November, 1945, referred to earlier. Although less than 100 men struck on that occasion, the strike within a week reduced the food supply of New York to a dangerously low point. Similarly unrealistic is the view that strikes producing serious emergencies are confined to public utilities and a few other industries. A strike of construction workers in a utility or even at an atomic-energy plant usually produces less serious consequences than a strike of the elevator operators in the office and apartment buildings of a great city. Verily, whether a labor dispute produces, or is likely to produce, a national emergency depends upon all surrounding circumstances.

Because such situations are so varied, it seems desirable not to attempt to define them in advance. The Congress cannot deal with them effectively as they arise. The only alternative is to vest wide discretion in the President.

The emergency provisions of the Taft-Hartley Act are now law, and there is no present likelihood of their repeal. They clearly should be strengthened as Senator Taft proposed in 1949. Emergency boards set up under the act should have power to attempt to settle the dispute and, failing in their efforts to that end, should have authority to make recommendations.

In some situations resort to these provisions may be the soundest method of dealing with a strike producing a national emergency. But to have no alternative will often prove inequitable and hazardous. Workers will deem it unfair to continue to work for 80 days at their old wages, particularly if the crisis develops long after their contracts have expired and while the employers continue to enjoy large profits. What could be done if the union officers in good faith tried to get the men back to work but if the workers en masse should stay out is not at all clear. Disraeli's maxim "Never expose the impotence of government" is worth remembering. Experience has demonstrated that injunctions do not ensure settlement of disputes, and the Taft-Hartley Act expressly provides that they shall stand dissolved after 80 days. If the workers then strike, the government is helpless to deal with the situation unless some new legislation is enacted—and Congress may not even be in session.

The wiser course is to authorize alternative methods of procedure, to be used as the particular situation may warrant. These might include, in addition to the Taft-Hartley procedure, authority for the appointment of special mediation tribunals or of fact-finding boards with power to make recommendations. Further, the courts might be authorized to stay strikes at the President's application, without prior necessity of appointing a board of inquiry. As Senator Taft also proposed in 1949, there should also be power to seize and operate strike-bound properties, under appropriate safeguards. If Congress deems it necessary to retain a voice in determining what action should be taken in particular emergencies, the President might be required to report what he does and Congress might be given power to nullify his action by joint resolution within a specified number of days.

All the measures suggested have, in fact, been utilized in the past. No great abuses have occurred, and the actions taken have been pretty effective in preventing serious harm to the public interest. The effective safeguards against abuse are the election of the President by the people, the Congressional control of the purse strings, and the now-established power of the courts to set aside the President's actions if unconstitutional.

Need for action is quite urgent despite the long record of few strikes in this country which have produced real national emergencies. This is the more true because of the present critical international situation. In such a situation our nation should not be left without means of coping with national-emergency strikes other than the provisions of the Taft-Hartley Act, which its principal author has himself recognized as being far from completely satisfactory.

CHAPTER 34 LABOR AND MANAGEMENT INFLUENCE ON SOCIAL CONTROLS

Kermit Eby   *University of Chicago*

THE activity of unions and employers to influence and control opinion in the different publics of our contemporary United States takes place within the framework of a compensatory state. That is, the two groups compete within the framework of a state where conflicting economic groups pressure for the favors of government and where government withholds or grants its favors with an ever-present consciousness of the necessity of staying in power. This is not a particularly new phenomenon. From the very beginning of our republic economic groups have struggled for the favors of the state. The significant new factors in the picture are the increasing size and power of the competing groups and the arrival on the scene of organized labor as one of the more powerful of these conflicting groups.

Pressure Groups and the Governmental Process

The working of this "compensatory" process can be illustrated by the way in which the President's Council of Economic Advisers functions. The Council, prior to preparing its report on the economic health of the nation, hears the evidence of the great economic pressure groups—labor, agriculture, and business—and occasionally even small business and consumer groups present their cases. Representatives of these interests appear before the Council and its staff and present their arguments for the payment of wage increases without price increases, for continuing subsidies for agriculture, or for correcting the unfairness of existing or proposed corporation taxes.

The Council hears the special pleaders, makes its own scientific investigation of the facts, writes its report, and transmits it to the President. The President then uses the material in the report as a basis for his message to Congress. But the President's message is a translation of the report, and his translation is determined not only by his responsibilities as President of the United States but by his role as the leader of the political party in power. In this latter role he must try to hold the loyalties of the groups which support him and his party, and in this as well as other messages he projects his party's program.

Similarly, the Taft-Hartley Act exemplifies an issue in which unions and employers have sought to influence public opinion and government action in their behalf. By employers it was represented as a bill to free labor, to preserve the worker's right of individual choice. Organized labor fought it as a bill to enslave labor. Its enactment represented the triumph in Congress of its supporters, but not necessarily a final triumph. It remains an issue, and both groups are still hard at work convincing the public that it is a "good" or a "bad" piece of legislation. At the last national political conventions both parties considered it, both parties heard arguments by the interested groups, and both parties gave it recognition as an issue in their platforms. Candidates find it necessary to take positions on the issue, and each takes what he hopes will be the most popular position. His position, he argues, is consistent with the public interest; his opponent's position is inimical to the public interest.

This identification of the special group's interest with the public interest is characteristic of the campaigns of all groups who seek to influence public opinion. This difference between business, labor, and agriculture appears in their contrasting definitions of the public interest and in their different notions about the way in which it is best advanced. Organized labor believes that it is in the public interest to lift the level of living for all by lifting the level of purchasing power of the organized workers and to organize the unorganized so that they may have similar privileges. They believe there is much to be done as long as income is presently so distributed (1950 census) that the lowest 20 per cent of income recipients in America receive 3 per cent of the total money income whereas the upper 20 per cent receive 47 per cent.

Other pressure groups define the public interest and its advancement differently. The farmer argues that agriculture is the backbone of the nation. How could we get along without food and fiber? he asks. Business insists that the nation's economic strength is dependent on the creation of jobs by the entrepreneur and by his consistent expansion of capital investment, produced through work and savings.

Each group is sincere in its own way, and each follows about the same routine in attempting to influence public opinion and legislation. Be it at the local, state, or national level, there are three major methods which are used to promote the interests of the special group: lobbying, mass media, and education.

Lobbying activities take several forms. Most commonly, lobbying provides a channel for communicating public opinion and the interests of special groups to legislators. By contacting congressmen and by appearing before legislative committees, the lobbyist supplies information to them pertinent to the interest of the group which he is representing. Frequently, much of the substantive information on bills introduced in, and passed by, national and state legislatures springs from the organizations which sponsor the legislation. Often bills are drafted by the lobbyist to be introduced by a legislator who is friendly to the special-interest group.

A second type of lobbying stresses the reaction of voters and focuses the legislator's attention on the support he will gain or lose by his stand. The third type of lobbying activity is the destructive kind, in which use is made of the "fix" and the "squeeze." What begins as wining and dining has been known to turn into outright bribery.

Both groups make use of the mass media—the press, radio, television, films, pamphlets, comic strips, etc. These media are generally used in a manipulative way. The typical full-page ad makes more use of large black type and loaded words than of sincere communications giving the public the facts. It is meant to sell, not to inform.

Another kind of influencing presupposes that the individuals who compose the public are capable of thinking for themselves, given the facts and the opportunity to consider them. This is more akin to education than to influencing, however, because it seeks to inform rather than to impress. Such education cannot be mechanical; it demands a person-to-person relationship between teachers and taught. It requires an opportunity to question and to disagree. Ideas cannot be sold. They are the outgrowth of discussion, of reading, and of the respect for another person's point of view which develops in the personal contact.

Given the foregoing tools, the influencing efforts of unions and employers are directed toward particular objectives. Each tries to win public support to promote its interest.

In these years of full employment labor disputes call forth some rather unusual appeals to the public. The employer appeals to the public as consumers; he argues that, in refusing to grant the union's demand for wage increases, he is protecting consumers against price increases. The union counters by saying that the employer's profits are enormous and that he could easily pay the wage increase without raising prices. Where the labor dispute is one in which government intervenes and either of the parties objects to the government action, an appeal is made to the public, as electorate, to "throw the rascals out."

In an election organized labor appeals for support for its candidate on the basis of his record and/or campaign promises on particular issues which make him "a friend of labor." As a friend of labor, it is assumed that he is a friend of the public. Employer groups never appeal for support of their candidate by claiming him to be "a friend of employers." Although his position may be exactly opposite that of organized labor, they will also claim that he is a friend of labor and, furthermore, that he is for free enterprise and the American way of life.

The objective of both groups in enlisting public support for particular legislation and governmental actions affecting labor relations is to strengthen their own group. Legislation or governmental action affecting labor relations is almost certain to affect their respective strength at the collective-bargaining table. Moreover, labor is concerned with securing social-welfare measures which will benefit its membership. Employers, on the other hand, are fearful that social-welfare legislation will increase their tax bill.

Organized labor has developed a growing understanding of economic cause and effect since 1932 and, particularly, since 1936 which has influenced its increased interest in politics. The top labor leaders and their intellectual advisers understand that the CIO grew up with Section 7A of the National Industrial Recovery Act, with the Wagner Act, and with Roosevelt and that the AFL doubled its membership under the same friendly aegis. The walls which have shored up the workers' security—the minimum wage, unemployment insurance, and old-age and survivors' insurance—are the walls of government.

The conditions under which collective bargaining takes place are set not only by legislation but by administrative action as well. In recent years contract negotiations have involved constant consideration of the cost of living. Inasmuch as it is the Bureau of Labor Statistics which measures changes in the cost of living, arguments have developed between unions and employers regarding the alleged biases of the Bureau's index. If changes in wage rates were to hinge on changes in the cost-of-living index, labor was concerned that cost-of-living increases not be understated. Their distrust stemmed from their feeling that the Bureau's statisticians were too dependent upon business sources for their facts. Under other circumstances employers might well charge bias in another direction.

The experts, the politicians, and the intelligentsia in the labor movement understand the nature of the compensatory state and the increasing number of decisions made at the top governmental levels. They also understand the nature of the American two-party system, in which conflicting economic groups struggle for the control of the party and its candidates, reconcile their conflicts around a common denominator of interests, and compete with their opponents for fulfillment of their aims.

Influencing Efforts by Labor and by Management

Organized labor seeks to operate politically in much the same manner as do other organized interest groups. It seldom is revolutionary to the extent that it wishes to change the established economic system or the ongoing rules of the political organization. Its ambition, instead, is to achieve ever-increasing security for its members within the political and economic structure as it exists. In the same manner as other economic groups, organized labor almost always identifies its own interest with the public interest. A representative of the labor movement keeps his peace of mind in proportion to his ability to convince himself that the interest of the group which employs him actually does advance the public interest. Spokesmen of the NAM, the Chamber of Commerce, and the Farm Bureau are sustained by similar convictions.

Irrespective of their conflict with each other, employers and unions are both concerned with securing the "good will" of the public. Employers, as sellers of products as well as buyers of labor, cannot afford to lose customers. Unions cannot afford to stir up ill will if they wish to have friends in legislatures who will protect and support their interests.

In their employment of the methods at hand to influence public opinion and action, both groups make use of the same machinery. Some of this machinery, however, lends itself more readily to use by one group than it does by the other.

Both labor and management participate in lobbying in its most constructive form. That is, both groups reach legislators and appear before legislative committees to give information on pending bills. An examination of the records of committee hearings over the past several decades shows an increasing representation of labor in these hearings. Moreover, labor now comes supplied with its own experts—lawyers, economists, statisticians, and the like—to match the experts who testify for business groups.

The second type of lobbying, which stresses the giving or withholding of support depending upon the yes or no vote of the legislator, is carried on differently by the two groups. Organized labor judges senators and representatives by their voting records in committee and by roll call on so-called labor bills. If the legislator fails to measure up to expectations, he is threatened with the withdrawal of support by labor's voting bloc. In reality, labor, even organized labor, does not vote as a bloc, and while the leaders may influence its vote, they by no means control it. While almost one-third of all families in America are "labor-union families," union members constitute one of the groups in the population with a low voter-turnout ratio. Moreover, in the last presidential election one out of three union members voted for the Republican candidate despite the recommendation by top leaders to support the Democratic candidate. Nevertheless, unions do organize political action committees, and they do work to get out the vote; they represent a formidable number, and their voting strength cannot be lightly dismissed.

Employers and business groups can point to no such voting group, but they have a particular advantage which not even a united labor organization can balance. They can offer or withhold another kind of support. The great game of politics in the United States is an expensive one. The man of average income cannot play it. He is too dependent upon contributions for the cost of his election, and it is here, as was so clearly indicated in the hearings on the Taft campaign, that big money talks. In fact, it often talks for men of independent fortunes, corporation executives, or the corporation lawyers who represent them.

The fix and squeeze, which are characteristic of the third and most destructive type of lobbying, also require sizable expenditure. It is this kind of political activity which undermines public morals and destroys public confidence. In a complex society such as ours, where economic advantage is avidly sought, more and more individuals and organizations look to government as a means of engineering this advantage—through grants-in-aid, government contracts, price supports, tax exemption, and the like. In the confusion which is Capitol Hill the uninitiated seek the help of the initiated, and money and liquor flow to bridge the gaps of calculated reason. Both the venal and the unsophisticated live in a world of influence. Both agree that the only way to get things done in Washington is through someone else and that "after all, the halls of Congress are too large and the mazes of the Pentagon too complex for the average person to comprehend." The danger stemming from such a philosophy is that the fix and the squeeze may become so firmly institutionalized in our culture, as they have in China, that they will threaten the very basis of our democratic processes, for in the last analysis the integrity of the law and the stability of our institutions is dependent on the integrity of the men who administer them.

But in groups whose motives are avowedly materialistic and whose resources make it possible for them to spend money in quantities, these practices provide a relatively easy means for reaching their goals. The moral patterns of a society which produces the fix and the squeeze are influencing the political strategy of increasing numbers of groups. Wining and dining are accepted; the 10-pound hams, the deepfreeze, and the mink coat may be condemned in political speeches, but they are all too often only winked at when the speaker's back is turned to his constituents. Thus even many men who represent organized labor today believe that, to be effective, they too must operate through cocktail parties and expense accounts. One is reminded of the reply of one author to another who complained that "The very rich are very different from you and me." His comment was "Yes. They have more money."

The fact that employers "have more money" gives them a decided advantage in employing the mass media. The full-page ad and the radio speech of the company executive when a strike is in progress are standard operating procedures for business. But they are expensive procedures, and those persons who pick up the checks in the labor movement know that they cannot compete with the great business organizations in these areas. Although the public-service responsibility of the radio stations compels giving time for the discussion of public issues, that time is often given when listeners are few. Furthermore, as was discovered in 1946 during the steelworkers' and other strikes, the purchase of too much space and time by unions to tell their story may have a negative effect. The public asks how, if the workers are as hard up as they claim, their unions can afford such big expenditures for radio time and ads.

There are other important reasons why the mass media lend themselves more readily to use by employer groups than to use by organized labor. Employer groups have no large membership base to which they can appeal and which, in turn, will reach others outside their groups. They must use these media to reach, if only at a superficial level, the public. While the public is undoubtedly influenced to some extent, there is good reason to believe that under many circumstances the mass appeal falls flat. From 1936 on, 90 to 95 per cent of the American press opposed Franklin Roosevelt. Americans are a very literate people; nevertheless, they elected Roosevelt to the office of President for four terms.

While with the CIO and CIO-PAC, I helped develop its public-relations program, following the precedents of the manipulator making use of the mass media. However, as I saw the program perfected, I lost faith in much that I had helped to develop. The reason is simple: I found such programs made little difference, and I found that genuine education, proceeding through the exchange of ideas in person-to-person relationships, repeatedly triumphed over the mass-media techniques. In 1944 CIO-PAC put out a minimum of 40 million pieces of literature—a maximum of 80 million—to help reelect Franklin Roosevelt. The AFL the same year put out little or no literature. On the basis of studies made since the election, it can be stated that approximately 71 per cent of the registered CIO voters voted Democratic while about 68 per cent of the registered AFL voters cast Democratic ballots. Forty million pieces of literature and a 3 per cent difference in the voting pattern!

Education versus Manipulation

In spite of such negative indications, the temptations for unions to use the mass media is a constant one. And to the extent that organized labor copies the techniques of the slick public-relations men employed by the wealthier organized interests, it neglects means of influencing political and social direction more in harmony with the structure of its organization.

It is in the third type of influencing, the more personal approach which involves two-way communication, that unions have a decided advantage. A good public-relations program for the labor movement is not too different from a good educational program within the union. The worker who has confidence in his union, who participates in it, and who has knowledge of its program is the natural interpreter of the union's point of view. And wherever he meets people he speaks up out of his confidence, thus personalizing its point of view. Particularly in times of full employment the American union member does not think of himself as an exploited proletarian. He, like many other Americans, thinks of himself as an integral part of the community, as a member of a political party, a church, or a parent-teacher association or as a Mason or an Elk—all those organizations that play so great a part in his life. It is this orientation that makes union members in a public-relations program for organized labor a more effective resource than purchased mass media.

Companies with a good record in their labor relations have found that friendly employees act not only as public-relations people for their product but as producers of general good will in the community. The company without such a good record can count on only the relatively few supervisory employees and perhaps on stockholders who know "its side of the story."

In working with their memberships, however, and at the same time appealing to the larger public, both union leaders and company executives in times of crisis are often caught in an ambivalent position by the very nature of the crisis. Union leaders must make a vigorous effort to secure what their membership demands, yet these demands must be reasonable if the public's support is to be gained. Similarly, company executives may find themselves reporting to their stockholders and investors that under their management profits are at a record level, at the same time resisting the workers' demands for wage increases in order to protect those profits, all the while appealing to the public on grounds that the workers' demands are unreasonable.

I stress this point because the whole public-relations programs of the conflicting groups cannot be understood unless it is seen that the public-relations program of an organized interest group is as much concerned with keeping the membership happy as it is with influencing public opinion by convincing the larger population that the group is behaving in accord with the general public interest.

Both parties to industrial conflict identify their organizational aims with human and national welfare. Business does not advertise that it is in business to make profits. It "makes possible the employment of hundreds of thousands." It "provides the dependable efficient . . . service so essential to the economic well-being and military strength of our nation."

When organized labor sets up a public-relations program, it too seeks to convince the public of its high moral purpose. In the CIO the center of its public-relations program was a mailing list made up of some 120,000 people from all over the United States. This list was broken up into some fifty-two categories consisting of teachers, ministers, political scientists, educators, reporters, radio announcers, organization heads, etc. They were mailed a consistent flow of literature interpreting the CIO's position on issues. In times of crisis—strikes and otherwise—the reasons for the CIO's direct action were accompanied with a personal letter attempting to identify the reader's interest and that of the CIO. Whenever replies to the literature were received from interested parties, their names were put on cards and classified according to states and Congressional districts. It was this list which became the nucleus of much of PAC when labor went into politics full tilt in 1944. The philosophy behind such organizing was clear-cut and previously defined—that person-to-person relations are more important in influencing opinion than a barrage of propaganda which can provide only the initial contact for establishing such personal relationships.

Such two-way communication is not only more effective, it is more consistent with democratic institutions which depend for their very life on a genuinely informed electorate participating in the decisions which affect them. As the conflicting economic groups grow larger and more powerful, more and more of the decisions are made by top-level experts and politicians. This trend will continue as long as people feel that they can do little or nothing to affect their destiny. It is the responsibility of leaders of the conflicting groups to involve their membership in decisions, to urge their participation, and to discuss all facets of the issues with them. The organizational press must do more than report; their columns should be open to a discussion of issues; letters-to-the-editor columns should find room for all the pros and cons. Such columns exist in all too few journals of the labor and business press.

Today business, labor, and agriculture are each convinced that domestic inflation is as great a threat to the stability of American institutions as foreign communism, but each group is contributing in its own way to the total that is producing inflation. Business wishes to continue to enjoy its present high profits, agriculture its price supports, and labor its wages. Each group charges the other with causing inflation, and not one of them is willing to support the higher taxes that would control inflation unless, of course, the higher taxes are levied on someone else. If the members of these same groups understood this inflationary process and could compare the losses they would suffer from inflation with the extra burden of taxation, there might be unprecedented agreement and pressure for Congress to raise their taxes.

Just as bargaining collectively in good faith resolves conflict more often than not and in the same way as the United Nations has helped opposing nations find a compatibility of interests, full, free, and informed discussion may well prove the only way for competing economic groups to find harmony. To the extent that manipulative techniques and purchased influence prevail, the conflict will be aggravated not lessened.

As I ponder the analysis I have set forth, I am afraid I have painted a negative picture. While it is possible that the public-relations man may be the herald of the unilateral press and that the manipulators and salesmen of unilateral media may be the forerunners of the dictators, I have pointed to a positive alternative—an educational program which gives men the facts and promotes an understanding of them. This alternative, furthermore, can then be stifled only by those who are careless of preserving their generation.

INDUSTRIAL CONFLICT IN OTHER SOCIETIES

ONE can surmise that there are certain basic similarities in employment relations in every industrial nation, democratic or totalitarian, socialist or capitalist. Presumably the desires and expectations of industrial managers are not entirely consistent with those of rank-and-file workers anywhere in the world. The clash of desires for self-expression and freedom of activity with the security motive must be universal, for example. Presumably also workers everywhere are discontented with their share of the world's goods.

On the other hand, there are clearly great differences between one nation and another in the means and possibilities of conducting overt conflict as a method of resolving controversy. Productivity and real earnings may be rising, stagnant, or declining. The domestic economy may be highly dependent on foreign commerce or relatively insulated from the international market. Wage and salary earners may be highly organized (as in Australia, Sweden, or Great Britain) or only moderately organized (as in Canada and the United States), or independent unionism, as we know it, may not exist, as in the communist nations. Further, the political and consumer-cooperative aims of the labor movement may be well developed or only rudimentary. There may be considerable reliance on legislation for regulating terms of employment, as in France and the Latin-American countries, or minimal reliance, as in Sweden and the United States. Finally, the right to strike may be unrestricted by law, somewhat modified, or abolished altogether.

Available statistics indicate that, where the right to strike is observed, there are great variations in the incidence of overt industrial conflict. Some international comparisons have already been noted in Chap. 1.

Within the scope of this volume it is not possible to examine all the influences affecting industrial conflict in the various countries nor to analyze the reasons for differences in strike activity. Instead, it was decided to deal with relationships between industrial conflict and the economic, political, and bargaining institutions in four countries—England, Nazi Germany, Soviet Russia, and Sweden. The countries and authors were selected to illuminate a somewhat different problem in each chapter.

Chester was asked to deal with the problem of industrial conflict in the British nationalized industries, such as coal, railways, and road transport.

Does the act of socialization extinguish any of the causes of industrial conflict? Was trade-union militancy tempered by the affiliation between the unions and the Labor Party while the latter was in power? In relation to the employees of a nationalized industry does the union serve increasingly as disciplinarian as well as bargaining agent; and if so, has a latter-day "shop-steward movement" developed among lower levels of leadership? Chester's account of developments during the past 8 years is of particular interest because it deals with the question of whether the basic character of unionism must change in a socialized industry. As Chester states, the inheritance from the past is a large one and no final judgment can be made after only a few years; but there is reason to believe that most of the original problems persist and that unions are reasserting their role as agencies of protest. Whether this would be possible in a predominantly socialist economy is a crucial question to be considered.

In the British nationalized industries private property was eliminated, but independent unionism was maintained. In Nazi Germany the opposite was true. Kelly describes vividly the abuses and discriminations committed in the name of the "leadership principle" after democratic forms and procedures were suppressed. We asked him to consider this question: What happens to industrial discontent when there are no means of communicating or expressing it, and what happens to industrial conflict when there are no labor organizations to prosecute it? Kelly concludes that worker resistance was slight and that a surface industrial peace was maintained but that while "the fascists seemed to avoid some of the problems encountered under democratic capitalism, they ran into others equally as complex. . . . The strike, lockout, and other outward manifestations of industrial unrest may be suppressed. But industrial strife will take other forms unless a sense of mutual respect and responsibility can be developed. . . ." As long as the dignity of human labor was not maintained and the leadership principle rather than equality was sought, it was inevitable that industrial peace would have to be by the sword. Even then, while the National Socialists ruthlessly suppressed strikes and other major forms of industrial conflict, they had a continuing and increasingly serious problem of deterioration in the quality of output and supervision.

Unlike Nazi Germany, Soviet Russia has retained a trade-union structure. But inasmuch as ownership of the means of production is deemed to rest with the workers and peasants, the official viewpoint does not recognize the possibility of industrial conflict except for that resulting from a survival of atavistic "capitalist consciousness." What then is the function of the Russian unions? Galenson points out that "the Soviet trade-union is neither in theory nor in fact primarily a representative of worker interests but rather a quasi-governmental agency predominantly engaged in nonpartisan activities on behalf of the state" and that "at least the higher bureaucracy within the trade-unions are more nearly civil servants than representatives of the workers. . . ." Wages and other conditions of labor are determined by the planning agencies and promulgated as law, while collective agreements merely rehearse the obligation of workers and managers to attain production objectives. An elaborate procedure has been established for adjudicating individual grievances over classification, overtime pay, fines and penalties, and so on, with the unions acting as appeals bodies if plant decisions are contested, but Galenson finds reasons for doubting its efficacy as a bargaining instrument. "Against an affirmative hypothesis," he states, "is the testimony of Soviet expatriates and the Soviet labor code itself, indicating the ever-present possibility of unpleasant consequences for the individual worker who considers his needs and desires superior to those of the state. . . ." This is what becomes of a trade-union movement in a totalitarian society regardless of the forms of ownership.

The chapters on Great Britain, Nazi Germany, and Russia deal with trade-unionism and industrial conflict in relation to economic and political systems. Peterson's chapter on Sweden deals with bargaining institutions. Peterson shows that centralization and self-government are the cornerstones of industrial relations in Sweden. Not only are employers and employees highly organized, but there is great concentration of power in the "peak" organizations, which have authority to develop national policy and enforce it upon their constituent units. Thus national agreements on job security, employment of women, works councils, and other problems have been developed, as well as consolidated wage-policy decisions which provide the framework for specific agreements throughout the country. Observing that the peace and quiet in the Swedish labor market have been notable in recent years, Peterson warns against the assumption that the same results would necessarily be obtained if Swedish practices were exported into a different environment. Nevertheless, the Swedish experience is of great interest in connection with two highly controversial issues in the United States: (1) Is multiemployer bargaining conducive to industrial peace, or should it be prohibited because it leads to intolerable industry-wide strikes? (2) Should a "national wage policy" (at one extreme) be encouraged as a device to facilitate high employment and stable price levels, or should bargaining be restricted to local plant units (at the other extreme) in order to eliminate "labor monopoly," or should bargaining units and "patterns" continue to develop in various sizes and shapes agreeable to the parties involved?

CHAPTER 35 INDUSTRIAL CONFLICTS IN BRITISH NATIONALIZED INDUSTRIES

T. E. Chester   *Acton Society Trust (London, England)*

In CONSIDERING the postwar experiments in nationalization in Great Britain, many observers are surprised at the number of strikes and go-slow movements and at the high figures of absenteeism: in the coal industry alone, there were about 1,600 small-scale strikes during the year 1950. Such observers point to the increasing manpower shortages, especially in the coal and railway industries (the Railway Executive has recently offered a bonus to employees for inducing new entrants to join the industry). They notice that the labor turnover in the nationalized industries is as high as that in private industries. From these facts, they often conclude that industrial conflict has by no means been lessened in nationalized industries and that, on the contrary, in some, such as gas and electricity, where industrial relations were satisfactory in the past, the situation has seemingly deteriorated.

The changing views held by the trade-unions apparently confirm these conclusions. The British trade-union movement, as is well known, has for many years been the foremost advocate of nationalization. Yet the Trades Union Congress of 1950 found time for only two resolutions on nationalized industries. The general secretary of the largest union, the Transport and General Workers' Union, went so far as to rule out further nationalization schemes as politically impracticable for the time being. At the recent annual general meeting of the powerful Amalgamated Engineering Union, a member of the national executive launched a bitter attack on the board of the nationalized electricity industry.

However, it would be an oversimplification to base a complete evaluation of nationalization on the unrest in these industries and the present attitudes of the trade-unions. Both these sets of facts have to be seen in the right perspective. Here it is pertinent to ask, Is this unrest caused by nationalization, and if so, what are the managements of the industries and the leaders of the trade-unions doing to remove its causes? In fact, it can easily be seen that the present situation is a complex of factors by no means all deriving from the very recent nationalization measures.

In the first place, the nationalization measures were not solely or even mainly designed to improve industrial relations. In some cases, the realization of the full aims of nationalization, for example, the integration of road and rail transport as laid down in the Transport Nationalization Act, was bound to involve an initial increase in industrial unrest. Secondly, industrial conflicts in the nationalized industries have, in many cases, been the result not of nationalization but of other economic factors and of the specific conditions prevailing in the industries.

To mention only a few economic causes: the serious material and capital shortages affecting British industry generally and, of even greater consequence, the postwar rise in prices which has continuously forced up the cost of living in postwar Britain. These factors, in conjunction with almost literal full employment, have created a new situation, which is baffling British management and calling for a new type of industrial leadership.

In addition, each particular industry has its own difficulties. The financial straits of the coal and railway industries go back a long way in British economic history, and wages in both these industries account for more than two-thirds of their total costs. Most of the nationalized industries are service industries, which are attractive enough in times of unemployment since they can offer steady jobs but are unable to hold their labor force in times of boom because statutory and other restrictions prevent a quick adjustment of prices to meet rising costs. The main exception to this generalization is the coal industry, where the high wages of today have not effaced the memories of wage cutting and almost continuous unemployment in the interwar years. How different would have been the attitude of the miners to a public board in the coal industry could it have guaranteed steady employment in the prewar period of slump.

Industrial conflicts are a projection of men's minds, and the act of nationalization can only modify traditional attitudes as it becomes institutionalized in new organizations and administrative actions. To take one example, bus drivers all over the world are prone to reject new time schedules because they are convinced that their employers aim to "put something across them." Is it really surprising that, after so many years of agitation against "exploitation," men continue to take the same attitude, even when the ownership of their company is transferred to a public corporation?

However, the act of nationalization was considered by many objective observers to be an indispensable precondition of any improvement of traditionally embittered industrial relations. In the coal industry, in particular, it was generally recognized that no steps taken by management to improve industrial relations could possibly have succeeded as long as the industry remained in private hands.

The first part of this chapter aims to show how the sponsors of the legislation approached the problem and how the new Boards are attempting to remove the causes of bad relations. The second part will then discuss the role of the trade-union movement, now inextricably bound up with the future of the industries.

Impact of Nationalization

Background. An analysis of the impact of nationalization on industrial conflict must be a study of the adaptation of human behavior in a changing environment, that is, a study of social change. Therefore it is first necessary to describe briefly the backgrounds of the nationalized industries, so that the organizational problems caused by nationalization can be understood.

The nationalized industries covered by this paper are the three fuel and power industries—coal, electricity, and gas—and the air and inland transport services. The last-named include the railways, all the passenger transport services in London, many of the provincial road passenger services, long-distance road haulage, canals, and most of the docks.[1] It is not proposed to include the steel industry since it has been nationalized for only a few months, and the new Government has decided to denationalize it in the near future.

The significance of industrial conflicts in these industries is shown by the fact that they employ nearly 10 per cent of the total working population of this country.

	Approximate number employed
I. *Fuel and power industries*	
Coal	765,000
Electricity supply	170,000
Gas	140,000
II. *Inland transport industries*	
Railways	610,000
London transport	98,000
Road haulage	80,000
Road passenger services	61,000
Miscellaneous transport services	50,000
III. *Air transport industry*	
Civil air transport	23,000

Before nationalization, most of these industries were predominantly of a small-scale character. The coal industry was operated by about 750 companies, electricity by about 560 private and municipal undertakings, and there were about 1,000 gas undertakings in the country. The new Road Haulage Executive had to be built up out of 3,000 small-scale private undertakings. Only the Railway Executive inherited large-scale organizations—the four main-line railway companies, established when the British railway system was reconstituted by the Government in 1921. Nationalization, which meant the compulsory amalgamation of all these undertakings at one stroke, was bound to lead to difficult problems in all fields of organization. This fact is of vital importance for an understanding of the attitude of management and men in the nationalized industries. Both found it difficult to reorientate their methods of working and ways of thinking from small-scaleness to large-scaleness.

It is obvious that such a problem of adjustment and adaptation needs time to work itself out, and the time so far available has been short—the gas industry, the most recently nationalized, has been $2\frac{1}{2}$ years under public ownership, and the first postwar public corporation, the National Coal Board, has been in existence for barely 5 years.

A further warning: the term "nationalized industries," as used in this paper, is a convenient label, but the reader must remember that this survey

---

[1] It should be noted that dockers in Great Britain are not employees of the nationalized industries discussed in this paper but come under the purview of the National Dock Labor Board.

deals with industries heterogeneous in their technical and economic character and with widely different cultures. Even the term "coal industry" can be misleading because the industry is, in fact, composed of a number of separate and divergent parts. How different, for example, has been the fate and the corresponding attitudes of the miners in South Wales, so hard hit by the inter-war depression, from that of the comparatively prosperous miners in the newer coal fields in Nottingham and Derbyshire.

Any generalizations found in this paper have to be interpreted with this proviso.

Policy of the Boards. All nationalization acts contain clauses designed to remove sources of industrial conflict. The most important provide for the following:

1. Appointment of trade-union officials to the Boards
2. Establishment of comprehensive negotiating machinery for wages and conditions
3. Establishment of machinery for what is now commonly termed "joint consultation"
4. Action by the Boards to improve the standard of personnel management, with special emphasis on the training and education of their employees

The impact of these measures on industrial relations will be analyzed in detail.

The provisions for appointing trade-unionists to the Boards were the outcome of a compromise reached within the trade-union and labor movements in the 1930's. After prolonged discussions, the idea was accepted that nationalized industries should be run by Boards of "experts" owing undivided loyalty, through the appropriate minister and Parliament, to the community as a whole. The proposal adopted in other countries, such as France, that the membership of the controlling boards should represent sectional interests was rejected.

The trade-union movement, however, insisted (see the Trades Union Congress's interim report on postwar reconstruction, 1944) that among the experts to be included on the Boards there should be experienced trade-union leaders. The vexed problem of divided loyalties was solved by making the appointed trade-union leaders sever all connections with their unions. In this way the trade-union movement hoped that the Boards would possess and act upon an understanding of worker attitudes, an understanding which was considered to be lacking in the board rooms of private industry.

It is in the National Coal Board that the practice of appointing trade-unionists to managerial posts has found its fullest expression. Here ex-officials of the biggest union, the National Union of Mineworkers, were appointed to all levels of management. Thus not only is the Board Member for Labor Relations the former general secretary of the union, but all Divisional Labor Directors and Area Labor and Welfare Officers come from within the ranks of this union.

Machinery for the collective negotiation of wages and conditions was not new for any of the nationalized industries; in nearly all of them, it had been built up to national level for the manual grades. The real significance of the new statutory provision lies in the fact that arrangements have been extended to cover practically all grades. Thus it is the declared policy of the British Electricity Authority to institute collective bargaining for all its officials, excepting only 150 chief officers. In fact, there is now an elaborate system of committees for the negotiation of salaries, wages, and conditions for management, technical specialists, clerical staff, and workers up to a salary level of 2,000 pounds at national, regional, and local levels.

In addition, all Boards have the statutory duty of establishing joint machinery with employees "for the promotion and encouragement of measures affecting the safety, health and welfare of persons employed . . . and the discussion of other matters of mutual interest . . . including efficiency in the operation of the services of the Board."

As a result, a further set of committees for "joint consultation" between management and men has been created, in most cases parallel to the existing machinery for negotiation. In view of the fear of the trade-union movement that such joint consultation might lead to "company unionism," great care was taken to bring the trade-unions into consultation. In all the industries, the employees' representatives on the national and regional consultative committees are officials of the recognized unions, and only at the local level do employees elect their own representatives by secret ballot. Even here the trade-unions carried the rule that only a member of a recognized trade-union can put himself forward for election, and in the coal industry, the National Union of Mineworkers has succeeded in getting the exclusive right to put forward lists of candidates through its own local branch, *i.e.*, the pit lodge.

Although the statutory provisions to improve the standards of personnel management were of a less formal character, it is perhaps in this field that the greatest changes have taken place, in view of the backwardness of many of the small-scale companies existing prior to nationalization. Now all the industries have central personnel-management departments. These departments are represented at the regional and area levels, but so far at least, very few personnel specialists have been appointed at the local level. On the contrary, there has been strong resistance to the idea of introducing personnel officers as assistants to local managers—particularly in the coal industry, where, notoriously, human relations have been at their worst.

In fact, personnel management, among other specialist newcomers to the organization of these industries, has yet to become a fully accepted department. Nonetheless, nationalization means that, for the first time, modern techniques in recruitment, staff statistics and manpower budgeting, and selection and training, as well as promotion schemes, are being slowly introduced. Indeed, all industries have by now developed policies for vocational training of all grades of employees, while forms of "human-relations training" for supervisory grades, sponsored by the Training within Industry department of the Ministry of Labor, are gaining wider acceptance. Real attempts are being made to create equality of opportunity for all employees. Noteworthy is the Coal Board's "Ladder Plan"—a full-scale combined training and promotion scheme. It is too early to judge such long-term measures, but they should not be overlooked. In recognition of the special responsibilities of large-scale public organizations, most Boards aim to give their employees a better knowledge of their industries, and various schemes of "industrial education" have been promoted, taking the form of summer schools or residential courses.

The seeming arbitrariness of disciplinary action has always been one of the chief causes of industrial conflict. In attempts to remove such impressions, nearly all the public Boards have laid down detailed disciplinary codes and have established formal procedures to guarantee justice and a fair hearing. Similar motives brought about "redundancy" agreements to regulate layoffs.

In addition to the progress in personnel management, there has been an undeniable improvement in working conditions. This is nowhere more conspicuous than in the mining industry, where medical schemes, dust control, and other measures destined to improve conditions in the mines have been widely introduced. The trade-unions pressed for the introduction of pension schemes, or the extension of existing schemes to all grades, where these were confined to office staff. The implications of such far-reaching pension liabilities were originally viewed with alarm by the Government, which asked the Boards to postpone negotiations. When, however, the manpower situation in the coal industry seriously deteriorated at the beginning of 1951, the National Coal Board, following the intervention of the Government, introduced a pension scheme for miners.

As to the level of wages, while wage increases have occurred in all the nationalized industries, wages have increased throughout British industry since the war, and it is very difficult to establish how far nationalization has changed the relative position of wage earners as compared with their fellow workers in the private sector of industry. Miners have probably done better than most other workers; railwaymen, not so well.

It was hoped that nationalization would facilitate the building of a more rational wage structure to provide fairer rewards and greater incentives. However, this has proved an intractable problem; tradition and prejudice are strong, particularly in the matter of long-established differentials, and to date, no serious attempt to change the existing customs has been made.

Role of the Trade-unions

Although the trade-union movement was one of the main sponsors of nationalization, it could not be expected that the transfer of ownership alone would extinguish traditional differences and rivalries within and between individual unions. While the industries are unified by nationalization, the unions in the industries remain numerous and diverse.

There are about 200 unions affiliated to the Trades Union Congress. Out of these, more than fifty independent unions have members in the nationalized industries, quite apart from two federations in the engineering and building trades, one of which has about twenty and the other some forty constituent unions. In no single nationalized industry are there fewer than a dozen unions represented (although their membership varies, for example, the National Union of Mineworkers enrolls the majority of workers in the coal industry). The unions include the largest single union in the country, the Transport and General Workers' union, with a membership of about $1\frac{1}{4}$ million, and at the other extreme, the National Society of Street Masons, Paviors and Road Makers, with a total membership of no more than 2,000. They vary from craft unions with a long tradition, such as the Associated Society of Locomotive Engineers and Firemen, to recently formed clerical unions. They include "industrial unions," such as the National Union of Railwaymen, with long-standing aspirations to organize *all* workers in one particular industry, and unions such as the Association of Supervisory Staffs, Executives and Technicians, set up to enroll specific grades from all industries. All these unions operate with a wide range of methods and differing policies and traditions.

The difficulties will best be appreciated if it is realized that such a variety of trade-unions means that (1) each industry has to deal with a large number of unions and (2) nearly all the unions have members in all industries. In such a situation, nationalization was bound to throw up new dilemmas. For example, the demarcation lines of recruitment between craft and general workers' unions have been shifted. The electricity industry recently had to cope with a long strike because a craft union insisted that a newly appointed electrician's mate should leave his original "general" union. Similarly, the conflicts between clerical and manual workers' unions have not diminished. Cases are known where clerical staffs opposed the granting of sick-pay schemes to manual workers, with the argument that these workers were irresponsible. On the other side, the National Union of Mineworkers has recently resolved to investigate the staffing establishment of the National Coal Board, because its members were convinced that too many easy jobs had been created for clerks.

This situation has become more complicated through the setting up of "managerial unions," with which the old established trade-unions find it difficult to establish a fruitful relationship. These managerial unions are one of the specific consequences of nationalizing whole industries under a single board. Junior managers and many specialists have become aware that these boards are their "sole employers" over the whole country; and they feel the need for some protective association. This has led to the creation of such organizations as the British Association of Colliery Managers, the Gas Officers' Guild, the Association of Managerial Electrical Executives, and the British Transport Officers' Guild. It seems that in many cases the old established unions are as suspicious of these managerial unions as they were of the former employers.

The trade-union movement is aware of these difficulties and a number of attempts have been made to coordinate policies. Various devices have been developed, such as collective representation, joint standing committees, and more permanent structures such as federations. It is often asked why the Trades Union Congress does not take a firmer line in disputes between unions. The answer is that this body has no compulsory power over its constituent unions and can only work through agreement and persuasion, which is, of necessity, a long-term process.

How far have the trade-unions been influenced by their association with a Labor Government and by the fact that former trade-union leaders are helping in the management of the industries? Despite the fact that the Labor Party derives a large part of its funds from the trade-unions, which sponsored nearly 140 Labor candidates at the recent election, it is easy to overestimate the extent of the political identification between the trade-unions and a Labor Government. It is traditional among the unions that the industrial side of the labor movement, which they represent, prefers to take its decisions independently of, and may thus differ from, the political side of the movement. In fact, it is an open question whether the existence of a Labor Government was an advantage or an embarrassment to the unions in the nationalized industries. Cases occurred where the unions, by invoking Government intervention, tried to overcome a refusal by the Boards to grant further concessions. On the other hand, it is also a fact that the trade-union movement accepted the wage freeze in 1948, and it was due to its loyalty to the Government that this standstill lasted until 1950. Similarly, in spite of opposition from the rank-and-file trade-unionists, the regulations making strikes illegal, passed as a wartime emergency measure in 1940, were in operation until August, 1951.

However, there is a growing feeling in the trade-union movement that the character of negotiations with nationalized industries is changing. It is often said that the unions negotiate nominally with the Boards but that the final decisions can be taken only with the approval of the responsible Minister, who sometimes has to consult with the Minister of Labor and with the Treasury. The British trade-union movement has resisted the formulation of a comprehensive wage policy, preferring to adhere to the traditional methods of bargaining to which its officials are accustomed. It appears that this attitude is beginning to change—but whether the change derives more from the nationalization process than from the simultaneous developments in planning the whole economy is difficult to say.

It is also hard to assess the influence of the trade-union officials now participating in management. Most Boards include only one trade-unionist, but there are more than a dozen unions in each industry. Thus the general secretary of the major railway union, the National Union of Railwaymen, was appointed to the Board of the British Transport Commission, the general secretary of the Association of Locomotive Engineers and Firemen became a Board member of the subordinate Railway Executive, while the third major union, the Railway Clerks' Association (now the Transport Salaried Staffs' Association) has no representation on the Boards. In view of the traditional disagreement between the National Union of Railwaymen and the other two unions, the danger inherent in the situation can be appreciated. Such difficulties are intensified when the unionist on the Board has to try to persuade his former colleagues to accept an unpopular policy decision.

It was assumed that the appointment of trade-union leaders to the Boards would reassure the workers that their point of view was being taken into account. Subsequent events have not altogether confirmed this assumption. The feeling is fairly widespread among the rank and file that a trade-union official who gives up his life's work and accepts a salary of 3,000 pounds—the salaries of even the highest-paid union officials in this country are not more than half this amount—soon becomes "out of touch." It is often said that he "has gone over to the other side." This, coupled with the increasing awareness that the trade-union movement has lost many of its most able leaders, has led to second thoughts on how the national Boards should be composed.

The joint consultative machinery was envisaged by the unions as a means of introducing greater "industrial democracy." It was believed that prior consultation on major decisions affecting the workers would not only prevent industrial conflict but would, at the same time, give the rank and file a greater feeling of belonging to their industry.

It was not expected that these conceptions would be translated into action without teething troubles. In many cases, this type of committee, intended to discuss constructively matters of common interest, was new to managers as well as to workers' representatives. The two sides had been accustomed to meet only when wages or grievances had to be settled "across the table." The consultative committees, especially those at local levels, have been working for only a short time, and it is therefore premature to assess their effectiveness as instruments for creating industrial harmony. Nevertheless, it is already clear that joint consultation can have far-reaching repercussions on trade-union organization and policy. It has presented the unions with a challenge and thrown into relief some of their weaknesses.

The unions demanded that the consultative machinery at national and regional levels should be reserved, in the main, for trade-union officials. These officials have wide experience in handling wage negotiations, but they do not necessarily possess the knowledge of economic, financial, and technical problems which is essential for a serious discussion of operational efficiency. It is not, therefore, surprising that even the best-organized joint consultative committees have confined their discussions to such topics as training and education, health and welfare, and safety.

National or regional committees are usually large bodies, as they have to represent a number of unions. But since most unions have members in many other industries, it proved difficult for them to provide sufficient officials to sit on all the committees. In addition, the same officials have to be available for the collective-bargaining machinery.

The joint consultative machinery has been built on a hierarchical structure, with centralizing tendencies. This narrows the scope of "effective" consultation between the local manager and his workers. Any constructive work which the new committees have been able to do has mainly performed at the top, that is, the national level.

Consultation at the top has been facilitated by the fact that good informal relations have developed between Board members, senior managers, and permanent trade-union officials, as a result of frequent contact. At the same time, there has been some suspicion among the rank and file that the officials were getting "too near to management." It is interesting to note that, in prewar days, unions were sometimes afraid that consultation might result in bringing management "too near to the men."

Recent studies have shown that the difficulties of introducing joint consultation as an effective force are not limited to organizing the machinery and making it work. It has proved exceedingly difficult to communicate results to the rank and file and to interest the mass of workers in the operation of even local committees. This problem of "reporting back" demands further and more detailed investigation.

In spite of some notable success in consultation—in preparing major reorganizations and even redundancy schemes—some trade-union officials are beginning to doubt whether they should take part in joint consultation at all.

Some trade-unionists maintain that joint consultation, by definition, leaves unaffected the prerogative of management. Hence all the discussions are "a waste of time," since management always has the last word. They point out that there is no provision for disagreements to be referred to independent arbitration as there is in the collective-bargaining system. Other trade-unionists maintain that the mere fact of joint consultation imposes too heavy a burden of responsibility on the unions—although all formal decisions are taken by management. If, for example, the National Union of Mineworkers representatives accept a Coal Board proposal that certain pits should be closed, what should be their attitude to rank-and-file members who do not accept this decision and go on strike?

The general secretary of the National Union of Mineworkers bluntly declared at the Trades Union Congress of 1949 that nationalization in a mixed economy—where about 80 per cent of industry remains in private hands—does not change the relationship of employers to employees, even if the employer happens to be a public Board.

But whether trade-union officials are prepared to admit any changes openly, there can be no doubt that the functions of the unions have been closely affected by nationalization. As one trade-union official put it, "Their old role as 'stirrers up' against an exploiting private employer is being slowly transformed to 'smoothers down.' " Certainly they face some difficult decisions. For example, if a union official is pressed by the rank and file to submit a wages claim which they believe to be opportune owing to staff shortages, where does his responsibility lie? Should he act in the traditional way and go on with the claim, or should he consider it his public duty to assist the corporation in making better use of existing personnel?

It is difficult, at this stage, to predict the line of development. One union put up a poster indicating a refusal to defend any member indicted of negligence in the performance of his duties. There is also the case of an immediate wage claim being submitted by the union for "increased responsibility" when a Board asked meter readers to explain its new tariff schedule to consumers. And in between is the example of the three major railway unions: in conjunction with a favorable wage settlement, they pledged themselves to the setting up of a special joint committee for increasing efficiency and improving productivity. In fact, however, little has been achieved by this committee to date.

The unions are also reluctant to let the Trades Union Congress act for them. At the recent Trades Union Congress, a resolution which would have allowed the general council to intervene in case of a stoppage of work in a nationalized industry was heavily defeated. It would have meant a constitutional revolution.

It can legitimately be asked whether the new role of trade-unions in the nationalized industries gives an opportunity for unofficial leaders to step in as did the "shop stewards" in 1917. In some industries, unofficial committees of shop stewards have achieved a powerful local influence, but their effectiveness has never been so strong as to become a serious threat to official leadership. There have been a number of unofficial strikes, and unofficial leaders have taken charge of certain works for a short period, but again it would be easy to exaggerate the total effect. On the whole, there have been very few breakaway movements, and fewer still have survived in organized form. There is an interesting example of the rank and file bypassing their union in the railways. Here a number of drivers persisted with a petition against the Railway Executive when their union refused to support the case, but this was caused mainly by the traditional loyalty of engine drivers to one of the old companies and had no political significance.

Certainly, the Communists have failed to increase their strength in the nationalized industries. Some unions, foremost among them the Transport and General Workers' Union, have been able to carry out full-scale purges of Communist officials. A few unions continue to be led by Communists, but even the largest of these still acts on traditional lines in the field of industrial relations. In one or two cases, this leadership was able to use existing genuine grievances for inciting or prolonging a strike. On the other hand, the Communist leaders of one union had to retract when they tried to affiliate the union to the Peace Council movement. A special general conference of the rank and file vetoed their decision, and affiliation had to be withdrawn.

The official trade-union movement has been strengthened by two very important provisions on the statute books. According to the various nationalization acts, access to the negotiating and joint consultative machinery is open only to unions officially recognized by the public Boards, and a recent amendment of the law on trade disputes has, in fact, left it to the discretion of the Minister of Labor to debar from industrial arbitration those unions which do not habitually take part in negotiations. As wages and conditions in the nationalized industries as well as in private industry remain of the first importance to the ordinary worker, unofficial unions which cannot promise effective action hold little attraction for membership.

Outlook

In a period of increasing social change, the British trade-union movement finds itself groping for new institutions to replace the old "authoritarian" system of management. One section of the movement, it is true, disappointed that nationalization has not fulfilled all expectation, looks for scapegoats and complains of excessive compensation payments to the former shareholders or of the continued employment of managers hostile to nationalization. But nationalization has resulted in some new thinking in the unions, chiefly in three directions.

First, the unions have to decide how to adapt their internal organization to new functions. Secondly, they have to agree upon the demarcation lines between unions and the role of the Trades Union Congress. Thirdly, and most important, the relation of the whole movement to the state and its projections —the nationalized industries—has to be reconsidered.

As to the first problem, two factors are the most relevant to union organization. The greater range of duties facing officials calls for different methods of selection and training; and the greater volume of work and the long-term aim of the unions—a democratic way of life in industry—call for greater participation of the rank and file in union administration. Many union officials would not admit this, but increasingly, matters formerly outside the scope of union activity must now be dealt with in the interests of the members. In nationalized industry, such matters are the organizational structure of the industry itself (is the public corporation the right form of organization, and is it compatible with industrial democracy?), how far and in what ways trade-union officials should participate in management, and what the union contribution to joint consultation should be.

Are the traditional methods of electing and appointing trade-union officials suited to these tasks? For example, trade-unions continue to neglect university graduates and offer salaries so low that it is often impossible to recruit the best men.

Further, it is clear that unions suffer the same disabilities as other large-scale organizations—overcentralization, remoteness from the man on the job, bureaucracy, and apathy. How can internal communications be improved and what institutional forms can be devised in order to retain the economic power of the large union without loss of initiative and enthusiasm at local level?

Unions are beginning to realize the implication of these problems and have taken some steps to tackle them. Many have established research units and training schemes. But the movement has no staff-training college of its own, in spite of the fact that it has an annual income of more than 12 million pounds and can dispose of funds amounting to 60 million pounds.

It was expected that nationalization would lead to a more rational organization of the movement, and some hoped that industrial unions would develop. This has not happened, though a few attempts have been made to coordinate the policies of different unions. There is unlikely to be a drastic change in the role of the Trades Union Congress, though it is possible that its functions may be extended to provide more common services. This would be an indirect way of increasing its influence, and in accordance with the tradition of the movement.

This is not to say that unions are likely to come closer to the state. There is an increasing consciousness of the contradiction between the orthodox socialist concept of the state and the reality in a democratic society where changes of the party in power are an inherent and essential feature. Under these circumstances, "nationalization" has a different meaning. Moreover, nationalization in conjunction with increased national planning means that nationalized industries are not free agents but are subject to the decisions of politicians and planners and to ministerial directives. Trade-unionists are not, therefore, prepared to sink their identity either into the state or into these new corporations, and they reaffirm the character of unions as voluntary organizations whose main purpose is to protect the interests of their members.

Conclusion

However fundamental the readjustments demanded of the trade-union movement may be, the task facing management is equally formidable. In the nationalized industries, management has first of all to sort out the internal problems of the new organizations. Secondly, if it wants to regain effective leadership, it will have to strive not only to provide better "functional" training and education but to produce better administrators, with a greater awareness of the "social skills." Thirdly, and most important of all for an improvement in industrial relations, is the realization by management that in these matters the initial responsibility is its own. It must be prepared to face a situation where the workers are still distrustful of its best intentions and uncertain of the future. It is a fact that the majority of British workers have yet to be convinced that full employment has come to stay, and the talk of some managers about "overfull" employment confirms them in their belief that management would welcome a return to the "old days."

A very little sober reflection should have shown all concerned that the act of nationalization alone could work no great changes. Industrial conflict can be said to center around three major issues: first, the allocation of jobs and the problem of employment and unemployment; second, the problem of authority, that is, who is to give orders and who is to take orders; and third, the division of the surplus, that is, how the profits of the work are to be divided.

Does nationalization settle these issues? In part, it answers the third question—but only in part. It converts equity shares into gilt-edged debentures and abolishes the highly paid sinecure directorships, but it does not settle the shares of different groups of employees or balance the needs of workers against those of consumers. The first two questions it does not answer at all. In short, nationalization of itself can have little positive effect. This is one of the chief reasons why its supporters have been disappointed by its short-term results.

The final and perhaps greatest lesson of nationalization in Britain has yet to be learned, namely, that even in a new organization no man starts with a clean sheet. Traditional attitudes persist and neither managers nor trade-unionists and workers are endowed with some magic power which enables them to settle their differences overnight.

CHAPTER 36 INDUSTRIAL RELATIONS IN NATIONAL SOCIALIST GERMANY

Matthew A. Kelly   *New York Employing Printers Association*

LABOR relations as practiced in Nazi Germany was an interesting if not tragic experiment in the state control of industrial conflict. All that is customarily cherished and protected in the relationship between labor and management in democratic countries was ruthlessly suppressed. Among the freedoms denied were the right of labor to organize freely and to bargain collectively for its economic security, the right of management to function in its own as distinct from the state interest, and the right of individuals to enjoy protective labor legislation freely and without fear of discrimination. In their place was substituted the basic tenet of National Socialism, to wit, that the individual's primary responsibility is to the state.

The Role of Labor and Management in the Nazi State: "Harmony through a Common Interest"

Under National Socialism the rights of the individual, if they can be called such, stemmed from the largess of the ruling group and were contrived to further the will of the state. This was evidenced in Hitler's concept of the role of labor and management in the industrial community.

In theory, at least, Hitler recognized the necessity for the assumption of certain social and economic responsibilities in the society he and the National Socialists would erect. On various occasions he stated that it was essential for employers to develop a sense of "social duty" and a respect for "human rights." Similarly the creation of a sense of responsibility to the entire "national community" was held to be the new and equally necessary role of workers in the National Socialist state.[1]

---

[1] Hitler's philosophy, general objectives, and attitude toward labor are touched upon in several places in *Mein Kampf*, New York, Reynal & Hitchcock, 1939. In general, these views are brought together and summarized in Vol. 2, Chap. 12, "The Trade Union Question," pp. 868–884. For background material, see also the discussion of Nazi philosophy and practices in the following two United States government documents: *National Socialism: Basic Principles, Their Application by the Nazi Party's Foreign Organization and the Use of Germans Abroad for Nazi Aims*, Washington, Division of European Affairs, Department of State, 1943 (the study is especially useful in bringing together all basic documents and directives issued by the National Socialist government); and *Fascism in Action: A Documented Study and Analysis of Fascism in Europe*, Washington, Library of Congress, Legislative Reference Service, 1947, esp. pp. 1–6, on the fascist philosophy, pp. 7–12, on the German political organization, pp. 68–105, on the organization of the Nazi economy, and pp. 119–130, on the status of labor in fascist countries.

It was the further belief of Hitler and the protagonists of this form of totalitarianism that, once this concept of responsibility and duty was embraced by labor and management, it would remove the necessity for "mass struggle." Thence labor and management could function in harmony under the protection and in the general interest of the state. In place of industrial conflict or, at best, the shaky compromise effected by divergent industrial groups under democratic capitalism, National Socialism would present a singleness of purpose shared by all elements in the state and mutually beneficial to labor, management, and the community alike.

The "Leadership Principle" in Industrial Relations: A Substitute for Labor-Management Equality

That Hitler's concept of human rights and social responsibility was a perversion of the rights traditionally cherished and protected in free democratic countries is apparent in the measures developed to further this objective under National Socialism. In industrial-relations matters the political philosophy that subjected individual rights to the supreme authority of the state was embodied in the "leadership principle." [2]

In a sense, the leadership principle may be said to have been the industrial-relations code of Nazi Germany. It replaced the principle of labor-management equality which had been a basic provision of the Weimar constitution in the German Republic that governed from the end of World War I to 1933.[3] As set forth in the Act for the Organization of National Labor, which was promulgated by the National Socialists on January 20, 1934,[4] the employers were designated as the "leaders" and the employees as the "followers."

The decisions of employers, as leaders, were held to be supreme in industrial-relations matters unless expressly modified by the laws of the state or the directives of its administrators. While it was the employer's obligation to carry out the directives and general objectives of the state and, hence, in a sense be a follower himself, his interests were accepted as being closely akin to those of the state and its interpreters, the officials of the National Socialist Party. The employee, on the other hand, with the primary responsibility of being a loyal follower, was wholly dependent upon the employer and in turn to the state since he was forbidden to organize and to seek to improve his economic condition through collective bargaining or collective action. It was through this form of "cooperation" among the "fellow members of the works community" that "harmony" was to develop in place of industrial strife in the Nazi state.

Although the lockout, like the strike, was looked upon as treasonable and outlawed as a willful act of self-interest against the greater interest of the

---

[2] E. B. Ashton, *The Fascist: His State and His Mind,* New York, Morrow, 1937, has an interesting analysis of the leadership principle in Chap. 4, esp. pp. 91–95, 110–116.

[3] For a discussion of this aspect of the Weimar constitution, see Nathan Reich, *Labour Relations in Republican Germany: An Experiment in Industrial Democracy, 1918–1933,* New York, Oxford, 1938, pp. 271–272.

[4] "Gesetz zur Ordnung der nationaler Arbeit," *Reichsgesetzblatt,* Part I (1934), 45. The National Labor Law is analyzed in some detail by C. W. Guillebaud, *The Social Policy of Nazi Germany,* London, Cambridge, 1941, pp. 20–36.

state, the employer as the leader and the "promoter of welfare" had a preferred position relative to that of labor. Yet the businessman's lot under National Socialism was far from an enviable one, and his preferred position proved
in practice to be more apparent than real. This is not immediately evident in
a comparison of Nazi economic institutions with those of democratic capitalism.
To all outward appearances the National Socialists retained the same structure of business organization and economic institutions as are present in the
free-enterprise system. To be sure, there was a superstructure of control. But
presumably individuals could form businesses and operate them as they saw
fit in response to known and anticipated consumer demand. Ostensibly private
enterprise was as much the core of the economic system of fascism as it was
of democratic capitalism.

But it is this very characteristic of fascism which plagues those who would
protect democratic capitalism against totalitarianism in any form. The fact
that fascism functions with the seemingly identical economic institutions of
the free-enterprise system makes it all the more insidious and, hence, in a
sense the most to be feared of the alternative economic systems. Far too frequently the economic institutions associated with the economic freedoms of
democratic capitalism are confusedly thought of as guarantors of freedom in
and of themselves. This apparent acceptance of the basic economic institutions
of the free-enterprise system lures the unsuspecting into giving fascism their
support. But as the sordid history of fascist growth shows, the nominal retention of the institutional structure of the capitalist economy enables fascism
to come about piecemeal and gradually until, like a malignant growth, it
envelops the system.

Despite the seeming reliance on private industry and the free-enterprise
system, the employer under National Socialism soon found enterprise only
nominally free. Through his "conversion" from an owner to a leader, the employer's business in a sense became an instrument of the state. In place of
the rights traditionally enjoyed in a free-enterprise system, the entrepreneur
operated under state-conferred powers only. In the development of an economic policy of the self-sufficient state, the interests of the state and business,
at least big business, were frequently found to be identical.[5] National Socialist
Party leaders and industrial magnates, where not the same individuals, seemed
to be inseparable.

This supposed affinity between the state's interest and that of business
was in sharp contrast to the more or less subservient role labor was called upon
to play in the Nazi system. Yet to construe this as evidence of the state being
run in the interest of the employer is to oversimplify what constituted the
basis of a very complex relationship. The tie-in between business and the state
was not unlike a marriage of convenience; while basically necessary, it lent
an air of respectability to the state's increasingly broad interference in individual enterprise. In the final analysis, however, business was in a preferred
position only when it functioned in the state interest. To be sure, the National

[5] For an interesting treatment of business under National Socialism see Robert A.
Brady, *The Rationalization Movement in German Industry*, Berkeley, University of Cali-
fornia Press, 1933. Also Ludwig Hamburger, *How Nazi Germany Has Controlled Business*,
Washington, Brookings, 1943.

Socialists commonly viewed business in a favorable light. But when, as in the case of small and nonintegrated business, the interests of the individual enterprise ran counter to the consolidations, mergers, and large-scale operations considered essential to greater national efficiency, the freedom of the employer to engage in enterprise was ruthlessly suppressed.[6] On the other hand, to contend, as some have,[7] that business suffered more under fascism than any other segment of society seems to slight to the point of ignoring the greater tragedy of the loss of more basic and fundamental individual liberties.

The Instruments of National Socialist Control of Labor

In addition to establishing the leadership principle, the National Socialists took other measures designed to give the state supreme control over labor relations. These are too well known to merit other than a brief mention by way of summary. The principal organizations and instruments for administering Nazi labor policy were the Trustees of Labor (*Treuhänder der Arbeit*), the German Labor Front (*Deutsche Arbeitsfront*, DAF), the Councils of Trust (*Vertrauensrat*), and the Social Honor Courts.

Trustees of Labor were appointed in each of the seventeen districts into which Germany was divided for administrative purposes by the National Socialists. The Labor Trustees were directly responsible to the Minister of Labor and had absolute control over labor relations in the area under their supervision. Their principal function was "to maintain industrial peace," and to this end they were authorized to issue rulings and directives with the force of law. In questions of disputes over general conditions of employment, matters which ordinarily would have involved the state mediation and arbitration boards in the Weimar Republic, the decisions of the Trustees of Labor were final. In fact, as indicated below, the economic terms of collective-bargaining agreements were replaced by the edicts of the Labor Trustees.

[6] The National Socialists issued many regulations and directives to promote mergers and encourage large-scale business. Among these were the stipulations requiring small companies with a capitalization of 100,000 marks or less to merge, refusing to authorize the formation of new companies unless capitalized at 500,000 marks or more, and prohibiting the purchase of corporate stock except in amounts totaling 1,000 marks or more in par value. The Reich Minister of Economic Affairs was empowered to force firms to join a cartel and to dissolve companies which persisted in "unbecoming conduct." The vast majority of rulings in this regard were levied against the small firm.

As a consequence of these efforts among other things, there was a net decrease in the number of German corporations under the National Socialists, with the incidence being concentrated among the smaller companies. At the same time there were increases in the average size of German corporations, the number of cartels, and the amount of corporate capital held by the larger companies. Although some of these changes were the product of the Depression, the majority were induced by the deliberate efforts at the rationalization of German industry. In the period down to 1938 alone the number of German corporations was reduced from 12,000 to 5,500. Companies with 5 million marks or more capitalization, however, decreased from 750 to 616 only. Moreover, the total corporate capital held by these larger corporations increased during this period from 56 to 77 per cent. At the same time the average size of German corporations increased from 3.7 million marks to 5.2 million marks.

[7] See, for example, Ashton's (*op. cit.*, p. 92) comments in this regard. In fairness to Ashton, however, it should be noted that he expressed these views without having had the benefit of observing developments in the National Socialist state after 1938.

The national labor law of 1934 required that wages and other conditions of employment be determined for each industry separately. However, by way of transition, the economic terms prevailing on April 30, 1934, in the pre-Hitler collective-bargaining agreements (*Tarifverträge*), were allowed to continue. It was estimated that there were some 9,000 collective-bargaining agreements covering approximately 10 million wage earners and 2 million salaried employees at the time.[8] In their place the Trustees of Labor issued so-called collective or *Tarif* regulations (*Tarifordnungen*). These were the instruments by which the state laid down wages, hours, and labor standards for German industry. Between 1934 and 1937 alone the Labor Trustees issued over 2,000 *Tarif* regulations, and by the end of the Nazi regime it was estimated that some 4,500 of them were in existence.[9]

The German Labor Front, as distinct from the Trustees of Labor, who were officials of the state government and the Ministry of Labor, was an organ of the National Socialist Party.[10] Its major objective was to reconcile the traditional and somewhat antagonistic views of labor and management with the social, political, and economic aims of the Nazis. In practice the German Labor Front served as an instrument for promoting National Socialist philosophy and propaganda among industrial groups. In this regard it was perhaps the most effective of the Nazi agents.

Unlike the Italian fascists, who tolerated the continuance of trade-unions but "bored from within" and imposed general restrictions so as to "direct" worker organizations along lines consistent with the state's objectives, the National Socialists forbade labor unions as such. At the time of their dissolution some 7 million wage earners and salaried employees were members of German labor organizations. The most influential of these was the Federation of Free Trade-unions supported by the Social Democratic Party. As his initial step in establishing the German Labor Front, Hitler dissolved the Free Trade-unions, confiscated their funds and properties, and arrested their leaders. The remaining unions were "coordinated" into one national labor organization open to wage earner and salaried worker, employer and employee alike. By decree this became in October, 1934, a "national organization of German workers of brain and brawn." The German Labor Front was officially declared an affiliate of the National Socialist Party in 1935.

Although membership in the German Labor Front was nominally voluntary, much pressure was exerted locally and nationally to secure members. Except for those who were specifically excluded, as, for example, "non-Aryans" and "foreign" labor, nearly all wage earners and employers became members. It was good politics, if nothing else, to join, and in the light of existing conditions it took strength and courage for an individual to refuse membership. The "dues" of employers were graduated according to size of plant, while wage earners paid 1.6 marks per month. By the end of the war the German Labor

[8] John P. Umbach, "Labor Conditions in Germany," *Monthly Labor Review,* 60 (March, 1945), 516.

[9] *Wages, Hours and Working Conditions of Industrial Labor in Germany,* War Department Civil Affairs Guide, July, 1944, p. 2.

[10] For a fuller discussion, see Ernest Hamburger, "The German Labor Front," *Monthly Labor Review,* 59 (November, 1944), 932.

Front claimed close to 25 million members and some 360 million marks in capital, exclusive of the properties of the pre-Nazi trade-unions and cooperatives which had been turned over to it shortly after their dissolution. All officials of the German Labor Front were appointees of the National Socialist Party.

In contrast to bona fide labor organizations, the principal activities of the German Labor Front were social and "cultural" rather than economic. The German Labor Front could not, even if it wanted to, change or influence the wages, hours, and other basic working conditions set by the Trustees of Labor. However, it did intervene in a limited fashion in industrial disputes by trying to get employers and wage earners to settle their differences in the plant rather than to certify them to the Labor Trustees and the Social Honor Courts for a decision. But the vast majority of the activities of the German Labor Front were directed at furthering National Socialist philosophy, aims, and programs among the working populace. Its "Strength through Joy" movement, "Beauty of Work" inspection system, and "Model Business" competitions were some of the more publicized of its activities along these lines.

Councils of Trust, or Confidential Councils, as they were frequently called, were authorized under the national labor law of 1934 to replace Works Councils. In the German Republic, the Works-council Act of 1920 had required councils of wage earners and salaried employees to be elected in all plants employing twenty or more workers. Although the works-council movement had drawn its support from many diverse and often antagonistic groups, it was in the main an expression of the principle of the equality of labor and management as set forth in the Weimar constitution.[11] And while the record of Works Councils in Germany was spotty—labor and management rarely combined the degree of cooperation, interest, ability, and responsibility necessary to effect the equality in day-to-day plant operations that the sponsors of Works Councils sought—they nevertheless provided workers, whether unionized or not, with the opportunity of helping, through democratically chosen representatives, to formulate shop rules, review dismissal cases, and share in the administration of the provisions of protective labor legislation and collective agreements.

In the light of the leadership principle and the National Socialist disdain for democratic rule, it was inevitable that the Councils of Trust were called upon to perform a wholly different function from that of the Works Councils of the Weimar Republic. Although Councils of Trust were "elected" by the workers in each plant, the list of nominees was selected by the employer and the German Labor Front. Inasmuch as no other candidates could be substituted, it was apparent that only "politically acceptable" employees served on the Councils of Trust. They were consulted on personnel matters and on industrial-relations questions involving factory rules and health and safety provisions. But like the German Labor Front, the principal task of the Councils of Trust was to appeal to the "honor" of the individual worker and to "promote the community spirit" in each plant. In time, however, the German Labor

[11] See C. W. Guillebaud, *The Works Council: A German Experiment in Industrial Democracy,* London, Cambridge, 1928; and Boris Stern, *Works Council Movement in Germany,* U.S. Bureau of Labor Statistics Bulletin 383, March, 1925.

Front took over the direction of the propaganda functions of the Councils of Trust and entrusted them to shop stewards whom they appointed in each plant. After this change the Councils of Trust became more and more the administrative agents of the Trustees of Labor. By this time they were appointed by the Labor Trustees, and their principal activity was supervising the rules and regulations which had been designed to increase production.

The National Socialists did not interfere directly with the system of federal labor courts which had been established by legislation in 1926. The courts, composed equally of employers and employees under a professional judge, who presided, continued to serve as the final arbiter of differences between workers and employers. But because of the "conciliation" activities of the Trustees of Labor, the Councils of Trust, and the German Labor Front, fewer cases reached the federal labor courts, and their role in minimizing industrial conflict was greatly reduced. In addition, the Nazis set up a system of Social Honor Courts in an effort to promote the "new society" and to punish those who "violated the Nazi spirit." These were separate and distinct from the federal labor courts and other legal tribunals. Although the Social Honor Courts were not designed to govern labor relations as such, their activities greatly affected labor and management in their dealings with one another. Many of the alleged violations of the spirit of the Nazi community were the very acts of independence which the Republic and democratic countries generally had considered essential to the preservation of free collective bargaining. The Social Honor Courts, among other functions, served as another instrument for imposing the will of the state in all industrial-relations matters.

The Nature of Control over Wages, Hours, and Labor Standards

As previously indicated, the general level of rates which prevailed at the time the National Socialists came to power was maintained as part of the state's economic policy. Inasmuch as these had been set forth in collective-bargaining agreements, they were minimum rates, and employers generally were not prohibited from paying more until war production was begun in earnest.[12] However, as with most minimum rates in periods of relatively low business activity and few job opportunities, they soon became the prevailing rate. From 1933 to 1938 average hourly rates remained virtually unchanged, being 67.6 reichpfennigs in 1933 and 67.9 in 1938.[13]

After July, 1938, following the seizure of Austria and the building of the Siegfried Line, the Trustees of Labor were empowered to set maximum as well as minimum rates. With the outbreak of war in September, 1939, a general wage freeze was ordered. In addition, the Trustees of Labor were authorized in October of that year to decrease bonus payments and other incentives wher-

---

[12] An exception was made to this general policy for the building and construction industry, where a general scarcity of skilled labor developed early. In an effort to curb labor pirating and prevent wage-price relationships from being upset, employers in this industry were forbidden to raise rates above the minima set in the *Tarif* regulations.

[13] Otto Nathan, "Consumption in Germany during the Period of Rearmament," *Quarterly Journal of Economics*, 56 (May, 1942), 366.

ever necessary. But despite the stabilization of the basic rate, there was some increase in earnings because of the greater use of the piece-rate system and of longer hours in particular.[14] Average hourly earnings rose from 70.7 reichpfennigs in 1933 to 78.9 in 1938.[15] Apparently this upward trend in earnings continued to the war's end, rising some 10 reichpfennigs in the period 1938 to 1944 alone. Yet the real wages rose little, if at all. Despite price control, the cost of living rose about 10 per cent—and this by government statistical reports which tended to undervalue increases in living costs. The actual rise in the cost of living was held to be considerably greater than the published figures, and along with the huge amount of compulsory wage deductions required by the state, this was a heavy burden for the average wage earner to bear.[16]

Industrial Peace and Full Employment: What Price?

Labor standards in National Socialist Germany were permeated with practices which were patently discriminatory and rancorous. For the most part these were the express product of National Socialist philosophy and labor policy. Discriminations against foreign labor and against individuals not of

---

[14] Earnings were also increased, especially in the early years of Nazi rule, through a loosening up of promotion policy and improvements in family allowances, vacations, and holiday-pay standards. The advantages these brought to the average wage earner were more than offset, however, by the virtual abandonment of protective labor legislation establishing the 8-hour day and by the introduction of an inverted piece-rate system. This last worked a particular hardship on the wage earner. It was encouraged by Nazi officials, and after 1939 its use became fairly general. Instead of adding to earnings in proportion to increased output, the inverted piece-rate system as practiced in Nazi Germany resulted in a standard of output being set which was held to be the norm, and all wage earners who failed to meet this standard were penalized by decreases in pay. Frequently a maximum of 125 per cent of the standard could be earned by those who exceeded the output norm. But this was subject to the proviso that earnings above the standard were to be paid only if they could be offset by proportionate reductions in the earnings of fellow employees who failed to meet the norm. There was, too, still another limit on individual earnings under the Nazi piece-rate system: regardless of the individual's output and where it stood in relation to the norm, earnings were not allowed to exceed the wage "to which the worker was accustomed." Under the strict discipline of Nazi controls of labor, the system seemed to work. It was introduced first in the building industry, the metal industries, and in all "homework." By the war's end this and other discriminatory wage practices were widespread in German industry generally. See the author's analysis of the problems Nazi wage practices and regulations presented to the Allied Control Council in the German occupation, "Allied Policy on Wages in Occupied Germany," *International Labour Review*, 55 (May, 1947), 351–371.

[15] Nathan, *op. cit.*, p. 366.

[16] See Maxine Y. Sweezy's critical analysis of the cost-of-living indexes used by the German statistical office, in *The Structure of the Nazi Economy*, Cambridge, Mass., Harvard University Press, 1941, pp. 200–201.

With respect to compulsory wage deductions, it is perhaps important to note that they rose from slightly less than 20 per cent of the average worker's income in 1933 to approximately 35 per cent by the end of the National Socialist rule. For an analysis of the wage earner's economic position under National Socialism generally, see Hilda Oppenheimer-Bluhm, *The Standard of Living of German Labor under Nazi Rule*, New York, New School for Social Research, 1943. See also Ludwig Hamburger's (*op. cit.*, pp. 63–65) analysis of the use of cost-accounting practices to limit the payment of wages above the minimum set forth in *Tarif* regulations.

the chosen race and ideology were carried into the work shop and into almost every phase of industrial relations and the economy generally.[17] Wage rates and overtime-pay standards, working hours, and general conditions of labor were all made less favorable for these employees. Labor camps and forced labor of all manner and kinds became increasingly widespread under the Nazi rule. For workers generally the necessity to register at government employment offices, carry employment cards, and comply with the numerous edicts stringently controlling the movement of labor and the right to change jobs virtually eliminated the freedom of occupational choice.[18] The Nazis saw fit to continue, at least nominally, the extensive social insurances, public-assistance programs, and other state benefits traditionally extended to German workers. But even here discriminatory practices were followed. Whenever it suited Nazi objectives, the social-insurance and public-assistance programs were modified to deny benefits to employees of certain racial, political, and religious groups or, on the other hand, to reward certain favored groups. For example, in December, 1936, the Nazis suspended the payment of pensions under the German old-age-and invalidity-insurance program to "persons engaged in activities hostile to the state." In the administration of public assistance special state aid was given members of the National Socialist Party who had fought in the League of Front Soldiers (Stahlhelm) in the political struggle to gain control of the state. The May, 1942, law on sickness insurance and maternity benefits specifically introduced racial discriminations and preferences. Foreign workers were not given the same unemployment compensation and relief rights as were extended workers generally. Even in the matter of increased children's allowances (Kinderbeihilfen) and family allowances generally in the wage structure, the act was more a reflection of a population policy which aimed at assuring the state of an increasing supply of future soldiers than one of humanitarianism as such.

[17] For a detailed discussion of labor standards under National Socialism, see, among others cited elsewhere in this study, Rene Livchen, "Net Wages and Real Wages in Germany," International Labour Review, 50 (July, 1944), 65–72, and earlier articles in issues of December, 1943, pp. 714–732, and August, 1942, pp. 136–165; Rene Livchen, "The Employment of Women in Germany under the National Socialist Regime," International Labour Review, December, 1941, pp. 617–659, and the succeeding study, March, 1942, pp. 286–296; G. Warburg, Six Years of Hitler: The Jews under the Nazi Regime, London, G. Allen, 1939; Vaso Trianovitch, Economic Development of Germany under National Socialism, National Industrial Conference Board Study 236, 1937, esp. Chaps. 1 and 2, which deal with the status and economic position of German labor under National Socialism; Otto Nathan, The Nazi Economic System: Germany's Mobilization for War, Durham, N.C., Duke University Press, 1944, esp. Chap. 7, dealing with Nazi control of labor; Harold Zink and Taylor Cole (eds.), Government in Wartime Europe, New York, Reynal & Hitchcock, 1941, esp. Chap. 4, "Wartime Theories and Policies of the Third Reich," by Professor Cole; and the Civil Affairs Guides, esp. Wages, Hours and Working Conditions of Industrial Labor in Germany, July, 1944, Old Age and Invalidity Insurance in Germany, June, 1944, War Pensions, Service Men's Dependents Allowances, Children's Allowances and Similar Programs of Public Aid in Germany, July, 1944, Sickness Insurance in Germany, July, 1944, Unemployment Compensation in Germany, July, 1944, and Economic Controls in Nazi Germany, February, 1944.

[18] In this connection see Sweezy, op. cit., Chap. 9; and Ludwig Hamburger, How Nazi Germany Has Mobilized and Controlled Labor, Brookings Institution Pamphlet 24, 1940.

The most repugnant aspect of the National Socialist experiment was the utter and complete disdain for the individual as such. In industrial relations this was reflected in the patent disregard for the dignity of human labor. It underlay Nazi labor policy and industrial relations programs whatever their form. Discrimination, wanton denial of basic freedoms, and the ruthless, arbitrary, and capricious suppression of certain groups, individuals, and institutions was its inevitable by-product.

While most people would not voluntarily pay the toll totalitarianism exacts in the form of the denials of freedom and controls enumerated above,[19] many were lulled into complacency by its apparent economic successes. The National Socialists achieved and maintained full employment, increased productivity and national income, and virtually eliminated overt expressions of industrial conflict.[20] This last would be likely to have an increasingly greater appeal in countries such as the United States where, because of the rapid growth of large unionism and big business, industrial conflict is no longer a local community problem.

The economic successes of the National Socialists were more apparent than real. Prior to World War II and the close scrutiny of fascist controls (this critique is equally applicable to fascist Italy and to National Socialist Germany), supporters of democratic capitalism were forced to contend that the disdain for the dignity of human labor and the denial of basic freedoms were too high a price to pay for the seeming efficiencies of this alternative economic system. But the war has altered this. Closer observation after the war indicated that the Nazi economy was no better equipped than ours to avoid the bottlenecks of industry and the so-called inconsistencies, inefficiencies, and basic weaknesses of capitalism.[21] While the fascists seemed to avoid some of

19 In this regard it was satisfying indeed to have been privileged to assist German labor and management to regain in the Occupation the many freedoms that had been wrested from them by the National Socialists. The eager spirit and the manner in which these rights were restored and Nazi discriminatory practices were eliminated were analyzed by Arnold Zemple, "The Labor Situation in Germany," *Military Government Journal,* Vol. 1 (February, 1948); Oscar Weigert, "Labor Relations in the U.S. Zone of Germany," *Monthly Labor Review,* Vol. 66 (April, 1948) (reprint serial R. 1921); R. Taylor Cole, "Labor Relations in Western Germany," *Visiting Expert Series No. 2,* OMGUS Manpower Division, October, 1948; and the author's article "The Reconstitution of the German Trade Union Movement," *Political Science Quarterly,* Vol. 64 (March, 1949).

20 Although there were no major strikes or lockouts under the National Socialists, there were some manifestations of industrial unrest and conflict. For example, Max Seydewitz, *Civil Life in Wartime Germany: The Story of the Home Front,* New York, Viking, 1945, pp. 167–193, reported some evidences of the hostility of workers in the winter of 1941–1942. There were some slowdowns in production, food protests, defiance of the German Labor Front in its demand for increased output, and inauguration of incentive pay systems and "wages based on performance." In the Ruhr there even were some sit-down strikes in protest against the heavy overtime and Sunday work loads. But in general worker resistance was slight. *Ibid.,* pp. 30–41; Guillebaud, *The Social Policy of Nazi Germany,* pp. 120–132; and Evelyn Lend, *The Underground Struggle in Germany,* League for Industrial Democracy Pamphlet Series, August, 1938, pp. 8–10—all analyze the reasons for this, citing in particular the split in trade-union ranks and the reliance on law rather than collective action to secure economic ends.

21 This became more and more apparent as Nazi officials were interrogated and institutions were studied firsthand at the war's end. My personal observations were largely limited to labor and manpower agencies. But apparently this condition was fairly general.

the problems encountered under democratic capitalism, they ran into others equally as complex. It is my firm conviction, based on something more than a casual acquaintance with the Sovietization of Eastern Germany as well as on a study of the Soviet Russian economic system, that this is true of totalitarianism in all its forms.

The strike, lockout, and other outward manifestations of industrial unrest may be suppressed. But industrial strife will take other forms unless a sense of mutual respect and responsibility can be developed. The notion in the National Socialist ideology that there is a common interest which can overcome labor and management differences has merit. But so long as the dignity of human labor was not maintained and the leadership principle rather than equality was sought, it was inevitable that industrial peace would have to be maintained by the sword. Even then, while strikes and other major forms of industrial conflict were ruthlessly suppressed by the National Socialists, they had a continuing and increasingly serious problem of deterioration in the quality of output and supervision. Even from a pragmatic point of view it cannot be conceded that Nazi labor and economic policy was more successful and efficient than that of democratic capitalism.

Fascism has been on the decline since the defeat of its major proponents and practitioners in World War II. But it is disturbing to note that the state control of industrial conflict, on the other hand, has been on the rise. The stringency with which labor-management relations today are controlled the world over gives cause for real concern. The parallel between fascist methods of controlling labor and those practiced by Soviet Russia and the communist satellite countries is well known.[22] But of even greater concern is the extent state control over labor relations has become the accepted policy in countries uniformly espousing individual freedom. That the state is obliged to enact "rules of the game" in the protection of its citizenry against the excesses of strong labor organizations, powerful management groups, or bilateral monopoly, as the case may be, is self-evident. The danger, however, is that such a goal will be deemed insufficient and that industrial peace will be sought at all costs. Extreme care must be taken to avoid giving succor to the very infringements of individual freedom and liberty we fought so hard to stamp out when practiced under a different name. Where industrial peace is obtained through stringent regimentation or elimination of labor's freedom to organize, through state control of wages, hours, and working conditions generally, and through compulsory arbitration, the price is prohibitive. It is perhaps well to review the Nazi experiment in its entirety from time to time, since for most of us it will serve to reinforce our rejection of the autocratic approach to the industrial-relations problem.

See the report of findings and conclusions on the National Socialist economy, based on the interrogation of high-ranking Nazi leaders and economists, by Frank D. Graham and J. J. Scanlon, *Economic Preparation and Conduct of War under the Nazi Regime,* Washington, War Department, Historical Division, Special Staff, Apr. 10, 1946.

[22] See, for example, the analysis of labor relations and policy in Soviet Russia by Walter Galenson in this volume. See also my article "Communism in German Labor Organizations," *Journal of Political Economy,* 57 (June, 1949), 213–226.

CHAPTER 37 SOVIET RUSSIA

Walter Galenson   *University of California (Berkeley)*

IT IS part of the ideological heritage of the Soviet state that the nationalization of industry, the transfer of the means of production from private to public ownership, will automatically eliminate labor disputes by removing their basic cause, class conflict. The failure to realize this ideal situation is attributed by Russian political theorists to human imperfection rather than to failure of the "objective" economic institutions. Lenin ascribed the lack of harmony evident in early Soviet industrial relations to "bureaucratic distortions of the proletarian state and the remains of the capitalist past and its institutions, on the one hand, and the political and cultural backwardness of the laboring masses, on the other." [1] Thirty years of Soviet rule have apparently not succeeded in extirpating "the remains of the capitalist past," for we find a recent authoritative Soviet treatise on labor law [2] saying:

> The basic cause of labor disputes in socialist factories and enterprises under conditions of gradual transition from socialism to communism [officially, the present developmental stage of Russia] is the survival of the capitalist consciousness among some citizens. This is manifested in bureaucratic distortion of labor law by the management of certain enterprises, which leads to violation of the rights of workers and employees, to complaints by them. The survival of capitalism is manifested also in the effort of some irresponsible, unscrupulous workers to give the state less work and to receive greater rewards. The selfish demands of such people, their failure to fulfill their obligations, produce labor disputes.

The official Russian view, then, is that labor disputes are not inherent in socialism (or communism) and that, once the "capitalist consciousness" disappears, all conflict will cease. But current Soviet practice clearly indicates no great faith in the arrival of this millennium. Once the necessary genuflections to dogma have been made, the problem of labor disputes is treated in a factual and detailed manner that indicates a prevalent belief in its permanence.

Allowable Area of Controversy

It is essential at the outset to delineate clearly the area within which labor disputes are permitted in the Soviet Union. Conflicts over economic interests,

---

[1] V. I. Lenin, *Collected Works*, Vol. 27, New York, International Publishers, 1927–1945, p. 149.
[2] N. G. Aleksandrov (ed.), *Sovyetskoye Trudovoye Pravo* ("Soviet Labor Law"), Moscow, 1949, p. 295.

that is, concerning the general level of wages and the number of hours worked, which in the West are the most prolific breeders of industrial strife, are not recognized as legitimate in Russia. Determination of the national wage bill and its allocation among industries and individual enterprises are functions primarily of the central planning authorities. We do not know precisely what role the trade-unions play in the performance of this vital economic function; their official authority is stated in the following manner:

> Both in the regulation of wages by collective agreement and in direct governmental regulation, an important role devolves upon the trade-unions. They participate in the consideration and the preparation of laws and decrees regarding wage questions, influence actively the level and the system of wages, exercise control over the correctness of wage organization, contend against inequities adversely affecting workers and employees and illegal overpayments and other distortions in the field of wages. The All-union Central Council of Trade-unions organizes the preparation by central committees of national unions of measures for establishing the proper wage differentials among various groups of workers; studies the measures developed for regulating wages at the inter-industry and district level; participates in the work of the State Planning Commission and the cabinet of the USSR; states its conclusions regarding projected wage regulations submitted by the ministries and the central trade-union committees to the Council of Ministers of the USSR. . . .[3]

But even if in practice the trade-unions exercise a greater authority over central wage determination than the above quotation seems to indicate, it must be remembered that at least the higher bureaucracy within the trade-unions are more nearly civil servants than representatives of the workers. And it is perfectly clear that at the enterprise level there is no opportunity for local union officials or individual workers to question the equity of the governmentally determined wage levels.

The only disputes that are permitted to come to light are those arising out of differing interpretations of the labor laws or of collective agreements. Of the two latter categories, disputes over legal rights are the more important, since it is by law rather than collective agreement that basic conditions of labor are regulated. The Soviet collective agreement has had a checkered career, and at present it bears little similarity to the instrument of the same name in the United States. Until the first 5-year plan in 1928 wages and other conditions were basically determined by collective agreement, but thereafter a progressive deterioration set in: beginning with 1931, agreement terms had to fall within limits set by higher governmental authority, and in 1935 collective agreements were abolished altogether. The practice of concluding collective agreements was resumed in 1947, but their purpose was now exhortatory rather than normative. "The level and system of wage payment is not established by collective agreements; they state the rates and systems approved by the government." [4]

Agreements are initiated by the central committees of the national unions in cooperation with the various industrial ministries. Typical agreements are

---

[3] A. E. Pasherstnik, *Pravovi Voprosi Voznagrazhdenia za Trud* ("Legal Questions Regarding Wages"), Moscow, 1949, pp. 207–208.

[4] *Ibid.*, p. 211.

sent to local unions and management, which are then supposed to adapt them to local conditions, with the participation of those employed in the plants. Soviet collective agreements include such matters as the obligations of labor and management to fulfill the state plan through raising labor productivity and reducing spoilage; agreement on the part of the union to train labor, to further "socialist competition," and to work for installation of piece rates wherever possible; and agreement on the part of management in regard to safety and health measures, housing construction, and other welfare measures.

> The collective agreement is an important instrument for the communist education of the masses. Accepting the obligations in collective agreements, workers, engineers, and employees are by that very fact obliged to adopt a communist attitude toward work, toward public property, to economize state goods, to strengthen labor discipline, to struggle against antigovernment tendencies, against grafters and idlers, habituating themselves to giving the state more and themselves less.[5]

The worker-welfare obligations of management occasionally give rise to dispute,[6] but essentially such a document does not lend itself to strife between labor and management at the factory level.

The only really significant source of labor controversy is alleged violation of the labor code by labor or management. Such disputes fall into the following major categories:

1. Disputes involving the application of the centrally determined wage scales. Attached to each local trade-union is a wage commission, which

> . . . systematically checks the wages of particular trades . . . brings to light the causes of incorrect wage relationships among particular categories of workers, and takes steps through factory and local union committees to eliminate these causes. The commission examines the correctness of the distribution of work and workers by grades, the extent to which workers and employees are being used according to their skill; participates in the preparation of rate-skill tariffs projected by management for submission to higher authority. . . .[7]

The precise role of the local union in wage setting varies by industry; in construction, for example, all work loads and piece rates are determined unilaterally by the government, whereas in other industries only minimum and maximum rates are set, with the precise determination left to local bargaining. Presumably, the greater the latitude allowed to the local people, the greater is the possibility of conflict.

An individual worker, as well as the local union, can initiate a wage grievance on the basis of misclassification or misassignment. It is obviously in ac-

---

[5] *Professionalniye Soyuzi* ("Trade-unions"), May, 1947, p. 20.

[6] For example, in one reported case the management had agreed to provide its employees with fuel for heating their homes, and a controversy arose over the price to be charged them. "The dispute was submitted to the appropriate ministry and the central committee of the trade-union, which decided to supplement the agreement by adding an obligation on the part of management to deliver wood to the families of servicemen, war invalids, women with minor children, and workers with large families at prices not exceeding those set by the fuel corporation, and to remaining employees, at full delivered cost to the enterprise." Aleksandrov (ed.), *op. cit.*, p. 297.

[7] Pasherstnik, *op. cit.*, p. 209.

cord with the advancement of production that workers be employed at their highest skills, and it is therefore of little wonder that the labor press frequently airs complaints of skill underutilization.[8]

2. Disputes involving subsidiary wage questions, including overtime pay, vacation pay, penalties for spoiled work, idle-time pay, and pay for the use of tools belonging to the worker. The law governing each of these questions is rather detailed, and there has been built up around the law a body of judicial interpretation.

3. Disputes relating to voluntary quits, discharge, and transfer. The voluntary movement of Russian workers is severely circumscribed, but if he leaves his job on legal grounds or is discharged pursuant to a reduction in force or to transfers, he may be entitled to certain payments, including severance pay and travel allowances. There may also be conflict over management's refusal to release a worker, as well as over entries in the labor book that every Soviet employee is required to have.

4. Disputes over fines and other penalties imposed by management for infraction of working rules. The Soviet code of labor discipline is a strict one, and there is ample room for controversy over alleged lateness, absenteeism, work of poor quality, and other violations. Certain offenses, such as persistent absenteeism or lateness, carry criminal liability, but these fall within the jurisdiction of the courts.

The foregoing are the major, though by no means the only, categories of labor disputes that are regarded as legitimate in Soviet industrial life. In general, they involve the individual in relation to his job, for collective or trade-union interests are considered to be identical with those of the employing enterprise and the state. The possible divergence of individual interests is recognized only because, even for a regime as totalitarian as the Russian, which has been able to utilize fiat as the basis for determining a broad range of major economic questions, it might well prove dangerous to suppress the many on-the-job grievances that arise in the course of the working day. The industrial worker, who provides the basic political support for the present Soviet government, may be better induced to accept dizzying shifts in economic and political policy and the ever-increasing work loads demanded of him if an outlet for the airing of individual inequities is provided. Grievances can often be adjusted at little or no cost to the economy, and in the long run their correction will probably result in economic gain in the form of a greater degree of voluntary effort. It is for these reasons that the Soviet authorities, no believers in individual freedom, have provided and publicized mechanisms for the adjustment of labor disputes at the factory level.

Machinery for Consideration of Grievances

The initial step in the processing of grievances is through the shop committee of the trade-union. In large plants the chairman of this committee and perhaps several of the members will be full-time trade-union officials, while in smaller shops the chairman will be a regular worker. Grievances are dis-

[8] See, *e.g.*, a letter entitled "I Want to Work as a Skilled Worker," *Trud*, July 13, 1951, p. 3

cussed with management, and it is reported that, in the great majority of cases, satisfactory adjustment is obtained. If such is not the case, the matter is submitted to the so-called Rates and Conflicts Commission, on which management and the local union are equally represented.[9] This body, which normally consists of four members, with a rotating chairmanship, is a conciliatory rather than an arbitration tribunal. Its meetings are informal, open to the public, and are always held outside working hours. Evidence may be presented either in oral or written form, depending upon the importance and the complications of the case being dealt with. There may be a separate commission for each department in large establishments.

The Rates and Conflicts Commission can only reach final decisions by unanimous vote. If unanimity prevails, a decision can be appealed only on the following grounds: (1) that the decision adversely affects conditions of labor stipulated by law or collective agreement; (2) that it sets a standard exceeding the maximum work load established by law or collective agreement; (3) that there has been some irregularity in the constitution or the jurisdictional exercise of the commission; (4) that the decision contravenes a judgment rendered by a court.

Appeals from decisions of the Rates and Conflicts Commission or cases in which no decision has been reached at the factory level normally go to the regional, the republic, and, finally, the national trade-union (although the People's Court has jurisdiction over certain cases). This peculiar procedure stems from the earlier period of Soviet history when conciliation commissions in the Ministry of Labor supervised the Rates and Conflicts Commissions. Upon the dissolution of the Labor Ministry and the transfer of its functions to the trade-unions, the appeals function also became lodged in the union organization. That this is considered perfectly equitable procedure provides one indication of the extent to which Russian trade-unions are regarded as governmental institutions.

For practically all disputes involving the determination of future conditions of labor and for most disputes involving alleged violation of law or contract, the Rates and Conflicts Commission is the obligatory tribunal of original jurisdiction. In the case of the latter type of dispute a worker may appeal to the People's Court, which is the lowest level in the regular judicial system, and in a very limited category of disputes he may take the case directly to the People's Court without the prior intermediation of the Rates Commission. However, nonjural disputes involving future labor conditions are not within the jurisdiction of the People's Court but can only be decided by the higher trade-union organizations.

There are no general statistics either on the number of disputes that arise or on the manner of disposition. Some doubts as to the militancy of local union officials in furthering grievances arise from the oft-repeated statement that in individual factories "there were very few disputes and that settlement was usually reached at the level of the works committee."[10] It was reported of

---

[9] A good deal of Russian labor literature is devoted to describing the structure and functions of this body. For a good summary, see D. V. Shveitzer, *Razreshenie Trudovikh Sporov v SSSR* ("The Adjustment of Labor Disputes in the Soviet Union"), Moscow, 1949.

[10] *Official Report of the British Delegation of Trade Unionists to the USSR*, 1951, p. 59.

one of the largest machine-tool plants in Russia, the Caliber Plant in Moscow, that only one case had been appealed to the higher trade-union body from the factory Rates and Conflicts Commission during the period 1944 to 1950.[11] One may well question the existence of appeals machinery which is used so infrequently or the degree of protection afforded workers by a union which is able to reach full agreement with management on practically every occasion. On the other hand, from frequent references in the labor press, one gains the impression that a not inconsiderable number of disputes reach the level of the Rates and Conflicts Commission.

Soviet Grievance Machinery in Practice

While the general outline of Soviet disputes machinery is clear, little is known about how it actually operates. At the risk of repetition, it should be remarked that the Soviet trade-union is neither in theory nor in fact primarily a representative of worker interests but rather a quasi-governmental agency predominantly engaged in nonpartisan activities on behalf of the state.[12] But it is also fair to say that the representation of workers in labor disputes is a not unimportant facet of its activities, though its efficiency in carrying out this function is somewhat questionable, as one may judge from the following incidents, which were abstracted from the Soviet trade-union press and appear to be not unusual.

One Soloviev was in charge of the nonferrous-metals stockroom of a Moscow automobile plant.[13] He was an active member of the trade-union shop committee and chairman of the union subcommittee covering the supply departments. At a union meeting he charged that the head of the plant supply department was inefficient in his management of metals, the result of which was that Soloviev was removed from his job, presumably as a disciplinary measure. After the Rates and Conflicts Commission failed to reach agreement on his plea for reinstatement to his regular job, he appealed to the central committee of the automobile workers' union, his appeal receiving the support of the secretary of the Communist Party unit in the supply department, Aframeev by name. The union upheld his plea and ordered his reinstatement.

But this did not terminate the dispute. Within 3 months not only Soloviev but Aframeev as well were discharged from employment, Aframeev for "taking advantage of his official position" and for "systematic nonfulfillment of his duties." As the reporter remarks, "They were determined to get him one way or another." Soloviev appealed this time to the People's Court and secured an order of reinstatement. Though he was elected plant organizer of the trade-union shortly after his return to the plant, he was discharged a third time and reinstated again by Court order and was apparently at work at the time the case was written up.

Aframeev, in the meantime, had appealed his discharge to the central com-

[11] *Report of the British Workers Delegation to Russia,* New York, SRT Publications, 1950, p. 47.

[12] The reader interested in the history and functions of Soviet labor unions may be referred to Isaac Deutscher, *Soviet Trade Unions,* London, Royal Institute of International Affairs, 1950.

[13] This incident was printed in *Trud,* Mar. 25, 1950, p. 2.

mittee of the union, which after two months of procrastination ordered him reinstated with back pay. However, within a few days the order was revoked. We are not told of Aframeev's final fate, although presumably he too was finally reinstated.

A third worker, one Gniteev, in charge of the chemical storeroom and also a member of the union shop committee, was discharged along with Soloviev for his support of the latter. He was unable to secure redress from the automobile union and carried his appeal to the highest trade-union body, the All-union Central Council of Trade-unions. The complaints department of this organization directed the automobile union to consider the grievance, which was finally done about 6 months after the discharge and after Gniteev had been reemployed as a foreman in the body department. The union issued an order holding Gniteev's discharge unlawful "because it was effected without prior consultation with the divisional and plant committees," but as the reporter caustically remarked, "What use was this decree?"

What emerges from this story is the seeming lack of interest shown by the automobile union in the discharge of its local officials and the impunity with which management was able to discipline workers who took seriously the exhortation to criticize inefficiency. The incident brings home the oft-noted impotence of a Soviet trade-union in dealing with a management that is successfully fulfilling its production quotas.[14] In the last analysis, court action proved more efficacious than union protest in securing redress. It is also interesting to note that not even Aframeev's Communist Party position stopped management in its determination to get rid of him.

It is also necessary to point out, however, that eventually management was obliged to reinstate the aggrieved workers and that the latter were able to, and did, avail themselves of the regular grievance machinery. Perhaps the public espousal of their cause by the trade-union press and their apparent vindication were due to the fact that they were victims of an endeavor to further efficiency and increase production. If instead they had been discharged for contesting a work load that they regarded as too high, it is doubtful whether the outcome would have been as favorable for them. Certainly there would have been much less newspaper indignation over their fate.

In another reported labor dispute [15] the manager of a Tashkent machine-tool plant had unilaterally changed the customary day of rest, depriving the workers of their legal day off, acting on the basis of a permissive decree issued by the Ministry of Machine Tools. Local action proved of no avail, and the matter was protested to the central committee of the Machine-tool Workers'

---

[14] In a recent analysis of the Soviet novel the following dialogue is quoted from a very popular novel published in 1947: "Usdeskin (chairman of the factory committee) . . . came to Listopad (manager) with a number of demands concerning working conditions in the factory.

" 'No, you stay out of these matters,' said Listopad. 'You leave all that to me.'

" 'Sorry, comrade manager,' said Usdeskin, 'but don't you know that this is a direct function of the trade union?'

" 'No, I don't,' said Listopad. . . 'It's your business to know what your functions are.' "

Alexander Gerschenkron, "A Neglected Source of Economic Information on Soviet Russia," *The American Slavic and East European Review,* February, 1950, p. 1.

[15] *Trud,* Apr. 15, 1950, p. 2.

Union, which discussed it informally with the Ministry and received the reply that the decree was based upon a decision of the Supreme Court of the USSR. The Ministry did not even dignify by a reply two subsequent protests formally filed by the union. The Machine-tool Union appealed to the All-union Central Council of Trade-unions for help and finally succeeded in having the decree revoked. However, the reporter noted that the plant in question was still operating on the legal holiday.

Again we witness the impotence not only of the local but of the national trade-union as well in the face of arbitrary and apparently illegal management action. However, there was in the last analysis a possibility of protest even in the face of a presumably laudable attempt by management to raise output. Of course, similar action by the management of a unionized enterprise in the United States would undoubtedly have led to direct action by the workers in protest. The Soviet grievance machinery serves to a certain extent as an imperfect substitute for the right to strike.[16]

A typical shop-committee chairman is described as interviewing from forty to fifty persons each day on matters ranging from complaints about housing to shop grievances.[17] In view of the great variety of trade-union functions, including administration of social insurance (except for unemployment insurance, which is not to be found in Russia on the theory that there is no unemployment) and the factory-inspection laws, this volume of activity is quite credible. It would appear reasonable that local trade-union officials are instrumental in adjusting informally the myriad of petty grievances that are to be found in an establishment which provides workers not only with jobs but in many cases with living quarters, retail shops, and social facilities as well.

There remains, however, the crucial question of whether there is sufficient substance in the Soviet labor-disputes procedure to convince workers that their individual rights and aspirations are being given adequate consideration, thereby creating the modicum of consent essential to the ultimate stability of the system. On this question there is little concrete evidence. Against an affirmative hypothesis is the testimony of Soviet expatriates and the Soviet labor code itself, indicating the ever-present possibility of unpleasant consequences for the individual worker who considers his needs and desires superior to those of the state. Raising a grievance would seem to require not a little temerity, and it may well be that much of the complaint that receives public expression is part of the vaunted campaign of self-criticism that is often a prelude to the removal of inefficient management. It is probably not farfetched to conclude that the volume of grievances and trade-union activity stand in inverse relationship to the degree of operating efficiency diplayed by management.

But having said this, one returns to the question of why the Soviet rulers have lavished so much care upon factory representation institutions if indeed they are but meaningless shells, for no amount of propaganda could hide from

---

[16] The Russians are fond of pointing out that, while strikes are perfectly legal, they never occur in practice, since no worker would think of striking against an enterprise in which he, as a citizen, has a property stake. Until 1928 there were in fact numerous official strikes, but since that time strike efforts have been treated as political offenses rather than as expressions of economic discontent.

[17] *Trud*, Aug. 20, 1948.

workers a gap between theory and fact that could be seen firsthand. It is one thing to convince workers that unemployed persons are dying of hunger in the streets of New York, and quite another to claim that a mechanism for the processing of grievances exists when in fact the worker cannot find it.

That the Russian trade-unions reflect predominantly the "production" point of view, that their major function is to stimulate the worker to greater efforts, is hardly open to question. But this is not inconsistent with the hypothesis that their "consumptionist" function is important as well. In the latter area their basic function would appear to differ considerably between the top and the bottom of the bureaucratic hierarchy. Whatever representation the worker gets as a consumer interested in higher wages and lower prices is exercised at the national level, to the extent (unknown) that trade-unions influence the formulation of plans. At the local level there can be no diversion of income, merely corrective action on behalf of the individual.

It is difficult enough where one has full access to the facts to evaluate the effectiveness of machinery designed to alleviate the type of labor dispute that the Russians deem within the "allowable area" of economic conflict. The difficulty is compounded many times in the case of Russia, where our only sources of information are the official press and the not disinterested accounts of expatriates. Yet by careful and continuing evaluation of the available bits of information and by the application of such knowledge as we have of the economic and psychological causes of labor disputes in our own country, we may eventually catch a glimpse of the reality behind the Russian façade and help provide an answer to one of the major problems of our time.

CHAPTER 38 INDUSTRIAL CONFLICT—SWEDEN

Oliver A. Peterson *   *U.S. Department of State, Brussels*

Two thousand Stockholm building workers found themselves out on strike in 1882 without a union and without leadership. Anton Nyström, a young doctor who had been active in behalf of the workers, was called upon to chair the strike meeting, and in the absence of organization and a strike fund he urged the men to go back to work rather than die of starvation. Nyström advocated organization, and believing in "the harmony of interests," he urged an organization including workers and their employers.

Since Swedish employer-employee relations of today appear to be even more peaceful than those in some other countries, the casual observer may get the impression that Dr. Nyström's ideas have prevailed at last. Such is not the case, however.

There are many reasons for the peace that prevails, not the least of them being a high degree of labor-management statesmanship based in large part on a healthy respect for the strength of the other side. The 15 per cent of the employers who are organized account for 80 per cent of the country's private payroll, and in general, their industry-wide agreements set the pattern for the small and more numerous unorganized employers who deal with the same unions. Industrial workers are over 95 per cent organized, and the white-collar group about 50 per cent.

In a country roughly the size of California and with only two-thirds of its population, the Confederation of Employers, or SAF—the dominant employer organization, with forty member federations—has a strike fund with a kronor equivalent of 15 million dollars,[1] plus legally collectible strike-fund pledges from its members totaling 50 million dollars. The Confederation of Trade-unions—LO, membership 1,315,000—has a capital of almost 7 million dollars, and the forty-four national unions report over 40 million in addition. The Central Organization of Salaried Employees, TCO, and its forty-six white-collar unions with almost 300,000 members report strike funds and capital totaling about 6½ million dollars. In other words, labor and management believe in leading from strength. While they have demonstrated a predilection for peace, they believe in keeping their weapons at hand.

There has been a marked decline in the use of these weapons since the signing in 1938 of the so-called Saltsjöbaden Agreement between LO and SAF on the handling of industrial disputes. In only 4 of the succeeding 12 years did

---

* Formerly Labor Attaché, American Embassy, Stockholm.

[1] Figures converted at 5.18 Swedish crowns to the dollar. An upward adjustment of a third would give a better idea of the size of these funds.

the man-days lost through strikes exceed 100,000, including the big metal-workers' strike of 1945. In the 12 years immediately preceding Saltsjöbaden there were, by contrast, only 2 with losses under ½ million man-days. The all-time low came in 1950, with 5,900 man-days. Wildcat strikes are very rare. Further statistical elaboration could hardly be accepted as final evidence of the superiority of Sweden's top-level collective-bargaining and union-management centralization. Periods of prosperity and depression and the mere numerical growth of trade-unionism, to mention only two factors, would combine to make such efforts futile. Part of the answer would be found in an examination of each situation, and a cursory review reveals numerous instances where strong central authority preserved the peace.

Regardless of the reasons for the declining strike curve in Sweden, a note of caution is in order for those who read oversimplified accounts of Swedish practices and lightly assume they can be exported readily to other countries. The country is small; it possesses an abundance of natural resources, including water power; and it is almost self-sufficient as to food. The population presents a good record of literacy; and in addition to a high degree of religious homogeneity, there is an almost complete absence of rural-urban tensions. It should be pointed out, too, that it is about 140 years since Sweden has been at war, a fact of no little importance to domestic prosperity and industrial peace. These facts are not given to explain the present low incidence of industrial conflict but to point up the utter lack of comparability with a country like the United States, which was just getting its adventurous continent-wide start at a time when little Sweden had already been in business for some centuries.

Collective bargaining and labor practices are both nationwide and highly centralized. But while an autocratic rule tends to provoke counterpressure and aggression, the Swedish labor market is largely self-governing, legislation amounting to little more than a codification of existing and tested practices; this provides one clue to the relative absence of industrial conflict in present-day Sweden. It is not uncommon for legislation to be based word for word on labor-management agreements.

Legal Framework of Industrial Relations

The Collective Agreements Act and the Labor Court Act, both passed in 1928, are no exception to this general principle, although both were opposed at the outset by organized labor as dangerous and unwarranted state invasions of the labor market. Their purpose was to provide for the peaceful settlement of disputes involving interpretation of collective agreements freely made by voluntary associations of employers and workers.

The Collective Agreements Act specifically prohibits direct action for the purpose of (1) settling disputes over the interpretation or existence of an agreement, (2) effecting changes in a still-valid agreement, (3) forcing acceptance, during the validity of a contract, of terms for a future contract, or (4) supporting an illegal strike or lockout undertaken by others.

Although these disputes may be submitted to private arbitrators, both labor and management increasingly favor adjudication by the Labor Court.

Labor, although originally opposed to the establishment of the Labor Court, has brought in over four-fifths of the cases.

Another law, the Collective Bargaining Act of 1936, broadened the principle of labor-market self-government. It further strengthened freedom of association and empowered the Labor Court to require an employer to recognize and deal with a union, one of the purposes being to extend to the white-collar field the principle of voluntary association long recognized for manual workers. Agricultural workers were among the last to achieve the right of association through open conflict, some 20 years ago. In 1935 a special commission had reported widespread employer opposition to the organization of salaried employees, and it was argued that in this field striking to secure recognition could cause particularly serious disruptions. The Collective Bargaining Act thus substituted civil action in the Labor Court for open conflict in the labor market.

Effect of Institutional Security

Basic to the Swedish approach is the assumption that workers and employers should be organized. National unions cannot discharge their full responsibility by dealing only with individual employers, nor can employers share responsibility with masses of unorganized and leaderless individuals. Visitors are often surprised to hear Swedish employers say that they don't want unorganized workers. In the light of this philosophy, and given the present strength of the unions, Swedish labor can look with relative equanimity on practices and regulations that spell only trouble under other circumstances.

The SAF constitution, for instance, requires all collective agreements signed by its members to contain a provision "stipulating the right of the employer to engage and dismiss workers at his own discretion; to direct and allot the work; and to avail himself of workers belonging to any organization whatsoever, or to none." This open-shop clause constitutes no real threat to the unions; only in the case of Sweden's scarcely 20,000 Syndicalists is it a source of irritation. The SAF may impose a heavy fine on any of its members violating this provision. The unions respect it and sign union-shop agreements only with non-SAF employers.

The SAF constitution also contains a limited blacklist provision: "During a strike or lockout no employer affiliated with the Confederation through any one of his enterprises may, against the decision of the Board, either directly or indirectly, extend work or any other support to labor involved in the strike or lockout, or otherwise affected by the dispute." These are fighting words where labor is still seeking status, but Swedish unions can afford to look upon the provisions as legitimate rules of the game. They have ample assurance that employers in general and organized employers in particular want a strong and responsible trade-union movement.

An even more striking example of labor's calm in the face of usually disturbing developments was afforded in the summer and fall of 1951 when central negotiations between the Nurses' Union and the public hospitals broke down and several hundred nurses prepared to strike. The government prepared a bill providing for compulsory arbitration of the dispute. and the King called a special session of the Riksdag to act on it. Passage of the bill was accepted by Social Democratic organized labor as a foregone conclusion and was averted only by a last-minute agreement between the nurses and the hospitals. Labor's attitude throughout was marked by the feeling that collective agreements *can* be arrived at and by calm confidence that compulsory arbitration would not become general. In a roughly comparable situation in 1947 an affirmative decision was taken on compulsory arbitration for policemen but was never actually invoked.

Functions of the Labor Court

The Labor Court and the Conciliation Service represent the state's chief participation in regulation of the labor market. With the exception of the union-recognition cases noted above, the function of the Court is to adjudicate disputes involving interpretation of collective agreements. Its decisions are final and binding. Workers found guilty of violating a collective agreement may be fined up to 200 kronor each, but there is no stated limit to a fine that may be imposed on an employer. Reliance is placed on union and employer top organizations to make Court decisions effective, one result being that they exhaust all possibilities of settlement short of court action. While recourse to the Court is a relatively simple and inexpensive matter for cases that clearly come within its jurisdiction, its greatest value lies in its mere existence. Important also is the speed with which the Court acts, decisions often coming in a matter of weeks.

The Court is composed of seven members appointed by the Crown. Two each are nominated by management and labor, and three, including the chairman, by the government. The chairman and vice-chairman must have legal training and juridical experience, and the third public member must be a recognized expert in labor relations. Members or their alternates usually disqualify themselves in cases where they have a direct business or trade-union interest. It is significant that with a court of this composition almost all decisions are unanimous.

The Court has no function in situations arising from fruitless efforts to draw up a collective agreement. It is here that the Conciliation Service may act on its own initiative or may be brought in by management or by labor. Both sides are required to take part in the proceedings, but they are under no compulsion to reach an agreement. If conciliation fails, labor is free to resort to strike or management to a lockout, a 7-day notice being required.

For the purposes of the Conciliation Service the country is divided into eight districts, each under a part-time conciliator. Interdistrict cases or cases involving seamen come under the jurisdiction of the Social Board, which may appoint a special conciliator or a commission.

In its active promotion of the present stabilization program the government has sought to head off stalemates of this kind. Most contracts come up for renewal around the turn of the calendar year, and in the current period of overfull employment and inflationary tendencies the government schedules a series of advance conferences separately with SAF, LO, and TCO for discussion of the general economic situation and to secure the widest possible agreement on the problems anticipated. Management and labor thus get down to collective bargaining with the chances of stalemate and eventual open conflict greatly reduced.

Social Legislation in Sweden

Other participation by the government in labor-market management comes mainly under the heading of social protection, including regulation of hours of work, night work, hazardous employment, homework, and employment of women. It is interesting to note in this connection that the minimum paid vacation is not a matter for collective bargaining in this self-governing labor market. Vacation with pay is considered a socially desirable and necessary institution, and the 2-week vacation legislated in 1938 is being extended gradually to 3 weeks in 1953, under an amendment adopted in 1951. Collective agreements provide for paid vacations beyond the minimum, especially for salaried employees. Reference should be made also to the extensive state, provincial, and municipal programs in the fields of health, housing, and general welfare—programs that do much to solve problems that carry the germ of open conflict. Potential labor-market disputes are thus transferred readily to the legislative arena in cases where labor dominates not only the national but also the provincial and municipal administrations. Labor and management are agreed, however, on keeping governmental participation to a minimum. Some years ago nonlabor Social Democrats favored legislation designed to improve the lot of agricultural workers. The "trade-union way" was chosen, however, and the Union of Agricultural Workers has enjoyed a remarkable growth in numbers and influence. As in other European countries the labor movement made ample use of legislation in its fight against feudalism, but the high degree of unionization has led to more direct dealing with employers in the solution of modern labor-market problems.

LO and TCO voluntarily extended the 1948 wage agreements through 1949 and then through 1950, while the labor government undertook to stabilize the price level through price controls and subsidies on certain consumer items. With devaluation of the Swedish crown in 1949 the subsidies became especially important and were extended beyond the original expiration date. Local wage adjustments brought manual labor through with no loss, and upgrading of individual white-collar workers, especially in state employment, achieved roughly comparable results for them. It is doubtful that a nonlabor government could have secured the agreements in the first place or carried them through with equal success.

Although the farmers now participate in the government, the Social Democratic Party remains dominant and, as the political arm of the labor movement, is relied on for legislative solutions of many social issues. For instance, rather than make pensions a matter of collective bargaining as in the United States, an effort is being made to establish a universal old-age-insurance program. Unemployment insurance is left to the national unions under state supervision and with some state financial support. Under legislation dating from 1916 employers are required to carry adequate workmen's-compensation insurance.

Development of Joint Relations

While LO and SAF reached an agreement as long ago as 1906 on freedom to organize, it is obvious that industrial peace was still to be achieved. Witness the general strike of 1909. The Labor Court and Collective Agreements legislation of 1928 represented notable forward steps, but it may be said that the present era of labor-management relations dates from the Saltsjöbaden Agreement of 1938 for the peaceful handling of disputes. A government committee had been asked to study a series of proposals for legislative action on labor disputes, and while the committee was still at work, LO and SAF undertook a program of their own.

The resulting LO-SAF committee met off and on for 2 years and drafted a detailed agreement on procedures for the limitation of industrial conflict, including the thorny problem of job security, which underlay many disputes. The agreement requires ample advance notice of layoffs or discharges and specifically prohibits direct action for the purpose of forcing small family enterprises to hire outsiders. Sympathy strikes and lockouts are permitted, but not when in support of action taken in violation of a contract. An important element in the agreement is joint union-management concern for the maintenance of vital public functions and services. Although not formally incorporated into the agreement, attached minutes state that, when needed, strikers will take it upon themselves to perform work essential in preserving the plant and its machinery as well as materials and goods on hand.

The agreement provides that either party to a dispute may request that it be taken up centrally by LO and SAF for speedy solution. A joint Labor Market Board—not to be confused with the Royal Labor Market Board—was established for this purpose. It has been noted that under the SAF constitution employers retain the right to hire and fire without regard to union affiliation, and the Labor Market Board finds its most difficult work in matters involving job security. As in the case of the Labor Court, the real value of the Board is the fact of its existence, and relatively few cases have actually come before it—only fifteen since 1938.

The Saltsjöbaden Committee, named from its meeting place outside Stockholm, has continued its work, drawing up formal agreements on in-plant safety (1942), vocational training (1944), labor-management committees or enterprise councils (1946), and time-and-motion studies (1948). In the spring of 1951 the Committee drew up an agreement establishing an LO-SAF council to work on the employment problems of women, the purpose being to increase the effectiveness of this part of the labor force. These agreements take the form of recommendations to affiliated unions and employer groups for inclusion in their collective agreements.

The agreement on labor-management committees is perhaps the most significant of these, such committees being very important in the local application of the other agreements. Although the committees are only advisory and function under the usual prohibition against touching wages and other matters reserved for union-management negotiation, they are often used on problems which in the United States are handled by shop stewards and foremen, workers finding them "ready channels to the top."

The white-collar organization (TCO) is also a party to the agreement on labor-management committees, its Foreman's Union and the Union of Clerical and Technical Employees in Industry being especially interested and active. Both LO and SAF have full-time staff members on this program, and the new SAF school at Yxtaholm devotes the major part of its year-round 5-day residence courses to work in this field. The residence schools maintained by LO and TCO also devote considerable attention to the labor-management committee program, and LO as well as its individual national unions gives special technical assistance to committee members on an *ad hoc* basis.

Over 3,000 Swedish firms now have committees, and almost 500 firms with less than twenty-five workers have single worker representatives under the program. Well over half of the LO members are involved. It is admittedly a hothouse development—the Communists call it hot air—but one that promises to yield real dividends. A more detailed discussion of the program is found in Charles Myers's excellent report, *Industrial Relations in Sweden,* based on an intensive field study in the fall of 1950.

The Swedes make haste slowly, and the preparation of these agreements was sufficiently protracted to permit consultation with a wide circle on both sides, and the required ratification by affiliates in each case was almost a foregone conclusion. The same is true of the industry-wide bargaining that characterizes the management of the labor market.

Concentration of Authority

Even when making allowance for the democratic forms maintained with relative ease in a small and quiet country, the observer is impressed by the extent to which authority is concentrated in the central employer and labor organizations. This is especially true of SAF and, on the labor side, more pronounced in LO than in TCO.

Reference has been made to centrally controlled strike funds and to SAF prohibition of certain employer actions in conflict situations. Further restrictions may be mentioned at this point. While the lockout is a perfectly legitimate weapon when there is no contract in force, any individual employer or member association ordering a lockout without SAF approval forfeits lockout benefits and may, in addition, be subject to a heavy fine.

An employer member is not eligible for strike benefits if he "has taken unjustified measures which impaired the position of the workers and thereby proved to have caused or furthered the strike." Nor is he eligible if he has "refused to take measures requested by the Board or the General Council with the purpose of preventing or ending the strike." The SAF constitution also provides heavy penalties for the signing of a collective agreement without SAF Board approval. Withdrawal from SAF is strictly governed by requirements of advance notice that may run as high as 18 months, and LO as well as SAF hold the employer to the terms of existing collective agreements. Any penalties imposed by the SAF on its members are legally enforceable.

Centralization of authority is not so pronounced in LO as in SAF, but it is nevertheless much greater than in the AFL or the CIO. In the past the LO constitution required central approval of any strike involving 3 per cent or more of a national union's membership, when LO financial support was desired. This requirement received a close second look when in the spring of 1951 the Municipal Workers' Union staged a network of pin-point strikes involving less than 3 per cent of its membership but paralyzing certain services in several cities. There was no noticeable demand for "a law," but at the LO convention in September, 1951, the constitutional provision was quietly changed with scarcely a reference to the Municipal Workers' Union. The restriction was tightened to the point where virtually no strike may be called without top LO approval. This is not forthcoming unless central LO and other efforts have failed to secure a peaceful settlement. While constitutional restrictions of this kind are important, the moral influence of the central authority remains dominant.

The 1951 convention also approved the establishment of a central Collective Bargaining Council, with the task of making a careful study of the wage situation, notably of wage relations between industries and groups of workers within industries, and of preparing the recommendations which the LO General Council usually addressed to the unions on the eve of a new round of wage negotiations. The Collective Bargaining Council would advise the Executive Board and, by delegation, perform some of its advisory functions during the collective-bargaining season. The actual establishment of the Council was left to the Board, which, as expected, decided to postpone action for the upcoming negotiations and perform those functions itself with somewhat greater firmness than in the past.

In November, however, the General Council instructed the Board to undertake central negotiations with SAF, the guaranteeing of real wages being the central issue. An agreement was reached after 2 months of negotiations. In addition to a guarantee of real wages in the form of reopening rights in case employers do not increase wages in line with stated cost-of-living increases, the agreement put ceilings on initial wage increases and set a 17-day deadline for the conclusion of individual supporting agreements, LO and SAF to take over any negotiations not completed. The deadline as well as the wage ceilings were included at SAF's insistence. Before entering upon negotiations on these issues, the LO Board consulted the presidents of the LO affiliates, who in turn secured the consent of the majority of union boards. Only five unions were reported in opposition. The final agreement took the form of recommendations to labor and employer affiliates, and some unions reached immediate agreement within its framework, thus avoiding the necessity of delegating authority to the LO Board for the handling of unsolved issues.

The agreement was unprecedented as an example of centralized negotiations and greatly reduced the likelihood of open conflict in the settlement of wage disputes.

Labor's attack on the problem of jurisdictional disputes has necessitated increasing centralization of authority, involving the abandonment of certain forms usually associated with maintenance of democratic processes. As a consequence very few jurisdictional disputes have led to open conflict, the LO Board resolving all disputes between LO unions and a joint LO-TCO committee handling cases involving unions of the two confederations. The line of demarcation between the white-collar and manual-worker fields is not always clear, and with a different federation organizing in each of these areas there are bound to be disputes. It is usual to find three unions in an industrial plant—the appropriate LO industrial union, the TCO Union of Clerical and Technical Employees in Industry, and the Foremen's Union, also TCO. While industrial unionism is general, it does not extend across the line separating manual workers from those in the technical and white-collar field.

LO jurisdiction in a plant is determined without regard to worker preference, the general rule being that jurisdiction goes to the union showing the largest number of workers in its field. A group of workers involved in an impending transfer of jurisdiction recently queried LO on the possibilities of a plant election, but this was rejected as being irrelevant to the question of providing the best possible union representation for the whole plant. The program works under an LO requirement that every affiliated national union maintain constitutional provision for the acceptance or release of members ordered transferred. A worker moving to a plant under another union jurisdiction readily has his membership transferred, and in the course of a year a national union may have a turnover of hundreds or even thousands without material net change in its total membership.

Another example of centralization in LO is the requirement that the board of an affiliated national union must have final authority on collective agreements or strike calls. Membership referenda or the votes of representative councils or other bodies within the union can be only advisory. The only exception to this is on the calling of a special convention of the union. This may be brought about by a two-thirds vote of the members participating in a referendum arranged on petition by a stipulated number of members, an arrangement rendered the more necessary by the practice of holding conventions at intervals ranging from 3 to 5 years. Three unions have had conventions called in this way in the past 10 years.

Peculiar to Sweden's advanced stage of union organization is an LO requirement on its unions that membership be open to any qualified worker. The only exceptions are workers who, as members, could be expelled for strikebreaking or other equally serious offenses against organized labor.

Centrifugal Tendencies among Employers and Unions

There are only occasional signs of employer or union dissatisfaction with the policies and practices described above. The story is still current of the employer who, some 10 years ago, notified his association that he contemplated withdrawal to the greater freedom of independent existence. He changed his mind when he learned that the association would thereupon be disbanded. Certain employers presently enjoying unprecedented prosperity in export lines prefer a decontrolled labor market with more freedom to compete for labor but are deterred by a realization of what could happen to the whole economy. Then too there is only relatively less prosperity in other lines, and the effects on labor of the accompanying overfull employment make it a matter of pure self-interest to hold employer lines intact.

Several years ago the Masons' Union considered withdrawal from LO and queried the other unions on the type of cooperation that could be expected in the future. They all replied that cooperative relationships were maintained only within LO. Since it was LO policy to consider workers in other groups— the Syndicalists, for example—as unorganized workers, the masons drew their own conclusion and remained in LO.

LO maintains its traditional "solidaric wage policy," which means relatively larger increases for the low-wage groups that had been slowest in joining up. The result has been a certain amount of dissatisfaction with the small spread between skilled and unskilled wages. LO policy is popular with the low-wage groups, but unions in a relatively strong position vis-à-vis the employers show a decided unwillingness to go along. These divisive tendencies are weakened, however, when the Social Democratic leaders of these unions find it difficult to take a position publicly in opposition to the stabilization program promulgated and supported by LO and other Social Democratic government leaders. Recalcitrant unions thus find themselves challenged by LO and by the government as well as by the SAF.

The Communists no longer advocate dual unionism—peace and unity are watchwords here, as elsewhere—but they have, of course, not distinguished themselves in the art of avoiding industrial conflict. They can be given credit, although they don't dare claim it, for instigating and more often merely fanning little disputes that may eventuate in wildcat strikes of a few hours' or days' duration.

Only two of their operations have reached serious proportions: the legally engineered Metalworkers' strike of 1945, which was settled for what had been offered before the strike, and the wildcat longshoremen's strike in the spring of 1951. The 1945 strike almost ranks with Prague as a cause of Communist decline in Sweden. It is not altogether impossible that, by deliberately refraining from vetoing the strike, the Social Democratic leadership of the union gave the Communists enough rope to hang themselves. Over 11 million man-days were lost that year, second only to 1909, when the general strike brought work-time losses to almost 12 million man-days.

The longshoremen's strike came in the midst of negotiations for a new contract and was based on a number of legitimate grievances that made it difficult for the parent Transport Workers' Union to press its initial and justified charge that the Communists were the instigators. It spread from the Communist-dominated local at Göteborg when ships were turned away and sought to unload at ports where, in spite of grievances, the longshoremen had remained loyal to the union leadership engaged in the negotiations. But the longshoremen were being asked to serve as hated strikebreakers, and their own grievances were a factor in obscuring the nature of the strike—a case of conflicting loyalties serving the purposes of dissident and disruptive elements.

The tendency toward more severe and far-reaching strikes under a centralized system carries with it its own remedy. Disagreements at different times between a number of local nurses' unions and their respective employers would have caused no great stir and, at worst, a few local strikes, but the entire government entered the picture when a national union arranged the resignations of a few hundred nurses in key positions. And in the case of the municipal workers it took the deliberate crippling of selected public services by a powerful national union to bring from LO an effective prohibition of such actions in the future.

Reasons for Continued Success

There are several reasons for top management and labor ability to prevent centrifugal tendencies from gaining mastery within their respective groups. In the first place, internal disagreements and misunderstandings are kept to a minimum by elaborate and detailed consultations and clearance on policies and actions. On the labor side national unions prepare for collective bargaining by submitting detailed reports to the membership and by the convening of a "collective-bargaining conference" at which all locals are represented in proportion to their size.

Secondly, there are the highly developed educational programs of the unions and the less extensive but highly effective educational work developed by SAF. Under the impact of this educational work individual workers and employers come to recognize the necessity of dealing centrally with the increasingly complex domestic and international problems affecting the Swedish labor market. Backing up the workers' education activity at residence schools for the development of effective leaders is the extensive LO pamphleteering and the network of thirty-five daily labor newspapers, most of which are subsidized by the labor movement. Prominent in this activity is a running fight on Communism and heavy emphasis on cooperation for increased productivity. The result of all this is a feeling of solidarity capable of resisting attacks from all sides.

In the third place, the very experience of working together within one's own organization and with the opposite side has a civilizing effect notably absent where management and labor have had little successful experience in this field. Far from tolerating fragmentation and return to conflict relationships, the Swedes contemplate even further centralization and coordination of efforts.

Next, centralization, once started, inevitably calls for further centralization and the weakening of dissident elements within opposing groups. LO was organized in 1898, and SAF became necessary, coming in 1902. SAF's answer to centralization in LO was more centralization, and even with the steps taken in 1950 LO has not caught up. In any event, a present-day LO union could no more defy SAF than could an SAF affiliate or single employer challenge LO.

In the fifth place, not only has the influence of Communist strike agitators declined most drastically in the years since the Prague coup—the Communists now control no more than about 100 of LO's almost 9,000 locals—but with it has declined the tactical need for the Social Democratic trade-union and political leaders to make concessions to potential rebels: the Communist vote dropped from 11.2 per cent of the national vote in 1946 to a mere 4.9 per cent in 1950. The forthcoming 1952 elections are expected to show an even lower figure, the stepped-up "cultural" campaign from the East being more than offset by developments such as the spy cases currently shaking the country and by the intensified anti-Communist drive of the Social Democratic Party.

An important factor also is the general class consciousness of employer and worker groups. Cooperation is the watchword among employers who have gone to the same few schools, sit on the same business and government boards, and belong to the same clubs. On the other side, the unions have a powerful hold in a group where relatively few individuals rise above the position of foreman, although the sons of workers are increasingly receiving advanced training essential to greater advancement.

Equally important is the general atmosphere of the country: racial, religious, historical, and social homogeneity and a calm temper throughout. The national temperament that has combined with a certain amount of good luck to keep Sweden out of shooting wars for 140 years is admirably suited to the maintenance of organizational discipline essential to industrial peace. Centralization is no more disturbing than is, by now, the idea of a king in a country governed by Social Democracy.

It may be noted in addition that Marxism never went very deep in Sweden, where socialist pioneers are noted for their contributions to the solution of immediate problems rather than for the development of socialist theory. Present-day labor leaders complain that their comrades in other European countries spend valuable time developing theories when they should be getting on with the job of building their unions.

Swedish employers simply do not comprehend the antiunion attitude of employers in many other countries, and it may be said that their approach to industrial relations is at once a cause and a consequence of Swedish labor's approach. There are those who fear that the Swedish labor movement doesn't have much more to live for and is settling down into a comfortable old age at a time when the world is demanding the vigor and enthusiasm of youth striving for goals far beyond immediate grasp. Whether or not there is a basis for this fear, it is obvious that, *for Sweden's particular problems and conditions,* the workers and their management friends are developing a set of practices well designed for the maintenance of industrial peace.

PART **5** *INDUSTRIAL CONFLICT:*
THE PRESENT AND THE FUTURE

The Editors

W E CANNOT safely extrapolate from the past and present to provide a preview of the future in industrial relations. This is particularly true because there are now in the making fundamental changes in environmental factors that may prove as important as any of the developments foreseeable in the light of present conditions. The forces that determine labor-management relations not only are changing but are as complex as the society itself. Neat predictions based on unstated and unanalyzed assumptions are worthless. In large measure the future of industrial relations is an unknown, an emergent still to be decided by changing influences only dimly discernible. A simple projection of current trend lines appears most precarious.

It seems much wiser to inquire what the major determining forces and changing conditions are which must be assessed and continually reassessed as the intricate socioeconomic processes of the world work their way onward. This is not to imply a blind historical necessity. On the contrary, the processes involve at every turn essential factors of human intervention that express the shifting values, beliefs, and goals of the people and organizations concerned. There is need for constant study and weighing of evidence to determine the impact of changing influences and to judge the directions in which efforts have to be exerted if desired results are to ensue.

Industrial Relations in a Changing World

In the following pages we call attention to several of the major areas of change in our era and the unanswered problems dependent upon these changes. Any significant prognosis regarding industrial conflict and labor relations must rest upon the best assumptions we can make, however tentative, about the course of our society—whether free, democratic institutions will survive and flourish, whether atomic war will overwhelm our civilization, what further transformations may soon be precipitated by science and technology, whether we shall avoid economic depression, what far-reaching changes are already occurring in our social organization and in the characteristics and distribution of our population, and the effects of mass media and other instruments of education, propaganda, and social control.

Merely to ask questions concerning these matters, surely not an unrealistic enterprise in the present-day world, is to note the ephemeral and even superficial nature of much of the thinking and research on labor-management issues. It also suggests deep-cutting doubts in regard to any confident analysis of what lies ahead. This healthy skepticism itself, it is hoped, may arouse our society to the deeper understanding so poignantly needed if we are to find our way successfully through the present ominous and confused period. Problems of industrial conflict inevitably merge with problems of peace, democracy, economic stability, and the "good life."

Later sections of this chapter will deal more concretely with the outlook for the near-term future of industrial relations. But first we shall sketch portions of the larger and more speculative picture of pervasive changes that must at least give pause to the venturesome social prognosticator.

The Atomic and Electronic Age. Particularly in the area of technology will we have to speculate on the broad scale. Science and technology have already put us on the frontier of the newest industrial revolution. We can dimly see the outlines of this revolution in the making, and what is already evident is startling.

The peacetime utilization of atomic power sources points immediately to the obsolescence of traditional industries furnishing the motive power for our industrial civilization. Think what can happen to the skills and the work forces of the coal mines, the oil fields, the hydroelectric plants, and the steam-generating plants. And what about the allied industries, the barge lines and the pipelines, the coal-hauling railroads and the coal-distributing firms? Where is this skilled and specialized work force going to be absorbed in the society, and at what cost? Will the technologically displaced smash the atom smashers as their forebears attacked the machines of the first industrial revolution? While this extreme reaction appears highly improbable, the social system must be prepared to absorb considerable initial shock of transformation and to control the rate of innovation so as to minimize its disruptive impact.

Fortunately or unfortunately, atomic power is only the beginning of the revolution. We can produce "thinking machines," servomechanisms that reproduce many of the routine features of man's mind. Translated into production processes, these electronic devices challenge the very usefulness of large segments of our working population. The utility of a man on the production line or in a production process has come increasingly to depend not upon his physical strength or muscular coordination but upon his mind, which controls and directs the proper responses demanded in working behavior. Now machines have the potential of doing some of the more rudimentary thinking tasks of man and of carrying on sequences of operations with a minimum of human intervention. The possibility of technological displacement of industrial workers is staggering. And how totally different will be the technological skills and training necessary to direct and maintain the new workerless production operations.

Are there any threads of continuity between the present and the atomic and electronic future? Is our concern for the present in industrial relations only the fumbling of a tradition-bound outlook that cannot comprehend the future almost upon us? Is industrial conflict even an issue for the future, or will it be swept aside as irrelevant and meaningless by the new industrial technology and its accompanying social system? Electronic controls have no personality, no attitudes, no motives, no urges, no group affiliations, no morals, no ideology. Will the new society take on the imaginative pattern of Bellamy's *Looking Backward,* that classic and delightful utopia in which human work shrivels to insignificance and other human activities flower? Or will the new machines ultimately conquer man in the form of "Rossum's Universal Robots," as suggested in Čapek's fantasy drama *R.U.R.?*

All our questions take on the breathless character of science fiction because their answers are highly speculative. We know that the changes are already upon us. We cannot be even moderately certain of the responses of our social system to the revolution in technology. Nor can we adequately set forth the time schedule—the rate of change or the particular segments of society that will be affected first. We can only guess that 10 years from now the prototype of the new machines will be in operation; that 20 years hence the revolution will be evident to the man in the street; and that 50 years in the future substantial portions of Western technology will have been revolutionized.

What about industrial relations? It seems obvious that we can anticipate a sharp increase of attention to problems of technological change and its possible impact. It is also possible in the more distant future that the management and labor power elite of the present will be supplanted and subordinated to a scientific and technical elite. Is it possible that worker groups will cease to have meaning in our society because there will be so little human work to be done and that other kinds of interest groups will be contesting for social power? The single virtue of raising these speculative questions is to suggest the importance of a broad perspective that will be necessary to probe the wonders and terrors of the atomic and electronic future in the field of industrial relation as well as elsewhere.

War and Peace. In a more contemporary vein we can examine one major implication of war and peace for industrial relations in the United States. The war, cold and hot, has polarized the world into Communist and non-Communist sectors. What is the probable impact of this polarization upon the course of union-management relations?

At least in the United States we can expect management and labor to make common cause of anti-Communism. Communism has never gained a mass following in this country. It has succeeded in gaining only a temporary foothold in the leadership positions of several labor organizations and in a few organized groups in the arts and intellectual fields. The pressures against public identification with the Communist ideology are many. Federal, state and local legislators are actively Red hunting; the organs of mass communications are filled with anti-Communist pronouncements; all the symbolic values of our society have been mobilized in the fight. What remains of a genuine Communist apparatus is already underground and serving a conspiratorial purpose for its masters.

The country is partially mobilized in the economic and military sectors and more fully mobilized in the ideological sphere. The central consideration has already become the defense of a homeland, of an ideology, of a way of life. More intensive mobilization of ideas and emotions, rather than less, can be anticipated over the long period of international tension that probably lies ahead. There is at least a possibility that home-front activities will more and more take their cue and fall into perspective in relation to the overriding demands of the fight against the external foe. If the threat of atomic war becomes more imminent, it can be anticipated that, in the interests of ideological and emotional national accord, organized labor will be asked, along with other organized groups, to contribute to social unity by accepting home-front inconveniences. Labor and management will be under pressure to minimize industrial conflicts that have any conceivable relation to the fight against Communism, and even where a strike or an industrial dispute seems remote from the cold war, every effort will be made to clothe it with such significance in the interests of resolving the dispute.

To the extent that war fears grow more acute, we can expect a synthetic unity between management and unions that is largely negative in character. It is only in the face of the larger threat of Communism and war that the parties to industrial relations will seek more rapid and ready resolution of conflict situations. In so far as hopes for a peaceful world settlement diminish, exceptional pressure for industrial strength and unity is likely to be exerted by government and by public opinion.

So long, then, as the hot and cold war defines the major dimensions of contemporary social policy, we can expect that industrial relations will be importantly affected thereby. In an atmosphere of temporary cooperation and self-sacrifice, of a fear of rocking the boat lest the enemy benefit thereby, the tempo and intensity of industrial disputes are likely to diminish. However, the longer the emotional and ideological mobilization continues as a response to the war atmosphere, the greater will be the difficulty of maintaining relative industrial peace. The evidence of the increasing industrial unrest toward the end of World War II is suggestive on this point.

The Social Structure. The population of the United States is increasingly to be found in urban areas. Each census has revealed a higher proportion of the population living in urban centers, until by 1950 almost two out of every three citizens lived in areas classified as urban. The transformation of our society from a rural to an urban orientation has had at least two consequences of significance to industrial relations: (1) The structural stability of the social system is usually affected by urbanization, and with it can come repercussions in industrial relations. (2) The elements that make for consensus at the level of sentiments and ideology are modified by the urban environment, and this too can have an impact upon industrial relations.[1] Since urbanization will continue to develop in intensity if not in extent, it will be important to examine these two general points.

The urban environment is one in which the traditional institutional associations and primary relations of the individual living a rural way of life are translated into relationships with other kinds of social units. It is in the urban environment that we find a vast proliferation of all kinds of groups having special and narrow interests. There is an organized group that stands ready to function in any nook and cranny of the individual's life. Where the rural man may belong to a church, a farmers' association, a political party, and a lodge, his urban brother is likely to add to these a large number of additional associations, more specialized and more superficial, that fill his life with group activity. It is perhaps suggestive to put the situation as follows: The broad

---

[1] Some of the summary ideas suggested here are considered more fully in the report of the Corning Conference. See Eugene Staley (ed.), *Creating an Industrial Civilization*, New York, Harper, 1952.

relationships with institutions of the rural man become the narrow segmentalized relationships with organized groups for the urban citizen.

The urban man is known to his fellows by the organizations of which he is a part. Indeed, it is through these organizations and group associations that one's position is largely defined in the social structure. As the late Prof. Louis Wirth suggestively noted, "What a man belongs to constitutes most of his life career and all of his obituary."

The union has the potential of being one of the central associations of the urban environment. It can provide a point of social identification in the anonymous urban world. Furthermore, the union can provide a social unit to which the individual can rally with some enthusiasm, since the union can be a primary agent for defining a man's relationship with his source of livelihood. The opportunity for the union to provide a central associational affiliation for its members and, through that, a "way of life" is largely an unrealized potential. Should this potential even partially be realized, the union movement would be substantially strengthened and the union, as one of the newer structural units of the social system, would play an increasingly central role. The social system has become sufficiently open so that interest groups can supplant institutional associations, like the church, as foci of loyalties and social action. Strong counterpressures, however, have operated to keep the labor union from becoming so central in working people's lives, especially in large cities. The dispersion, heterogeneity, and divisive forces among union members, the competing attractions, and the narrow economic interest traditionally represented by the union—all impose serious interferences. It remains problematic whether unions will come to occupy a more rounded and significant place in the life of its members.

Our second major point about the urbanization of the population is that this modifies the basis of consensus among the citizens of the society. The urban environment is the mart of new ideas where the traditional is minimized or, at least, thrown into sharp relief and contrasted with innovations. The very narrowness of interests around which groups form contributes to the possibility of new ideas being advanced. Indeed, the unique idea, the different mode of phrasing an idea, may become the rallying point for a group, as with the "isms" of the arts or sectarianism in religion. The vast physical mobility of our population, with millions of our people constantly on the move between states, between their rural birthplaces and their urban job opportunities, and between the older industrial centers and the new, makes for greater opportunity of exposure to new ideas and a higher probability that the traditional ideas will be weakened in their hold upon the individual.

The urban environment is experimental in character, producing few permanent new ideas, but trying many and discarding the failures. In this experimental, heterogeneous environment the sense of community is likely to be minimized. The common sentiments and common understandings (the sociologist's "folkways") that serve to define the participants in the community and its boundaries have difficulty in developing. In short, community-wide consensus develops only with difficulty, and its place is largely taken by interest-group consensus, which is often much narrower in coverage of ideas and number of participants.

We can expect a great deal more social invention in the field of industrial relations because of the minimum dependence upon tradition and the experimental character of the urban community. Just as "fringe benefits" were an untried experiment only a few short years ago and have now become standard, so can we expect other developments and inventions to arise in collective bargaining and personnel administration. Likely areas of development are annual wages, humanizing industrial engineering, new procedures for building morale, and motivation and codetermination of the firm's policies, just to mention a few of the more obvious possibilities. It seems safe to predict that there will be a high rate of invention of new ideas and new techniques in the industrial-relations field.

The Changing Sociopolitical Scene. That we live in a period of rapid change and social uncertainties has become a truism. The unsettled sociopolitical temper of the times is in major degree a consequence of the ongoing technological revolution, the international tensions, and the population shifts discussed in preceding pages. These, along with other historical influences, have produced confusion and contradictions in public opinion and an ambiguity of political values and trends. Yet it is these very political changes in the making that must profoundly affect the course of labor relations.

It cannot be too often repeated that what labor and employers feel impelled to do in their relationships is determined not by simple economic necessities—by gains or losses of given magnitude, by imperatives which external situations impose—but by the perceived impact of the changes in relation to what people have come to desire and expect, to feel "right" and "fair." These aroused wants and beliefs depend on currently accepted social interpretations and on what types of social action are sanctioned, what symbols are popular, what leadership is available, and what group pressures operate most forcefully. In a very real sense the road ahead for industrial relations will be determined by what the public comes to believe, by political ideals and ideologies, and by the values and social philosophy that prove most appealing. And it is precisely here that the uncertainties of prediction appear most formidable.

Consider a few of the current unresolved alternatives with which American minds are struggling. Who can solve the following problems with confidence: whether we are entering a period in which we shall have expanded or curtailed freedom for social change and experimentation; whether the trend will be toward increasing thought control, conformism, and anti-intellectualism or whether the pendulum will swing in the opposite direction; whether we are moving toward greater amounts of genuine democratic participation and sharing of power or whether these are pretty words which will mask the use of "administrative skills" and new techniques of persuasion or manipulation by sophisticated elites; whether or not—and to what extent—the control of the opinion-forming industry will be one-sided, permitting propaganda to exert its power unchallenged by counterpropaganda; and whether the political drift is to be in a conservative or liberal direction, whether toward "socialism" or "fascism" or neither. Then add the question of what happens in all these respects in event of a third world war—or in case "merely" of an economic depression.

All such questioning we believe supports at least these two conclusions for present purposes: First, it dictates utmost caution in thinking that we know which road lies ahead for industrial relations. The second conclusion is that, in considering the course of industrial relations, the whole big social picture needs to be kept in view and the changing picture must be constantly appraised and reappraised in order to judge (1) what is likely to be around the next corner in respect to industrial conflict and (2) what efforts are appropriate either to advance or to block the perceived trend.

The changing sociopolitical scene is, of course, both cause and effect of labor and management activities. While industrial-conflict behavior is largely dependent on the thought patterns and on the formal and informal social controls of the society, these beliefs and social pressures are themselves affected in significant measure by the active participation of unions and business in the sociopolitical process. Organized labor and management compete for public approval, political favor, and desired governmental actions as well as for direct industrial objectives. In this competition it can scarcely be questioned that the business viewpoint, the social interpretations and values congenial to management, are the ones predominantly circulated. Since the media of mass communication are preponderantly in the hands of businessmen and depend on the support of management interests (advertisers), this tends almost inevitably to be the case. Moreover, influence in support of management philosophy, aims, and outlook must be reckoned with in many other quarters—schools and colleges, churches, political parties, everywhere that the prestige and power of wealth are felt. In all these directions labor unions and their allies exercise a certain amount of offsetting influence. One of the profoundly important uncertainties of the period ahead is the question of how strong and effective these balancing propaganda, educational, and political programs will prove to be.

We shall return to the far-reaching implications of these considerations in the final chapter. At this point our concern has been simply to suggest as major determinants of industrial relations the vast importance of the sociopolitical climate and the conscious influences exerted in manipulating it.

Extension of the Collective-bargaining System

These next sections are written on the assumption that no drastic social changes will occur during the near-term future. They deal with labor-management relations as they now exist and as they are currently being modified. Obviously, in the context of the preceding pages, the reader is warned to regard this depiction of what lies ahead as most tentative and subject to important reservations in terms of the changed conditions that may occur over the longer period.

One possible course for the future is the further extension of the collective-bargaining system along its present lines. If we assume no drastic social changes, it seems likely that this will occur, regardless of whether alternative courses (such as greater government participation) are followed at the same time. What specific developments in collective bargaining as a means of handling issues and controversies between labor and management can be expected during the next decade or so?

Sooner or later there will probably be another spurt in union membership, which tends to grow jerkily with intervening periods of stability or decline. There have been four spurts of union growth thus far in the 20th century: (1) 1900–1904, when membership reached 2,073,000; (2) 1916–1920, with a peak of 5,048,000; (3) 1936–1938, when the total reached 8,000,000; and (4) 1940–1944, at the end of which there were an estimated 13,750,000 union members. At the end of 1952 official membership claims aggregated 15 to 16 million, but the real total was probably smaller. Of course, there is no proof that additional waves of organization will take place, but this seems probable because at least 65 per cent of all wage and salary earners are still nonunion, including most office workers, salespeople, agricultural laborers, and financial employees.

Another aspect of growth would be in the scope of collective agreements. There was a time when bargaining was confined primarily to general wage changes and closed-shop commitments. Today's bargaining, in contrast, leads to elaborate written agreements, often covering the most intimate details of wage administration, complex systems of conditional employment rights, manifold overtime- and premium-pay provisions, retirement benefits, and various types of insurance. Up to now it has never been possible to obtain agreement on a set of "management prerogatives" which are exempt from bargaining; and while there is no strong tendency for unions to seek to bargain over prices, production levels, and other matters outside the field of personnel administration, neither is there any indication that a saturation point has been reached within the personnel area—witness the insistent demand for guaranteed wage or employment provisions.

Jurisdictional patterns will probably be further stabilized over the years. Although official jurisdictional claims of unions still overlap greatly and although there is little likelihood of an amalgamation between AFL and CIO, nevertheless there has been a pronounced "settling" of bargaining rights since the early 1940's. The only significant change in recent years is that some of the left-wing unions have been dismembered and various right-wing unions have picked up the pieces. Otherwise one seldom sees a large bargaining unit shifting from one union to another today, although this was common in the early years of the Wagner Act. The AFL Seafarers' Union has the West Coast, the CIO Maritime Union has the East Coast. The Machinists have some airframe plants, the Automobile Workers have others. No large plants have dropped or changed their union affiliations under the decertification procedure of the Taft-Hartley Act; several "no-raiding" agreements between unions have been signed; and both the AFL construction unions and the CIO have established machinery for determining jurisdictional disputes. These developments have been facilitated by the continued spread of "union-security" clauses; by 1952 more than 60 per cent of workers under union agreement were covered by union-shop, closed-shop, or preferential-hiring arrangements, although some of these were technically illegal. The *de facto* stabilization of bargaining rights, should it continue, will be conducive to more peaceful union-management relations, since interunion rivalry has pronounced unsettling effects.

Labor-management relations will doubtless continue to "mature" as the parties accumulate more experience in dealing with each other. Maturity in industrial relations is a difficult concept to elucidate. It seems to be compounded of attitudes which are conducive to harmonious coexistence, procedures and practices which are productive of agreement, and a habit of self-reliance which is generated by success in solving problems jointly. Considering the large measure of accommodation between employers and unions in many major industries (such as rubber, autos, clothing, and West Coast longshoring) since the 1930's, it is reasonable to expect similar adjustment elsewhere, provided that circumstances are at all favorable. Sometimes maturity comes only after painful experiences: relations in the auto industry improved notably after the General Motors strike of 1945–1946; and similar improvement can be hoped for after the steel debacle of 1952, which was the fifth major controversy to be thrown in the government's lap by the parties in that industry since 1940.

In the process of accommodation numerous supposedly irreconcilable conflicts of principle have been reconciled. Some 40 years ago Robert F. Hoxie, a pioneer student of the labor movement, concluded that trade-unionism and scientific management were incompatible. Since then job evaluation, time study, employee merit ratings, and other appurtenances of scientific management have been absorbed into the collective-bargaining system, and today we seldom hear of any alleged incompatibility. In fact the scientific management of 1912 was not compatible with the trade-unionism of 1912, but both have changed greatly in the meanwhile. At one time unionism was regarded as a serious threat to industrial discipline, and discipline did break down in many newly organized plants. But where industrial relations have matured, discipline has been reintegrated into collective bargaining. Concepts of due process and consistency have been introduced, and on the other hand, many employer concepts of shop administration have been accepted in union circles. This is particularly true as to various obligations of an employee—to render continuous service during the period of an agreement, to meet established production standards, to obey instructions from supervision, and to observe shop rules. Even the age-old controversy over union security is yielding to compromise as various modifications of the union shop are devised in order to meet employer objections and still satisfy the union's purposes.

Hoarse cries of "sellout" have generally pursued those firms and unions which have taken the lead in the accommodative process. The garment unions have been attacked for promoting piece-rate methods of payment in the 1920's, United States Steel for recognizing the Steelworkers in 1937, Ford Motor for granting the union shop in 1941, the Automobile Workers for signing a long-term agreement in 1950, and General Motors for adopting the "annual improvement factor" in 1948 and again in 1950. But collective bargaining cannot prosper if theories or principles are followed to their logical conclusion, because it is a device for smudging differences of principle rather than preserving them. It can be expected that today's "irreconcilable conflicts" will eventually meet the same fate as those of a generation ago.

To point out that compromise is a form of progress and that many issues are eventually resolved is not to predict that peace and quiet will settle down upon the labor-management community. Indeed there is no reason to believe that this will occur. Old issues and conflicts are superseded by new ones, which are drawn into the shifting flux of power relationships between unions and firms and within the labor movement. Discontent is the normal condition of mankind, and the demands which workers can make upon the economic system are potentially limitless. One should not suppose, for example, that the type of "health-and-welfare" plan presently included in many collective agreements will be deemed satisfactory for any long period of time. Power relations between labor and management are inherently unstable and are constantly unsettled by changes in technology, market relationships, public opinion, executive personnel of companies and unions, general business conditions, political power, legislation, and judicial interpretation. As Prof. Blumer [2] stated some years ago, "We deceive ourselves and perhaps engage in wishful thinking when we regard this shifting flow of relations in industry as temporary and transitory, to be followed by a shaking down of relationships into a permanent orderly system."

Moreover, despite the working of the "iron law of oligarchy" within union organizations, which facilitates hegemony of entrenched leadership groups, revolts and secessions do occur, as indicated by recent experience in the Textile Workers Union.

> No leadership is eternal and no social structure unchanging. . . . As the corroding influences in the course of time take their toll of the established leadership, new potential leaders begin to press from below for preferred positions. If entrance to the cadre of the élite is not altogether closed . . . then that society [or union] experiences an orderly peaceful development. . . . If the door to leadership opportunities is closed shut, however, then violence and revolutions ensue.[3]

One cannot define at this time the issues and problems on which the power struggles of the future will turn, but that there will be such issues, problems, and struggles is the lesson of history.

Personnel Administration as a Solution to Conflict

The problems of preventing industrial conflict or keeping it within bounds and of maintaining organizational harmony and morale—these are generally considered major responsibilities of management. Running an enterprise means not only getting out the day's production but also keeping human relations on an even keel. Traditionally, enlightened executives have felt that it was up to them alone to work out the best answers to these personnel problems. Now under new pressures exerted by unionism and increased governmental controls, the question is how management can adapt its procedures to the new conditions and how effectively it can work with unions in achieving satisfying and productive human conditions in industry. Those phases of personnel management and of welfare activities which have utilized more or less paternalistic methods are almost certain to be less successful in the present period. New emphasis is bound to be placed upon programs by which management and labor unions jointly determine procedures for avoiding conflict and for dealing

---

[2] Herbert Blumer, "Sociological Theory in Industrial Relations," *American Sociological Review,* Vol. 12 (June, 1947).

[3] Joseph Rosenfarb, *Freedom and the Administrative State,* New York, Harper, 1948, pp. 106, 108.

with it. The question of central interest here is the extent to which management's efforts, both the programs it carries on independently and those in which the union participates, will provide answers to the problem of industrial conflict.

Corporations are devoting ever greater attention to personnel administration—and, especially in recent years, to problems of human relations. These management activities are based on the premise that productive efficiency and, hence, the survival and profitability of the business depend in significant degree on the morale of the work force. "Productive efficiency" here refers not only to the performance level of workers but to labor turnover, absenteeism, grievances, waste and sabotage, strikes, and every other expression of apathy or hostility that interferes with the organization's effectiveness. The activities cover a wide range: employing qualified workers and seeing that they are properly trained and supervised, that their pay is satisfactory, and that they have suitable hours, conditions of work, and arrangements for health and safety; giving employees opportunities for personal development and advancement, steady work, and agreeable relations with fellow employees and bosses; seeing that they can voice their ideas and their grievances and have these fairly dealt with and that they can feel themselves part of a good and useful organization; and seeing that facilities are available for recreation, welfare, and counsel and help in meeting personal problems.

Any such listing as this represents one way of looking at personnel management, but it omits the key element of "personnel spirit." Just about everything that management does has its impact on attitudes and human relationships within the organization and, hence, makes for greater harmony or greater conflict. Personnel-minded executives learn to consider every policy and act from the standpoint of how it will affect employees, whether it will make sense to them and be acceptable or whether it should be done in a different manner. They are alert to the hopes and fears of working people; they try to deal with them as rounded human beings. The separate personnel practices are likely to succeed or fail to the extent that this spirit prevails.

Personnel management typically proceeds on the assumption that the interests of employer and employee are fundamentally harmonious. While it is accepted that serious strife arises at times over wages and other terms of employment, this is considered unnecessary and something to be prevented by more effective personnel administration, including good treatment in respect to basic employment conditions. It is now quite generally accepted that human-relations programs are never a substitute for sound economic relationships. Geraniums in the plant windows and a turkey for Christmas do not make up for substandard pay. According to this conception, then, it is management's responsibility to treat employees fairly and well, within the limits of its ability to do so, and to have the employees understand that the company is doing all it can for them. It is contended that, by working together wholeheartedly for the good of the enterprise, employer and employees will both benefit. The viewpoint is that of the enlightened executive trying to run the organization smoothly, by persuasion and by timely adjustment of differences rather than by exercise of arbitrary authority.

Where strong unions exist, management's personnel activities must be such that they can stand up under union questioning and attack. Employees must be kept satisfied in order that neither basis nor excuse will be provided for new union demands. This task becomes more difficult as the workers feel more independent and as their expectations are aroused by union promises and union accomplishments. Management's persuasions lose some of their strength since they are now offset by the union's arguments. These consequences occur whether the union is already in the plant or stands outside waiting to organize the employees when a favorable opportunity arises. The new position of unions means that, even where they play no direct part, personnel management is under constant pressure to meet the union challenge.

As these last observations indicate, management's attempts to mitigate industrial conflict by means of personnel administration and the human-relations approach do not escape the problems imposed by labor's and management's divergent aims. The question here is not whether, in spite of some differences of viewpoint and objective, both groups can perceive beneficial effects from enlightened personnel procedures. We are asking, rather, whether these activities contain an effective answer to industrial conflict. They may produce valuable results in terms of the health, welfare, and advancement of employees as well as contribute to productivity and yet fail to reduce conflict. It is possible, indeed, for employer actions to exacerbate dissatisfaction and conflict. And it is also possible for conflict to be decreased in a manner that represents not improved understanding and constructive, accommodative adjustments between the parties but management's achievement of a position in which it can dominate industrial relations and prevent effective pressing of opposed demands.

The possibilities of conflict arising with respect to management's personnel activities may be seen more concretely if we consider the usual orientation of the personnel philosophy. We shall mention four such roots of conflict. First is the fact that management's basic aim of securing employee loyalty to the company readily, if not necessarily, leads to competition with the union for the worker's primary support and allegiance. Efforts to create high company morale easily merge into attempts to make employees "management-minded" in a manner that implies no opposition of interests and no need for the union. A wedge is inserted between union members and union leaders, and management tries to appear responsible for beneficial changes rather than letting the union receive credit.

A second emphasis that comes into conflict with the usual labor-union position is the stressing of *individual* motivation as against group security and group gains. Personnel administration, in its attention to individual differences, reward for merit, and personal competitive achievement, tends to play down objectives central to the union's purposes—protection and advancement for the whole group of employees and for all similar workers over the long run as well as immediately.

A third contrast is present in management's focus on employee relations in the company and on matters under its control, while the union is concerned equally with industry-wide improvements and with economic and political conditions affecting labor as a whole.

The fourth element of personnel philosophy to be mentioned in this connection is the contention that management's right to manage should remain unchanged, or as nearly unchanged as possible. The union's increasing involvement in personnel matters is ordinarily resisted as long as it can be, and each new "encroachment" is accepted only as the pressures of the situation require.

The amount of emphasis on these management aims, as opposed to union objectives, differs greatly from company to company and from year to year. In weighing management programs from the standpoint of their effects on industrial conflict, we may distinguish at least four main types of situation:

1. Management continues to oppose the union (whether already "recognized" or not) and uses its personnel administration as an instrument to weaken the union, to win (back) the workers, and if possible, to get rid of the union.

2. Management accepts the union and makes no attempt to undermine or weaken it but conducts its personnel activities as fully as possible "on its own," with as little "interference" from the union as it can manage.

3. Management accepts the union, encourages collective bargaining in respect to personnel policies, and welcomes some degree of joint participation by the union in personnel operations.

4. Management accepts the union and tries to develop union-management cooperation in respect to a wide variety of functions pertaining to improvement of production as well as to personnel matters.

The first of these four alternatives is now rarely practiced or advocated in the main centers of American industry. In smaller concerns, in areas where labor organization remains weak, and in certain other special cases, personnel administration may be thus utilized as an adjunct in the effort to avoid or destroy unions. This type of employer approach successfully reduces conflict under those special circumstances where the unions at least temporarily withdraw in defeat and the company is able to hold the allegiance of its employees. With the general growth and acceptance of unions, this path to industrial peace seems destined to remain a minor side road. While in particular contexts it may bring relative freedom from conflict, this achievement either depends on accepting accommodations arrived at through conflict waged elsewhere (living up to pattern-setting situations) and, hence, does not imply general diminution of conflict, or it results from local governmental and public-opinion support for antiunion tactics. There seems extremely little probability that sentiment against unions will become widely or strongly enough expressed to make "union busting" a major attempted solution to the problem of industrial conflict. But the possibility is certainly not one to be entirely dismissed.

The last of the four relationships listed above is still more limited at present. Comprehensive and genuine union-management cooperation plans have been confined to smaller companies and are usually entered into by management only under conditions of economic stress and obvious need for the union's assistance in meeting production or financial problems. No tendency is observable for these plans to be adopted by the main stream of large-scale American industry. This is not to say that there is no increase in "cooperative" arrangements for handling specific matters such as layoffs, pensions, accident prevention, etc. (these efforts fall into category 3 of the fourfold classification), nor does it refer to programs of employee (not union) cooperation unilaterally introduced by management as techniques for improving workers' satisfaction and morale (these are parts of management's personnel- or employee-relations procedures and usually would belong under category 2). While the scattered instances of success where true union-management cooperation is involved do represent interesting curtailments of conflict, this successful pattern cannot safely be extrapolated to industry as a whole for several reasons: (1) The cooperation plans, to start with, presuppose the existence of special conditions favoring the acceptance of harmonious solutions and of willingness to make concessions. Moreover, continued cooperation usually rests on demonstrated financial advantages over competitors who do not have cooperation plans—which presents the interesting question of what would happen if cooperation were to spread to most of industry so that the exceptions become the rule. (2) The cooperative situations are ones where peaceful relations are maintained partly because wage patterns and other basic matters are established elsewhere as a result of conflict. (3) In most labor-management situations one or the other party or both are deterred from cooperation programs by fear of long-run effects on their relative power positions. Management representatives fear that they will sacrifice rights and freedom of action or be accused of such sacrifice; union leaders fear the charge of sellout and the actual or alleged loss of the union's fighting strength.

Situations of types 2 and 3 in our classification are the main present labor-relations contexts within which personnel administration is carried on in large organizations. In the absence of systematic evidence we can merely suggest what appear to be reasonable speculations as to the impact of personnel work on industrial conflict under these two sets of relationships. When management operates as independently of the union as it can (category 2 above), we would expect conflict to be reduced to the degree that management is able to gain from employees general acceptance and support of its point of view. This would imply the absence of a labor union willing and able to press the aims of employees in opposition to those of management or, at least, the existence of superior power and influencing effectiveness on the part of the company vis-à-vis the union—and, presumably, it would also imply a favorable sociopolitical atmosphere for promulgating management's philosophy. Conversely, if labor organizations are active and influential in the particular situation or in the larger economic and political environment, then management's attempts to cultivate loyalty and harmony by unilateral employee-relations activities that bypass the union are likely to provoke resentment and to increase conflict.

Here again, moreover, we face the grave question of whether mitigation of conflict is a sound social objective if the peace is imposed from above or is "put over" by means of one-sided controls. If the aim is peace with justice, a peaceful relationship that provides for growth and adjustment to change, we may well ask whether the parties must not each participate sufficiently in the control of the relationship to ensure that its interests are fully represented and that neither party is constrained to accept the dictates of the other. To the extent that this doctrine of democratic rights pervades the thinking of unions and the public, it becomes doubtful that management can achieve industrial peace by personnel administration that aims to avoid union participation. Adherence to this doctrine, however, is itself a changing matter and one difficult to assess. Consequently, we have to recognize that the development of employee relations along lines that not merely seek freedom from conflict but provide methods at the same time for constructively facing and resolving conflict will depend upon the whole society's structure of attitudes and beliefs regarding democratic participation and the role of labor unions as instrumentalities of such participation.

The long-term trend seems to be toward a wider acceptance of labor organizations as part of an emerging system of representative government in the sphere of industrial relations. This trend would point to the kind of employee-relations context suggested in category 3 of our earlier classification—an expansion of collective bargaining in respect to personnel policies and increased participation by the union in personnel operations. What can one say as to the effects of this type of personnel development on industrial conflict? Principally this, that the answer is bound up with the effects of collective bargaining in general. In so far as collective bargaining is made to work successfully as a procedure for dealing with opposed interests and divergent aims, personnel functions conducted within this same framework may likewise be expected to find appropriate accommodations. Personnel programs jointly controlled by management and union may, in turn, contribute positively to smoother, more peaceful bargaining through fostering a more friendly spirit, a recognition of common as well as opposed interests, and an increased sense of responsibility on the part of union representatives. It seems clear, however, that the partnership arrangement still contains divisive elements of the kind earlier discussed and that no necessary or automatic decrease in conflict derives from such efforts.

Whether personnel and human relations activities do, in fact, make for peace or conflict depends upon how they are conducted and how they are perceived by the people affected. The procedures must be appropriate to the current attitudes and expectations of employees, union officials, and public. In the present period it has become especially unlikely that the more superficial forms of employee-relations work can operate effectively to remove conflict. Oppositions of working people to particular management policies cannot be talked out of existence or dismissed as matters of interpersonal misunderstanding. Disharmonies cannot be treated as though there is nothing involved that a tactful management and a good battery of personnel techniques will not cure. Personnel administration functions as one component in the entire labor-management relationship; its results are determined by the satisfactoriness of that whole relationship. And the whole includes prominently the pattern and the spirit of collective bargaining in the particular company and in the industry, as well as the economic and political conditions affecting the position of labor generally.

Specific personnel programs that are successful at one time and place may fail dismally at other times and places. The social interpretations that are current, the expectations that are aroused, and the subtle implications and overtones of management's moves often become the decisive factors. For these reasons constant reference to the sentiments of employees and to the position of union leaders is indispensable. The selfsame human-relations activities may meet with enthusiastic response or may be damned as paternalistic, calculating, and manipulative. While the difference sometimes lies in the activities themselves, it is in great degree a product of the prevailing values and philosophy, of the structure of sentiments upon which the activities impinge. Even highly desirable benefits may provoke dissatisfaction and conflict if they come through processes that are distasteful to workers. Independent effective participation by their own organization may itself become a vital goal—with all the implications this participation carries for future protection and further advances. Such considerations suggest the probability that the future of management's personnel efforts will largely be determined by the basic outlook that emerges in the society as a whole as to what is fair and just in regard to the control of management-worker relations and in regard to the role of unions as participants in this process.

Government Intervention

Another possibility to be examined is that government will participate ever more actively in the sphere of industrial relations. We have noted the extensive degree of participation which already exists. Government polices industrial conflict by prohibiting some practices (*e.g.* discriminatory discharges and secondary boycotts) and by regulating others (*e.g.* picketing). It provides a peaceful procedure for certifying and decertifying unions as bargaining agents. It endeavors to maintain production when it fears that interruption would create an emergency. It undertakes to limit wage increases and settle industrial disputes in periods of war. It prohibits the parties from adopting some terms of employment deemed contrary to public policy (*e.g.* the closed shop and featherbedding provisions). It affirmatively requires other terms of employment deemed essential to public policy (*e.g.* minimum wages). Finally, the government organizes insurance systems to provide against various economic risks (*e.g.* unemployment compensation and old-age insurance) and endeavors to provide jobs in periods of unemployment.

In discussing the likelihood of greater or lesser government activity in the future, we must take note of the situation in 1954. Current opinion is running strongly against public intervention in industrial conflict as well as in other phases of economic life. Strong preference is almost universally expressed in favor of handling issues and problems privately. While there are good reasons to fear undue concentration of authority in Washington and excessive reliance on government at any time, it is wise to recognize certain special reasons for the unusual vigor of antigovernment sentiment at the present time. We have come to the end of a 20-year period in which doubtful questions as to the advisability of government action were generally resolved in the affirmative; and a recoil was inevitable. Federal handling of major industrial disputes has often worked out badly in recent years, with the 1952 steel case a particular fiasco. Wage and price controls are currently in disrepute, probably because they were unwisely continued in effect after the need had evaporated. Moreover, the fact is that the occasion for government intervention in matters affecting employment is at a low ebb. The level of employment has been high for many years. Much progress has been made in reducing the incidence of poverty; labor-management relations are relatively stable, with no significant organizing conflicts in progress. Most firms have been sufficiently well off to grant wage increases and other benefits large enough to satisfy most unions. Certainly the government has contributed to the present situation through reform measures and through war and defense spending. Nevertheless, the situation, regardless of its causes, is one in which government activity is naturally deprecated.

There have been other periods, such as the 1920's, during which the need for public intervention was weak and, in consequence, antigovernment sentiment was strong. When conditions changed, ideas did likewise. This suggests that the growth of government activity in the United States has not really represented the unfolding of any formal ideology but instead a response to problems and pressures demanding attention. So it is likely to be in the future. It is also worth noting that government intervention in the labor market has increased at the same time as collective-bargaining arrangements have expanded. The two are discordant in an ultimate sense, but history is careless of ultimates. Thus it is postulated in the theory of collective bargaining that private decisions are superior to imposed solutions and that the collective-bargaining system must be protected against outside interference; yet there would probably be less collective bargaining today had there not been outside interference a few years ago. Therefore, while specific private solutions are often an alternative to specific public solutions (for example, in the field of health insurance), further government intervention in general is not incompatible with the further development of collective bargaining in general.

It should not be assumed that particular regulatory measures, once enacted or adopted, will necessarily be eternal. At one time the labor injunction was used by Federal and state courts as a device for meddling in thousands of industrial disputes. The Norris-LaGuardia Act of 1932 and similar state legislation virtually foreclosed the use of the injunction until it was revived on a limited scale in the Taft-Hartley Act. Certain of the regulatory provisions in the Taft-Hartley Act have worked poorly and may be abandoned sooner or later. It is widely believed, for example, that a rigid statutory procedure for handling "emergency disputes" is inadvisable. The prohibition on closed shops in the Taft-Hartley Act has been generally circumvented in traditional closed-shop industries; it might be preferable to permit the parties to adopt whatever form of union security they might agree upon and to require that basic civil rights be observed within unions. In our present stage of development "refusal to bargain" could well be omitted from the list of unfair employer and union practices, since the provision is difficult to administer and probably unnecessary once the labor movement has organized to a position of strength. Emergency wartime wage controls and dispute-settlement procedures have been adopted twice and dismantled twice.

It is unlikely, however, that the total amount of government intervention in the labor market will diminish greatly. In this respect the United States will probably continue to stand in the middle group of countries, with the government playing a more active role than in England or Sweden but a less active role than in France or Germany.

Economic, political, and military developments will largely determine the future course of government policy on industrial conflict and related problems. Another depression would induce measures to maintain purchasing power and increase employment; another wave of strikes, like that which occurred in 1945–1946, might stimulate repressive legislation, such as the proposal to prohibit multiemployer bargaining; and it goes without saying that another military emergency would occasion government controls across the board. Much will depend on the success or failure of private arrangements for handling problems. The railroads were nationalized in World War I but not in World War II. The difference was not one of doctrine but of practical necessity. Local provision for the unemployed was supplanted by a national relief program in the Depression, not because of any theoretical objection to local provision but because it broke down. And so it is in industrial relations. If private programs for meeting the cost of medical care are successful, they will survive; otherwise public health insurance will be adopted, regardless of doctrinal difficulties.

One more variable should be mentioned. Government activity is seldom neutral in its effect on conflict situations, and the precise impact of future policies will depend on the political balance between labor and management. Labor had greater political strength in 1933 and 1937, management in 1947 and 1953. Their relative power in 1963 will strongly affect the government's program for dealing with industrial conflict and with the issues involved in conflict.

CHAPTER 40 CONCLUDING INTERPRETATIONS

A. THE UNDETERMINED FUTURE
OF INDUSTRIAL CONFLICT

Arthur Kornhauser

T HESE final comments may well begin with the reminder that industrial conflict has its psychological roots in the beliefs people hold regarding their own interests and the ways in which their goals can best be achieved. Many industrial
workers in our society are not fully satisfied with the rewards and the conditions
of their employment and with their lives as wage earners. Even among those
who are not actively dissatisfied, large numbers believe that they can better
their position through organized pressures as well as by individual efforts.
Correspondingly, many owners and managers feel that they cannot live and
work as they should, that they cannot satisfactorily perform their functions of
operating profitable and enduring enterprises, if they submit to the pressures
and acquiesce in the expanding demands of working people. In this basic sense,
it appears that, in a free society, there is no end to industrial conflict.

The extent and nature of the conflict, its intensity, and the ways it is
manifested and resolved depend upon the influences that shape people's desires
and expectations, the gratifications and deprivations they experience, the social
sanctions for particular kinds of conflict behavior, the disapproval of other
types, and the social machinery evolved for dealing with conflicts. The future
course of industrial conflict must be estimated with due reference to all these
complex social determinants. Students of labor affairs inevitably differ in the
weight they attach to the several influences and in their reading of expected
change or absence of change in these influences.

Two principal orientations can be distinguished among the diverse views:
One stresses the trend toward progressively more stable, regularized, institutionalized industrial relations, in which conflict is dealt with in a steadily more
orderly manner. The other view emphasizes the dynamic factors that constantly
produce new strains in modern society, new turns to group power relations;
it points to the changing, emergent quality of personal motivations and of institutions and accordingly sees industrial conflict itself undergoing irregular
changes and unruly phases—encountering lulls and accelerations and shifts of
direction rather than proceeding along an established course. Obviously there
are many degrees and variations of these two views and many intermediate
positions, but the simplified contrast will serve to bring into focus some important unsettled questions about the future of labor-management relations.

The first view seems to be growing in popularity, that is, the belief that union-management relations have now entered a period of maturity and stability, under businesslike collective bargaining arrangements, and that this relationship is destined to undergo smooth progressive improvement. Some social scientists go farther and see a drift toward unification of management's and labor's efforts, leading to greater and greater cooperation, teamwork, and harmony. Under both these conceptions, government is assigned a relatively minor role. Unions are perceived as fitting into the industrial system as it now is, with no essential change in the organization of industry or the power positions of the parties. There is much to support these views. The extension of stabilized collective bargaining to ever larger sections of American industry has certainly represented a major trend in labor-management relations. It is reasonable to suppose that continued institutionalization along present lines may, indeed, prove to be the main course of the future. This thesis, in explicit or implicit form, runs through large portions of the present book. It is wise, nevertheless, to recognize that this emphasis may be overdone, to the neglect of other quite different developments affecting industrial conflict.

A contrasting interpretation holds that forces are at work in our society which may disrupt current patterns of labor-management relations and produce conflict over an expanded range of political as well as economic issues. Not that the growth of collective bargaining will cease or diminish in importance, but it needs to be seen in a larger sociopolitical setting. According to this view, there are no fixed goals or "proper" areas of concern for labor; working people's organizations will adapt to the wants and expectations of their members and to the dominant internal and external pressures affecting the group and the leaders at the time. Similarly, management, if conditions are favorable, will employ a dynamic strategy and endeavor to improve its position by changing some of the rules of the game which are currently in effect. The labor-management conflict relationship, it is suggested, is such that it will tend to break through any fixed, neatly circumscribed limits. Both the forces within industry and those in the larger society tend constantly to create new strains and set up new tensions. Moreover, the day-to-day conduct of union-management affairs increasingly extends into the community—in the form of educational, propaganda, public-relations, and political efforts by both parties. To confine discussion of industrial conflict to the direct dealings between managements and unions *in industry*, according to this conception, is bound to produce a false and misleading picture of the processes at work. Industrial conflict is still *industrial* conflict even when the battle is waged on the political and communications front.

The central aim here is to call attention to the challenge presented by this second interpretation, since the considerations that it stresses tend too often to be neglected. The questions asked in this section are intended particularly to suggest that the future in respect to industrial conflict may not be so settled as much present-day thinking pictures it.

In many labor as well as management circles, it is unpopular to point to divergent group interests, problems of changing power relations, and the importance of political action in industrial affairs. Such emphasis smacks of class consciousness and foreign labor movements. Within this climate of values, there is a disinclination to weigh possible alternative conceptions of organized labor's role in reference to industrial conflict. To raise questions like those that follow in this section is often viewed as equivalent to *advocating* the unpopular position. What is less clearly seen is that failure to raise the questions is equally to be an advocate—but of the accepted "going" views. It is not my purpose to plead a case for any particular interpretation or any particular path to be taken by union-management relations. It *is* my intention to advocate open-minded weighing of alternative futures for industrial conflict, the influences making for one or another trend, and the considerations that may lead people to choose one course or another.

That one's own value premises affect the points he elects to stress is undeniable. But this is a universal phenomenon. A principal purpose of this section, in fact, is to point up the value issues that all must face in pursuing studies of labor-management relations and in arriving at answers in regard to industrial conflict. To ignore the issues is to adopt a restrictive frame of reference that itself goes far to predetermine the conclusions.

It should be clearly stated that the aim here is not to predict what *will* happen any more than it is to prescribe what *should* be. No implication is intended that only one answer can be given to the questions asked below. The questions are rather to suggest that the future of industrial conflict is in significant measure undetermined and that we must be wary of social-science predictions that assume a fatalistic continuation of whatever trends are now exhibited. More analytical studies of psychological and social determinants are required. The following questions simply indicate some of the factors to be taken into account in such further studies.

1. Will the economic demands of workers and their organizations remain within "reasonable" boundaries, and will unions accept a role of "mature," "responsible," businesslike negotiating, with power relations and rules of the game remaining essentially as they are; or is it to be anticipated that labor groups from time to time will try to break through the fences and seek to change the rules and relative power positions by resort to tests of strength? The question is really whether an essential function of unions is to push for gains that reach beyond those that can be achieved without coercive influence; whether, by its nature, a union is impelled to press for "more" when in a strategic position to do so; and, hence, whether strong unions are likely indefinitely to fit into a relationship of prolonged stability.

The question is not whether new points of dispute will occur between unions and companies; this is assumed to be true. It is also certain that many of the new issues and demands will be amicably settled through bargaining, with or without an occasional well-controlled and not too damaging strike. But the all-important additional question is whether "fighting" issues will continue to arise which may *not* be handled so smoothly. Will unions and managements try to reach for gains that cannot readily be accommodated within the existing collective-bargaining system? Will battles occur to change old norms and assumptions governing the relations of the parties? Will there be struggles over reforms that transcend businesslike bargaining in particular companies? A philosophy of settled and stabilized relationships implies a continuation or, at most, a gradual evolution of laws, regulations, and assumptions concerning collective bargaining; but such a philosophy might not survive efforts to change the old norms drastically.

2. Are working people and their organizations likely to confine their demands to the familiar economic gains, or will their aims expand and produce increased conflict over noneconomic demands that management will perceive as threatening its prerogatives and freedom of action? If further economic gains from the individual firm should grow less obtainable and if changing conditions accent intangible social and personal deprivations, the latter could assume new saliency and emerge as new sources of contention. What we know of human motivation—the variety and complexity of wants, their constant redefinitions and shifts of intensity under changing social influences, and the manifold interferences they encounter—strongly suggests a continued tendency for demands to spread and give rise to new conflicts. In a society which attaches central importance to its democratic values and which insistently stresses ideals of personal worth and human dignity, individual development and self-expression, and rights of equal treatment and participation, it appears probable that unsatisfied aspirations will continuingly be aroused that may be channeled into pressures for industrial change—change beyond that dictated by economic considerations and beyond that willingly tolerated by management except under compelling pressures.

Most important, perhaps, is the question of whether demands will grow for effective participation in decisions and sharing of responsibility at the work-group level. Will there be demands for increasing independence and democratic rights in industry to parallel those enjoyed as citizens in the community? And beyond the confines of the shop, will the future witness expanding expectations in regard to social-security measures, medical care, and improved opportunities for education, housing, recreation, and whatever else the common man may come to feel is his due? Will such expanding demands or the prospect of their occurrence bring countermoves by business to restrict and "contain" unions—moves that in turn may precipitate new conflicts?

3. A further set of questions may be asked in regard to influences affecting unions as institutions: Will the public and political pressures of the years ahead tend to make for continued "limited-function," job-centered unionism or for a broadened range of aims and activities? Traditional business unions, working directly in the self-interests of their members, run athwart the interests of various other groups. The problem becomes more serious as unions grow larger and more powerful. The union is feared and damned for its militancy and social irresponsibility; it is viewed by many as a selfish interest group that threatens the general welfare. As such it becomes a political target and is likely to be subjected to stricter political control in the "public interest."

The question then arises whether the union, under such pressures from public opinion and government, must either retreat from vigorous pursuit of its aims or advance by expanding its activities to make them better accord with what the unorganized public conceives to be the common welfare. This latter course might mean a type of unionism that would continue to work for direct economic benefits for its members but would strive at the same time to help members meet their personal and social needs, in and out of industry, and would join with other groups to secure governmental and community action in the interests of all working people. The possibility is suggested that labor organizations may increasingly come to believe that, by extending the unions' horizons and functions, they can escape the politically vulnerable position created by the pursuit of narrow self-interested objectives under the conditions of their new size and strength. Conditions in the larger society may induce major labor groups to adopt the view that the wise course for them is to battle not merely each for its own special group but for the welfare of working people and the society as a whole. There are many signs that this changed outlook has already impressed itself on the thinking of important labor leaders.

4. A final question, which I believe deserves vastly greater attention than is usually accorded it, has to do with public opinion and the social values that are held in respect to labor-management relations. The questions may be stated in this way: To what extent will organized labor increase its efforts to balance and offset what many labor leaders believe to be a predominantly business-oriented control of the news, ideas, and interpretations that are circulated? Will influence exerted by business in shaping public opinion through control of mass media and through pressures on schools, clergymen, writers, and other opinion leaders be felt as a serious threat to labor unions, their continued growth, and their bargaining effectiveness? If so, will this aroused concern lead labor organizations to attempts to combat the one-sided influences, as they see it, and to provide the public with other information and alternative views more favorable to union efforts and to social changes in the interests of working people? In a word, may we expect to see intensified industrial conflict on the level of political action and psychological warfare? Will sophisticated labor and business leadership increasingly perceive their long-run relations as largely determined by public opinion (including workers' opinions) and its political expression, and will their conflicting goals, accordingly, be sought largely through contending efforts to win moral approval and support in the public mind?

These questions of how greatly labor-management relations are affected by the prevailing value structure, thought patterns, and social outlook of the times and of how these orientations are influenced and changed may turn out to be the most crucial considerations determining the course of labor relations. Yet it is these very matters that are ignored or assumed to remain constant in many over-all prognoses concerning labor-management affairs. From the standpoint of organized labor, the issue is whether emphasis on the collective-bargaining function alone, without attention to public opinion and political influence, might mean that bargaining would tend more and more to be conducted within an atmosphere and a legal framework thoroughly in accord with management views and devoted to preserving management rights unmodified. If unions should become the predominant power in public influence, the shoe would, of course, be on the other foot—but the essential fact would remain that basic elements of industrial conflict would be carried on outside the industrial sphere. The question, then, is whether organized labor and employers will feel that collective bargaining is not enough and that it is only as dependable as the state of opinion, law, and politics permits it to be.

For labor leaders, these same issues may take this form: Will labor leaders predominantly strive to gain prestige and power by winning *public* support—frequently in opposition to corporations—or by winning acceptance and backing of the companies with which they deal? Will working people and the public see the latter type of relationship as effective, realistic labor leadership, supportive of the American way of life, or will it be stigmatized as "sellout," weakness, and "collaboration?" Either *could* happen. It will presumably depend on future economic and political conditions—and especially on the social interpretations that become current. The latter brings us back once more to the importance of the ideas that are communicated in the society, the values that are inculcated, and the alternative views that are circulated.

Not only labor-management relations but the course of our sociopolitical life in general may be determined in great measure by the answers to these questions having to do with public opinion. From a broad social standpoint, the question is whether large-scale corporate business and organized labor will, each in its own interests, exert influence curtailing and balancing any disproportionate concentration of social power in the hands of the other. The exercise of such offsetting group influence may well be indispensable if freedom of inquiry and discussion is to flourish, if our society is to search freely for new and better answers to our social and economic problems, and if nonconformist thinking is to be encouraged or even tolerated when it takes directions distasteful to an established elite.

The foregoing questions point to some of the social and psychological factors that may prominently influence the course of industrial conflict. Analysis of the influences, rather than leading to fixed predictions, emphasizes that the future is still in the making. Industrial-relations trends will depend upon the shifting forces at work and on the emergent aims, convictions, and action programs they evoke. The task of inquiry and reflection is to help delineate the alternative roads open, the influences favoring one or another alternative, and the probable consequences of moving in each direction. In the light of such knowledge, it is for the groups concerned (potentially this includes everyone) to choose the road they prefer to follow and, within the limits of their democratically exercised power, to try to shape social policy accordingly.

In addition to underscoring the indeterminateness of the road ahead, our analysis again calls attention to the fact that conflict of aims is deeply rooted and enduring and that it is an essential feature of the employer-employee relationship, viewing industry as a whole. The opposition stems from the firm determination of those at the top of the economic pyramid to protect their interests (and the general welfare as they see it) against the threatening gains of working people striving for a larger share of the good things of life—including a greater measure of participation and influence through labor organizations and through government.

To suggest, however, that industrial conflict may continue to wax and wane, to break out of each newly achieved period of equilibrium, to spread to fresh areas of contention—to mention these possibilities is by no means to deny that industrial conflict has been undergoing significant constructive changes. A great deal of evidence reported in this book and elsewhere testifies that orderly procedures for dealing with conflict have been on the increase and that resort to violence has sharply declined. It is reasonable to anticipate a continuation of this long-run tendency for union-management conflict to grow more institutionalized, more fully subject to formal and informal social controls. But this is not to forecast harmony in the more general relationships of organized labor in the society. The trend toward more strictly controlled conflict may indeed enlarge the areas of controversy, since it acutely raises the wider questions of who controls the social controls and whether industrial relations are being institutionalized in a pattern less congenial to one side than to the other. In short, conflict relations may tend to subside on the industrial front while becoming more intense in regard to political issues and efforts to win public support and favorable governmental action.

A main thesis here is that industrial-conflict trends cannot be properly appraised if they are viewed only in the perspective of direct union-management dealings and disputes over economic and job-centered gains. While it seems reasonable to believe that the future may witness gradual extension of union activities into the government of industry, with an accompanying development of constructive collaboration between unions and management (though with continuing conflict as well), at the same time, struggles over social policies and political power intimately affecting union-management relations may become the new storm centers.

It has been suggested that pressures are operating that may impel unions to pursue their goals on the broad sociopolitical scene as well as in industry itself. The future role of unions and, hence, the outlook for labor-management relations are likely to depend on how citizens as a whole come to answer the basic question: Are strong labor unions, independent and able to exert economic and political influence opposed to that of big business, essential for the nation's democratic progress? Are expanded union activities needed as a check on business power in the decisions of industry and government, or does a satisfactory balance now exist? If such questions are answered in a manner that implies a continuation of group conflict, then that condition may have to be accepted as part of a vigorous democratic process. The goal must then be conceived not as labor-management harmony but as progressive improvement in which all people's interests are fully represented.

Since so much of this book concerns itself with the organized and formal expressions of conflict between unions and employers, it should again be emphasized that there is need for giving full recognition to the many other manifestations of conflict between working people and the owners and managers of industry. In weighing alternative interpretations of trends, there is scant justification for looking only at organized union and management activities. A wide range of informal, unorganized, and individual conflict behavior remains. These larger dimensions of conflict behavior were explicitly noted in Chap. 1.[1] Even if formal union-management relations were to be thoroughly regularized and handled in the most peaceful and cooperative manner, industrial conflict would persist in other of its myriad forms. Directly or indirectly, individuals will find expression for their frustrations and hostilities and their unfulfilled aspirations—both those engendered by their industrial situations and those displaced upon industry. Unless our institutions undergo revolutionary changes, much of the dissatisfaction and effort for group im-

[1] See pp. 14–15.

provement will continue to be directed against the owners and managers of industry. The basic problem will exist as long as there are felt oppositions of interests and goals arising from people's differing economic roles in the industrial society.

Finally, I believe that we must recognize the heavy responsibility upon social scientists who deal with a problem such as that of industrial conflict. The fact cannot be sidestepped that social scientists not only describe, analyze, and interpret; they inevitably also influence the processes which they report. Wittingly or unwittingly, those who write a book like this have some impact on the interpretations that are accepted in the larger society and on the social behavior that ensues. Scholarly writings become part of the context that helps sanction or condemn conflict and that leads the public to believe in harmony and cooperation or to look further and ask what price harmony; to feel that a satisfactory balance has been reached and that industrial rights and power relations should be maintained essentially as they are or that processes of change should go forward to more satisfying accommodations of divergent interests. It is reflections like these that have dictated efforts throughout this volume to look at industrial conflict from different standpoints and with frequent warnings against too hasty or too firm commitment to particular answers. The search for better answers is a never-ending one. Acceptable conclusions will be those hammered out by the whole society.

B. PROSPECTS OF INDUSTRIAL CONFLICT—A PREDICTION

Robert Dubin

AFTER taking into account all the larger influences that play on the uncertain future of industrial relations, as set forth particularly in the previous chapter, it is still worth making a specific prediction about the future of industrial conflict. Life goes on. Society has continuity. The past and present do contain at least some of the seeds of the future. While straight extrapolation may be pointless and misleading, a prediction based upon a model of the future social system can be very much in order. For a sociologist in particular, concerned as he is with the stabilities and regularities of social life, there is almost a compulsion to see the scientific task as requiring a prediction. This involves "sticking one's neck out" even at the risk of being wholly inaccurate. But if the tools of social analysis are useful, then the scientifically constructed models of the future social systems should give us the basis for predicting the state of one of the secondary sets of social practices, namely, industrial conflict.

The general prediction for industrial conflict is: measured by the length and intensity of strikes it will show relative stability in the next several decades. What follows suggests the outline of the analysis that leads to this conclusion.

It has been one of the underlying themes of the chapters in this volume that industrial relations in the United States have become regularized or institutionalized. In the whole range of topics and areas dealt with, this idea emerges over and over again. In some areas, such as union-management cooperation, the experimentation has been limited and the efforts either tentative or dictated by special pressures or circumstances. In other areas, such as wage and salary administration (to take but one example), elaborate practices have grown up that are widely adopted and denote highly developed institutionalized behavior. Regardless of the uneven development of regularized practices in industrial relations, the fact remains that formalized union-management relations, collective bargaining, and the various facets of personnel administration have become integral parts of commercial and industrial operations.

In a long-run forecast of American industrial relations, we must, therefore, start with the knowledge that we are considering a set of institutional practices that are an integral part of an unfolding social development. It is no longer a matter of whether or not these developments can be turned on or off at will. They are built into the organizational and social system of industry. The advent of a new political administration will not produce startling innovations in the industrial relations area simply because the new party in power

527

represents an employer or a labor point of view. It is notable, for example, that the Taft-Hartley law was formally and functionally a revision and modification of the Wagner Act; it was built upon it. The sort of intentional redirection of the emerging trends in industrial relations through legislation, for example, that many management partisans have repeatedly asked for is impossible, short of tearing down not only the practices objected to but also a host of related practices.

In a very literal sense, the advent of widespread collective bargaining in American industry has produced (1) the invention and adoption of many new subsystems of behavior for management representatives, for union leaders, and for rank-and-file workers and (2) the modification of existing behavior systems to bring them in concordance with what was happening in union-management relations. At any given moment in time, these behavior systems are in relative equilibrium. All the people involved in these stabilized systems of behavior have various kinds of reasons for maintaining the stability. This is another way of saying that, when a system of social practices becomes even partially routinized, there arise strains toward perpetuation of these practices.

It follows, then, that there are two broad lines along which industrial relations and its accompanying conflicts can develop: (1) There is the possibility of increasing institutionalization either (*a*) as a development of the parties directly involved in relatively private systems of collective relations or (*b*) as a consequence of governmental intervention in the interests of social stability in the larger society. (2) Other developments that seem more remote will be considered which might involve the destruction of labor unions and the elimination of industrial relations of the present sort as a familiar part of the American scene. Let us first consider the further routinization of industrial relations.

If further routinization of collective bargaining and industrial relations is a major trend of the future, what influences seem to point toward primary direction of this at the hands of the parties involved?[2] The answer to the question of the primacy of the influences based upon private decision making takes into account the complexity and specialized nature of industrial relations. From the previous chapters, it should be clear that the many facets and areas of industrial relations are complex. Special knowledge and insight at the operating plant level may be required to carry on activities successfully in this area of human behavior. It is not enough that one has to know something about the seniority principle, for instance. To make a successful application of the principle entails special knowledge of the production processes and departmentalization of work in a given company as well as of the distribution of length of service of its employees and the natural units of operations at any given percentage of capacity operation. It is this combination of highly technical knowledge and familiarity with the known conditions at the operating

[2] When the primary direction of the evolution of industrial relations is in the hands of the parties involved, the developments which occur will come as a consequence of private decisions. Since these private decisions usually take into account the whole gamut of developments in the society, it should be clearly understood that "human relations in industry" is not a synonym for institutionalization. Practices can become institutionalized in situations of discord, distrust, compromise, and partial satisfactions as well as under circumstances of faith, hope, love, and charity.

levels that makes it highly probable that the institutional practices of industrial relations will be the product of management and labor working out their adjustments at the plant level.

Let us consider the alternative of far-reaching government intervention into the industrial-relations area. Is it possible to standardize the content of industrial relations to the degree necessary to make uniform Federal or state laws the basis for more or less uniform and widely adopted practices in this field? Or, in the other direction, is it possible to have such complex laws and administrative regulations that they will cover every possible special and unique situation? The answers to both of these questions seems to be largely in the negative. Variations in Federal labor-relations laws, through time, and among state laws, at a given time, suggest the improbability of uniformity. The wartime experience with complex administrative direction of union-management relations is equally suggestive of the diminishing returns from pursuing this course.

But what, then, comes to be the role of the government in industrial relations? Does governmental intervention have a role here in either establishing, maintaining, or limiting the industrial-relations practices developed either collectively or unilaterally by labor and management? It is worth repeating what has already been said in this volume. The governmental concern with collective bargaining will continue to hinge on the issue of overt conflict and its limitation. As long as industrial conflict remains relatively private—*i.e.,* does not have an immediate and direct impact upon the public—the limited areas of governmental regulation will continue in vogue. Thus strikes are always a likely subject of governmental concern, but wage-payment systems are less probable subjects of government regulation, since the conflict over them can be carried on relatively privately with no overt break in the ongoing production processes.[3]

As long, then, as the relations between management and labor continue to move in the direction of developing greater regularities and of being incorporated in behavior systems whose structure and processes are acknowledged by both parties, it is probable that the role of government will continue to be limited to policing overt conflict.

It is necessary to take into account other developments previously noted in Chap. 39. Suppose totalitarianism, red or black, engulfs our society. It seems scarcely necessary to point out that industrial relations as we know them in America would undergo profound alterations. The examples of Germany, Italy, and Russia are instructive on this score. Free trade-unions would disappear and organizations called unions would become organs of the state. Free collective bargaining would also disappear. Many of the personnel practices of a free society would be replaced by those grounded in a philosophy of force and restricted freedom, in the interests of the state. In short, there would be a sharp discontinuity with the past, reflecting a society-wide change in values and institutions.

---

[3] There are, of course, important legislative areas affecting labor relations, such as minimum wages, industrial safety, workmen's compensation, old-age and survivors' insurance, and unemployment compensation. While legislative action in these areas affects the social milieu within which collective bargaining occurs, it does not deal directly with union-management relations nor with the practices that result.

At the level of technology, the developments noted in Chap. 39 may introduce just as important discontinuities in the development of industrial relations as do politicosocial revolutions. The whole basis of earning a living in our society may be transformed by atomic power, electronics, and related developments. It is difficult to see how many of the practices of the preatomic era can successfully be carried over into the postatomic era. The extent of the discontinuities and the upheavals caused by the new technological developments will be a consequence of the rapidity of their introduction and the ability of the society to adapt itself readily to the changes. Some hold the belief that American society is presently highly flexible and adaptive and that it is perhaps the most capable, among Western societies, of rapidly transforming itself into an atomic-era society with a minimum of social dislocation.

A general forecast for industrial conflict, then, is that, measured by the length and intensity of strikes, it will show relative stability. Governmental pressures to limit and control overt conflict will operate in this direction. Furthermore, the institutionalizing processes will tend to enlarge the areas of nonviolent conflict (where negotiation substitutes for direct force).

This prediction is based upon the rather static assumptions that the sociopolitical structure of the society remains relatively unchanged and that the technological base of industry undergoes only slow and easily assimilated modification. If either of these assumptions about the relatively easily assimilated rate of change in our society is wrong, then there is the possibility of vastly increased industrial conflict.

Should totalitarianism be the wave of the future, then industrial conflict can readily become a weapon of insurrection and, ultimately, of revolution in either a fascist or communist development. If our technology advances in an uncontrolled fashion to produce major dislocations in our society (including mass unemployment and permanent obsolescence of lifetime skills), then blind revolt may be at least an initial reaction, accompanied by a much higher volume of overt conflict. But these postulates of abrupt change rather than more gradual modification in the social institutions simply represent another way of declaring that the basic institutions of our society (the governmental structure and the economic system) are so brittle and fragile that their future is uncertain. If this is so, then it becomes futile to attempt prediction of a much more secondary set of institutional practices, such as industrial relations, which are dependent upon the underlying and basic institutional arrangements. However, there seems to be sufficient evidence pointing to the vitality of the underlying institutions of our society to justify predictions about industrial conflict on the basis of relatively static assumptions concerning these basic social institutions.

C. CONCLUDING OBSERVATIONS

Arthur M. Ross

Inasmuch as the trends and tendencies which relate to industrial conflict have already been summarized in Chap. 39, I believe that a short concluding statement on my part will be sufficient.

1. Conflict is one of the substances out of which human society is built. Nation and nation, employer and worker, seller and buyer, parent and child, student and teacher—all are dependent on each other, but it would be fatuous to claim that their interests are entirely harmonious. Without conflict of interest there would be little need for law and government and little social change, constructive or otherwise.

2. Conflict being normal and natural, it should wherever feasible be recognized frankly for what it is and permitted to come to the surface where some kind of resolution can be achieved. Where the free expression of conflict is unfeasible it may be suppressed. A healthy society will act to prevent itself from being destroyed but should not conclude too hastily that destruction is threatened.

3. Whether a particular method of prosecuting conflict is to be deemed normal or pathological depends on the facts and circumstances and is not a matter of absolute principle. Modern war is pathological not because it represents international conflict but because of the carnage and destruction. Most strikes are not pathological for the reason that the resulting damage is ordinarily tolerable. Some strikes accomplish constructive results which could not be achieved otherwise. This should not be taken as generally advocating strikes, however. Certainly, as a general proposition, nonbelligerent resolutions of industrial conflict, avoiding resort to economic force, are to be preferred.

4. With the growth of a massive and integrated technology, stronger and more inclusive organizations, and more effective means of communication, the destructive potentialities of industrial conflict have greatly increased; but the real impact has been kept well within bounds. Doubtless this is to be explained by the creative development of collective bargaining, modern social legislation, and other means of handling the issues in controversy.

5. It is desirable that employers and workers understand each other, but it should not be expected that communication—singular or plural, one-way or two-way—can cause genuine diversity of interests to disappear. With better understanding, it often develops that no real basis for controversy exists. Just as often it becomes apparent that the basis is deeper and broader than was formerly appreciated.

6. Similarly, it is desirable that personal relations at the work place be

amiable, since workers and supervisors must spend a great deal of time in each other's presence. There is no reason why industrial life should be any more unpleasant than it has to be. Moreover, work is accomplished more effectively where personal relations are good. It should not be supposed, however, that conflicts of interest will disappear if the privates on the front lines—workers and supervisors—can be taught to get along with each other. I see no great harm in "human relations" and do not regard it as a devious conspiracy against the pursuit of rational self-interest, although the exaggerated claims and pretentious terminology are often irritating and the need that people always agree with each other is greatly overdrawn.

7. The art of industrial statesmanship is to minimize the need for suppression. Suppression must be on someone's terms—those of the employers or those of the labor organizations or those of the state. Limited forms of conflict may be suppressed in a democracy, but total suppression requires totalitarian methods.

8. Conflict between employers and workers is expressed in the industrial, political, and opinion spheres. The second and third of these modes of expression are nonbelligerent. The first may be either belligerent or not; that is, it may be resolved with or without economic force. Whether all three or only the first should be defined as "industrial conflict" is a matter of terminology. I prefer to limit the term so that it applies to the employment relationship, but it cannot be denied that industrial, political, and propaganda controversies are closely related.

9. Particular industrial conflicts are all eventually resolved. One of the great virtues of collective bargaining in its various forms (including the strike) is that it permits the formulation of limited issues which are amenable to resolution and blurs over large differences of principle which can never really be settled. This, of course, is revolting to those who will settle for nothing less than "basic solutions."

10. Another great virtue of collective bargaining is that it permits the compromise or reconciliation of divergent interests. Again this is abhorrent to those who are wedded to absolute justice as they see it, but I regard it as a virtue because it seems fairer and makes for a smoother functioning of society. Aside from this, no great normative merit should be assigned to the compromise solutions which are developed, since the notion of "equal bargaining power" is only a pleasant fiction. The terms of compromise depend on the relative strength and determination of the contending parties, the sanctions available to them, and the current social norms and are not necessarily better, in any absolute sense, than another set of terms might have been. On the other hand, it is wise to be skeptical of confident definitions of the "public interest," standing above and apart from special interests.

11. Emphasis on the creative achievements of collective bargaining and modern social legislation should not be construed as an argument that industrial relations have arrived on a plateau of permanent stability, as a denial that difficult new issues will arrive in the future, or as a disinclination to recognize that important social and economic change will emerge in the resolution of these issues. Certainly, many of the issues will spill over into the political sphere. I do not think it possible at this time to distinguish between demands

which will be directed against the employer and those which will be directed against the government, but the question is an interesting one to speculate about.

12. Neither is it possible, in my opinion, to foresee the exact character of the social and political developments which will occur as technology, power relations, concepts of equity, and methods of prosecuting conflict change. The traditional issue of public versus private ownership of the means of production is no longer the crucial one. Tell me whether or not peace will be kept, economic stability maintained, and democratic values and institutions largely preserved, and I will make a prediction as to the future course of labor-management conflict. Otherwise I prefer to wait and see.

INDEX

DATE DUE

MAR 3 0 '66			
MAY 26 '76			
MAR 14 1984			
GAYLORD			PRINTED IN U.S.A.